The Whole Baseball Catalogue

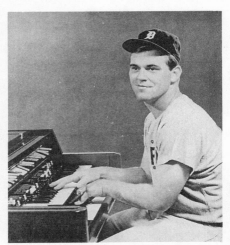

The Whole BASEBALL Catalogue

Edited by
John Thorn and Bob Carroll
with David Reuther

A Baseball Ink Book

A Fireside Book • Published by Simon & Schuster Inc.
New York / London / Toronto / Sydney / Tokyo

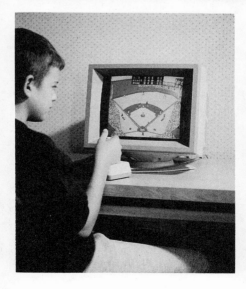

A BASEBALL INK BOOK

FIRESIDE
Simon & Schuster Building
Rockefeller Center
1230 Avenue of the Americas
New York, New York 10020

FIRESIDE and COLOPHON are registered
trademarks of Simon & Schuster Inc.

Manufactured in the
United States of America

The Whole baseball catalogue / edited by
John Thorn and Bob Carroll with David
Reuther.
    p. cm. — (A Baseball ink book.)
    "A Fireside book."
    1. Baseball—United States—Miscel-
lanea. I. Thorn, John, date.
II. Carroll, Bob (Bob Newhardt)
III. Reuther, David.
IV. Series.
GV867.3.W56 1990
796.357'0973—dc20   89-49090
                      CIP

ISBN 0-671-68347-0

10 9 8 7 6 5 4 3 2

"Grapefruit League Sweeteners" by Eliot
Cohen appeared originally in *Major
League Monthly*; it is reprinted courtesy
of the author.

"Cactus League Pricklers" by Ed Connolly
appeared originally in *Major League
Monthly*; it is reprinted courtesy of the
author.

"Ticket Taker Talks Technique" by Bill
Doyle, copyright © 1979 The Associated
Press, was originally published by *The
Holyoke Transcript-Telegram*; it appears
here courtesy of The Associated Press.

"The Long Goodbye" by Eric Nadel, copyright © 1984, was originally published in
Sport; it appears here courtesy of the author.

"Postcards from Fantasy Camp" by Ted
Lutz, copyright © 1985 The Washington
Post, was originally published in *The
Washington Post* as "Follow That
Dream"; it appears here courtesy of The
Washington Post and the author.

"Hal Hempen's All-American Dream" by
Joseph M. Schuster, copyright © 1987,
was originally published in *Sport*; it appears here courtesy of the author.

"What I Learned in School Today" by
Scott Shuger, copyright © 1987, was
originally published in *Sport*; it appears
here courtesy of the author.

Picture credits appear on page 355.

For our children—
The Thorns: Jed, Isaac, and Mark
The Carrolls: Hoss and Cathy
The Reuthers: Kate and Jacob

List of Contributors

Bob Carroll	BC	John McManus	JM
Merritt Clifton	MC	Terry Moffatt	TM
Eliot Cohen	EJC	Eric Nadel	EN
Neil Cohen	NC	Curt Pesmen	CP
Liz Comte	LC	John Rolfe	JR
Bob Condor	RC	Jon Scher	JS
Ed Connolly	EC	Stuart Schreiberg	StS
Keith Dunnavant	KD	Joseph M. Schuster	JMS
Jeff Elijah	JE	Barry Shapiro	BS
Brian Harris	BH	Scott Shuger	SS
John Hanc	JH	James K. Skipper	JKS
Lloyd Johnson	LJ	Robert Smith	RS
Jack Kavanagh	JK	Dan Schlossberg	DS
Danny Knobler	DK	John Thorn	JT
Stefanie Krasnow	SK	Glen Waggoner	GW
Tim Kurkjian	TK	Sydney Waller	SW
Bill Ladson	BL	Miles Wolff	MW
Lew Lipset	LL	Bob Wood	BW
Ted Lutz	TL		

Acknowledgments

Despite the appearance of only two names on the cover, *The Whole Baseball Catalogue* is very much a team effort. Besides the thirty-seven writers whose initialed credits follow their segments of this book, there is a legion of elves (and some full-grown human beings) who prop up the editors and make their labors respectable.

First among equals, as with all Baseball Ink productions, is David Reuther. This book would not have come together in twice the time without his ability to manage a mob that was large, temperamentally diverse, and geographically remote.

Another veteran of previous Ink Wars is Marc Cheshire, itinerant designer and production whiz, who has made this thing look like a real book, rather than the name-address-and-telephone directory it might easily have become. After *Total Baseball* Marc swore he'd never do another big baseball book, but we dazzled him with visions of riches and fame.

The improbably named Gypsy da Silva brought her flashing eyes and nimble feet—and, more important, her gift for organization—to the final months' flurry of galleys, page proofs, photo captions, etc. Coordinating fact checkers, proofreaders, and indexers, she was there when we needed her. The same must be said of Judy Eskew of TSI Graphics, who handled our interminable stream of faxes and Fed Ex shipments with aplomb, courtesy, and unfailing professionalism.

Margaret Miller was responsible for the picture research, fact checking, marketing contacts, and sundry emergencies. Margie, ya did good. Her right-hand woman was Jennifer Harkins, who also worked wonders daily.

Our editor was the estimable Jeff Neuman, who played an active role in shaping this book from initial concept to last-minute typo. His unceasing care in diverting us from mine fields and trip wires is a model of—and we know he'll wince at our expropriation of the Mets' gloriously illiterate slogan—editing like it oughta be.

Scott Kurtz, our copy editor, was his customarily thorough and eagle-eyed self; but Scott's exploits go beyond pushing commas and civilizing barbarisms—his first-rate knowledge of baseball was indispensable. Our valiant if harried band of proofreaders and indexers consisted of: Andrew Attaway, Carol Catt, Sean Devlin, Ruth Elwell, Barbara Hanson, Caron Harris, and Ted Landry. Others who provided invaluable assistance with the editorial process are: Bill Deane and Tom Heitz of the National Baseball Library; and Neil Cohen, Lloyd Johnson, Curt Pesmen, Jack Kavanagh, Larry Green, and Eliot Cohen, whose contributions went beyond their signed pieces herein.

Photo gathering was a bear of a project, and we called upon old friends and colleagues Mark Rucker, Barry Halper, Mike Aronstein, and Mike Saporito; Dan Bennett and Pat Kelly of the National Baseball Library, who one day will answer a call from us without groaning; Miles Wolff of *Baseball America*; Tom Gilbert at Wide World; John Grabowski of Western Reserve; Marla Miller of Major League Baseball Properties; Debra Reid of The Farmers' Museum in Cooperstown; Tom Stevens of the *Providence Journal*; and Hal Bergan of The Summer Game. We also received outstanding cooperation from the firms and individuals whose baseball-oriented products and services are on display in this book.

We have left off our list of *thank-yous* the many good folks at Fireside, from Dan Farley on down, whose work on this book is just beginning as we begin to relax. But if past is prologue, then, thanks a million. And we have not mentioned our merry band of writers, figuring that they have had a page all their own. But guys, this book's for you.

John Thorn & Bob Carroll

Contents

VII. SEVENTH-INNING STRETCH

VIII. POSTGAME HIGHLIGHTS

IX. CLUBHOUSE

Introduction

If a catalogue covering the whole *earth* could be contained within a single paperbound volume (by Stewart Brand and the folks at Portola Institute), why devote a book very nearly its size to baseball, a subject that occasions not a moment's thought among a billion Chinese? One answer is that America's national pastime is slowly but surely becoming a global passion. Another is that baseball elicits feelings from some fans (and all too many writers) of mystical union and holistic hoohah that permits one to regard the 108-stitched cowhide sphere as a pretty good stand-in for Mother Earth.

But the best reason for *The Whole Baseball Catalogue*—really, the only acceptable one for a book that is designed for use—is the need for it. The boom in baseball shows no signs of abating, and the merchandising of baseball goods and services has simply exploded. Shopping has become a job, and sometimes a treacherous one; not all of baseball's purveyors march behind the banner of quality and value. This book is a centralized source of information about a vast area of baseball—from backyard batting cages to fantasy camps to rotisserie leagues—not encompassed by any other source. A consumers' guide to the baseball marketplace, the *Catalogue* offers candid reviews and advice by a staff of baseball experts; specialized information for dedicated fans and all those who work in baseball (or hope to);

and an abundant affection for the grand old game.

Do you wonder what features to look for in lights for your town's Little League field? Would you like to take a course in baseball history for college credit? How about arranging a summer-vacation tour of baseball shrines and historic spots? Or starting your own fan club? Publishing your own baseball book or newsletter? Trying out for big-league scouts? We'll tell you how to do it.

Who are the top baseball entertainers, mascots, and speakers—and how do you get one to come to an event you're planning? What are the best buys in table-baseball games? The best wurst at any big-league park? You get the idea: no mere directory of names, addresses, and telephone numbers, this book is chock full of opinions, offered by folks who've done their homework.

As with any book of this scope, we have had to scramble to provide up-to-the-last-minute information. Phone numbers change. Companies—especially the single-entrepreneurial outfits that offer some of the quirkiest and most appealing products—move or fade from view. Prices rise, and sometimes even drop. New releases, as in computerized baseball games, bump older versions from the shelves. In some details, it could be said this book was out of date as soon as we finished it (which is why we are staying abreast of the market, anticipating a clamor for a *Second Whole Base-*

ball Catalogue); still, you can rely upon the vast bulk of the data and recommendations herein to steer you straight.

You can't order the goods and services in this book directly from us, nor can we assure you of satisfaction or even courteous service. We are not allied with any of the merchandisers listed in this book in any way, nor are we beholden to them. Product samples and information have been gratefully accepted, but only with the understanding that we were putting up no *quos* for those *quids*. If purveyors of goods or services screw up, obtain a remedy by letting them know about it . . . but also let us know (care of the publisher), so that we can reconsider our recommendations in the next edition. Likewise, if you know of some firm or individual (even yourself) who has a baseball product to sell or a story to tell, write; we'll pay attention if not cash dollars.

If you wish to know whose prose you are enjoying at a given point in the book, look to the end of the entry for the writer's initials, and check against the List of Contributors that precedes the Introduction. You'll note that some chapters were entirely (or very nearly so) the work of one writer, while others are jigsaw jobs. In any case, we are responsible for any errors, omissions, or lapses in judgment or taste.

John Thorn & Bob Carroll

The Whole Baseball Catalogue

CHAPTER 1

Take Me Out to the Ball Game

American popular music has sung of American baseball from early Tin Pan Alley to Frank Sinatra and Bruce Springsteen. Both baseball and pop music reflect what we like to think is the American way of life. Both grew up with America, and America grew up with them.

In 1858 representatives of twenty-five amateur baseball teams from northeastern cities organized the first rudimentary league, the National Association of Base Ball Players. No one tried to set that mouthful to music, but the same year J. Randolph Blodgett, a player on the Niagara Base Ball Club of Buffalo, published the first piece of music devoted to baseball—"The Baseball Polka." By 1860, bands were oom-pah-pahing at the ballpark—particularly on Opening Day, the Fourth of July, and in championship games—playing popular tunes before the first pitch, between innings, and while the crowd filed out. Sometimes the players themselves entertained with song hits as well as base hits. In 1869 when the all-professional Cincinnati Red Stockings were compiling their unbeaten season, they did it to their own theme song. Before each game they'd line up at home plate and with hats in hands would sing it to the crowd.

During the late 1920s and early 1930s, Kansas City jazz musicians and Kansas City Monarch baseball players of the Negro Leagues enjoyed a close relationship. "We went to see them play during the day, and they came to hear us play at night," Count Basie said. Louis Armstrong sponsored a semiprofessional team of black players during the 1930s in New Orleans. And during the big band era of the 1940s, several of the better known bands, including Cab

Baseball Music

Center field —from Joltin' Joe to Willie, Mickey, and the Duke

Calloway, Tommy Dorsey, and Harry James, had their own softball teams that sometimes played for charity at major league stadiums.

Musicians could raise money for charity, but they couldn't live on alms. By the 1940s cheaper organists began replacing expensive large bands at the ballpark, although small combos still moved around the grandstand from inning to inning entertaining the crowd. When the cost of even that kind of live entertainment became prohibitive, disc jockeys fed electronic music through a public address system. Nevertheless live sound lives today each time broadcaster Harry Caray leads the crowd through "Take Me Out to the Ball Game" during the seventh-inning stretch of every Cub home game.

The paths of baseball and popular music have crossed many times over the years. Harry Frazee, Bing Crosby, and Joe E. Brown were major league club owners, and in 1917 Al Jolson held shares in the St. Louis Cardinals. Gene Autry, of course, currently owns the California Angels. On the other side of the ledger, Rube Marquard, Doc White, and George Moriarty composed baseball songs, as did Mrs. Lou

Gehrig and such media giants as Ring Lardner and Ernie Harwell. Babe Ruth, Ty Cobb, Christy Mathewson, John McGraw, Lou Gehrig, Marquard, and Waite Hoyt either sang or danced in vaudeville acts. The St. Louis Cardinal "Gashouse Gang" teams of the middle 1930s featured the Mississippi Mudcat Band led by Pepper Martin and Dizzy Dean.

In more modern times, 1950s pitcher Maurice "Mickey" McDermott once sang with Eddie Fisher at Grossinger's resort in the Catskills. Arthur Lee Maye, a 1960s outfielder, was the lead singer of an early rock group called Maye and the Crowns. For a brief time Denny McLain was a hot nightclub act playing the organ. Ball players who have made at least cameo appearances on baseball recordings include Willie, Mickey, but alas, not the Duke.

Although baseball music has been with us longer than the Chicago Cubs, no one has bothered to define exactly what it is. (Baseball music, that is; definitions of the Cubs vary.) Consequently you never know for sure in what form diamond ditties may appear.

The first and most obvious type is music with lyrics about some aspect of the game: players, teams, umpires, fans, parks, the game itself, the love of it, and so forth. Instead of "June-moon-swoon," it's "sun-fun-home run."

A second category consists of instrumentals. They have baseball in the title or are dedicated to a particular player, team, or some aspect of the game. Of course, when you hear them played, you have no idea they are related to baseball unless you are familiar with the title or dedication. Or see the illustration on the cover of the sheet music or album. Or read the liner

Baseball's Tin Pan Alley leads straight to the Bronx and Yankee Stadium.

notes. Or are standing next to some bozo who says, "Yep, those oboes are the Mets' infield!"

A third category is made up of songs that use baseball as a metaphor but really are not about any action that takes place on a ballfield. Characteristically they are popular love songs of the "I'm-leading-the-league-in-heartache-'cause-I-keep-striking-out-with-you" ilk.

A fourth type of baseball song includes those tunes that have no relationship to baseball except that they were written or sung by someone associated with the game. An example would be "Dear Old Home of Childhood," a 1911 Top-Forty candidate by the forty-game winner of 1908, Big Ed Walsh.

Finally there are the songs that have no intrinsic relationship to baseball except that they have been chosen by a team as a theme song. The '79 Pirates "We Are Fam-i-lee'd" all the way through the World Series.

One thing that just about all baseball songs have in common is what they are *not* and what they do *not* say. While baseball and popular music both reflect the American way of life, the same cannot be said for the music of baseball. Other popular music recognizes the social issues of the time: depression, war, changing sexual mores, civil rights, women's rights, and so forth. Baseball music rarely if ever touches on these topics.

Moreover, baseball music ignores baseball issues. There are no baseball songs about integration, free agency, the Players' Association, strikes, drug use, or escalated salaries. There isn't even a song titled "I Was a Designated Hitter on AstroTurf."

By focusing on the glory and past traditions of the game and celebrating its heroes and events, baseball music takes us outside the realm of reality. Maybe that's its function. Maybe that's the way it ought to be. —JKS

Babe Leads the Hit Parade

No player ever symbolized the national pastime more than George Herman Ruth. Naturally the Babe is the player most often immortalized in American popular music, though it's a safe bet that the songwriters hoped "immortality" would rub both ways.

Ruth deserves a discography all his own.

The first tune dedicated to him, "Batterin' Babe," was published in 1919 when he was still with the Red Sox. Several songs celebrated his career with the Yankees. A third group almost twenty years later mourned his death in 1948. Then, when Hank Aaron broke Ruth's home run record, the Babe was fondly recalled in the sentimental tune, "Move Over Babe (Here Comes Henry)" by Ernie Harwell and Bill Slayback.

A Selected List
of Babe's Most Forgettable Hits

"Batterin' Babe" (1919)
"Oh! You 'Babe' Ruth" (1920)

"Babe Ruth: He Is a Home Run Guy"
(1923)
"Along Came Ruth" (1925)
"Babe Ruth! Babe Ruth!" (1928)
"Joosta Like Babe-A-Da Ruth" (1928)
"Babe" (1947)
"Our Bambino" (1948)
"Safe at Home (The Mighty Babe Is)"
(1948)
"Move Over Babe (Here Comes Henry)"
(1973)

It's hard to see why "Joosta Like Babe-A-Da Ruth" failed to be a biggie. (Remember how much fun it used to be to ridicule immigrants' accents?) And "Babe Ruth: He Is a Home Run Guy" sure seems to have the makings of a standard. But, as with all baseball songs, the Ruthian numbers couldn't achieve Ruthian numbers on the pop charts. Even Irving Berlin got only a loud foul with his 1925 "Along Came Ruth." But then the Babe didn't get a hit every time up either. —JKS

Musical Murderers' Row

Even without playing a single Babe Ruth song, an enterprising disc jockey can spin a lineup to turn any major league manager green with envy. (Tommy Lasorda turns Dodger blue-green.)

Here are our starters in the field. Uh-one, uh-two . . .

- Willie Stargell—First Base. "Willie Stargell" (Al Perry; Love UR-2019, circa 1977).
- Jackie Robinson—Second Base. "Did You Ever See Jackie Robinson Hit That Ball?" (Count Basie and His Orchestra; in *The Complete Count Basie: Volume 19*, Ajazz 409). Also on 45-r.p.m. single (RCA Victor 47-2990) and on 78 r.p.m. (RCA Victor 20-3514), both 1949. Originally recorded on 78 r.p.m. by the Buddy Johnson Orchestra, Ella Johnson, vocal (Decca 246765, 1947).
- Ernie Banks—Shortstop. "Ernie's Tune" (Wanna WR 45814, circa late 1950s). The lyrics include "It's a beautiful day, let's play two" and other Banks-isms.
- Pete Rose—Third Base. "Charlie Hustle" (Pamela Neal; Free Flight 11557, 1979) presents Rose, to a disco beat. Also available on 33⅓ laserdisc (Free

Flight JM-11555).
- Stan Musial—Left Field. Take your pick: "Stan the Man" (Steve Bledsoe; Scope J90W-7522, 1961) or "Stan the Man" (Marty Bronson; Norman 543, 1963). Same Man, same title, different songs.
- Willie Mays—Center Field. "Say Hey, The Willie Mays Song" (The Treniers). Mays joins in the vocals and Quincy Jones directs the orchestra. On both 78 r.p.m. (Epic 9006, 1954) and 45 r.p.m. (Epic 5-90066, 1956).
- Hank Aaron—Right Field. "Hammerin' Hank" (Blast Furnace Band; Clintone CT-012, 1973). One in a long line of songs commemorating Aaron's assault on Ruth's record.
- Johnny Bench—Catcher. A whole album! *One Step Along the Way* (Terry Cashman; Lifesong 8140, 1983). A tribute to Bench and the Reds on Bench's retirement. Songs include "The Big Red Machine" and the title track, subtitled "The Ballad of Johnny Bench."

Speaking of "benches," what a bench a tuneful team could boast!

- Joe DiMaggio. "Joltin' Joe DiMaggio" (Les Brown Orchestra, Betty Bonney,

Vocal; Columbia 38554, Okeh 6377, 1941). The old 78 about the man and his 56-game hitting streak.
- Roberto Clemente. "The Ballad of Roberto Clemente" (Paul New; BBB Records 233, 1973). Honoring Clemente after his death in a plane crash on New Year's Eve, 1972, while bringing supplies to earthquake victims in Nicaragua.
- Mickey Mantle. "I Love Mickey" (Teresa Brewer; in *Miss Music*, Coral 37179, 1956). A cute ditty from Mantle's Triple Crown year, in which the Mick, himself, answers back, "Mickey Who?"
- Carl Yastrzemski. "Yastrzemski Song" (Jess Cain; in *The Impossible Dream*, Fleetwood FCLP-3024, 1967). A tribute to the Red Sox left fielder in *his* Triple Crown season.
- Maury Wills. "Ballad of Maury Wills" (Maury Wills; Dot 45-16529, circa 1962). The moral is: I know it's wrong to steal, but . . .
- Thurman Munson. "Playing Catch with the Babe" (Jess DeMaine on 45 r.p.m.; Thurman 82579, circa 1979). A memorial to the Yankee catcher after his death in a plane crash.

You could put together a pretty good

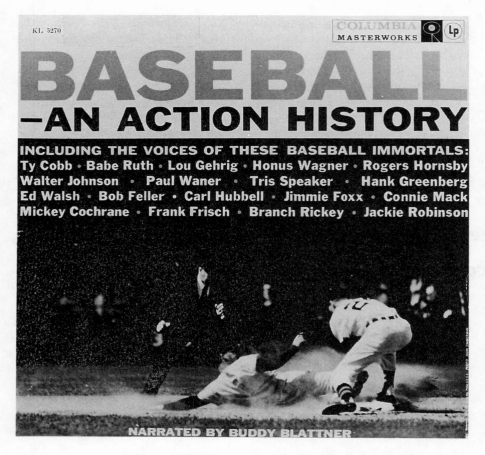

KL 5270

COLUMBIA MASTERWORKS ℗ Lp

BASEBALL
—AN ACTION HISTORY

INCLUDING THE VOICES OF THESE BASEBALL IMMORTALS:
Ty Cobb • Babe Ruth • Lou Gehrig • Honus Wagner • Rogers Hornsby
Walter Johnson • Paul Waner • Tris Speaker • Hank Greenberg
Ed Walsh • Bob Feller • Carl Hubbell • Jimmie Foxx • Connie Mack
Mickey Cochrane • Frank Frisch • Branch Rickey • Jackie Robinson

NARRATED BY BUDDY BLATTNER

pitching staff of musical treasures too. Alphabetically, here's a five-man starting rotation.

- Catfish Hunter. "Catfish" (Joe Cocker; in *Stingray*, A & M SP-1374, 1976). Blues tribute to Catfish Hunter by Bob Dylan and Jacques Levy.
- Sandy Koufax. "Dandy Sandy" (Jimmy Durante; in *Sound of the Dodgers*, Jaybar, circa 1966).
- Phil Niekro. "Hey Niekro Polka" (Jimmy Stun; Starr 1448, 1984). Thanking Atlanta for giving the Ohio-born Polish boy to the Yankees for nothing.
- Gaylord Perry. "Ballad of Gaylord Perry" (Wong; Freedom, circa 1977).
- Warren Spahn. "Warren Spahn" (The Blackholes; Blackhole Records 0604, circa 1979).

And in the bullpen:

- Dwight Gooden. "Dr. K" (Dwight Gooden and the MCL Rap Machine; Vine St. 004, 33⅓-r.p.m., 12-inch single). A rap record.
- Mickey Lolich. "Roly Poly Mickey Lolich" (The Fans; Marquee MQ-447, 1968). Kidding him about his physique.
- Denny McLain. "Maestro of the Mound" (Bull Pen; Fleetwood, 1968). Yes, 31-win seasons are worth singing about.
- Johnny Podres. "Johnny Podres Has a Halo 'Round His Head" (A. Swift; Jubilee 45-5222, 1955). Particularly after he pitched the Dodgers to a World Series championship over the Yankees.
- Fernando Valenzuela. "Fernando" (Stanley Ross; Horn NR-10A, 1981). One

of several songs inspired by Valenzuela in his rookie year.

Of course, someone might quibble that there's not a true relief pitcher on our staff. Oddly, no one seems to have recorded such potential hits as "Please, Mr. Wilhelm, Knuckle Down" or "It's a Relief When Sutter Suits Up." And it would be stretching things to include the Beatles' "I Saw Your FACE" or Frankie Laine's "Song of the Wild GOOSE." And what's that song about "icy FINGERS up and down my spine"? Never fear. Our All-Star manager will still get the best out of the bullpen.

- Earl Weaver. "Earl of Baltimore" (Terry Cashman; Lifesong 45112, 1982). Also available as a 33⅓ laserdisc (Lifesong 8138).

And last, but not least, we even have a song about an owner:

- Charlie Finley. "Charlie-O the Mule" (Gene McKorm; Bilin B5-2200).

Of course, with Charlie-O in charge, Catfish might opt to free-agent to another label.   —BC

Big Hits at the Ballpark

Baseball music doesn't always start out as baseball music. Odds are John Denver wasn't thinking about the 1974 Baltimore Orioles when he recorded "Thank God I'm a Country Boy." And Kool and the Gang probably weren't enjoying a victory by the 1981 Oakland A's when they made "Celebration." But both tunes became team theme songs.

In fact, starting way back, a few baseball teams appropriated popular tunes as their own. Several songs became so associated with a team for a season, or with baseball in general, that they qualify as baseball music.

The first tune to make that crossover was "Tessie You Are the Only, Only, Only" (1915). It became (with special lyrics) so much the theme song of the 1915 Red Sox that Boston fans marched into World Series games singing it. In 1967 another Red Sox team, one that was not expected to play in the World Series, adopted "[To Dream] The Impossible Dream" from the musical *Man of La Mancha* as its theme song. Alas! A Series win has been impossible for the Bosox since Tessie's heyday.

Willie Stargell's constant clubhouse playing of Sister Sledge's "We Are Family" led to its becoming the 1979 World Champion Pirates' theme song. During a 1977 game between the Royals and the White Sox, Chicago organist Nancy Faust played an old 1960s song by the group Steam, "Nan Na Hey Hey Kiss Him Goodbye." For some inexplicable reason it was picked up by the crowd and rapidly became what one writer called "The 'Marseillaise' of the South Side of Chicago." Unlike other theme songs, this one has remained popular and has spread to other locations and even to other sports.

Such fan-driven theme songs have an authenticity (and popularity) unknown to the producers of those embarrassing team fight songs packaged for the tone-deaf and often accompanied by a videotape of singing ball players demonstrating why they'll never play Vegas.

On the flip side, there is one popular tune—actually an old nursery rhyme set to music—that is strictly taboo at the ballpark. After a controversial umpire decision in a 1988 South Atlantic League game at Greensboro, North Carolina, the public-address announcer was ejected from the premises by the men in blue when he broke into a crowd-rousing rendition of "Three Blind Mice." —JKS

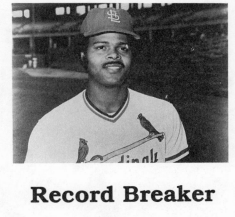

Record Breaker

Tom Seaver once said that some pitches have "trouble" written right there on the baseball and that as soon as you let the ball go, you wish you could have it right back. Apparently the same is true when it comes to ball players making record albums.

Warner Fusselle, announcer for Major League Baseball Productions, compiler of the recent anthology *Baseball's Greatest Hits*, and a baseball music collector, tells of the time he heard that Reggie Smith, while in Japan playing for the Yomiuri Giants, had recorded an album. He called Japan to get a copy.

"I heard nothing from the record company or the team," Warner recalls. "Then I get this call from Smith himself. He asks me, kind of gruffly, 'What do you want my record for?' I tell him, 'I'm a collector, and I heard you had this record, and I wanted to buy it.'

"But that wasn't good enough for Reggie. 'What are you gonna do with it?' "

Warner throws up his hands, exasperated even in the retelling.

"I said, 'Well, I thought I might listen to it if it was all right.' I thought he was going to come after me with a baseball bat."

Fusselle finally did get a copy of the record. He listened to it. And then he understood why Smith had been so protective of his work.

Says Warner: "It was awful." —NC

Sheet Music—Not for Musicians Only

Almost none of the sheet music written prior to 1906 was ever recorded. Evidently, it belonged to its own era—the kind of era the collector, the music historian, or the hardcore musician can most relate to. Still, there is baseball history here for all fans.

Sheet music was the first widely distributed baseball collectible. The value, then as now, was as much in the illustrations on the cover title page as in the music itself.

Since the sale of baseball songs and music has always been limited, publishers issued sheet music with attractive covers often in color to entice purchasers. Many of these covers now have historic value because they show how the game, its players, and its fans were portrayed in that day. Most notable are some of the earliest

pieces that had color lithograph covers: "The Base Ball Polka" (1858), "The Live Oak Polka" (1860), "Home Run Quick Step" (1861), "The Base Ball Quadrille" (1867), "Home Run Polka" (1867), and "Silver Ball March" (1869).

Most pieces of pre-1900 baseball music were instrumentals for dancing or marching and dedicated to a particular team. For example, the "Home Run Polka" (1867) was dedicated to the famous Nationals of Washington, DC, who made baseball's first extended road trip. The "Silver Ball March" celebrated the Lowells of Boston, who usually won the silver ball trophy in New England in the 1860s, and the "Una Schottische" did the same thing for the Una ball club of the Boston area in the 1870s. The "Union Base Ball Club March"

(1867) commemorated the champions of Missouri, and "The Red Stocking Polka" (1869) recognized the first professional team, formed in Cincinnati.

"The Bat and Ball" and "Baseball Fever" (1867) were the first baseball songs with written words, and the former was the first to mention baseball as the national game. Other songs extolling the virtues of baseball include: "Hurrah for the National Game" (1868), "Baseball Song" (1874), and "Base Ball" (1883). "Slide Kelly Slide" (1889), "Clancy Wasn't in It" (1890), and "Husky Hans" (1904) were the first songs to refer to players—Mike "King" Kelly, Buck Ewing, and Honus Wagner, respectively.

"Who Would Doubt That I'm a Man?" (1895), pictured a woman dressed in a

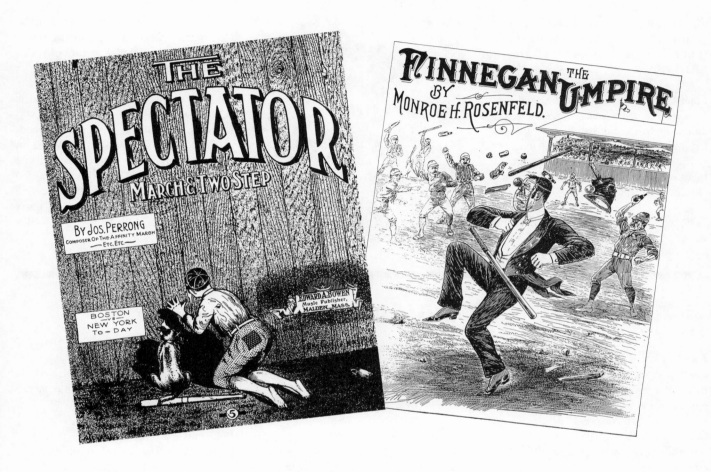

baseball uniform on the cover, and "The Umpire Is a Most Unhappy Man" (1905) was the first song to recognize the plight of the men in blue. Spectators were first emphasized in "The Base Ball Fan" (1892). Finally, songs referring to or using the dialect of ethnic groups were fairly common before the First World War. "Brother Noah Gave Out Checks for Rain" (1907) had a color illustration of blacks playing baseball. "It's Great at a Baseball Game" (1906) was geared toward a German audience, "The Day I Played Baseball" (1878) an Irish one, and "Jake! Jake! The Yiddishe Ball Player" (1913) the Jewish population.

The period 1905–1920, but especially 1907–1914, was the "Golden Era" of baseball sheet music. About 80 pieces were published, more than equaling everything up to that time. While "Take Me Out to the Ball Game" was the only real hit, it was during this span of years that such well-known figures in the music business as Harry von Tilzer, Irving Berlin, Noel Coward, and George M. Cohan tried their hands at baseball songs and failed to produce one home run among them. Speaking of losers, it was also during this period that Harry Frazee, owner of the Boston Red Sox, decided to sell Babe Ruth to the New York Yankees in order to finance his musical comedies, including *No, No, Nanette.*

Unlikely participants in the musical sweepstakes included several baseball figures. In 1908 two-thirds of the Chicago Cubs' famous double-play combination, Joe Tinker and Johnny Evers, found out what happens when you don't leave things to "Chance." Their song "Between You and Me" was a double dud. Sportswriter Ring Lardner and Chicago White Sox pitcher Guy "Doc" White combined to produce "Little Puff of Smoke, Good Night" (1910), and "Gee It's a Wonderful Game" (1911). Detroit third baseman George Moriarty was responsible for the words to "I Can't Miss That Ball Game" (1911) and "Remember Me to My Old Gal" (1912). The latter's only relationship to baseball was the sheet music cover, which featured pictures of pitchers Cy Morgan, Chief Bender, and Jack Coombs, heroes of the 1911 World Series. (Using baseball to boost sales was a common publisher's gimmick.) Rube Marquard got into the act when he participated in a vaudeville skit

I LOVE MICKEY

Words and Music by
TERESA BREWER · RUTH ROBERTS · BILL KATZ   Price 50c

WILLOW MUSIC CORP.   GRAND MUSIC CORP. 1619 Broadway, N.Y.

with actress Blossom Seeley, whom he later married. One of the results was a tune (and a dance step) called "The Marquard Glide" (1912).

After 1920, the quality, quantity, and importance of baseball sheet music diminished significantly and progressively. Undoubtedly this was due to the ever increasing influence of the recording industry. With few exceptions, songs worthy of comment were recorded, and thus are treated elsewhere in this chapter.

There are, however, three pieces of post-1920s baseball sheet music worth calling attention to, for their historical value.

"Bucky Boy Hit of Uncle Sam's Follies" (1925) has a particularly distinctive cover. In addition to the center picture of Washington player/manager Bucky Harris, a girls' baseball team is shown across the bottom, and women with bats form the side panels. "Baseball Blues" (1931) was reportedly sung before and after the broadcast of games over radio station WCFL in Chicago. In 1935 Mrs. Lou Gehrig became another in the long line of women who have been involved in baseball music. She collaborated with Fred Fisher on "I Can't Get to First Base with You."   —JKS

So You Wanna Write a Fight Song?

As you know, your ball club desperately needs a fight song. Only that last bit of motivation is required to ensure a pennant. So what are you waiting for? Get out your pencil (or crayon) and inspire 'em. Every music-loving player and fan will hereafter speak your name with reverence.

Okay, so you can't write music. Never fear! Even if you don't know the difference between a G-clef and a G-string, you can always steal the tune from some existing ditty. And think of the fun you'll have waiting for that nasty letter from ASCAP's lawyers!

The lyric's the thing. "Ol' Man River" would just be *duh-duh-da-da* without its lyric. It's your fighting words that'll spark your team from fourth place to first.

A few helpful hints:

Think positive! Your team's fans never boo—or have cause to.

Think '27 Yankees! Maybe your team couldn't hit its weight after a summer on Oprah's diet. Nevertheless, their lethal bats bring fear and trembling to opponents.

Think arrogant! All your opponents are sniveling cowards anyway. That's not a

drum in your rhythm section, it's the other team's knees knocking together when they're playing agin' your guys.

Think rhyme! All right, this is a little tricky. If you're not careful, you'll show some originality—sure death for a fight song. Fortunately, we here provide some *do* and *don't* phrases to rhyme with common baseball terms.

old ball game
DO: "glad you came" or "Hall of Fame"
DON'T: "Steinbrenner's to blame"

three strikes, you're out
DO: "cheer and shout" or "circuit clout"
DON'T: "Early Wynn's gout"

crack out a single
DO: "sets us a-tingle"
DON'T: "ol' Casey Stingle"

hit for a double
DO: "foes are in trouble"
DON'T: "pitcher's beard stubble"

bang out a triple
DO: use "three-base hit," which rhymes

with lots of stuff
DON'T: try to rhyme "triple" with obscure references to Jim Ripple or Pete Gray

over the fence
DO: "fans are tense"
DON'T: "ball flew hence" (too literary)

double play
DO: "happy day," "make 'em pay," "hooray," or "say hey"
DON'T: "make us gay" (subject to misinterpretation)

If you really get stuck, you can always save the day by adding "OH" onto the end of your rhyming words, as in "wild pitch-OH" rhymes with "Incaviglia-OH" or "hit for the cycle-OH." This goes especially well with a calypso beat, and it even allows you to refer to your favorite player's new contract, as in "two-comma-oh-oh-oh-comma-oh-oh-OH."

Just remember, your team needs your word power more than a new power hitter-OH. Go, team, go!

Think first place! (Rhymes with pennant race.)   —BC

The Strange Case of "Take Me Out to the Ball Game"

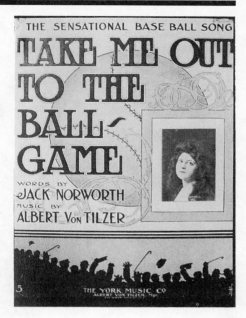

The screwiest thing that ever happened to baseball music is "Take Me Out to the Ball Game."

For starters, it's a song written by two men who had never seen a major league game nor had any interest in the sport. Yet it's become the national pastime's national anthem. That's about as likely as Johann Sebastian Bach penning "Did Your Mother Come from Ireland?"

"Take Me Out to the Ball Game" (1908) was the work of Jack Norworth and Albert von Tilzer, two successful music professionals. Von Tilzer was the brother of the reigning kingpin of Tin Pan Alley, Harry von Tilzer. Norworth would eventually write some 2,500 other songs, the next-best-remembered being "Shine On, Harvest Moon."

Norworth wrote the lyrics for the song during a half-hour New York City subway ride, getting the idea from an advertisement suggesting customers take in a baseball game at the Polo Grounds. Ride the subway today and the only lyric you can think of is "Help!"

After von Tilzer composed the music, Norworth introduced the song in his act at the Amphion Theater in Brooklyn. The audience reacted with all the enthusiasm usually accorded the reading of the last meeting's minutes, and Norworth figured he'd bombed. The song went into his trunk but came out three months later, when he was booked as the ninth act on a big vaudeville bill at the famed Hammerstein's Victoria Theater. To his surprise several performers before him, including acrobats, had incorporated "Take Me Out to the Ball Game" into their acts.

A hit was born.

Just why the song has enjoyed such lasting popularity is harder to explain than why the sky is blue. "Stardust" it ain't. Artistically there were better baseball songs before and after it. Loads! The verses are less than memorable and today are all but forgotten. Probably less than one half of one percent of all baseball fans even know there ARE verses. They recount the story of Katie Casey, a girl crazy over baseball. When her beau asks her out to a show, she declines by saying (the chorus), "Take me out to the ball game."

It is only the chorus that we remember; not one fan in a stadiumful can sing you the whole song. (In case you want to be that one fan, the full verse is offered below.) Even here, critics have called the words "crude" rather than clever and implying a curious "'Alice in Wonderland' logic." But the words, if but "pop stuff," are singable, and the waltz music swings, if waltz music can be said to swing.

Katie Casey was baseball mad,
Had the fever and had it bad;
Just to root for the hometown crew,
Ev'ry sou, Katie blew.
On a Saturday, her young beau,
Called to see if she'd like to go,
To see a show but Miss Kate said, "No,
I'll tell you what you can do":
Take me out to the ball game,
Take me out to the crowd,
Buy me some peanuts and cracker jack,
I don't care if I never get back,
Let me root, root, root, for the home team,
If they don't win it's a shame.
For it's one, two, three strikes, you're out,
At the old ball game.

Certainly the song benefited from the torrid three-way National League pennant race of 1908, finally won by Chicago over New York and Pittsburgh by one game. And the use of film slides illustrating the song and sheet music in nickelodeons throughout the country contributed to its initial success. But neither reason accounts for the lasting popularity of "Take Me Out to the Ball Game," since four other baseball songs were published the same year with the same advantages, including a quite similar and clever ditty, "Take Your Girl to a Ball Game," by George M. Cohan and others.

For whatever reasons, Norworth and von Tilzer's creation became an American folk classic; only "The Star Spangled Banner" and "Happy Birthday" have been sung more often in the United States.

There have been many recordings of "Take Me Out to the Ball Game"—some good, some not so good, some you wouldn't wish on a tax collector. I consider the most memorable renditions to be:

- Edward Meeker (Edison Cylinder 10139, 1908).
- Frank Luther, Zora Layman, Century Quartet (Decca Album A-120-3210, 1939).
- Tony Martin (RCA 20-4216, 1951).
- Harry Caray (Churchill LR 7714, 1978).
- Steve Goodman (Red Pajamas 1001, 1981).   —JKS

That Other Tune
They Play at the Ballpark

Why is it that we play "The Star-Spangled Banner" before every baseball game? As Ken Smith pointed out in the old *New York Daily Mirror*, "Macy's and Gimbels don't play 'The Star-Spangled Banner' when they open their doors every morning."

The National Baseball Library in Cooperstown can't document the earliest playing of "The Star-Spangled Banner" at a ball game, but chances are it was played irregularly at best in the early years of baseball. *Any* music was heard irregularly—there was no recorded music, and bands were available only on special occasions like the Fourth of July or Opening Day. Even on those days, there's a better-than-even chance they weren't playing

Francis Scott Key's opus; other patriotic tunes like "Columbia, the Gem of the Ocean" were more popular.

"The Star-Spangled Banner" didn't officially become our national anthem until March 3, 1931, when President Herbert Hoover signed Public Law 823. But President Woodrow Wilson proclaimed as much in 1916. And our first documentation of the playing of the anthem at a baseball game comes from *The Sporting News*, which reported that "The Star-Spangled Banner" was played by bands hired to perform on Opening Day as early as 1917, and that it was played at the World Series that year as well. But, though recorded music had made its debut, public address systems were still a thing of the future. Teams

weren't about to hire bands to play at every game.

However, by the end of the 1930s the man with a megaphone gave way to the man with a microphone. The National Baseball Library's best guess is that the practice of playing the National Anthem before every game began shortly thereafter, probably as a patriotic salute with the start of World War II. By the end of the war, the playing of the anthem had become a common practice, and it stuck.

Not that the custom hasn't been without controversy. Jose Feliciano's folk/blues rendition before the fifth game of the 1968 World Series between St. Louis and Detroit got the purists riled up. (Marvin Gaye did the same for the NBA at its 1983 All-Star Game, with a hand-clapping soul interpretation.)

In 1972, during the Vietnam era, the Kansas City Royals announced the National Anthem would not be played except on Sundays and special occasions, because, as owner Ewing Kaufman said, so many people were not showing the proper respect when the anthem was played. One hundred twenty-four indignant letters and seventy-five emotional phone calls later, the anthem was restored.

The music critics were back following the '85 Series (St. Louis–Kansas City). After Reba McIntyre, Melba Moore, Glen Campbell, the Oak Ridge Boys, Jennifer Holliday, Lou Rawls, and the Gatlin Brothers all took their turn at the anthem, a Missouri legislator tried to introduce a law that would require anthem singers to stick to the traditional version or not sing it at all. (It wasn't clear whose style he objected to.)

Why do we play "The Star-Spangled Banner" before ball games? Patriotism, yes. Perhaps it also has something to do with the fact that before Key added the words, the tune of "The Star-Spangled Banner" was that of an old British drinking song. What could be more natural than for all to rise, sing the anthem, have a beer, and, "Play Ball!"   —NC

Critic's Choice: The Early Years

Take me (*scratch*) to the ball (*scratch, scratch*) . . ."

The appeal of baseball recordings from the era of cylinders and 78-r.p.m. ten-inch discs is more to the brain than to the ear. But if you have the opportunity to listen to the selections mentioned below, they'll prove rewarding both as historical artifacts of baseball music and for what they reveal about the culture and society of those days. Cylinders and 78s are not all dry history though; particularly in the later years, you'll find a couple of finger-popping tunes as well. This period lasted from 1906 until the early 1950s and the introduction of the 45-r.p.m. seven-inch single and the 33⅓-r.p.m. twelve-inch long-playing record.

Although there was a wax recording of "Slide Kelly Slide" as early as 1893, it was not widely distributed, and some consider the first disc about baseball to be "Jimmy and Maggie at a Baseball Game," which was recorded on cylinder in 1906. "Take Me Out to the Ball Game" (1908), eventually became the chartbuster of this era, but several other early discs are also worth noting.

"Brother Noah Gave Out Checks for Rain" (1907) is important for several reasons. First, it acknowledges blacks' interest in baseball at this early date, albeit not in a very flattering manner. Second, it indicates how early baseball terminology (rain checks) had begun to be part of our popular language. Third, it is an example of a form of music, quite acceptable to the white population for sixty years after the Civil War, that poked fun at blacks through the use of stereotyped dialect on the recordings and caricatures on the sheet music which portrayed blacks as poor, stupid, and lazy. Despite the negative reactions this type of song may provoke

almost eighty years later, one stanza is still entertaining. A black church deacon attempts to justify baseball by reference to the scriptures.

Eve stole first and Adam second;
St. Peter umpired the game.
Rebecca went to the well with a pitcher,
while Ruth in the field won fame.
Goliath was struck out by David;
a base hit made on Abel by Cain.
The Prodigal Son made one home run;
Brother Noah gave out checks for rain!.

"Brother Noah" was not the only song of the day that referred to an ethnic group. On the surface, the 1911 tune "They're All Good American Names" would not seem to have anything to do with baseball. Yet the chorus acknowledges the game's indebtedness to those of Irish descent by reciting the names of players and managers:

Jennings and McGann, Doyle, and
    Callahan.
Hanlon, Scanlon, Kirk, and Donlin,
Devlin, Keeler, Walsh, and Conlin.
Joe McGinnity, Shea, and Finnerty,
Farrell, Carroll, Darrell, and McAmes
Connie Mack and John McGraw
all together shout hurrah!
They're all good American names.

A third song, now almost entirely forgotten, "Bobby the Bomber" (1918), is of historical interest. It tells the story of Bobby, a baseball pitcher who joins the Army and tosses bombs at America's foes as accurately as he hurled strikes across the plate. It is one of the few songs that relates baseball to events taking place outside the game.

Another tune in this genre is "Eleven

More Months and Ten More Days," released in 1929. One stanza, supposedly sung by a prison inmate, goes:

Now we play once a week
And you should see the score
Ev'ry player steals a base—
There's lots of folks would like to come
And see us when we play
But they've built a wall around the place
To keep the crowds away!

The bulk of the baseball music of the 78 era celebrated the game itself ("The National Game March," "Baseball, Baseball," "Baseball Polka"), saluted teams ("The Cubs on Parade March," "Follow the Dodgers," "Battling Boston Braves," "Fightin' Phils"), and glorified the personalities ("Grand Old Man of Baseball" [Connie Mack], "Did You See Jackie Robinson Hit That Ball?" "Doby at the Bat").

Only two baseball songs of the entire era had any real popularity, but both were, in my opinion, among the top baseball songs of all time.

The first dates from 1941 and calls attention to Joe DiMaggio's fifty-six-game hitting streak, "Joltin' Joe DiMaggio." Couched in the big-band style of Les Brown, with a swinging vocal from fourteen-year-old Betty Bonney, it is as enjoyable today as it was almost fifty years ago.

The second, "Say Hey," with Willie Mays clowning with the Treniers, was recorded in 1954 and bridges the gap from the 78 era to that of 45s and also from Tin Pan Alley to rock and roll. I can't quite put my finger on why, but the tune sticks with you; perhaps it is because of the "Say Hey."

Both songs can be hunted down in the 78 pile of an old record store, but they're also available on the album *Baseball's Greatest Hits.* These old-timers are music to this old-timer's ears.   —JKS

Critic's Choice: The Modern Era

The modern era of baseball music was ushered in by the development of the 45-r.p.m., seven-inch single—a format ideally suited to the production of low cost, low demand, limited-distribution recordings. Bang! Musicians of all types began mixing a little of their favorite sport in with their art, making musical variety the order of the day.

Baseball music today—at least the kind to be listened to as music rather than as a partisan ritual—is less likely to be music aimed directly at a baseball audience than music that uses baseball as a theme in works written or performed for audiences with particular musical tastes.

Jazz is represented by such instrumentals as Count Basie and Oscar Peterson's "Home Run," André Previn and Russ Freeman's album *Double Play*, and Art Lande's "Round Tripper."

"Brown-Eyed Handsome Man" is a rhythm-and-blues tune as delivered by both Chuck Berry and Jerry Jaye.

Shorty Warren and his Western Rangers put "The Mighty Mickey Mantle" in a country-western motif.

John Fogerty's "Centerfield" and Warren Zevon's "Bill Lee" are straight rock songs.

Frank Sinatra's superb ballad "There Used to Be a Ball Park" is in the best tradition of Tin Pan Alley.

Classical baseball music? Charles Ives' solo piano piece "Some Southpaw Pitching" is the only classical composition with a baseball title ever recorded (small matter that it is close to unplayable). The only baseball opera, and it has yet to be recorded, is William Schuman's *Casey at the Bat* (1954), which is revived regularly by the Glimmerglass Opera Company of (where else?) Cooperstown, New York.

The modern era is loaded with songs celebrating the game of baseball and its teams and players, but an important development has been the introduction of songs of personal nostalgia about baseball. Sinatra reminisces about the demise of Ebbets Field in "There Used to Be a Ball Park," but with a little imagination it could be Forbes Field, Crosley Field, the Polo Grounds, or any other late and lamented ballpark.

The songs by Fogerty and Bruce Springsteen recall baseball in their teenage days. In Springsteen's "Glory Days," it is meeting an old friend who used to be a great pitcher. In his song, probably autobiographical, Fogerty pleads with a coach to put him in "Centerfield." In "My Favorite Spring," Tom Paxton is a one-time big league pitching prospect who hurt his arm, but can still reflect fondly on his past and now sees that same promise in his young son. In "Right Field," sung by Peter, Paul, and Mary, a boy laments that he is not a good player and is forced to play right field because that's where the least action is expected.

Dave Frishberg in "Van Lingle Mungo" recalls his youth in the Minnesota Twin Cities area by simply reciting the names of former major league players. More recently, Terry Cashman's "Talkin' Baseball" does the same thing for each of the major league franchises except Seattle. His "Willie, Mickey, and the Duke" is a classic.

And, there is another tune that must be mentioned. "A Dying Cub Fan's Last Request" is a spoof on the inept play of the Cubs by Steve Goodman, who was in fact dying from leukemia at the time of the recording—entertaining, but also moving.

For me these songs represent the best baseball music of the modern era. They transcend a time-space framework and allow listeners to conjure up their own trail of memories.

A second development, though far less stirring, is the production of team songs for promotional purposes: "Oriole Magic," "Go Go Phillies," "Let's Go Go White Sox," "Hang On Blue Jays," "Go Cubs Go." They are distributed on a local or at best regional basis, usually for a (thank God!) short period of time. Their musical value is low—on a par with when the plumber dropped his tool box down the back stairs—and for obvious reasons, they receive little attention from anyone in the baseball community who doesn't have a rooting interest in that team. How many fans in Los Angeles wake up singing Montreal's "Les Bus Squad?"

A third theme found in the modern era songs is a tendency to focus on specific events. This occurs as early as Phil Foster's 1956 "Let's Keep the Dodgers in Brooklyn." Other songs commemorate pitcher Denny McLain's thirty-one victories in 1968 ("Maestro on the Mound"), George Brett's pine-tar incident ("Pine Tar Wars") and Pete Rose's quest for 4,000 hits ("Pete's Hit Record").

Three events evoked not one, but a series of songs: the sudden and tragic death of Roberto Clemente in December 1972; Henry Aaron's 715th home run, breaking Babe Ruth's record; and, perhaps the most interesting, the rapid rise of Fernando Valenzuela to hero status in the early 1980s.

My choices for the best of the lot are: Jim Owen's "Roberto's Gone," Bill Slaybeck's "Move Over Babe (Here Comes Henry)," and F. Sternwheeler's "Fernando de Sonora."

Finally, special mention must be made of the first baseball compact disc, *Baseball's Greatest Hits*, which was issued on the Rhino label in April 1989. It includes seventeen baseball songs from the modern era plus five other cuts of interest to baseball fans. There is also a shorter version on LP. It is a gem and a must for all baseball fans. We owe a debt to all those responsible for producing it, including the compiler, Warner Fusselle.

Discography

- *Baseball's Greatest Hits* (Various Artists; Rhino CD R2 70710, 1989). This album contains 18 cuts, 13 of which are baseball tunes (the rest are comedy and recorded history). The LP version includes "Take Me Out to the Ball Game," Doc and Merle Watson; "Joltin' Joe DiMaggio," Les Brown and Betty Bonney; "Say Hey (The Willie Mays Song)," The Treniers; "Van Lingle Mungo," Dave Frishberg; "D-O-D-G-E-R-S Songs (Oh, Really? No, O'Malley)," Danny Kaye; "Move Over Babe (Here Comes Henry)," Bill Slayback; "Take Me Out to the Ball Game," Bruce Springstone; "Love Is Like a Baseball Game," The Intruders; "Willie, Mickey, and the Duke," Terry Cashman; "A Dying Cub Fan's Last Request," Steve Goodman; "Baseball Dreams," The Naturals With Mel Allen; and "Baseball Card Lover," Rockin' Ritchie Ray.

  The compact disc includes these additional numbers: "Did You Ever See Jackie Robinson Hit That Ball?" Count Basie and Taps Miller; "The Land of Wrigley," Stormy Weather; "The Ball Game," Sister Wynona Carr; and "We Are the Champions," Big Blue Wrecking Crew.
- "Bill Lee." Warren Zevon in *Bad Luck Streak in Dancing School*, Asylum 5E509, 1978.

- "Brown-Eyed Handsome Man." Chuck Berry, Chess 1635, 1958. Jerry Jaye, Hi-2139, 1968.
- "Centerfield." John Fogerty in *Centerfield*, Warner Bros. 1- 25203, 1985.
- *Double Play*. Andre Previn and Russ Freeman, Contemporary 57001, 1957.
- "Dying Cub Fan's Last Request, A." Steve Goodman on *Affordable Act*, Red Pajamas RPJ-002, 1981.
- "Fernando de Sonora." F. Sternwheeler, Mystic Sound MS-45-505, 1981.
- "Glory Days." Bruce Springsteen on *Born in the U.S.A.*, Columbia QC-38653, 1984.
- "Go Cubs Go." Steve Goodman with the Chicago Cubs Chorus, WGN 784, 1984.
- "Go Go Phillies." The Umpires, Jacylyn 101, circa 1965.
- "Hang On Blue Jays." 1983 (cassette tape released by radio station CHFI, Toronto, Canada).
- "Home Run." Count Basie and Oscar Peterson on *Satch and Josh Again*, Pablo 2210-802, 1977.
- "Les Bus Squad." Tommy Hutton, Quality Records Q238IX, 1980.
- "Let's Go Go White Sox." Captain Stubby and the Buccaneers, Drum Boy 121, circa 1959.
- "Let's Keep the Dodgers in Brooklyn." Phil Foster, Coral 9-61840, circa 1957.
- "Maestro on the Mound." Bull Pen. Fleetwood, 1968.
- "Mighty Mickey Mantle, The." Shorty Warren and His Western Rangers, Gametime Records 45-102.
- "Move Over Babe (Here Comes Henry)." Bill Slayback, Karen 714, 1973.
- "My Favorite Spring." Tom Paxton in *Up and Up*, Mountain Railroad MR-52792, 1979.
- "Oriole Magic." Perfect Pitch 003001YA, 1980.
- "Pete's Hit Record." Gale Watson, Genius, 1985.
- "Pine Tar Wars." C. W. McCall, AFR 001839, 1984.

Baseball's Greatest Hits (Rhino Records)

Not Music, but an Incredible Simulation

For high schools, colleges, and even minor league teams that can't afford to torture their fans with a real organist, Bill Heald believes he's developed the next best thing: the organist in a can. Well, a cassette actually, and four of them to be exact. All you need is an auto-reverse dual-cassette player, a public-address system, and Heald's *Baseball Blips* tapes, and you can rouse a crowd with a chorus of "Take Me Out to the Ball Game," whip them into a frenzy of trumpeted "Charges," or sedate them with a ten-minute organ solo during a rain delay.

Heald is a keyboard player and baseball fan who wanted to combine his two loves. Since he opened shop in '87, he's found plenty of takers across the country, all the way up to the Double-A Scranton/Wilkes-Barre Barons.

Heald does his work with a keyboard synthesizer, conjuring up trumpet and organ sounds to be played between pitches and after great plays; he has longer musical effects for between innings, some popular songs, and, of course, the national anthems of the U.S. and Canada (in two keys).

The starter set costs about $40. For more information you can reach Heald at Stanley Sound Productions, 1100 Cleveland Street, Suite 900, Clearwater, FL 34615; (813) 442-4971.   —JKS

- "Right Field." Peter, Paul, and Mary in *No Easy Walk to Freedom*, Gold Castle 171001-1, 1986.
- "Roberto's Gone." Jim Owen, Ace of Hearts 0476, 1973.
- "Round Tripper." Art Lande in *Hardball!*, The Great American Music Hall GAMH-2702, 1987.
- "Some Southpaw Pitching" (Charles Ives). James Sykes on *Ives' Piano Solos*, Folkways 3348, circa 1955; Alan Mandel in *Complete Piano Works of Ives*, Desto 6458/61, 1968.
- "Talkin' Baseball." Terry Cashman on *Talkin' Baseball—American League*, Lifesong 8136, and *Talkin' Baseball—National League*, Lifesong 8137, 1982.
- "There Used to Be a Ball Park." Frank Sinatra in *Ol' Blue Eyes Is Back*, Reprise FS-2155, 1973.
- "Van Lingle Mungo." Dave Frishberg in *The Dave Frishberg Song Book, Vol. 1*, Omnisound N-1040, 1981.

Where to Find Them

You really have to want it badly to be a successful collector of baseball music, particularly if you're after a pre-LP song.

Baseball enthusiasts haven't kept track and catalogued baseball songs. The music industry doesn't use baseball as a category, nor do librarians. Some baseball songs were recorded privately and never copyrighted. Others were made for only local or regional distribution and escaped national attention—for example, songs about semipro or minor league players or teams. Many of the 45-r.p.m. recordings about baseball were produced by small independent labels whose lifespan was short and cataloging next to nonexistent. Finally, even major record labels released 45-r.p.m. recordings without including information on the performers and release dates.

Don't lose hope. Below are some people, places, and ideas which should prove useful in getting further information on baseball recordings, on purchasing the discs themselves, or on possibilities for taping.

- The Library of Congress, Washington, D.C. 20540, is the copyright deposit library for the United States and therefore the largest repository of sound recordings—over 1,600,000. The holdings, however, are not even separated by musical genre, let alone broken down by category such as baseball. Therefore, it is wise to know what you want by title, artist, and year of issue. It is a site for serious research, not browsing.
- Berklee College of Music, 150 Massachusetts Avenue, Boston, MA 02125. The library holds a large collection of jazz, rock, and pop recordings.
- Popular Culture Library and Audio Center, Bowling Green State University, Bowling Green, OH 43402. This library is devoted entirely to popular music and contains 300,000 recordings, including 800 cylinders. The personnel are particularly knowledgeable and helpful to those with needs concerning popular music.
- The Music Information Center, Chicago Public Library, 78 E. Washington Street, Chicago, IL 60602. The library contains a special Recorded Sound Collection of Popular Music and Culture.
- National Baseball Library, P.O. Box 590, Cooperstown, NY 13326. The library does own baseball recordings, but as of this writing they have not been catalogued. It may be worth browsing to discover what is there.
- The New York Public Library's Music Division and Museum of the Performing Arts at Lincoln Center, 111 Amsterdam Avenue, New York, NY 10023, has a vast collection of pop music recordings. But again, this is another library which is

difficult to use if you don't know exactly what you are searching for.

There's never been a great demand for retailers to "think baseball," so you won't find any record stores (new or used) that separate baseball recordings into a special stack. My suggestion is to haunt every possible place used records appear, from record dealers to flea markets, from thrift shops to liquidation sales. Another way is to pick up a copy of *The Record Collector's International Directory* by Gary S. Felton (Crown Publishers, Inc., One Park Avenue, New York, N.Y. 10016; $8.95), which lists over 1,000 dealers and stores carrying rare and discontinued records. Felton notes which dealers are willing to run searches for desired titles or to notify you if the title comes in.

Then there are the following nice people, who are knowledgeable about baseball recordings, have collections, and are willing to share information:

- Mike Brown, Brown, Koff, and Fried, Inc., 14 West 23rd Street, New York, NY 10010.
- Richard Miller, 200 Avenue of the Americas, New York, NY 10013.
- Warner Fusselle, c/o Major League Baseball Productions, 1212 Avenue of The Americas, New York, NY 10036. —JKS

The Family of Baseball, as interepreted by Sister Sledge and the Pittsburgh Pops, Willie Stargell.

CHAPTER 2

Lights, Turf, Tarp

Football *Stadium*—movements in precise lockstep, masses of faceless warriors, tier upon tier of cloned onlookers, inhuman, cold, sterile.

Basketball *Arena*—conflict, heated gladiators, bellicose rabble, sweaty, messy, smoky, humid.

Ah, but baseball *Park!*

Frolicking competition, gamboling sportsmen, cheerful gathering, clean air, balmy breeze, green grass—joy!

More than with any other sport, the baseball field is a part of the game. In his book *Green Cathedrals*, Philip J. Lowry describes a ballpark as "a sanctuary for the spirit, a haven where the ghosts of Babe Ruth, Josh Gibson, Ty Cobb, Satchel Paige and so many other greats continue to roam among their modern-day counterparts." That's as true for the adult remembering Ted Williams from the grandstand of Fenway Park as it is for the kid invoking Jose Canseco on a sandlot in Oakland.

To love baseball is to love watching the present chase the past. Every time Canseco tags one for the stratosphere, he's inching one step closer to Mays, Ruth, and Aaron. We can sit back and compare the accomplishments of today's stars to those of their predecessors because each is playing under the same set of rules. The length between the basepaths, the dimensions of the ball, the distance from pitcher to batter, the circumference of the bat are the same now as they were in Ruth's day.

Only the ballparks have changed, and the effects of those changes are subtle and the subject of much debate. Once, every site had its own unique stamp. Crosley Field had its left field hill. The Polo Grounds had the cavernous center field

The Stadium

Even the dirt has to come from somewhere, not to mention the seating, the scoreboard, the backstop, and . . .

where Willie Mays would later work his magic. Griffith Stadium in Washington had that peculiar rectangular shape. Ballparks were compact, intimate hosts made only for baseball. They breathed open air and wore real grass.

But most of the structures of that era were razed in the name of progress long ago. There are only four parks left where Ruth hit home runs. Baseball is inching ever closer to the day when statistics will be its only link to the past.

A funny thing happened on the way to

expansion in the 1960s. Baseball lost its intimacy. The leagues got bigger, and for some reason so did the ballparks. Progress demanded that places such as the Polo Grounds, Ebbets Field, and Crosley Field, parks with obvious engineering flaws, bad sight lines, and lots of character, be replaced by the sterile, cookie-cutter forms of Atlanta–Fulton County Stadium, Three Rivers Stadium, and Riverfront Stadium.

The multiuse facility may have been municipal pragmatism at its best. But it was baseball at its worst. The resulting architectural mutant was neither a baseball park nor a football stadium. It was a rectangular peg trying to fit both round and square holes. Oh, but the sight lines were perfect. There were none of those old-fashioned columns to obstruct your view. Only distance.

"In a matter of six or seven years, virtually the entire baseball universe was remade into something sterile and nondescript," observes John Pastier, a contributing editor to *Architecture Magazine* and a leading designer of the stadiums of the 1990s, including Baltimore's everything-old-is-new-again park in progress. "The trend was to build them out in the suburbs, where parking was plentiful and crime was low. But they didn't realize what they were losing: baseball's character."

Aging treasures like Fenway, Comiskey, Wrigley Field, and Tiger Stadium are national landmarks. These are baseball parks. They were built into cities, not around them. They exude character, not sterility. Walk into a ballpark and know that Ruth played there! That's something special only baseball can offer, that unique feeling that the game you're watching is part of a bigger picture. —KD

The Inside on the Insides

There's a difference between buying groceries for a family of four and going food shopping for the United States Army. Assembled below are our listings of top companies providing the goods and services it takes to build and maintain ballparks, and all their vital stats. Included are those who outfit the major leagues and those who specialize in slightly smaller jobs.

Lighting a major league ballpark can cost over $2 million. Maybe you'll never have to buy enough bulbs to light up Comiskey Park. But won't you feel better about paying your own light bill knowing theirs comes to about $50,000 a month?

Lighting

The process of lighting a ballpark has evolved from haphazard guesswork to computer-aided specificity. What used to take engineers months of work over a hot sliderule, computers now do better in a twinkling. Lighting designers feed in a gaggle of numbers defining the dimensions of the park, the environment surrounding it, and the desired effect. Out pop how many Mazdas, where they're situated, and where they're aimed.

A good thing too. The demands of television necessitate perfect lighting at major league parks. But even at the high school level, a poorly aimed lamp can blind a pitcher working from the stretch or a batter swinging for the fence.

HUBBELL LIGHTING
2000 Electric Way
Christiansburg, VA
(703) 382-6111
Contact: George Brammer, lighting specialist

Hubbell has installed plenty of bright lights in the big-city ballparks. But for every major league job, the firm lights a dozen high school, college, or minor league parks. Some of its bigger jobs, such as Riverfront Stadium, Dodger Stadium, and Anaheim Stadium, involved installing up to 1,000 metal halide fixtures of 1,500 watts each and carried price tags in excess of $1 million. Average life for each light: 3,000 hours. Designing and lighting a high school or college field can cost as little as $25,000. The company usually spends about four weeks creating a customized lighting design.

GENERAL ELECTRIC LIGHTING SYSTEMS
3010 Spartanburg Highway
Hendersonville, NC 28793
(704) 693-2198
Contact: Fred Dickey, lighting engineer

General Electric, the company which boasts proudly in television commercials about ushering in the era of night baseball half a century ago, seemed to come full circle by lighting Wrigley Field in 1988. "They came to us with a special request: no lights in the outfield," says GE lighting engineer Fred Dickey. "So we worked around that and positioned them at different angles."

GE's lighting systems division also participated in the recent relightings of the Hubert H. Humphrey Metrodome and Veterans Stadium, two projects that offered the most challenging problem in lighting design: serving the two-headed monster of the multipurpose stadium. Light configuration must be such that fixtures are aimed to be effective for both football and baseball, no easy trick. This drives the price from the $1 million range to as high as $1.5 million. Such stadiums take 600 to 900 1,500-watt fixtures, each in excess of 550 volts. Smaller, less costly, and less demanding fields are a growing part of GE's business, however.

Scoreboards

The first scoreboards were little more than bulletin boards with tacked-on numbers. Those early placard models gave way to solenoid relays, which gave way to today's microprocessors with no moving parts. But at the major league level, the word "scoreboard" has grown passé. Most big league teams, and a growing number of minor league and college teams, now have "matrix boards" which show color replays, flash messages, and, almost as an afterthought, tell the score.

MITSUBISHI AMERICA
5757 Plaza Drive
Cypress, CA 90630-0007
(714) 220-2500
Contact: John Cunningham, national sales manager

Mitsubishi unveiled its Diamond Vision, the first large screen video display, at the 1980 All-Star Game in Dodger Stadium. Sixteen major league parks, including Shea Stadium, Atlanta–Fulton County Stadium, and Jack Murphy Stadium, now have their own. Each board is custom-made, and an average 24-foot-by-32-foot structure costs about $3 million installed. The biggest? The Astrodome's, 26 feet by 35 feet.

Mitsubishi warrantees each unit for one year. The life of the average lighting board is 20,000 hours. Depending on the size of the unit and the range of its applications, it can take from two to nine people to operate it during a game. Alas, a number of specialized uses have sprung up in recent years, including the unbelievably popular Dot Races game at Arlington Stadium.

SONY CORP.
Sony Drive
Park Ridge, NJ 07656
(201) 930-1000
Contact: Steve Burk, promotion mgr.

Sony Corp. entered the color matrix board market in 1985. The JumboTron installed in Anaheim Stadium cost about $5.5 million, with annual maintenance charges of about $130,000.

GENERAL INDICATOR CORP.
All-American Scoreboards Div.
413 South Main Street
Pardeeville, WI 53954
(800) 356-8146
Contact: Velda Allen, sales manager

The traditional scoreboard lives on for the lower end of the marketplace. All-American Scoreboards is a leading supplier for high school, college, and minor league ballparks unable to spend millions.

Remember when all the games at Wrigley Field (opposite) were played under the sun and scoreboards told only the score?

Much of the company's business is done directly with soft-drink companies, who buy products to donate to schools in return for free signage.

All boards are run by microprocessors, with no movable parts. The most basic board, with only items such as home and visitor score and inning, costs as little as $1,200. The most expensive, with those basics plus inning by inning scoring, costs as much as $11,000. Standard boards can be delivered in less than six weeks. Custom orders need 8 to 10 weeks lead time.

Other scoreboard manufacturers on this end of the market include:

FAIR-PLAY SCOREBOARDS
Box 1847
Des Moines, IA 50306
(800) 247-0265

GSC SPORTS, INC.
600 N. Pacific Ave.
San Pedro, CA 90733
(213) 831-0130

SPECIALTY INSTRUMENTS CORP.
Box 153447
Irving, TX 75015
(214) 790-1810

Screens, Nets, and Backstops

The same contraptions that keep so many foul balls out of your hands also keep them out of your molars.

In recent years, the big trend in field-boundary restraints has been away from chainlink and toward fish net. The nylon surface of fish net is more durable and gives a softer bounce of the ball back into play.

BSN CORP.
P.O. Box 7726
Dallas, TX 75209
(800) 527-7510
Contact: Toni Bradford, asst. sales mgr.
BSN custom-manufactures backstops

Pitching Machines

Next to pitch variety and control, the nicest thing about pitching machines is they never get tired and sit down in the shade or get mad and go home.

Pitching machines have been around since the 1890s when a Princeton professor came up with a little smoothbored cannon that he insisted could "throw" drops, curves, and whatever. The speed of the pitch depended on the size of the powder charge, and the boom of a mediocre fastball was enough to put a helluva hitch in your swing. Most of today's machines use some sort of rotating-wheel setup, quiet enough not to scare your Little Leaguer.

The JUGS machine, whose manufacturer of the same name claims to outsell all competitors combined by four to one, "pitches" with a matched set of rotating, pneumatic tires set on a tripod. By adjusting the angle and speeds of the tires, you can get the machine to throw anyplace in your strike zone at anywhere from Tommy John to Nolan Ryan velocity. It'll toss any kind of curve, or even split-finger fastballs and knuckleballs. Or, it can spit out grounders, line-drives or pop-flies for infield or outfield practice.

About fifteen companies manufacture

pitching machines, so shop around. Hillerich & Bradsby puts out one called the "Slugger Trainer" for a suggested team price of only $270. Obviously aimed at the Little League market, one of its selling points is the "only variation in pitches . . . is vertical." Translation: no curves or changing speeds. Curvemaster, which performs many of the same tricks as the JUGS machine for about the same price, comes equipped with wheels, so you can move it around the infield. The Curvemaster folks say most of their rigs are used indoors.

You probably figure most of the machines go to teams, but JUGS says they do two or three setups a week for individuals who want to sharpen their kids' batting eyes or maybe get in a few licks themselves. You can have the whole package shipped to you for about $3,000: pitching machine ($895 to $1,350, depending on the sophistication of its pitch selection); automatic ball feeder ($225); and installation, framework, and net for a 70′ × 12′ × 14′ batting cage ($1,230). If you want to save a few bucks, buy the pipes for the batting cage locally, but do get some kind of enclosed cage if you have neighbors within home-run distance.   —BC

and screens and the netting that goes with them for all baseball levels. It sells a portable backstop usually purchased by high schools and colleges that weighs 522 pounds and is bounded by 14-inch galvanized steel. That model is 18 feet wide, 12 feet deep, and 14 feet high, takes 600-ply netting, and sells for $1,350. Big Boy, its larger backstop used by major and minor league teams, weighs 450 pounds, is 17 feet wide, 18 feet deep, and 12 feet high, and costs $3,990. Netting on both backstops is guaranteed to withstand 300 pounds of pressure. (Safe up to Sid Fernandez!) BSN products are used through-

out the majors. The company also manufactures outfield fences.

PUTTERMAN & CO., INC.
4834 South Oakley
Chicago, IL 60609
(800) 621-0146
Contact: Joan Koza, vice president
Putterman custom-makes nets to fit existing hardware. The basic nylon is a 1¾-inch knot-resistant nylon that will withstand 300 pounds of pressure. In addition to fitting backstops, Putterman also manufactures netting for batting cages. The basic cost is 50 cents per square foot. A

lead time of four to six weeks is needed for most jobs, since all are custom orders.

Seating

The days of splinter-ridden wooden bleachers are as distant as nickel soft drinks. Most of the seats in modern major league ballparks are of the straight-back theater variety, made either of cast iron, aluminum, or plastic. Aluminum bleachers are still common in the outfield and upper-deck cheap seats, and in numerous college and minor league stadiums.

AMERICAN SEATING COMPANY
901 Broadway NW
Grand Rapids, MI 49504
(616) 456-0600
Contact: Al Meyer, vice president, production

The Grand Rapids company, which has been in the business since the 1920s, bills itself as the nation's leading provider of spectator seating. And indeed eighteen of the twenty-six major league ballparks contain seats designed, manufactured, and installed by American Seating. American's designers work with a stadium's architect to customize orders to fit certain geometric specifications, a process that can take up to one month. Production then can take another month to two months, with installation lasting from one to four weeks, depending on the size of the job. American's basic painted plastic seat lists for $60 to $70 installed.

AMERICAN DESK, INC
P.O. Box 6107
Temple, TX 76503
(817) 773-1776
Contact: Gene Pemberton, director of special projects

American Desk offers a slightly higher-priced model that is popular among minor league and major league spring training facilities. Its Model 2552, which comes in sizes from 19 to 22 inches high, sells for $110.75 plus a basic $10 installation charge. This Texas firm is the only major

player to dip its product in an acrylic paint, which it says reduces fading. Most clients start talking about design specs five to six months in advance, and the company usually needs seventy-five days lead time to process a job. Past jobs include the Oakland-Alameda Coliseum, Arlington Stadium, Jack Murphy Stadium, and Veterans Stadium. Most recently, American Desk installed new seats at Buffalo's refurbished Pilot Field.

SOUTHERN BLEACHER CO.
P.O. Box 1
Graham, TX 76046
(800) 433-0912
Contact: Steve Mazzanti, sales representative

Southern Bleacher works at the lower end of the seating market, specializing in manufacturing and installing aluminum bleacher seats at high school, college, and minor league parks. Jobs range from $50,000 to $1 million-plus. The basic no-back bleacher runs $80 to $90 installed. One of the firm's recent jobs was installing 5,000 seats at Thurman Munson Memorial Stadium in Canton, Ohio, home of the Canton-Akron Indians (Double-A). Cost: $800,000. All bleachers are custom made. Southern needs four to five months lead time to install the average order.

Also dealing in bleacher seating are:

ALENCO, INC.
615 Carson
Bryan, TX 77801
(409) 779-7770

ALUMNEX
1617 N. Washington Street
Magnolia, AK 71753
(800) 643-1514

Tarpaulins

Sometimes it rains.

Baseball's vulnerability to the elements made tarpaulin an inevitable invention, and an invaluable one. The biggest nega-

tive about tarps has always been their massive weight, and the fact that it took the better part of an infantry division to roll them out. But that, too, is changing, as increasingly lighter surfaces are being developed and installed.

COVERMASTER, INC.
100 Westmore Drive
Unit 11-D
Rexdale, Ontario, Canada M9V5C3
(800) 387-5808
Contact: Larry Moreland, vice president

Fifteen spring training facilities and two big league parks protect their infields with Covermaster's polyethylene plastic blend. All covers are custom woven from 12-inch panels. About three weeks lead time is needed. The average cost of a 160-foot-by-160-foot major league cover is about $5,000, and it should last for about five years. The same tarp weighs about 1,000 pounds.

PUTTERMAN & CO., INC.
4834 South Oakley
Chicago, IL 60609
(800) 621-0146
Contact: Joan Koza, vice president

Putterman's tarps are used by a number of major league teams, including the Cincinnati Reds, Milwaukee Brewers, and Los Angeles Dodgers. The company pioneered a new dip-coated vinyl tarp that weighs as little as 300 pounds for a standard 160-by-160 cover. All of its big league clients continue to use the polyethylene tarps, which last longer. But Putterman insists the new vinyls are the wave of the future, especially for colleges and minor league teams that don't have big grounds crews. Cost of the polyethylene is 18 cents to 32 cents per square inch, while the newer vinyls cost from 36 to 42 cents per square inch.

Turf

Artificial turf was a novelty when AstroTurf was first installed in the Astrodome in 1966. But today it's the surface of choice for eleven major league ballparks and countless minor league facilities. There is, however, a growing affection for natural surfaces that act like artificial grass.

ASTROTURF INDUSTRIES
809 Kenner St.
Dalton, GA 30720
(404) 272-4200
Contact: James Siegle, sales manager
AstroTurf has fought off a myriad of challengers to remain on top of the industry it spawned. All of the major league stadiums with artificial turf have AstroTurf, and the company boasts that it has installed 60 percent of all artificial surfaces.

AstroTurf consists of a top layer of grasslike blades on top of a perforated pad of open graded asphalt. The bottom is lined with gravel. Installation costs vary wildly. On the high end, the Hubert H. Humphrey Metrodome ($1.35 million) and Veterans Stadium ($2.1 million) cost so much because of sophisticated irrigation systems. On the low end, Gately Stadium in Chicago, a high school field, cost just $600,000. The most recent turf installed at the Astrodome, the "magic carpet" with separate retractable fields for football and baseball, cost $3.2 million.

GRASS SERVICES CO.
44 MacArthur Rd.
Pueblo, CO 81001
(719) 544-4511
Contact: L. C. Meade, president
Prescription Athletic Turf (PAT) only *sounds* plastic. It's real grass, hailed as having all the benefits of artificial turf without many of its drawbacks. Developed by Purdue University agronomy professor William H. Daniel eighteen years ago, PAT is based on a complex irrigation system. It utilizes a thick peat-and-sand base over a network of drainpipes. Suction pumps draw water from the sand into a plastic liner. The water can then be pumped back into the roots and grass. Installation is much cheaper than synthetic surfaces—

$250,000 to $550,000. And yearly maintenance costs of $30,000 to $100,000 are cheap by natural grass standards. Denver's Triple-A Diablos play on the surface at Mile High Stadium; so do the Braves at Atlanta–Fulton County Stadium.

PACIFIC SOD CO.
305 West Hueneme Rd.
Camerillo, CA 93010
(805) 488-4478
Contact: Tony Prater, customer service manager
Pacific Sod grows and sells Bermudas and bluegrasses for major league and minor league teams. Dodger Stadium uses its TifGreen Bermuda blend, and Jack Murphy, Anaheim Stadium, and the Rose Bowl have recently switched to a new blend called Santa Ana Green. The company grows the grass on its grounds for five to six months, then transplants it into a stadium's field. After five to six weeks in the ground, the grass is considered strong enough to absorb daily use. An average job costs about $40,000.

Architects

As you might expect, the number of firms catering to the ballpark part of the industry is relatively small—there are only so many major and minor league teams. As for design, everyone wants something different, but the trend is away from the multipurpose stadium that became fashionable in the 1960s. Baseball owners seem to be telling architects that smaller is better. They want smaller seating capacities in a more compact shape that minimizes the number of foul-territory seats—bringing the fans closer to the action—while keeping good sight lines.

HELLMUTH, OBATA & KASSABAUM (HOK)
323 W. 8th Street
Suite 700
Kansas City, MO 64105
(816) 221-1576
Contact: Earl Santee, associate
HOK is the nation's leading ballpark and

stadium design firm. Currently the Kansas City–based firm is involved in four major baseball projects: the new Comiskey Park, scheduled for a 1991 completion; the downtown baseball facility in Baltimore (1992); the Florida Suncoast Dome in St. Petersburg (1990); and the planned baseball-only stadium in San Francisco (1994). Only the Suncoast Dome is bucking the baseball-only trend. HOK also designed the new Pilot Field in Buffalo, N.Y.

HOK architects design a blueprint to fit specific needs, but most projects take on at least some characteristics of an HOK model featuring unobstructed seating. Pinpoint seat configuration is done mostly by computers over a three- to four-month period.

OSBORN ENGINEERING
668 Euclid Avenue
Cleveland, OH 44114
(216) 861-2020
Contact: Dale Swearingen, vice pres.
Osborn designed many of the first great stadiums. The short right field at Yankee Stadium, the long center field at the Polo Grounds, the oblong-shaped Griffith Stadium, all sprang from Osborn blueprints. Recently the firm has been more involved in structural analysis and renovation of old parks, including Chicago's Wrigley Field and Cleveland Municipal Stadium, than in designing new ones.

In Chattanooga, Tennessee, the local government brought Osborn in to restore the old look of its aging minor league park. The firm responded by designing a new concourse with an old look, complete with circa 1930s oil-derrick lighting fixtures and enhanced arch work, and by exposing the riveted structural steel that had been covered decades earlier.

Contractors

While there are no companies that concentrate on baseball facilities alone—the jobs are too rare to build an entire business on—several do handle stadiums and sports field construction.

HUBER, HUNT & NICHOLS
2450 South Tibbs Ave.
Indianapolis, IN 46241
(317) 241-6301
Contact: Mike Kerr, executive vice president

Huber, Hunt & Nichols was the general contractor on the recently completed Florida Suncoast Dome, a $70 million contract, in St. Petersburg. In the past the firm built Riverfront Stadium in Cincinnati and Three Rivers Stadium in Pittsburgh. The company does more arena and football construction than baseball because those jobs are more frequent. Miami's Joe Robbie Stadium was an HHN project. When they come along, however, baseball jobs are among the firm's prime contracts. The Suncoast Dome, which St. Petersburg is using to try to lure an expansion franchise to Tampa Bay, included more than 25 subcontractors and a total of 400 men working more than 2½ years.

TURNER CONSTRUCTION
11 South Lasalle
Chicago, IL 60603
(312) 704-0770
Contact: Trygve Olibersen, vice pres.

Turner has built several major league spring training facilities as well as handling renovations and additions to existing major league ballparks. Recent renovations include Wrigley Field and Tiger Stadium. At Wrigley, Turner built a new press box and 67 new luxury skyboxes.

SPORTSFIELDS, INC.
P.O. Box 615
Blue Island, IL 60406

HOK designed this gem of a ballpark for the Buffalo Bisons, the Triple-A affiliate of the Pittsburgh Pirates. With seating for 19,500 fans, Pilot Field is large enough for minor-league play but will be expanded to hold 40,000 fans if Buffalo lands a big-league expansion team.

(312) 371-0917
Contact: James Walsh, president

Sportsfields builds the field itself for little league, high school, college, and pro interests. The firm designs, landscapes, and irrigates the field and installs fencing. The average job can take as little as a few weeks and can range from $25,000 all the way up to $100,000. Recent projects include the White Sox' spring training facility in Sarasota, Florida, and the UCLA diamond.   —KD

Through the Years

Ballparks have come a long way. The first enclosed ones in the mid to late 1800s were small, wooden, one-level structures of little distinction. Then in the early years of this century, after a number of costly fires, cities began to build structures of steel and concrete, which facilitated larger and more ambitious stadiums. But even as the grandstands got bigger, architects were able to keep the fans close to the field. Proximity for all was more of a priority than making sure that every seat was a good seat. As a result, the shapes of stadiums varied wildly as builders tried to conform to the buildings surrounding the sites. The opening of Yankee Stadium— "The House that Ruth Built"—on April 18, 1923 set the pace for an entire generation, with its three decks suspended by a series of columns.

But as much as the introduction of columns would shape stadium construction for that generation, figuring out how to get rid of them would play a key role in altering the next. Cantilevered upper decks first appeared in Washington's D.C. Stadium (later renamed RFK Stadium) in 1960, an advancement that allowed the multipurpose stadium craze to catch on just in time for baseball's great expansion. Suddenly just about every city building a new stadium was spurning the old-time baseball park for one of those saucer-shaped wonders that could host football

and baseball. Only Dodger Stadium bucked the trend.

"At about the same time, three different companies were building stadiums in Atlanta, St. Louis, and Pittsburgh, and they all came out looking like one copied the other," said Dale Swearingen, vice president of Cleveland-based Osborn Engineering. "Of course, no one copied anyone. I guess that's the odd thing about that whole era. All those cities asked for a multipurpose stadium that could be all things to all people, and what each of those companies came up with was essentially the same because there's only so much you can do in drawing a straight line from baseball to football."

The introduction of indoor baseball with the Astrodome in 1966 forever changed the game. But the latest and most profound architectural change came with the completion of Royals Stadium in 1970. Unlike the saucers, this was a true baseball facility, with perfect sight lines and immaculate landscaping. Like many of them, it was placed out in the middle of nowhere. Today, many in baseball consider it the perfect example of a modern ballpark.

"Royals Stadium is our model," said Earl Santee of Hellmuth, Obata & Kassabaum (HOK), which designed it. "It is the old-time pure baseball facility with all the modern conveniences the Polo Grounds never had."

Architectural Magazine's John Pastier disagrees. "It's still a stadium predicated on great distances and unobstructed vision, and one of those is bad," he said.

"One thing that really bothers me about it is there are no fair-territory outfield seats."

But the number of seats, if not their quality, no doubt altered baseball's conventional wisdom. Royals Stadium seats just 40,655, second lowest in the American League. Sixties' thinking was that bigger was better. But owners who built or leased those 55,000-seat caverns learned two things: the game's intimacy was lost with all those seats, and besides, they almost never sold out anyway.

"I've always said the perfect baseball stadium was open-aired and had 45,000 to 48,000 seats," says Giants' owner Bob Lurie, whose team now plays in 58,000-seat Candlestick Park. "I've fought about this for a long time. I think anything bigger causes a case of diminishing returns. You're only going to drive the fans away.

And who's going to sell that many seats?"

It's no coincidence that two of the smallest parks in the game are among the oldest. The people who built Wrigley Field (38,040) and Fenway Park (33,583) before World War I knew what they were doing. But the next generation had to find out the hard way. And baseball's heritage suffered at their hands.

Pastier, who grew up watching games at the Polo Grounds and now marks the progression of architectural trends, put it simply: "How many stadiums are left where Babe Ruth hit a home run?" he said. "Baseball, which has changed so little in the last century, has let almost all of its great arenas be pushed aside in the name of progress. And that's very sad."

Sadder still would be letting the remaining treasures—Wrigley, Fenway, Tiger

Stadium—fall into disrepair.

"As much as we try, we can't recreate an old ballpark," Swearingen said. "We can dress it up and play off the nostalgia kick, but we can only go so far. Those old parks are part of our national heritage that we should protect."

You want sad? Fifty years from now, some unfortunate fans will be waxing nostalgic about Atlanta–Fulton County Stadium and going on about how great architecture should be preserved.

Save the saucer?   —KD

Brooklyn! Baseball! Once upon a time the two were one. The Williamsburg section provided baseball's first enclosed ballpark; in Brownsville the great Cincinnati Reds first tasted defeat; and in Flatbush—let's just say that there used to be a ballpark there.

The previous spread depicted Dodger homes old and new. This pairing shows two formerly contending new homes for the Chicago White Sox. Below is HOK's Florida Suncoast Dome in St. Petersburg, which came within a cat's whisker of whisking the White Sox away from the Windy City. Although Chicago retained the Sox by committing to the new Comiskey Stadium sketched in above, the 43,000-seat Suncoast Dome is not likely to be without major-league ball for long: Atlanta could use a regional NL rival.

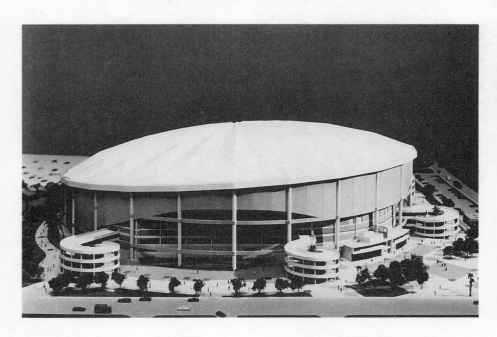

Ballparks of the Future

Character is on the comeback trail.

The future of baseball ballparks probably will bring less emphasis on searching for something new than on recapturing something old. The Baltimore Orioles and local government officials are using words like "intimacy" and "character," with a noticeable absence of "versatility," in their plans for a new, 45,000-seat downtown ballpark. The new park, to be completed by 1992, will be an asymmetrical figure built to fit the configuration of the surrounding business district, much in the same way Wrigley Field conforms to its neighborhood. The new Comiskey Park in Chicago, set to be completed in time for the 1991 season, promises to keep many of the old stadium's charms. And in San Francisco, Giants' owner Bob Lurie is talking about the "cozy" park he expects to inhabit by 1994.

The forward-into-the-past thinking already has been tested at the minor league level, most notably in Buffalo's new $56 million Pilot Field. The 19,500-seat facility, completed in 1988, was built to conform to the dimensions and decor of the surrounding downtown historical district. Kansas City–based architectural firm Hellmuth, Obata & Kassabaum (HOK) created a neoclassic park in the spirit of Ebbets Field and Connie Mack Stadium. The exterior is dominated by exposed arches and walls lined with marble tiles set into precast concrete to match nearby buildings.

"We didn't go in there with the intention of building an old-time ballpark," said HOK's Earl Santee. "We built a modern park with all the conveniences fans have come to expect. But we did some things that gave it a traditional, old-time baseball feeling at the same time. It was a case of aesthetics not getting lost in providing all the modern nuances."

The White Sox' plan also is to move forward while clinging to tradition.

"We intend to have a modern park, but we're loading it with the feel of the old one, which is the feel of the White Sox themselves," said Terry Savarise, vice president–operations. "That includes stuff like arch work from the old times to go with great sight lines made possible by modern technology."

A more radical departure was suggested by Chicago architect Philip Bess, who designed an imaginary, site-specific project he called "Bill Veeck Park." It showed the advantages of a smaller, baseball-only facility. Bess used the site of the new Comiskey Park for his imaginative creation, tailoring the distances to his outfield fences to the available space instead of forcing a characterless symmetry. Left-handed hitters would love his 334-foot right field power alley and right-handed batters curse his 406-foot "Death Valley" in left, but baseball played in "Veeck" would have the same unique quality found in old parks like Fenway.

Bess's "Veeck" would not be an island in the middle of a huge parking lot, as are so many current stadiums. Adjacent neighborhoods could be protected by the use of linear parking to the north and east—again adapting his design to the existing site.

The nostalgia movement is not embraced by all. Domed stadiums, which are about as contrary to baseball tradition as vendors selling sushi, continue to encroach in less tradition-minded cities. In St. Petersburg, the Florida Suncoast Dome is ready as soon as that city gets a team. And Toronto's new SkyDome offers several innovations.

The SkyDome has a retractable roof, a hotel with seventy-seven rooms overlooking the field, a health club, and several McDonald's franchise locations. Original plans also called for a theater and an indoor golf facility.

This mall-like atmosphere is not lost on the rest of baseball.

"The latest thing is making the area underneath the stadium have all the features and looks of retail stores," Santee said. "It used to be that you'd go to a ballgame and all you could get were a hot dog and a beer. But those days are gone. You can get it all now."

So Mom gets a touch-up at the hairdresser and buys a new pair of shoes at Foot-World. Dad browses at the bookstore, stops by the pub for a beer, gets a new woofer at Radio Shack. The older child watches *Rocky VII*, and the baby spends the afternoon in Day-Kare. They're halfway home before they notice they forgot to go to the ballgame. —KD

Even the Dirt Has to Come from Somewhere

Jim Kelsey gets all the dirt. His firm, Partac Peat Corp., provides the clay-and-sand mixture used by 9 major league clubs, 46 minor league teams, and more than 150 colleges. It goes by the name of Beam Clay.

"It's not just whatever comes out of the ground," Kelsey says. "It's a fine mixture that's processed and shredded to the right consistency. And we can even match colors—red, orange, or brown—to suit a particular diamond."

Kelsey furnishes dirt of several different mixtures. A 50-pound bag of hard-packed clay used for the pitcher's mound sells for $7. At that rate it costs about $35 to recondition a mound. Adding an eight-inch coat to an entire infield costs about $2,000. Kelsey also offers separate mixes for the batter's and coaches' boxes and on-deck circles.

What makes his dirt so special?

Kelsey won't reveal any secrets, but he does allow that the stuff is pulverized, ground up, run through screens, and shredded. Then sand is added, and the new mix is run through screens again.

Partac is located in Kelsey Park, Great Meadows, NJ 07838. Or you can call Jim Kelsey at (800) 247-BEAM, (201) 637-4191 in New Jersey. It's a dirty job, but . . . well, you know the rest. —KD

Why the Grass Is Greener

So you thought ball players were pampered? Take a look at where they wipe their feet.

Growing and maintaining a field of grass for a ballpark is a painstaking, year-round process that often begins in a nursery. Grass is grown to maturity, transplanted into the field in February or March, and manicured daily by a large crew of grounds keepers. The average cost of an annual resodding falls in the $30,000-to-$50,000 range for about 110,000 square inches.

Two basic types of grass are used in the major leagues: Bermuda on the West Coast and bluegrass on the East Coast and in the Midwest. The Bermuda grasses are trimmed low, usually to about ½ inch high. The bluegrasses are cut higher, to 1½ or even 2 inches.

The Dodgers use a Bermuda hybrid called TifGreen, while San Diego's Jack Murphy Stadium and Anaheim Stadium recently switched to Santa Ana Green, a new, softer Bermuda strain that holds up better for multipurpose stadiums. Both hybrids go dormant in temperatures under 40 degrees, which translates into three or four months of the year in California.

"We've used some form of Bermuda since Dodger Stadium was built," says Dodgers head grounds keeper Al Myers. "TifGreen withstands heat during the late months. It tolerates the abuse it's given and it doesn't require much watering. I think it's the perfect baseball turf."

But stadiums in cold-climate cities can't use Bermudas, because they would stay dormant through much of the season. As a result, most continue to experiment with bluegrass blends. "The bluegrass goes dormant, too," points out Orioles' head grounds keeper Pat Santarone. "But not for as long as Bermuda."

All baseball grasses must meet certain criteria. They must look good, drain well, and prove durable over a season of abuse.

"It's a little more complicated than growing grass in your backyard," Myers points out. "But it involves the same principle."   —KD

Pop-Ups

Some things to look for between innings at the ballgame.

- **Anaheim Stadium** (Angels): Those two thin black lines running from the left field bullpen to foul territory are TV cables, not the San Andreas Fault.
- **Arlington Stadium** (Rangers): Called Turnpike Stadium before the Rangers arrived in 1972, this is one of two major league parks (the other is Dodger Stadium) that you enter from the top. The field is built below the level of the surrounding parking lot.
- **Astrodome** (Houston): Two seats in the upper deck in left field are marked by drawings of a cannon and a rooster. Astros Jimmy (The Toy Cannon) Wynn and Doug (The Red Rooster) Rader hit two of the only three balls to ever reach that mark. A third seat might have been marked by a hawk. Visitor Andre Dawson is the only other player to claim the feat.
- **Atlanta–Fulton County Stadium** (Braves): Chief Noc-A-Homa's teepee has been moved several times without incident since its installation in 1967, but the two times it was *re*-moved (late in 1982 and early in 1983) the actions were solely responsible for Braves losing streaks. Of course, some cynics have tried to blame the Atlanta pitching.
- **Busch Stadium** (St. Louis): The statue of Stan Musial outside the stadium since 1968 could still outhit most National League batsmen. Home plate was transferred from the old Busch Stadium. The tarp rose along the first base line and attacked Vince Coleman, causing him to miss the 1985 World Series.
- **Candlestick Park** (San Francisco): Candlestick Point got its name from the jagged rocks and tall trees that rise out of the nearby swampland. Often cold, with

the worst winds in baseball! Dress warm and watch out for flying baseballs, peanuts, pillows, papers, and people.

- **Cleveland Stadium** (Indians) hosted the largest crowd in American League history in 1954, when 84,587 came out to see the Tribe play the Yankees. No one has ever hit a homer into the center field bleachers. The Tribe's 1948 pennant was publicly buried in center behind the low outfield fence in August 1949.
- **Comiskey Park** (Chicago White Sox) is the oldest park still standing in the majors (at least until the new Comiskey is finished). It was built in 1910, two years before Fenway Park and Tiger Stadium, four years before Wrigley Field, and thirteen years before Yankee Stadium. Griffith Stadium, Crosley Field, Ebbets Field, and Braves Field (Boston) all opened after Comiskey, and all closed before.
- **County Stadium** (Milwaukee): Terrific tailgate parties in the lot are often better than the games. Try the bratwurst. The park has the most precisely measured right field foul line; the surveyor's mark on the pole reads "315.37."
- **Dodger Stadium** (Los Angeles): In 1963 the mound was lowered from 15 inches to 10 inches. Opposing teams maintain it is still the highest mound in baseball.
- **Fenway Park** (Boston): There are two vertical series of what seem to be dots and dashes on the left field scoreboard in Fenway Park. They are, in fact, Morse code for Tom and Jean Yawkey's initials.
- **Hubert H. Humphrey Metrodome** (Minneapolis): The forty-foot canvas curtain in right field masks seats that are opened out for football.
- **Jack Murphy Stadium** (San Diego): Because of the configuration of the stands near the foul poles, it's possible for an outfielder to catch a foul ball out of sight of the umpires.
- **Memorial Stadium** (Baltimore): In 1966 *(Cont. p. 30)*

But Turf Is Putting Down Roots

Artificial turf has been through the mower the last two decades. Players and fans alike have tried to cut it down to size using a twin blade: It adds injuries, it takes away from the nature of the game.

But it's here to stay for one simple reason: grass won't grow indoors.

That may sound blatantly obvious now, but it wasn't so in 1966. The builders of the Astrodome had to learn the hard way. The operators of the world's first indoor stadium had already reconciled themselves to the notion of playing baseball on dirt after the grass they planted refused to grow. But then Astros' owner Judge Roy Hofheinz came across an article describing Monsanto's experiments with a nylon knitted fiber. Desperate, he convinced Astrodome officials to offer the so-called Eighth Wonder of the World as artificial turf's first guinea pig.

Some players are convinced that the extra pounding their bodies take on the turf can shave years off of careers. Artificial surfaces have long been linked to increased injuries, especially torn knee ligaments occurring when a player's foot locks in the turf. A 1985 study conducted by sports injury expert Dr. James Garrick, founder of San Francisco's Center for Sports Medicine, found that about 25 percent of all serious knee injuries occur when a player makes a sudden change of direction—most commonly on turf.

Turf's supporters counter that beyond turf toe and other unique-to-turf hurts, injuries caused by the surfaces are minor and not out of line with those that occur on grass.

The indoor stadiums have no option. And for multipurpose stadiums such as Three Rivers in Pittsburgh and Cincinnati's Riverfront, having synthetic grass is the pragmatic thing to do when you have to serve both football and baseball masters.

But then there's Royals Stadium in Kansas City. A true baseball park, it's lauded for having perfect sight lines, immaculate landscaping, and that intimate feeling reminiscent of the old days. And it just happens to be the only true baseball park with artificial grass. —KD

Frank Robinson blasted Luis Tiant for the only homer to go completely out of the stadium. Try the great crabcakes!

- **Kingdome** (Seattle): Large speakers hanging from the ceiling and roof are in play. Several balls have hit on high and been caught for outs, and at least two fouls went up, stuck, and never came down. They were ruled strikes.
- **Riverfront Stadium** (Cincinnati) was a pioneer among ballparks: the first to paint metric distances on the outfield walls. Home plate came from the old Crosley Field.
- **Royals Stadium** (Kansas City): Yes, those are waterfalls out there behind right center; the stadium's not leaking.
- **Shea Stadium** (New York): Mets fans say the scoreboard in Shea Stadium is the largest in the majors: 86 feet high and 175 feet long. Anti-Mets fans are asking for a recount. The loudest nonfan noise in baseball comes from jumbo jets taking off and landing at La Guardia Airport just beyond right field.
- **SkyDome** (Toronto): The roof can be opened or closed in twenty minutes—in other words, between pitches for many major league hurlers.
- **Stade Olympique** (Montreal): A plaque dedicated to an infielder who played for the Triple-A Royals of the International League in 1946 is apparently the only memorial to a minor leaguer in a major league park. And a foreigner too! His name was Jackie Robinson.
- **Three Rivers Stadium** (Pittsburgh): The plaque that showed where Babe Ruth hit his 714th home run is in the Allegheny Club. Alas, it shows nothing; the ball was hit in Forbes Field.
- **Tiger Stadium** (Detroit): The sign above the entrance to the visitors' clubhouse in Tiger Stadium reads, "No Visitors Allowed." The 125-foot flagpole just to the left of the 440-foot mark in center is in play all the way to the top.
- **Veterans Stadium** (Philadelphia): Yet another transplanted home plate, this one from Connie Mack Stadium. The field looks like Riverfront, Three Rivers, and Busch, but the boo-birds make it sound like Philly.
- **Wrigley Field** (Chicago Cubs): Ivy didn't appear on the walls of Wrigley Field until 1937. A hit by Bill Buckner once became lost in the ivy as he circled the bases for a home run. The ground rules now say that a ball stuck in the vines results in a ground-rule double, but if the ball comes out, it's in play.
- **Yankee Stadium** (New York): The original monuments, in center field, honored Lou Gehrig, Babe Ruth, and Miller Huggins. Today they are joined beyond the fence by plaques for, among others, Joe DiMaggio, Mickey Mantle, Casey Stengel, Joe McCarthy, Thurman Munson, and Pope John Paul II. Some of these men did not own, manage, play, or work for the Yankees.

—KD

Softball Comes In from the Cold

It's January. The temperature is twelve degrees and there's a foot of snow on the ground. Ready for a game of softball? Indoor softball?

In the last three or four years, a handful of entrepreneurs scattered across the country have begun building indoor softball facilities in an attempt to siphon off some of a softball boom that has seen the number of people playing the game grow from 25 million in 1978 to almost 50 million today. Interest is growing so fast that thousands each year don't play because they can't find a field. Softball entrepreneurs, who took the lead from local governments to ignite a privatization boom in the mid-1980s, have learned that it's hard to make a profit on something used only six or seven months a year.

But there were all these indoor tennis

facilities lying around, left over from that sport's bust. And some businessmen, such as Mark Littleton of Homerun Indoor Softball in Columbia, Maryland, got the idea to convert them into indoor softball fields. Instead of paying at least $2 million to build from scratch, they can pick up an old tennis facility cheap and spend as little as $400,000 on conversions.

The entrepreneurs make their money by charging teams $400 to $600 for a 10- to 15-week season and by selling concessions.

The emerging indoor game is a shorter, faster kind of softball. The dimensions of the field and various rules are dictated by the size of the facility. Outfield fences, usually 8 feet high and 300 feet away for the outdoor game, often are as high as 12 feet and as short as 75 feet indoors.

"It's a game for line-drive hitters," says Bill Plummer of the Amateur Softball Association. "It's a faster game and an easier game from a hitting standpoint, but I don't think it's a better game."

The indoor game does fill a void for those players who want to play softball year-round. But it remains to be seen whether the entrepreneurs who build the facilities can convince them to keep playing inside when the ground is dry and the air is warm. Though it's hard to attach a figure to this emerging segment, no more than a few thousand are thought to be playing the indoor game.

"It's never going to replace the conventional outdoor game," Plummer says. "It's just a phase." And if it doesn't pan out, there'll probably be some indoor stadiums on the market real cheap just in time for someone else to think they're getting a bargain. Tennis, anyone?   —KD

In days of old when men were cold, they struck up a game of baseball on ice (left), a pastime that would have been perfect for Lonnie "Skates" Smith. Today indoor softball is the hit of the hot-stove league, that time when fans look back to such fabled ballparks of old as New York's Polo Grounds, shown above.

Firsts at the Ballpark

- **Admission Charged:** All Star N.Y. vs. Brooklyn at Fashion Race Course, Long Island, 1857. The price was a whopping 50 cents.
- **Enclosed Ballpark:** Union Grounds, Brooklyn, 1862,
- **Turnstiles:** 1878.
- **Concrete and Steel Stadium:** Shibe Park (later known as Connie Mack Stadium) in Philadelphia, 1909.
- **President to Throw Out First Ball:** William Howard Taft, in Washington, 1910.
- **Game in Yankee Stadium:** April 18, 1923.
- **Public-Address System:** Polo Grounds, 1929.
- **Night Game in Organized Baseball:** Independence, Kansas, in the Western Association, April 28, 1930.
- **Use of Publicly Owned Stadium for Major League Game:** Cleveland Municipal Stadium, 1932.
- **Park to Host an All-Star Game:** Comiskey Park, July 6, 1933.
- **Major League Night Game:** Crosley Field in Cincinnati, May 24, 1935.
- **Night No-Hitter:** Ebbets Field, June 15, 1938, as Johnny Vander Meer pitched his second consecutive no-hitter in the ballpark's first night game.
- **Domed Stadium:** Astrodome in Houston, 1965; also first stadium with artificial turf playing surface.
- **World Series Game Played on Artificial Turf:** Baltimore at Cincinnati, October 10, 1970.
- **Night World Series Game:** Baltimore at Pittsburgh, October 13, 1971.
- **World Series Played Indoors:** St. Louis at Minnesota, October 17, 1987. —KD

CHAPTER 3

The Science of Staying in the Lineup

Kirk Gibson limped to the plate in the bottom of the ninth of Game 1 of the 1988 World Series, favoring both of his legs. When he then drove a three-two pitch from Athletics' reliever Dennis Eckersley over the fence to give the Dodgers a crucial Series win, he still couldn't hide his pain. Gibson circled the bases of the Oakland–Alameda County Coliseum, punching his right fist into the night air and inventing the Home Run Hobble.

Indeed, one of the most dramatic home runs in baseball history had its genesis in an unlikely, unromantic place—the visitors' cramped training room. For there earlier that same day Gibson had climbed up and laid his six-three, 210-pound body on the rectangular, tan, six-foot by two-foot padded training table, offered up his sprained right knee, and received two crucial injections.

On the advice of Dodgers' team physicians Dr. Frank Jobe and Dr. Michael Mellman, Gibson was injected with cortisone and Xylocaine to try to blunt the pain. This was not your everyday baseball training treatment for a sprained knee ligament, but Gibson was no amateur and this was no Saturday softball game. Still, although the pain subsided, it didn't vanish. And the fact that Gibson had pulled his left hamstring the week before in the National League Championship Series against the New York Mets didn't help matters. Gibson was a bag of aches and throbs in big trouble.

Unlike players of previous eras of baseball history, players today look for minor miracles from the health professionals employed by their clubs. The living, breathing, aching million-dollar-a-year ma-

Inside the Trainer's Room

From liniment to whirlpool, on up through ergometers, keeping fit makes dollars and sense

chines expect their athletic trainers to be nothing less than wizard mechanics. And hundreds of times during the season the trainers succeed—not with injections generally, but with techniques such as massage and ultrasound, the kind of treatments that last season enabled San Francisco's Kevin Mitchell to shed his bandages of spring training and get off to a torrid start.

Trainers are the first to arrive at the park and often the last to leave. Their salaries are less than untested rookies' and yet their decisions can add up to (or cost a team) a pennant. From stretching exercises and taped ankles to massages, emergency splinting, and ice-downs, the trainers' work is wide-ranging but largely unseen. Then too, every season it seems they take on more responsibilities.

Inside some of the leading training rooms of the modern era of major league baseball you can find computerized fitness machines called Orthotrons that cost more than $40,000. These devices allow for safe training and rehabilitation of tricky joint injuries and measure precisely how much strength or range of motion a player has in his leg or shoulder.

"This machinery is important," says Jeff Cooper, head trainer of the Philadelphia Phillies, "because it gives you information in black and white. If a player says he is 90 percent recovered, I can say, 'You're not,' and show him the printout." Still, adds Cooper, "We make our living with our hands."

Athletic training in baseball, on balance, has made huge strides since the days of prescribing a couple of aspirin for a Babe Ruth hangover or giving Ralph Kiner a liniment rubdown. In fact, if you go way back, you'll find that some baseball managers used to double as trainers too. In 1886, for example, when Chicago manager Cap Anson decided to take his preseason team down to Hot Springs, Arkansas, he did more than simply sweat the beer and poundage out of his players. He actually inaugurated the tradition of annual spring training camps down south. He pushed his players into hot baths and sent them on strenuous hikes with walking sticks up hills. (They took batting practice too.)

Unlike many of their counterparts of old, today's pro baseball trainers are college-educated, licensed, and experienced. They are certified by the Greenville, North Carolina–based National Athletic Trainers Association (NATA); they are also members of an elite group of trainers, the Professional Baseball Athletic Trainers Society (PBATS).

As such, pro baseball trainers routinely utilize machines that sound as if they belong on the starship *Enterprise*: machines like hydrocollators, Cybex isokinetic exercisers, and upper-body ergometers. Then too, trainers employ dozens of preventive measures (such as exercise cycling and flexibility exercises) to keep the athletes in

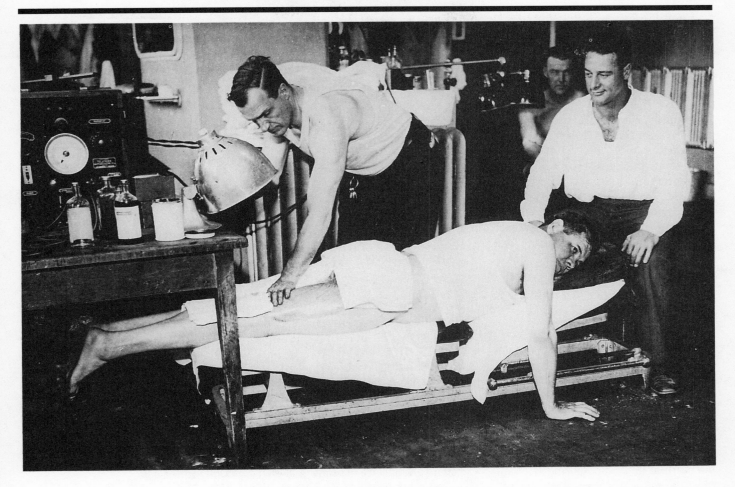

tune month after month during the grueling, 162-game schedule.

Just as important, or perhaps more so, after an injury the trainer serves as the crucial link between the team physician and the player. Pro athletes, on a daily basis, "need a threshold with which to monitor their progress," says Pat Croce, a member of NATA (he's the trainer of the Philadelphia Flyers) and a physical therapist who has worked with Mike Schmidt during the off-season since 1985. More often than not, the day-to-day guardian of a ball player's conditioning is his club's training staff.

In the rest of this chapter, you'll tour a typical professional baseball trainer's room and get a look inside the mysterious black bag you often see trainers lug onto the field when a ball player suddenly goes down.

In most cases trainers will suggest modifications for Little League, high school, and college players gleaned from exercises and equipment of the pros. For as big

league baseball trainers will tell you, it's not great equipment that makes strong players. It is instead dedication—and respect—for the athletic bodies so often punished in play.　　　　　—CP

Horse liniment, lamps, and massage were hot stuff in the training rooms of the Babe's time. Lou Gehrig, of course, needed scarcely an aspirin over 2,130 consecutive games.

Inside the Trainer's Room

While pro baseball players live their lives variously as heroes, bums, and public figures, there's one place they all retreat to when they crave privacy—the trainer's room. Both American and National League rules prohibit reporters from entering or conducting interviews in the training rooms. And for good reason! Serious work is going on inside.

What follows is a lineup of equipment and products you'll find in professional trainers' rooms around the major leagues.

Some of it you might find mysterious; some of it borders on the sublime. (And some of it might seem just plain simple.) You'll also find information on how the machines and supplies work—as well as where they can be found.

Because of the specialized nature of the equipment, in each case we've provided information on the supplier most often named by major league trainers; in some cases, at the trainers' suggestions, we've included an alternate supplier. Prices are approximate, but they are based on what a high school or small-college trainer would be quoted.

In some instances exercises without equipment can substitute for expensive machinery. Or they may be called for when a team is on the road. In all cases, remember that when an injury occurs, no trainer or piece of equipment can substitute for a doctor's diagnosis. Trainers are professionals, not magicians.

Ice Machine

"This is the most important piece of equipment in the room," says Jeff Cooper, head trainer of the Philadelphia Phillies since 1981, as he scooped up a handful of freshly made Veterans Stadium crushed ice to display. "If I only had a $2,500 budget, I'd get a crushed ice machine and towels." Cooper's not kidding. The lowly ice machine, not nearly as impressive looking as a Nautilus, Universal, or Cybex fitness station, has nevertheless done more for pro baseball players over the years than any other single piece of equipment.

"You've simply got to have one," says Paul Grace, the trainer who's in charge of certification for all members of the National Athletic Trainers Association.

"In spring training," says Cooper, "the first thing we do on arriving at the stadium at 5:30 A.M. is to make ice towels. We make 'em up and store them in ice chests." Considering how many players—and especially pitchers—are used in spring games as they're warming up for a new season, it's necessary for trainers to have chests full of ice towels at the ready all day. Unlike the regular season, it's normal for pitchers and players to play only one or two innings.

Ice is wrapped around sore shoulders, knees, thighs and backs to help reduce the pain of overuse and inflammation. But it isn't just used to treat injuries. Ice also provides stimulation for blood flow and natural healing. Some teams, like the Los Angeles Dodgers, use ice-and-plastic-bag

combinations, but most trainers prefer towels or bandages and ice. There's simply less waste.

KOLD-DRAFT, INC.
div. of Uniflow Manufacturing Corp.
1525 E. Lake Rd.
Erie, PA 16511
(814) 453-6761
Cost: $1,500–$3,000

FERNO ILLE
div. of Ferno-Washington, Inc.
70 Weil Way
Wilmington, OH 45177
(800) 733-3766
(513) 382-1451 in Ohio
Cost: $4,500 for icemaker/freezer/water dispenser

Cryo Therapy Cup

Okay, not every coach, trainer, or player can afford a $3,000 ice machine. And even if you can, what do you do when your team has an away game? You use an ice machine alternative—in this case, ice in a cup.

Like a homemade Popsicle, this inexpensive ice device allows you to freeze water in a reusable plastic cup. The cup won't crack in the freezer and it has a sticklike handle.

Trainers for years have used ice frozen in paper cups with Popsicle-stick handles to get ice directly on a tired and sore arm or shoulder. But the paper doesn't rip off the ice cleanly and easily. And because paper cups aren't considered "equipment," they often go unpacked or forgotten on the road.

It took a guy from Harvard to invent the Cryo Therapy Cup—and it's not named that because the cold makes you cry. *Kryos,* from the Greek, means "icy cold," and that's good for a ball player's muscles or joints when the hurt hits.

SPORTSWARE WEST
1320 Panchita Place
Santa Barbara, CA 93103

(805) 962-7454
Cost: $5 per cup

CRYO THERAPY INC.
Box 415
Monticello, MN 55362
(800) ICE-5722
(612) 295-5455 in Minnesota
Cost: $3.00 including postage

"Magic" Wands

These hollow, light, white plastic tubes, about as long as a duffer's putter, are technically called "wands." Any magic they perform in stretching ball players' arms, shoulders and backs originates in the exercises supervised by an orthopedic doctor, trainer, coach or physical therapist.

The wands are simple in design, and allow athletes to stretch their trunks, upper and lower backs, and rotator cuffs through a wide range of motions. (Some pro trainers say broomsticks can serve a similar function.)

One wand exercise for the rotator cuff, for example, calls for the athlete to lie on a training table on his back, then to grasp a

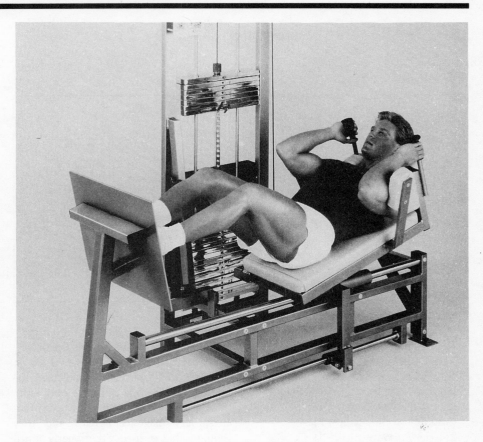

"T" wand with both hands. (The throwing hand, say, holds the "T" end; the other hand holds the bottom.) With one hand straight back above the head and the other hand set out straight to the side, the athlete presses from the "T" through the wand into the other hand, which offers resistance. The wand is held in this manner for an eight count and then released. Then hands are switched. By varying the arm and shoulder positions and resistance, a player works out the four muscles of the rotator cuff: the infraspinatus, subscapularis, teres minor, and supraspinatus.

Dr. James Andrews, the orthopedic surgeon who operated on Ron Guidry of the Yankees and Mike Schmidt of the Phillies, speaks highly of the wands if they are used regularly (with other exercises) under professional supervision.

The wands are available through:

DON COURSON ENTERPRISES
P.O. Box 4093
Birmingham, AL 35206-0093
(205) 836-3113
Cost: $5 each

Exercise Cycle

Every pro trainer will tell you: the arms are the glory limbs in baseball, but the legs provide the power. The exercise bike provides the seat for ball players to get their own wheels turning.

Exercise bikes are great for warmups, trainers add, because they don't stress the knees as running can, and they come in extraordinarily handy during cold or wet spells and during dismal rain delays.

Caution though: athletes must make certain the seat is adjusted properly for their height. If the knees are hyperextended (fairly locked) at the downstroke of each pedaling rotation, the knee joints will be stressed over time and may be prone to strain or injury. Make sure the knee is just slightly bent each time you pedal.

Five minutes is a good warmup period;

fifteen gives you an aerobic workout if you're pedaling with intensity. (And remember to strap your feet into the pedals: that way you can pull the pedals on the upstroke, working the hamstrings in the back of the thighs.)

QUINTON INSTRUMENT COMPANY
2121 Terry Ave.
Seattle, WA 98121
(800) 426-0347
(206) 223-7373

CYBEX (Fitron Cycle)
division of Lumex Inc.
2100 Smithtown Ave.
P.O. Box 9003
Ronkonkoma, NY 11779
(800) 645-5392
(516) 585-9000 in New York state
Cost: $1,600–$3,300

Training / Taping Table

Some say it's the "pitcher's mound" of the training room, and that's not a bad analogy. It's centrally located, to be sure, and everything starts from here. Pregame tap-

The leg press, by Cybex.

ing, diagnosis, massage, joint rotation exercises and checks under the watchful eye of the trainer, postgame tape cutoffs, rubdowns, and ice wrapping all commence at the trainer's table.

The standard size is six feet by two feet; however, some trainers prefer narrower widths so they can work both sides of the table without moving the body. There's no medical reason why the tables always seem to be *brown*-padded leather, but then again, you don't see many fielders sporting purple mitts either. Brown looks right in these rooms—serious brown, with sturdy legs that can stand up to a squirming, 225-pound Steve Balboni.

PROFEX MEDICAL PRODUCTS
1521-F E. McFadden Ave.
Santa Ana, CA 92705
(714) 541-4969
(Also: P.O. Box 16043
St. Louis, MO 63105
[800] 325-0193
[314] 727-2996)
Cost: $200–$600

Incline press

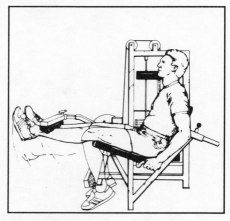

Leg extension

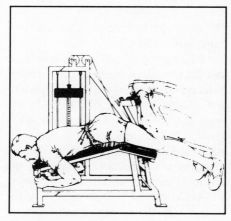

Leg curl

MICRO BIO-MEDICS, INC.
7177 South Third Ave.
Mount Vernon, NY 10550
(800) 431-2743
(914) 699-1700 in New York
(Also: Micro Bio-Medics, Inc.
211 Harbor Way
South San Francisco, CA 94080
[800] 241-6555
[415] 589-6037 in California)

Micro Bio-Medics is a medical supply brokerage. All twenty-six major league teams, as well as many minor league and major colleges and universities order their training supplies through one of their two offices.

Whirlpool (Upper and Lower Body)

Whirlpools aren't complicated pieces of training equipment, but neither are they benign. Trainers will tell you that whirlpools are fine for relaxation, but are not to be used immediately after an injury.

A common misconception among amateur athletes is to say, "Hey, Gary Carter soaks in one." He does, but Carter and other pros don't use them to treat or condition their bad knees or elbows. Ice (and compression) is the modality of choice after an injury. The heat, hot water and relaxation come later, up to 48 hours later, and then, only under the supervision of

the trainer, doctor, or rehab specialist.

Frustrated trainers say there's a reason modern oval whirlpools look like the troughs horses drink from—a lot of horses' asses misuse the tubs even today. Jacuzzi jets may feel great, and they should—that is, if they're properly aimed and properly prescribed.

FERNO ILLE
division of Ferno-Washington, Inc.
70 Weil Way
Wilmington, OH 45177
(800) 733-3766
(513) 382-1451 in Ohio
Cost: $1900–2700

JACUZZI WHIRLPOOL BATH
P.O. Drawer J
Walnut Creek, CA 94596
(800) 227-0710
(415) 938-7070 in California
Cost: $2000 for an institutional model

Hydrocollator

When you think "hydrocollator," think heat pack. This rectangular, electric, metal device, about the size of a TV/VCR stand made for a twenty-inch television, holds hot water and warms heat packs. The heat packs, filled with heat-retaining silicon pellets and wrapped in a sturdy fabric exterior, are used more commonly in rehabili-

tation than for injury prevention. (Fortunately, you don't need to buy the entire unit to benefit from it in rehab. The company will sell you the hydrocollator packs alone and tell you how to heat them up in water on the stove at home.)

Open the top of a hydrocollator heating unit and you'll see steam rising from the pack-filled water basin. Grab a pack, heft it—it's about the size of a knee sock—and you can immediately understand how the 140-degree heat travels into the body and penetrates deep into the musculature. It's not scorching heat, but it's authoritative heat.

"We always use ice first, immediately," Phillies' trainer Jeff Cooper will remind you. The heat isn't applied to sore joints until, typically, forty-eight hours after an injury occurs. And even then it is used in conjunction with ice, massage, and rest. The hydrocollator unit, while important, is only part—a pinch runner, say—of the healing team.

CHATTANOOGA CORP.
101 Memorial Drive
P.O. Box 4287
Chattanooga, TN 37405
(615) 870-2281
Cost: $255–$2,345 for main unit (heat packs can be purchased separately: $8–$12 per pack, depending on size; $100 per set)

Lateral raise

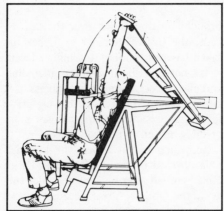

Shoulder press

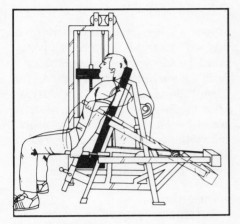

Tricep extension

Weight Machines

It used to be that baseball lore spoke of weight training as a negative thing for ball players. It used to be that a lot of players didn't train properly with weights. But that's finally changing, as elite-level players move to year-round conditioning for baseball.

The Cincinnati Reds generally are credited with being the first major league team to incorporate a series of weight-training machines, back in the mid-1970s. In previous baseball eras, the trouble wasn't with the weights themselves, but rather how they were being employed. Players were looking for bulk and strength, without regard for flexibility.

Trainers today will remind you that the more you train for strength—using free weights or weight machines such as Nautilus or Universal—the more you need to stretch. One complements the other. To avoid stiffness players are generally advised to use light weights and perform a lot of repetitions when they lift.

In 1989 the San Francisco Giants combined two new Universal weight machines with the hiring of a year-round fitness and nutritional consultant, Mackie Shillstone of New Orleans. Shillstone previously had trained Will Clark and Matt Williams of the Giants, as well as former heavyweight champion boxer Michael Spinks.

Don't look now, but the trainer's room is starting to get crowded.

UNIVERSAL GYM EQUIPMENT, INC.
P.O. Box 1270
Cedar Rapids, IA 52406
(800) 553-7901
(319) 365-7561 in Iowa

NAUTILUS, INC.
P.O. Drawer 809014
Dallas, TX 75380
(800) 874-8941
(214) 490-9155 in Texas

EAGLE FITNESS SYSTEMS BY CYBEX
division of Lumex Inc.
2100 Smithtown Ave.
P.O. Box 9003
Ronkonkoma, NY 11779
(800) 645-5392
(516) 585-9000 in New York

Dumbbells

Despite the influx of high-tech fitness machines into training rooms across the country, some of the most important, sport-specific weight work that's done in baseball is done with dumbbells. (No cracks, please.) And despite the presence of bulging bicep players like Brian Downing and Jose Canseco, light weights are often the best weights to use, trainers say.

Most trainers have a full complement of metal dumbbells on hand, ranging in weight from eight pounds to sixty pounds. But most of the work is done with the eight- to twenty-five-pounders. The reasons? Repetitions and safety. There's no magic formula, of course, but when the NL and AL trainers got together and wrote a book on baseball fitness, they stressed that baseball players using dumbbells to work the shoulders should aim for about twenty-one repetitions (three closely timed sets of seven reps for various exercises).

There's also an unwritten rule among pro pitchers that during the season they use ten-pound dumbbells rather than the twenty- or twenty-five-pounders in order to build stability in the arm and shoulder as opposed to building muscle bulk. Infielders and outfielders can benefit from the hurlers' experience. Most shoulder injuries in baseball are a result of repeated stress being placed on the shoulder and its rotator cuff. The rotator cuff muscles, then, act as "brakes" to decelerate the throwing arm that's whipping violently through the air and across the body.

When trainers talk about using dumbbells off the diamond, they advise players to use them to work on their "range of motion," "internal and external rotation," and "flexion" of their joints. It's important to have a proper program to work from, they add, one that is designed by a professional, because you don't want to sacrifice flexibility for newfound strength. As San Diego Padres trainer Dick Dent observes, when discussing weight training, "A stronger pitcher may last longer on the mound, and a better-conditioned fielder may gain a little extra range and more velocity on his throws, thus preventing more hits."

YORK BARBELL
Box 1707
York, PA 17405
(800) 358-YORK
(717) 767-6481 in Pennsylvania
Cost: $25–$479, for an Olympic set.

IVANKO BARBELL CO.
P.O. Box 1470
San Pedro, CA 90733
(213) 514-1155

UBE Ergometer

Perhaps more than any other machine brought on the market over the last decade, the UBE Ergometer by Cybex has taken baseball training to a higher level.

It's not that the machine is incredibly complex. In fact, some fitness experts have described it as, basically, a bicycle crank for the arms. Still, the mechanism is incredibly helpful to baseball players.

According to Pat Croce, the Philadelphia physical therapist who worked with Mike Schmidt after his 1988 shoulder surgery, the UBE is "great because, unlike dumbbells or rubber tubing, you can increase the resistance on the arm and shoulder muscles. And you can go in both directions, forward and back." Push forward and you work the chest, the pectorals, and triceps. Pull up and you work the deltoid, biceps, and trapezius muscles. And you also work the muscles of the rotator cuff.

"[For a simple aerobic workout] most players prefer the bike," though, says Jeff Cooper, the Phillies' head trainer. "They don't realize how much work it is to work the UBE. They're more used to cycling."

The UBE ergometer.

CYBEX (See p. 39.)
Cost: $2,390 plus $140 freight

**Cybex II Orthotron,
Biodex Multi-Joint System Machine**

These devices not only tell trainers who are the strongest and weakest players on a team, they also allow trainers to peer inside the body (in a way) without surgical intervention. *(Cont. p. 39.)*

On the Trainer's Wall

NATIONAL ATHLETIC TRAINERS ASSN.
Mary Edgerly, admin. coordinator
1001 East 4th Street
Greenville, NC 27834
(919) 752-1725
This nonprofit organization founded in 1950 offers accreditiation for professional trainers, sets standards, and evaluates those seeking to become athletic trainers in the U.S. Players' associations for Major League Baseball, as well as for the NFL and NBA, now require new trainers to be certified by NATA. NATA certifies about 700 new trainers each year.

PROFESSIONAL BASEBALL ATHLETIC
   TRAINERS SOCIETY
President: Charlie Moss

Head athletic trainer, Boston Red Sox
Fenway Park, 4 Yawkey Way
Boston, MA 02215
(617) 267-9440
In 1988 the major league trainers opened up PBATS membership to the trainers working for minor league affiliates of the pro clubs, making this the largest athletic training organization serving a professional sport. Its purpose is to provide a continuing-education program for athletic trainers at all levels of professional baseball to keep them current in injury-management techniques.

And on the Bookshelf

Last year, PBATS, along with writer Lee

Lowenfish, authored *The Professional Trainers' Fitness Book*. Each chapter is dedicated to a particular area of baseball training and is written by a different big league trainer. There are also photographs of various training techniques, exercises and stretches. It has its rough edges—at least one trainer complained of having to write a chapter out of his area of expertise—but it is the first comprehensive look at the state of the art.

*The Professional Trainers' Fitness
   Book*
Warner Books
P.O. Box 690
New York, NY 10019
Trade paperback, $12.95   —CP

The Cybex II and Biodex measure how an athlete's muscles are balanced, how an "agonist" muscle (i.e., quadriceps) stacks up against its "antagonist" counterpart (i.e., hamstring). This enables a doctor and trainer to prescribe a specific series of pre-season, postseason, and in-season exercises to bring a particular athlete's muscle groups more in line.

Let's look more closely at the example above: the common hamstrings-quadriceps imbalance of the thigh muscles. From Rickey Henderson to Keith Hernandez on the speed continuum, baseball players year in and year out have lost important playing time because of muscles that were out of balance. The explosive power of the quadriceps muscles in front can easily pull the thinner, cordlike hamstrings in back.

"When Mike Schmidt first came here in 1985," says Pat Croce, "it was scary." Schmidt's legs were stiff and woefully out-of-balance. "He was missing twenty to thirty games a season."

Schmidt's teammate in his final year, speedy outfielder Bob Dernier, thinks he knows another reason why more trainers are ordering machines such as the Cybex II and the Biodex. "It tells them when we're worn out."

These fitness-rehabilitation machines, then, put numbers on athletes' arms, legs, thighs, and shoulders. Now they've got some body stats to go along with their batting averages, RBIs, and ERAs.

CYBEX 340 MULTI-JOINT SYSTEM
Cybex, division of Lumex Inc.
2100 Smithtown Ave.
P.O. Box 9003
Ronkonkoma, NY 11779
(800) 645-5392
(516) 585-9000 in New York state
Cost: $41,990; an alternative machine with fewer functions but similar principles is about $9,990

BIODEX MULTI-JOINT SYSTEM
Biodex Corp.
49 Natcon Dr.
Shirley, NY 11967
(516) 924-9300
Cost: $44,900

—CP

Inside the Black Bag: A Selected Listing

Take a look inside a pro trainer's black medical bag and the first thing you'll see is order. "One common denominator among major league trainers," says Kent Biggerstaff, head trainer of the Pittsburgh Pirates, "is that most of us could go into our medicine kits in a dark room and pull out in an instant exactly what we need."

Tape, Bandages

Very often the first thing trainers will pull out of their black bags is athletic tape (for the ankles, elbows, or knees) or flexible bandages—sleeves—that slip over joints and provide a modicum of support.

Aside from the various 1/2- and 3/4-inch tapes commonly found in sporting goods shops or drugstores, pro trainers use miles of elasticized tape during the season. It provides a bit of a stretch with the support. Then, too, there are specific "knuckle bandages" and "fingertip coverlets," both of which do a fine job of protecting highly mobile, sensitive digits that are a crucial part of a ball player's arsenal.

Biersdorph "Elastoplast" elastic tape, Johnson & Johnson tapes and bandages:
CRIPPS FIRST AID AND MEDICAL
   SUPPLY
102 Weldon Parkway
Maryland Heights, MO 63043
(314) 567-9908
Cost: $3 and up
Cripps is another medical supply brokerage which deals mostly with smaller clients: high schools and some colleges.

JOHNSON & JOHNSON PRODUCTS
Customer Service
501 George St.
New Brunswick, NJ 08903
(800) 631-5259

Aspirin, Acetaminophen, Ibuprofen

From Excedrin to Tylenol to Advil and beyond, these pain-killing pills and tablets are stored in training rooms in containers big enough that they wouldn't fit on the shelves of your local Walgreen's.

We're not talking high-tech here, and neither do the trainers when it comes to analgesic tablets. But they do talk high volume. Every player's got his own preference, and so the list of brands in most training rooms is about as large as the list of active players on the pitching staff. On the amateur level, a two- or three-brand selection will suffice.

VARIOUS LOCAL DRUG STORES
(See also listings elsewhere in this section for Cripps First Aid and Medical Supply, and Micro Bio-Medics, Inc., for bulk orders and prices.)

Ethyl Chloride
("chloroethane" instant
pain-relief/freeze spray)

As soon as the Mets' Darryl Strawberry gets hit on the wrist by a fastball from, say, Todd Worrell of the Cardinals, two things happen. First, Strawberry flings his bat down and begins a charge to the mound—or at least he badmouths the guy who just

No, these are not punt-return men. In baseball fashion, eyeblack is in.

nailed him. Second, when he gets to first base, the Mets' trainer, Steve Garland, will sprint to the bag and spray ethyl chloride on the skin that's starting to swell.

"For a bad bruise, the spray isn't going to do much," says another certified athletic trainer who prefers to go unnamed here. "It's only temporary. In fact, if it's a deep muscle bruise in the back or the thigh, the spray isn't really effective; it's only topical. We trainers call it a 'TV time-out' because, let's face it, you've got to do something when you go out there. And how'd it look if you just went out there and massaged it a little bit?"

Still, this can of colorless, flammable, volatile liquid spray is found in every major league team's trainer's kit (and in all of the minor league trainers' kits too). And it does relieve pain for at least a minute or so. A doctor's prescription is required before ordering it.

GEBAUER CHEMICAL CO.
9410 St. Catherine Ave.
Cleveland, OH 44104

(800) 321-9348
(216) 271-5252 in Ohio
Cost: About $8 per 4 oz. cannister
(Also available with prescription at some local drug stores.)

Ben Gay, Sportscreme, Capsolin (Analgesic Balm)

No, it doesn't have to "smell bad to work good," but it does have to feel hot on the body, trainers say. And among the mysterious ingredients that go into the hottest of the arm/shoulder balms, Capsolin, is an extract from hot red peppers.

To be honest, trainers question the true value of the topical creams, because after all, if there's muscle or joint pain, it's well below the outer layer of the skin, the epidermis. And it's deeper than the next level of skin, the dermis. No matter how "hot" the balm, it's not going to penetrate all the way into the joint. So along with a little muffling of pain, a lot of what's going on here is the placebo effect. "But you gotta have it," trainers say nonetheless, "because the players always ask for it." (Think "ice" if you're serious, modern trainers add.)

For Ben Gay, Sportscreme:
VARIOUS LOCAL DRUGSTORES

For Capsolin:
PARKE-DAVIS CONSUMER HEALTH
　PRODUCTS, WARNER-LAMBERT, INC.
201 Tabor Rd.
Morris Plains, NJ 07950
(800) 524-0818
(201) 540-2000 in New Jersey
Cost: $10 per tube

Scissors and Cuticle Scissors (for hangnails, etc.)

The primary purpose of scissors, as far as trainers are concerned, is for removing tape from ankles, elbows, or other joints. Even if, as some pro trainers lament, the players always seem to be asking to borrow a pair to snip stray leather laces off of their gloves.

Knuckleballers and other pitchers also frequently ask trainers for scissors to manicure their fingernails. A hangnail on the index finger of someone's pitching hand may not sound serious, but it could greatly affect the moundsman's delivery.

And speaking of control, the Phillies' Jeff Cooper says, "I don't let anybody borrow my scissors. They're with me, on my belt, at all times. I may go through a pair a year, but I don't give them out. I'm the son of an electrician and I learned: 'Never lend your tools.' I keep a spare pair in the trainer's kit." Most trainers also stock an array of scissors, some for toenails or special foot gear.

MICRO BIO-MEDICS, INC.
717 S. Third Ave.
Mount Vernon, NY 10550
(800) 431-2743
(914) 699-1700 in New York state
(Also: Micro Bio-Medics, Inc.
211 Harbor Way
South San Francisco, CA 94080
[800] 241-6555
[415] 589-6037 in California)
Cost: Complete selection, $10 and up

Eyeblack/Sun Glare

Players like third baseman Mike Pagliarulo consider this gooey black wax that they smear under their eyes a part of their uniform. If there's a day game, the eyeblack goes on, even if the clouds are three miles thick.

It's not superstition to the players who swear by the stuff—it's physics. Dark colors absorb light; light colors reflect it. And ball players want the sun's rays to be absorbed or reflected away from their eyes when they're calling for a pop-up or fly ball. Old-time players would use lamp black (the soot from oil lamps) before companies started producing this stuff in a tube.

There's a good bit of conflicting opinion as to whether the stuff works in places like the Houston Astrodome or the Minneapolis Metrodome, but that doesn't mean it gets left off the face when it's time to play ball indoors. It goes on as automatically as the National Anthem before the first pitch.

CRAMER PRODUCTS
P.O. Box 1001
Gardner, KS 66030
(800) 255-6621
(913) 884-7511 in Kansas
Cost: 3 oz. tube, $4.75
(Also available at major full-line sporting goods stores.)

Massaging Oil

On any game day, trainer Ken Biggerstaff will likely be wearing a T-shirt in the Pittsburgh Pirates clubhouse that reads: "Lots of treatment; no sympathy."

Biggerstaff spent fifteen years in the minor leagues before landing in Pittsburgh in 1982, and in doing so he has massaged thousands of tired, hurting, shell-shocked pitching arms and shoulders. He had the shirts printed up after he massaged his 6,000th or so bruised ego.

Today he massages mostly with Albo-lene cream, which he favors over baby oil or Dermassage, another popular product, because the cream "liquifies very quickly." It also cleanses the players' skin—unlike baby oil, which irritates some players. Despite his T-shirt, Biggerstaff says, "I'm a firm believer that pitchers need extra care because pitching [200 or so innings a season] is such an unnatural act. In that respect we baby them a little with extra massage."

CRIPPS FIRST AID AND MEDICAL
    SUPPLY
102 Weldon Parkway
Maryland Heights, MO 63043
(314) 567-9908
Cost: $3 and up
(And at various local drugstores.)

NORCLIFF THAYER, INC.
    (Albolene Liquifying Cleanser)
Beecham Products
P.O. Box 1467
Pittsburgh, PA 15230
(800) 245-1040
(412) 928-1000 in Pennsylvania

Antibacterial Solution, Hydrogen Peroxide (for strawberries, abrasions, etc.)

It almost goes without saying, but trainer Biggerstaff will say it anyway: over a 162-game schedule plus spring training, "we get a lotta cuts and scrapes."

Besides the generic, antibacterial hydrogen peroxide preparation available at any local drugstore, baseball trainers often use a solution called Betadine. This is a povidine-iodine mix that is applied by spray or gauze to a cleaned, still-stinging cut or abrasion (caused by sliding or an artificial turf "burn"). It goes on after the hydrogen peroxide and before an antibacterial ointment such as Bacitracin.

CRIPPS FIRST AID AND MEDICAL
    SUPPLY (See above.)
Cost: Hydrogen peroxide: about

$ .54 per bottle; Betadine povidine-iodine: about $7 per bottle
(Also available at local drugstores.)

Hypodermic Needle and Syringe, Fluid-Draining Needle (for knees, elbows, etc.)

Though it's certainly true that major league training rooms have surgical needles and syringes on hand, National Athletic Trainers Association (NATA) guidelines do not allow trainers to give injections.

That is the job of the team physician, or another doctor if a club is on the road. That's not to say that pro trainers don't give injections on occasion, but when they do they are operating in risky territory.

"A syringe is a prescription item," says Ernie Nelson, a certified trainer in the New York area who also works at a medical supply brokerage firm. "We can't even sell a needle unless it's a prescription item from a doctor."

For supplier and cost, consult your doctor or team doctor.

Ice Pack/Frozen Gel ("Blue Ice")

When it's not convenient to lug an ice-making machine around, a trainer can use portable frozen gel packs to reduce pain and the swelling of an injury. Most of these packs on the market are made of a malleable blue substance covered in clear plastic. Roughly the size of a paperback book, there are gel pacs that must be kept in the freezer and others that will simply turn cold when snapped.

Over the past few years, the makers of athletic and elastic bandages have come out with bandages with sleeves that hold frozen gel packs nicely against the limb or joint. As far as Little Leaguers or other young players are concerned, an added feature to look for is the nontoxicity of the gel product (in case the plastic pack splits open).

CRAMER PRODUCTS
P.O. Box 1001
Gardner, KS 66030
(800) 255-6621
(713) 884-7511 in Kansas
Cost: About $10 per dozen packs

MUELLER SPORTS MEDICINE, INC.
One Quench Drive
Prairie du Sac, WI 53578
(800) 356-9522
(608) 643-8530 in Wisconsin
Cost: $10 and up per dozen packs

Sunglasses

On top of everything else, big league trainers are responsible for making sure the right lenses shade the right pairs of eyes.

It's not as simple as it looks. "There are two kinds of frames and four shades of green lenses," says Jeff Cooper of the Phillies. "Sometimes the guys will choose the darkest shade (No. 4) for spring training in the Florida sun, and then they want to change it when they come up north." Other players find they want to switch to a different shade by midseason. The days are longest then, and the sun glances off fielders' eyes at different angles than in spring or fall. Again, it's up to the trainers to switch the lenses and properly store them. Between and during games, the glasses are stored (by players' numbers) in a pocketed container that looks a lot like a long, fold-up cotton towel with twenty-eight slots. Everybody's got his own precisely fitted pair.

"Some guys got bucketheads and some got pinheads," Cooper muses. "And after a day game I physically stand in the dugout and take them off the players." The lenses are made of sturdy polycarbonate, Cooper says, not only for longevity but also "so they bounce off the back of the dugout better."

VISION MASTER, INC.
3972 Warrensville Center Rd.
Cleveland, OH 44122

(216) 283-8381
Cost: $32–$37 per pair
(For less expensive, nonprofessional models, go to any large sporting goods store.)

Eyewash/Contact Lens Solutions

One of the strangest cases of a baseball player being disabled occurred during spring training in 1974, at Mesa, Arizona. Without warning one day, outfielder Jose Cardenal took himself out of the Cub lineup because, he said, his eyelashes were stuck together.

Cub manager Whitey Lockman was dumbfounded. So were Cardenal's teammates. But his eye was indeed stuck until an eyewash solution and a good night's sleep finally loosened up the lashes.

The much more common use of saline solution, sterile water, boric acid, and other eyewash solutions occurs when the swirling dust of the infield gets in players' eyes, disrupting play as well as their vision. Trainers keep an eyecup and eyewash solutions on hand for moments like these.

In recent years they've also begun stocking several brands of saline and cleaning solution for players who wear contact lenses (while following ophthalmologists' prescriptions). While the players clean and store their lenses daily, the trainers keep a spare pair for each player in the clubhouse and on the road.

BAUSCH & LOMB
Personal Products Division
Rochester, NY 14692-0450
(716) 338-6372
Cost: $2.50 and up for saline solutions; about $9 per bottle for sterile water

To catch the ball, it is wise first to see it. Kevin McReynolds and Lenny Dykstra, then of the New York Mets, both with their shades down, prepare to emulate the Bruise Brothers. If Billy Loes had worn shades in the 1952 Series, would he have "lost that grounder in the sun"?

Surgical Tubing (for flexibility exercises, workouts on the road)

Barry Weinberg, the Oakland Athletics' trainer, may share the bench with two of the strongest sluggers in the American League—Jose Canseco and Mark McGwire—but he often favors workouts with skinny rubber bands instead of heavy, weighted barbells.

These flesh-colored strips of latex surgical tubing can do much more than make great slingshots. "Pitchers use them to loosen their shoulders," Weinberg says, "and other players use them for rehabilitation and to maintain flexibility throughout the season." By pulling on the high-strength tubing in various ways, players can give their arm and leg muscles intense, controlled resistance. More important, under a trainer's or physical therapist's guidance, they can target specific, hard-to-reach muscles in and around a knee or shoulder.

And amateur players don't even need to get the official kind. "Fifteen years ago I used to use bicycle tire tubing," says Weinberg. "Now they put a fancy name on it, like Sport Cord, and make a lot of money on it." Trainers also like to use surgical tubing on the road because it's easy to pack and carry—and players can work with it on road trips in their hotel rooms. Or when they watch TV.

MICRO BIO-MEDICS, INC.
717 South Third Ave.
Mount Vernon, NY 10550
(800) 431-2743
(914) 699-1700 in New York state
(Also: Micro-Bio-Medics, Inc.
211 Harbor Way
South San Francisco, CA 94080
[800] 241-6555
[415] 589-6037 in California)
Cost: $29 per 50-foot roll of
¼-inch latex

LIFELINE INTERNATIONAL
(Lifeline Gym)
1421 South Park Street
Madison, WI 53715
(800) 553-6633
Cost: $50

Fluid Replacement Drinks (Gatorade, Exceed, H₂0.)

Although you don't normally think of water as baseball equipment, it plays an invaluable role in the trainer's arsenal during the long hot summer. Because games are often played in 90-degree-plus weather, the dangers of heat cramps, heat exhaustion and heatstroke hover over clubs constantly.

Dick Martin, head trainer of the Minnesota Twins, says it is commonly accepted that more than any other nutritional factor, dehydration causes athletic performance to decline.

Trainers repeatedly tell their ball players they should drink about ten ounces of water before a game and then ten ounces

every twenty minutes or so thereafter to perform at peak efficiency. The makers of brand name electrolyte/carbohydrate drinks for athletes have done a great job of marketing over the past fifteen years, but the truth is baseball players don't need those fortified drinks as much as marathon runners do. That's not to say that both don't sweat profusely, but baseball is not an aerobic exercise. Gatorade or other drinks such as Exceed have certainly made inroads into almost every pro clubhouse, but they've done so as "luxury" drinks.

One more reason that water is the drink

of choice among major leaguers: After a called third strike it's simply not as satisfying to fling a quart container of Gatorade six feet as it is to wind up and slam your open fist against the defenseless dugout water fountain. Then take a sip and cool off.

GATORADE THIRST QUENCHER
division of Quaker Oats Company
P.O. Box 9001
Chicago, IL 60604-9001
(312) 222-7111

EXCEED
distributed by Ross Labs
625 Cleveland Ave.
Columbus, OH 43215
(614) 227-3333

—CP

Tough Guys Finish Early

You've heard all those "be-an-Oriole" stories about how the old-timers used to rub a little dirt and tobacco juice on compound fractures and go right on playing.

According to legend, if a priest didn't give a guy last rites, he didn't come out of the lineup. What the stories don't tell you is how many careers were ended prematurely by the old-time combination of macho malarkey and prehistoric prescriptions. Rotator cuffs were just as fragile then as now.

In fact, Joe Borden, the winning pitcher in the very first National League game back in 1876, finished that premier season as the team groundskeeper when his arm, as they used to say, "died." Maybe with an "arm transplant," *à la* Tommy John, Borden could still have been pitching when the 60′ 6″ distance came in.

You've got to wonder what modern care and treatment might have done for Hall of Famer George Sisler. The "Sizzler" lashed out a major-league record 257 hits in 1922 while batting .420, his second .400 season. But then he missed the entire 1923 season with a sinus infection that affected his sight. After that he was a "good" hitter but nothing like he'd been before. If antibiotics had been invented a little sooner, we might have had to rewrite the record book. —BC

Ron Guidry's arm is in an ice bucket to constrict blood flow from the capillaries that broke around his elbow.

ice cold shower in the morning. But it can become an acquired taste for players like sore-armed pitchers who recognize its soothing, anesthetic effects. "My pitchers can't wait to ice down after a game," says Starr. The same pain-killing effect enables the trainer, in the case of an injury, to put the troubled limb through range of motion exercises to determine the extent of the problem.

Ice is really just one part of a first-aid response to sports injuries that goes by the acronym RICE: rest, ice, compression, elevation. That means the injured area should first be immobilized, that ice should be fastened to the injury to help speed the healing, and that the injured area should be raised, on a chair or bench, to help facilitate blood flow.

Although no trainer worth his smelling salts would ever apply heat to a fresh injury (it could increase swelling), there are many who will use "contrast" therapy, after twenty-four hours, for certain joint injuries and for contusions of the thigh and lower back. Contrast is a mode of therapy in which ice and heat—in the form of heat pads, or even a whirlpool bath—are rotated every three to five minutes. "It dilates and constricts the vessels and allows more blood to flow into the injured area," explains Gene Gieselmann, head trainer for the St. Louis Cardinals. Still, he cautions, "As soon as the injury occurs, you use ice."

How to use it is another question. Some trainers go for chemical bags, the prepackaged "blue ice." But Starr, for one, doesn't recommend these as part of the normal first aid kit. He points out that the bags can break and chemicals can leak out, causing inflammation. He maintains that ice packs or good, old-fashioned ice cubes wrapped in a towel are just as effective. If no improvement is evident after twenty-four hours, X rays are advisable.   —JH

First Response: Ice and "RICE"

What's the first thing to use on the aches, pains, and sprains of baseball? Well, ice is nice. RICE is even better. But heat just isn't cool.

Start with ice. That's what most professional baseball trainers do whenever there's swelling involved. That may sound strange, since the objective is to increase blood flow to the injured area—get the old blood out and new blood in. Wouldn't ice have a chilling effect on that process?

"That's the biggest misconception [about ice]," says Cincinnati Reds head trainer Larry Starr. "Initially you will get constriction of the vessels. But if you continue to apply ice, your body will respond by trying to elevate the temperature and increase blood flow."

Just think about what happens when you make a snowball in your bare hands. "Your hand turns red," says Starr. "That red is blood. It's the body reacting to cold."

Still, as any red-blooded (or warm-blooded) player knows, the big problem with ice is that it feels about as good as an

---

DISCLAIMER: CONSULT YOUR DOCTOR FIRST

On this and the following pages you'll find suggestions for various training programs and exercises, as well as treatments for various injuries and ailments. The instructions and advice presented on the following pages are in no way intended as a substitute for medical treatment or advice. Consult your doctor before begin-

ning any of the programs suggested here, especially if you have any serious medical condition or are taking medication.

The authors, editors, and publisher of this book disclaim all responsibility for any injury or illness that may result from employing any treatment or exercise program described in this book.

A Life-Saving Play

On July 30, 1988, first baseman Greg Walker was fielding ground balls before a night game against the California Angels. Suddenly he was down, without warning, collapsed on his back on the ruddy-brown clay of the infield. Walker had suffered a rare seizure, and his body began convulsing out of control. He shouted for help, and shortstop Ozzie Guillen sprinted over to him.

Guillen tried to calm Walker, but Walker shook him off violently. Guillen later said, "I've never been so scared." The call went out to Herman Schneider, the White Sox trainer since 1979. He bolted from his clubhouse office to first base, and saw Walker turning blue and slipping into unconsciousness. Schneider tried to use an "oral screw" to force Walker's mouth open, but it was clenched shut. He then used a pair of scissors to help force Walker's teeth apart.

Instinctively Schneider reached down Walker's throat and was able to pull his tongue out of his windpipe. In doing so Schneider saved Walker's life. He then rode with him to the hospital, where doctors determined that the seizure was probably caused by a rare infection that had invaded Walker's brain.

When the incident hit the news wires, the Epilepsy Association criticized Schneider's actions, insisting that people don't really swallow their tongues. They got no support from Walker or any other White Sox player.

"If Herm doesn't do what he did, Greg's gone," said Sox manager Jim Fregosi.

"When I got to him," Schneider told Chicago writer Bob Verdi, "on a scale of one to ten, he was nine-plus dead."

On April 5, 1989, the White Sox' Opening Day boxscore showed Walker back in the starting lineup, going two for five against the California Angels.   —CP

The Five Most Common Baseball Injuries, and How Not to Get Them

A general manager once asked Oakland A's trainer Barry Weinberg how a team could have an injury-free year. You'd need two things, Weinberg replied. Healthy players. And luck.

Well, players have gotten healthier in recent years. Or at least stronger and leaner. A study by the Cincinnati Reds found that between 1981 and 1989 the average weight of a player increased from 189 to 205 pounds, while his average body fat declined from 15 to 10 percent.

But all the weight training in the world can't change the way the ball bounces—or the way it's thrown, pitched, or swung at. Let's face it: the human body was not designed by Abner Doubleday. Over the course of a 162-game season, virtually every major league player requires some kind of treatment for some kind of injury, from broken bones to blisters.

The most common are the so-called "soft tissue" injuries. These are the strains and sprains, the overuse/abuse injuries, the infamous "itises" (as in bursitis and tendinitis) that afflict the tendons, cartilage and ligaments that bind and support muscle and bone.

Torn Rotator Cuff

The most commonly injured part of a ball player's body is his shoulder. Weinberg estimates that over 40 percent of all baseball injuries are shoulder-related. Specifically they're related to the four muscles that make up the most famous part of the baseball anatomy: the rotator cuff. "The primary job of the rotator cuff muscles," explains Toronto Blue Jays trainer Tommy Craig, "is to act like the parachute on a dragster. They slow down the arm."

And, like a fraying shroud of nylon that has had to put the breaks on one too many funny cars, the rotator cuff muscles of a ball player also begin to wear out as they're used again and again—throw after throw, game after game, season after season.

What eventually develops is what surgeon Frank Jobe calls "rotator cuff disease." It's a cycle of weakness, pain and loss of range of motion in the arm. Then tendinitis (inflammation) sets in, scar tissue forms and eventually the muscles tear. "It's a slow, insidious process," says Craig. But it's not just veterans who are affected. Cincinnati Reds trainer Larry Starr sees Little Leaguers with potential rotator cuff problems. "They abuse their arms," says Starr. "A kid pitches a seven-inning game, throws for an hour later, and then pitches again the next day."

If overuse and abuse is what causes rotator cuff disease, what cures it should be obvious: rest. "I don't care how advanced we get in sports medicine," says Milwaukee Brewers trainer John Adam, "we can't substitute for rest."

Preventing the problem demands a little more activity on the part of the player and his coaches. First and foremost, it takes conditioning to keep the muscles strong

Six Steps to a Healthy Rotator Cuff

The rotator cuff muscles are to baseball—in terms of use and abuse—what the knees are to football. After a regular weight workout (see page 48), trainer Tommy Craig of the Blue Jays recommends performing a medley of exercises for the rotator cuff muscles of both shoulders that was developed by the American Sports Medicine Institute and is called the "Essential Six." They're performed with five-pound weights for two to five sets of ten to fifteen repetitions per set.

1. *Shoulder Abduction:* Stand with your elbow straight and hand rotated outward as far as possible. Raise your arm to the side of your body as high as possible. Hold for two seconds and then lower.

2. *Shoulder Abduction with Internal Rotation:* This motion is often compared to pouring water out of a can. Stand with your elbow straight and rotate your hand inward as far as possible. Raise your arm to eye level at a 30-degree angle. Hold for two seconds.

3. *Prone Horizontal Abduction:* Lie facedown on a table with your arm hanging down over the edge. With your hand rotated outward as far as possible, raise your arm out to the side, parallel to the floor. Hold for two seconds, then lower.

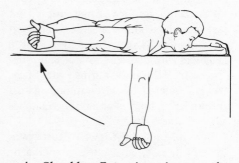

4. *Shoulder Extension:* Assume the same position, facedown on the table, arm hanging over the edge, with hand rotated outward. Raise your arm straight back, parallel to the table. Hold for two seconds, then lower.

5. *90-Degree External Rotation:* Lie facedown with the forearm extended over the edge of the table at a 90-degree angle and your elbow on the edge of the table. Keeping your shoulder and elbow fixed, raise your arm to a point parallel to the table. Hold for two seconds, then lower.

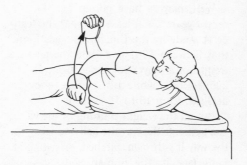

6. *Side-Lying External Rotation:* Lie on your side, with your elbow bent at 90 degrees. Keeping your elbow fixed, raise your arm to a point perpendicular to the table. Hold two seconds, then lower.

—JH

and balanced and stretching to keep them supple (see the exercises opposite). It also means icing down the arm after a game, massage, and, of particular importance to younger players, good mechanics and form.

Pitcher's Elbow

Another overworked and thus oft-injured part of the body is the elbow. Actually it's a problem that could be shared by Mats Wilander and Matt Keough. Tennis elbow and pitcher's elbow are essentially the same ailment: an inflammation of the muscles and joints of the elbow that can even affect the ulnar nerve at the base of the elbow. It's an overuse injury sometimes aggravated by poor mechanics or even by a pitcher trying to work on a new pitch. The symptoms are swelling, discomfort, and, when the nerve is affected, numbness and tingling in the elbow. The treatment is RICE (rest, ice, compression, elevation).

Lower Back Pain

The New York Yankees lost two of the best hitters in the game—Dave Winfield and Don Mattingly—to back injuries during the 1988–89 seasons. Winfield had a herniated disk that required surgery. Mattingly missed some games and was relegated to a DH role in others because of back problems he has had since high school.

The Yankees don't play on artificial turf, but that could be one factor in what some trainers see as an overall rise in the number of back (as well as knee and hip) injuries in recent years. Whatever the turf, it's the infielders and catchers who get the brunt of the lower back problems, with all the crouching and bending they do, but, as outfielder Winfield's case shows, no player is immune.

The symptoms for lower back injuries are discomfort, difficulty in bending over, and numbness or tingling down the legs, which often, but not always, indicates a disk problem. Mattingly described his ailment as "a sudden stiffness across the bottom band of my back."

For that kind of lower back problem, heat packs or ice treatments are helpful. Best of all, according to Seattle Mariners trainer Rick Griffin, are fifteen- to twenty-minute sessions in a whirlpool. Some of that time might well be spent doing the abdominal crunches and hyperextensions that can help prevent back injuries.

Knee Injuries

In recent years, knee injuries have moved up on the list of the most common baseball maladies. Starr knows why. "I'm going to get some heat from my general manager for saying this," he says, "but it's Astro-Turf." Specifically it's players running on AstroTurf, an unforgiving surface that may lead to chondromalacia—a degenerative condition that affects the soft tissue surfaces of the knee. The symptoms are swelling and loss of range of motion. The treatment is RICE. But if a ligament is damaged all that a player can do is strengthen the muscles around the knee with weight training and hope for a trade to a team that plays on the stuff cows eat.

Common Wrist Sprains

The scenario for yet another common baseball injury is an all-too-familiar one for the Brewers' John Adam. A player slides into second, puts his hand down to the base, and comes up holding his wrist. "It's the dreaded wrist sprain," says Adam. "You X-ray it a million times. Nothing. But it's still sore. He can't swing a bat. It begins to affect his throwing. A check swing drives him through the roof. He wants you to tape it tighter and tighter. By the time his fingers turn blue, he realizes it's not working. Meanwhile, your GM is yelling at you, 'Make it better.' The answer? Rest. You just have to shut it down."

Or you can just put your hands up while you slide. That's the best way to prevent the dreaded, common wrist sprains. —JH

Oddball Injuries

Even proper technique, rest, strengthening, and stretching can't prevent one common class of injuries. "Balls hit guys, guys hit guys," says Oakland's Weinberg. "It's part of baseball. You get hit by a pitch or a foul tip. You run into somebody at first base." The result: a contusion. The treatment: RICE. The way to prevent it: take up another sport.

Less predictable are the injuries that come in cycles for no apparent reason, to the chagrin of players, trainers and coaches alike. One year Weinberg had four players injure the oblique muscles on the side of the torso. Another year he had three wrist fractures. In 1988 he had four facial injuries sustained by players who ran into each other. In an average season he might see only one, if any, of these problems.

Seattle's Rick Griffin, working with a team that always has long distances to travel for games, treats many stiff necks of players who fall asleep on the plane with their heads turned to the side. He's also encountered numerous shin splints, which are easily prevented by wearing proper shoes. "It's strange when you consider the amount of money these guys make," says the Mariners trainer. "But they won't spend it on shoes. One guy eventually got a stress fracture in his leg because he refused to buy a good pair of running shoes. He had an endorsement contract with a shoe manufacturer and insisted on waiting for them to send a free pair. He waited too long."

You might not travel to your games by plane or have a shoe contract. But you should have the common sense to work at the conditioning and take the preventive steps necessary to minimize the risks of most baseball injuries.

In other words, get yourself healthy and good luck will naturally follow.   —JH

Stretching: Preventive Medicine

Whether you're playing first base or running your first race, the guidelines for warming up are the same. But try to get ball players to believe that.

"It's all kind of foreign to them," notes John Adam, head trainer for the Milwaukee Brewers. "When I tell my guys, 'Okay, let's warm up,' they throw the ball around the infield for a few minutes and say, 'All right, my arm's loose. I'm ready.' "

But of course, a loose arm does not a warmed-up body make. A proper warmup for baseball begins not with pepper or even pushups, but with three to five minutes of aerobic-type activity: running in place, jumping rope or even the old jumping jack exercises you used to do in high school gym class. This elevates the body temperature and gets you ready for flexibility drills: a fancy name for stretching.

This can be as simple as an individual player swinging the bat, loosening the arms and legs, and stretching out the areas that feel tight to him. Or it can be as regimented and exotic as the Oakland A's stretching sessions, which are led by a *tae kwon do* black belt and done to music.

"The most important thing," says A's trainer Barry Weinberg, "is for players to learn how to stretch, why they stretch, and how stretching can help them."

How it can help should be as clear as the hamstring pulled by a leadoff hitter as he tries to leg out a hot grounder on a cold muscle. Muscles that are warmed up and flexible aren't as likely to snap, crackle, and pop a player off the field and onto the injured list.

Learning how to stretch isn't hard either. A few simple rules should suffice. Stretching shouldn't hurt. It should be done gradually and carefully—none of that bouncing around like you're in an aerobic dance class, please. And it isn't competitive. "If you can't touch your toes— and I can't," says Weinberg, "you're still going to get the same benefits as somebody who can." Just stretch as far as you can while feeling tension, but not pain. Hold it for 10 to 20 seconds and repeat. Your body will tell you when it's ready.

A player's position will dictate what areas require special stretching attention. For example, a catcher is going to be more concerned with his hip and groin than an outfielder, who'll be concentrating on those legs, which can get awfully stiff standing around out there.

Whatever you do, make sure you do it gently and gradually. Don't be lackadaisical, but don't get as worked up in your warmup as Cardinal rookie Geronimo Pena did last year during a spring training game. Pena broke his wrist while swinging a weighted bat in the on-deck circle.

—JH

Weight Training, Baseball-Style

When Rick Griffin arrived in Seattle as the Mariners' head trainer, he found that there were no weight-training facilities for the players to use. "I was appalled," says Griffin. "The coaches told me you can't lift and play ball. 'You'll get tight,' they said. 'You won't be able to throw correctly.' "

Eight years later, the pendulum has swung to the other extreme. Now teams not only have weight training facilities, but special coaches to help the players use them. Now managers like former Yankees skipper Lou Piniella complain that players are spending too much time in the weight room. Now, barbell boys like Jose Canseco of the Oakland A's and Kirby Puckett of the Minnesota Twins are the prototypical sluggers in the game.

What happened? The tradition-bound baseball establishment finally realized what coaches and athletes in almost every other sport, from football to water polo, have known for years. A stronger athlete is generally a better athlete, and the best way to build strength and power is through the use of weight training.

We're not talking about bench-pressing Volkswagens here—or about five-hour, Schwarzeneggerian training sessions. This is baseball, not bodybuilding—and the weights are a means to an end. "We're not looking to just develop large muscles," says A's trainer Barry Weinberg. "We never lose sight of the fact that the game is played with a ball and a bat." But that ball can be thrown harder and farther, that bat can be swung with more authority—and for more seasons—if the men doing it are stronger.

Getting that power edge is achieved by lifting regularly, three or four times a week, working all the muscle groups and practicing strict form on the movements, whether you're using old-fashioned dumbbells or high-tech, computerized resistance machines.

The following is a basic program developed by trainer Tommy Craig for the Toronto Blue Jays that he believes can be used by players at all levels. This is a three-day-per-week program (Monday-Wednesday-Friday or Tuesday-Thursday-Saturday) that works all muscle groups. The amount of weight that can be comfortably

handled will vary from individual to individual. As Craig advises his players, consult an instructor at your local gym to help you find the right weight and to show you how to perform these exercises properly. Add weight gradually. A good rule of thumb might be that once eight reps is easy, add five to ten pounds of weight.

DAYS 1 AND 3
Leg Press, 3 sets of 10 repetitions
Leg Extension, 3 x 10
Leg Curl, 3 x 10
Calf Raise, 1 x 15
Bench Press, 2 x 12
Flys, 2 x 12
Shoulder Press, 2 x 12
Deltoid Flys, 1 x 12
Rows, 1 x 12
Pulldowns, 1 x 15
Dips, 1 x 15
Triceps Pushdowns, 3 x 10
Pushups, 2 x 10

DAY 2
Leg Press, 1 x 12
Leg Extension, 1 x 12
Leg Curl, 1 x 12
Calf Raise, 1 x 15
Chest Fly, 2 x 10
Shoulder Press, 2 x 10
Deltoid Flys, 2 x 10
Rows, 2 x 10
Pullover, 2 x 10
Bench Dips, 2 x 10
Dips, 1 x 10   —JH

Iron Arms

Joe McGinnity of the Giants pitched complete game victories in both ends of three doubleheaders during August 1903.

Ed Reulbach, Cubs, blanked Brooklyn twice on September 26, 1908.

Joe Oeschger, Boston Braves, and Leon Cadore, Brooklyn, battled for 26 innings to a 1–1 tie, May 1, 1920.   —BC

Don't Wait Till Next Year: Off-Season Workouts

Time was, baseball players used the off-season to escape the rigors of playing baseball. Today, baseball is a year-round proposition. Professionals are expected to arrive at spring training in as good or even better shape than they were the previous season.

Milwaukee Brewers trainer John Adam says, "I've had some players who've never worked out in the off-season. They're the guys about whom people end up saying, 'Hey, whatever happened to so-and-so?' "

What happened is that they got out of shape and consequently had to get out of baseball. Such a fate can be avoided by a sensible, structured off-season program. Indeed, as trainer Tommy Craig of the Toronto Blue Jays points out, rest and a healthy diet are two important components. The other four, more active ingredients are daily flexibility exercises (stretching), endurance work, strength training, and skill work.

"We are a quick, short duration, highly explosive sport," says Cincinnati Reds trainer Larry Starr. For endurance, he believes in fast-paced two- or three-mile runs, three or four times a week, or a speed workout like the one trainer Rick Griffin uses for the Seattle Mariners—six to eight 300-yard sprints with a minute of rest in between; or, if winter weather keeps you indoors, the fifteen- to twenty-minute cardiovascular training sessions that Craig's Blue Jays do on stationary bikes, Stairmaster machines (a fixture in most health clubs), or even jump ropes.

Off-season, Griffin and a group of Mariners meet three times a week at the Kingdome to lift weights. They, like most other ball players, work all body parts with a special emphasis on the rotator cuff muscles of the shoulder.

Finally, don't neglect skill work in the off-season, but don't overdo it either: Work on fundamentals two or three times a week, but keep it light. Throw, don't pitch. Swing the bat to loosen up, not to reach the fences.

It's hard for intense, highly competitive individuals to play any game without giving it 100 percent—thus risking injury. Don Mattingly's contract forbids him to play racquetball or basketball in the off-season. But you can. Just don't play games with your off-season conditioning program.   —JH

CHAPTER 4

Tools of the Trade

The baseball is primary.
Without a ball, the bat is kindling, the glove is a bloated mitten, and the base an obese pincushion. Without a ball, World Series crowds could cheer only pantomimes in flannel and pinstripes. Without a ball, our national game would be base-*standing-around*.

But though the ball is elementary, essential, intrinsic, and indispensable, discussions of the sphere *sine qua non* always seem to start and stop with one question: how much rabbit is in it this year?

The alleged bunny quotient is tied to each season's home run totals. When homers fly with the regularity of rain on the roof, everybody says the ballmakers left the gate to the hutch open. As soon as homers go down, the makers are accused of bunnicide.

Not so, say the ballmakers—Rawlings since 1977; Spalding for about a hundred years before that. (Rawlings also made balls for Spalding from 1968 to 1974.) Baseballs, they say, have changed less in 118 years than footballs or basketballs. Since 1872, the baseball has weighed 5 ounces and measured 9 inches in circumference. If you let it go at that, you figure the horsehide Ozzie Smith blasts over the Busch Stadium fence is the same as the one Home Run Baker earned his nickname on. But wait a minute. We all know there's a big difference between smacking 5 ounces of vulcanized cottontail and clubbing 5 ounces of Silly Putty. It's what's inside those 9 inches of horsehide circumference that counts.

Well, if you're going to get technical, says Rawlings, the outside has been made of cowhide since 1974, when then-Com-

Bat, Ball & Glove

Do today's balls have more bounce to the ounce? Do aluminum-bat wielders eat quiche?

missioner Bowie Kuhn discreetly authorized the switch. It wasn't big news except to Secretariat.

And the size and weight *can* make a difference, says Rawlings, dredging up 3-ounce, 8½-inch-circumference baseballs from the 1840s. Games sometimes saw more than 100 runs scored until they changed the rules in 1846 to the winner being the first team to get 21. So there! Still, Rawlings admits, inside that undersized ball was a melted rubber center covered by wound wool, and that had an effect on its liveliness.

Okay, but in 1854 balls ballooned to 5½ or 6 ounces and a circumference up to 11 inches without changing the contents. The resulting thud was so dead that four years later rulemakers scratched the "out on first bounce" rule.

The ball shrank a little in 1860, and then in 1872 the size was standardized at 5 to 5¼ ounces and 9 to 9¼ ounces, the same as today. Rawlings suggests that the ball could be as lively as a Vegas party in the nineteenth century, citing the 142 homers the Chicago White Stockings (today's Cubs) hit in 1884. Don't believe it. Chicago played in a band box that year. The left-

field foul line was 180 feet; right field was 196; and center was all of 300. Those dimensions would make a Reggie Jackson out of Michael Jackson. In 1885 the White Stockings moved into a real ballpark and their homers fell to 54, which was still nearly 30 more than any other National League team.

They not only played with a deceased baseball in the nineteenth century, they also liked it like that. One New York manufacturer advertised "our professional dead balls . . . are made of all yarn without rubber and are the deadest balls made." That was handy to know in the days when the hometeam had to provide the ball. If you had pitching and fielding but couldn't hit a lick, you wanted your baseballs to arrive in a box marked "R.I.P." The National League tightened the rules on balls, but no one seriously compares the nineteenth-century rock with today's rocket.

In 1900 Spalding tried a cork-center ball, but it didn't work because the surrounding wool yarn swelled after the thing was stitched. In 1910 they got it right. The cork was reduced and covered with a layer of rubber. Home runs in the majors went up from 271 in 1909 to 359 in 1910 and 512 in 1911. That sparked the first real rabbit-ball criticisms, but the pitchers defused that by developing shine balls, emery balls, and so on. By 1912 homers were down to 438.

The next big brouhaha over bunny baseballs came in the early 1920s, when home run totals shot way up again. Ball makers plead no *mea culpa* on that, blaming the ban on the spitball and other freak pitches along with a change in attitude that saw batters trying to emulate Babe Ruth.

According to Rawlings, the only change

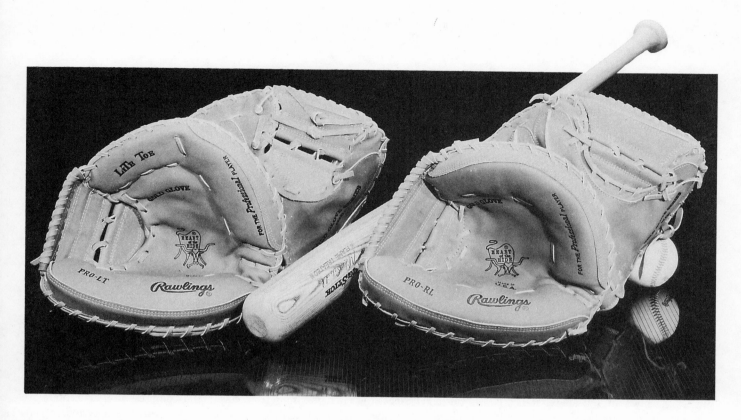

in baseball specs since Taft was President has been the replacement of the old cork center with a *cushioned* cork center, which was introduced in 1931. They start with a small sphere of composition cork molded inside a couple of layers of rubber. The inside layer is made up of two hemispheres of black rubber, sealed with a cushion of red rubber. The outside layer is red rubber. Major league homers actually dropped from 1,565 in 1930 to 1,068 in '31 and didn't surpass the 1930 total until 1940.

Rawlings will wax poetic about the three-wool-and-one-cotton windings that surround the baseball's cushioned cork center. They get a charge out of citing temperature and humidity controls. All that yarn is cemented (but not *rubber-cemented*) to keep it from lumping up and then is covered by cowhide cut in two fat eights. After 108 stitches and the Rawlings and major league stamps, the balls are ready to roll—literally. Each ball gets fifteen seconds of machine rolling to work out any kinks.

It's important that the seams not be too high or too low because it's primarily air resistance that makes a curveball possible. Some rabbit fanciers have suggested that tightening the stitches can make a ball more lively. That appears unlikely, but tighter stitches might flatten seams, thus straightening curves. Rawlings denies any change in stitching.

A certain number of baseballs (Rawlings says a "statistically representative sample") never get to the ballpark. They're tested by shooting them out of an air gun at 85 m.p.h. against a board wall 8 feet away. The rebound has to be 54.6 percent of the original velocity, give or take 3.2 percent.

As far as Rawlings is concerned, the balls that today's umpires douse before a game with Lena Blackburne's Baseball Rubbing Mud (to cut the shine) are just the same as the baseballs Red Ruffing used to throw to Bill Dickey. Blaming an unusual increase in gopher balls on rabbit balls is a red herring, so stop beating a dead horse; look elsewhere for the snake in the grass, says Rawlings. For example, the homer binge of Maris, Mantle, and the rest

In 1876, when fielders were barehanded, one fielding chance in six was flubbed; today it is two of a hundred. Here's why.

of the American League in 1961 can be pinned on AL expansion, which watered down major league pitching. Add two new teams, you add twenty Triple-A pitchers. Other bursts of boomers can be blamed on weather, changes in fences, or stricter rule enforcement. Grandma used to accuse the space program, insisting it was "them things they're shooting up."

Curing Rabid Rabbits

Major league pitchers remain unpacified. No matter what Rawlings claims, pitchers think they're handling live bombs. Moreover, they'll tell you a little more rabbit juice is added almost every season. They attempt to defuse the ball by subjecting it to certain trauma not sanctioned by the rule makers.

The spitball gets the press, mainly because it sounds like something out of Ty Cobb's day. Aside from being unsanitary, it

violates the rule about applying illegal substances to the ball. A fastidious pitcher can get around the health code by using something else that's wet in place of spit, but he still has the illegal substance problem. Actually hardly anyone complains about spitballs except a few fussy umpires and several hundred batters. Although it's thrown like a fastball, it behaves like a fast, wet knuckleball. The pitch slides spinless off the dampened fingers. As it approaches the plate, its lack of rotation coupled with air resistance on the seams causes it to drop unnaturally.

When a pitcher "doctors" a baseball, he's usually doing more than spitting on it. He can make a pitch dip, swerve, or even sail by roughing the cover (like with a nail file), scuffing it (with perhaps a belt buckle), or gouging it (maybe a tack stuck in a glove). Unlike spitballs, doctored pitches usually spin, but air resistance is still a pitcher's best friend. The trouble with doctored pitches is that almost no one can be absolutely certain where

they're going to go. And that includes most of the guys who throw them. Batters and others who hold life sacred get a little nervous about 90-m.p.h. missiles that follow untraditional and unpredictable courses.

But don't expect the Pitchers' Union to apologize. Until Rawlings' baseballs have lead centers wrapped in caulking compound, pitchers are going to complain

about rabbits—and to exercise their own surgical procedures as preventive therapy.

Prices and Such

The suggested retail price for an official major league baseball is $10.25. The major leagues pay Rawlings a little less. After all, they go through about 45,000 dozen balls—more than a half million—each season. If it's a wet spring, that number is even higher.

Most of the balls used in every game of baseball, from the Little League to the majors, feature the same type of construction. A few used in youth leagues have smaller than standard circumferences. And some manufacturers offer rubber- and vinyl-covered models too.

For indoor training, balls with nylon covers and compressed cloth centers are available. Markwort's orange-colored Tuff-Lite baseball is excellent for practice in the late evenings.   —TM

The Bats: The Lighter They Are, the Harder They Fly

Remember when you were a kid and it was macho to swing the heaviest bat available in your pick-up game? You probably thought the bigger your lumber, the farther you'd hit the ball. Well, you were wrong, and your ego may have kept you from being your block's Reggie Jackson or Ralph Kiner or Babe Ruth. (Just how old *are* you?)

The only advantage you got from a bigger bat was a bit more hitting surface. That's not worth the bat speed you lost trying to swing your telephone pole. See, it's *bat speed* that determines how far a batted ball goes. Major leaguers swing through the strike zone at an average of seventy m.p.h. But for every m.p.h. faster they swing, they can pick up an extra five feet on their drives. That's why today's power

hitters favor bats with smaller barrels— they can get 'em around faster and add yards to line drives.

The flip side is that a lot of swings that might have produced fouls with a bigger-barreled bat will miss the pitch completely. Homers go up, but so do strikeouts.

The speed thing also explains the advantage of corked bats. Simply bore an 8-inch hole in the top of a bat, tamp in cork, and camouflage the hole with a sanded plug. You get rid of about 1.5 ounces of weight, and for every ounce lost you can swing one m.p.h. faster. The extra distance can change a warning-track out into a home run.

The cork, by the way, does nothing to increase distance on its own. The only advantage of cork is that it's lighter than

the wood it replaces. Styrofoam would be better, and empty space best of all. The trouble with a hollow bat is that it would shatter just about every time the bat made contact with the ball.

Naturally, a corked (or hollow) bat is illegal as all hell, but tell that to some batter who's sure the pitchers are feeding him doctored baseballs. Every time a hitherto powderpuff hitter reaches the stands, somebody wants to put his bat under an X ray. The only corker caught recently was Billy Hatcher, then with the Astros. Billy was nabbed *in flagrante de-cork-o* when his bat shattered, showering the infield with bottle stoppers.

Although corking can get a player suspended, one legal way to cut the weight on a bat is to take a cup of wood out of the end. That's why almost all the bats you see big leaguers use today are "innies" instead of the "outies" you used as a kid.

Another legal weight reducer is a thin handle, but that also makes for more broken bats.

You've gotta wonder how many homers Babe Ruth would have hit if he'd known this stuff. The Babe used a thick-barreled 36-inch "outie" weighing 42 ounces, an inch longer and 9 or 10 ounces heavier than most major leaguers use today.

Specs

According to major league baseball rules, a bat shall be a smooth rounded stick (no paddles), not more than 2¾ inches in diameter at the thickest part (no piano legs). Heinie Groh (1912–1927) was famous for his "bottle bat," which was simply untapered from the end to about eighteen inches from the knob. He said it gave him better control and a larger hitting surface. Groh had a .292 lifetime batting average, but he managed only 26 homers over his career, no doubt in part because the bottle shape hindered his bat speed.

Nobody will ever try to touch a baseball with a ten-foot pole because the maximum allowed length is 42 inches. That last rule is academic because no one would want to swing a bat that long. According to Hillerich and Bradsby, the biggest producer of bats, the record is Hall of Famer Al Simmons' (1924–1944) 38-inch pillar. The shortest bat, they say, belonged to Wee Willie Keeler (1892–1910), who hit 'em where they ain't with a 30½-inch toothpick. The key for any batter is to be able to reach the whole strike zone. Keeler batted with a closed stance and crowded the plate; Simmons stepped away from the plate,

Eggs in the henhouse? Op art? These bats create a monolithic impression, but the beauty of baseball's basic implement lies in its variety—that for a true hitter, a fraction of an inch or an ounce makes all the difference in the world.

"putting his foot in the bucket."

There aren't any restrictions on bat weight. Reds outfielder Edd Roush (1913–1931) used a 48-ounce log and Reds second baseman Joe Morgan (1963–1984) swung a 30-ounce wand. Roush hit 67 home runs in nineteen years; Morgan 268 in twenty-two. Most major leaguers use 32- to 34-ounce bats today.

All major league bats must be made of one solid piece of wood or formed from a block of wood consisting of two or more pieces of wood bonded together with an adhesive in such a way that the grain direction of all pieces is essentially parallel to the length of the bat. Any laminated bat must contain only wood or adhesive except for a clear finish. Any kind of wood is permissible, but American white ash grown in Pennsylvania or New York is favored as the best combination of strength and light weight. A hundred years ago hickory was popular.

No colored bat may be used in a professional game unless approved by the rules committee. Blacks and browns are okay, but you'd have trouble getting a pink bat into play. Reggie Jackson advocated the use of dark bats for night games because, he said, fielders had more trouble seeing the ball come off the bat.

For the record, that indentation on the end of the bat that's so common today can be up to an inch in depth, but it can be no wider than two inches and no less than one inch in diameter and must be curved.

The bat handle may be covered or treated with any material including pine tar to improve the grip, but such material cannot extend for more than eighteen inches from the bat end. Any such material, including pine tar, which in the umpire's judgment, extends beyond the eighteen-inch limitation shall cause the bat to be removed from the game. In case you've forgotten, this was the cause of the George Brett "Pine Tar Incident" in 1984. Brett's homer against the Yankees was wiped out by the umpire when Yankee manager Billy Martin spotted pine tar more than eigh-

teen inches up his bat. Eventually the commissioner gave Brett his home run, ruling that any such nit-picking had to be done *before* a player batted.

Make Me a Bat

In 1884 eighteen-year-old "Bud" Hillerich lathed the original "Slugger" for Pete Browning of the Louisville Eclipse team. Ol' Pete was such a butcher in the field that he'll never make the Hall of Fame, but he was a *serious* batsman who averaged .341 over thirteen major league seasons. Soon other players were getting their bats in Louisville, and in 1894 the "Louisville Slugger" trademark was registered. Today, Hillerich and Bradsby claims to cut down 20,000 trees a year, most from their own forests, to manufacture 1.5 million Louisville Sluggers for professional players. Well, figure a pro will go through an average of seventy-two bats a year.

Actually 200,000 trees are cut, but the rest of the wood goes for bats you can buy in a sporting goods store. A problem is on the horizon. As metal bats increase in popularity, companies like Hillerich and Bradsby have less use for the wood deemed unsuitable for professional bats. This would seem to leave any company hoping for a profit no option but to lower its standards for wood used in professional bats.

The wood is cut into billets which are forced-air-dried in kilns for six to eight weeks. Then, at the factory, the billets are lathed into shape, sanded, and passed through a flame to harden the surface and accentuate the wood grain. A colored wood filler is applied to open the pores and make the bat an attractive color.

Remember how they always told you to keep the trademark up? That's legitimate. The trademark is stamped on the flat side of the grain so the bat, when held with the trademark up, will make contact on the edge of the grain where the bat has maximum strength. Amazing how many major leaguers ignore that! At H & B they'll tell you Yogi Berra hit so consistently with the trademark facing the pitcher, they finally started stamping his trademark on the side. At least, that's the story.

The bats that are available in sporting goods stores aren't very different from those used by pros, although a lot more care is put into the manufacturing of big league bats. At Louisville Slugger, bats bound for the big leagues are hand turned on lathes by master woodworkers at a rate of about one every fifteen minutes. Bats that are sold at retail outlets are produced on machine lathes that shape them in about eight seconds.

Retail, the bats go for about $20, while the company loses a little money on those made specifically for big leaguers, which go for about $16.50 per. Of course, the company's reputation as bat maker for the big leagues makes their selling of retail bats possible.

H & B makes about 300 different professional models, although they have specifications for 20,000 models on file. Even then, some big league hitters aren't completely satisfied. Some players rub their bats with soda pop bottles or bones to close the pores and strengthen the wood. Most wood experts say any advantage gained by rubbing a bat is mostly to a player's confidence. Other players have been known to take a knife to their bats, whittling down the handle to give bats a faster whip.

The company has lots of legends about picky major league hitters.

Babe Ruth once rejected a load of bats as "not worth a damn." Later he relented and accepted the batch, one of which was used for his sixtieth homer in 1927.

Ted Williams, a real fanatic, sent back a shipment because the handles weren't right. Sure enough, when workers measured them, the handle width was off by 5/1,000ths of an inch.

They say Frankie Frisch (1919–1937) would hang his bats in a barn to cure them like sausages. Eddie Collins (1906–1930) buried his bats in dung heaps to "keep them alive." When playing in San Francisco, Bobby Murcer (1965–1983) stored his

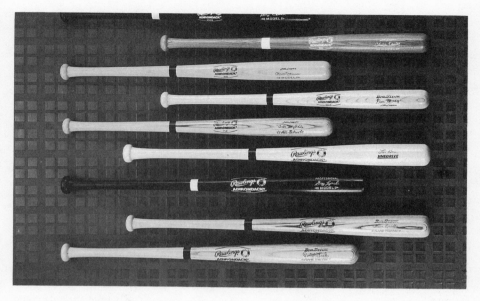

bats in the clubhouse sauna to protect them from the cold. Richie Ashburn would sleep with his bats, but only on the road.

Perhaps Orlando Cepeda had the strangest fixation. He was convinced that each bat contained only one hit in it. As soon as a bat gave it up, Cepeda would give up on the bat. Cepeda had 2,351 hits in his major league career, and that doesn't count exhibitions and postseason games.

Pass Me the Home Run Cream

Batters can get all kinds of accessories from grip tape to pine tar rags. Grip tape costs about $3.50 for fifteen yards. You can

also purchase replaceable grip such as the Totes Supergrip or the Tourna-Grip for $6 or $4.50 respectively. The Totes Supergrip has a tacky outer surface and is also padded to reduce bat sting. The Tourna-Grip absorbs sweat to reduce slippage during the swing.

Pine tar rags cost about $2. An extra bottle of tar costs about $6. If you don't like to grab a sticky rag, you can spray your bat handle with Stick-Um, an aerosol pine tar spray from Worth.

Sure, as a kid, you wound your bat with adhesive tape and spit on your hands. But did *you* have a million-dollar contract riding on how many hits you got? —TM

Batting Helmets

For a lot of years, most big league hitters thought batting helmets were "sissy." At least that's what they said. Still, you didn't hear a whole lot of complaining when rules were written making helmets mandatory for everyone.

In 1971, Rule 116 of the official rules of baseball said that all players should wear a helmet and that Class A and Rookie League

players should wear helmets with ear flaps. Over the next couple of years, the ear-flap rule was extended to cover AA ball, then AAA, and finally every player in the major leagues.

A typical helmet features a polycarbonate alloy shell and two-ply pads of foam. One side of the foam liner absorbs the energy of the ball. The other side of the foam allows a snug fit to prevent the helmet from spinning on the head after wiffing a pitch, or bouncing while running the bases.

The one thing that all the helmets used in real games share is a NOCSAE approval stamp. NOCSAE is an independent testing firm that sets standards for sports equipment like baseball and football helmets. If you don't see a NOCSAE stamp (usually molded into the outside surface of the helmet's shell), don't wear it. Also, as all helmet makers insist, don't use a helmet if the shell is cracked or deformed or if the interior padding has deteriorated or been modified. Also be careful about painting helmets. Some paints can be detrimental to the integrity of the materials used in the helmet.

Professional league baseball helmets can cost as much as $43. Helmets approved for play through college level cost about $19. And for Little League play, a NOCSAE-approved helmet is available for about $16.

Here are some tips to use when fitting a helmet, according to Athletic Helmet Inc.:

1. Measure head circumference and match to helmet size on sizing chart.

2. Fit the helmet squarely on the head. The width of two fingers measures the proper distance between the bridge of the nose and the helmet's bill extension. The bill must not ride down across the face to obstruct vision, nor ride too high to expose the forehead.

3. Center the earholes over the ear.

4. The rear sides of the helmet should extend to cover and help protect the critical mastoid process area.

5. The back of the helmet should extend down to cover the occipital region. —TM

Helmets worn by the A's, 1937.

Ping!

Most major leaguers reacted negatively when Peter Gammons' article predicting the inevitability of metal bats in the majors appeared in *Sports Illustrated* (July 1989). Most registered concern over baseball's sacrosanct record book or ballplayers' safety, but Jack Clark of the Padres mentioned the sound made when metal hits baseball and hoped, "Maybe they can just use it in the American League."

Aluminum bats are illegal in major league baseball but popular in college and little leagues. They're more expensive than wood bats—as much as $150 per—but they last so much longer they're a better investment. You can crack a wood model in your first at bat; an aluminum bat's good for about 500 hits before it develops metal fatigue. Manufacturers also say that aluminum bats can be made to exact specifications better than wood. Incidentally, they're not solid aluminum. A metal shell is filled with foam. Traditionalists hate aluminum bats mostly because of the sound they make hitting a ball, although manufacturers claim the new ceramic and carbon composite bats make the old satisfying sound you get from wood.

Of more importance: Would metal bats make current record books obsolete, and are they safe on a major league level? Both questions stem from a more basic premise—that the ball flies farther and faster off a metal bat. The theory holds that a lighter metal bat can be swung faster than a heavier wood model. Therefore, when a batter connects, the ball goes farther.

Aerospace engineers at Mississippi State disagree. In tests conducted with bats from Worth, Spalding, and Easton, they saw the ball flying farther when hit by a wood bat—so long as the ball was whacked at the bat's point of optimum impact, the so-called "sweet spot."

However, there is another factor at work here. The "sweet spot" on an aluminum

Ten Great Original Bat Models
(or, They Just Don't Make 'Em Like That No More)

1. *The Shot Heard 'Round the World Warclub* was used in 1951 by Bobby Thomson. It turned Ralph Branca into a celebrity and gave Russ Hodges the chance to yell "The Giants Win the Pennant!" thirty or forty times.

2. *The Forbes Field Lightning* was swung by Pittsburgh's Bill Mazeroski to end the 1960 World Series. This bat convinced Ralph Terry that golf was really his game and ensured that baseball's best-fielding second baseman would be remembered for something else instead.

3. *The Handicapped Hammer* was favored by Kirk Gibson in the opening game of the 1988 World Series. Unusually effective for batters who must swing from the hips because their legs are out of order.

4. *The Fenway Farewell* was Ted Williams' weapon in his final major league at-bat. Although criticized as an old model, this bat still had one last home run in it.

5. *The Bottle Model.* The untapered barrel made this the strangest-shaped bat ever when Heinie Groh brought it to the plate. Rumor was he had trouble keeping it away from Hack Wilson, who kept trying to uncap it.

6. *Old Reliable's Reliable* was the model used by Tommy Henrich to win the 1949 Series opener with a homer off Don Newcombe and kick off a decade-plus of Yankee heroics.

7. *The Tommy Holmes Heartbreaker* produced the RBI single that handed Bob Feller a two-hit, 1–0 loss in the 1948 Series opener after Rapid Robert had picked winning-run Phil Masi off second to the satisfaction of everyone but umpire Bill Stewart.

8. *The Direction Is All Special.* In the tenth inning of the first game of the 1954 World Series, pinch hitter Dusty Rhodes used this club to smash an awesome 260-foot fly over the Polo Grounds' right-field wall and make Willie Mays's earlier catch of Vic Wertz's 425-foot drive to center *really* mean something.

9. *The Mr. October Labor Saver* was the most efficient bat ever. In the 1977 Series finale, Reggie Jackson waved it three times on three pitches and produced three homers.

10. *The Mighty Midget* was an eighteen-inch model used by three-foot, seven-inch Eddie Gaedel in his lone at-bat for Bill Veeck's 1951 Browns. Although now illegal for baseball, it's still perfect for propping open windows on a warm summer day to let in fresh air.   —BC

bat is about twice the size of that on wood. Secondly, when a batter hits the ball with the handle of the bat, the bat usually shatters and the ball pops to an infielder. A handle-hit off an aluminum bat will go over the infielder's head, and a Bo Jackson might even put it in the stands.

Nevertheless, say the engineers, aluminum would contribute a few more home runs but not a dramatic increase. Batting averages would also rise, but don't expect everybody to become a .300 hitter. The power of aluminum bats is overstated.

Oddly, traditionalists who worry over the purity of the record book seem to ignore the non-bat factors that have dropped batting averages since the hitting heyday between the World Wars. Then, .350 seasons were common and .400 not

unknown. Night games, increased use of relief pitchers, and larger ballparks make it much tougher for modern batters to top the magic .300. On the other hand, the DH and artificial turf have worked to the hitter's advantage.

While records can be compared, safety is a matter of opinion. Players in the field, particularly pitchers, have been getting hit by batted balls since Al Spalding's day. Remember, pitchers in the early days stood 45 feet away—with no glove. Would Dizzy Dean have suffered *multiple* broken toes if Earl Averill had used an aluminum bat?

All the paranoia by batters and pitchers is meaningless, of course. Unless the record book is turned completely upside down and pitchers are knocked off like Martians in an arcade game, aluminum

bats are going to be in the majors. Probably in the next decade.

Tree lovers will rejoice, but the reason for the rise of metal has nothing to do with a wood shortage. Jack Hillerich explained the rock-bottom reason to Gammons: "A wood bat is a financially obsolete deal. If we were selling them for $40 instead of $14 (minor league) and $16.50 (major league), then we'd be making a sensible profit. But we aren't. We can't charge that much."

As soon as the bat companies say no more wooden losses, professional baseball will have no choice but to go along. Or do you think you can find a team owner who'll swallow the cost of manufacturing his own bats just for the sake of keeping a tradition?   —BC

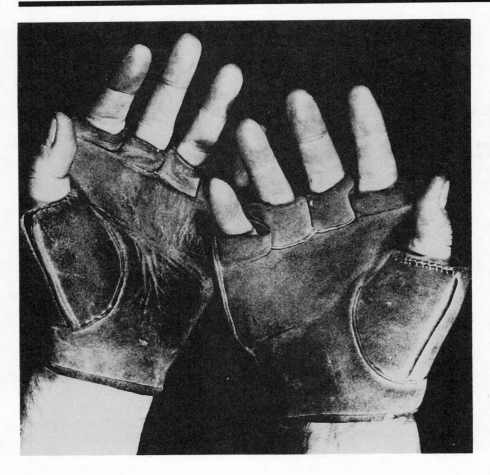

Gloves: Where Would Ozzie Be Without a Cow?

Ball players first put on gloves for protection. Doug Allison, who caught for the first all-professional team, the Cincinnati Red Stockings, had a saddlemaker sew him a mitt in 1869, but it was an idea before its time. When Charles Waitt of St. Louis took to the field in 1875 wearing a thin, flesh-colored glove similar to those sported by buggy drivers, he got a very hefty razzing by fans and players alike. It just wasn't manly.

Nevertheless, when overhand pitching became the norm in the 1880s and the ball began flying off bats at higher speeds, more and more players began donning gloves. Some of them even wore two—thin things with a smidgen of padding on the palms and the fingers cut off to allow for throwing. At about this time, Buck Ewing, a catcher for the New York Giants, became the first to use a "pillow-type" mitt.

The last player to refuse to wear a glove through his whole career was Jeremiah Denny, a third baseman who played until 1894. Actually he had a pretty good reason. Denny normally threw right-handed, but he was ambidextrous and could get his toss away as a lefty when a close play demanded it. A glove would have taken that part of his game away.

You've seen pictures of players around 1900 wearing those funny, puffy little gloves that look like they'd make catching a baseball as easy as grabbing a basketball with tweezers. At best, you probably thought they were quaint. Remember, the idea was still to protect the hand, not to facilitate fielding.

Rawlings introduced the "Sure Catch"

glove in 1912, a one-piece model with sewn-in finger channels. It looked perfect, if you had a hand like a duck's foot. A ball player finally took matters into his own—uh—hand. In 1920 Bill Doak, a Cardinals pitcher, went to Rawlings with the idea of a laced pocket in the crotch between the thumb and index finger, creating a natural pocket for the first time.

With the Doak model, gloves shifted from being hand protectors to ball trappers. You'll be a long time looking for a fielding record (other than most errors) set before the development of modern gloves.

Since 1920, nearly all the innovations, improvements, and variations in fielders' gloves—three-finger gloves, six-finger gloves, two-piece webs, laced fingers, and increased size—have been designed to make it easier to catch the ball. Even gloves built with nylon backs that are supposed to keep a player's hand cooler can be said to help fielding by making it more comfortable. Next they'll be putting in mini–air conditioners!

Gloves are made about the way you'd figure. The pieces are cut out of cowhide according to dies, then sewn together while the thing's inside-out with welting (an extra chunk of cowhide) over the seams. Then the whole thing is turned rightside-out and the padding is added. The final shape is pounded into it over a hot forming iron. The whole thing takes two cows and God knows how many workers.

A rainbow of colors is now available. White is out for pitchers because it's confusing, but you can get gloves in orange, burnt-orange, black, red, blue, yellow, an endless range of browns, and multicolored. No hue will help you win a Gold Glove, but you might as well look spiffy even when you boot one.

The Drudgery of Cleaning Up

Up until 1954, fielders left their gloves lying on the grass when they went in to bat. And every once in a while a batted ball would bump into a dormant glove and set off in a new direction. Rule makers finally got tired of this and put in a rule that the gloves had to be carried into the dugouts.

This was an earlier, more innocent time; so as far as we know, not a single player asked for a bonus to cover his new responsibilities or asked that his contract be renegotiated with a Teamsters' rep present.

Why Not?

Maybe you've seen a home run heading blissfully for the stands and wondered why some outfielder didn't sail his glove into the air in hope of knocking the ball down. There are lots of good reasons, like he'd probably miss or his glove might get knocked into the stands and stolen. But the real reason is it's against the rules and the batter would be awarded a home run anyway. As a matter of fact, if a fielder throws his glove and hits any batted ball on the field, even a bunt, the runner gets three bases.

On the other hand, if the fielder stops a batted ball by throwing his cap or shoe, the runner gets only two bases. You're probably asking yourself, "What's the difference?" So are we.

How Much?

Well, let's see. Um, the cost of cowhide is going up all'a time. And then there's technology involved in nylon backs and such. That costs, buddy. And don't forget the welting. Uh, add in dyeing the glove chartreuse and stamping Smead Jolley's name on it. Oh, and tax. Hmm. Well, it comes to less than you'd spend on a two-day trip to Cleveland.

Gloves in Rawlings' Gold Glove series range in price from $197 to $254. Mizuno's MZ GPT5, a popular pitcher's glove, costs $198. Catcher's mitts and first baseman's gloves are similarly priced. Rawlings catcher's mitt model R Pro-Klta costs

$253. Mizuno's MZ GFB6 first basemen's mitt costs $205.

Of course, gloves are available for considerably less money. MacGregor offers adult-size gloves for as low as $60. Markwort offers fielder's mitts for $48. Kid-sized gear is even cheaper. Mizuno's youth-sized gloves cost between $31 and $49. Markwort offers youth-sized gloves for as low as $24. But you can really save money if your kid's a DH.

How Big?

There really are major league glove regulations, but sometimes you have to ask if anyone pays any attention. We've all seen outfielders wearing gloves that look like they're out to trap wolverines. Actually the idea of bigger is better seems to have passed its peak. Too many outfielders had to practically crawl into their gloves to retrieve the ball.

Infielders' gloves (except for those of first basemen) have always been smaller than outfielders', just because they had to get the ball away fast. Generally the smallest glove on the field belongs to the second baseman.

The specs on gloves are:

- *First base:* No more than 12 inches from top to bottom or 8 inches across the palm. Web no more than 5 inches high or 4 inches wide.
- *Fielders:* No more than 12 inches from tip to heel or 7¾ inches wide, as measured from the inside seam to the outside edge of the little finger. Web no more than 4½ inches at the top.
- *Pitchers:* All one color (no white or gray). Otherwise the same as fielders' gloves.
- *Catchers:* No more than 38 inches in circumference or 15½ inches from top to bottom. Web no more than 7 inches across the top or 6 inches to the base of the thumb.

The Tools of Ignorance and Other Stuff

Every year manufacturers come up with new protective devices, but the DL's seem

Early gloves (see left) were designed merely for protection. The gloves below feature buttons that relay electronic signals between pitcher and catcher!

to keep getting longer. It's probably just that some injuries are taken more seriously now than in the old days when a guy was told to spit some tobacco juice on it and go play. A lot of careers were ruined by aggravating this or that.

Anybody can see that the catcher needs extra protection, so he ends up squatting back there looking like a mini-Sherman tank. Except for a helmet and the plastic strip that hangs down from his mask to protect his throat, Benito Santiago wears the same stuff today that Benny Bengough wore in 1920: shin guards, chest protector,

and mask. Santiago's big advantage is that the equipment is lighter and stronger now.

They used to call the catcher's getup the "Tools of Ignorance," the idea being that only an idiot would play a position that consisted mostly of catching high-speed objects and blocking runners coming hell-fer-leather. The phrase went out of use the first time a catcher signed for a million bucks.

One thing, it costs more to be a catcher than just about anything else in baseball except a season-ticket holder. Top-of-the-line equipment runs about $48 for a mask,

$39 for a chest protector, $80 for shin guards, $65 for a helmet and $6 for a neck protector.

Other protective equipment includes batter's leg guards ($25) to keep those annoying fouls from smashing shins and ankles and sliding pads ($25) so the only strawberry will be in right field for the Mets.

One piece of athletic equipment that no baseball player should be without is a protective cup and supporter. Make sure your kid wears one; your grandchildren will thank you.   —TM

And Now, Wearing a Cunning Flannel Bodice . . .

Picture this: Nine men dressed in long, navy blue trousers, webbed belts, white shirts, and straw hats. What are you looking at? The Supreme Court's annual picnic? Hopefuls in the Old MacDonald Look-Alike Contest? The men's chorus from *Oklahoma!*?

Heck no. It's the New York Knickerbockers baseball team, circa 1850, decked out in their uniforms—the first ball club to have everyone dress up the same. Maybe your first thought is that they're *not* wearing knickerbockers. (The club name came from a term originally applied to descendants of Dutch settlers in New York.) Second, you realize that they must have been very uncomfortable. It hurts to think of them running or picking up grounders in those getups. Sliding? Forget it!

The Knickerbockers, who put together the first real set of playing rules—four bases and like that—considered baseball a gentlemanly game and dressed accordingly. If they had models, they were English cricketeers. In fact, a couple of years later, the straw hats were set aside for cricket caps. By then, most teams that aspired to anything better than pickup status were wearing uniforms that would have been

smashing at Miss Elizabeth Abercrombie's lawn party.

The first baseball team to wear clothes that actually aided their performance was the Cincinnati Red Stockings. As the first all-professional team, they had a real interest in anything that would help them win ball games and keep getting paid. Their innovation? Knickerbockers! Or knickers, as we usually call them. If you think about it, it would have been kind of silly to call them "Red Stockings" if they wore long trousers covering their hose. When they came on the field wearing those odd knee britches, folks snickered. But after they'd toured the country undefeated in 1869, no one thought the Red Stockings or the red stockings were funny-looking at all. Within a year or so, every ball team had knickers. By the 1880s you could even see men wearing knickers as street clothes.

It took a while for players to get out of high collars (sometimes with ties!) and long sleeves, but that too began to come on in the 1880s. Sleeves started creeping up and soft sun collars appeared. Black uniforms became an "in" thing late in the decade, probably because of the success of the New York Giants in their black duds.

One really strange innovation was tried by the Detroit Wolverines in 1882—different color uniforms for each position. The first baseman, for example, wore a jersey, belt, and cap in red-and-white stripes, while the center fielder was in red and black. Just why the owner thought this was a good idea is unknown. Couldn't he remember who played where? And what happened when players switched positions? Did they have to switch uniforms too?

The players hated looking like a decorator's showroom and the idea was dropped by June.

Pictures of ball players in the 1890s show them in outfits that are certainly recognizable as baseball uniforms. The most obvious differences from today are the high collars, beanie caps with bitty bills, and high-top shoes. Less obvious: the uniforms were wool. How'd you like to try that for a day game in Texas? You could get the whole outfit, including stockings, cap, and belt for $12.50.

By the first decade of this century, some teams had different home and road uniforms. Sleeves in many cases were up to the elbows. The most distinctive thing about uniforms eighty or ninety years ago was how much of them there was. Shirts and pants were blousey, baggy, billowy, and just plain too big, like everybody was auditioning for a White Cloud commercial. You can imagine a grounder getting lost in the folds of an infielder's uniform while a runner circles the bases.

Ball clubs first began wearing team nicknames on their uniforms during the teens, though not all teams of course; city names and initials were still more common. The reason nicknames didn't get on uniforms earlier was probably because teams were constantly changing their nicknames until a few years into this century. Among the real oddities about baseball are that the Cubs were originally the White Sox (or White *Stockings*, to be technical), and the Atlanta Braves started as the Boston Red Sox/Stockings. For a while, you could wake up any morning and find your Superbas had become the Dodgers. By the end of the teens, most of the clubs had nicknames they'd hold onto. Even the Phillies, although they tried for years to be the Blue Jays.

Also during the teens, most teams started wearing those funny baseball socks they still wear. You know, the stirrup socks on the outside and the white socks underneath. The story goes that Cleveland second baseman Nap Lajoie got spiked in 1905 right through his full-length blue stocking. The dye from the sock got into the wound and he developed blood poisoning as a result. So somebody came up with the idea of wearing colored stirrup socks over white *sanitary hose* as a preventative measure, and by the next decade everybody went for it. Frankly, if there ever was any logic to stirrup socks, it's long past. Especially now that the style is to stretch the stirrups up and the pants legs down until only a thin strip shows. But baseball is a traditional game, and if they want to go on looking silly around the ankles, that's their business. Just as long as they don't bring back straw hats!

The Yankees started wearing pinstripes in 1915.

You could buy a whole 1923 uniform for $30; teams got a $5 discount.

Baseball uniforms between the world wars looked just about the way they do today, only a lot baggier. (The Pillsbury Dough Boy Look didn't go out until the 1960s, when tailored uniforms became the

thing.) Piping around the neck and sleeves became common. Zippered shirts appeared in the 1930s. Numbers went on the backs and were standard by the '30s. Something that's hard to keep straight is that Christy Mathewson pitched for the Giants until 1916 and was called "Big Six" but never wore the number. The original "Big Six" was a famous New York firetruck. (No, Christy wasn't a relief pitcher either.)

In the 1950s a couple of ideas were tried without much success. Hollywood and Fort Worth in the minors had short affairs with Bermuda shorts. The players blushed and went back to long pants as soon as they could. The Pirates wore batting helmets in the field for a time, making the team look as bad as it played. Toward the end of the decade, Cincinnati and Pittsburgh sported sleeveless shirts with long-sleeved T-shirts underneath. They reminded you of some old guy who threw his bib overalls on over his long johns. The sleeveless idea was apparently inspired by Reds first baseman Ted Kluszewski, who had upper arms like something that should be cured in a smoke house and cut off his sleeves to facilitate movement and terrify pitchers.

The first team to go all double-knit was the 1970 Pirates, who timed their sartorial splendor with the opening of Three Rivers Stadium. With tailoring, 1960s uniforms became tighter. Shirts tapered at the waist. Pants went in at the hips, thighs, and across the knees. Pants were worn longer and bloused at the calf rather than at the knee. Uniforms became lighter and more colorful until you got to today's rainbow hues. Some teams put players' names on the backs for fans who can't count. In the mid-1970s, the White Sox tried to resurrect the Bermuda shorts idea but succeeded only in leading the league in knees. Oddities like the Pirates' painter caps in

Baseball fashions of 1870, showing a knickered Cincinnati Red Stocking, a jockey-capped New York Mutual, and more.

the late 1970s–early '80s were tried and found wanting.

A uniform today costs $100 to $125 for the real thing, cap and socks extra.

Shoes will cost extra, too. And every player needs at least two pairs: for natural and for artificial surfaces. Major leaguers usually have extra pairs of shoes, but they also often work out endorsement deals that provide them with freebies.

For natural surfaces (the stuff that cows eat), players can still wear the traditional metal spikes. These won't do for artificial surfaces (the stuff that even goats won't eat) because they'd punch holes and because they really don't grip the stuff. For playing on plastic, players use shoes with special cleats. Ty Cobb would be heartbroken that he couldn't file them into lethal weapons.

You may remember Nippy Jones, the guy in the '57 Series who got an important Hit-By-Pitch when his black shoe polish showed up on a white baseball. Ol' Nippy would have trouble today when many shoes are white. Actually, you can get footwear in a variety of colors and combinations. No problem, the top part isn't leather anymore; it's stuff that "breathes," like Dynalite.

A Little Help

If you grew up playing schoolyard baseball, with a cracked bat and a coverless ball both held together by adhesive tape and the only glove lent to the kid playing first base, you probably get the giggles when you hear about the extra folderal major leaguers need to ply their trade. You sure didn't need batting gloves, sliding gloves, and stuff like that—just enough bricks for home and three bases, and it was "Play ball!"

But put things in perspective. If you went 0 for 25 in a schoolyard game, the worst that could happen was you'd be picked last the next day. Go 0 for 25 on a major league level and you could wind up in Columbus.

So major leaguers look for any edge they can get. If a hunk of kangaroo hide, padding, and spandex makes a bat feel more comfy in their hands, it might result in six more hits a season. And six hits can raise a batting average ten points and a contract $250,000. As a matter of fact, even if they only *think* a glove might help, it might help. Confidence, you know.

Before you snicker, giggle, or guffaw, just remember, you can't really know the other guy's situation until you've slid a mile in his glove.

Most "special" baseball gloves are about the same as gloves designed for other sports: leather front and nylon/spandex mesh back. Some feature an extra-wide wrist band to absorb perspiration. Better-made batting gloves have precurved fingers which make it easier to grip the bat. Spandex gussets between the fingers can make them more breathable and comfortable.

Markwort makes a glove called the Power Swing that has a strap from the thumb across the backs of the fingers. It's sup-

posed to make it easier to get the bat around and also reduce strain on the wrist and arm. You can get it left- or right-handed for $12. The fashion-conscious can cover the other hand with a matching glove for $9. If you don't want to go all the way but still dread the heartbreak of bat sting, spend $6.20 on Direct Protect, a pad that slips over your thumb and cushions your grip. Baserunning gloves have extra padding on the palms.

Catchers (and other fielders) can buy a padded glove to wear inside their mitts— sort of a glove for a glove—for $15. You can even pad individual fingers with a variety of special pads that run from $1 to $3 each. So far, nobody's marketing a joint pad for inside the finger pads that go inside the padded glove that fits inside the fielding glove. But stay tuned.

Call 'Em Like You See 'Em!

Plate umpires used to crouch behind a big balloon chest protector. No more. The well-dressed (and well-protected) ump now wears his padding inside his uniform. It's lighter, more flexible; it's also more costly.

Available body armor includes a body protector; throat protector; shoulder caps; upper leg, knee, and shin pads; and a mask. For about $150 an ump can be fully outfitted for a game or a joust. Then add in a ball bag ($6), ball-and-strike indicator ($20), and plate brush ($30).

Well, after all, he *can't* brush off the plate with a broom from Goodwill. What would people say?

Sunglasses

One of the scariest moments ever on a major league diamond happened to Mookie Wilson in a spring rundown drill when he was smashed in the face by a thrown ball. His sunglasses shattered, sending glass particles into his eye. His career could have ended at that moment, but fortunately there was no permanent damage.

According to the eye-care specialists (and common sense), the best kind of sunglasses to wear for almost any kind of sports, but especially baseball, are those made with plastic lenses, preferably polycarbonate plastic. Polycarbonate is super tough and shatterproof, while offering all of the optical quality of glass. It's best if the lenses and the frames are made from one piece of plastic. But if not, the frame should be made from a nylon or plastic and be designed so that the lenses will not pop back into the eye if struck by a ball.

Flip-up sunglasses are not generally made with all-one lenses and frames, but at all costs, avoid glass.

More Stuff

There's no end to the products available for making baseball a better and more expensive game.

You can soften your glove with a variety of oils and unguents. Or you can mold a nice pocket into a new glove with a doodad that sits in the pocket and holds the fingers closed. Old-timers could only stick in a baseball and tape the glove shut, poor dears.

You can tutor your batting stride with a Stride Tutor, which attaches at the ankles and limits the length. (Or you could try it with an old piece of clothesline.) There are also batting tees for sale.

To practice fielding or pitching, you can buy a contraption that looks like a net trampoline turned on its side that will bounce a thrown ball back to you. One with a strike zone outlined in red is available from Rawlings for $26.

It's been a while since we've seen that "throw curves" gadget advertised. Remember? The tricky little device you could

hold in your hand and throw—they said—any kind of curveball. It used to be in all the magazines. We could never figure out why anyone would want one since it'd be illegal in a game.

Any respectable ball club will carry equipment in special bags. Hey, none of that going to the food store for spare cartons! There's ball bags, bat bags, helmet bags, and "other stuff" bags that run anywhere from $30 to $65. Bags for individual players' equipment go for $25 to $35.

Even though a ball club has ninety zillion regular bats lying around, it'll also want a supply of fungo bats. These are long, thin bats to use in hitting practice balls to outfielders and infielders. They'd never stand up to pitched balls, but they're perfect for a coach to hit fungos. If you don't know, a "fungo" is what you call that action where the batter tosses the ball a few feet in the air and then hits it out as it falls. Fungo bats are light enough to swing all day but can pop deep flies. They're available in wood or aluminum.

If measuring pitches as "fast," "pretty fast," and "never saw it" isn't specific enough for you, radar guns are available. The AMTECH sports radar gun, costing $780, comes complete with battery pack, charger, and tuning fork. It measures pitch speeds from 10 to 200 miles per hour.

Two hundred! Nolan Ryan has only been over 100 a couple of times! Well, hope springs eternal . . .   —TM

The umpire watching Ted Williams hit (opposite page) is wearing the chest protector favored by arbiters in the AL long after their NL counterparts adopted a model that permitted them to bend more . . . and thus the birth of the "low strike" call in the senior circuit. On this page, the man behind the dark glasses is Dodger outfielder Casey Stengel.

CHAPTER 5

The Lefty Groves of Academe

If you always felt that you could have been an A student if only baseball were taught in school, then you may want to dust off your lunchbox and head for the classroom. For although you can't exactly get a degree in baseball, you can now study it in a college classroom, either toward a career in sports management or in one of an increasing number of sports history courses.

Sports management or administration is one of the hottest fields of study on campuses today. You can find it at well over one hundred colleges and universities, in the undergraduate and graduate (master's and Ph.D.) variety. The latest estimate is that 15 percent of the off-field jobs in sports are currently held by people with sports management, sports adminstration, or business degrees—a number that most certainly is growing.

Because of its "boom" nature, sports management is the Wild West for American colleges. There is no such thing as accreditation right now, although the movement for that is afoot. So there are outlaw programs in those hills, schools that jumped on the bandwagon by taking a regular phys ed program that was suffering from sagging enrollment, tacking on a couple of sports management courses, and calling it a degree program. That kind of activity has made professional ball clubs wary about hiring graduates from other than the top, more established schools. There are also some seven thousand students enrolled in some kind of sports management program (men outnumber women two to one), so the competition for jobs is fierce. Fortunately there is more to the job market than the twenty-six major

Baseball 101

The college of baseball knowledge is no trivial pursuit— barroom experts need not apply

league ball clubs, and many graduates find themselves working at the college level or at the health club around the corner. (For more on Jobs and Baseball, see Chapter 17.)

Let's assume for the moment, however, that you're not planning on a career in sports management. Nevertheless you'd like to take a course in baseball history to (a) learn more about your favorite game, (b) review your already strong knowledge of the national pastime, or (c) prove to yourself that you know more about baseball than any college professor. If you enroll in one of the better baseball history courses, you should be able to satisfy reason *a* or *b*, but you may not get the answer you're expecting for *c*.

On the other hand, a baseball history course may not be available to you. A general sports history course may satisfy you, especially if you're interested in other sports as well. Just don't expect to talk baseball at every session. In a good course, you'll learn something about boxing, basketball, and black athletes, to mention only three other B's. A poor course—and there are some lulus—can drive you up the wall. One baseball fan enrolled in a

course supposedly about the history of sports in America, only to discover that, as taught, it was a history of the local hockey franchise. —NC

You're Taking What?

When you sign up for a sports history course, one of the hardest things is explaining why to your friends and family. They're likely to accuse you of spending your semester reading batting averages and looking at bubble gum cards. "Oh, sure," they'll snicker, "when you go looking for a job, the first thing an employer is going to ask you is who won the 1908 World Series!"

They miss the point.

"A course in the history of baseball is not going to make you any more employable than a course in the history of women or a course in the history of industry," says Professor C. Robert Barnett of Marshall University. "A sports history course is not vocationally oriented. It's not like taking a computer course where you can say, 'All right, if I take this course I'll have these specific skills which will qualify me for these four jobs.' But the kind of information you get from it gives you a better understanding of the American experience."

Professor David Q. Voigt of Albright College emphasizes the same point. According to Voigt, "Any student contemplating entering a sports or baseball history course should first ask, 'Does it bear on my understanding of my own culture, my own country?' In other words, does this show the relevance of sports or baseball to American life? Does it fit the subject of sport into the mainstream of American life?

"I try to do that with my course 'Base-

ball in American Culture.' I try to show how aspects of American culture are reflected in baseball. Otherwise I think the course could get to be just antiquarian—just out there by itself with no concern for relevance. The best books on Japanese baseball attempt to show how, through baseball, you can learn more about these mysterious Japanese. There are a lot of American topics you can pick out and see in baseball their mirror image—unionism, racism."

As an example of how pervasive sport is in American society, Voigt offers: "I wrote an essay on sex and baseball. I grew up in an era when you didn't refer to sex blatantly, but you could do it obliquely through baseball with phrases like 'I didn't get to first base with her' or 'I struck out.' Baseball does mirror the changing sexual attitudes in America, like the morality back in the nineteenth century. And this can be seen in such ways as how ladies were

treated at the ballpark. Getting rid of Ladies' Day, I think, is an egalitarian step."

Barnett adds, "One reason I like my students to take a course in sports history (or baseball history) is they get a sense—a reflection of a lot of American ideals, an understanding of where we've been in our American society. For example, the treatment of blacks in baseball reflects much of the treatment of blacks in American society, particularly the idea of segregation from the 1880s until 1946 with the development of 'separate but equal' baseball leagues. The emergence of Jackie Robinson reflected the growth of integration. For a lot of students it can help them understand what racism, segregation, and discrimination were about in American society."

Another thing you should be aware of: trivia and history are not interchangeable. You may be proud of knowing Lonnie Frey's 1940 batting average, but don't ex-

Reporters like Fred Lieb and Damon Runyon (second and third from left) could not have dreamed that their daily filings would one day be studied in universities.

pect it to get you any points on the final exam. No doubt you'll learn many fascinating tidbits, but your professor wants you to show him what happened and *why*. Then if you want an A, you'd better be able to fit it into the wider context of American history. Trying to understand baseball's history through mastery of trivia is like trying to understand the American Civil War through Mrs. Lincoln's dress size. Knowing about the Reserve Clause will be more important than knowing the reserves on the '69 Mets.

As for the suspicion that some critics raise, that a sports history course might be nothing more than a string of anecdotes and trivia, Barnett says, "One thing I always tell students on the first day of class is that they will learn a certain amount of trivia. Educated people are expected to know some trivia, so it can stand you in good stead in social situations. There probably should be a course in French called 'A Few French Phrases That Will Carry You Far.' The other thing is they'll be able to go to the orange squares in Trivial Pursuit without trembling."

But, he points out, the use of anecdote and trivia in the classroom is primarily illustrative. You may know a hundred great Lefty Gomez stories, but only five of them will help you understand baseball in the 1930s. "For example, everyone's heard the Babe Ruth story in which he was told the raise he wanted would give him a higher salary than President Herbert Hoover's, and Ruth responded, 'Well, I had a better year.' Taken alone, it's amusing, but it also illustrates the importance America placed on sports in 1930, when an athlete could be better paid than the President. It also makes a good introduction to the Depression, for, in fact, Ruth *did* have a better year than Hoover."

A baseball history course will not teach you to play first base like Keith Hernandez or even raise your batting average .001. We're talking academics here. You will be required to read about baseball, write about baseball, and think about baseball. If you're not asked to do those things, you're wasting your time and money.

Voigt is adamant that his course will challenge students. "When I began, I felt a compulsion that this would not become a Mickey Mouse course. The potential for so much derision is there. I determined to have term papers, readings, presentations, outside speakers. This course was one I guarded closely. I wanted to make sure they weren't going to make it into a joke. I tell the students, we wouldn't be doing them any favor if we let them get by with no substance.

"Any course should be a challenge, but something like baseball . . . back when I did my first dissertation, it was considered the toy department, almost too frivolous.

Career Advancement

Many major leaguers have gone on to successful careers in academia as college baseball coaches and teachers. But after winning 94 games for the Braves and Red Sox from 1896 to 1901, pitcher Edward Morgan "Ted" Lewis taught public speaking and English at Harvard, Columbia, Williams, and Yale before settling in at Massachusetts State College in 1911. From 1927 until his death in 1936, he was president of the U. of New Hampshire. At his funeral, former teammate Fred Tenney was a pallbearer and Robert Frost read poetry.   —BC

You had to defend it, show that sports as an institution could be treated along with other institutions like family. Not that I think baseball is on the level of family, but it's up there."

"One thing that's very important," says Barnett, "is that undergraduates can use the material of sports—an area of high interest—to develop skills in research, interpretation, evaluation, and presentation. Then these skills will carry over into other academic areas.

"For example, I teach kids to write book reviews and television reviews. They learn not only to synthesize but to interpret. If they can take a book on Jackie Robinson or a period of baseball history and do that, they can apply the same skills to a work on Lincoln or the rise of the labor movement. They start from an area of strength, an area they understand, and then step into an academic approach.

"The pennant race of 1912 will arouse a student's interest sooner than the Tariff Act of 1912."

Voigt admits there are still doubters in academia, but adds quickly, "I think you get a lot of support from fellow-traveling scholars. There's an organization, the

North American Society of Sports History (NASSH), that's more academic than, say, SABR. It provides a chance for people who teach sports history courses to get together and share common problems."

Barnett notes that the traditional idea of the absentminded professor completely absorbed in the pursuit of some arcane knowledge doesn't apply here. "You aren't likely to spend much time learning the ins and outs of the history of billiards in a sports history course. In the early part, the rise of sports, you'll hear about some sports that are no longer popular today— bear baiting, for example. But, particularly when covering the years after World War II, a sports history course is likely to focus on many units—television, black athletes, women athletes, and so on. Because of that broad range, the major sports are stressed—baseball, for example.

"If we're going to understand where we are, we must know where we've been. The best way to learn history may be to experience it, but that's out of the realm of possibility in most cases. History is the collected experience of a society. Understanding history is understanding those experiences, and sports are a classic part of the American experience."   —BC

Your Chance to Ask the Questions

Accreditation is the usual way academics ensure consistency of quality in degrees offered by institutions of higher learning. After all, you'd want to know that someone with a medical degree from Acme Tech had to at least take the same courses as the fellow who got his degree from Harvard.

The sports management field feels it isn't ready yet for accreditation—it's too expensive, the field's too young, the market will shake itself out, they say. Still, in order for students to protect themselves against schools simply putting up a shingle and passing off regular physical education courses as a sports management major, the National Association for Sport and Physical Education suggests that would-be students ask some questions before choosing a program.

The best approach when considering an individual course in baseball or sports is to ask students who've taken it to evaluate it. Another good idea is to talk to the professor, and, if possible, get a copy of his syllabus. And, while it's not a perfect match, you can get some insight into the quality of an individual course in baseball or sports history by learning about certain aspects of the program.

1. *General information about the program:* What admission standards are required (undergraduate GPA, standardized exams)? Is there an interview required? How many students are admitted? What's the ratio of part-timers to full-timers? What's the degree conferred? What's the title of the program?
2. *Physical resources:* What type of learning resources are there (books, periodicals, monographs, computer software, etc.)? Where are these learning resources located? (Better programs have their own library or resource center.)
3. *Financial assistance:* Are there work-study programs available for students? Part-time positions? Graduate assistantships? Fellowships? Scholarships?
4. *Opportunities for practical experience:* On campus, can students work or intern in the department of athletics, intramurals, campus recreation, physical education? Off campus, are there high schools, colleges, commercial clubs, professional teams? (In a rural area, a school can have a fine academic program but can't give the students additional experiences. Some sports management schools have no affiliation with intramurals or on-campus athletics.)
5. *Human resources:* What are the number of faculty with primary responsibility in the area of sports adminstration? What are the specialized subject areas of these faculty? What type of research interests do these faculty have? Are there courses taught by faculty from other academic units—business administration, education administration, journalism, telecommunications? What enrichment activities are available: guest lectures, workshops, symposia, off-campus visits?
6. *Curriculum:* How many hours are necessary for the completion of the degree program? How many hours are specifically focused on sports management/sports administration content? Is there a research methods course required? Is there a project or thesis requirement? Is there an internship requirement?

The NASPE also has issued voluntary guidelines that identify the areas that ought to be covered in the undergraduate and graduate programs. The organization's Task Force on Sports Management Curricula suggests the following courses are critical to an undergraduate sports management program: accounting, marketing, management, computer applications, sports marketing, sports law, sports management, sports foundations (sports history, philosophy, ethics, psychology, and/or sociology) and the internship.

Keep that in mind when choosing a program. —NC

Undergraduate Sampler: St. Thomas University (Miami, Florida)

Program: St. Thomas launched the first undergraduate sports administration program in 1973. (A master's program was added in 1977, but we will focus on the undergraduate program here.) It is located in the division of Business, Economics, Sports, and Travel (after all, this is Miami). Graduates receive a bachelor's degree in sports administration.

Philosophy: Both the undergraduate and graduate programs emphasize the teaching of management skills. Except for two management courses, all courses are specific to sports. "You'll learn the theories as they relate to a team rather than a K-Mart store."

Student Body: 75–80 students (45–50 at the graduate level).

Curriculum: Besides the liberal arts requirement (a core of courses, including accounting, economics, news reporting, communications), the sports administration required courses are introduction to sports administration, sports financial management, legal aspects. Electives include stadium and arena management, public relations, psychology, principles of leisure services.

Internship: Students are encouraged to develop their own internships through the help of a faculty coordinator. "We encourage them to start networking as soon as they get here."

Extras: Professors are also professionals in the field: in sports marketing, law, management, and psychology. —NC

What I Learned in School Today

Some people snicker at the idea of classes in sports management—and sometimes they're right.

The first thing you notice is the size of the students—the majority fill the door frame. And as they peel off their letter jackets and warm-ups, you can see they're mostly body-by-Nautilus. More than a few straggle in on crutches, their knees or ankles heavily taped. The buzz of preclass conversation comes to a halt as the lecturer takes his place at the front of the room. He's Will Perry, assistant athletic director at the University of Michigan, and today's topic is "Licensing Athletic Logos."

After stating that logo fees are an increasingly important revenue source for athletic departments, producing $112,000 in fees at the University of Michigan last year, Perry tries to give his subject some theoretical underpinning by distinguishing various forms of licensing. At each stage of his presentation, he tries to evoke a response from the thirty-odd students, most of them varsity Michigan athletes. But his efforts are in vain. When he asks, "Can anybody give me an example of regulating something by a license?" the football, basketball, hockey, baseball, and volleyball players are silent. Things are so dead there's not even a show of hands when Perry asks in desperation, "Does anybody here have a driver's license?"

It's like a scene from *Back to School.* But it's just another session of PE 402— "Sports Management and Marketing"—an upper-level phys ed course at the University of Michigan.

Michigan has the largest athletic department in the country. It enjoys a clean reputation and is also one of only a dozen big-time schools that has never been put on probation by the NCAA. Still, a few years ago, the Michigan physical education program was removed from the School of

Education and given unique status as a "division," reporting directly only to the provost and a university vice president. School officials say this was done to provide more options for students interested in sports management.

The PE division's most popular offering with jocks is a concentration in "sports management and communications." More than half of the students in this major are athletes on scholarships. The new administrative arrangements have made it tough for outsiders to learn what goes on, say, in such courses as "The History and Sociology of Human Movement," "Personal Exercise," or "Organized Camping." Which is why, in the fall of 1986, I decided to attend one such course from start to finish.

There were a couple of good reasons for choosing PE 402. Not only was it a four-credit upper-level course, but it also featured guest lecture appearances, and one of the two regular lecturers was Don Canham, the athletic director himself.

The class lectures are held on Mondays, Wednesdays, and Fridays from 9 to 10 A.M. Canham is never very animated in the class. He looks down at his notes a lot. He mumbles. He's fond of bromides, often spending blocks of time on such mottos as "If one cannot manage time, one cannot manage anything"; "Set reasonable goals"; or "Talk to the janitor."

Canham's dress is usually country-club casual—howling green sports jacket, canary slacks. Between his attire and the shorts and muscle T-shirts favored by the students, it's hard to keep in mind this is a for-credit college class. It looks more like the club director briefing his caddies before the Labor Day tournament.

There are four quizzes given during the term. Along with some legitimate questions are others such as these: "Athletic administrators should be primarily con-

cerned with two (2) groups; name them." (Answer: players and coaches.) "At the Michigan Stadium a spectator can be readmitted to the game if he has a hand stamp visible." (Answer: false.) "What are the two main elements in a computer system?" (Answer: hardware and software.)

And on those occasions when class time is spent on potentially interesting topics, little analysis or explanation is attempted. When Canham addressed Title IX, the federal law passed in 1972 requiring equal opportunity for women in physical and other education programs, he said, "I was in favor of the bill, but the problem arose when HEW said 'equal opportunity' means 'equal money spent.' That's nonsense. We spend a million and a half dollars on football. I was in Washington and I asked these clowns, 'Does that mean I have to spend a million and a half dollars on women's sports?'"

When UM business manager and former women's softball coach Bob DeCarolis talks to our class about financial operations, he rarely strays from locker-room analogies. "Financial projections," he explains, are "like the predictions that come out at the beginning of the season saying Michigan is going to be number two."

There is no required reading for the course. In fact, there are no regular assignments at all. Only once is a book even *mentioned* in class—that's when Bill Cusumano, the other regular instructor, cites Curt Flood's autobiography.

One recurrent theme of PE 402 is that the athlete's problems and deficiencies are invariably caused by someone else. "The most discriminated-against person in the university is the athlete," Canham says. For a change, his audience takes notes eagerly. "The growth of the NCAA is one of the most disappointing things I've seen in my career."

Susan Monaghan, a recent UM grad and the daughter of Detroit Tigers' owner Tom Monaghan, was a PE 402 classmate of mine who thinks the class didn't do her

Graduate Sampler: Kent State University (Kent, Ohio)

Program: Kent's is a graduate-only program. 36 hours—32 hours of course work and 4 hours of internship. Graduates receive a master of arts in physical education with a concentration in sports administration (some other schools, like Ohio University, offer a masters in sports administration). Philosophy: "We ask students to consider the level at which they want to work—high school, Division I, Division III, professional, or commercial, and the focus they want to take—sports information, media relations, comptroller, facility manager. We're trying to get people to begin to focus their careers."

Student Body: 40–45 students a year. About 15 are part-time. Night and summer classes are available. Majority of students come with interest in working in the collegiate area. Range in age includes students right out of undergraduate school to 36 years old.

Curriculum: The school requirement in the masters program includes a research course and an ethics course. Then there are 18 hours of sports administration courses (approximately six courses), including an internship, leadership theory, marketing, and law. Other courses can be selected to suit your area of specialization (facility management, issues in sports, selection and development of personnel). Also required are 12 hours of related, support study: two intradisciplinary electives (within the school but outside the sports administration courses) from a list that includes sports sociology, psychology of

coaching, athletic training, and exercise physiology. Also, two interdisciplinary (outside the school) electives from a business college, college of education, or school of journalism. There is a thesis option.

Internship: Students are encouraged to pursue internships according to the level at which they want to work, the part of the country they want to work in, and what they perceive to be their entry-level position. Then they're encouraged to network like mad, remembering that "it's not important who you know, but who knows you."

Extras: Because of Kent's proximity to

If the Kent State athletic program is not exactly a ticket to playing a pro sport, the sports-administration program is a winner. And the field is a fertile one, as the business of sport seems to provide new opportunities each year.

Cleveland, Akron, Youngstown, and Canton, and cooperation from the athletic department and intramurals program, the school currently offers twenty-two graduate assistantships.

Doctoral Program: Housed in the college of education. Students receive a Ph.D. in education administration with a minor in sports administration.   —NC

wrong. She's now working full-time for the Tigers in the front office.

"We learned a lot," she says in retrospect. "We got hands-on, firsthand information. We learned a little bit about

a lot of sports."

"Mr. Canham is unbelievable," says Steve Galetti, chairman of the department of sports management and communications, when asked to comment on PE 402.

"Some kids don't take as much advantage of this as others."

Whatever value the class actually offers, many of the students don't reap the benefits. Throughout the term absenteeism and lateness are rampant; stony silences bury almost every attempt at participatory discussion.

One day Cusumano mentions how *Brown v. the Board of Education* eventually opened up college athletics. He's well into his explanation when he finally feels all the dead stares. "Uh, does anybody know what *Brown v. the Board of Education* is?" Utter silence. Finally one lone guy—a hockey player, a *Canadian*—raises his hand.

Campus "names" tend to be among the 15 or 20 students cutting class each day. The teaching assistant for the course, Pat Aviotti, spends much of his time checking up on the whereabouts of his "boys."

Paul Jokisch, a one-time basketball player who became a starting split end, doesn't come to class at all until four weeks into the semester. When he finally does appear, Bill Cusumano turns to Aviotti and says, "Pat, would you put together a package of all the material we've covered so far and make copies of it for Paul?" Word of the poor attendance gets back to coach Bo Schembechler, who reportedly confronts the offenders at a team meeting: "Is that a bunch of dumb asses to miss a class with the athletic director?"

"We monitor class attendance in our division closely," Galetti says in defense of PE 402. "Maybe the missing kids were on athletic trips." They were not.

And even when these guys show up, some of them roll in half an hour late, looking groggy. On Linemen's Row against the back wall, as the guys park their crutches, pop their morning sodas, and break out the Copenhagen, a tackle explains the prevailing attitude to a visiting lecturer. "We just come back here and go to sleep—we already know what he's talking about."

Among the most noticeable features of the lax class environment is the widespread cheating that occurs during tests. I routinely see students whispering answers to each other or consulting the notebooks they've left open at their feet or directly beneath their exams. Furthermore, every quiz is preceded by several periods where Cusumano all but stamps his feet as he serves up actual test material. By the end of the term, it's not surprising to hear Cusumano promise, "In discussion section tomorrow we'll try to skate you through the final exam."

Pat Aviotti monitors the final exam all by himself, and whenever a student calls him over to ask a question, cheating flares up behind his back. Aviotti eventually notices that offensive guard Mike Krauss is openly leafing through the notebook at his feet, and Aviotti invites him to sit in the front of the classroom. As Krauss takes his new seat, he smiles at Aviotti, who does not in the least smile back.   —SS

A Baseball Course

Any student who walks into David Q. Voigt's "Baseball in American Culture" class at Albright College (in Reading, Pennsylvania) expecting to get by with a cursory perusal of the *USA Today* sports page is in for a shock.

For starters, there's a textbook, and it's required reading from cover to cover. Voigt has penned his own critically praised histories of baseball, and his *Baseball: An Illustrated History* provides the backbone of his four-and-a-half-week course. "B. in Am. Cul." is an interim semester course, offered during January between Albright's two regular semesters.

For supplementary material, the Macmillan *Baseball Encyclopedia* and *Total Baseball* are on reserve at the school library, and there are some seventy-five books on baseball in the 796.357 section.

Voight also recommends *The Sporting News, Sports Illustrated, Baseball Digest*, and several other magazines for further reading.

Two-thirds of a student's grade will be based on two tests, a midterm and a final. "Test" is the operative word, not "quiz." A typical Voigt test consists of fifty short-answer questions (true-false or multiple choice), five questions to be answered in factual, complete sentences, and an essay question. An example of the latter requires students to come up with six points to explain the statement, "Baseball (major league) is a long-established institution that mirrors changes and trends in the culture at large."

Attendance is factored into the grade, but largely negatively. Although perfect attendance is a plus, more than two unexcused absences will count against a student. And when Voigt has a speaker in, any absence must be excused. Don't expect the professor to look kindly on a vague "I wasn't feelin' good." What does your doctor say?

A final third of the grade is based on a student's "presentation." This can be handled orally (a day is set aside near the end for oral presentations) or as a written paper. A written presentation must be a minimum of eight pages in length, based on at least three sources, and footnoted. The paper must cover a topic of interest in baseball—a subject that fits into the mainstream of baseball history and, Voigt stresses, *the larger framework of American culture*. He expects at least one paragraph in the paper to justify the importance of its subject, and the quality of the student's writing will also be taken into consideration.

Among the topics Voigt suggests for presentation:

1. Book reviews (he'll provide a recommended list)

2. Baseball issues (race, unionism, sexism, and outside influences such as war, depression, media, etc.)

3. Changing character of fans (some suggested types: ballpark fans, collectors, trivia nuts, statistical nuts)

4. Changing major league game (focusing on owner-player relations, scouts, umpires, officials, etc.)

5. Subcultures of major league baseball (minors, Negro majors, college baseball, women's majors, softball, little league, etc.)

6. Literary baseball (focusing on novels by writers such as Roth, Malamud, Coover, or films such as *The Natural*)

Book reviews demand more than a mere retelling. Students should be able to expand on a major topic, using illustrations, then conclude by commenting on the book's significance to the course and to the history of major league baseball. Although students can nominate their own choices, Voight suggests the following eight as fitting the significance criteria:

- Roger Angell, *Five Seasons: A Baseball Companion*
- G. H. Fleming, *The Unforgettable Season*
- Roger Kahn, *The Boys of Summer*
- Kevin Kerrane, *Dollar Sign on the Muscle*
- L. Lowenfish and Tony Lupien, *The Imperfect Diamond*
- Ron Luciano and David Fisher, *The Umpire Strikes Back*
- Robert W. Peterson, *Only the Ball Was White*
- Jules Tygiel, *Baseball's Great Experiment: Jackie Robinson and His Legacy*

Voigt admits that a student choosing to go the oral route may have an easier row to hoe, so long as he can avoid stage fright. One of the professor's pet concerns is getting young people up on their feet to face an audience. An oral presentation should not exceed fifteen minutes, but students should be open to questions from the floor at the end of the presentation.

Four speakers are imported during the course to supplement Voigt's lectures. Examples might be a retired major league umpire, a former player in the Negro leagues, a noted author, and an expert on Japanese baseball.

Voigt, who is anything but the stereo-

No major American event failed to touch baseball; here, pregame drills in WW I.

typical droning mumbler, covers the whole range of baseball history in his lively lectures, starting with the formation of gentlemen's club teams in the 1840s and ending with last year's World Series winner. He'll spend extra time on such key areas as the creation of the Reserve Clause, the formation of the American League, the integration of blacks, and the effects of expansion, but still manages to touch on oddities like the Merkle "boner" and Bill Veeck's midget. His words are often illustrated with slides and short films. Voigt, whose method is Socratic rather than Sock-It-to-'Em, encourages students to chime in when they have significant questions or points to make.

Students successfully completing "Baseball in American Culture" may not qualify as "experts"—"informed fans" might be more accurate—but they'll never look at baseball or American culture in quite the same way. The best part, says Voigt, is when a student who's already received his grade comes up to him and says, "Gee, I never knew there was so much to baseball!"   —BC

Sports History

An increasing offering in history departments in colleges and universities around the country is sports history, often in the form of social studies ("Sport and America" is a common course title). Courses exclusively devoted to baseball are still rare but are popping up more and more. On the following pages you'll find a selected listing of schools (arranged by state) that offer courses in baseball history or courses in sports history taught by scholars who have a special interest, or are conducting their own research, in baseball history. Another source of information about the study of sports history is the North American Society for Sport History (contact: Professor Ron Smith, c/o Department of Exercise and Sport Science, Penn State University, 101 White Building, University Park, PA 16802, [814] 865-2416).

ARIZONA

Arizona State University
Tempe, AZ 85287
(602) 965-3151
James E. Odenkirk, Professor, Health and Physical Education Dept.
  Special Interest: American Culture and Baseball.
  Courses Taught: History of Physical Education and Sports. (undergraduate); Historical Basis of American Sports (graduate).
  Member, NASSH, SABR.

ARKANSAS

University of Arkansas
Ozark Hall-12
Fayetteville, AR 72701
(501) 573-3001
Timothy P. Donovan, Professor of History.

  Special Interests: History of Baseball; Sports Heroes in American Society.
  Current Research: Sports Heroes in the 1940s.
  Course Taught: History of Sports in America.

CALIFORNIA

California State University, Hayward
Hayward, CA 94542
(415) 881-3037
William G. Vanderburgh, Professor, Department of Kinesiology and Physical Education.
  Special Interest: U.S. Sports (1850–1900).
  Course Taught: History of Sports.

California State University, Stanislaus
801 West Monte Vista Avenue
Turlock, CA 95380
(209) 667-3238
Samuel O. Regalado, Assistant Professor, Department of History.
  Special Interests: Latin Americans in American Professional Baseball, Their Acculturation and Assimilation Process, 1871–1981; Baseball in the Los Angeles Barrios During the Post–World War II Period.
  Course Taught: American Sports History.
  Member, NASSH.

Humboldt State University
Arcata, CA 95521
(707) 826-4536
Albert J. Figone, Associate Professor, Dept. of Health and Physical Education.
  Special Interest: Relationship of Social, Political, and Economic Factors to the Development of Sports During the 1920s.

  Current Research: The Construction of Candlestick Park in San Francisco; Warren G. Harding and Babe Ruth.
  Course Taught: History of Sports.
  Member: NASSH, SABR.

St. Mary's College of California
St. Mary's Road
Moraga, CA 94707
(415) 376-4411
Paul J. Zingg, Professor of History and Dean.
  Special Interests: Baseball Parks; College Baseball; Baseball in Film and Fiction.
  Course Taught: Research Seminar in American Sports History (undergraduate).

San Francisco State University
1600 Holloway Avenue
San Francisco, CA 94132
(415) 338-1141
Eric Solomon, Professor of English.
  Special Interest: Baseball Fiction by Jewish Authors.
  Courses Taught: Sports Fiction; Sports Journalism; Baseball History and Literature.
  Member, SABR.
Jules E. Tygiel, Professor of History.
  Special Interests: Baseball, Jackie Robinson, the Negro Leagues.
  Courses Taught: Century of Sports; History and Literature of Baseball.
  Member, NASSH, SABR.

COLORADO

Metropolitan State College
1006 11th Street
Denver, CO 80204
(303) 556-3175/3113
Thomas L. Altherr, Professor of History.
  Special Interest: Nineteenth-Century Baseball History.
  Course Taught: Sports in America.
  Member, SABR.

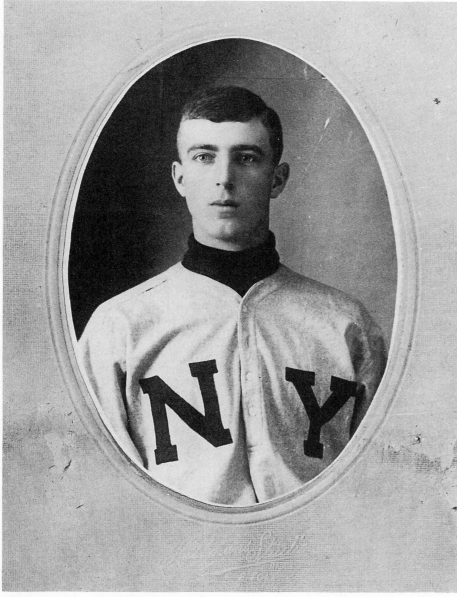

Fred Merkle was only 19 when his blunder cost the N.Y. Giants the 1908 pennant.

Northeastern Illinois University
5500 N. St. Louis Avenue
Chicago, IL 60625
(312) 794-2836
Steven A. Reiss, Professor of History.
  Special Interest: Urban Sports.
  Current Research: Professional Baseball
    and Social Mobility, 1880–1960.
  Courses Taught: History of American
    Sports; Readings in Sports His-
    tory; Seminar in Sports History;
    Sports in the Contemporary World,
    1931–present.
  Member, NASSH, SABR.

INDIANA

Indiana University Southeast
4201 Grant Line Rd.
New Albany, IN 47150
(812) 945-2731, ext. 371
John E. Findling, Professor of History.
  Special Interests: Baseball in Louisville
    and Chicago; Sports Biography.
  Current Research: Biographies in *Bio-
    graphical Dictionary of American
    Sports.*
  Course Taught: American Sports Histo-
    ry Colloquium.
  Member, NASSH.

Purdue University
University Hall
West Lafayette, IN 47907
Randy W. Roberts, Associate Professor,
  Department of History.
  Special Interest: Biography, American
    Sports—1945 to Present.
  Course Taught: American Sports (un-
    dergraduate).

IOWA

William Penn College
2314 Ridgeway Avenue
Oskaloosa, IA 52577
(515) 673-1110
David L. Porter, Shangle Professor of History and Political Science.

FLORIDA

University of Central Florida
P.O. Box 25000
Orlando, FL 32816
(305) 275-2224
Richard C. Crepeau, Professor of History.
  Special Interests: Baseball; Intercolle-
    giate Athletics.
  Current Research: Rise of Intercolle-
    giate Athletics in Catholic Universi-
    ties.
  Course Taught: Sports in America.
  Member, NASSH, SABR.

ILLINOIS

University of Illinois/Urbana-Champaign
119 Gregory Hall
810 S. Wright Street
Urbana, IL 61801
(217) 333-2352
Thomas B. Littlewood, Professor of Jour-
  nalism.
  Current Research: Biography of Arch
    Ward, *Chicago Tribune* Sports Editor
    (1930–1955).
  Course Taught: Sports Journalism.
  Member, NASSH, SABR.

Alexander Cartwright put out fires when he wasn't busy inventing baseball.

Special Interests: Baseball.
Current Research/Publication: Editor, *Biographical Dictionary of American Sports* (four volumes).
Courses Taught: American Sports History; History of Baseball.
Member, NASSH, SABR.

KANSAS

Kansas State University
Manhattan, KS 66506
(913) 532-6765
David K. Wiggins, Associate Professor, Physical Education.
Special Interest: Black Athletes in American Sports.
Courses Taught: History of Sports; Minority Groups in Sports.
Member, NASSH.

KENTUCKY

University of Louisville
Louisville, KY 40292
(502) 588-6641
Lawrence W. Fielding, Professor of Physical Education.

Special Interests: Civil War; Sporting Goods.
Recent Publication/Presentation: "Hillerich and Bradsby."
Courses Taught: History of American Sports; Rise of Institutionalized Sports in America.
Member, NASSH.

MICHIGAN

Michigan State University
East Lansing, MI 48823
(517) 353-9261
Peter D. Levine, Professor of American History.
Recent Publication: A. G. Spalding and the Rise of Baseball.
Course Taught: History of Sports in America.
Member, NASSH, SABR.

MINNESOTA

Normandale Community College
9700 France Avenue S.
Bloomington, MN 55431
(612) 896-4506
John C. Chalberg, Instructor.
Special Interests: Baseball History; Sports Journalism; Impact of the Cold War; Television and Sports.
Current Research: Sports Autobiographies.
Recent Publications/Presentations: Sandy Koufax; Bill Veeck.
Member, SABR.

MISSOURI

University of Missouri—St. Louis
8001 Natural Bridge Road
St. Louis, MO 63121
(314) 553-5690
Charles P. Korr, Professor of History.
Special Interest: History of Major League Baseball Players Association.
Courses Taught: Sports and Society; Sports and Social History.
Member, SABR.

University of Missouri—Kansas City
Office of Continuing Education
4900 Troost
Kansas City, MO 64110
(816) 276-2736, ext. 18
W. Lloyd Johnson.
Special Interest: Baseball—The Early Years.
Course Taught: History of Major League Baseball.

NEBRASKA

University of Nebraska
Oldfather Hall
Lincoln, NE 68588-0327
(402) 472-2414
Benjamin G. Rader, Professor of History.
Special Interests: American Sports.
Recent Publication/Presentation: Television and Sports, Sports in the Nineteenth-Century U.S.
Course Taught: History of Sports.
Member, NASSH.

NEW JERSEY

Union County College
20 Rainier Road
Fanwood, NJ 07023
(201) 709-7176
Lawrence D. Hogan, Professor of History.
Special Interest: Negro League Baseball.
Course Taught: History of Sports in America.
Member, SABR.

NEW YORK

Manhattan College
Riverdale, NY 10471
(212) 920-0217
George B. Kirsch, Chairman, History Department.
Special Interests: Nineteenth-Century American Sports, Cricket and Baseball.
Recent Publication/Presentation: As-

pects of Nineteenth-Century Baseball.
Courses Taught: American Studies; Sport and American Society.
Member, NASSH.

State University of New York at Cortland
119 Old Main, Cortland, NY 13045
(607) 753-2723
Ann M. Scanlon, Professor of History.
Current Research: History of Professional Sports Franchises.
Course Taught: Sports as a Big Business: A History.

State University of New York at Oneonta
Oneonta, NY 13820
(607) 431-2404
Williams M. Simons, Associate Professor of History.
Special Interest: Jews in Sports.
Course Taught: Athletics, Society, and History.
Member, SABR.

NORTH CAROLINA

North Carolina Wesleyan College
Rocky Mount, NC 27804
(919) 977-7171
Leverett T. Smith, Professor of English.
Special Interest: Literature of Baseball.
Courses Taught: Sports in America; Baseball in American Life.
Member, NASSH, SABR.

University of North Carolina at Greensboro
209 Forney Building
Greensboro, NC 27412
(919) 334-5432
Richard A. Swanson, Dean, School of HPERD.
Special Interest: Sports in the United States, 1865–1940s.
Course Taught: History of American Sports and Physical Education (graduate).

OHIO

Capital University
2199 E. Main Street
Columbus, OH 43209
(614) 236-6204
Harry Jebsen, Jr., Dean, College of Arts and Sciences.
Recent Publication/Presentation: Integrating Sports History into the American History Survey.
Courses Taught: Sports History; Sports Journalism.
Member, NASSH, SABR.

Miami University
Phillips Hall
Oxford, OH 45056
(513) 529-2702
Alan G. Ingham, Associate Professor, Sociology.
Current Research: Relocation of Professional Sports Franchises.
Course Taught: Sports and Modernization.
Member, NASSH.

OREGON

Oregon State University
Corvallis, OR 97331
(503) 724-3244
Michael V. Oriard, Associate Professor, Dept. of English.
Course Taught: American Sports Literature.
Member, NASSH, SABR.

PENNSYLVANIA

Albright College
Reading, PA 19612
(215) 921-2381
David Q. Voigt, Professor of Sociology/Anthropology.
Special Interests: Major League Baseball; Labor History in Minor League Baseball.
Recent Publication: Baseball: An Illustrated History.

HELP!

Confused? Need some guidance? The sports management field has two associations that serve it. Give them a holler and let them serve you, too. The National Association of Sports and Physical Education (a division of the American Alliance for Health, Physical Education, Recreation, and Dance) has taken on the role of curriculum certification and accreditation. Its president is Dr. Annie Clement, of Cleveland State University, who is also a member of the North American Society for Sport Management.

NASSM focuses on the dissemination of information and research about sports management theory and practice through an annual conference and publication of *The Journal of Sport Management* (published by Human Kinetics Publishers, PO Box 5076, Champaign, IL 61820; 217-351-5076). NASSM's president is Dr. Bill Sutton from Ohio State. Past president is Dr. Carl Schraibman from Kent State. See listings under each school for addresses and phone numbers.

Not all sports management courses are worthwhile, clearly. Indifferent instructors and students abound, so *caveat emptor.* —NC

Courses Taught: Baseball in American Culture; Sociology of Leisure and Sports.
Member, NASSH, SABR.

Chatham College
1609 Beechwood Blvd.
Pittsburgh, PA 15217
(412) 422-7962
Rob Ruck, Assistant Professor of History.
Special Interests: Black Community; Baseball in the Caribbean.
Course Taught: History of Sport.
Member, NASSH, SABR.

Penn State University
101 White Building
University Park, PA 16802
Ronald Smith, Professor, Dept. of Exercise
and Sports Science.
  Courses Taught: History of Sports in
  American Society; Western Literature
  and Sports.
  Member, NASSH.

TENNESSEE

East Tennessee State University
Box 22990A
Johnson City, TN 37614-0002
(615) 929-4339
Robert J. Higgs, Professor of English.
  Course Taught: The Literature of
  Sports.
  Member, NASSH.

TEXAS

Lamar University
Beaumont, TX 77710
(409) 880-8516
John M. Carroll, Professor of History.
  Special Interests: Nineteenth-Century
  Baseball.
  Course Taught: History of American
  Sports.
  Member, NASSH, SABR.

Texas Christian University
Box 32872
Fort Worth, TX 76129
(817) 921-7240
David L. Vanderwerken, Professor of En-
glish.
  Course Taught: Sports in Modern Amer-
  ican Literature.

Texas Tech University
Lubbock, TX 79409
(806) 742-3744/3355
James W. Harper, Associate Professor/
Director of Honors, Dept. of History.
  Special Interests: Baseball; Sportscast-
  ing; Sports as a Reflection of Society;
  Biography.

Current Research: Biographical Stud-
ies; History of Sportscasting and
Sportswriting.
Courses Taught: History of Baseball; A
Mirror of America; History of Sports
and Recreation in the U.S.
Member, NASSH, SABR.

UTAH

University of Utah
Salt Lake City, UT 84112
(801) 581-6121
Larry R. Gerlach, Professor of History.
  Special Interests: Baseball History; Race
  and Gender in Sports.
  Current Research: History of Baseball
  Umpires.
  Recent Publication/Presentation: Race
  and Ethnicity in Baseball
  Course Taught: History of Sports in
  America.
  Member, NASSH, SABR.

WEST VIRGINIA

Marietta College
415 Columbia Avenue
Williamstown, WV 26187
(304) 375-7611
Eugene C. Murdock, Professor of History
Emeritus.
  Current Research: Transcribing Inter-
  views with Old-Time Baseball Players,
  1910–1940.
  Course Taught: Sports in American
  Life.
  Member, SABR.

CANADA

Mount Royal College
4825 Richard Road, S.W.
Calgary, Alberta
Canada T3E 6K6
(403) 240-6511
Gary A. Koroluk, Instructor, Physical Edu-
cation Department.
  Current Research: Sports Literature.
  Course Taught: Philosophy of Sports

Baseball's Lettered Man

Perhaps baseball's most intellectual player was catcher Moe Berg, who put in 15
major league seasons between the World
Wars. Berg was a *summa cum laude* grad
of Princeton. After his death in 1972 the
world learned he'd also been a master spy
for our government.

Only Berg would have described the
catcher as "the Cerberus of baseball." In
an *Atlantic Monthly* article in 1941, Berg
wrote, "With Montaigne, we conceive Soc-
rates in place of Alexander, of brain for
brawn, wit for whip." His subject? Lefty
Grove's decision to throw a forkball to
Heinie Manush!   —BC

(Historical Perspective).
Member, NASSH.

Seneca College
1750 Finch Avenue East
Willowdale, Ontario
Canada, M2J 2X5
(416) 491-5050
William A. Humber, Chairman, Continu-
ing Education.
  Course Taught: Baseball Spring Train-
  ing for Fans.
  Member, NASSH, SABR.

University of Western Ontario
London, Ontario
Canada, N6A 3K7
(519) 679-2111, ext. 5485
Robert K. Barney, Professor, Physical Edu-
cation.
  Special Interests: American Sports and
  Physical Education, Baseball in
  Early Nineteenth-Century Ontario,
  Canada.
  Course Taught: Sports in America: A
  Historical Perspective.
  Member, NASSH, SABR   —NC

Baseball in American Culture, Final Exam

Bet you never saw an exam like this land on your desk in school. Highlights from an exam given in Professor David Voigt's class, "Baseball in American Culture," at Albright College in Reading, PA (answers on the following page). Don't panic; we haven't included any of the essays.

1. Which word best describes the way major league baseball came about? (a) invention (b) discovery (c) creation (d) evolution.

2. Which early form of organized baseball won out? (a) the Massachusetts game (b) the New York game.

3. Prior to the Cincinnati Reds of 1869, no ball player was ever paid for playing baseball. True or false?

4. The first professional league was the (a) National Association of Base Ball Players (b) National League (c) National Associaton of Professional Base Ball Players (d) American Association.

5. During the National Association era (1871–1875), all but one of the pennants went to the (a) Philadelphia Athletics (b) Boston Red Stockings (c) Cincinnati Red Stockings (d) New York Mutuals (e) New York Giants.

6. Beer sales and Sunday ball were promotional gimmicks used by which league in the 1880s? (a) American League (b) Players League (c) American Association (d) National League.

7. Making a player contract with one major league team for an indefinite period was achieved by the (a) re-entry draft (b) National Agreement (c) Players League (d) reserve clause.

8. Concerning the geography of major league baseball in the nineteenth century, it was (a) continental (b) limited to eastern and old northwestern regions (c) limited to northern and southern regions.

9. In monopolizing major league baseball in the nineteenth century, the National League eliminated all but one of these rivals: (a) American Association (b) American League (c) Players League.

10. "Official" recognition of major leagues and minor leagues is contained in (a) the reserve clause (b) syndicate baseball (c) national agreements (d) the National Commission

11. The Chicago "Black Sox" players were judged guilty and expelled under which code of law? (a) baseball law (b) civil law.

12. The nineteenth-century superstar whose $10,000 sale to Boston excited fans was (a) Pop Anson (b) Charley Radbourn (c) King Kelly (d) Harry Wright (e) Al Spalding.

13. Which of these stars holds the most batting titles? (a) Cobb (b) Ruth (c) Wagner (d) Kelly.

14. The "Czar of Baseball" who made the American League into a thriving major league was (a) Ban Johnson (b) Harry Wright (c) Branch Rickey (d) Chris von der Ahe.

15. The nineteenth-century innovator who codified rules, edited journals and histories, and devised the modern box score was (a) Harry Wright (b) Henry Chadwick (c) Al Spalding (d) John Ward (e) Chris von der Ahe.

16. Branch Rickey is best associated with which form of talent recruiting? (a) the farm system (b) the bonus baby era (c) purchasing players from independent minor league operators (d) the rookie free agent draft of 1965 and afterward.

17. The National Agreement of 1903 recognized which league as major? (a) the American Association (b) the Players

The Boston Red Stockings featured Al Spalding and the (landbound) Wright brothers.

League (c) the National League (d) the American League (e) the Federal League.

18. Baseball law differs from civil law in that baseball law was able to deny freedom of movement to players by such devices as blacklisting and the reserve clause. True or false?

19. Once the white majors accepted black players, the owners of the Negro major league clubs made hefty profit windfalls from sale of their players to the majors. True or false?

20. Old-time players (those prior to 1920) enjoyed freedom of movement and better salaries during those times when invading major leagues tried to win acceptance. True or false?

The Answers

Allow five points for each correct answer. How'd you do?

1. (d) evolution.
2. (a) Massachusetts game.
3. False.
4. (c) National Association of Professional Base Ball Players.
5. (b) Boston Red Stockings.
6. (c) American Association.
7. (d) reserve clause.
8. (b) limited to eastern and old northwestern regions.
9. (b) American League.
10. (d) National Commission.
11. (a) baseball law.
12. (c) King Kelly.
13. (a) Cobb.
14. (a) Ban Johnson.
15. (b) Henry Chadwick.
16. (a) the farm system.
17. (d) American League.
18. True.
19. False.
20. True.　　　　　—NC

Three baseball paradigms for students: the heroic Branch Rickey, the obsessed Ty Cobb, and the naive Joe Jackson.

CHAPTER 6

Live the Fantasy

A few years ago, on a 40-degree mid-March morning, four friends and I left New York City and headed off by railroad to Neptune, N.J., a town filled that day with all the dreariness you'd expect of winter in a South Shore resort area. We rented a Winnebago and pointed it south.

By the next afternoon we were sitting in the grandstand in Municipal Stadium in West Palm Beach watching the Braves play, our shirts off, cold beers in hand, baking in 80-degree sunshine. Then it was out to the beach for a swim, a night game at Fort Lauderdale Stadium to see the Yankees, and on to a campgrounds in the Everglades. The next morning, after an airboat ride, we were off to Vero Beach and a day at Dodgertown.

So began our week-long odyssey of spring training. We saw eight games in six days, all over the state—Tampa, Miami, West Palm Beach, Vero Beach, Sarasota. We learned the joys of hot showers and cold sodas while cruising down the open road. We slept at campgrounds, swam in the ocean, ate catfish and hush puppies in Yeehaw Junction. For a week we lived only for the next ball game.

It was like being an eight-year-old on summer vacation again. Only better.

We were pulled over by the police only once (just a warning in Palm Beach; we should have known better—we *were* tacky in our "recreational vehicle"), and we spent maybe $400 apiece for everything, including the R.V., tickets, camp grounds, beer, and food. (Breakfast is the best meal in Florida—especially at Skyway Jack's on the Gulf Coast.)

We left on a Sunday morning—why not wait till the last minute?—and headed

Camps and Tours

Whether you're a prospect or a suspect, it's all here: tryout camps, summer leagues, umpire schools, and more

home so that we could all get back to work on Monday. Twenty-four hours later, we were back in Neptune. But we couldn't go back to work, not yet. We spent the morning hanging around a truckstop, talking about the trip and having our reality readjusted.

Seeing spring training by Winnebago.

Taking a bus tour across America, ballpark by ballpark. Playing baseball ten hours a day in summer camp. Stepping up to the plate to face Sandy Koufax in fantasy camp. These aren't just dreams anymore; they are realities. And they're yours for the asking, if you've got the time and the money—fantasies, after all, generally don't come cheap.

Welcome to the dream machine. This chapter is about getting up from the audience and onto the screen, of passing through the looking glass and being with your heroes.

As baseball's popularity has exploded, entrepreneurs have devised more and more ways to cater to the fans' desire to touch a part of the game. Travel agents now specialize in arranging tours to spring training or personalized road trips so you catch your team's away games. You can take bus tours to major league and minor league cities all summer (there's even one for teenagers). Or cruises during the winter along with ball players and their wives.

If you're more player than spectator, you can follow the dream through life. From instructional baseball camps for Little Leaguers to high schoolers and beyond, to summer leagues and tryout camps for college prospects and would-be bigleaguers, to umpire schools and on to fantasy camps, the consolation prize for most of us.

On the pages that follow you'll find information about all of these adventures. You'll also get an inside look at an umpire school, spend a weekend at one kid's big league tryout and a week at a fantasy camp. You'll even get tips on how to beat the traffic at spring training. If you can go there, it's in here.   —NC

Camps and Schools

Don't expect summer camp babysitting here or instructors just throwing out the equipment bags and letting the kids play. Although some of these organizations call themselves camps, others schools, and still others "academies," the approach is the same: these are teaching programs aimed at helping beginning players develop better skills, and advanced players win college scholarships or possibly gain pro careers. Below, you'll find those camps that have national reputations and draw kids from all over the country and abroad. Some are summer programs, some are held in Florida over the winter. You can choose a week or, if you're lucky, stay the whole summer.

BO BELCHER'S CHANDLER BASEBALL CAMP
PO Box 395
Chandler, OK 74834
(405) 258-1720
Contact: Tom Belcher, camp director.
Ages: Boys 8–18.
When: Five two-week sessions June through August, plus a one-week session devoted to hitting only. You can attend one or more sessions.
Where: Chandler, OK, halfway between Oklahoma City and Tulsa.
Cost: Rates range from $225 for one week and $395 for two weeks up to $455; they are set according to demand, and start lower in June and peak in August.

Facilities: Summer camp setting on sixty-four wooded acres, housing in redwood cabins, cafeteria-style food. Five lighted fields, pitching machines (including curveball machines), batting nets, radar gun, and video instruction.

Tom Belcher is a former All-American pitcher from the University of Texas who pitched in the Mets organization in the early sixties (the camp was founded by his father, a local newspaperman and publicist, in 1958). The camp's coaching staff varies from eight to ten, depending on the number of campers attending a particular session. But Belcher is the guru: all coaching is done according to his blue book of prescribed practice techniques.

A typical day begins at 8 A.M. and ends at 10:30 P.M. and includes morning and afternoon practice and instruction sessions, and games at night. Campers are divided into Pee Wee (8–10 years olds), Midget (11–12 years old), Prep (13–14 years old) and Senior (15–18 years old), and work out on fields whose dimensions suit their own. The atmosphere is rustic, quiet, and dedicated to baseball, but Belcher adds that more important than the baseball instruction, "My major concern is to assure that our program is developing, through baseball, a more determined and confident boy."

BUCKY DENT'S BASEBALL SCHOOL
490 Dotterel Road
Delray Beach, FL 33444
(407) 265-0280
Ages: 8–23.
When: Open mid-December through April, and mid-June through August. Students can pick one week or more
Where: International Sports Village in Delray Beach, 30 minutes north of Fort Lauderdale.
Cost: Live-in student, one week is $425, two weeks $825, each additional week $385. Day student, one week is $200 in winter and spring, $140 in summer; two weeks $385 and $270; each additional week $150 and $100.

Facilities: Training site is Miller Field Complex: six fields, two batting cages, bullpen area. Housing complex is 15 three-bedroom, two-bath condo units. Also rec/dining room, two lighted batting cages. Added attraction is Little Fenway, a new field with a 37-foot replica of the Green Monster, built to commemorate Dent's 1978 playoff home run.

The only school with condominium housing, and the most celebrity-oriented of the bunch. Dent, of course, is the manager of the New York Yankees and the 1978 World Series MVP, but his involvement is limited once the season begins. President Larry Hoskin, a former Yankees scout, has been running baseball schools since 1974. The staff consists of former and current professional baseball people, like former Yankee pitcher Gil Patterson. (Instructor/camper ratio is 1/12.) Guest lecturers have included Don Mattingly, Andre Dawson, Tommy John, Ron Guidry, Don Baylor, and Ted Williams. Weeks that feature active big leaguers can be sellouts, so apply well in advance.

Major league scouts come by to check out prospects, but usually, if a kid shows talent, the school will suggest colleges where he'll be able to play. Hoskin reports he has helped over 200 boys get college scholarships and professional contracts.

DOYLE BASEBALL SCHOOL
PO Box 9156, Dept. SN
Winter Haven, FL 33883
1-800-443-5536 outside Florida
813-293-8994 in Florida and Canada
   Contact: Jim Zerilla, scouting director.
   Ages: All ages.
   When: Eighteen weeks a year in Florida: two weeks over Christmas, February 1 through mid-April, one week in June, two in July, two in August. Also two- to five-day satellite schools in spring and summer around the U.S. and Canada.
   Cost: $520 per week, including Doyle College Evaluation System (see below); otherwise, $420. Room, tuition, and meals included.

Facility: Orlando Sports Complex, adjacent to Twins spring training site. Four fields, two with lights. Hotel housing.

The Doyles are an intense baseball family. Denny (Phillies, Angels, Red Sox) and Brian (Yankees, Oakland) Doyle are former big leaguers. Everyone else teaching here has either played professionally at some level or coached in college or scouted (the instructor/student ratio is 1/25). The school is in its eleventh year of operation. It started full-time after Denny was released by the Red Sox in December 1978.

The evaluation system? Players are evaluated and graded as they would be by a scout. Kids under fifteen are instructed on skills to work on when they return home; players over fifteen have their reports mailed to over three hundred colleges. "We've been very successful with our evaluations," says Zerilla. "Colleges tell us they're very honest and accurate."

FLORIDA PROFESSIONAL BASEBALL
SCHOOL/BIG LEAGUE BASEBALL CAMP
PO Box 461
Snapper Creek, FL 33116
(305) 382-2205 or (718) 946-9827
   Ages: 8–21.
   When: Christmas week through the end of April, and summer sessions, mid-June through August; one or more weeks.
   Where: Ft. Pierce, Florida (winter), Montclair State College, Montclair, New Jersey (summer).
   Cost: $395 per week, including motel or dormitory accommodations and meals. $295 for each additional week.
   Facilities: In Florida, four major league–quality fields leased from St. Lucie County; motel accommodations. In New Jersey, three regulation fields, two with lights, one utility field; dormitory accommodations. Meals included. The Florida school is for guys who want to make their high school or college teams or better their skills to get into pro ball. The New Jersey camp draws younger kids: Little League and Babe Ruth League age, with a few high school players.

Owner Lou Haneles is a former minor league owner and manager and one-time coach at City College in New York. Chief instructor Vince Pica is a former big league scout with the Reds and Expos. The school, in some form, dates back to 1947, and has seen some fifteen grads go on to the majors.

"We're the oldest baseball school in the world," says Lou. "Seven or eight of the current schools were started by guys who used to work with us."

THE JIM RICE PRO-BASEBALL
SCHOOLS
PO Box 66479
Dept. SN
St. Petersburg, FL 33706
(800) 552-HITS
   Contact: Pat Jano, director.
   Ages: 8–24.
   When: One or more weeks, year round except May and September.
   Where: On the beach in St. Petersburg, Florida.
   Cost: $385 per week.
   Facilities: All major league spring training facilities—use Al Lang Field, Busch Complex, Huggins Field, Payson Field. Personalized videotaping is available for an extra $75. Students room at efficiency apartments on the beach; menu includes fresh seafood.

Jano, a former professional player with the Braves and Cardinals, used to own the Doyle camp, was bought out there, and went into business here with the Red Sox' Rice, whose involvement is limited to some guest instruction and the use of his name. Still, over twenty-five current or former players are affiliated with the school, including Ron LeFlore, Tito Landrum, Wade Boggs, Wayne Garrett, Joe Sambito, and Steve Renko. Scouts are also invited to observe students that Jano feels have big league potential.

Students are classified according to age and ability; there is one instructor per every 8–10 kids. The baseball day starts at 9 and goes to 4 P.M., with instructions in the morning and games in the afternoon, leaving some time for swimming, water-skiing, etc. Evening activities include talks with major league players, baseball films, and reviewing videos of the day's work (and visits to Cardinal night games at Al Lang Field during spring training).

MICKEY OWEN BASEBALL SCHOOL
PO Box 88
Miller, MO 65707
(417) 882-2799 (off-season)
(417) 452-3111 (May–August)
Ken Rizzo, administrator
Ages: 8–19.
When: May through August, six one-week or two-week sessions for 11–19-year-olds; one-week sessions only for 8–10-year-olds. Also a one-week intensive special session for 11–19-year-olds at the end of August.
Where: On eighty acres of Ozark countryside, twenty-five miles west of Springfield, Missouri, and forty-six miles west of Joplin.
Cost: 8–10-year-olds, $395; 11–19-year-olds (two weeks) $565; special session: $450. Early bird discounts available, including free airfare from Newark.
Facilities: Six professionally groomed fields, four of them lighted; four lighted batting cages, seven pitching machines, color videotaping with instant replay and slow motion. Students bunk in oak cabins by age group with a counselor on hand. Students also eat by age group, home-cooked meals, served cafeteria style.

Mickey Owen, the former big league catcher, started the school in 1959. It is now run by Joe Fowler, the school director, a Missouri high school baseball coach, and adminstrator Ken Rizzo, a former All-Big Ten catcher at Wisconsin who has been associated with the school since 1960. Students are grouped by age: 8–10, 11–12, 13–14, 15–19 (also 15–16 and 17–19 when enrollment permits). Instruction and drills all day, games and batting cages at night. Students will play 15–20 games in two weeks. No celebrities, just a lot of

hard work on fundamentals. "Our focus of instruction is always on nurturing skill development and on understanding the game, and not on determining the best players or on instilling the drive to win."

PHIL WILSON'S SHO-ME BASEBALL CAMP
Star Route 4, Box 198-A
Reeds Spring, MO 65737
(417) 338-2603
Ages: 13–23.
When: In summer, six two-week sessions from Memorial Day to about August 20. Also one week over Christmas vacation.
Where: Branson resort area near Reeds Spring, thirty-five miles south of Springfield (summer). Dodgertown, Vero Beach, Florida (Christmas).
Cost: $325 for one week; $595 for two weeks. Covers room and board and all instruction.
Facilities: Basic summer camp setup, with dormitory housing, recreation room, swimming pool, dining room, kitchen, four baseball diamonds, batting cages.

Phil Wilson coached in the Big Eight conference for ten years as an assistant and head coach at Kansas State. The camp is thirty years old, and he's been there since 1958. His emphasis is on teaching kids who want to use baseball as a way to earn a college scholarship. The staff is mostly college coaches with a couple of longtime high school coaches.

For distractions, Table Rock Lake, home to a summer series of country-and-western concerts, is nearby, as is Silver Dollar City, an 1880s theme park.

"PLAY BALL" BASEBALL ACADEMY
PO Box 48558
Ft. Lauderdale, FL 33338
(305) 776-6217
Contact: Fred Ferreira.
Ages: 8–23.
When/Where: One week or more. Fort Lauderdale, mid-December through Labor Day; Buzzards Bay, Massachusetts (Cape

Cod), July through August.
Cost: Full-time, $385 (one week) to $1,385 (four weeks); commuter students, $175 (one week) to $625 (four weeks).
Facilities: In Florida, Plantation Central Park, an eight-diamond baseball complex. On Cape Cod, the Massachusetts Maritime Academy. Personal evaluations on videotape (thirty minutes) available for $75. Dormitory-style accommodations. Batting cages, weight room. Camp president Fred Ferreira is a former Yankees scout; camp director Randy Kierce is a Montreal Expos scout. Regular instruction is provided by local high school and college coaches. There are some celebrities here; guest instructors include Ozzie Guillen, Tony Fernandez, Andre Dawson, and Mike Pagliarulo. Campers play in their own age group (8–12, 13–15, and 16–23), and all receive evaluation reports. Ferreira, well respected in the scouting world, will respond to talent when he sees it: he'll make college scholarship recommendations or call in pro scouts for a look. After-school activities in Florida include a dip in the Olympic swimming pool; in Massachusetts there are trips to Fenway Park.

LITTLE LEAGUE SUMMER CAMP
PO Box 3485
Williamsport, PA 17701
(717) 326-1924
Age: 9–15.
When: Two-week programs, July through August.
Cost: $350.
Where: Camps in Pennsylvania, Texas, Florida, and California.
Facilities: There are 10–12 boys in a cabin and 2 counselors, a sleep-away camp setup with "tasty meals, prepared with modern food service equipment" . . . so you know we're talking cafeteria-style food. For baseball facilities, see below.
A typical day: up at 7 A.M. for breakfast, then down to the field to work on your position all morning. Free time and lunch, then a game in the afternoon. Late afternoon brings more free time for swimming

or work in the batting cages. Dinner, movies, showers, and lights out at 10 P.M. Whew!

You don't have to be a member of a Little League team to attend. There are no guest instructors, no big names here. The staff consists of college students who are majoring in phys ed or play on college baseball teams. Each camp is a little different:

- The camp at Hillsgrove, Pennsylvania, called Green Acres, is in its twentieth year and is limited to boys 10–12 who need extra guidance in fundamentals. Enrollment is limited to 112 boys per session. It's in a country setting: fish-filled streams, deer, hiking, outdoor-type activities. Four two-week sessions.

- The Williamsport, Pennsylvania, camp, around for twenty-eight years, is at the site of the Little League headquarters and World Series in north central Pennsylvania, surrounded by the Bald Eagle Mountains. The forty-five-acre complex includes Little League Senior League fields, swimming pool, etc. Plus games are played daily at the World Series Stadium. Three two-week sessions.

- The San Bernardino, California, camp is at Little League Western Regional headquarters. Campers are teamed in age groups 10–12 and 13–15. Games are played at lighted Al Houghton Stadium, plus a new regulation-sized field for campers 13–15. Two two-week sessions.

- The St. Petersburg, Florida, camp is open to boys in age groups 9–12 and 13–15. The camp uses Al Lang Memorial Stadium facilities, including fully equipped dressing rooms. Three two-week sessions.

- In Waco, Texas, the Mickey Sullivan Little League Summer Camp for boys 9–15 is held on the campus of Baylor University, where Sullivan is head baseball coach. He supervises the instruction and checks everyone out. An individu-

ized report on each camper is sent to parents following each camp session. Three one-week sessions, $250 per week.

For campers in need of financial help, each year Little League Baseball offers the Robert H. Stirrat Summer Camp Scholarship, which pays round-trip transportation and tuition costs. It's open to all boys of camp age (10–15). To apply, they should write an essay of one hundred words or less about their impressions of and suggestions for Little League Baseball and submit them to Stirrat Summer Camp Scholarship at the Little League Baseball address above.

JACK AKER BASEBALL
PO Box 1222
Port Washington, NY 11050
(516) 883-5628
   Ages: 6 to college.
   Cost: $395.
   When: One week at the end of August.
   Where: Racquet Lake Camp in New

George Steinbrenner thinks some of his Yankees ought to consider signing up.

York's Adirondack Mountains, sixty miles west of Lake George and sixty miles north of Utica.

Facilities: Racquet Lake Camp is a sleep-away camp established in 1916. Baseball facilities include three diamonds (one lighted), lighted batting cages, and additional practice areas. The usual sleep-away camp facilities: waterfront with boats and swimming, videotaping equipment, lighted tennis and basketball courts, indoor recreational facilities.

An intensive one-week instructional program, directly supervised by Aker, the former major league pitcher, who is involved in all of the instruction himself. Limited to 100 campers. Aker, who set up minor league spring training programs for Cleveland, will conduct camp as an exact replica of spring training, except that games will begin on the first day. Each day, ten hours long, will include general demonstrations of techniques and discus-

Instruction in the tools of ignorance.

sions of strategy, small group instruction position by position, batting and fielding practice—and at least one ball game. Aker's selling point is that his is the only camp where a former major leaguer actually does the day-to-day teaching, "not college players or high school coaches or occasional big league guest instructors." Aker won't be doing it all alone, though; the counselor/camper ratio is 1/10. (Aker also does private instruction; see below.)

SAN DIEGO SCHOOL OF BASEBALL
4688 Alvarado Canyon Road
Suite Q
San Diego, CA 92120
(619) 583-7372

Contact: Jim Garrett.

Ages: 5 to college age.

When: Private lessons year round; four-day Christmas camps, December 20–23, 27–30; summer camps, July–August. Wide variety of specialized programs (see below).

Where: Various locations around San

Diego County.

Cost: Varies according to program.

Facilities: Batting cages on-site for individual instruction. Camps held at various college campuses and other facilities around county. Most are day camps; live-in option means hotel accommodations with burgers/chicken-type fare.

The school was started in 1970 by, among others, former big leaguers Roger Craig and Bob Skinner; current owners include Tony Gwynn and Alan Trammell. A variety of programs are offered:

- Pee-wee program for 5–7-year-olds focuses on teaching basic, beginning skills, like how to throw and catch.
- Christmas camp features Gwynn-Trammell Hitting School, conducted at Del Mar Fairgrounds' Exhibition Hall, with fourteen batting cages going at once. Guest instructors have included Willie Stargell, George Brett, Mike Scott, and Robin Yount ($199 for day students, $319 for live-in).
- Father/son camp is a four-day/three-night event with hotel accommodations and tickets to a Padres game; both learn fundamentals together ($568 for the pair).
- Pro and college evaluation camps, also with live-in accommodations, are four full days with both instruction and scouts on hand to observe. (Four-day/three-night, live-in accommodations are $339; five full-day program, $199; four half-day program, $99).
- Specialty camps: hitters and pitchers, infielders and outfielders, all-offense (hitting, baserunning).

Private Tutoring

ROD CAREW'S BASEBALL SCHOOL
1961 Miraloma
Suite D
Placentia, CA 92670
(714) 524-9600

Contact: Marilyn Carew.

Ages: 9 to Major League.

Cost: $40 per half hour, semiprivate;

$80 per hour, private. Five-lesson minimum.

Facilities: The school is set up in 7,500 square feet of warehouse space in an industrial park in Placentia, near Anaheim. The dirt is real dirt, the same as the stadiums. The pitching mounds have the same slope as big league mounds. The lighting is Mercury lighting, so that kids see all of the ball. There are eight batting cages, open only to students. All lessons are videotaped; students get homework. And there is a separate area for parents to sit, to keep them out of trouble.

Seven-time American League batting champion Rod Carew does all the hitting instruction, with the help of instructors who teach fast-pitch softball for girls, and two who teach baseball pitching. Cages and mounds are set up so that students will hit and pitch from the distance appropriate to their level of play. Says Rod's wife Marilyn, who oversees the business end of things, "Rod wanted a school for the serious student who wanted to learn, not a recreation center. For $200 you can get instruction with Rod Carew. If your kid wanted to play piano, where would you send him so that he could become a concert pianist?" Recent major league clients have included Gerald Young, although the pros usually like to keep their visits quiet.

JACK AKER BASEBALL
PO Box 1222
Port Washington, NY 11050
(516) 883-5628

Ages: 6 through college.

Cost: $90 per hour for individual instruction; group lessons and clinics also available.

Facilities: In winter, indoor at closest batting ranges around Long Island; in summer, he will make house calls and conduct lesson at nearest playground or high school field.

You may remember Aker as a relief pitcher with the A's, the Seattle Pilots, the Yankees, the Cubs, and the Mets in the

1960s and '70s, and as a minor league manager in the Mets and Cleveland organizations and the Indians pitching coach in 1986 and '87. He's the man who sent Ron Darling, Jody Davis, Jeff Reardon, Cory Snyder, and dozens of others to the big leagues. He's been giving private lessons in every aspect of the game in the Greater New York area since late 1988. Besides individual instruction, Aker will also give group lessons with, for example, an entire team or just the pitching staff. He will also give clinics for 20–30 people and coaching clinics for Little League coaches. (Aker also runs a summer camp; see above.) —NC

Critic's Choice

Any college baseball coach worth his chaw will have his own on-campus summer baseball camp. It's just too good a money-making opportunity for a coach or college to pass up. If you're planning to stay local and make use of one of these camps, here are a few things to remember. First, be sure that instruction and drilling are emphasized. Of course there should be plenty of practice games, but they should be secondary to the teaching process. Also, make sure that the camp divides the kids according to age group, as finely as possible, so that a 15-year-old doesn't have to stand around while a 10-year-old learns to throw strikes, and that the 10-year-old isn't intimidated by having to work with the older kids.

If you have the money and inclination to go anywhere for the best instruction, college coaches and pro scouts recommend the Doyle and San Diego schools most highly for intensive short-term instruction. For more summer camp–like settings, Phil Wilson's camp and the Little League camps (for younger kids) receive high marks. —NC

Summer College Leagues

A halfway house for college ball players between summer camp and professional ball, the summer leagues allow a full schedule of competition against top college talent, supervised by local college coaches and played under the watchful eye of professional scouts. Participation is by invitation and/or recommendation of your college coach. From the fan's point of view, the games are top drawer. Contact the individual leagues for schedule information. We list the leagues in our order of preference.

CAPE COD LEAGUE
PO Box 2200
Orleans, MA 02653
(508) 896-6653
President: David Mulholland.
    Clubs in Bourne, Brewster, Chatham, Cotuit, Falmouth, Harwich, Hyannis, Orleans, Wareham, and Yarmouth.

GREAT LAKES LEAGUE
PO Box 1121
Bowling Green, OH 43402
(419) 354-5556
Commissioner: Lou Laslo.
President: Ron Miller.
    Clubs in Bowling Green, Cincinnati, Columbus, Lima, Muncie, Toledo.

SHENANDOAH VALLEY LEAGUE
PO Box 2246
Staunton, VA 24401
(703) 885-8901, 886-1748
Commissioner: David Biery.
    Clubs in Front Royal, Harrisonburg, Madison, New Market, Staunton, Waynesboro, Winchester.

JAYHAWK LEAGUE
5 Adams Place
Halstead, KS 67056
(316) 835-2589, 283-4591
Commissioner: Bob Considine.
    Clubs in Amarillo (Texas); Clarinda and Red Oak (Iowa); Hays, Hutchinson, Liberal, and Wichita (Kansas); and Nevada (Missouri).

ATLANTIC COLLEGIATE LEAGUE
130 Colony Avenue
Park Ridge, NJ 07656
(201) 391-9376
President: Jerry Valonis.
    Clubs in New Jersey, New York City, Pennsylvania, Brooklyn, and on Long Island.

CENTRAL ILLINOIS COLLEGIATE LEAGUE
603 Normal Avenue
Normal, IL 61761
(309) 557-6318
Commissioner: Mike Woods.
Director: Tom Lamonica.
    Clubs in Danville, Decatur, Fairview Heights, Lincoln, Jacksonville, Springfield, Twin City.

NORTHEASTERN COLLEGIATE LEAGUE
905 Ontario Street
Schenectady, NY 12306
(518) 372-5296
Commissioner: Hank Caputo.
Director: Jim Burke.
    All clubs in Upstate New York: Auburn, Broome, Cohocton, Cortland, Rome, Schenectady, Syracuse.

SAN DIEGO COLLEGIATE LEAGUE
948 Jasmine Court
Carlsbad, CA 92008
Commissioner: Jerry Clements.
    Eight clubs in the San Diego area.
—NC

Team Camps

The big league teams listed below still conduct one or two tryout camps during the year. Some are one-day affairs, others two-day (the second only for callbacks). In addition, scouts will often conduct regional camps in their part of the country. The format of the camps is similar to the one described on the facing page.

Many clubs hold a tryout camp during spring training. Players should be realistic if they are going to invest the money for a trip to Florida or Arizona. One plus is that teams usually stagger their tryout camp days so you can schedule a number of tryouts with a number of teams over a week or so. Camps are open to anyone except where indicated. (Addresses and phone numbers can be found in Chapter 13.)

ATLANTA BRAVES
When: Starting in mid-June for two to three weeks.
Where: In Atlanta, regionally around the country.
Contact: Braves scouting director Paul Snyder at end of May for schedule.

BALTIMORE ORIOLES
When: Summer.
Where: Regional camps held by scouts around the country.
Contact: Doug Melvin, special assistant to the president and general manager, for dates and locations.

CHICAGO CUBS
When/Where: Regional camps only, conducted by local scouts.
Contact: Scouting office in Chicago.

CHICAGO WHITE SOX
When/Where: In Sarasota, Florida, just before opening of spring training; also scouts around country conduct regional tryouts which they advertise locally.

Contact: White Sox scouting department late January for schedule.

CINCINNATI REDS
When/Where: One camp in late January at spring training complex in Plant City, Florida. Others are regionals around the country during the summer.
Contact: Wilma Mann in scouting department.

DETROIT TIGERS
Who: Players 16–23.
When/Where: Ten camps in June and July, mostly in Detroit with a couple "outstate" (Traverse City). Produces more "follows" than signings.
Contact: Tigers scouting office in mid-May for schedule.

HOUSTON ASTROS
Who/When/Where: Two camps a year. One in Kissimmee, Florida, during spring training, open to any player who has completed eligibility, whether high school, junior college, or college. One in Houston in June (pre-draft), open to everyone except American Legion players or players drafted by another team the previous year.
Contact: Dan O'Brien, scouting director.

MILWAUKEE BREWERS
When: Summer.
Where: One camp in Milwaukee and one in each minor league city: Denver, El Paso, Stockton (California), Beloit (Wisconsin), and Helena (Montana).
Contact: Dick Foster in scouting department; dates announced late April.

MINNESOTA TWINS
Who: High school graduates under 24.
When/Where: Two two-day camps (with callbacks only on second day). Both in

June: one at Metrodome, the other at the spring training complex at Orlando.
Contact: Terry Ryan, scouting director.

MONTREAL EXPOS
Who: By invitation.
When/Where: One during spring training at minor league complex at West Palm Beach; one at Olympic Stadium during summer. Others are held by regional scouts throughout the country.
Contact: Don't call; they'll call you.

PHILADELPHIA PHILLIES
Who: Open.
When/Where: A dozen camps from mid-June to mid-August, in Delaware, Maryland, Pennyslvania, and New Jersey.
Contact: Minor league office (by mail) for sites and dates.

PITTSBURGH PIRATES
Who: By invitation (but you can get an invitation by calling up and asking for one).
When/Where: One week before spring training camp opens in Bradenton, Florida; also a pre-draft camp in June. Scouting supervisors also conduct regional camps across the country, as well as in Puerto Rico and the Dominican Republic.
Contact: Pirates minor league office for name of local scouting supervisor, or watch for announcement in local paper.

SEATTLE MARINERS
When/Where: Around the country during the summer by regional scouts, who will often advertise in local newspapers.
Contact: Scouting office in Seattle.

ST. LOUIS CARDINALS
When/Where: One tryout in St. Petersburg, just prior to the opening of minor league spring training camp. The other in St. Louis around mid-June.
Contact: Minor league office.   —NC

Big League Tryout Camps

The days of the old bird-dog scout beating the bushes and uncovering an unknown 18-year-old phenom who stands 6'6" and throws 95 m.p.h. are over. Nowadays, by the time that kid's hit high school, he's been entered into the computer system and is being monitored and measured against other kids his age and size by every big league organization and major college program in the country.

But there's hope: some still get away. If you feel you are undiscovered big league material, and you're old enough to sign a contract but still young enough to be worth the development expenses (25 is about the cutoff, but there are always exceptions), major league baseball wants you—at least for a look.

The Major League Scouting Bureau runs tryout camps around the country for all of professional baseball, but several clubs run their own camps as well. It's mostly for public relations for the club, but once in a while they'll sign someone. All you need is a glove and shoes; they'll take care of the rest.   —NC

The Major League Scouting Bureau conducts 55 tryout camps each year that are open to players ages 16–25. Each year 4,000 players are showcased, anywhere from 100 to 300 in each camp. The camps have been around for the last fifteen years.

All twenty-six major league teams subscribe to MLSB; some send their own scouts to cover these camps. MLSB will send reports to all teams on players it feels have major league potential.

Here, according to MLSB director Don Pries, is how it works.

DRILLS: All players are timed in the 60-yard dash. Arm strength is evaluated by throws from the outfield and infield posi-

tions. There is infield practice and usually a game that follows. Pitchers throw in the bullpen and are graded on a radar gun. For a pitcher to make it out of the pen and into the showcase game, he must throw at least 83-84 mph.

What They're Looking For From . . .

- *Catchers:* Arm strength, agility and quickness, ability to receive, aggressiveness plus leadership.
- *Infielders:* Arm strength, agility, quickness, speed, soft hands, instinct, and hitting ability (especially from the corners, says Pries).
- *Outfielders:* Arm strength, speed, instinct, aggressiveness, hitting ability.
- *Hitters:* Strength, bat speed, plane of swing, absence of fear, aggressiveness, top-hand extension, and follow-through.
- *Pitchers:* Arm strength, velocity, movement, and a curveball with tight rotation; free arm action and proper delivery, with complete extension on follow-through (basically a live, quick arm, aggressiveness, and the ability to concentrate).

Scouts miss prospects because the radar gun didn't register high enough, but the adage is, "you can't teach speed." The five fastest (semi-official) clockings are:
Bob Feller, Indians, 107.9 MPH, 1946
Nolan Ryan, Angels, 100.8 MPH, 1974
J. R. Richard, Astros, 100.0 MPH, 1978
Walter Johnson, Nats, 99.7 MPH, 1914
Jim Maloney, Reds, 99.5 MPH, 1965

As a result of these tryouts, Pries says, major league teams will sign a total of twelve to twenty-one players each year. A "follow" tag will be put on another hundred players, whose progress will be monitored as they return to high school or college. Pries says that about eight players discovered in the fifteen-year history of MLSB have gone to spend some time in the big leagues.

The camps are held in June and July, and are spread around the country: large cities and small towns, territories MLSB has previously found to be the most fertile. A schedule of the tryout camps is ready around mid-May. If you're interested in giving it a shot, write to Don Pries at the Major League Scouting Bureau, PO Box 10129, Newport Beach, CA 92660. —NC

An All-American Dream

You can only chase a dream so long," Hal Hempen says. "If you don't get it, you don't get it, and you have to go on to other things."

Hempen's dream is to play major league baseball, but he is starting to wonder if it's getting close to the time to move on to the other things. He's twenty-one now; next month he'll be twenty-two. After that comes twenty-three, then twenty-four.

So Hempen has come to Busch Stadium in St. Louis for the Cardinals' annual open tryout camp. It's two days in June when anyone with a glove and the dream can show up to prove himself to a handful of major league scouts. If you have it—IT— there's a contract for Johnson City, one of the Cardinals' rookie league teams. If you don't, you go home.

Hal Hempen grew up in Carlyle, a small town among the farms and coal fields of southern Illinois. He looks like a boy from the farm: reddish, angular face, broad jaw, a thick fullback's neck. He was always a big kid—six feet tall before he got to high school; six-three, 220 pounds now. Like all big kids, he became a pitcher, a right-hander who blew away the hitters. This spring, as a senior relief pitcher at Southeast Missouri State University, he struck out 61 in 45 innings on his way to a school-record eight saves. The Cardinals invited him to their predraft camp this year, but they didn't pick him.

So this is it. He's given up the chance to work at construction this summer—good money—to attend tryout camps. It might not be his last shot, but how many more will there be?

Can it get any hotter? It's in the eighties by nine on the first morning. By noon it will be 90. Waves of heat rise from the turf.

Tom McCormack, the Cardinals' supervisor of scouting for the Midwest, stands along the first base line, watching over 140 players, making notes on his clipboard.

You have to wonder about a lot of the guys out here. Many are out of shape; some seem afraid of the ball. Some are regulars here, guys who come out every year, thinking that something has happened since last June—some talent finally awakened.

In the first round of the tryouts a player's chance for glory comes down to a few seconds. For a fielder it's his time in the sixty-yard dash and three throws to grade his arm. One race, three throws, and you make the cut, or you don't and you go home without even getting a chance to bat.

For pitchers, it's a simple question of velocity. Each throws in the bullpen against a radar gun. To make the cut a pitcher has to top 80. Few throw that hard; some barely make 60 miles an hour.

But Hempen's pitches hit the catcher's glove with a sharp smack, the unmistakable sound of a ball thrown with authority and velocity. "How fast is he?" someone asks. The gun reads 86, 82, 87, 86; a litany of competence in the midst of rampant inability.

After the first round, more than half of the players have been cut. For those who make it, there is a short game this afternoon and then a second cut. The survivors will be back tomorrow for another game.

Hempen pitches to two batters in the afternoon game. The first goes to no balls, two strikes before grounding out. The second batter strikes out.

Hempen is not satisfied. "I should have struck out the first hitter," he says, shaking his head, fidgeting, fastening and unfastening the same snap on his warm-up jacket, "But I let up on a fastball with two strikes on him."

But McCormack is impressed. "He has good arm strength," he says. "I like his velocity. His mechanics worry me a little

bit. He throws across his body too much. Tomorrow, we'll get a better look at him."

The second day is mercifully overcast. McCormack is only interested in looking at four players, including Hempen. Shortly before the game starts, Lee Thomas, then the Cardinals' director of player development (now with the Phillies), comes down to the field to watch him. Hempen doesn't know who he is but knows he is someone to impress because he wears a tie and jacket.

This is it. Hempen sprints to the mound. He strikes out the first batter, throwing fastballs. The second hitter flies out to shallow right field. Hempen looks strong. The third batter singles to center. Ignoring the runner on first, Hempen strikes out the last man and sprints off the mound.

For the second inning, Thomas asks Hempen to throw his slider and split-fingered fastball. He does not look as sharp. He goes to two balls, two strikes on the first batter before getting him to pop to second, then goes to 3 and 0 on the second batter.

"Blow it in, son, smoke it," yells his father, who has taken the day off from his job as a crane operator.

Hempen gets the last two batters out on ground balls and he sprints off the mound.

That's it. He's finished throwing. In the dugout he worries about two pitches that got away from the catcher and rolled to the screen. They broke more than he expected, he says. But all he can do now is sit and watch the other players. "I just have to wait and see if they talk to me," he says.

The Cardinals signed Hempen that afternoon. He was the only one who was offered a contract. He reported to Johnson City on June 12.　　　　—JMS

(Editor's note: Hal Hempen's dream ended a year later on May 23, 1988, when he was released from Hamilton, the Cardinals' Short-A team in the New York–Penn League.)

Umpire Schools

Hard work, intensive study and drilling, and a high rate of failure—all for a shot at a job that starts at less than $2000 a month and will land you in the backwoods of professional baseball. You gotta love it.

The Brinkman School and the Wendelstedt School are literally the only places to go if you're serious about becoming a big league umpire. They feed their top students directly into the minor league job pipeline (see sidebar). Another school, the New York School of Umpiring, which had operated in the summer months, was at best in some state of suspended animation

as of this writing. Of the 195 umpires working minor league baseball in 1988, 103 came from Brinkman and 90 from Wendelstedt.

These are teaching facilities and as such have no special requirements to attend. Minor league baseball, however, does require a high school diploma, good eyesight with or without corrective lenses, and that you be a reasonable weight for your height and frame (you know who you are).

Have no illusions. Only the top twenty or so graduates from each school get job referrals.

JOE BRINKMAN UMPIRE SCHOOLS
1021 Indian River Drive
Cocoa, FL 32922
(407) 639-1515
Contact: Karen Brinkman.
When: The Brinkman School is a five-week program that begins shortly after January 1 and runs to the first week in February.
Cost: $1,775, includes lodging, three meals a day, and instructional materials.
Where: Cocoa Expo, former spring training home of the Houston Astros, a full baseball facility.

Who teaches an ump to say "Stee-rike"?

The school has been in existence since 1969; the Brinkmans came in at the end of 1981. There are 13 instructors, all of whom are working umpires in professional baseball. Brinkman, of course, is a senior American League umpire. The average age of the students is 25; their number varies between 100 and 150 per session.

During the course, students spend 57 hours per week under direct supervision; they are expected to spend another 10–15 hours on their own, studying or working outside games.

Students who are not recommended for jobs are not encouraged to come back and try it again next year. "This is a very emotional experience," says Karen Brinkman, Joe's wife and chief lieutenant. "It is not like going out and buying a tire."

HARRY WENDELSTEDT SCHOOL FOR UMPIRES
88 South St. Andrews Drive
Ormand Beach, FL 32074
(904) 672-4879
   Contact: Harry Wendelstedt.
   When: A five-week program (six days per week) that begins shortly after the first of the year and runs through the first week of February.
   Where: Exposville Complex in Daytona Beach, Florida, a five-field facility.
   Cost: $1,300, includes double occupancy at the Days Inn motel. Meals are not included. Repeating students receive a $100 discount.

Wendelstedt, of course, is a National League crew chief and senior umpire. All staff members are working professional umpires, including five major league arbiters. The school was founded by Al Somers, who started the first umpire training school.

One hundred fifty classroom hours are required to graduate. Students must score 70 percent or better on exams and evaluations to qualify for consideration for pro ball.

Homework

Both schools require incoming students be well versed in the rules:

The Sporting News
Official Baseball Rulebook
P.O. Box 56
St. Louis, MO 63166

The Umpire's Handbook
By Joe Brinkman and Charlie Euchner
Viking Penguin
299 Murray Hill Parkway
East Rutherford, NJ 07073   —NC

Only the Tough Turn Pro

After a would-be big league umpire completes umpire school, his next stop on the gauntlet is the Major League Baseball Umpire Development Program, run by executive director Ed Lawrence in St. Petersburg, FL.

"We develop umpires for the major leagues," Lawrence explains. "We recruit, assign, and develop all 196 minor league umpires."

Lawrence's candidates come from the top graduates of the umpire schools—about 50 a year are chosen. Prospects then undergo a ten-day evaluation course. Of those who survive, half are placed instantly in short-A or rookie league jobs, and the remainder are placed on a reserve list, from where they are likely to be called in the first year. From there it's another long road to the big leagues.

Starting salary for first-year umpires is $1,800 per month, long-A is $1900, Double-A $2,000, Triple-A $2,400. Major league umpires start at $25,000–$30,000 and can reach well over $100,000 after twenty years. And we're not even talking about the $160 per diem allowance and flying first class.   —NC

Relief Umpire

In 1935, when ump Red Ormsby went down with heat prostration between games of a White Sox–Browns doubleheader, in stepped a Chicago benchwarmer who did so well he decided to go into it full time. In 1941 he was hired by the National League, where he stayed for 27 seasons. In 1974 he was named to the Baseball Hall of Fame. His name: Jocko Conlan.   —BC

Fantasy Camps

Eat, drink, laugh, and play ball with (pick one) Dodger, Giant, Yankee, Cardinal, Cub . . . greats. The camps are one week long, and the idea is to simulate spring training for the fan. Although it varies slightly between camps, the general routine is to have tryouts the first day to divide the players into teams that will be managed by one of the team legends. The following days see instruction in the morning followed by games between teams in the afternoon, culminating in a game between the campers and their heroes at the end of the week. Evening activities include dinners, watching team highlight films, talking more baseball, and, finally, an awards banquet. Generally, all camps will provide you with a uniform

with your name and number to keep, an autographed ball, a team photograph, and often a videotape (usually of all the campers; although some provide a personal highlight film at an extra charge). Most meals (light clubhouse lunches, often barbecue dinners) are included—but not the bar bill. You can expect to find between 60 and 120 other campers at a successful camp.

This business is divided into the Big Guys, who have contracted with several teams to run their camps and provide them with a share of the profits, and the Little Guys, who run one camp with players from their own favorite team, generally without an official business relationship with the ball club. The former pride them-

selves on state-of-the-art camps and efficiency, the latter on spontaneity and personal involvement. The Dodgers operate their own camp.

Everyone has been in business for at least a few years; and the field is neatly split up with no competitors vying for the same team's fans. Let's face it, you're going to pick a camp because you love the team.

THE ULTIMATE ADULT BASEBALL
CAMP
c/o Los Angeles Dodgers
Dodgertown
PO Box 2887
Vero Beach, FL 32961
(800) 334-PLAY outside Florida

(407) 569-4900 in Florida

Contact: Sheryl Enlow.

When: February, just before opening of spring training; and in November.

Where: Dodgertown, Vero Beach, FL.

The Dodgers run two different camps: the one in February features all Hall of Famers (Ernie Banks, Catfish Hunter, Willie Stargell, Ted Williams, Don Drysdale, Duke Snider) and costs $4,395; the other, in November, is with all Dodger greats (Snider, Drysdale, Carl Erskine, Wes Parker, Dave Lopes, etc.), and also runs $4,395. Both take place, along with lodging and recreation, on the grounds of Dodgertown, a true adult playground with all the Dodgers' baseball facilities plus tennis courts and two golf courses.

SPORTSWORLD
5764 Paradise Drive
Suite 7
Corte Madera, CA 94925
(415) 924-8725

Contact: Bonnie Legg, Executive Camp Director.

Providing camps for the San Francisco Giants, Minnesota Twins, Milwaukee Brewers, and San Diego Padres, and currently in negotiation to run camps for several additional clubs.

When: January–February, April–May.

Where: Mostly at spring training facilities of the clubs, in Florida or Arizona.

Cost: $3,400.

Each camp is handled separately out of Sportsworld offices, but they all follow the same general format described above. Sportsworld also runs corporate camps. They will put together a camp for a company's employees that will feature their favorite players and Hall of Famers with no particular team affiliation.

Sportsworld boss Max Shapiro is one of the giants in this field; he ran his first camp back in '83 and has run well over twenty since.

DREAM WEEK
Carriage House

PO Box 115
Huntingdon Valley, PA 19006
(800) 888-HERO

Contact: Ken Byck.

Camps for the Baltimore Orioles, Cincinnati Reds, Cleveland Indians, Kansas City Royals, New York Mets, Philadelphia Phillies, Pittsburgh Pirates, and more on the way.

When: Late January, early February.

Where: Spring training sites of the teams.

Cost: $3,195.

Another of the titans battling for this business, Dream Week head honcho Norman Amster prides himself in being a baseball purist: not only do you use the actual spring training site, but you use the actual team trainers, clubhouse personnel, and batting cage operators—so that besides the former big league stars there are plenty of grizzled old baseball characters running around to add atmosphere. Each camp is self-contained, but one day during the week players from one camp will take a road trip—on official minor league buses, of course—to play players at another camp, sort of a fantasy Phillies vs. the Pirates.

**RANDY HUNDLEY'S OFFICIAL
BIG LEAGUE BASEBALL CAMPS**
605 North Court, Suite 205
Palatine, IL 60067
(312) 991-9595

Camps featuring Chicago Cub players and combined camps featuring Cubs and St. Louis Cardinals players.

When: January and April (before and after spring training).

Where: At Cubs spring training complex in Mesa, AZ.

Cost: $2,995.

Hundley is the originator of the fantasy camp concept (see sidebar) and the only former big leaguer who runs his own camp. Make of that what you will. *He* believes it provides him with unique insights into how to recreate the experience of spring training for campers. The camps

tend to be smaller, with 60 campers divided into teams of nine or ten players rather than other camps' squads of twelve players. That means more time in the game, less time on the sidelines. All campers must be thirty or over. Hundley's camps are not officially connected with the Cubs or the Cardinals.

SPORTS FANTASIES, INC.
19111 West Ten Mile Road, Suite A21
Southfield, MI 48075
(313) 353-5643

Contact: Jerry Lewis.

Camps featuring Detroit Tiger players, particularly from 1968 and 1984 teams.

Where: Henley Field in Lakeland, FL; camp uses Tigers spring training home, Marchant Stadium, for the final game.

When: Early February.

Cost: $2,700.

Lewis (the apparel salesman, not the comedian) is a Tiger fan, and partner Jim Price was a former backup catcher on the 1968 Detroit team. Lewis runs it as a fan instead of as a businessman. "Fantasy Camp is not a week, it's a lifetime," he says. He has an alumni association and sends out a monthly newsletter, holds luncheons, and schedules twenty hardball games a year. Ernie Harwell does the voice over and interviews on the videotape. Two women were scheduled to attend the 1990 camp. The camp is not affiliated with the Detroit ball club.

THE SOX EXCHANGE
PO Box 145
Montpelier, VT 05602
(802) 223-6666

Contact: Stuart Savage.

Camp featuring Boston Red Sox players.

When: One week, beginning last Sunday in January.

Where: Red Sox spring training facility in Winter Haven, FL.

Cost: $3,450 (including airfare from New England, double-occupancy at Winter Haven Holiday Inn, clubhouse lunch, and most evening meals).

Savage, another fan-turned-entrepreneur, generally brings out about nineteen ex-players, two for each team of campers. Ted Williams even turns up for a couple of days; everyone else stays the entire week, including Bill Lee, Jim Lonborg, Frank Malzone, Bernie Carbo, Luis Tiant, Rico Petrocelli, and Johnny Pesky. The camp basically takes over the hotel; there's even a kangaroo court, run by Dick Radatz and Gary Bell, with fines going to support the Jimmy Fund in Boston. Savage also runs some alumni events, including special days at Fenway Park and an occasional game later in the year. Last year it was between Red Sox camp veterans and Dodger camp veterans.

THE MICKEY MANTLE/WHITEY FORD FANTASY BASEBALL CAMP
PO Box 68
Grayson, KY 41143-0068

(606) 474-6976 or (212) 382-1660

Contact: Wanda Greer.

Camp featuring former Yankees players.

When: Two one-week camps, usually the first two weeks in November,

Where: New York Yankees spring training complex in Fort Lauderdale, FL.

Cost: $3,650 (including airfare from New York, single-room hotel accommodations, two meals daily—lunch, catered to the ballfield, is tuna salad or crab meat salad, not hot dogs and hamburgers). Enrollment is limited to 72 per week and generally sells out by June, we're told. Campers are divided into six 12-man teams and play each other all week long, under the direction of the likes of Mantle, Ford, Hank Bauer, Ralph Houk, Enos Slaughter, Johnny Blanchard, Moose Skowron, and Catfish Hunter. Besides the usual loot, campers receive a Yankee uniform with the

number of their choice, a fantasy camp jacket, a personalized Louisville Slugger, and a pair of baseball shoes.

The fantasy finale on Saturday pits the former Yankee Heroes, with Whitey on the mound, vs. the Campers at Fort Lauderdale Stadium before a crowd of real people (they get in free). —NC

How It All Began

In the beginning, there was Randy Hundley, the former Cubs catcher, out of baseball after a stint of managing in the minor leagues, frustrated at having to go on his knees to the Winter Meetings in search of a job, working at a children's camp in a Chicago suburb.

"One day a fellow came to speak to the kids about the importance of education," says Hundley today. "He got there early, so I put him into a baseball game with some of the kids. He had such a great time that a week later he suggested we do a camp for adults. My partner asked if I could get some former players to come out. I said no, not if we did it locally."

A great idea was slipping away, but then the light bulb went on in Hundley's head. "I thought, if we could go to Arizona and do a spring training camp like in the big leagues, the players would come. And we'd make it just like a big league camp, so that the people who signed up would feel just like they were on a big league roster."

Charging what was then the astronomical sum of $2,295 for a week's fantasy, Hundley signed up 65 people for the idea's debut, in January 1983, and he had to turn many others away. The rest, as the man says, is history.

"I always felt that once February rolled around every male daydreamed about going to spring training and playing baseball," says Hundley. "It just seemed unfair that some guys got to go and others didn't." —NC

Postcards from Fantasy Camp

Day 1

I come straight from a business meeting to the Clearwater, Florida, site of Dream Week and the Phillies' spring training headquarters and arrive at the Quality Inn on Saturday night. It's both comforting and amusing to see the "Welcome Dreamers" sign on the motel marquee and pictures of the Phillies dominating the lobby. I also stumble across the twenty-four-hour whirlpool that will became so critical to my ability to function over the next seven days.

The charter from Philadelphia carrying most of the fifty-nine campers arrives about 2 P.M. today. We receive our room assignments and go to unpack. I'm a little nervous about meeting the complete stranger who will become my roommate for the week. I'd debated paying extra for a single room but had been persuaded "to do it the way the regular ball players do."

My roommate Ralph is a jeweler, a skilled craftsman with valuable hands.

Knowing this, it strikes me now how delightfully consistent with the spirit of the week that Ralph is going to play catcher, a position not exactly distinguished for delicate treatment of fingers.

We head over to Carpenter Field, the Phillies' training complex, to try on our uniforms. Within minutes, usually reserved adults are transformed into giggly kids. I sit in front of my locker, don the burgundy-and-white uniform, and trade hats to get the right size—as the "real" world fades and the fantasy begins.

We walk onto the field at the complex. Having played, as I recall, a brilliant short-stop years ago for Carleton College in Minnesota, I am anxious to see whether I can still make the throw to first base from deep in the hole. Now the distance seems so great that I can barely see first base, let alone heave a ball over there. I leave the field wondering if I should even try to play shortstop.

Soon after returning to the motel, folks are out in the parking lot loosening up

arms and tongues. Some returnees from last year (approximately 15 or 20 percent of last year's participants have come back) are entertaining the rookies with last year's highlights. I join the group and find I can barely throw the ball fifty feet.

At a welcoming reception tonight, the introduction of each ex–major leaguer brings back special memories. When pitchers Jim Bunning and Chris Short are recognized, my mind snaps back to 1964. Back then I had to keep my Philadelphia-bred Carleton roommate from slitting his throat as each day yielded a new horror story.

Day 2

As we do every day, Ralph and I get up early and walk over to Lenny's ("Best breakfast in Clearwater"). I wonder if the waitress ever gets tired of wearing Phillies' hats and shirts.

We have to be in uniform and ready to start training by 10. Because it's raining—the only rain we have during our week—morning instruction is held inside. We break down by position, with Ralph joining the catchers while I remain with the infielders. We focus on making the double play and our instructors are Larry Bowa, Bobby Wine, and Tony Taylor.

Bowa, still a starter for the Cubs after many years in Philadelphia, is doing Dream Week for the first time; Wine and Taylor are returning from last year. As with all the pros, they impress with their enthusiasm and energy. During their week, Bowa skips lunch to work in the batting cage with one of my colleagues; Taylor comes in early to teach the intricacies of cut-off plays; Wine is an indefatigable leader. The pros clearly make the week.

After we dine on a standard clubhouse lunch of soup and sandwiches, the weather clears. Infielders practice double plays. Probably nothing develops a sense of teamwork and camaraderie quicker than turning over a quick 6-4-3. I concentrate on trying to tag second base with the proper foot. The lesson will have application in my softball league, although advancing age has pushed me toward the first base/designated hitter role.

My first time in the batting cage is rough. I have no timing and barely make contact. Following the day's drills, the pitching machine stays on. I get forty extra swings and start to feel comfortable.

Walking into the clubhouse after working up a good sweat playing ball in sunny 70-degree weather, I feel fifteen years younger.

Day 3

Waking generates a special suspense at Dream Week. You just don't know how your body is going to function as you take that first step out of bed.

Morning drills start with baserunning instruction. After looking us over, former Phillies great Richie Ashburn, now part of Philadelphia's broadcasting team and overall Dream Week manager, stresses the key principle of Dream Week baserunning: "Don't get hurt."

Infielders then move on to fielding pop-ups. In keeping with Ashburn's concern for our physical well-being, they should have issued helmets. As I try to follow the speck of a tiny ball against the bright Florida sun on this cloudless, windy day, all I can think of is how the words "hit in the nose by rapidly descending spheroid" will look on my health insurance claim form.

Following lunch, we prepare for our first intrasquad games. After watching us work out yesterday, the coaches drafted four fifteen-person teams. Each afternoon, we play a six-inning game against another squad.

My team, coached by Tony Taylor and former Phillies coach Maje McDonnell, is matched against the Bowa/Short Cubs. Ralph is catcher for the Cubs and I start at shortstop for Tony's Tigers.

Even though the Florida Instructional League umpires are told to use a wide strike zone, having a pitcher who can throw strikes is a prized asset. Today, our starting pitchers are wild, and we fall behind 7–0. We rally furiously, only to lose, 9–8, when two baserunning blunders eliminate the tying and winning runs. Good thing we had that morning baserunning lesson.

The only Cubs pitcher to throw near the plate to me is Bernie, a gynecologist with a good curveball. Ralph accurately assumes I am expecting a fastball on a 2-1 pitch; Bernie's curve fools me and I tap weakly back to the mound.

An enjoyable and necessary ritual is lounging around the motel whirlpool, recounting highlights of the day's action. I visit it three times a day.

Day 4

Ralph and I decide to go to optional morning batting practice. The pitching machines are supervised by Homer, a patient and cheerful fellow. His advice—"You've got two more, young fella"—becomes the camp motto for me. As the days go on, my hands hurt so badly from making poor contact that these words generate feelings of relief, not disappointment. Still, it just doesn't seem big league to skip valued swings in the cage because your hands hurt. Misguided machismo, I'm sure.

Each morning at 10 the entire group gathers to review the highlights of the previous day's action, a great opportunity for spirited banter between coaches and players. A hitting award is given to Jack, the feisty sixty-two-year-old second baseman on my team, for his perfect day at the plate yesterday.

The first morning drill is on sliding. Bowa points out that my hands were on the ground as I slid, a practice that could curtail my ability to process paperwork. After lunch, our team takes pregame batting practice with a twenty- to thirty-m.p.h. wind blowing out to left field. As a right-handed hitter, I figure this is my chance to hit one out (left field is 340 feet,

dead center 410). Despite Taylor's fat pitches, the best I can do is about 335 feet. Once a warning-track hitter, always a warning-track hitter.

Our team's hitting dominates today's game. I get lucky my first time up and line one down the right field line on an 0-2 pitch. With the right fielder shaded toward center, I have no excuse but to keep going to third. Upon arrival, I look desperately for a portable oxygen mask.

Our 15–4 victory and one by Bobby Wine's team in the other game, leave all four squads tied with 1–1 records heading into tomorrow's semifinals. You can feel the tension building in the postgame whirlpool assembly.

Day 5

My lusty hitting is mentioned during the discussion of yesterday's highlights. At this point, my batting and fielding averages are both about .500.

Before morning drills, we do our daily calisthenics, led by a staff member well suited for the role of inspirational sadist. It's a scene of funny-shaped bodies contorted into ridiculous positions, with the sunny silence punctuated by moans of agony. Still, I look forward to it.

We lose the semifinal game 1–0, with the final out coming on a line shot to right with the tying run in scoring position. I do get a chance to field a ball deep in the hole at shortstop. Much to everyone's amazement, I throw the guy out.

Day 6

The disabled list is growing. Trainer John Fierro's room begins to look like Grand Central Station, and there are several guys I wouldn't recognize today if they weren't wearing an ice pack. Nothing serious, however.

We play our final game in the morning so that the pros and other staff can play in the afternoon. By this point in the week, we are short on pitchers, especially since we want to save our good pitchers for tomorrow's big game against the pros.

This situation gives me a chance to do something I've always fantasized about—pitch in organized competition. (My secretary will confirm that I dictate from the stretch position.) I go in at the start of the third inning with a 4–2 lead. Eight of my first nine pitches aren't even close to the strike zone.

Finally, I get the ball over and start having fun. It begins to feel like pitching Wiffle Ball twenty-five years ago in my backyard, trying to hit the corner of the chair that served as the strike zone. I get the "W" and a fantasy fulfilled.

After lunch, the staff and those pros arriving early for the game Saturday play a group of Dream Weekers. As a Minnesotan, it is a particular thrill for me to hit against Jim Kaat. He looks just the same as he did twenty years ago when he pitched the game that clinched the pennant for the Twins. He lays one in there and I bounce to third.

Day 7

Ralph and I head over to the training complex for the last time. Our task is to dress, clean out our lockers, and go to Jack Russell Stadium, home field for the Phillies' spring training games and site of today's action.

The format for today's benefit game is to have each of the four Dream Week squads play a four-inning game against a pro team. My team will play the third game.

There are about 1,000 people witnessing the action on a gorgeous day. Many are relatives of the campers. Chris Wheeler, one of the Phillies' announcers, does a full play-by-play of the game on tape. He also taped interviews with all fifty-nine campers during the week.

I stand behind the batting cage while the pros take hitting practice. They enjoy seeing each other again, and their chatter makes it seem like a real game.

For the first two games, the pros capitalize on wildness by Dream Week pitchers and slipshod fielding to obliterate the campers by a combined score of 24–2.

As our team warms up for our four-inning stint, we see big Art Mahaffey warming up for the pros. All during the week, we've been told that Mahaffey, a right-hander for the Phillies in the early 1960s, throws hard and doesn't like to get hit. Since each of us is likely to get only one plate appearance, I shift my fantasy from hitting a shot to avoiding a strikeout.

My chance to hit comes in the first inning. As a result of one hard-hit and one wind-blown single, there are runners on first and third with two out.

Mahaffey's first pitch is far quicker than anything I have seen all week, a strike on the outside corner. I make up my mind to swing at the next pitch regardless of location. It looks as if it's headed for the same spot as the first one, and my late flail sends the ball toward right field. Jim Bunning's playing an extremely shallow right field; the ball goes over his head. I cruise into second base to the glee of the assembled multitudes.

With excellent pitching and fielding, we hold the pros scoreless the first two innings, even producing a 6-4-3 double play. The pros then take over and we lose 5–1.

Completing the day, Ralph's team goes into the last inning trailing by only 2–1 and manages to get the tying run in scoring position with one out. Faced with the prospect of continuing this hot day in the sun, pitcher Claude Osteen responds to pressure from his pro colleagues by retiring the next two hitters with some wicked pitches not previously seen at Dream Week.

The closing banquet tonight is well attended by families and friends. Art, one of our Philadelphia lawyers, speaks for many of us when he says, "I hurt all over and I've never felt better."   —TL

Tours

A collection of selected unusual trips—for the true baseball adventurer.

JAY BUCKLEY'S MAJOR LEAGUE BASEBALL TOURS
PO Box 213
LaCrosse, WI 54602-0213
(608) 788-9600
Contact: Jay Buckley, director.

For the serious baseball fan who doesn't mind riding the bus and sleeping in motels, Buckley organizes bus tours of major league cities during July and August. Each are nine-day excursions (two weekends and the week), and last year he did six (five headed east: New York, Boston, Montreal, Cooperstown, etc.; one headed southwest for ten days: Kansas City, Houston), hitting every park east of the Rockies and reaching Cooperstown on five of the six trips, and taking in seven to nine games per trip.

The cost is about $540 (a little more for the ten-day southwest trip) and includes bus transportation (in a Greyhound-style coach, equipped with rest room and VCR to show baseball movies), tickets to all games and Halls of Fame, and motels every night (double occupancy, usually Red Roof Inns or Motel 6's). "We get in late and leave early; there's not a lot of time for lounging around the pool." Indeed, between two and eleven hours each day are spent traveling on the bus. Time is allowed, however, for sightseeing in cities like Boston, Philadelphia, New York, and Montreal. Each bus carries forty-seven people, some trips take two buses, and each trip has two hosts: Buckley, a middle school principal, and usually his son or daughter.

A typical trip from one summer—Saturday: California at Milwaukee; Sunday: Detroit at Chicago White Sox; Monday: New York Mets at Philadelphia; Tuesday: Minnesota at Baltimore; Wednesday: Cleveland at New York Yankees; Thursday: St. Louis at New York Mets; Friday: Cooperstown; Saturday: Milwaukee at Cleveland; Sunday: Philadelphia at the Chicago Cubs. Nine days, eight games, thirteen teams, eight parks. Cost: $535.

GEORGE AUERBACH'S TEEN CARAVAN
41 German Mills Road
Thornhill, Ontario
Canada L3T 4H4
(416) 731-1862
Contact: George Auerbach.

Auerbach, a Toronto junior high and high school science teacher, has been running travel/camping camps for kids for almost twenty years. Included in his program now is a twenty-one-day Baseball Caravan in August for fans thirteen to sixteen years of age. His idea is to combine baseball and the great outdoors.

Kids travel by air-conditioned, restroom-equipped bus, stay in hotels/motels, or camp out in KOA campgrounds. Best of all, they attend major league and minor league baseball games—nineteen of them last year. There is about 250 miles of travel each day. Each trip can accommodate 20–40 kids plus four adult staffers. Cost is $1,375, including all admissions, food, everything but souvenirs. Sidetrips are taken for such sights as the Arch in St. Louis and the Hillerich & Bradsby bat factory in Louisville.

The trip starts in Toronto, goes to the Midwest, and then to the East. Last summer, it went on to Chicago, Des Moines, Madison, WI (one of the highlights, says Auerbach, was to see the Muskees and get a tour of their park), Kansas City, St. Louis, Cincinnati, Baltimore, Milwaukee, New York, Boston, and Syracuse.

W. LLOYD JOHNSON
205 West 66th Street
Kansas City, MO 64113
(816) 822-1740

Johnson, a baseball historian and former executive director of the Society for

American Baseball Research (SABR), runs a February trip to the Caribbean World Series, trips to spring training in Florida (to follow the state heroes, the Cardinals and Royals), and a minor league tour. The Spring Training trip is $400 (airfare not included) for seven days, seven nights, and seven games, including hotel (Days Inn, double occupancy), game tickets, and a ballpark lunch. In addition, there are stadium tours and sidetrips to visit with baseball personalities Johnson has dug up around Florida.

The minor league trip is to New York-Penn League cities plus Cooperstown, seven games in seven ballparks via minibus. This also runs about $400, airfare not included. (The cost of the Caribbean World Series trip was unsettled at press time.) You'll get all the baseball history you can soak up. Space is limited to 20–25.

BASEBALL FOR PEACE
P.O. Box 8282
Woodland, CA 95695
(916) 661-1659
Contact: Jay Feldman.

Quiz: Who has not signed up for the tour?

Feldman, active in over-thirty baseball, has for four years run Goodwill Baseball Tours to Nicaragua, with a team of 15–20 thirtysomethings. The tour goes for about ten days and includes a visit to the Nicaragua World Series (if the trip is in April; the timing can vary) as well as a schedule of games against various *campesino* teams. Cost is about $1,300 and $200 reserves a spot (first come, first served). But there is no lying on the beach. This is baseball as a political statement. "We're saying it's better to play baseball than fight wars," says Feldman. He's been working on a similar trip to the Soviet Union.　　—NC

Spring Training/ Road Trips

Our calls around both leagues showed that each team has a favorite travel agency that handles its own needs. And calls to those travel agencies showed that any one of them would be happy to book a booster on a trip anywhere he wanted to go. But only a handful were specialists who each season put together travel packages to spring training or weekend trips to watch the team on the road in-season.

Most offer a choice of hotels for spring training (deluxe and first class), and will take care of tickets and transportation to and from the ballpark. Expect anywhere from 200–400 fellow maniacs on the spring training tours, and 50–100 on the road trips. All prices noted are double-occupancy.

EAST TOWN TRAVEL
765 North Broadway
Milwaukee, WI 53202-3673
(414) 276-3131 in Wisconsin
(800) 822-3789
Contact: Jonathan M. Harper.
East Town follows the Brewers everywhere, with seven spring training trips, five in-season trips, and a January cruise to the Caribbean. Your host is Jim Ksicinski, visiting clubhouse manager and baseball raconteur. Arizona Spring Training trips range from weekend getaways ($379–$509), week-long departures ($679–$1,099) and Easter Week specials ($689–$1,179)—all inclusive (including game admissions). In-season road trips are by air/deluxe coach, and range from $199 for a weekend hop to Minnesota to $559 for 4 days in New York and Cooperstown.

TRAVEL MERCHANTS
333 Hagenberger Road
Oakland, CA 94621
(800) 458-2448
Contact: D'Ann Ford.
Travel Merchants runs three six-night tours to spring training sites in Arizona, ranging from $450 to $600. Fully escorted tours (price includes tickets, first-class hotel accommodations, car) center in Scottsdale (Giants) and run buses to Mesa (Cubs and Brewers), Phoenix (A's) and Tempe (Mariners). In-season road trips include seven night trips to New York–Boston ($1,395, including theater tickets) and Toronto–Montreal–Cooperstown.

CRIMSON TRAVEL
2 Center Plaza
Government Center
Boston, MA 02108
(617) 742-8500
One- and two-week trips to see three or six Boston Red Sox games at Winter Haven. Prices range from $459 to $1,100, and can be upgraded to improve hotel accommodations, add a rental car, and obtain passes to Disney World. Game tickets and transportation to the ballpark included.

KOBELT TRAVEL SERVICE
1350 E. Touhy Avenue
Des Plaines, IL 60018
(312) 297-7960
Contact: Tor Saile.
Eight- and fifteen-day tours to Mesa, Arizona, to see the Cubs, include airfare, accommodations, and tickets to four and eight games, respectively. And your hosts are Jim and Jan Piersall. Prices range from $997 per person for one week to $1,879 for two. Choice of two hotels, one in Scottsdale, one in Mesa. In-season trips have included long weekends of Cubs baseball, June–September, in St. Louis, New York, San Diego, Los Angeles, Philadelphia, Montreal and Cincinnati; and week-long excursions to watch baseball in California.

CARDINAL TRAVEL INC.
217 Village Square
Hazelwood, MO 63042
(314) 895-1010 in Missouri
(800) 325-4133
Contact: Joe Hoerner.
Hoerner, the former Cardinals pitcher turned travel agent, follows the birds. A late March week in spring training includes five games at Al Lang Field, hotel accommodations in St. Petersburg (from $695 to $725), plus he can bring out the Cardinal personnel for a cocktail party. In-season booster weekend trips include San Diego, Pittsburgh/New York, two in Chicago, and two right in St. Louis. Prices range from $225 (Chicago) to $899 (New York).

BARNEY RAPP TRAVEL
505 Carew Tower
Cincinnati, OH 45202
(513) 381-7277
Contact: Herb Reisenfeld.
Rapp handles the arrangements for the Cincinnati Red Rooters Club, this year making its thirty-fifth spring training tour. The week-long trip holes up in Tampa and makes bus excursions to Plant City for Reds games, Tarpon Springs, Cypress Gardens, Busch Gardens or Epcot Center, and the Boardwalk & Baseball theme park. But the highlight is the players' banquet. Cost by air is $900; by Greyhound bus, $845; and by your own car, $670. Rapp will put together in-season tours: last year, they arranged a three-day trip by motorcoach to Cooperstown for Johnny Bench's induction into the Hall of Fame ($350 per person); and a three-day weekend bus trip to Chicago sponsored by the Rosie Reds fan club ($260 triple occupancy).

CARRIER'S TIGER SPORTS TRAVEL
PO Box 5128
Dearborn, MI 48128
(313) 562-6810
Contact: Pat Carrier.
The lion's share of Patricia Carrier Enterprises' travel business is done with the Tigers. Since 1980 she has been putting together week-long trips to see the team in Lakeland (she now does three separate weeks in March), and now has expanded that to include weekend trips in-season to every city in the American League (coincidentally, the same weekends that the Tigers are in town, and at the same hotels). Several trips have an air/drive option, so prices vary widely. As an added perk, for an additional $25 per person (minimum twenty people) Carrier will put together a cocktail party or continental breakfast with a Tiger player in any city on her schedule.   —NC

Cruises

Not the easiest way to commune with your favorite ball player (although he is a captive audience three miles out on the high seas); it's a big boat and there generally are a half dozen to a dozen players and 400 or 500 fans. Still, it's a good marketing move by the cruise lines (no, you don't have the boat to yourself) and a free ride for the players and team personnel. As for you, you generally get to pay full fare. These things tend to come and go; the teams and cruise lines are equally mercurial when it comes to making money.

NEW YORK METS
Promotion Department
Shea Stadium
126th Street and Roosevelt Avenue
Flushing, N.Y. 11368
(718) 507-6387

The Mets have regularly run a January cruise from New York City to the Caribbean and back, ten days, for $1,600–$1,900 per person. Last time they brought thirteen players, coaches, and broadcasters, who traveled with 480 fans. Planned activities include photo and autograph sessions, seminars, clinics, and a softball game in Barbados.

EAST TOWN TRAVEL
765 North Broadway
Milwaukee, WI 53202-3673
(414) 276-3131 in Wisconsin
(800) 822-3789
Contact: Jonathan M. Harper.

East Town sponsors the Milwaukee Brewer Fan Fun Cruise (with three players and manager Tom Treblehorn) in January. The price tag is $1,395–$1,495 per person for a week in the Eastern Caribbean, with chalk talks, schmoozings, meals with players, on-board Wiffle Ball, and on-island softball.

CARDINAL TRAVEL INC.
217 Village Square
Hazelwood, MO 63042

(314) 895-1010 in Missouri
(800) 325-4133
Contact: Joe Hoerner.

Hoerner brings out five or six active Cardinal ball players plus team personnel for a week-long cruise that leaves from Fort Lauderdale and sails around the Caribbean on the Holland-America Line. Prices range $1,297–$1,750 per person. Activities include photograph and autograph sessions with Cardinal players, and gift presentations of team memorabilia and parties.

DAN SCHLOSSBERG
c/o Skybox Baseball Cards
517 South Livingston Ave.
Livingston, NJ 07039
(201) 740-0060

Schlossberg, a baseball writer and memorialist, generally puts together two tours a year with former players and Hall of Famers. Trips in the past have included a cruise on the Bermuda Star Line from San Diego to the Mexican Riviera (with the romantic Clyde King, Bill White, Ralph Branca, and Jay Johnstone), and one from New Orleans to Key West, Cancún and Cozumel (with former Cubs Gary Matthews, Phil Regan, and Gene Oliver). Other trips, some on the *QE II*, have included Billy Williams, Ferguson Jenkins, Jim Kaat, Monte Irvin, Ernie Harwell, Bob Feller, Stan Musial, and Eddie Mathews. Some are four-day weekends, others week-long, generally in January and February. Prices are set by the cruise line and were unavailable at presstime.   —NC

Spring Training Sites

For the do-it-yourselfer who wants to find his own way around spring training, a bit of advice: Due to the popularity of spring training, ticket prices were expected to rise at presstime and availability of tickets on game day is doubtful, so be sure to call in advance, even to order tickets well in advance. Workout times generally are 10 A.M., game times 1–1:30 for day games; 7–

Dreams Come True

It's every fan's fantasy to be sitting in the bleachers and have the manager of the home team come over and ask him to play. The most successful fantasizer was George McBride, who, on September 12, 1901, was recruited from the stands to start at shortstop, for Milwaukee. True, McBride *was* a minor-league player whose South Dakota team had finished its season. And the Milwaukee management *did* suggest that he bring his glove to the park, just in case. What makes McBride unique was that he went on to play 1,658 *more* major league games before retiring in 1920 as one of baseball's best-fielding shortstops.

7:30 for night games. At last check, prices were running $6–$8 for box seats, $4–$6 for reserved, and $3–$4.50 for general admission. Seniors and kids under twelve will usually get a break. Schedules are generally available from some clubs as early as November, and tickets can often be ordered as early as December.

Here are the sites to see (with recommendations noted), arranged for your traveling convenience.

GOLD COAST (Southeast Florida)

ATLANTA BRAVES
Municipal Stadium
715 Hank Aaron Drive
West Palm Beach, FL 33401
Ticket Info.: (407) 683-6100

BALTIMORE ORIOLES
Miami Stadium
2301 N.W. 10th Avenue
Miami, FL 33127
Ticket Info.: (303) 635-5395
Seedy but atmospheric—former home of the Miami Marlins. Satchel Paige pitched here at the age of fifty-three.

LOS ANGELES DODGERS
Holman Stadium
4001 26th Street
Vero Beach, FL 32960
Ticket Info.: (407) 569-4900

Dodgertown merits a special note; it is like a resort for baseball people: the players live there, the brass hold meetings there; there are golf courses and tennis courts—not to mention several baseball diamonds. The complex is huge—it used to be a naval training base—and visitors can roam around to watch infield practice on one diamond, hitting practice at the batting cages, or just to watch the players moving from site to site in a very low-key, easygoing atmosphere.

MONTREAL EXPOS
Municipal Stadium
715 Hank Aaron Drive
West Palm Beach, FL 33401
Ticket Info.: (407) 689-9121

NEW YORK METS
St. Lucie County Sports Complex
525 N.W. Peacock Blvd.
Port St. Lucie, FL 34985
Ticket Info.: (407) 879-7378
A spanking new, state-of-the-art facility with one of the world's largest collections of chain-link fence. So don't expect to get too close to the players; Mets P.R. man Jay Horwitz barely lets the press have that opportunity.

NEW YORK YANKEES
Fort Lauderdale Stadium
5301 NW 12th Avenue
Ford Lauderdale, FL 33309
Ticket Info.: (305) 776-1921
As you might expect, some of the highest prices around. Expect to pay at least $10 for a reserved seat, although you can find a spot in the bleachers for a few dollars less. And you'll find the usually military-style atmosphere we've come to expect from Steinbrenner & Co. But a beautiful ballpark.

NO COAST

BOSTON RED SOX
Chain O' Lakes Park
Cypress Garden Blvd.
Winter Haven, FL 33880
Ticket Info.: (813) 293-3900
Yes, you can see Ted Williams giving hitting tips to the Red Sox, minor leaguers and major leaguers alike.

DETROIT TIGERS
Joker Marchant Stadium
Lakeland Hills Blvd.
Lakeland, FL 33801
Ticket Info.: (813) 682-1401

HOUSTON ASTROS
Osceola County Stadium
1000 Osceola Blvd.
Kissimmee, FL 32743
Ticket Info.: (407) 933-5500

KANSAS CITY ROYALS
Baseball City Stadium
I-4 and U.S. 27
Haines City, FL 33844
Ticket Info.: (800) 826-1939
(800) 525-8233 in Florida
A Felliniesque baseball experience. The ballpark is the centerpiece of Boardwalk & Baseball, the theme park that includes an amusement park, games of baseball skill, and other family-style attractions. If you have small children and your wife isn't into baseball, you might be able to escape to a game for a few hours—if you can block out the screams from the roller coaster.

MINNESOTA TWINS
Tinker Field
287 Tampa Avenue South
Orlando, FL 32855
Ticket Info.: (407) 849-6346

GULF COAST

CHICAGO WHITE SOX
Ed Smith Stadium
12th and Tuttle Streets

Sarasota, FL 34237
Ticket Info.: (813) 953-3388

CINCINNATI REDS
Plant City Stadium
1900 S. Park Road
Plant City, FL 33566
Ticket Info.: (813) 752-1878

PHILADELPHIA PHILLIES
Jack Russell Stadium
800 Phillies Drive
Clearwater, FL 34617
Ticket Info.: (813) 442-8496
No phone ticket orders.

PITTSBURGH PIRATES
McKechnie Field
17th Avenue West & 9th Street West
Bradenton, FL 33508
Ticket Info.: (813) 748-4610

ST. LOUIS CARDINALS
Al Lang Stadium
180 2nd Avenue S.E.
St. Petersburg, FL 33701
Ticket Info.: (813) 894-4773

TEXAS RANGERS
Charlotte County Stadium
2300 El Jobean Rd.
Port Charlotte, FL 33948
Ticket Info.: (813) 624-2211

TORONTO BLUE JAYS
Grant Field
311 Douglas Avenue
Dunedin, FL 33528
Mail: PO Box 957
Dunedin, FL 34697
Ticket Info.: (813) 733-9302

CACTUS LEAGUE

CALIFORNIA ANGELS
Angels Stadium
Sunrise & Barristo Roads
Palm Springs, CA 92263
Ticket Info.: (619) 268-9686,
(213) 410-1062, (714) 634-1300

Gloriously situated with a mountain for a backdrop behind home plate. The Angels spend their first month of spring training working out at Gene Autry Park, 4125 E. McKellips, Mesa, AZ 82505; (602) 830-4137. They only play road games until the middle of March, when they move to Palm Springs to play their home schedule.

CLEVELAND INDIANS
Hi Corbett Field
Randolph Park
Tucson, AZ 85726
Mail: PO Box 27577
Tucson, AZ 85726
Ticket Info.: (602) 791-4266

CHICAGO CUBS
HoHoKam Park
1235 N. Center Street
Mesa, AZ 85201
Mail: PO Box 261
Mesa, AZ 85201
Ticket Info.: (602) 964-4467

MILWAUKEE BREWERS
Compadre Stadium
1425 W. Ocotillo Road
Chandler, AZ 85248
Ticket Info.: (602) 821-2200

OAKLAND ATHLETICS
Phoenix Municipal Stadium
5999 E. Van Buren
Phoenix, AZ 85008
Ticket Info.: (800) 829-5555

SAN DIEGO PADRES
Desert Sun Stadium
Ray Kroc Baseball Complex
Avenue A at 35th Street
Yuma, AZ 85364
Mail: PO Box 230
Yuma, AZ 85364
Ticket Info.: (602) 782-2567

SAN FRANCISCO GIANTS
Scottsdale Stadium
7402 E. Osborne Rd.
Scottsdale, AZ 85251

Cactus League Pricklers

From the left-side of the country, some tips on getting around Arizona in the spring.

- Leave the rain gear home. You'll never hear raindrops on the rooftop—an occasional fact of life in Florida—that signal the cancellation of the day's game and a dreary afternoon at the laundromat or dollar movie.
- Attend camp before the exhibition games begin to collect autographs and meet the players. Cuts haven't been made, vacations have just ended, and the guys are in a relatively relaxed, friendly mood.
- Eat at Bill Johnson's Big Apple Restaurants in Phoenix, featuring old west barnyard decor, and waitresses who wear

guns. For those seeking baseball ambience, there's Harry (Caray) and Steve's (Stone) Chicago Grill in Mesa; for high rollers, the Pink Pony in Scottsdale.
- Check out college ball at Arizona State and Grand Canyon College in Phoenix, or the University of Arizona at Tucson. Most games are at night and don't conflict with the major leaguers, a busman's holiday for those who can't get enough.
- Cross the border into Nogales or Tijuana. You won't be in Kansas anymore. Don't let Toto out of sight.
- See democracy at its most lenient in Palm Springs, the late March home of the Angels, which is ruled by Mayor Sonny Bono.

—EC

Ticket Info.: (602) 230-9112
Probably the only real charmer among ballparks down here, complete with redwood stands and a hand-operated scoreboard. See it while you can—if it's not too late already.

SEATTLE MARINERS
Tempe Diablo Stadium
2200 W. Alameda
Tempe, AZ 85282
Ticket Info.: (602) 438-8900 or
(602) 829-5151

—NC

Grapefruit League Sweeteners

Spring training's popularity has become its worst enemy. Although the camps and exhibitions remain significantly more intimate than a Saturday night at Shea Stadium, increased spring attendance has robbed the event of spontaneity. With that in mind, we offer these inside tips on the art and science of spring camping in Florida from sun-ripened veterans.

- Focus on seeing teams, not ballparks. Winter Haven and Vero Beach are worth a special trip, but most other sites aren't.
- Avoid team hotels. The stars don't stay there and the rookies can't afford them. You may find the team physican, but that's about it. One exception is the Tigers' Holiday Inn headquarters in Lakeland, where Sparky Anderson spends many late afternoons knocking a golf ball around the backyard and holding court.
- Bed down close to the ballpark. Traffic in many areas is abysmal. You'll want to arrive at the park early, so stay close and spare yourself hassles. This point especially applies to the twenty-mile Pinellas County corridor from St. Petersburg to Dunedin. The relatively short distances might tempt you into trying to cover all area clubs from one spot, but you'll wind

up spending a lot of time in traffic on infamous Route 19. This Suncoast spine is a nightmare of traffic lights, construction, and cars. Speeds over twenty miles per hour are virtually unknown during normal hours. If you want to see a lot of parks, plan on seeing a lot of motels as well.

- Practices usually aren't worth the trouble. Many of the newer complexes restrict fan access to a single field, so you don't have the opportunity to roam. Intrasquad games can be a lot of fun, but batting practice and fielding drills get old very fast. Unless you're a serious autograph seeker, practice is a bore. When your team is on the road, don't count on the fellows they've left behind to provide an exciting day at the fields. The Red Sox are an exception to the rule because you can still see Ted Williams teaching hitting to young players in the morning.
- Start early. The Teddy Ballgame show, pregame practices, and B-games can start as early as 9 A.M. When you get there, roam around as much as possible to find the best action before settling in.
- Plan your Sarasota excursion in advance. For reasons not obvious to the casual visitor, Sarasota is a tough place

to find a motel room, especially on weekends, and is comparatively pricey. Unprepared travelers will find themselves canvassing the black stocking district and telling the desk clerk they want a room for the whole night. The new complex may seduce you into a Sarasota stop. If you can resist, you'll avoid headaches; if you can't resist, make reservations.

- Bring rain gear and some warm clothes. The weather in Florida is great, sometimes. Night games can be breezy and it does rain, sometimes just enough to make watching miserable but playing tolerable. (In the event of a rainout, call other nearby sites for possible backup games. Storms are often local.) Expect a day or two of precipitation per week, leading to abundant mud around camps, and evening temperatures that may dip below 50 degrees, plus chilling breezes.
- See college baseball. University of Miami's Mark Light Stadium hosts many of the northern powerhouses during March under the lights. In Lakeland, see the Florida Southern Moccasins, a perennial Division II power that also plays a lot of night games, some at Joker Marchant Stadium, the Tigers' spring home.

—EJC

CHAPTER 7

What Mom Didn't Throw Away

Your collection of baseball memorabilia can begin so naturally, you hardly notice. You go to a ball game and come home with the ticket stub tucked in your pocket. Before bed you put your change and your keys on the bureau, and there's that stub. Weeell, you toss it in the top drawer. It'll be there to remind you of the fun you had tonight at the ballpark. You're a potential ticket-stub collector. Perhaps you've also brought home a scorecard, or a yearbook, or a pennant. Aha! The cornerstone for a collection has been laid. It may take a couple more trips to the ballpark before you begin to think of your hoard as your "collection," but you're on your way to the point where the salvaged treasures become more important than the game you go to.

It's time to consider the parameters.

How to collect? What to collect? The key word is *collect*. Only the independently wealthy can collect *everything*. Everyone else (us) has to pick a specialty—or a specialty within a specialty. Ticket stubs, programs, pins, autographs, baseball stamps; you name it. If it's not tied down or breathing, it's collectible.

Most kids start with baseball cards, collecting the cards of players on their hometown team or the biggest modern-day stars. Eventually they may expand their cache into complete sets of current-day players. Adults—or older kids, if you will—do the same thing, collecting the cards of players who were the stars when they were young. Some grown-ups are fortunate enough to still have the cards they saved in their youth. If those precious pieces of pasteboard exist, resurrected collectors may want to fill in items they missed back then. Alas! All too often the

Cards and Collectibles

How to collect? What to collect? What's it worth? Have fun—this ain't Wall Street

story is "Mom threw out my cards." The total value of kids' card collections trashed over the years by zealous moms at spring-cleaning time would pay off the national debt.

Many collectors choose to build a collection of memorabilia based on one team. Others collect items from a certain era. Historians may choose to collect the written word—that is, publications. Some ambitious historians have tried to obtain a card or a photo of everyone who ever played baseball on the major league level, a nearly impossible task. Some collectors choose to collect cards depicting players of their own ancestry. Considering the variety of collectibles, the possibilities are almost infinite.

Where to find these treasures? The most obvious places are trade (or hobby) papers and shows, but sometimes the most obvious are not always the cheapest—or the most pleasing. Many collectors will tell you the fun is in the hunt; everything else is secondary. Hunting can be the best way to collect—it's certainly the cheapest and most rewarding. Searches of garage sales and flea markets have resulted in remarkable discoveries for many. Don't be

ashamed to tell friends, relatives, and business acquaintances you collect baseball items—you never know when it will pay off. If they give you a funny smile, tell them about the T206 Honus Wagner card.

The list of people for whom collecting has paid off contains as varied a group as you'll find at a baseball game. A Chicago-based American Airlines pilot has three storage areas filled with nothing other than bound editions of newspapers with baseball material. He waits for his retirement when he will become a baseball memorabilia dealer. Scott Forst, a former player in the Brooklyn Dodger organization, sells his own artwork along with baseball memorabilia. When he retires from the New York Police Department, he'll become a memorabilia dealer full-time.

Edward C. Wharton-Tigar, a British mining magnate, has one of the largest collections of tobacco cards in the world, including the largest known group of the 1880s Goodwin Old Judges. In fact, Wharton-Tigar has an example of nearly every tobacco card issued in the world. His collection has been given to the British Museum for future display.

A friend of Wharton-Tigar's, Jefferson Burdick, is considered to be the father of modern card collecting. Burdick, from his home in Syracuse, New York, accumulated a massive collection not only of baseball cards, but of all trading cards, post cards, trade cards, and general paper ephemera. He was a reclusive clerk who dedicated his life to the study of cartophily. In the 1940s, he helped to create the American Card Catalog (more on that later), which remains the bible of the hobby. Burdick's collection can be seen by appointment in the print division of the Museum of Modern Art.

The attraction of baseball memorabilia is not restricted to unknowns. Some celebrities have also been caught by the bug. Keith Olbermann, a nationally known television sports anchor in Los Angeles, has been collecting cards for more than twenty years. CBS Sports's Brent Musberger can often be seen roaming the aisles of card shows. Former player and broadcaster Joe Garagiola is an avid collector of tobacco and gum cards from the 1930s. Sports author Peter Golenbock (*Dynasty*, *The Bronx Zoo*) had a passion for autographs when he penned several articles about that subject in a now defunct trade paper called *The Trader Speaks*.

One dealer brags that he was a high school dropout and brags even louder that baseball cards have made him a millionaire. Indeed, there are quite a few who have seen their collections grow from personal passions to million-dollar holdings. The flip side of the incredible influx of people buying baseball memorabilia is the number of longtime collectors selling off what they've treasured for years because the idea of holding items that valuable is frightening.

It's easy to get hooked on baseball collecting. But beware. There have been cases where a single innocent purchase has resulted in a lifetime addiction.   —LL

Collectibles and Memorabilia

The objects people collect and the way they collect them reflect their own creativity and imagination. Still, a little direction never hurt. The sources of baseball collectibles and memorabilia that follow were chosen for their experience, knowledge, and credibility (not to say that someone who isn't listed isn't credible). We've also tried to provide geographical balance and have listed our people in alphabetical order by state, to make them easier to find. Addresses and phone numbers are provided under the source's main area of business.

Shows

Baseball card shows or conventions are a relatively new concept. They started in the 1970s and have reached the point where it is impossible for a collector to leave his house on a weekend and not find a show within a half hour's drive. Most of today's shows take one of two approaches—the old-fashioned style, where the dealers and the memorabilia take precedence; or the newer concept, which features ball players signing autographs in the hope of attracting big crowds.

Some of the best shows in the country, including both styles, are listed below, arranged alphabetically by states. Contact the individual show promoters for exact dates and details.

BOB WILKE
See "Stores" for address.
Wilke runs a major show every March in Arizona during spring training. It's a weekend show, giving people time to also hit the spring training camps.

GAVIN RILEY
19008 S. Cecelia Pl.
Cerritos, CA 90701
(213) 865-4549
With three other Southern California collectors, Riley has been running this show, one of the first, every Memorial Day and Labor Day weekend at the Disneyland Hotel. This is an old-guard show with a baseball star or two.

GARY NAGLE
Baseball Card World

16 Broadway
Kissimee, FL 32742
(407) 846-3429
Nagle promotes several small shows a year in Florida. (There is no one big show in the state. No one to date has picked up on the idea of combining one with spring training.)

BRUCE PAYNTER
Windy City Sports
2759 Porter Ct.
Glenview, IL 60025
(312) 205-0342
Paynter's major shows in Chicago usually feature a big-name ball player and some of the nation's better dealers.

WAYNE MILLER
10632 Little Patuxent Pkwy.
Suite 300
Columbia, MD 21044
No autographs, no frills. Only better dealers and better cards.

JIM HAWKINS
4217 Highland Rd.
Suite 225
Pontiac, MI 48054
(313) 363-7694
This former sportswriter runs three shows a year at varying locations in the Detroit area. They usually feature star players.

GLORIA ROTHSTEIN
P.O. Box J
Highland Mills, NY 10930
(914) 928-9494
A long time promoter who has gotten into baseball memorabilia shows, Gloria does several shows a year in the New York and New Jersey area. One called the International, held in White Plains, New York, in August, stands out and is well worth attending. Rothstein runs both types of shows; last year she did a theme show with the 1969 Mets.

PHIL LACHMEIER
1067 Benz Ave.

Cincinnati, OH 45238
(513) 251-1626
A small show; but one of the oldest in the country and one of the best. Held the first weekend in November. No stars.

BOB SCHMIERER
P.O. Box 37
Maple Glen, PA 19002
(215) 628-4969
One of the old guard, Schmierer's is a long standing show dating back to the late 1970s; it is generally considered to be one of the best collectors' shows. In fact it's probably the number one old-fashioned card show in the country. Schmierer usually features former Phillie players. Three shows a year—in March, May, and September.

RICH HAWKSLEY
See "Stores" listing for address
Hawksley runs two major shows in the St. Louis area, usually in May and November. Each features big name players. Hawksley also conducts several smaller shows during the year.

LARRY DLUHY
Sports Collectibles of Houston
5308 W. Bellfort
Houston, TX 77035
(713) 723-0730
Dluhy always features a star or two at the several excellent shows he runs in the Houston area.

WANDA MARCUS
Arlington Sportscards
2304 W. Park Row
Arlington, TX 76013
The promoter of the sixth National Convention runs several shows in the Dallas area—with stars.

Stores

There's a good chance you'll find a baseball card store in any shopping center. However, the following lists some of the better *(Cont. p. 106.)*

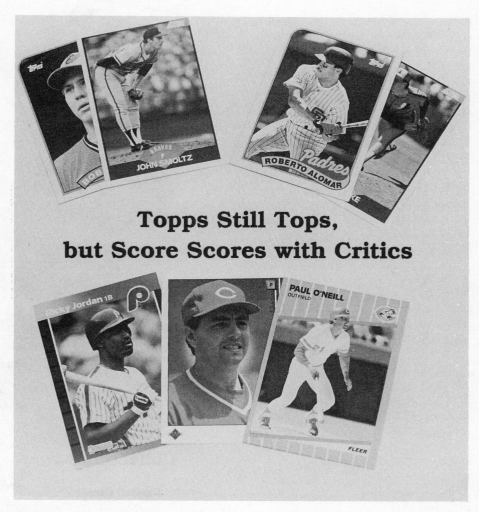

Topps Still Tops, but Score Scores with Critics

According to an article in the April 21, 1989, *Wall Street Journal*, Topps controls about 50 percent of the baseball card market it's dominated since 1952. The net sales of the four top card makers—Topps, Donruss, Fleer, and Score—totaled more than $250 million in 1988, with a 20–30 percent rise expected in 1989.

Although exact figures are jealously guarded, the *Journal* reported that Topps maintained its top spot—half the market—with an expanded line of supplementary cards and better distribution. Donruss, which controlled about 25 percent of sales in 1988, also benefitted from strong marketing. Its parent company, Leaf Inc., makes such kid staples as Good 'n' Plenty, Milk Duds, and Heath Bars, giving their sales force well established contacts all across the country.

Fleer and Score nearly split the remaining market, with Fleer holding a slight lead. But Score is on the rise. In its first two years of cardmaking, its cards, featuring game-action color photos, better paper, and well-written card backs by a former *Sports Illustrated* writer, have been voted the best by hobby publications. Although that bids fair for Score's future, hobbyists don't have the final say. It's what the kids like that counts. Card makers say that children in the seven-to-twelve age bracket account for 75 to 90 percent of all sales.   —BC

stores in the country. All are owned by knowledgeable collectors and dealers who have spent several years in the hobby. Most will also sell through the mail.

THE SHOEBOX
Bob Wilke
515 E. Camelback Rd.
Phoenix, AZ 85012
(602) 263-0593

SPORT COLLECTORS STORE
Pat Quinn & Don Steinbach
9 S. LaGrange Rd.
LaGrange, IL 60525
(312) 354-7970

AU SPORTS
Audre Gold
3328 1/2 Dempster
Skokie, IL 60076
(312) 679-8310

HOUSE OF CARDS
Bill Huggins
2411 University Blvd.
Wheaton, MD 20902
(301) 933-0355

HALL'S NOSTALGIA
25 Mystic St.
Arlington, MA 02174
(617) 646-7757

RICH HAWKSLEY
1212 Lanvale
St. Louis, MO 63129
(314) 843-9366

CARDS FOR COLLECTORS
Ron Oser
Roosevelt Mall
2327 Cottman Ave
Philadelphia, PA 19149

FIRST BASE
Gervaise Ford
231 Webb Chapel Village
Dallas, TX 75229
(214) 243-5271   —LL

Collectibles

Baseball Cards

Baseball cards are the cornerstone of the baseball memorabilia hobby. Most dealers get started with newer cards and as they gather more experience move on to the antiques. Because cards have been issued since the late nineteenth century, dealers will invariably start specializing in a specific area. Possibilities include the Topps and Bowman era; the 1930s gum era; nineteenth-century tobacco cards; twentieth-century tobacco cards; other turn-of-the-century cards. All of the dealers listed below have some knowledge in all of these fields, but they are listed in terms of their specialties.

Collector-dealers who specialize in older cards:

MARK MACRAE
Box 2111
Castro Valley, CA 94546

LOU CHERICONI
43 Clifton Ct.
Walnut Creek, CA 94595
(415) 934-3382

JOHN SPALDING
5551 Fern Dr.
San Jose, CA 95124
(408) 264-5530

RICH STROBINO
1030 Second St.
Santa Rosa, CA 95404
(707) 527-7310

PETER GILLEENY
Rt. 2 Box 1133-76

The 1911 Turkey Red set of 126 cabinet cards at the left may be the hobby's most beautiful. The cards are known in the hobby as "T3"s.

Fruitland Park, FL 32731
(904) 728-4819

BARRY SANDERS
4022 Whistling Forest Ct.
Lilburn, GA 30247
(404) 972-6354

KEITH MITCHELL
1332 Golden Valley Rd.
Bettendorf, IA 52722
(319) 355-3421

DAN McKEE
214 Parkholme Circle
Reistertown, MD 21136
(301) 833-2613

JIM REID
336 Annursnac Hill Rd.
Concord, MA 01742

CHARLES CONLON
117 Edison
Ypsilanti, MI 48197
(313) 434-4251

BARRY SLOATE
231 Clinton St.
Brooklyn, NY 11201
(718) 855-7513

WALTER HANDELMAN
5 Ascot Ridge
Great Neck, NY 11020
(516) 482-0089

LEW LIPSET
New York, NY
See "Press Pins" listing.

CHARLES COLLECTORS CORNER
Charlie Hosan
100 D West 2nd St.
Hummelstown PA 17036

RON OSER
Philadelphia, PA
See "Stores" listing.

PAUL POLLARD
112 Kenbridge Pl.
Lynchburg, VA 24502
(804) 239-5839

LARRY FRITSCH
735 Old Wausau Rd.
Stevens Pt., WI 54481
(715) 344-8631

Dealers specializing in post–World War II cards, including the most popular: Topps, Bowman, Donruss, and Fleer.

STEVE BRUNNER
1308 Cypress Ave.
Glendora, CA 91740
(818) 963-9717

GEORGIA MUSIC
Dick DeCoursey
P.O. Box 490331
Atlanta, GA 30349

TOM HENNINGSEN
P.O. Box 158
Prospect Heights, IL 60070

KEITH MITCHELL
Iowa
See listing for older cards, above.

FRANK LUCITO
760 Barbe St.
Westwego, LA 70094
(504) 348-1451

BILL GOODWIN
5456 Chatfield
St Louis, MO 63129
(314) 892-4737

BRANSON McKAY
22 Stonecroft Dr.
Hampton, NH 03842
(603) 926-1568

Scandals Can't Dim Collectors' Interest

The various scandals surrounding Pete Rose, Wade Boggs, and Steve Garvey apparently have had no effect on the enthusiasm of dedicated collectors. Last year the tenth annual National Sports Collectors Convention, held in Chicago, drew more than 34,000 fans and collectors, despite the bad publicity Rose was reaping on the sports pages. Event chairman Bruce Paynter told *USA Today* that prices of Rose cards and memorabilia were unaffected by Pete's problems. "There's no taking away what Pete did on the field," he said.

Hot items: cards of Giants' sluggers Will Clark and Kevin Mitchell.   —BC

SCORE BOARD
Phil Spector
100 Dobbs Lane #206
Cherry Hill, NJ 08034
A public company—its shares are traded on the over-the-counter market—that deals in baseball cards.

MIKE GORDON
680 Speedwell Ave.
Morris Plains, NJ 07950
(201) 540-0004

BASEBALL CARDS FOREVER
Richie Chapetto
79 Broadway
Hicksville, NY 11801

SCOTT SNYDER
44425 Telegraph Rd.
Elyria, OH 44035
(216) 322-7001

ROGER NEUFELDT
7868 S. Western
Oklahoma City, OK 73139

MIKE WHEAT
468 Baldwin Road
Pittsburgh, PA 15205
(412) 921-7644

RON OSER
Philadelphia, PA
See "Stores" listing.

BILL HENDERSON
2320 Ruger Ave., BLK-2
Jamesville, WI 53545

LARRY FRITSCH
Wisconsin
See listing for older cards, above.

Collectors specializing in baseball-related postcards and Exhibit cards:

GAVIN RILEY
California
See "Shows" listing.

BOB THING
Box 450
Skowhegan, ME 04976
(207) 474-5820

JIM REID
Massachusetts
See listing for older cards, above.

DAN EVAN
110 West Lake Dr.
Brandon, MS 39042
(601) 992-2681

LEW LIPSET
New York
see "Press Pins" listing.

RICH HAWKSLEY
St. Louis, MO
See "Shows" listing.

Help for Hackers

Need help in keeping your card collection organized? Compu-Quote (818-348-3662) now offers a program for your personal computer (MS-DOS or Apple) that will both catalogue your collection and assess its value.

Push the right keys and you'll get a report on the current market value of each of your cards (updates are available yearly at a nominal cost), plus the total worth of the whole batch. Additionally the program lists the date and price of each item bought or sold, profit percentage, and the cards needed to complete your collection.

Now if they only had a program that would tell you where you can find that 1952 Mickey Mantle!   —BC

RAY MEDEIROS
P.O. Box 10
Wauna, WA 98395
(206) 857-7331

Autographs

Autographs have become a big business, with major league superstars known to walk away with upwards of $20,000 for a few hours spent on a weekend signing their names. Even with the most willing signers, the bottom line is at least $10 for a signature. As a result, today's stars are wary of imploring kids, figuring they're out for a quick buck.

The amount of money being transacted has brought foul play (counterfeits, forgeries) to the field of autographs. Here, perhaps more than in any other area of baseball memorabilia, there is a need to know your subject and be familiar with the person from whom you're buying.

Prices for older autographs can vary greatly, depending on what was signed. Documents (such as a contract) are gener-

ally considered to be the most desirable item (they're counterfeit-proof). Signed letters are also highly sought, as are signed photos. At the bottom of the scale are "cuts" and 3 × 5 cards where a player just signed a card or his signature was "cut" from another document. Another major consideration in determining a price is when the player died. A premature death (Jackie Robinson, Roberto Clemente, Roger Maris) will mean higher values, while the autographs of all-time greats (Joe DiMaggio, Mickey Mantle) will be worth nominal amounts as long as they are around and willing to sign.

Autograph collectors steer away from autographs on paper—especially those that have been personalized ("To Randy from Mickey Mantle")—preferring autographed equipment, especially balls. Prices for balls will not only depend on who signed, but to whom they signed and what their relationship was.

Sample prices for autographs can vary widely. A Babe Ruth signed ball is worth from $1,000 to $2,000, one by Lou Gehrig even more. The simplest autograph, a "cut" signature of Ruth or Gehrig, is worth $500. Other sample prices for player cuts: Jackie Robinson $100, Frank Robinson $3, Roberto Clemente $75, Ty Cobb $50, Joe DiMaggio $10, Roger Maris $25, Cy Young $100, Ross Youngs $250.

Autographs are probably second only to cards in their popularity to baseball collectors. However, nothing can match their complexity and the knowledge required. The following dealers specialize in all forms of autographs:

MIKE GUTIERREZ
4357 Alla Rd. #5
Marina Del Rey, CA
(213) 306-7400

MARK JORDAN
821 SW 12th Place
Ft. Lauderdale, FL 33315
(305) 525-8593

(Cont. p. 110.)

Where It's Been: A History of Card Collecting

Baseball cards date back almost as far as baseball, all the way to the 1860s, when they took the form of various types of early photographica—tintypes (a photo on tin); *cartes de visite* (small photos mounted on cardboard): and cabinets (usually 4-by-6-inch photographs mounted on a cardboard backing). Gradually they evolved into trade cards (elaborately designed handouts advertising a product or service).

The earliest mass-produced cards were issued in the late 1880s as inserts to cigarette packages. One of the most widely known distributors was New York's Goodwin & Company, a tobacco concern which produced a massive 500-plus-player issue called Old Judge. Portraying players from the National League, American Association, Western League, International League, Pacific Coast League, and the Players League, this photographic issue was the first to try to document most, if not all, of the players of the time. In addition, most of the players could be found in anywhere from two to nineteen different poses.

Also from this era—and even more popular with nineteenth-century collectors—are considerably smaller card issues produced by the same Goodwin & Co. along with fellow tobacco companies Kimballs and Allen & Ginters. All three produced magnificent color-lithographed cards of champions in sets of fifty. Each set contained from four to ten baseball players. There were a few other issues in the 1890s, the most significant being a forty-eight-card issue by the Mayo Brothers in 1895, but generally issues subsided to just a few for several years, particularly after several of these tobacco companies merged to form American Tobacco.

In fact, the next boom in baseball cards didn't come until twenty years later, just before 1910, when the American Tobacco

One of the game's earliest and rarest cards is this carte de visite *of the Forest City of Rockford team of 1871, notable as Cap Anson's "rookie card."*

Company produced their famous "White-Bordered Set," consisting of over 400 baseball players. The set is now commonly known as T206 and features the hobby's most famous and valuable card, the Honus Wagner. ATC, which produced several other issues, began running into competition from candy companies, who were giving children a means of getting the same kind of cards their dads were getting in cigarette packages. In addition, sporting periodicals such as *Sporting Life* and *The Sporting News* began producing cards as subscription incentives.

This fabulous era tapered off with the arrival of World War I (1917), and card

issues were rare until the early 1920s, when the American Caramel Company and others resumed their production. The early 1920s also saw the introduction of the strip card, a strip of paper (of poor quality) that usually featured drawings of players, side by side. In 1921 the "Exhibit" card, so called because it was manufactured by the Exhibit Supply Company, was born in Chicago and gained prominence in vending machines from Coney Island to the West Coast. Exhibits, probably the first baseball card to be sold purely as a card, were produced annually until 1966.

On to the 1930s and some of the most popular cards ever issued. The leader was the Goudey Gum Company of Boston, which produced a 240-card set bearing its name which became nearly as popular as the American Tobacco Company's T206 set. Some of the other companies that produced cards in the decade were started by executives who left Goudey, all operating out of New England. Firms such as George Miller, DeLong, and U.S. Caramel each made a single contribution to the annals of baseball cards. The National Chicle Company also produced an extremely popular set called Diamond Stars with a "Pop Art" style. A Philadelphia company called Gum, Inc., became a regular issuer of baseball cards in the late 1930s, producing its "Play Ball" series from 1939 to 1941. The '30s era ended, a bit late, in 1941, once again with the start of a world war, and card sets of 1942–1947 were rare, aside from Exhibits, team-issued picture packs, and a couple of ice cream issues from the West Coast. But when the drought ended this time, it was for good. The Bowman Gum Company of Philadelphia started issuing card sets in 1948 and the Topps Gum Company followed just two years later.

Bowman led off with a simple forty-eight-card black-and-white issue. Its popu-

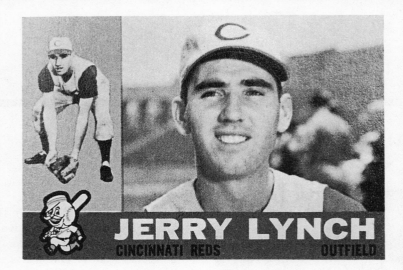

JERRY LYNCH
CINCINNATI REDS   OUTFIELD

larity led a year later to a colorized 240-card issue. More popularity led to more advancement—1950 brought full color and 252 cards. The succeeding two years brought greater numbers of cards, reaching an all-time high (for Bowman) of 324 in 1951. That '51 issue is the most popular Bowman set with collectors today because it includes the rookie cards of Mickey Mantle and Willie Mays.

Though Topps was experimenting before, 1952 was the year it exploded on the scene. The 1952 Topps issue has become famous for its "high numbers,"—that is, its last series. It was the custom then to issue cards in series, with a new series coming out approximately every month during the baseball season. Because the last series would have the shortest life span, over the years it has proven to be the most valuable. It was especially so in 1952. Topps saved many local New York heroes (including Jackie Robinson, Roy Campanella, Leo Durocher, Pee Wee Reese, Bobby Thomson, and Mickey Mantle) for that series. Hobby folklore has it that the 1952 Topps high numbers "never made it out of the East," that a large percentage "went to Canada," and that "they only went to other parts of the country in 1953."

Topps had made its presence felt quickly. Bowman's set diminished from 324 cards to 252 as players had to choose to sign contracts with one company or the other. Ted Williams was on Bowman cards exclusively until 1954, when he appeared for both companies. The Bowman card had to be withdrawn and was replaced by a sec-

ond card of Jimmy Piersall. The 1954 Bowman Williams card is considered to be one of the hobby's rarest modern-day cards. Following its 1955 issue, Bowman gave way to Topps, and the Brooklyn-based company had things pretty much to itself until the '80s. Topps' sets grew from a beginning run of 52 cards to the current 700-plus issue.

Not that Bowman or Topps ever had a complete exclusive. In the 1950s, potato chip companies such as Dandee issued a set featuring some hometown Cleveland Indians and some other selected players. Bell Brand Potato Chips featured the Los Angeles Dodgers for four years shortly after their arrival in Southern California. Baseball is synonymous with hotdogs, and that product was a healthy participant with Stahlmeyers, Hunter Wieners, Kahn's Franks, Peters Meats, and Wilson Wieners all issuing cards, usually as part of their package backing.

Post Cereal produced cards on the back of their cereal boxes for four years, and a Philadelphia gum company named Fleer issued card sets for four years. The last of these sets in 1963 came with cookies because only Topps could issue cards with gum. Fleer would reemerge in 1981. Then along came Donruss, Score, and Upper Deck to provide more cards than even the most dedicated card collector ever dreamed about. Today the number of companies manufacturing cards or buying them from a manufacturer to help sell their products is at an all-time high.

—LL

DAN GINSBURG
121 East Bonefish Circle
Jupiter, FL 33477

RICHARD BINDER
620 65th St.
Downers Grove, IL 60515
(312) 964-7502

JACK SMALLING
2308 Van Buren
Ames, Iowa 50010
(515) 232-7599

JOE SPERLING
43 Mays Landing Rd.
Somers Point, NJ 0824
(609) 653-1883

RICHARD SIMON
215 E. 80th St.
New York, NY 10021
(212) 988-1349

Sheet Music

There is a small group of baseball memorabilia collectors who specialize in sheet music and records pertaining to baseball. It can be a songsheet from *Damn Yankees*, the original music to "Take Me Out to the Ball Game," or instructional records used to advertise clothing. (See Chapter 1 for a selection of available baseball music.)

Prices for sheet music can vary greatly. Age, rarity, the illustration and artwork on the cover, and historical significance are all part of it. A piece of sheet music with Ty Cobb on the cover is worth $500. A nineteenth-century piece can be worth $1,000, even more if it's in color. Twentieth-century pieces with photographs or illustrations of players are worth $100 and up. Generic pieces from early in the century are worth about $50.

MIKE BROWN
12 Yorktown Rd.
East Brunswick, NJ 08816
(201) 254-0080

PEREZ-STEELE GALLERIES
Frank Steele
Box 1776
Ft. Washington, PA 19034
(215) 836-1192

Publications

One of the most extensive fields of baseball memorabilia is reserved for the written word. Material is extensive, easily available, and can be tailored to a collector's needs. A complete collection of all that's available would fill the Astrodome.

The first baseball guides were put out in the 1860s by Beadle. They were followed by the DeWitt Guides. These two companies produced the only annual guides until 1878, when Spalding published the first of an annual series which ran until 1941. Reach also issued an annual guide which ran concurrently with Spalding. *The Sporting News, Baseball Magazine,* and various smaller publishing concerns made sure there was no shortage of statistical material on the national game.

Some publication collectors try to obtain World Series and All-Star Game programs which date back to the first of these classics. Then there are newspapers, books, and yearbooks. Prices for periodicals can vary as widely as the types of periodicals themselves. World Series programs from before 1920 are almost all at least $1,000 and up, while more recent programs can be bought for less than their cover price. All-Star programs range from hundreds of dollars for the first ones to a few dollars for more recent editions. Yearbooks from the 1950s are $50 and up, proportionally less for later ones. Pre-1900 guides sell for $100 and up.

Dealers specializing in publications include:

BILL WHITE
400 18th St.
Ocean City, NJ 08226
(609) 398-6485

Me and the Man

The day before I learned the value of autographs, we put on ties and jackets and grabbed a bus down to the Schenley Hotel where the Cardinals stayed when they were in Pittsburgh. Robbie and I were barely old enough for acne, but with our ties, he explained, we'd look like we were registered at the Schenley to the hotel people.

We stood on the porch in the June sun waiting for the Cardinals to come from breakfast, carefully eyeing anyone male and under fifty. I secretly hoped someone would mistake us for ball players; when you're fourteen in a tie, you always think you'll pass for twenty.

Pretty soon Ray Jablonski, Steve Bilko, and Ferrell Anderson came out on the porch. Bilko was demonstrating something about his batting stance to Jablonski. Robbie accosted them courteously with his book; they signed and went back to pantomiming home runs. I leaned against the porch rail and gawked with aplomb. Real ball players!

More players arrived, doing ball player things like talking, yawning, and picking their teeth. After Robbie got their signatures, he walked over to me.

"Have you seen . . .?" he began. Suddenly he yelled so loud it must have rattled the scoreboard at Forbes Field a block away. "There's *Stan Musial*!"

Sure enough, across the porch, walking no more than a few feet above the ground, was Stan the Man. He threw up his hands in an oh-not-again gesture, but he was smiling.

"You'll have to leave." The hotel man suddenly beside us was firm. We started down the steps, spies caught stealing the plans.

"Wait a minute. Would you like me to sign that?" Musial was at the top of the steps; Mr. Hotel frowned. Robbie scampered up with his book. I apologized for not saving autographs.

I still remember our conversation.
Stan: "Are you going to the game?"
Us: "Un-huh."
Stan: "Great."

I can't remember saying thanks, but I must have. I hope I did.

The next day, when I told everybody Musial had talked to me, they nodded like I was explaining a fish that got away. And that's when I learned why it was important to get an autograph.

But he really *did* talk to me. Honest.

—BC

B & E COLLECTIBLES
12 Marble Ave.
Thornwood, NY 10594
(914) 769-1304

RON OSER
Philadelphia, PA
See "Stores" listing.

JERRY BLANK
235 Arlington Rd.
Flourton, PA 19031
(215) 233-5060

JEFFREY MILLER
323 W. Sterigere St.
Norristown, PA 19401

Celluloid Pins

Celluloid or plastic pins date back to the 1890s. These are the plastic pins that would be sold outside the ballparks, sometimes with ribbons attached. Earlier pins were issued with gum, tobacco, and bread.

Celluloid pins are a relatively safe collectible as there have been no reports of counterfeiting. Some collector-dealers who are interested include:

TOM REID
526 Franklin Ave.
Nutley, NJ 07110
(201) 748-4299

ROGER STECKLER
175 East 74th St.
New York, NY 10021

LEW LIPSET
New York
See "Press Pins" listing.

TOM GUILFOILE
405 Lloyd St.
Fond du Lac, WI 54311

Press Pins

In the last few years the press pins issued by the host team at the World Series or All-Star Games have emerged as interesting collectibles. Press pins date back officially to 1911, although there have been reports of earlier ones. In most cases, of course, there have been two press pins for each World Series. Three exceptions were the World Series of 1921, '22, and '23 between the Yankees and the Giants. All of those games were played in the Polo Grounds, so only one pin was issued.

Besides World Series press pins, the more sophisticated collect "phantoms," pins made in anticipation of a World Series appearance for a team that never got there. Today ball clubs have tried to eliminate the expense of making unusable pins by leaving off the year or marking them with a generic designation such as the "35th World Series."

The first All-Star Game pin was issued in 1938, five years after the first All-Star Game. No pins were issued the following two years. They were back again in 1941, 1943, and have been produced annually

A Question of Priorities

Thurman Tucker.
Walt Judnich.
Allie Clark.
Bob Kennedy.
My aunt from Cleveland gave me a ball signed by all the Indians in September—a real Spalding and real signatures, not one of those fake balls with printed signatures they sold at the ballpark. My aunt knew someone who knew someone.
Hal Peck.
Larry Doby.
Eddie Robinson.
I put it on the table beside my bed. In October the Indians beat the Braves in the World Series. Sixth grade let me listen to only the Saturday and Sunday games.
Joe Gordon.
Hank Edwards.
My signed ball stayed on the table through football season. I played fullback. I didn't like basketball—I was too short— but the signed ball kept me focused on spring.
Johnny Berardino.
Joe Tipton.
Bob Lemon.

Ken Keltner.
April at last. Saturday! Chuckie brought his bat out. Bill had a new glove. I had my old one. Mickey owned a baseball.
Steve Gromek.
Bob Muncrief.
Sam Zoldak.
But with the score 23–17 in the second inning, Chuckie fouled Mickey's ball into a storm drain. We sat down at home plate, faced with the whole afternoon and no game. "Maybe I'll get another ball for my birthday," Mickey said. His birthday wasn't until June!
Russ Christopher.
Eddie Klieman.
Don Black.
"I know where I can get a ball," I said, climbing to my feet. The Indians would probably win the Series this year too. And my aunt was still in Cleveland. "There's one on the table beside my bed."
Dale Mitchell.
Satchel Paige.
Lou Boudreau.
Gene Bearden.
Bob Feller . . .   —BC

since 1946. A newer press pin that has won immediate acceptance by collectors is the one given out at the annual Hall of Fame inductions. That pin was introduced in 1982.

Collectors of press pins have to be aware of counterfeits and "restrikes"—copies that are made after the fact, using the original mold. These can be more difficult to spot than counterfeits.

The value of genuine press pins will vary with their age. Those from before 1920 will run several thousand dollars apiece. Pins from the 1920s will hover around $1,000; those from the '30s and '40s between $300 and $800; and pins from the '50s in the low

hundreds. More recent pins, from the '60s on up, generally will range from $60 to $80.

The scarcity of press pins has made it difficult for a dealer to specialize in this collectible, but here are five who do:

SCOTT FORST
New York
See "Ticket Stubs" listing.

KEN SLATER
1712 Pacific Coast Highway
Redondo Beach, CA 90277
(213) 316-1388

ROGER PAVEY
606 Cedar Hill Rd. N.E.
Albuquerque, NM 87122
(505) 292-5794

LEW LIPSET
P.O. Box 137
Centereach, NY 11720
(516) 981-3286

JIM JOHNSTON
512 Jones Street
Titusville, PA 16354
(814) 827-7129

World Series and All-Star Rings

Every player on the roster for a World Series or an All-Star Game gets a ring. Most players would never part with them, but for various reasons some do, and a small group of collectors will reward them handsomely.

As a general rule, World Series rings will sell for more than All-Star Game rings and winners will bring more than losers. And the bigger the name engraved on the ring, the more it's worth. There has been a documented case of a Lou Gehrig ring from the 1920s going for $8,000; today that ring or Ruth's would bring over $20,000. The attractiveness of the ring can be another factor. The 1977 Yankees ring has "NY" cast in diamonds; even one that belonged to a no-name player would be worth $4,000 to $6,000.

Collectors should watch out for salesman's samples being passed off as the genuine article. And remember that rings are also given out to a team's front office people—they're worth a lot less.

KEN SLATER
California
See "Press Pin" listing.

GEORGE LYONS
19 Baylor Circle
White Plains, NY 10605
(914) 948-6466

The Babe is collectible, from wristwatches and bats to candy wrappers and underwear.

Uniforms and Equipment

Some people feel that the tools of the trade—uniforms, balls, bats, masks, shin guards that actually were used in games—are the only items worthy of being collected. The ball that Roger Maris hit for his sixty-first home run in 1961 made the person who caught it famous. The ball Hank Aaron hit to break Babe Ruth's record would be a prized possession. Any ball that can be tied, without question, to an historic event is going to be worth a lot of money. Likewise for bats and uniforms.

Uniforms from the last few years are fairly prevalent. But all, especially flannels from the 1950s and '60s, will bring at least a couple of hundred bucks. Stars' will bring considerably more, and those of major Hall of Famers (Mantle, Mays, Musial, Williams) will be in four figures. A uniform that was worn or a piece of equipment used when a no-hitter was pitched or a record was broken can be worth five figures if it's a big enough event (the bat Pete Rose used to pass Cobb reportedly brought six). Word is that when Gaylord Perry won his 300th game, he wore a different uniform in every inning so he would have nine chances to sell the historic garment.

Two concerns face any prospective uniform/equipment buyer: that the item is authentic and that it is coming to him by legitimate means. The uniform collector has to be knowledgeable himself and know whom he's buying from.

STAN MARKS
8337 E. Fairmount Ave
Scottsdale, AZ 85251

DICK DOBBINS
P.O. Box 193
Alamo, CA 94507
(415) 935-7130

LEN LUSTIK
2305 Portland Ave.
Rochester, NY 14617

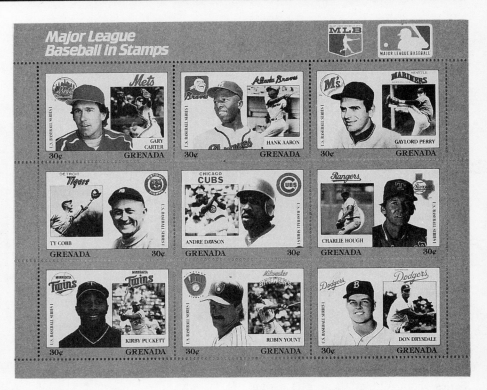

GEORGE LYONS
New York
See "Rings" listing.

SPORTS WAREHOUSE
Robb Wochnick
11865 S.W. Tremont
Portland, OR 97225

MURF DENNY
Box 127
Brule, WI 54820

Stamps and Related Items

Two hobbies are said to "cross" when a collectible can apply to either one of them. All of the stamps the United States Postal Service has issued with baseball subject matter are cross-collectibles. In addition some dealers are creating cross-collectibles by producing special-event covers that tie a stamp (not necessarily a baseball stamp) to a memorable baseball event with a postmark.

A cover is a combination of a stamp on an envelope. A first-day cover is a stamp on an envelope that is postmarked with the first day of issue of the stamp. On that day only the town of issue can use that date (the recent Lou Gehrig stamp was issued

These handsome stamps may be used for postage from the island nation of Grenada; for more info, see page 125.

out of Cooperstown). Event covers are commemorative affairs, where any stamp can be used, but the postmark represents a historic date. A dealer-collector will then have some kind of cachet (engraving or design) put on the envelope to commemorate the event of the day. An autograph is sometimes an added attraction.

This type of collecting (on the basis of pure philately) can be very inexpensive (often just the cost of a stamp). Here are some dealers who specialize in this type of baseball collectible:

KEN SLATER
California
See "Press Pins" listing.

GATEWAY STAMP CO.
Tom Wiley
P.O. Box D
Florissant, MO 63031
(314) 838-7549

SCOTT FORST
New York
See "Ticket Stubs" listing.

HISTORIC LIMITED EDITIONS
John Zaso
Box 400
Williston Park, NY 11596

Ticket Stubs

Ticket stubs are one of the oldest collectibles. They're still relatively inexpensive; thus they've experienced a recent surge in popularity. Regular game stubs from the last thirty years can still be found for just a few dollars, championship playoff games for about $10–$15, World Series games for $15–$25, and All-Star Games for $20–$40. Go farther back and they'll get more expensive. A stub from Larsen's perfect game goes for about $150, Ruth's "called shot" game for over $200.

DAN BUSBY
327 East Main
Gas City, IN 46933
(317) 674-3158

HOWARD HAIMANN
10 Park Pl., Room 309
Morristown, NJ 07960
(201) 239-8921

SCOTT FORST
10 Mara Rd.
Huntington Station, NY 11746
(516) 549-1510

LEW LIPSET
New York
See "Press Pins" listing.

RON OSER
Philadelphia, PA
See "Stores" listing.

A ticket from Game 6 of the 1977 World Series, in which Reggie Jackson hit three homers on three pitches, will be more desirable than an ordinary Series stub. But don't ignore tickets from special events or even regular games.

Hobby Publications

The growth of a hobby is always related to the strength of its publications. At this writing baseball memorabilia was being served by no less than four publications being issued at least monthly, and a number of monthly and annual price guides.

BASEBALL HOBBY NEWS
4540 Kearny Villa Rd.
San Diego, CA 92123
(619) 565-2848
$18 for 12 monthly issues.

BASEBALL CARD NEWS
P.O. Box 2510
Del Mar, CA 92014
(619) 755-2811
$17.95 for 26 biweekly issues.

SPORTS COLLECTORS DIGEST
700 E. State Street
Iola, WI 54990
(715) 445-2214
$32.95 for 52 weekly issues.

TUFF STUFF
P.O. Box 1637
Glen Allen, VA 23060
$17.95 for 12 monthly issues.

Annual Price Guides

Baseball card collectors can choose from at least two annual price guides. *The Sport Americana Baseball Card Price Guide* has been produced annually since 1979 under the direction of Dr. Jim Beckett. In addition to the annual guide, Sport Americana also produces a collectibles book which lists and gives prices on other baseball memorabilia.

The second price guide is produced by Krause Publications and has been produced annually since 1987.

Krause has also produced a more detailed catalog listing additional issues.

STATABASE
Jim Beckett
Suite 110
3410 Midcourt
Carrollton, TX 75006
   Sport Americana Baseball Card Price Guide, $12.95
   Sport Americana Price Guide to Baseball Collectibles, $12.95

KRAUSE PUBLICATIONS
700 E. State St.
Iola, WI 54990
   Standard Catalog of Baseball Cards, $24.95
   Sports Collectors Digest Baseball Card Price Guide, $13.95

Monthly Magazines and Price Guides

The rapid rise and change in baseball card prices, which have been likened to stock-market fluctuations, have created the need for more current price information than can be provided for in the annual guides. Three firms provide monthly guides which vary in presentation from no frills (*Current Card Prices*) to prices and advertising (*Baseball Card Price Guide*) to magazine style with feature stories and commentary (*Beckett Monthly*):

BECKETT BASEBALL CARD MONTHLY
Suite 110
3410 Midcourt
Carrollton, TX 75006
(214) 991-6657
$18.95 for 12 monthly issues.

BASEBALL CARD PRICE GUIDE
700 E. State St.
Iola, WI 54990
$17.95 for 12 monthly issues.

CURRENT CARD PRICES
P.O. Box 480
East Islip, NY 11730
(516) 277-7664
$21.95 for 12 monthly issues

Other Reading Material

The growth of the hobby has brought with it a hunger for more information. The following books specialize in memorabilia, but this shouldn't be considered an exclusive list. You may also find information in unexpected places. More and more books are using baseball memorabilia to illustrate their text, and many of the yearbooks being produced for and by major league teams are using baseball cards to illustrate the team's history. (See also Chapter 9.)

The Encyclopedia of Baseball Cards. A planned six-volume work which, when complete, will provide data on every baseball card set known to be issued. Comes with an abbreviated price guide.
   Vol. 1. *Nineteenth-Century Cards*, $11.95
   Vol. 2. *Early Gum and Candy Cards*, $11.95
   Vol. 3. *Twentieth-Century Tobacco Cards*, $12.95

Classic Baseball Cards. A tabletop book that illustrates more old cards (in color) than any book ever has.
Warner Books, New York, NY 10103
List $79.95

Topps Baseball Cards. Every regular Topps baseball card from 1951 through 1985 reproduced in color. Annual updates available.
Warner Books, New York, NY 10103
List $79.95

The Baseball Address List. The address of nearly every living ball player.
Jack Smalling
2308 Van Buren
Ames, IA 50010
(515) 232-7599

Non-Paper Sports Collectibles Price Guide by Hake and Steckler. Lists nonpaper baseball collectibles, especially celluloid pins.

Hake's Americana
P.O. Box 1444
York, PA 17405

Miscellaneous Supplies

You'll need plastic sheets, boxes, storage files, and holders for your cards. Here are some of the firms that provide these related services. Several sell less expensive reprint sets of rare issues.

DEN'S COLLECTORS DENS
P.O. Box 606, Laurel, MD 20707
Reprint sets, plastic sheets, albums, memorabilia books, publications

WAYNE MILLER
Maryland
See "Shows" listings for address.
Glass display cases.

ROTMAN PLASTIC SHEETS
4 Brussels St.
Worcester, MA 01610
(508) 791-6710
Plastic sheets, cards by the case, books.

ENOR CORP.
5 Tenakill Park
Creskill, NJ 07626
(201) 871-3710
Plastic sheets, albums.

BAGS UNLIMITED
53 Canal St.
Rochester, NY 14608
(716) 436-9006
Plastic bags, boxes, plastic holders

BALL FOUR
Box 19696, West Allis, WI 53219
(414) 383-1280
Lucite card holders, boxes, plastic sheets, albums, storage boxes, ball holders.

Insurance

With baseball card prices soaring it was

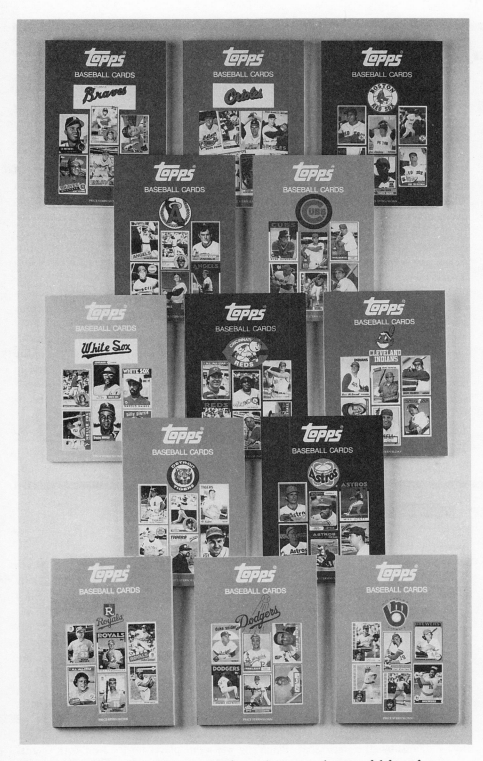

These books depict all the Topps cards for each team and are useful for reference.

only a matter of time before insurance companies started making coverage available for collectors. As might be expected there are variables for collectors and dealers, items stored in safe-deposit boxes or safes, houses with alarms, etc.

AMERICAN PHILATELIC INSURANCE PLAN
W. D. Walker
10405A Stevenson Rd.
Stevenson, MD 21153
(301) 486-5500

CORNELL & FINKELMEYER
P.O. Box 210
Wapakoneta, OH 45895
(419) 738-3314

The Card Companies

Not that there's any point in writing to them (they're not going to send you the cards you need), but our listings wouldn't be complete without the companies that have made most of this possible—the gum companies that produce the cards, with or without gum.

TOPPS GUM CO.
254 36th St.
Brooklyn, NY 11232

FLEER CORP.
10th & Somerville
Philadelphia, PA 19141

DONRUSS
P.O. Box 2038
Memphis, TN 38101

SCORE
Major League Marketing
25 Ford Rd.
Westport, CT 06880

UPPER DECK
1174 North Grove St.
Anaheim, CA 92806

—LL

Where It's Going: One Collector's Opinion

Although its roots reach back over one hundred years to the artistic cards of that historic era, the card market of today revolves around later issues—those from the post–World War II era (which includes the '50s) and from the present day—which have been the subject of incredible price rises. These have been well documented in newspapers, magazines, and on television. "Baseball cards are the best investment in the world" is what's written between the lines.

Watch it!

The effects of both growth and the greed have manifested themselves in the collection of baseball memorabilia. Prices have risen, sometimes by astronomical percentages. One would hope that the price structure would be governed by the laws of supply and demand, but unfortunately it is twisted by hype and manipulation.

One of the basic factors of card value is the condition or grade of a card. The normal conditions for cards five years ago were "Mint," "Excellent," "Very Good," "Good," "Fair," and "Poor." These grades still exist; however, the first grade, "Mint," has been subdivided into "Gem Mint," "Mint," "Near Mint," "Near Mint plus," etc. It's similar to the grading that was introduced into the coin hobby in the 1980s before that hobby's sizeable price decline. It's created an unstable market, easily manipulated by dealers who buy Near Mint cards and sell them as Mint. Just a few years ago a card was Mint if it looked as if it just came out of the gum package. Today, that's not sufficient. The card has to be well centered (have equal borders on all sides) and be void of printing creases or lines or gum stains on the back.

Another factor that's overlooked in assessing today's card market is the simple economics factor of supply and demand. Although the companies producing these pieces of cardboard won't even tell us how many they're producing, it's fairly evident that today's baseball cards are produced in the millions, if not billions. Considering the number of companies, saying there aren't enough cards to go around is like saying the Sahara is running short of sand. Even combining the entire circulations of the hobby press, the resulting number is a small percentage of the number of cards produced of just one player. At a cost to the manufacturer of less than a penny apiece it's hard to justify a resulting price, for selected players, of quarters, let alone dollars.

The card market only appears to be a means to endless profits in prosperous times. In truth an inevitable recession will correct much of this. Knowledgeable collectors and dealers note the changes in the availability of cards at card shows and in the hobby press. Other collectors and dealers watch interest rates, discretionary income, and other economic indicators.

—LL

These MVPS Are in the Cards

It's fairly well known which are the rarest and most valuable cards in the hobby today: the T206 Wagner, Plank, Doyle, and "Magie"; the 1933 Goudey Lajoie; and the 1952 Topps Mantle. But why they are so valuable is another story.

Though not even remotely the hobby's rarest card, the T206 Honus Wagner is certainly the most valuable, reportedly being sold for $100,000 (unsubstantiated) in mint condition. Guesstimates place a hundred copies of the card in existence, a fairly substantial number compared to many other cards, but a mere pittance compared to the many thousands of other T206s that exist and the popularity of the set. The rarity of the Wagner has generally been attributed to the great Pittsburgh Pirates shortstop's insistence that it be withdrawn. He feared his young, innocent fans might think he advocated smoking. On the other hand, Wagner's appearance on other tobacco cards makes a more likely reason for the unwillingness of the American Tobacco Company to pay him a fee for his appearance.

The T206 Eddie Plank card also is mysteriously difficult to find. The theory on Plank is that the photographic plate broke. But judging by the fact that Plank's appearance on other tobacco teams is scarce, it's more likely that Eddie felt the same way as Hans.

Sherwood Magee's card has a more apparent reason for its scarcity. Originally the American Tobacco Company spelled Magee's last name "MAGIE." The error was corrected quickly and the faulty card became a rarity. Why it was corrected is another interesting question as there are many other spelling errors in the same set that were left untouched.

Finally among the T206 rarities there's the card of Larry Doyle. Actually there are five cards of Larry Doyle in T206. Doyle was a fine player for the New York Giants, and his card carried the usual "N.Y. Nat'l" designation except for one card which was designated only "N.Y." This in itself was merely an interesting curiosity until that same card was found with "N.Y. Nat'l." Then it became a major rarity. In fact, it is the rarest of the four T206 rarities, but it does not approach the Wagner card in value.

Closing out the group of the hobby's six most valuable cards are the 1933 Lajoie and the 1952 Topps Mantle. The Lajoie is the only valuable card where a clear explanation for its rarity is available. When the Goudey Company issued their historic 1933 set, the cards were numbered to 240. Collectors would go to their grocery stores regularly to see if Goudey had released the next group of 24 cards. After a while it became apparent that number 106 not only wasn't available, it wasn't going to be produced. Collectors, who can get fanatical about completing a set (it's no different now then it was over fifty years ago), complained to the company. And Goudey, knowing the collector was the ultimate source of its income, decided to produce a card to fill the spot. So in 1934 as part of the last series of the year Goudey manufactured a 25-card sheet (5 rows of 5 columns) instead of the standard sheet of 24 cards (4 by 6). The additional card was of Napoleon Lajoie with the number 106.

The card, though indicating 1933 on the back, was clearly produced in 1934, as indicated by its design characteristics. What's more, the selection of Lajoie, whose career was long over, was a curious one.

Goudey distributed the card, via the mail, to anyone who requested it. The card was never distributed to retail outlets; therefore the "1933" Goudey no. 106 Lajoie card was never subjected to the usual handling most cards receive and can usually be found in excellent condition.

—LL

What Condition Is Your Condition In?

If you just came across an old shoebox full of baseball cards in the attic, relax, you may not be as rich as you think. In today's skyrocketing card market it is no longer enough to have *the* card; you need it in Mint condition. Cards are graded by dealers and collectors according to the shape they are in. The grading, in turn, affects the value. If a Mint card is worth 100 percent value, an Excellent card is worth 75–90 percent of that value, a Very Good card 50 percent, a Good card 25 percent, a Fair card 10 percent, and a Poor card less than 5 percent. Here, according to *Beckett Monthly,* is how to tell how your cards make the grade:

MINT: A card has no defects, no signs of wear. Look for sharp corners, even borders, original gloss or shine on the surface, sharp focus of the picture, smooth edges and white borders.

EXCELLENT: A card with very minor defects. An Excellent card should look Mint until you examine it closely. Then, any of the following flaws would lower its grade: very slight rounding or layering at some of the corners, very small loss of original gloss, minor wear on edges or slight unevenness of borders.

VERY GOOD: A card that has been handled but not abused: some rounding at the corners, slight layering or scuffing, slight notching on the edges. It is okay for a Very Good card to have a very light crease if it is barely noticeable.

GOOD: A well-handled card: rounding and layering at the corners, scuffing at the corners and minor scuffing at the face, notching at the edges.

FAIR: Rounding and layering at the corners, brown and dirty borders, frayed edges, noticeable scuffing on the face. A heavily creased card can be classified as Fair at best.

POOR: An abused card. Often some major physical alterations have been performed on the card. This is the lowest form of card. It has value as a collectible only as a filler until a better condition replacement can be found.

—LL

For What It's Worth

A comparative sampling of values of popular cards (in Excellent-Mint condition):

N162 Goodwin Champion	$300.00
N162 Goodwin Champion Anson	1,500.00
N172 Old Judge Common card	90.00
N172 Old Judge Anson	900.00
T206 Common card	35.00
T206 Wagner	90,000.00
T206 Plank	9,000.00
T206 Doyle	15,000.00
T206 "Magie"	7,000.00
T206 Cobb	850.00
E145 Cracker Jack Common 1915	55.00
E145 Cracker Jack Cobb 1915	2,000.00
E145 Cracker Jack Jackson 1915	1,600.00
M101-4 Babe Ruth (Rookie)	1,500.00
R319 Goudey Common Card	40.00
R319 Goudey Ruth	3,000.00
R319 Lajoie	10,000.00
R320 Goudey Gehrig	1,750.00
R334 1939 Play Ball Joe DiMaggio	1,000.00
R334 1939 Play Ball Ted Williams	1,000.00
R335 1940 Play Ball Joe DiMaggio	1,500.00
R336 1941 Play Ball Ted Williams	700.00
1948 Bowman Common Card	12.00
1951 Bowman Common Card	13.00
1951 Bowman Mickey Mantle	5,500.00
1951 Bowman Willie Mays	1,600.00
1952 Topps Common Card	20.00
1952 Topps Andy Pafko	900.00
1952 Topps Mickey Mantle	6,500.00
1952 Topps Bobby Thomson	175.00
1952 Topps Eddie Mathews	1,500.00
1954 Bowman Common Card	5.00
1954 Bowman #66 Ted Williams	2,100.00
1954 Bowman #66 Jimmy Piersall	100.00
1954 Topps #1 Ted Williams	500.00
1957 Topps Sandy Koufax	300.00
1957 Topps Brooks Robinson	300.00
1963 Topps Pete Rose	600.00
1969 Topps Mickey Mantle	150.00
1969 Topps Reggie Jackson	250.00
1971 Topps Pete Rose	45.00
1971 Topps Steve Garvey	75.00
1989 Topps Common	.03
1989 Topps Greg Jeffries	2.50

Walter Johnson is not as pricey a Cracker Jack card as Joe Jackson, Ty Cobb, or Christy Mathewson; all are tough to find without caramel stains. The T206 Eddie Plank is rare and precious for the same reasons as the Honus Wagner card. The 1911 T3 (Turkey Red tobacco) features old Cy Young at the end of the trail. The truly rare Goudey Lajoie card, though marked "1933" on the back, was produced in 1934. (See the Ruth card at the right for the correct 1933 format.)

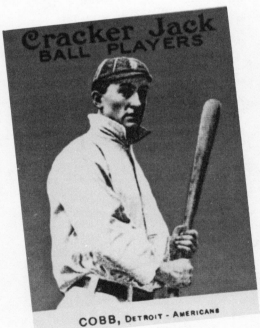

The Code of Collectors

We've been using the expression "T206" to describe tobacco cards from 1910. You may wonder where that designation came from.

The American Card Catalog was created in the late 1940s and was revised several times until the last version was published in 1968. Jefferson Burdick, generally considered the father of card collecting, was responsible for the historic work, which has created codes for almost all the card issues of the last one hundred years.

The system was simple enough. It chose a letter to designate a type of card and that letter prefixed a numerical code. For example:

"T" = Twentieth-century tobacco cards
"E" = Early gum and candy cards
"R" = Post-1930 gum cards
"B" = Felt (blanket) issues
"F" = Food issues
"PC" = Postcards
"P" = Celluloid pins
"W" = Miscellaneous issues
"C" = Canadian issues

The absence of a letter before the code was meant to indicate a nineteenth-century tobacco card, though now an "N" is generally used as the prefix for that type of card. The numerical code, however, is arbitrary, its logic known only to Burdick.

—LL

Babe Ruth cards always command a premium; this example is from the 1933 Goudey set. The Honus Wagner card above from the T206 set is the King of Kard Kash, with a reported sale in the six figures. The E145 Cracker Jack card of Ty Cobb is a beauty, though awfully tough to obtain in Excellent-Mint condition. And the Allen & Ginter's card of shortstop Jack Glasscock, one of the first mass-marketed baseball cards (1886), is priced surprisingly low, considering its scarcity.

MLB-Licensed Collectibles

Today Major League Baseball Properties, operating under the aegis of the Commissioner of Baseball, licenses nearly 400 firms to use official baseball logos in marketing everything from beach umbrellas to frozen food. The 1989 listings appeared under eight categories:

• The Diamond Collection—merchandise actually used by major league teams.

• Apparel—T-shirts, sweaters, night shirts, travel bags, and other items bearing team logos.

• Headwear and sporting goods—including hats, caps, towels, and even baseball golf bags.

• Accessories—from ties and watches to beach umbrellas.

• Household products—sheets, linens, aprons, clocks, and telephones, etc.

• Gifts and novelties—mugs, key chains, baseball parking signs, buttons, plus autographed and painted baseballs.

• Toys, games, and school supplies—featuring a variety of games and toys, including figurines of active players.

• Extra innings—trading cards and stickers, posters, photographs, reproductions of newspaper headlines about baseball, and foods served in containers emblazoned with baseball logos.

You can decide what to buy and where to buy it however you want, but you're better off if you can really see and touch the goods; everything looks great in the ads. To guarantee the quality—even if it means paying a higher price—the best bet is a personal visit to a gift shop sanctioned by Major League Baseball or its affiliates.

To serve the rocketing national demand for baseball items, Major League Baseball plans to open 100 stores across the country by 1993. The first of these, the Padres Clubhouse, opened for business in Escondido, California, in 1989. Featuring the motif of the nearest big league team, the stores will offer collectibles, souvenirs, apparel, and limited-edition memorabilia. Each store will tenaciously emulate a big league stadium setting, with a home plate in the doorway, artificial-turf carpeting, and ballpark audiovisual effects.

W. C. Bradley Company, a Columbus, Georgia, concern that also operates Sports Fantasy stores, will finance and operate Major League Baseball stores. Locations will be chosen to avoid conflicts with such team-operated outlets as those in Cleveland, San Francisco, and Pittsburgh.

Baseball concessionaires also maintain gift shops and souvenir stands inside big league ballparks. These are not to be confused with the fly-by-night vendors you see setting up their wares in ballpark neighborhoods before or after games (especially after dark). Because these quick-buck artists market baseball logos without the required license, most have been forced off the streets by Major League Baseball. Those that are still around persist in selling merchandise that is often cheaper but (almost) invariably inferior to that found in ballparks, authorized baseball stores, and shops that sell products licensed by Major League Baseball Properties.

For further information, write:
Major League Baseball Properties
350 Park Avenue
New York, NY 10022

Hall of Fame Souvenirs

The National Baseball Hall of Fame and Museum, located in the upstate New York hamlet of Cooperstown, has an extensive collection of souvenirs, many of them timed to coincide with such special events as the annual induction ceremonies or milestone anniversaries (such as the Hall of Fame's fiftieth birthday in 1989).

In May and June, when school groups swarm, the Hall of Fame's gift shop does big business in pens, pencils, pennants, key chains, magnets, baseballs, and other lower-price souvenirs for visiting students.

In July and August, the Hall's busiest months, T-shirts and sweatshirts suitable for all ages and sizes of both sexes are bestsellers, according to merchandising director Jeffrey D. Stevens. He tries to offer styles and colors that appeal not only to the fashion-conscious teenager but also to older, more tradition-oriented fans. About 25 percent of the available products reflect current major league baseball wear, while the remaining 75 percent involve baseball nostalgia and the Hall of Fame. Special T-shirts for both the annual induction cer-

emonies and the next day's Hall of Fame exhibition game often sell out, while commemorative induction pins are also extremely popular.

A special inductee bat program, guaranteed only through subscription, provides 500 bats for sale on induction weekend and another 500 for subscribers. Bats for years prior to 1988 were produced in limited-edition quantities of 500.

To mark the fiftieth anniversary of the Hall on June 10, 1989, a limited edition of 2,500 first-day Hall of Fame stamp covers were printed to coincide with the introduction of the Lou Gehrig stamp in Cooperstown. Those cachets were sold only in the Hall of Fame's gift shop. A special fiftieth-anniversary Hall of Fame shirt was also prepared for the occasion. The Hall of Fame gift shop also sells books and videos, stuffed animals, mugs, tankards, wearing apparel, and even Christmas tree ornaments—all with a baseball motif.

A full-color catalog is available from Baseball Gifts, National Baseball Hall of Fame & Museum, P.O. Box 590A, Cooperstown, NY 13326.   —DS

Tomorrow's Antiques

The variety of items offered by mail through hobby-publication display ads is so vast that it practically spans the entire alphabet. Consider the following:

• *Art*—Living Legends, a continuing series of oil portraits of living baseball greats by artist Ron Lewis (a limited edition of 5,000 plus 50 numbered press sheets) is available for $28 per set of four from Capital Cards, 1482 86th St., Brooklyn, NY 11228 (tel. 718-232-6400).

• *Bats*—laser-engraved commemorative wood baseball bats (World Series, All-Star Game, first Wrigley Field night game, etc.) and personalized baseball bats, both Pro Model 125 Series Louisville Sluggers, are available for $32.95 postpaid from Pro Insignia, P.O. Box 255, Cottage Grove, MN 55016 (tel. 800-533-0726).

• *Books*—Topps Baseball Cards books, distributed during ballpark promotions over the last two years, have been updated to include all through 1988 by Price Stern Sloan Publishers, 1900 East Sacramento St., Los Angeles, CA 90021 (tel. 800-421-0891).

• *Caps*—Wool signature caps, containing player signature and team logo on the front and printed player name and number on the back, are offered for $21.95 postpaid by AJD Company, 3301 Castlewood Road, Richmond, VA 23234 (tel. 804-233-9683).

• *Clocks*—Photos of Jose Canseco, Orel Hershiser, Darryl Strawberry, and other stars—or 8″ × 10″ photos submitted by customers—form the centerpiece of wood-framed, battery-operated clocks available for $34.95 ($5 less for those using their own photos) from Spectrum Sports, P.O. Box 291-R, Jericho, NY 11414 (tel. 718-641-7145).

• *Flannels*—Accurate reproductions of vintage jerseys, caps, and jackets, including those from the minor leagues and Negro Leagues, are available from Ebbets Field Flannels, Inc., P.O. Box 23010, Seattle, WA 98102 (tel. 206-329-3487), or Sports Locker, P.O. Box 2307, Rohnert Park, CA 94928 (tel. 707-584-1290).

• *Greeting cards*—A dozen greeting cards with a baseball theme are offered for $11.95 per set, including mailing envelopes (or two for $20.95), from Wishful Thinker, P.O. Box 8006-B, Long Island City, NY 11101 (sample: outfielder leaping over wall to snare potential home run over greeting, "You're the best catch I ever made").

• *Jerseys*—Authentic jerseys, jackets, and caps, plus other items, are available from Sports Corner, 73 Village Drive, Ormond Beach, FL 32074 (tel. 904-673-2823).

• *Models*—Large, full-color model kits (16" × 20" × 3"), good for table-top games or display, are available of Wrigley Field, Tiger Stadium, Fenway Park, and Ebbets Field for $21.95 postpaid from Bauer Diamonds, P.O. Box 11, Burdett, KS 67523.

• *Music*—The National Pastime Orchestra has recorded a CD called *A Century of Baseball in Song* for The Sporting News Collection, in conjunction with CC Entertainment (tel. 612-641-0714).

• *Photos*—8" × 10" photo prints of stars from the '50s and '60s are available for $3 postpaid from Hall of Fame Autographs & Promotions, 61 Pleasant St., Spencer, MA 01562 (tel. 508-885-9213).

• *Posters*—Among numerous firms that offer posters is Sports Poster Impressions (P.O. Box 201, New York, NY 10028, tel. 800-847-4150), which has commissioned artists Terrence Fogarty and Joseph Catalano to create more than two dozen different baseball personalities, past and present, in an 18" × 24" format, unmounted or laminated on a ready-to-hang wood plaque ($9.95 postpaid unmounted or $29.95 postpaid, laminated); a selection of unmounted baseball posters is also available for $4.95 each from Texas Sportcard Company, 2816 Center St., Deer Park, TX 77536 (tel. 713-476-9964).

• *Radio Caps*—Information on AM/FM baseball radio caps is available from EBJ Associates, 117 West Harrison Bldg., Suite 640-E162, Chicago, IL 60605.

• *Signs*—Full-color, embossed tin advertising signs, reproduced from originals promoting Ted's Root Beer (Ted Williams) and Pinch-Hit Chewing Tobacco (Babe Ruth), can be purchased for $15 postpaid from Card Collectors Bull Pen, 55 Urbana St., Cranston, RI 02920.

• *Statues*—The old Hartland statues, produced long before baseball took to licensing its products, have increased in value so much that the price range for those in mint, snow-white condition varies from $100 for the relatively common Eddie Mathews to $700 for the hard-to-find Dick Groat (SportsCards Plus, 14038-T Beach Blvd., Westminster, CA 92683, tel. 714-895-4401).

• *Stamps*—The complete set of 81 different baseball player stamps, issued by the Caribbean island of Grenada in 1988, is available for $16.95 postpaid from Herrick Stamp Company, P.O. Box 219, Lawrence, NY 11559 (tel. 516-569-3959); first-day covers are $29.50 postpaid.

• *Ties*—Cloth neckties with a realistic bat shape and natural-looking wood-grain pattern, plus team logo (all 26 clubs available) are offered for $21 postpaid from Lucky 13, P.O. Box 23636, Richfield, MN 55423.

• *Z Silk Cachets*—Historic Limited Editions (P.O. Box 400, Williston Park, NY 11596) has printed a separate series of sports envelopes commemorating highlights of New York Mets, New York Yankees, and Brooklyn Dodgers history; series on special moments (Rose passes Cobb, Seaver's 300th win, Raines wins All-Star Game, etc.); and a continuing series on special events, with covers postmarked at event site (prices vary).

Of all noncard baseball collectibles, figurines may be the most popular—probably because they are handsome items that can be purchased at relatively inexpensive rates. Sports Impressions Products, available from a network of authorized dealers, include more than two dozen hand-painted figurines and even more commemorative plates. The average price of both the figurines, which stand seven inches high on a wood base, and the gold edition autographed plate, with 10 1/4 inch diameter, is $125 (David Epstein's Sports Collectibles, P.O. Box 4553, Metuchen, NJ 08840, tel. 800-343-1256).

—DS

Don't Touch That Wastebasket!

DAMN! all that stuff your mother (or you) threw away when you were a kid! You'd be rich today! Some things to think about:

Collectibles are man-made things. Best of all might be something made by human hands *and* in limited quantities, like William Arlt's one-of-a-kind handsewn vintage baseball caps, from Negro League teams to pre-1920 barnstormers (Cooperstown Ball Cap Company, Box 1003, Cooperstown, NY 13326, 607-264-8294).

But collectibles can also be mass-distributed stuff any reasonable person would normally pitch out. What about junk mail? You could make a terrific collection of mailers from all the fringe suppliers of baseballiana featured in this book. *Tip:* Look for your images of sports heroes in odd, disposable places—inside bottle caps, on political banners, in underwear ads.

Or save the first issue of any book that might go into new editions. Like *The Whole Baseball Catalogue.* In fact, why don't you write to the publisher *demanding* a new edition? Please . . .

—BC

Fine art postcards make for fine collectibles; this photograph by Robert Houser is described below.

Fine Art by Mail

There's really only a handful of places from which you can order fine art baseball-related prints, posters, and other objects on a retail basis. On the other hand there are dozens of outlets for sports posters; these usually commemorate a particular player or team. The subject matter is dominant and treated in a competent popular style, but usually breaks no new ground in terms of baseball or art. These are available at your local sports centers. The following listing offers a selection of some of the more interesting and unusual multiple objects out there.

Cards

A packet of nine beautifully printed postcards is available from the Contemporary Arts Center in Cincinnati Museum Store. The postcards feature works by contemporary artists who are included in "Di-amonds Are Forever," and present a nice range of baseball/fine art imagery. The collection can be ordered by writing:

Contemporary Arts Center
115 E. 5th St.
Cincinnati, OH 45202
(513) 721-0390

Baseball "Card" Portraits

Sets of sixteen baseball "card" portraits of the Chicago White Sox were produced in 1986 to commemorate the seventy-fifth anniversary of the Chicago White Sox and the seventieth anniversary of the Renaissance Society in Chicago. The wildly interpretative portraits are by some of the most interesting Chicago-based artists of our time, including Gladys Nilsson, Jim Nutt, Ed Pashke, and Hollis Sigler, and come sixteen to the set. A poster compilation of the Chicago White Sox Baseball Card Por-

traits is also available.

The Renaissance Society
5811 South Ellis Ave.
Room 418
Chicago, IL 60637
(312) 962-8670

Also available by mail order is a small but eloquent image of an old-time baseball glove from the late 1920s or early '30s by artist-photographer Robert Houser. The matted, varnished photograph is beautifully printed (skone-toned method) and is suitable for framing. The original photograph was included in "Grand Slam!"—an exhibition mounted at Gallery 53 Artworks in Cooperstown, across from Doubleday Field, in 1989, the year of the Hall of Fame's fiftieth anniversary.

Gallery 53 Artworks
P.O. Box 118
Cooperstown, NY 13326
(607) 547-5655

Posters and Limited-Edition Prints

Artist Scott Mutter has created a mail-order business to handle the distribution of his quirky photo montage *Fans Shed Light*. The image depicts fans, coaches, and umpires doing precisely that (shedding light) at Wrigley Field in this amusing print. Posters are available individually and in larger quantities from:

Scott Mutter
P.O. Box 1316
Park Ridge, IL 60068
(312) 823-1856

A new outfit called The Summer Game is producing one or two excellent limited-edition prints. Their publishing philosophy is that "the feelings and memories inspired by baseball deserve to be expressed vividly through the visual arts." Currently available is *McGraw Watching*

Travis Jackson by Lance Richbourg, whose masterpieces featuring baseball have gained wide recognition. Other limited-edition prints on 100 percent rag, acid-free archival-quality paper are available.

The Summer Game
2433 University Ave.
Madison, WI 53705
(608) 233-7950 or (800) 356-4600

Limited-edition prints commemorating the fiftieth anniversary of the founding of the National Baseball Hall of Fame are available from the Hall of Fame Gift Shop. The print is by Janet Munro, a well-known contemporary folk artist whose style includes bright colors and a charming "primitive" style. The print can be ordered from:

The National Baseball Hall of Fame
Gift Shop
P.O. Box 590
Cooperstown, NY 13326
(607) 547-9988

More artwork related to baseball is also available in Cooperstown. The Walker Gallery/National Pastime not only specializes in baseball memorabilia, but also attempts to present the many aspects of baseball in a wide variety of media. This business offers both reproductions and original works of art including beautifully executed limited-edition etchings by Deborah Geurtze.

The Walker Gallery/National Pastime
81 Main St.
Cooperstown, NY 13326
(607) 547-2524

An outfit which has been dealing in sports art for over a decade has a booming mail-order business based in Manhattan which specializes in limited-edition offset lithographs. The artists—W. Feldman, J.

Lance Richbourg's McGraw Watching Travis Jackson *is available from The Summer Game.*

Golinkin, and A. Jurinko—primarily offer artwork featuring popular stadiums and beloved ballparks such as *Wrigley Field* and *Yankee Stadium Revisited.*

Bill Goff Inc.
P.O. Box 508
Gracie Square Station, NY 10028
(212) 794-747

A poster version of Lance Richbourg's *Campanella/O.K. Harris Gallery* painting is also available.

Graphique de France
46 Waltham St.
Boston, MA 02118
(617) 482-5066

West Coast artist Tina Hoggatt has created a portfolio of eight striking linoleum cuts called *Eight Ball Players from the Negro Leagues.* The limited-edition prints are hand-printed. Available from:

Davidson Gallery
313 Occidental Ave. South
Seattle, WA 98104
(206) 624-7684

T-Shirts

Two especially nice T-shirts featuring contemporary art are available from the Baltimore Museum of Art and Gallery 53 Artworks in Cooperstown. The Baltimore T-shirt reproduces a painting of Willie Mays in the air, making his famous '54 World Series catch, by artist Ron Cohen. The New York State Museum T-shirt, carried by Gallery 53, reproduces a linear Aztec-inspired portrait of ball players by artist Karl Wilson called *Looking for a Curveball in Cuernavaca.* The original artwork for both of these museum shop T-shirts is in the traveling exhibition "Diamonds Are Forever: Artists and Writers on Baseball."

Baltimore Museum of Art
Museum Shop
Art Museum Drive
Baltimore, MD 21218

Gallery 53 Artworks
118 Main St.
Cooperstown, NY 13326
(607) 547-5655

Tale of the Tapes

How's this for a doubleheader to listen to? In the first game, the Dodgers lead into the ninth inning until Bobby Thomson cracks the homer that wins the pennant for the Giants. In the second game Don Larsen pitches the first and only World Series no-hitter. Sound good?

John Miley can hear those games in the basement of his Evansville, Indiana, home any time he wants. Or he can opt for any one of the other more than 500,000 tape-recorded sports events in his collection. Most are highlights he's excerpted, but for important contests like the Larsen no-hitter, he has the complete game.

Miley started capturing football and baseball games on an old wire recorder as a boy in the 1940s, but he didn't save the recordings. It wasn't until nearly thirty years later, after he'd done some radio work himself, that he returned to his hobby. In 1973, he read that a man in New York claimed to have a recording of the entire Thomson home run game. Miley contacted him and soon they were exchanging tapes of sports events. Over the next few years, the tape-exchange network continued to expand. By 1977, when his hobby was detailed in a *Sporting News* article, Miley had nearly 100,000 tapes, including about 300 complete games.

Once word of his collection got out, he began hearing from people all over the country, offering to do tapings in exchange for other tapes. He even has one helper in Germany and another in Panama. Today, Miley has a highlight tape of nearly every major sports event of the last sixty years.

Despite the growth of his tape collection, Miley insists it is not first or even second among his priorities. "For me, family and friends come first, then work [he's an officer in three local corporations], and then my hobby." Nevertheless, he usually puts in four to six hours a day in

Baseball Restaurants

Another good, although undiscovered, source of memorabilia is the baseball restaurant.

Shortly after it opened in 1987, Mattingly's 23, owned by Yankee slugger Don Mattingly and located in his hometown of Evansville, Indiana, found that patron demand for souvenirs mandated the inclusion of a gift shop. That shop, selling T-shirts and a variety of other souvenirs, grew so fast that it soon expanded into the mail order business. Under the direction of Nancy Batsell, a distributor for Sports Poster Impressions, the Mattingly's 23 gift catalog now includes satin jackets, pennants, T-shirts, coffee mugs, sports bags, menus, and other merchandise carrying the red-and-white restaurant logo. It is available for $1 from Sports Order Center, P.O. Box 20228, New York, NY 10028 (tel. 800-847-4150).

Another all-time Yankee favorite, Mickey Mantle, makes frequent appearances at Mickey Mantle's Restaurant and Sports Bar, 42 Central Park South, New York, NY 10019 (tel. 212-688-7777). T-shirts, matchbooks, jackets, and even some of the baseball artwork on the walls are available for sale.

Among other noted restaurants with a baseball flavor are Rusty Staub's Rusty's, on Manhattan's fashionable Upper East Side, and Bobby Valentine's, in Stamford, Connecticut.   —DS

his basement "studio" boiling down long tapes to a few minutes of highlights. Naturally, major events warrant longer versions.

He admits that with more tapes coming in every day, he's so busy "just trying to keep up" that he seldom finds the time to listen to them after the first play-through. He foresees the day when he'll shut down. "Then I'll have time to listen to them at my leisure."

To join his tape network, write to: John D. Miley / P.O. Box 5103 / Evansville, IN 47716-0103.   —BC

The Babe Ruth of Collecting

The possessor of the world's best baseball memorabilia collection is the president of a paper-products business in northern New Jersey. Barry Halper is also a minority owner of the New York Yankees, and those kinds of contacts haven't hurt.

Halper's home is a virtual baseball museum, right down to a doorbell which chimes "Take Me Out to the Ball Game." Rooms set up especially to display baseball memorabilia overflow into the hallway, so hundreds of autographed (usually personally inscribed) photos accent the halls.

There is a nearly complete card collection. Every World Series and All-Star program, including ones from the nineteenth-century. An excellent book collection enhanced by first editions and signed copies. A complete press pin collection. Equipment, sheet music, advertising, jewelry—they're all there, all outstanding collections by themselves.

The collection that really stands out, though, is the uniforms, which are housed in a hidden compartment behind a wall operated by remote control. When a but-ton is pushed, an "Old Gold" advertising piece, featuring Babe Ruth, slides down toward the floor revealing a clothing rack much like what you might find in a dry cleaning store. Another button starts the conveyor belt. Over 800 uniforms, including almost all the great names in baseball history, are there.

The Halper collection has been compared to Cooperstown. But to the baseball memorabilia collector, there's really no comparison.

—LL

CHAPTER 8

Playing Indiana Jones

You don't have to drive to Cooperstown, New York, to spend a day with baseball history—although you certainly should whenever you get the chance. Whether you're a fan planning an outing with the family or a student of the game looking for a place to do research, no matter where in North America you are there's probably a treasure box of baseball history somewhere nearby—local halls of fame, ethnic halls of fame, sports museums, general museums, and even public libraries that feature baseball. And the contents of their collections will surprise and delight you.

For example, the Cleveland Public Library offers one of the largest collections of player biographies—over 2,000 of them. Want more? The Chicago Public Library has the personal papers of early pitching great and later sporting goods magnate Albert G. Spalding, as well as those of the founder of the National League, William Hulbert. The Oregon Sports Halls of Fame has a collection of memorabilia from such homeboys as Dale Murphy, Rick Wise, and Mickey Lolich. San Diego has done the same for Ted Williams, Ohio for Cy Young, and North Carolina is finishing up a hall of fame that will honor the likes of Catfish Hunter, Rick Ferrell, Enos Slaughter, Buck Leonard, and Hoyt Wilhelm. Dizzy Dean has his own museum in Mississippi and Burleigh Grimes one in Wisconsin. And of course there's the Babe Ruth Birthplace (along with the Baltimore Orioles Museum and the Maryland Baseball Hall of Fame) in Baltimore.

On the following pages you'll find some forty halls of fame, museums, and baseball archives along with descriptions of their

Finding Baseball Treasures

A baseball Baedeker of museums, libraries, shrines, and other roadside attractions

baseball collections, and nitty-gritty stuff like where to find them, their hours of operation, and the price of admission.

If your personal travels happen to bring you close enough for a side trip, there are also some twenty roadside attractions listed—sites where baseball history was made or is being made. And if the spirit

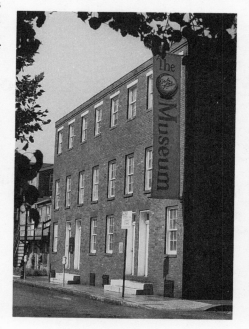

moves you, you'll also find the locations of the grave sites of all the baseball Hall of Famers who have passed on to that great ballpark in the sky. Plus a few odds and ends to keep in mind on your travels.

But if there's any place that's worth a special trip, it's the National Baseball Hall of Fame and Museum at Cooperstown. Even if you've walked the hallowed gallery of inductees before, you'll find some surprises: new exhibits devoted to Women in Baseball, the Negro Leagues, Olympic baseball. And just up Main Street is the National Baseball Library, the guardian of the official record of the game.

So get out the map, crank up the radio and hit the road. There's baseball history out there waiting to be discovered.

Halls of Fame, Museums, and Archives

The following listings (arranged by state) include museums and archives that are either completely devoted to baseball or include sizable baseball material in their sports collections. Besides addresses, phone numbers, hours of operation, and admission, you'll find some idea of what to expect when you get there. Generally it's a good idea to call first before you begin your journey. Like fame itself, some of these Halls of Fame are here today and gone tomorrow.

In addition you might want to contact the Association of Sports Museums and Halls of Fame, 101 W. Sutton Place, Wilmington, DE 19810, (302) 475-7068. The Association, founded in 1971, serves as a forum for directors/curators of sports museums and halls of fame, and can provide

additional information about sports museums and their locations.　　　—LJ

California

UCLA Film and TV Archives
Research Center
1015 N. Cahuenga Blvd.
Hollywood, CA 90038
(213) 206-5388, TV/Film Research Center
(213) 462-4921, Radio

Contact: Andrea Kalas, TV & Films, or Ron Staley, Radio.

Collection: Baseball collection includes taped radio World Series games from 1934 to the present, baseball movies, Sports Dynasty collection, and others. The Center services scholars, authors, media, and just plain fans. Baseball clips from the Hearst News Reel Collection are available for commercial use or for viewing by the general public.

Hours: Mon.–Fri. 9 A.M.–5 P.M.
Admission: Free.

AMATEUR ATHLETIC FOUNDATION
2141 W. Adams Blvd.
Los Angeles, CA 90018
(213) 730-9600

Contact: Wayne Wilson.

Collection: The sports research library has 20,000 volumes including 1,500 videos, several hundred baseball titles, 40,000 historical photographs, 2,000 Olympic publications. The Library performs on-line data-base searches. The microfilm collec-

The Babe Ruth Museum contains exhibits on Baltimore baseball as well as the Bambino.

tion includes the Avery Brundage Collection; the *New York Clipper*, 1853–1924; *The Sporting News*, 1886–1946; *Sporting Life*, 1883–1917; *Spalding Guide*, 1878–1900, *DeWitt's Guide*, 1869–1885; *Beadle's Dime Player*, 1860–1881; *Baseball Tribune*, New York, 1887. *Baseball Magazine* issues from 1909 to 1949 and the *Los Angeles Daily Times* from 1930 to the present are available in hard copy.

Hours: Mon.–Fri. 10 A.M.–5 P.M., Sat. 10 A.M.–3 P.M.

Admission: Free, although a call in advance is recommended.

INTERNATIONAL JEWISH SPORTS HALL OF FAME (U.S. office)
11500 W. Olympic Blvd.
Suite 303
Los Angeles, CA 90064
(213) 276-1014

The museum is located in the Wingate Institute for Physical Education, Student Union Building, 3rd Floor, Tel Aviv—Haifa Road Netanya, Israel.

Contact: Dr. Uriel Simri, excutive director.

Collection: International Jewish athletes, both amateur and professional, in an Israeli setting. Koufax and Greenberg memorabilia dominate the baseball exhibit. The Pillar of Achievement honors Moe Berg. Extensive research facilities are available in the Wingate Institute.

Hours: Contact the museum on arrival for details.

Admission: Free.

NATIONAL LIBRARY OF SPORTS
180 West San Carlos St.
San Jose, CA 95113
(408) 287-0993

Collection: Located in the San Jose Public Library, the research collection features extensive runs of sports periodicals, programs, and baseball books.

Hours: Mon. 6 P.M.–8 P.M., Wed. 5 P.M–8 P.M., Sun. 12 noon–3 P.M.

Admission: Free.

SAN DIEGO HALL OF CHAMPIONS AND SPORTS MUSEUM
1649 El Prado
San Diego, CA 92101
(619) 234-2544

Contact: Frank Kern.

Collection: Hall of Champions features Ted Williams, Bob Skinner, Gavvy Cravath, Deron Johnson, Ray Boone, Bob Elliott, Don Larsen, and Earle Brucker. The San Diego Padres–funded "History of Baseball in San Diego" begins with the 1936 Padres and continues to the present day National League Padres. A computer exhibit lists statistics for every major

league Padre player. Special attractions include a Ted Williams exhibit and a Diamond Vision video of the Thumper, as well as audio tapes of such significant events in baseball history as Bobby Thomson's 1951 home run.

Hours: Mon.–Sat. 10 A.M.–4:30 P.M., Sun. noon–5 P.M.

Admission: $2 adults; $1 seniors; members of military, and students with ID; $.50 for 6–17-year-olds, free under 6.

District of Columbia

LIBRARY OF CONGRESS
101 Independence Ave., S.E.
Washington, DC 20540
(202) 287-5522

Contact: David Kelly, Reference Librarian; Allan Teichroew, Manuscripts Division Reference.

Collection: In the Manuscripts Division, the Arthur Mann and Branch Rickey Pa-

The Sports Resource Center (part of the Amateur Athletic Foundation) offers more than microfilm readers and clip files.

pers relate to the integration of organized baseball. Mann was a sportswriter who did extensive research on Rickey and his considerable influence on baseball. The Seller and McGranery Papers consist of case files, correspondence, court transcripts, and briefs which relate to the Baseball Monopoly Case of 1954–1962 that went to the Supreme Court. The John Kieran Collection consists of correspondence, columns, and notes from the famed *New York Times* baseball writer. In other divisions are baseball-related photographs, newspapers, recordings, and periodicals.

Hours: Mon.–Sat. 9 A.M.–9 P.M.
Admission: Free.

Georgia

GEORGIA SPORTS HALL OF FAME
1455 Tullie Circle, Suite 317
Atlanta, GA 30329
(404) 634-9138
Contact: Sidney Scarborough, executive director.
Collection: Biographical information on 200 inductees, covering baseball as well as all other sports, both amateur and professional.
Hours: Mon., Wed., and Fri. 9 A.M.–3 P.M. But call first.
Admission: Free.

Illinois

CHICAGO HISTORICAL SOCIETY
North Ave. & Clark St.
Chicago, IL 60610
(312) 642-4600
Contact: Archie Motley.
Collection: The 1873–1889 personal papers and ledger books of Al Spalding and William Hulbert are the outstanding features of the research collection at the Society.
Hours: Mon.–Sun. 9:30 A.M.–4:30 P.M.

Admission: $3 adults, free on Mondays.

CHICAGO SPORTS HALL OF FAME
223 W. Ontario
Chicago, IL 60610
(312) 943-3086
Contact: Jack McHugh, executive director; John May, collection coordinator.
Collection: Outdoor Hall of Fame plaques that feature Chicago-area athletes.

NATIONAL ITALIAN-AMERICAN SPORTS HALL OF FAME
2625 Clearbrook Dr.
Arlington Heights, IL 60005
(312) 437-3077
Contact: George Randazzo, president.
Collection: The twelve-year-old Hall of Fame features memorabilia from over 200 inductees, including 19 major league baseball players. The collection includes items such as Ron Santo's Gold Glove, Joe Di-Maggio's jersey, Ernie Lombardi's uniform, and Joe Garagiola's uniform and broadcasting microphone. Electronic exhibits and touch-screen monitors offer sports and motivational messages from Italian athletes. The new building on Clearbrook Drive will open in 1990; contact the Hall of Fame for more information.

NEWBERRY LIBRARY
Special Collections Dept.
60 W. Walton St.
Chicago, IL 60610
(312) 943-9090
Collection: The library contains the J. Francis Driscoll collection of baseball sheet music and songsheets.
Hours: Open to scholars by appointment only.
Admission: Free.

Indiana

INTERNATIONAL BASEBALL ASSOCIATION
Pan American Plaza, Suite 490

201 S. Capitol Ave.
Indianapolis, IN 46225
(317) 237-5757
Contact: David Osinski, exec. director.
Collection: The limited research collection has documents that pertain to international baseball federations and some statistics of international amateur competition. In English and Spanish.
Hours: Mon.–Fri. 8:30 A.M.–4:30 P.M.
Admission: Free.

NOTRE DAME SPORTS AND GAMES RESEARCH MEMORIAL LIBRARY
University of Notre Dame
South Bend, IN 46556
(219) 239-5252
Collection: An extensive archive collection of artifacts, books, and periodicals, featuring the Red Smith Collection and Correspondence.
Hours: Open by appointment only.
Admission: Free.

Maryland

BABE RUTH BIRTHPLACE AND BALTIMORE ORIOLES MUSEUM, MARYLAND
216 Emory St.
Baltimore, MD 21230
(301) 727-1539
Contact: Mike Gibbons or Greg Schwalenberg.
Collection: What else? Babe Ruth memorabilia, plus those of other Maryland baseball players, including Home Run Baker, Jimmie Foxx, Lefty Grove, and Judy Johnson. Also artifacts of Bugle Field, an 1895 mascot's uniform, a photo library, and a research library with the official scorebook of the Orioles, 1954–1970, and Ruth's first game scorebook. There are audiovisual exhibits and a film of Ruth's life narrated by a young Mike Wallace.
Hours: Apr. 1–Oct. 31, Mon.–Sun. 10 A.M.–5 P.M.; Nov. 1–Mar. 31, Mon.–Sun. 10 A.M.–4 P.M.
Admission: $3 adults, $2 seniors, $1.50 children.

Massachusetts

BOSTON PUBLIC LIBRARY
Dartmouth Street at Copley Square
Boston, MA 02117
(617) 536-5400
Collection: In the Print Collection the McGreevey Baseball Collection contains 225 rare photos and paintings from 1870 to 1914. The collection once belonged to the organizer of the Royal Rooters cheering section, 'Nuf Sed McGreevey.
Hours: Mon.–Thurs. 9 A.M.–9 P.M., Fri.–Sat. 9 A.M.–5 P.M., Sun. 2 P.M.–6 P.M.
Admission: Free.

NEW ENGLAND SPORTS MUSEUM
Christian A. Herter Park
1175 Soldiers Field Road
Boston, MA 02134
(617) 997-7111
Contact: Dick Johnson, Curator.
Collection: Highlights New England-area sports, both amateur and professional, through videos, sculptures, and paintings. For those interested in a basketball diversion, a major attraction is a lifesize wood carving of Larry Bird by Armand LaMontagne.
Hours: Wed.–Sat. 10 A.M.–6 P.M., Sunday 12 noon–6 P.M.
Admission: $2 adults, $1 children 13 and under, free to seniors and children under 5 with adult.

Michigan

AFRO-AMERICAN HALL OF FAME
600 Randolph
Detroit, MI 48226
(313) 838-2202
Contact: Wanda Anderson.
Collection: Hall of Fame Gallery honors inductees from all fields including baseball. Research materials from area Negro Leaguers are available. Inductions are held annually in September.
Hours: Mon.–Fri. 8 A.M.–5 P.M.
Admission: Free.

DETROIT PUBLIC LIBRARY
5201 Woodward Ave.
Detroit, MI 48202
(313) 833-1722
Collection: Burton Historical and Ernie Harwell Collections cover the Detroit Tigers and broadcast history.
Hours: Mon.–Sat. 9:30 A.M.–5 P.M., except Wed. 9:30 A.M.–9 P.M.
Admission: Free.

MUSKEGON AREA SPORTS HALL OF FAME
430 W. Clay Ave.
Muskegon, MI 49443
(616) 894-2923
Contact: Dick Hedges, president.
Collection: Located in the Muskegon County Museum, the collection features baseball and all other sports, amateur and professional, plus exhibits on former big league player Frank Secory and manager/coach Jack Tighe.
Hours: Mon.–Sun. 9:30 A.M.–10 P.M.
Admission: Free.

Missouri

ST. LOUIS SPORTS HALL OF FAME
Busch Stadium
St. Louis, MO 63102
(314) 421-6790
Collection: St. Louis-area sports—Olympic, amateur, and professional—are the featured items of interest. Special displays honor August A. Busch, Jr., Bob Gibson, Lou Brock, Stan Musial, Dizzy Dean, and Rogers Hornsby. The Cardinals' World Series trophies are exhibited. A "Jack Buck, Voice of the Cardinals" broadcasters' display is located next to the Hall of Fame Theater.
Hours: Mon.–Sun. 10 A.M.–5 P.M., and open until 11 P.M. on game nights (game ticket required).
Admission: $2 adults, $1.50 children.

THE SPORTING NEWS
1212 N. Lindbergh Blvd.
St. Louis, MO 63132

(314) 993-7727
Contact: Steve Gietschier, archivist.
Collection: The research collection consists, of course, of *The Sporting News,* American and National League day-by-days, *TSN*-published *Official Records, Guides,* and *Registers,* photographs, plus a major and minor league player clippings file.
Hours: Mon.–Fri. 8:30 A.M.–5 P.M. Appointment recommended.
Admission: Free.

New York

THE NATIONAL BASEBALL HALL OF FAME AND MUSEUM
P.O. Box 590
Main St.
Cooperstown, NY 13326
(607) 547-9988
Contact: Bill Guilfoile, public relations.
Collection: Where to start? On the first floor, a life-size wood sculpture of Babe Ruth greets vistors as they enter the museum. The Cooperstown Room, with the IBM interactive video presentation, and the Great Moments Room, with nine-foot blowups, complement the Hall's fabled gallery of inductees. On the second floor, over 1,000 artifacts, photos, and memorabilia present the history of the game from its earliest forerunner in ancient Egypt to today's teams and players, including a display showing the evolution of equipment. Also on the second floor are the Negro Leagues and All-Star Games exhibits. The third floor features Ballpark and World Series Rooms. Babe Ruth, his voice, his locker, his bowling ball, his life and times are arranged to pay homage to baseball's greatest player. The collection of historic baseball cards includes the Honus Wagner T206 tobacco card. Uniforms, baseball music, minor leagues, and youth baseball complete the presentation—for now; expansion seems to be always going on.
Hours: Summer hours (May 1–October 31), Mon.–Sun. 9 A.M.–9 P.M.

Winter hours (November 1–April 30), Mon.–Sun. 9 A.M.–5 P.M.

Admission: $5 adults; $2 juniors (7–15 years); group rates available.

NATIONAL BASEBALL LIBRARY
P.O. Box 590
Cooper Park
Cooperstown, NY 13326
(607) 547-9988

Contact: Tom Heitz, librarian.

Collection: 5 million newspaper documents, 200,000 player data cards, 125,000 photographs, 15,000 baseball books, 2,000 pamphlets, 400 videotapes, 300 motion picture reels, hundreds of old radio broadcast tapes, and sheet music, among other things, have been donated. These materials document the game from 1840. The most notable collections are the papers of Abraham G. Mills, president of the National League 1883–1894; papers of Garry Hermmann, chairman of the National Commission 1903–1921; and the John Tattersall Collection of Boxscores 1876–1966. Every official, Negro Leaguer, umpire, and player has a file. There are also subject and team files as well as photography files. Not to mention complete runs of

Baseball Digest, *Baseball Magazine*, *Sport Magazine*, team publications, media guides, yearbooks, microfilm of *The Sporting News*, *Sporting Life,* and several reels of nineteenth-century major league city newspapers. If you're researching baseball, this is the place to come. Lee Allen, deceased historian of the Baseball Hall of Fame, wrote several of his highly readable books from this library. Baseball's official records, called "Day-by-Days," are held in the Library's underground storage facility.

Hours: Mon.–Fri. 9 A.M.–5 P.M. Appointment recommended.

Admission: Free.

NEW YORK PUBLIC LIBRARY
General Research Divison
5th Ave. and 42nd St.
New York, NY 10018
(212) 340-0849

Contact: Robert Quartell, librarian.

Collection: The Spalding Collection was a personal gift from Albert Spalding's widow in 1921. It consists of 3,000 books and pamphlets, 102 periodicals, over 600 photographs, and 30 original drawings. Spalding incorporates the libraries of Harry

A prime attraction of The Sporting News Archive is its card file of minor-leaguers.

Wright and Henry Chadwick and dates from 1845 to 1914. The Swales Collection was donated by ornithologist Bradshaw H. Swales and represents his lifelong hobby of collecting baseball records. The collection consists of 460 volumes, 37 pamphlets, 26 periodicals, 39 folders, major and minor league rosters, 144 scrapbooks, as well as *Baseball Magazine* 1908–1928, and *Sporting Life* 1883–1917. In 1946 Leopold M. Goulston donated his baseball collection in memory of Leo J. Bondy, vice president and treasurer of the New York Giants, who died in 1944. The collection is mostly pictorial but contains some books and pamphlets which make important contributions to the history of baseball. The 1822 *Les Jeux des Jeunes Garçons* and the 1834 *Book of Sports* both portray bat-and-ball games for juveniles. Both books predate the Abner Doubleday version of baseball's immaculate conception in the fields of Cooperstown in 1839. Swales also donated complete sets of Old Judge and Sweet Caporal nineteenth-century baseball cards.

Hours: Mon.–Sat. 9 A.M.–9 P.M.

Admission: Free.

North Carolina

NORTH CAROLINA HISTORY MUSEUM
109 E. Jones St.
Raleigh, NC 27601
(919) 733-3894

Contact: Jackson Marshall.

Collection: The museum serves for now as the home of the North Carolina Sports Hall of Fame. Exhibits include artifacts and memorabilia from the Hall of Fame inductees. A research collection consists of inductees' photographs and biographical files.

Hours: Tues.–Sat. 9 A.M.–5 P.M., Sun. 1 P.M.–6 P.M. Hours subject to change when new museum building opens in 1992 (see below).

Admission: Free.

This is Mecca for students of America's grand old game—the National Baseball Library in Cooperstown, New York.

sports history. The first project is to erect a bronze heroic-sized statue of Bob Feller in front of Municipal Stadium.

GREATER CLEVELAND SPORTS HALL OF FAME FOUNDATION
Cleveland Convention Center
1220 E. 6th St.
Cleveland, OH
(216) 781-0678
Contact: Robert Buseby, president.
Collection: Plaques of inductees are presented in the hallway of the Cleveland Visitors Bureau and Convention Center.
Hours: Varies, generally same as convention center.
Admission: Free.

OHIO BASEBALL HALL OF FAME
Lucas County Recreation Center
2901 Key St.
Maumee, OH 43537
(419) 893-9481
Contact: Kathleen M. Gardner, curator.
Collection: The collection features Ohio Hall of Famers (particularly Cy Young) as well as documents and memorabilia from the Cincinnati and Cleveland professional baseball teams, 1869 to the present.
Hours: Summer hours (April 1–September 30) Mon.–Fri. 10 A.M.–8 P.M., Sat.–Sun. 12 noon–8 P.M.; winter hours (October 1–March 31) Mon.–Fri. 10 A.M.–5 P.M.
Admission: $1 adults, $.75 seniors, $.50 children under 12.

THE WESTERN RESERVE HISTORICAL SOCIETY
10825 E. Blvd.
Cleveland, OH 44106
(216) 721-5722
Contact: John J. Grabowski, curator.
Collection: The society features a depository of over 1,000 glass negatives of pho-

NORTH CAROLINA SPORTS HALL OF FAME
3316 Julian Drive
Raleigh, NC 27604
(919) 872-9289
Contact: Bob Willis, executive director.
Collection: The museum will be completed and open to the public in 1992. Exhibits will feature collections of memorabilia from North Carolina Baseball Hall of Famers Enos Slaughter, Jim Hunter, Rick Ferrell, Buck Leonard, and Hoyt Wilhelm. Other natives, such as Gaylord Perry, Jim Perry, Roger Craig, Clyde King, Whitey Lockman, John Allen, Smoky Burgess, Tommy Burnes, Jack Coombs, Alvin Crowder, Wes Ferrell, Billy Goodman, John Lewis, Burgess Whitehead, Tom Zachary, and Ernie Shore, have made sizable donations. A library and archive are planned.
Hours: To be announced.
Admission: Free.

Ohio

CLEVELAND PUBLIC LIBRARY
325 Superior Ave.
Cleveland, OH 44114
(216) 623-2860

Contact: Thelma Morris, Social Sciences Department.
Collection: The Cleveland Baseball Collection began life as the Charles W. Mears Collection in 1944. Throughout a career as an advertising executive, Mears collected continuous runs of *The Sporting News*, *Beadle's Dime Player*, *New York Clipper*, *Sporting Life*, *DeWitt's Base Ball Guide*, *Baseball Digest*, and the Chadwick manuals. Mears also wrote and collected player biographies, and they're all here. There are 2,000 volumes and 1,320 items in this collection, all of which are on microfilm. In 1985 a Cleveland baseball fan donated scrapbooks on the 1946–1983 Indians to the library and the name of the Mears Collection was changed to the Cleveland Baseball Collection.
Hours: Mon.–Sat. 9 A.M.–6 P.M., Sun. 1 P.M.–5 P.M.
Admission: Free.

CLEVELAND SPORTS LEGENDS
P.O. Box 21163
Cleveland, OH 44121
(216) 381-5976
Contact: Morris Eckhouse, executive director.
Collection: The organization was established to preserve and promote Cleveland

tos taken by *Cleveland Plain Dealer* photographer Van Oeyen. From 1910 to 1940, Van Oeyen created some of the finest, most detailed portraits of American League players ever made. The Smithsonian Institution put together a traveling exhibit of his photos. Only a couple hundred of the Western Reserve glass negatives have been made into prints. The Society is still seeking a benefactor to complete the printing of their negatives.

Hours: Appointment recommended.
Admission: Free.

Oklahoma

OKLAHOMA AMATEUR SOFTBALL ASSOCIATION HALL OF FAME
2801 N.E. 50th St.
Oklahoma City, OK 73111
(405) 424-5266
Contact: Bill Plummer.
Collection: The outdoor sculpture, "Play at Home" by Leonard McMurry, greets visitors to the museum and the Research Center fills their brains with doctoral dissertations on softball, rulebooks, guides, videotapes, and books. The museum honors the national champions of the American Softball Association and all softballdom. There is also a players Hall of Fame.
Hours: November to February, Mon.–Fri. 9 A.M.–4:30 P.M.; March to October, Sat. 10 A.M.–4 P.M., Sun. 1 P.M.–4 P.M.
Admission: $1 adults, $.50 children.

Oregon

OREGON SPORTS HALLS OF FAME
Portland, OR 97204
Contact: Stan Link, executive director.
Collection: The museum houses memorabilia from 187 inductees, including 19 baseball players. The research collection consists of local newspaper clipping files on all inductees. Special exhibits feature Portland Beavers uniforms, Dale Murphy's Gold Glove, and Rick Wise's bat. Honored ball players of note are Johnny Pesky, Bob-

by Doerr, Rick Wise, Ed Basinski, Pete Ward, Mickey Lolich, Ad Liska, Wes Schulmerich, and Larry Jansen.
Hours: Mon.–Fri. 10 A.M.–3 P.M.
Admission: Free.

Pennsylvania

AFRO-AMERICAN HISTORICAL AND CULTURAL MUSEUM
7th and Arch St.
Philadelphia, PA 19106
(215) 574-0380
Stan Arnold, archivist.
Collection: Museum and Research Archive consists of oral history, tapes, materials on the Hilldales and Philadelphia Stars, photographs of black baseball from 1912 to 1950, and clippings, files of area players. The Lloyd Thompson–William Cash Collection, a recent acquisition, features Hilldale scorebooks, statistics, schedules, and correspondence. A special collection of biographical material from Ed Bolden, manager of the Stars, gives an inside look at the running of the black baseball team.
Hours: Mon.–Fri. 10 A.M.–6 P.M., Sat. 10 A.M.–5 P.M., Sunday 12 noon–6 P.M. Research Archive by appointment only.
Admission: $3.75 adults (admission to the Archive is free).

LITTLE LEAGUE MUSEUM
Rt. 15 South
Williamsport, PA 17701
(717) 326-3607
Contact: Cindy Stearns.
Collection: The museum features highlights from the fifty-year history of the Little League. Special collections are memorabilia of major league players from their Little League days, photos, and 2.5 million Little League team rosters. A hands-on exhibit features batting and pitching cages with video replay.
Hours: Every day except Thanksgiving, New Year's, and Christmas.
Admission: $4 adults, $2 seniors, $1 children 5–13, free under 5, discount for

groups, families, and AAA members.

SPORTS IMMORTALS MUSEUM
807 Liberty Ave.
Pittsburgh, PA 15222
(412) 232-3008
Contact: Joel Platt, director.
Collection: Still on the drawing board at press time, Platt intends to use his own vast personal collection to create an international exhibition of over one million mementos from all sports, especially those of Hall of Famers. Decade-by-decade audiovisual display cases will trace the development of sports in American society. Definitely call first.

South Dakota

PETTIGREW MUSEUM LIBRARY
Siouxland Heritage Museums
131 N. Duluth Ave.
Sioux Falls, SD 57104
(605) 339-7097
Contact: John Rytarik.
Collection: Historical data on the Northern League, one of baseball's grand old minor leagues, which covered the Dakotas, Minnesota, Wisconsin, and part of Canada and lasted from 1902 to 1971.
Hours: Tues.–Fri. 9 A.M.–5 P.M., Sun. 1 P.M.–5 P.M.
Admission: Free, donation requested.

Texas

TEXAS SPORTS MUSEUM AND HALL OF FAME
I-35 and University Parks Drive
Waco, TX 76701
(817) 756-2307
Contact: Charles McCleary, executive director.
Collection: The collection covers Texas high school sports state champions and features a Hall of Fame of outstanding players and coaches.
Hours: Sun.–Fri. 1 P.M.–5 P.M., Sat. 10 A.M.–5 P.M.
Admission: Free.

Wisconsin

BURLEIGH GRIMES MUSEUM
Clear Lake, WI 54005
(715) 263-2042
   Contact: Charles T. Clark.
   Collection: The museum/home houses memorabilia of rascally pitcher Burleigh Grimes, the last legal spitballer.
   Contact the museum for hours and admission information.

Canada

CANADIAN BASEBALL HALL OF FAME AND MUSEUM
P.O. Box 4008 Station A
Ontario Place
Toronto, ONT M5W 2R1 Canada
(416) 597-0014
Bruce Prentice, president.
   Collection: The museum features Canadians in baseball, starting with the premier 1838 game in Beachville, Ontario, and continuing through the original Maple Leafs from Guelph and the 1877 International Association Champion Tecumsehs from London, Ontario. There is also a Frank Chance 1905 autograph model Spalding bat and a Philadelphia Blue Jay pennant (Phillies in 1943). Live batting and pitching cages enable the visitor to stretch his arms and legs, and get a feel of the game.

SASKATCHEWAN SPORTS HALL OF FAME
2205 Victoria Ave.
Regina, SASK S4P 0S4 Canada
(306) 780-9200
   Contact: Margret Sandison, executive director.
   Collection: There are 200-plus inductees representing thirty different sports, including softball champions Laura Malesh, Bonnie Baker, and Arlene Noga. Exhibits include uniforms and equipment.
   Hours: Mon.–Fri. 9 A.M.–5 P.M., Sat.–Sun., noon–4 P.M.
   Admission: Free

SASKATCHEWAN BASEBALL HALL OF FAME
P.O. Box 524
North Battleford, SASK S9A 2Y1
Canada
(306) 445-8485 home
(306) 446-6266 office
   Contact: David Shury, president.
   Collection: This home museum features photographs and an extensive library. The ninety-two inducted players include two teams, the Saskatoon 1980 Canadian Senior Championship team, and the 1895 Moosejaw nine who were winners of the first territorial playoffs. Major league players are Reggie Cleveland, Dave Pagan, and Aldon Wilkie.
   Hours: By appointment only.   —LJ

The Western Reserve Historical Society has some great and seldom seen baseball images.

Roadside Attractions

Some are new, some are crumbling, some are marked only by simple plaques. For others you'll just have to use your imagination, and remember, as Old Blue Eyes crooned, there used to be a ballpark . . . (Arranged alphabetically by state.)

FLORIDA: BASEBALL CITY. The baseball fan who wants a glimpse of the national pastime's future should see Baseball City, the Florida home of the Kansas City Royals, and the prototype modern spring training facility. Located at the intersection of I-4 and US-27, the stadium is an ultramodern facility (it even has its own broadcast tower), located on the grounds of the Boardwalk and Baseball amusement park. Both the Florida State League (Class A) Baseball City Royals and Rookie League Boardwalk Royals use the grounds as home field during the summer baseball season. The broadcast tower enables the Royals scouting staff in Kansas City to watch Florida State League and Rookie League games on in-house television.

ILLINOIS: CHICAGO. What once was Lake Front Park, the home of the 1880s Chicago White Stockings, is now a small downtown park next to the Public Library at the crossroads of Michigan Avenue and Washington Street. Looking toward Randolph Street, one can imagine a 196-foot right-field fence. In 1884 Ned Williamson lifted 27 home runs over the short porch, the all-time mark until Ruth blasted 29 round-trippers in 1919.

Although 1060 W. Addison Street was the address on the driver's license of Elwood P. Blue of Blues Brothers fame, that's also the address of Wrigley Field. You should visit Wrigley before Harry Caray retires. It is an experience to sprawl in the stands, sip beer, keep score on the major leagues' only 25-cent scorecard, and listen to Harry belt out, "Take Me Out to the Ball Game" during the seventh-inning stretch.

At Elm Park, Elm Street, and Greenbriar Lane in Glenview, Illinois, those who remember the All American Girls Professional Baseball League of the 1940s and '50s can once again see women's hardball being played. The players of the American Women's Baseball Association have been battling there since 1988.

A trip to Chicago would not be complete without a visit to Graceland Cemetery, where William Hulbert, the founder and second president of the National League, lies buried beneath one of baseball's most attractive grave markers. You'll know it by the large stone baseball perched on top of a pillar.

IOWA: Outside of Van Meter, just south of Exit 113 on I-235 is the farm, barn, and field where Robert William Feller learned to throw his Hall of Fame fastball. His dad, William Andrew Feller, was a frustrated ball player who transferred his dream to his son. Many have tried, but few tried as hard as Mr. Feller, who even built a ballpark, then called Oak View Park, on his land so his son would have a place to play.

While in Iowa, you might like to see Cap Anson Park in Marshalltown or the city park in Garner, where Billy Sunday, former Chicago White Stocking of the 1880s, held his first tent revival in 1895. Billy, who quit baseball after the season of the Players' Revolt in 1890 in order to join the Moody Bible Institute, went from the cornfield town of Garner to a world-famous career as an evangelist.

MARYLAND: BALTIMORE. In a shabby tenement in the roughest section of town, the greatest baseball player who ever lived came to Earth from Krypton to live and tend bar and play baseball. While in Baltimore, George Herman Ruth, Jr., resided at 216 Emory Street, where he was born, and at St. Mary's Industrial School for Boys, where his parents consigned him at the tender age of seven. The Babe Ruth Museum has brought respectability to a section of town that was already seedy at the time of Ruth's birth, February 6, 1895. Those who wish to participate in an unforgettable celebration should show up for Babe Ruth's annual birthday party.

MISSISSIPPI: JACKSON. Amid the antebellum homes where Southern belles hid sweet potatoes in the dung patches to keep the Yankees from stealing them, one of baseball's all-time characters is honored by his own museum. Next door to Smith-Wills Stadium on Lakeland Drive is the Dizzy Dean Museum. Diz made plans at his death to transfer his trophies, ball, gloves, microphone, and memorabilia to Jackson from Wiggins, Mississippi, where his wife Patricia had turned the Dean home into a museum. It is open from 11 A.M. to 6 P.M. Tuesday to Saturday, and from 1 P.M. to 5 P.M. on Sunday.

Deanophiles also might consider taking a trip to Okema, Oklahoma, where the Great One grew up, pitched his first baseballs, and first "slud" into bases. Okema is in east central Oklahoma on I-40, just west of Henryetta. While you're in town, you can also check out the birthplace of Woody Guthrie.

MISSOURI: KANSAS CITY. On February 13, 1920, at the Paseo YMCA, located at 18th and Paseo, the National Association of Colored Professional Base Ball Clubs was founded. Rube Foster called a meeting of owners of several Midwestern black teams and sportswriters from black newspapers to create a league of black-owned baseball teams based on the same structure as the major and minor leagues. His hope was that it would pave the way for black champion teams to eventually play

A whole museum devoted to Jay Hanna Dean—better known to a nation of admirers as Dizzy—now who'd-a thunk it?

Cristo mountain ranges. Some of the Dodgers' most talented players have passed through this city that is named for a Portuguese war admiral. A side trip that features no baseball but great scenery is up the Rio Grande from Albuquerque to Santa Fe and Taos. (Remember Coronado searching for the Seven Cities of the Cibola League?)

NEW YORK: COOPERSTOWN. Through the Susquehanna valley, up Highway 80 past Oneonta, home of the Class A Yankees, is located the picture-postcard town that is the home of the National Baseball Hall of Fame and Museum. The Mills Commission, a group of baseball historians who were charged in 1905 by Albert Spalding to discover an American origin of baseball, chose Cooperstown as the point of baseball's immaculate conception. A glance down Main Street and you'll feel that if baseball *wasn't* invented here, it should have been.

The village today is still a nineteenth-century town. The Fourth of July is celebrated at Bump's Tavern on the Green of the Farmers' Museum by the reading of the Twelve Toasts by toastmaster Tom Heitz (the chief librarian of the National Baseball Library). The New York State Historical Society contains file folders on each piece of property in town. There are even regular games of townball, an 1800s precursor of baseball.

Other sites of interest, baseball and otherwise, are Lake Otsego, the headwaters of the Susquehanna; Doubleday Field, with the statue Sandlot Kid, home to the semipro Macs; James Fenimore Cooper's grave; the Farmers' Museum, with the Cardiff Giant; the opera house, which regularly produces William Schuman's *Casey at the Bat,* and the Fenimore House, which features one of the finest collections of 1820–1850 American art.

the winner of the white leagues for the true world's championship. The Western Division became the Negro National League. Foster, the father of Negro League Organized Ball, was elected to the Baseball Hall of Fame by the Veterans' Committee in 1981.

NEW MEXICO: ALBUQUERQUE. Albuquerque Sports Stadium is the first and only drive-in ballpark. In 1969, this stadium was built to accommodate 10,610 fans and 102 vehicles. An outfield parking terrace 28 feet above the playing surface was built to permit drive-in baseball. At one dollar per adult, automobiles, vans, motorcycles, pickups, and motor homes pull in to watch Dodger games. A mobile chuck wagon serves as the concession stand. Located at Stadium and University Boulevards, just off I-25, the park offers a panoramic view of the Jerez and Sangre de

NEW YORK CITY. Baseball had its non-Doubleday beginnings on the isle of Manhattan. The Knickerbocker Base Ball Club played in the vicinity of Madison Square Garden in 1842, and moved progressively north until the price of Harlem real estate forced the Knicks to move across the river to Hoboken, N.J., where Elysian Fields became an antebellum baseball mecca. Heinz Foods now occupies the property. A marker on Hudson Street at 11th Street in Hoboken commemorates baseball's earliest days.

The Ansonia Hotel on Broadway and 74th Street in Manhattan was the site of the September 21, 1919, clandestine gathering in Chick Gandil's room that led to the throwing of the 1919 World Series, the end of the National Commission, the establishment of a commissioner of baseball, the disgrace of Charles Comiskey and Ban Johnson, and the banning for life of eight prominent Chicago White Sox players, at least one of whom was a sure-fire Hall of Famer, Joe Jackson.

NORTH CAROLINA: DURHAM. Durham Athletic Field, a half mile off I-85 in downtown Durham, not only is the site of the hit film *Bull Durham,* but it is also where the Durham Bulls' owner Miles Wolff has recreated the heyday of the minor leagues, recapturing the atmosphere of a bygone era and promoting like a latter-day Bill Veeck. Wolff has been so successful, in fact, that the club was planning to build a larger ballpark to accommodate its ever-increasing following. However, the Durham Athletic Field will remain, to be used by the town for other baseball activities.

OKLAHOMA: HARRAH. Can you name the smallest town that has produced two members of the Baseball Hall of Fame? Harrah, with a population of 2,897, is the birthplace of Paul and Lloyd Waner, "Big Poison" and "Little Poison" (.333 and .316 lifetime B.A.) for more than a dozen years with the Pittsburgh Pirates. A marker outside of town boasts of their beginnings.

Stones of the Pioneers

Baseball had its first pilgrimage site by the 1860s, when a reverent trip to the grave marker of Jim Creighton in Brooklyn's Greenwood Cemetery became a necessary ritual for the true believer.

Creighton, a great pitcher and outstanding hitter for Brooklyn's amateur Excelsior Club, was called out by the Great Umpire because he swung too hard at a pitch, a lesson for today's power hitters. He ruptured his bladder and eventually died from internal bleeding on October 18, 1862, at the tender age of twenty-one years, seven months, and two days. (Alas! If he'd have hit to right, he'd be alive today!)

Creighton's Excelsior teammates, mourning their loss, erected a monument to their fallen leader in Greenwood Cemetery. It still stands and is easy to spot: it's high as a Little League pop-up and features crossed bats, a base, a cap, and a scorebook. Nothing ostentatious, of course.

While you're in the neighborhood, you might want to visit the grave of Henry Chadwick, the celebrated Father of Baseball and the first man to chronicle the game, who is also buried in Greenwood.

Chadwick's marker was purchased by the major leagues, whose teams had paid a pension to the ancient scrivener in his declining years. A nice touch was to lay stones at the four corners of the plot, each carved in the shape of a basebag, including the buckled belt to secure it to the underlying post.   —LJ

CANADA: BEACHVILLE, ONTARIO. This Canadian crossroads village happened to be the site of an 1838 recorded baseball game that is celebrated as the first recorded game in Canada and in North America. The record of this game came fifty years after it was played, when a doctor who had participated published a letter in an 1888 edition of the publication *Sporting Life*. In 1988 the Canadian Baseball Hall of Fame erected a marker on the 1838 site, which is in Beachville just off Canadian 401, near Woodstock and London. Those interested in baseball north of the border should visit the Canadian Baseball Hall of Fame at Ontario Place in Toronto.   —LJ

PAIGE ISLAND
DEDICATED IN HONOR OF
SATCHEL PAIGE
"?"   X   1982

Hall of Fame Grave Sites

Name	Burial Site
Alexander, Grover C.	Elwood, St. Paul, NE
Anson, Adrian "Pop"	Oakwoods, Chicago, IL
Averill, Earl	G.A.R., Snohomish, WA
Baker, Frank	Spring Hill, Easton, MD
Bancroft, Dave	Greenwood, Superior, WI
Barrow, Edward	Kensico, Valhalla, NY
Beckley, Jake	Riverside, Hannibal, MO
Bender, Chief	Ardsley Park, Ardsley, PA
Bottomley, Jim	I.O.O.F., Sullivan, MO
Bresnahan, Roger	Calvary, Toledo, OH
Brouthers, Dan	Wappingers Falls, NY
Brown, Mordecai	Roselawn, Terre Haute, IN
Bulkeley, Morgan	Cedar Hill, Hartford, CT
Burkett, Jesse	St. John's, Worcester, MA
Cartwright, Alexander	Nuuanu, Honolulu, HI
Chadwick, Henry	Greenwood, Brooklyn, NY
Chance, Frank	Rosedale, Los Angeles, CA
Charleston, Oscar	Floral Park, Indianapolis, IN
Chesbro, Jack	Howland, Conway, MA
Clarke, Fred	St. Mary's, Winfield, KS
Clarkson, John	Mt. Auburn, Cambridge, MA
Clemente, Roberto	Body never recovered
Cobb, Ty	Village, Royston, GA
Cochrane, Mickey	Cremated, ashes over Lake Michigan
Collins, Eddie	Linwood, Weston, MA
Collins, Jimmy	Holy Cross, Buffalo, NY
Combs, Earle	City, Richmond, KY
Comiskey, Charles	Calvary, Evanston, IL
Connolly, Tommy	St. Patrick's, Natick, MA
Connor, Roger	Old St. Joseph's, Waterbury, CT
Coveleski, Stanley	St. Joseph, South Bend, IN
Crawford, Sam	Inglewood Park, Inglewood, CA
Cronin, Joseph	St. Francis Xavier, Centerville, MA
Cummings, Candy	Aspen Grove, Ware, MA
Cuyler, Kiki	St. Ann's, Harrisville, MI
Dean, Dizzy	Bond, Bond, MS
Delahanty, Ed	Calvary, Cleveland, OH
Dihigo, Martin	Cienfuegos, Cuba
Duffy, Hugh	Old Calvary, Mattapan, MA

Name	Burial Site
Evans, William	Noilwood Mausoleum, Cleveland, OH
Evers, John J.	St. Mary's, Troy, NY
Ewing, Buck	Mt. Washington, Cincinnati, OH
Faber, Red	Acacia Park, Chicago, IL
Flick, Elmer	Crown Hill, Twinsburg, OH
Foster, Rube	Lincoln, Chicago, IL
Foxx, James E.	Flagler Memorial, Miami, FL
Frick, Ford	Christchurch Columbarium, Bronxville, NY
Frisch, Frank	Woodlawn, Bronx, NY
Galvin, James	Calvary, Allegheny, PA
Gehrig, H. Louis	Cremated, Kensico, Valhalla, NY
Gibson, Josh	Allegheny, Pittsburgh, PA
Giles, Warren	Riverside, Moline, IL
Gomez, Vernon	Novata, CA
Goslin, Leon A.	Baptist, Salem, NJ
Greenberg, Henry B.	Hillside, Los Angeles, CA
Griffith, Clark C.	Ft. Lincoln, Suitland, MD
Grimes, Burleigh A.	Clear Lake, Clear Lake, WI
Grove, Robert M.	Memorial, Frostburg, MD
Hafey, Chick	St. Helena, St. Helena, CA
Haines, Jesse J.	Bethel, Phillipsburg, OH
Hamilton, Billy	Eastwood, South Lancaster, MA
Harridge, Will	Memorial Park, Skokie, IL
Harris, Bucky	Pittston, PA
Hartnett, Gabby	All Saints, Des Plaines, IL
Heilmann, Harry	Holy Sepulchre, Southfield, MI
Hooper, Harry	Mt. Calvary, Santa Cruz, CA
Hornsby, Rogers	Hornsby Bend, TX
Hoyt, Waite	Spring Grove, Cincinnati, OH
Hubbard, Cal	Milan, MO
Hubbell, Carl	Meeker, OK
Huggins, Miller	Spring Grove, Cincinnati, OH
Jackson, Travis	Waldo, Waldo, AR
Jennings, Hugh	St. Catherine's, Scranton, PA
Johnson, Ban	Spencer, IN
Johnson, Walter	Union, Rockville, MD
Joss, Adrian	Woodlawn, Toledo, OH
Keefe, Timothy	Mt. Auburn, Cambridge, MA
Keeler, Willie	Calvary, Queens, NY
Kelly, George	St. Dunston's, Millbrae, CA

Name	Burial Site
Kelly, Joe	New Cathedral, Baltimore, MD
Kelly, King	Mt. Hope, Boston, MA
Klein, Chuck	Holy Cross, Indianapolis, IN
Klem, William	Graceland Memorial Park, Miami, FL
Lajoie, Nap	Cedar Hill, Daytona Beach, FL
Landis, K. M.	Cremated, Oakwood, Chicago, IL
Lindstrom, Fred	All Saints, Chicago, IL
Lloyd, John	City, Atlantic City, NJ
Lombardi, Ernie	Mountain View, Oakland, CA
Lyons, Ted	Big Woods, Vinton, LA
Mack, Connie	Holy Sepulchre, Philadelphia, PA
MacPhail, Larry	Elkland Township, Cass City, MI
Manush, Heinie	Memorial, Sarasota, FL
Maranville, Rabbit	St. Michael's, Springfield, MA
Marquard, Rube	Hebrew, Baltimore, MD
Mathewson, Christy	City, Lewisburg, PA
McCarthy, Joseph V.	Mt. Olivet, Tonawanda, NY
McCarthy, Tommie	Old Calvary, Mattapan, MA
McGinnity, Joe	Oak Hill, McAllister, OK
McGraw, John J.	New Cathedral, Baltimore, MD
McKechnie, Bill	Manasota, Sarasota, FL
Medwick, Joe	Saint Lucas, St. Louis, MO
Nichols, Kid	Mt. Moriah, Kansas City, MO
O'Rourke, Jim	St. Michael's, Bridgeport, CT
Ott, Mel	Metairie, New Orleans, LA
Paige, Satchel	Forest Hills, Kansas City, MO
Pennock, Herb	Union Hill, New York, NY
Plank, Ed	Evergreen, Gettysburg, PA
Radbourn, Hoss	Evergreen, Bloomington, IL
Rice, Sam	Cremated
Rickey, Branch	Rush Township, Stockdale, OH
Rixey, Eppa	Greenlawn, Milford, OH
Robinson, Jackie	Cypress Hills, Brooklyn, NY
Robinson, Wilbert	New Cathedral, Baltimore, MD
Roush, Edd	Montgomery, Oakland City, IN
Ruffing, Red	Hillcrest, Bedford Heights, OH
Rusie, Amos	Washelli, Seattle, WA
Ruth, Babe	Gate of Heaven, Hawthorne, NY
Schalk, Ray	Evergreen, Chicago, IL
Simmons, Al	St. Adalbert, Milwaukee, WI
Sisler, George	Cremated, Oak Grove, St. Louis, MO
Spalding, Albert	Cremated, Byron, IL
Speaker, Tris	Fairview, Hubbard, TX
Stengel, Casey	Forest Lawn, Glendale, CA
Thompson, Sam	Elmwood, Detroit, MI
Tinker, Joe	Greenwood, Orlando, FL
Traynor, Pie	Homewood, Pittsburgh, PA
Vance, Dazzy	Stage Stand, Homosassa Springs, FL
Vaughan, Arky	Alturas, CA
Waddell, Rube	Mission Burial Park, San Antonio, TX
Wagner, Honus	Jefferson Memorial, Pittsburgh, PA
Wallace, Bobby	Inglewood Park, Inglewood, CA
Walsh, Ed	Forest Lawn, Pompano Beach, FL
Waner, Lloyd	Rose Hill, Oklahoma City, OK
Waner, Paul	Manasota, Sarasota, FL
Ward, John M.	Rural, Babylon, NY
Weiss, George	Evergreen, New Haven, CT
Welch, Mickey	Calvary, Queens, NY
Wheat, Zack	Forest Hill, Kansas City, MO
Wilson, Hack	Rosehill, Martinsburg, WV
Wright, George	Holyrood, Brookline, MA
Wright, Harry	West Laurel Hill, Bala Cynwyd, PA
Yawkey, Thomas	Cremated, Cambridge, MA
Young, Cy	Methodist Church, Peoli, OH
Youngs, Ross	Mission Burial Park, San Antonio, TX

Nine Great Graves Worth Visiting

1. Jim Creighton's gaudy monument in Brooklyn's Greenwood Cemetery is one of baseball's earliest pilgrimage sites. The grave is now roped off, but you can take photos.

2. The Henry Chadwick monument, also in Brooklyn's Greenwood Cemetery, is a fitting tribute to the man who was known as the "Father of Baseball."

3. National League Founder and President William Hulbert is by a graveside monument in Chicago's Graceland Cemetery. The stone baseball etched with the names of National League teams is impressive. Note also the marker's location between notable industrialists Pinkerton, of detective agency fame, and Pullman, who invented the railroad sleeping car.

4. Ever wonder where Old Orioles go to die? The nucleus of the most famous nineteenth-century baseball team is buried together. New Cathedral Cemetery in Baltimore is the final resting place of Bobby Mathews, Ned Hanlon, Joe Kelly, John McGraw, and Wilbert Robinson.

5. Satchel Paige, who was bigger than life when he played ball, has an appropriately large grave marker. Paige Memorial, on its own grassy mound in Kansas City's Forest Hill Cemetery, is one of the largest structures on the grounds. Zack Wheat is also in the same cemetery.

6. The Ty Cobb mausoleum in Royston, Georgia, is a massive monument, fitting for the greatest hitter and no-nonsense competitor who ever played baseball.

7. In the Comiskey mausoleum, located in Calvary Cemetery in Evanston, Illinois, one can pay homage to three owners of the White Sox—Charles Lewis Comiskey, Dorothy Rigney Comiskey, and Charles A. Comiskey.

8. Louis Sockalexis, one of the earliest American Indian baseball players, is buried in the picturesque cemetery on Indian Island in the Penobscot River, outside of Old Town, Maine.

9. The fact that Babe Ruth lies in the Gate of Heaven Cemetery in Mount Pleasant, New York, shows that God really is a baseball fan and wanted the immortal Babe nearby. The Westchester County cemetery is also the last home of many famous Americans, including James Cagney, Sal Mineo, Fred Allen, Dorothy Kilgallen, and Mayor Jimmy Walker.   —LJ

A Monumental Catch

The next time you're in Washington, D.C., take a moment to stand at the base of the Washington Monument and look up. The monument doesn't commemorate the career of any of the six Washingtons who've played big league baseball (George had a good arm, but he never made it to the majors), but it does have a special place in the history of the game.

No sooner was it dedicated in February 1885, than H. P. Burney, a clerk at Washington's Arlington Hotel, began persuading National League players who stayed there that a ball could be caught from the Monument's peak of 500 feet. He found several players who were willing to at-

tempt the feat, but all of them failed.

Nevertheless Cap Anson of the Chicago White Stockings argued that it could be done and convinced White Stocking catcher William (Pop) Schriver to make the attempt on August 23, 1894. (Take a sec and imagine Don Zimmer asking Damon Berryhill to risk life and limb doing something so harebrained. Ah, the good old days!)

Lee Allen in his book, *The Hot Stove League*, recounts the tale:

"A party which included Frank Bennett, manager of the Arlington [Hotel], Burney, Anson, and such Chicago players as Clark Griffith, Walter (Jiggs) Parrott, Scott Stratton, George Decker, and Bill Hutchinson went out to watch the fun. Their first job was to proceed without the knowledge of the Monument's officials, watchful guardians of the shaft who took a dim view of such stunts.

"Schriver was immediately impressed with the magnitude of his task, and most of the players in his company were skeptical of any success. Griffith was chosen to drop the ball from the north window, about five feet below the peak. He let the first one go, and Schriver stood aside, watching to see if it bore a hole about ten feet in the pavement. Instead, it merely bounced high enough to be a high strike. Schriver then took heart, and when the signal was given for the second ball, he was ready. He staggered around, but managed to trap the ball neatly in his big glove, and was jubilant over his success. But by this time the Monument cop was onto the game and flew into a monumental rage, talking menacingly of arrests. But the players cajoled him into a more amiable mood, and the group departed safely."

Charles (Gabby) Street is often credited as the first man to catch a baseball thrown from the Washington Monument, but he didn't do it until several decades later. By then the big, white obelisk had already become a monument to, among other things, the fact that—especially among baseball players—boys will be boys. —LJ

Seven Must-See Places

1. The Babe Ruth Museum near the waterfront in Baltimore, Maryland, gives the tourist a vivid picture of the less than humble beginnings of baseball's greatest player and number one showman.

2. Lake Front Park at Michigan Avenue and Randolph Street, in downtown Chicago, is located across from the Public Library and above the Grant Park underground parking garage. Use your imagination to visualize the 180-foot fence in left field, and a 196-foot fence to the right field foul pole. The Chicago White Stockings played the 1883 and '84 seasons in the cozy confines of Lake Front Park and hit a nineteenth-century record number of home runs there.

3. Sculptor Douglas Tilden produced the bronze life-sized statue of an unknown nineteenth-century ball player that stands in Golden Gate Park, San Francisco. Seeing the statue is as good a reason as any to visit San Francisco, one of America's most pleasant cities.

4. Pittsburgh's Forbes Field is preserved in pieces. Home plate is encased in glass on the first floor walkway of the University of Pittsburgh library. The left field wall, where Mazeroski's homer sailed over Yogi Berra's glove to win the 1960 World Series, is in the Pittsburgh Pirates' front office at Three Rivers Stadium. A plaque marks the spot where Mazeroski's home run left the old ballpark. The center and right field brick walls still stand, along the base of the flag pole in Forbes Quadrangle. The Honus Wagner statue has been moved to the stadium entrance at Three Rivers.

5. Any baseball fan near Chicago should take the time to visit Comiskey Park and Wrigley Field and to watch games at these two stadiums. One of the glories of watching baseball is to imagine that Walter Johnson is on the mound instead of Shane Rawley. Imagination runs wild in Comiskey where the fans saw Jackson, Weaver, Felsh, Gandil, and Risberg before they went to an Iowa cornfield to play ball.

6. Nickerson Field in Boston, Old Braves Field.

7. The centerfield plaques honoring Babe Ruth, Lou Gehrig, Miller Huggins, and Thurman Munson at Yankee Stadium have long been must-see items for Yankee lovers. They make an equally inspiring sight for Yankee haters, since they symbolize the glory of the Yankees' distant past.
—LJ

Roll Over Jefferson

Former big leaguers have taken their place alongside ex-Presidents as namesakes for the nation's public schools. Okay, there are *more* Lincolns, Madisons, and Jeffersons, and none of the Washingtons honor Claudell, but seven schools have been named in memory of Roberto Clemente, including three in New York City alone. However, there is only one Steve Garvey Junior High.

- Roberto Clemente Elementary School, 250 E. 164th, Bronx, NY.
- Roberto Clemente Public School 73, 557 Pennsylvania Ave., Brooklyn, NY.
- Roberto Clemente Public School 15, 333 E. 4th, New York, NY.
- Roberto Clemente Middle School, 360 Columbus Ave., New Haven, CT.
- Roberto Clemente Middle School, 5th & Luzerne Sts., Philadelphia, PA.
- Roberto Clemente Primary School, 434 Graham Ave., Paterson, NJ.
- Roberto Clemente High School, 1147 N. Western Ave, Chicago, IL.
- Jackie Robinson Intermediate School, 46 McKeever Pl., Brooklyn, NY.
- Jackie Robinson Intermediate School, 1573 Madison Ave., New York, NY.
- Jackie Robinson Middle School, 150 Fournier St., New Haven, CT.
- Steve Garvey Junior High School, 340 N. Harvard, Lindsay, CA.
- Lou Gehrig Intermediate School, 250 E. 156th, Bronx, NY.
- Gil Hodges School, 2515 Avenue L, Brooklyn, NY.
- Walter Johnson High School, 6400 Rock Spring Drive, Bethesda, MD.

Claire Ruth unveils the plaque in center field by which the Babe joined predeceased mates Lou Gehrig and Miller Huggins in Yankee Stadium immortality.

The Man Who Would Make Casey

MIGHTY C[A...]

Both world-renowned sculptor Mark Lundeen and Topeka contractor John F. McGivern II had two things in common. They'd both played football at Nebraska's Kearney State College and they both felt a sense of unfulfilled promise from their sports careers. (Don't we all?)

"Based on my own frustrating experiences, and those of a lot of other athletes, I decided a few years ago to do a bronze statue of a sports figure who symbolized failing in the clutch, but doing it in style," says Lundeen. "The poem 'Casey at the Bat' immediately came to mind."

Fifteen seven-foot Caseys now dot the American baseball landscape. The mustachioed slugger at the Baseball Hall of Fame is a major attraction. Other Caseys guard the lobbies of banks in Kansas City, Missouri, and Topeka, Kansas. Former Royals' relief ace Dan Quisenberry recited "Casey at the Bat" at the Kansas City unveiling. The team of Lundeen, McGivern, and financier James Cole have now cast a fourteen-foot bronze Casey. The asking price is *one million dollars* for a genuinely unique piece of baseball Americana. So, if you've got a bare spot on your lawn . . .   —LJ

Some Notable Baseball Statues

Hank Aaron, Fulton County Stadium, Atlanta

Ty Cobb, Fulton County Stadium, Atlanta

Connie Mack, Veterans Stadium, Philadelphia

Stan Musial, Busch Stadium, St. Louis

Phil Niekro, Fulton County Stadium, Atlanta

19th-Century Player, Golden Gate Park, San Francisco

Babe Ruth, Baseball Hall of Fame, Cooperstown

Sandlot Kid, Doubleday Field, Cooperstown

Honus Wagner, Three Rivers Stadium, Pittsburgh

Ted Williams, Baseball Hall of Fame, Cooperstown

Ten Items We'd Pay to See in a Museum

1. *The Base That Bonehead Merkle Never Touched.* The 1–1 tie it produced had to be replayed to decide the 1908 National League pennant winner.

2. *Dizzy Dean's X-rays.* After the Diz had been skulled in the '34 World Series, they inspired the famous headline "X-Rays of Dean's Head Show Nothing."

3. *Bob Feller's War Years Statistics.* Where are those 20-win seasons he lost during WW II but that everyone always credits him with—in their hearts?

4. *The Continental League Schedules.* Everyone knows Branch Rickey's brainchild helped push the majors (screaming and kicking) into expansion, but could we have some details on this famous, yet ethereal, organization?

5. *How to Bat* by Eddie Gaedel. The 3′7″ midget batted only once before he was ruled ineligible, walking on four pitches.

The world never learned what he might have done over a full career. He could have revolutionized the game.

6. *Billy Martin's Dirt.* Why haven't some of those tons of fresh earth Billy the Kid kicked on umpires' shoes been enshrined somewhere?

7. *Ike's Scouting Report.* Dwight David Eisenhower played a few games in the 1908 Kansas State League before attending West Point. Let's see the scouting report that caused him to drop his baseball career. Bet he couldn't hit a curve.

8. *The Marion Team's Financial Records.* Considering Warren Harding's scandal-ridden administration, we'd love to see the ledgers for when he owned his hometown Marion, Ohio, baseball team in the Ohio State League. Creative bookkeeping, anyone?

9. *Jake Ruppert's Favorite Picture.* The

1925 New York Yankees were joined in spring training by a convivial chap who horned in on most of their after-hours escapades. At the gregarious guy's request, the carousers even posed for a picture. The unknown character turned out to be a private detective hired by Yankees' owner Ruppert to follow the club's partyers. Ruppert hung the picture in his office, but where is it now?

10. *The Other View of the Pickoff Play.* Sure, we've all seen the picture of Boudreau catching Masi off second in the '48 Series, but there must be a photo somewhere that shows what umpire Stewart saw when he called him safe. There *must* be! Stewart couldn't have been that wrong, could he?   —BC

A disciplined hitter, Eddie Gaedel watched four balls go by, then trotted to first.

Adventures in Scholarship

You've probably been asking yourself, "What is the oldest baseball research library in North America?" You probably think it's the National Baseball Library, founded in Cooperstown by the National Association on July 9, 1939. Think again! The Baseball Research Bureau was founded in the summer of 1938 in Toledo, Ohio, by then thirty-year-old Ralph LinWeber. The Bureau, like the National Baseball Library, still functions and remains where it was originally opened.

When Jackie Robinson broke into the major leagues with the Brooklyn Dodgers, many writers and historians claimed that he was the first black man to play at the major league level. LinWeber, knew better because he'd just completed the *Toledo Baseball Guide, 1883–1943*. His fifteen years of research into the 1,340 players listed in the *Toledo Guide* turned up two black brothers, Moses and Welday Walker, who had played for Toledo's American Association team in 1884.

After his Toledo history, Ralph began working on records for the revised *Barnes Official Encyclopedia of Baseball* that had originally been published by Turkin and Thompson in 1951. He received a letter from Ford Frick, then commissioner of baseball, commending him for his work in baseball research.

LinWeber is especially interested in deaf players, and his research goes beyond the introduction of umpire signals as a courtesy for Dummy Hoy and John McGraw's coaching signs at third for Dummy Taylor. (McGraw demanded that his New York Giants learn American Sign Language to communicate with Taylor, and the players began using the silent language to talk to each other on the playing field.) His files of biographical data are worthy of any large archive.

The Bureau Library consists of *Guides* dating back to the 1880s, *Baseball Magazine*, *Baseball Digest*, *The Sporting News*, rare books, photographs, and a card file of everyone who was ever associated with Toledo baseball.

Admission is by appointment only. You can write to Ralph LinWeber at 1916 Cone St., Toledo, OH 43606.

—LJ

Diamonds Are Forever

The first major league show on baseball was organized by New York State Museum in association with the Smithsonian Institution Traveling Exhibition Service. Called "Diamonds Are Forever: Artists and Writers on Baseball," the exhibition opened in Albany in 1987 and will be touring the U.S. and abroad through at least 1992.

Peter Gordon, lead curator for the show (and a former artist), says: "What is it about baseball? Why does the sport hold, as Wilfrid Sheed has written, 'a reserved seat in the American psyche'?

"A group of us at the New York State Museum had wanted to do an exhibition about baseball for quite some time, but with what theme? We tossed ideas back and forth . . . but no one theme caught our imagination.

"Then, in 1985, I came upon an excerpt from John Updike's famous essay, 'Hub Fans Bid Kid Adieu.' The piece deals with Ted Williams, his last game at Boston's Fenway Park, and especially his last time at bat—in which he hit a home run. Growing up in New England at that time, I remembered that game. The event was part of *my* experience, just as it was a part of Updike's, but his insight into that moment transformed it and made my experience and memory of it something wholly new.

"Yet isn't that the job of artists? They take those experiences that many of us have and transform them into something new—into paintings and poems and essays that challenge, delight, or touch us so deeply that we're convinced there's magic

Edward Pfeffer; *Lance Richbourg, 1987.*

Pastime, *by Gerald Garston, 1984; this painting, done in oil on canvas, became the exhibition poster of the traveling show, "Diamonds Are Forever."*

going on out there. That 'transformation' by the artist is not just technique, it's something more. The artist has that rare ability to make the ordinary extraordinary, to help us see and experience with 'new eyes.' I knew that our baseball exhibition had to be about the artist's and writer's personal insight into baseball—not the art or social historian's analytical view of the same.

"Two and a half years, lots of research, and many phone calls later, the exhibition 'Diamonds Are Forever: Artists and Writers on Baseball' opened at the New York State Museum with 116 works of art and 29 excerpts of writing. (The book, published by Chronicle Books, San Francisco, includes more writing.) That was September 1987. The exhibit is now scheduled to tour through July 1992 and maybe even longer.

"Lately there seems to be an explosion of baseball-related culture! And since 'Diamonds Are Forever' was done earlier, we thought we'd take credit for inspiring this outpouring. Well, okay, maybe not. The truth is that baseball has *always* been a subject rich in ideas and imagery for creative artists. I'm not about to try to 'define' what it is about baseball . . .

"Just think of your *own* experience— and you'll know the answers."

For information on where you can see the show, call Peter Gordon, Coordinator of Exhibitions at the New York State Museum at (518) 438-6975, or write to Peter Gordon, Coordinator of Exhibitions, New York State Museum Offices, 60 Commerce Ave., Albany, NY 12206.   —SW

The Fine-Arts-Look-at-Baseball Show

To view a wide range of original works of art depicting the many aspects of baseball, time your trip to Cooperstown to catch the Annual Fine-Arts-Look-at-Baseball exhibition organized by Gallery 53 Artworks, a small nonprofit arts space located on Main Street across from Doubleday Field.

The show takes place each summer, mid-July through late August, and features innovative sculptures, paintings, etchings, drawings, and more by both well-known and emerging artists. Most of the pieces have never before been exhibited, and they usually display a wide range of creative points of view, from the humorous to the startling.

For information contact Gallery 53 Artworks, 118 Main St., Cooperstown, NY 13326 or call (607) 547-5655.

—SW

CHAPTER 9

Baseball's Bulletin Board

The editor of the *Daily Birdcage Liner* won't print your letters. The host of "Let's Call'n Bitch" hangs up on you. The other Concerned and Cranky Citizens hiss you down at meetings. Don't worry! You can still get your Message to Mankind. Start a newsletter.

The world awaits.

Whether you want to save the whales, waste the polluters, preserve motherhood, or monitor and modify Saturday morning cartoons, there are like-minded people out there checking their mailboxes every day to see what you—or someone like you—has to say about their favorite subject. Thanks to the efficiency of the post office and the low cost of word-processing and photocopying, the whole country is networked by an underground mailroad of unpublished fact, unvarnished truth, unsupported theory, and unsolicited opinion on just about any subject you can name.

In this chapter, we'll name Baseball.

Baseball newsletters are at an all-time high in quantity and quality—or, at least, attractiveness. At the moment we write this, we count more than fifty out there. Many won't last—newsletters are the butterflies of the news world—but, by the time you read this, there might be fifty new ones. It's fall-off-a-log easy to start a baseball newsletter, but break-your-back hard to keep it going.

How Easy?

Eeee-zy. On the simplest, lowest level, you merely type up your deductions, meditations, or postulations re the subject baseball and give it a catchy title like *Diamond*

Newsletters and Periodicals

The brotherhood of fan: who's publishing what, and how you can get in the act

Doodles or *Base Knocks*. (There's no law that a newsletter *must* be typed. In fact, we've seen some that were handwritten, but people tend to take you more seriously if they think you can lay aside your Bic and manipulate a Smith-Corona. A computerized word-processor with justified margins is even more impressive, and you can save money on the next step.) Then you run off a few dozen copies on Ye Olde Xerox, and mail it to your friends and anyone else you think might give a tinker's doggone. Be sure you encourage some sort of response, like end with, "Write and tell us what you think about this," or, "Let us know if you agree."

Then go about your life normally while you wait.

Since just about everyone likes to be asked his opinion, you'll get some letters back. Edit out the dull stuff ("How are you? I am fine. I take pen in hand to . . . ") and type the good ones up with your replies. Nice phrases for replies are "Good point, Ralph, but . . . " and "Your letter leads us to an additional observation, George . . . " That way, you get to reiterate or amplify *your* ideas, which was why you started this newsletter in the first place.

Also, it's time to begin expanding your readership. Before you send out *Designated Hearsayer, No. 2*, put in a note asking for names and addresses of others who might be interested in receiving your newsletter.

And again you wait.

Right about now, you (the real *you* reading this article, not the prospective *you* writing a newsletter) are probably wondering who's paying for all this? You are—the *you* writing the newsletter. We'll tell you how much in a minute; right now, we'll simply point out that you're going to have to shell out of your own pocket to get started.

For the first two issues, it's been mostly fun. You've gotten some things off your chest you've wanted to see in print for years. And it's kind of heady typing "Editor" after your name.

Now comes the crunch.

If by the third issue of *Basebawling* you've already said everything you wanted to say when you started, you probably don't have a future in newsletters. But even if you're still percolating with great new ideas, the time spent writing them, printing or copying them, addressing envelopes, and mailing them—all on a regular basis—may be becoming more than you care to afford. And the cash investment's going up too because by now your original fifty mailees have sent you X-number of new names and addresses.

In case you feel like bailing out now, you probably should. It's going to get worse. Send out a little note that begins, "Due to previous commitments, unforeseen circumstances, and unexpected factors, *Base Lines* will no longer . . ."

However, if you're plucky and feel lucky,

just ducky. Start getting issue number three ready.

Quick question: Should you mail new readers of *Infield Flyer* copies of earlier issues?

Quick answer: It increases your time and cost, but it will help secure permanent readers. You'd be surprised how many out there will stay with you because they are building a complete set.

Paying the Price

It's possible you can offset some of the cost of producing your newsletter by selling advertising. But don't count on it. Some guys in Syracuse used their backgrounds in advertising to sell ads during the seven years they produced *Baseball News*. They had each issue paid for by the time it was printed. You, however, probably don't have Mad Ave experience and you're starting with a small readership so you can't charge much to print a plug. Besides, with all the time you're spending getting *Facts and Fungoes* published, do you really want to go around begging businesses for ads?

You'll probably have to rely on subscriptions.

If you don't have your own copier (or a kind-hearted boss), you're going to spend at least $20 to copy a four-page newsletter fifty times. If you're sending 100, it's usually cheaper (about 25 percent) to have them printed. Give the printer camera-ready pages. Do *not* have him typeset unless you own a couple of oil wells.

At a very minimum, you'll pay for postage, which means if you sent out fifty each time, you've spent $25 on stamps. Anyway, counting envelopes, you can probably get out your first two editions of *The Pinch-Pitcher* to about fifty people for a total cost of under $75. But your costs rise as your subscribers increase.

What if you get up to 500 subscribers?

By the fourth or fifth issue of *The Up-Shoot*, you should ask for money. Explain that, as much as you enjoy producing this interesting and informative piece of art,

you can no longer afford to contribute *both* your time and treasure. You're perfectly willing to go on breaking your back for your readers' edification, but they'll have to share the cost. Ask that they contribute X-number of dollars for X-number of future issues.

Here are some tips:

- In figuring your potential, do *not* expect all your present readers to send checks. People are funny that way. Give the non-check-senders a second chance in one more issue and then bid them farewell.
- In deciding how much to ask for, remember you've already invested a few shekels and will still probably operate at a loss for the next several issues.
- Don't bite off more than you can masticate in promising future issues. If you've been mailing monthly or every six weeks, don't suddenly promise to go bi-weekly. On the other hand, be sure to live up to whatever you do pledge.
- Ask for some nice, round number—$5, $10, $12. Just because you think you can do this for $8.63 per reader is no reason to figure *that* close to the bone.
- You'll get better results (although it will cost more) if you include a separate card to fill in name-and-address and a self-addressed envelope. The less your reader has to do to send you a check, the more likely you are to receive one.

What It Costs

As we said, you'll still probably lose money on the next couple of issues, and you're unlikely ever to reach anything like a minimum wage for your time, but there are some ways to increase your return.

Obviously, you can save a jereboam of money by running the pages off on your PC printer and then collating, stapling and folding them yourself, but that can take forever, especially as the number of subscribers goes up. You'd best forget copying machines too and go to commercial printing. It saves all that time slugging dimes

into the machine and cuts you quite a break on the per-unit price.

Here are some very ballpark prices for printing a four-page production, according to our friendly local ink-stained drudge:

No. Copies Each Page	Per Page (8½ × 11)	Per-Unit Cost (four pages)	Total Cost Per Issue
100	$ .08	$ .32	$ 32.00
500	.04	.15	75.00
1000	.03	.12	120.00

You can save a few bucks by having your four-page newsletter printed front-and-back on two sheets, and that'll look better, too. But, unless you're a glutton for punishment, you'll spend a few dollars more having the sheets collated, stapled and folded by the printer. You can get a better price on envelopes buying them by the thou and even have your return address and mailing permit number printed on them for a nominal cost. (You don't *have* to use envelopes, but folded and stapled pages sent through the mail tend to arrive looking like apprentice confetti.)

You don't even want to think about addressing all those envelopes by hand each issue. You can buy stick-on address labels in rolls and run them through your PC printer. Lacking a PC, you can type up sheets of addresses and have label sheets run through a copying machine.

Addressing, stuffing, and licking a thousand envelopes takes time, but you can probably find a teenager in the neighborhood who'll do it for a modest fee. Recruiting your own family as unpaid volunteers month after month can lead to editor-cide.

If you're sending at least 200 or more pieces, you can apply to the post office for a bulk mail permit, which can save you a bundle. As a matter of fact, if you get *close* to 200, buy the permit and send the extras to yourself; you'll still save.

To use a mailing permit from the post office ($50), all 200-plus pieces must be the same size and weight and you'll have to sort them into stacks according to zip codes and then bind them with gum bands. Still, you get the per unit price down to 10–12 cents instead of 25.

All right, what's it going to cost to send out 500, four-page newsletters every month? With tax, about $225 a month, or $2,700 a year. Add in miscellaneous costs like paper, typewriter ribbons, extra stamps, extra printings (i.e., return address envelopes), phone calls, gasoline (unless you walk everywhere) and you're looking at $3,000. You can make expenses if every one of those 500 subscribers sends $6, but you'd better ask for $12 to cover unforeseen difficulties (your PC breaks down!), unresponsive subscribers, bum checks, free samples, complimentary copies, and your costs next year while you wait for your subscribers to re-up.

What It Takes

The more attractive you can make *Personal Innings* without upping the cost, the better. You'll pay extra for special paper or ink, so that may not be the way to go. Two-color productions are out of your price range right now.

Concentrate on layout. If you don't know anything about it, read a book or take a class, but some easy things to start:

- Avoid a "jammed" look by leaving some white space (healthy margins and perhaps a space between paragraphs if your type is small).
- Break up long articles with sub-heads. They encourage and guide readers.
- Use headlines that vary but are bigger than your normal type. You can buy rub-on letters at any art store.
- Use columns rather than spreading your articles clear across the pages. Justified right margins look more professional as long as the space between words isn't too huge.

Illustrations are nice, but photos may not reproduce well. More important, any

photo you'll see in a book, magazine, or newspaper is copyrighted. Forget them. Unless you have your own cache of photos, hunt around for a local amateur artist who'll give you some line drawings just for the pleasure of seeing them printed.

Actually, anything you want to reprint from another source is protected by law. That doesn't mean you can't call up the author/artist/photographer and tell him your hard-luck story ("We're just starting, and we have no budget, and only a few readers . . . "). A lot of nice guys will let you reprint for a by-line. Some won't.

The single, most-necessary, can't-do-without, absolute *must* for a successful newsletter is a dedicated, hard-working, and reasonably competent publisher/ editor—you. Besides working your whatevers off, you must communicate with the reader, grab his attention, and get him involved. Partly you do it directly with your editorials and articles; partly you do it indirectly through reader-written articles you choose to grace your pages.

Readers can provide a cornucopia of information to make your newsletter interesting, but not all of them can spell, punctuate, type, or present their ideas coherently. Be prepared to edit, rewrite, delete, and pad. And, when your pages are still bare, you'll write something provocative yourself to fill the space.

What you're really pushing here isn't just news and not just a letter. It's a hybrid—new information, as filtered through your personality.

And, you're going to ask people to pay for it.   —BC

Newsletters

All newsletters in this section have been reviewed for content. An attempt has been made to present the best side of the information and features of each newsletter. Unless otherwise stated, the size is the standard 8 1/2″ × 11″. Contact the editors of these publications for more information.

The Annual Baseball Letter
1690 Northpoint St.
San Francisco, CA 94123
Bob McGee: Editor.
Subscription: Free to Friends of Bob McGee.
Description: A free-association, open letter to one of Bob McGee's friends appears to be chosen each year as the annual baseball letter. Between flirtations with almost every female and counting Mexicans in the stands at Dodger Stadium, the editor gives off a cheery "God Bless America and Baseball" message. A night spent with former major leaguer Dave Heaverlo fails to reveal any universal truths but does sound enjoyable. To read this newsletter is to eavesdrop into someone else's world.

The Autograph Review
305 Carlton Rd.
Syracuse, NY 13207
(315) 474-3516
Jeffrey W. Morey: Editor/publisher.
Subscription: $9.95 per year for six issues.
Description: This newsletter is for those who want to buy and sell autographs. Sample article: A Rube Waddell human interest story of how a real fan went to San Antonio, looked at local newspapers, and made a pilgrimage to the grave site.

Baseball Briefs
4424 Chesapeake St. NW
Washington, DC 20016
(202) 362-6889
L. Robert Davids: Editor/publisher.
Subscription: The 4-page letter is free while the supply lasts. Send a self-addressed, stamped envelope.
Description: Davids, the founder of the Society for American Baseball Research (SABR), began putting together a zestful year-end baseball report a few months before SABR was established in 1971. After a seven-year hiatus, Davids brought back his *Baseball Briefs* in 1981. The editor describes baseball events of the year and relates them to past events.
Examples: "George Brunet, who finally retired in 1985, played thirty-three years of organized ball and appeared in 992 games, 324 in the majors and 668 in the minors. Sixteen pitchers have appeared in more. Oddly only one Hall of Fame pitcher, Iron Man McGinnity, toed the slab more times than Brunet."
"When Ricky Henderson scored 146 runs in 143 games he became the first player since 1939 to average more than one run per game in a season. [1939 was] the year Jimmie Foxx scored 130 runs in 124 games. Babe Ruth did it six times. The only National Leaguer in this century to accomplish the feat is Chuck Klein."

Baseball for Peace Newsletter
P.O. Box 8282
Woodland, CA 95695
(916) 795-2770
Jay Feldman: Editor.
Subscription: Free to supporters of the Baseball for Peace Movement.
Description: A decidedly left-leaning publication that sponsors annual baseball tours of Nicaragua. If the information is to be believed, the Baseball for Peace Movement has done more to foster better cultural relations with the Ortega government than ten years of official diplomacy.

Stay tuned to the Central American baseball scene with this newsletter.

Baseball Hall of Fame Newsletter
P.O. Box 590
Cooperstown, NY 13326
(607) 547-9988
Bill Guilfoile: Editor.
Subscription: The quarterly publication is included with a $25 membership in the Hall of Fame Club.
Description: This slick, four-page newsletter is full of information about the Hall of Fame, including museum acquisitions, new exhibits, activities at the Hall, and news about Hall of Famers.

Baseball Insight publications:
Baseball Insight Pitcher and Team Report and *Baseball Insight Log Book*
Parrish Publications
P.O. Box 13727
Portland, OR 97213
(503) 244-8975
Phil Erwin: Editor and manager.
Subscription: Published every Wednesday during the baseball season since 1982; 26 issues plus an annual (see below). $119.00. Trial subscription: $35.00 for 6 issues plus the current annual.
Description: This is the racing form of baseball newsletters: pages and pages of raw data chronicling teams' and pitchers' past performances. It advertises itself on the front page as providing "Inside Stats for Serious Fans," but comes clean on the back page when it alludes to "handicapping information, not ordinary newspaper stats," and that it's been "read by writers, touts, handicappers, and wise bettors for seven years." It's not going to tell you whom to bet on or offer a betting system. Readers are encouraged to use the information provided to draw their own conclusions and "determine in advance the winners of every baseball game on the schedule." Sample: For the upcoming week, Erwin provides each team's schedule along with detailed performance statistics: home/away, righty/lefty, day/night, grass/

turf, bullpen ERA, defensive runs, pitchers' start/win ratios, pitchers' ERA home/road, day/night—for his last three starts, versus this week's opponents, last year, and over the last three seasons combined. One issue a page called "Extra Page" innocently lists all ballpark dimensions. Directly below each is a number to call to find out the up-to-the-minute weather report in each big league city. This is a newsletter about betting.

Baseball Insight Pitcher and Team Report. Published annually, in March for the coming season, it provides complete team and starting-pitcher past performance stats. 72 pages. Included with every *Baseball Insight* subscription.

Baseball Insight Log Book. Lists every game played last season by every team, by date, with information on opponent, won-lost, home/away, day/night, starting pitcher, bullpen work . . . 84 pages. $9.95 plus $1 postage and handling.

Baseball Our Way
Our Way Publications
3211 Milwaukee St., #1
Madison, WI 53714
(608) 241-0549
Dale Jellings: Editor.

Subscription: An 8-page newsletter for $9.00 per year (10 issues), published irregularly.

Description: This comes from a baseball fan with a typewriter, access to a copying machine, and some encouraging friends. From the logo drawing of a couple of boys playing ball to the last line, "We do second-rate rags best," it's a vegetable stew of comments about players and their dubious contributions to the success of their teams. Sample: "Charlie Kerfeld of the Astros (1986) wore his George Jetson T-shirt under his uniform every time he pitched well during the first weeks of the season. Some players eat chicken. Some worship space cartoons."

Basewoman
P.O. Box 2292
Glenview, IL 60025
(312) 729-4594
Darlene Ann Mehrer: Editor and publisher.

Subscription: 4-page monthly publication for $20 per year.

Description: This "Newsletter of Women in Baseball" by the founder of a women's hardball team is biased toward women, but is the best coverage of women in baseball's front offices, and of women in professional and amateur baseball.

Men who want to know what the other sex is thinking may want—or need—to subscribe.

Cable/Television Sports
250 E. Hartsdale Ave.
Hartsdale, NY 10530
(914) 472-7060
Dantia Quirk: Editor.

Subcription: $275 per year (52 issues).

Description: If you are in the business of media sports, this newsletter is a must. A media-oriented newsletter, it offers an inside look at the mushrooming business of sports media.

California League Newsletter
P.O. Box 5061
San Mateo, CA 94402
(415) 345-2907
William Weiss: Editor.

Subscription: Free to those involved with baseball.

Contact the editor to see if you qualify to receive it free.

Description: Weekly updates of California League news from the historical perspective of Bill Weiss, a fifty-year veteran of organized ball. Sample: Two Stockton players both hit for the cycle in a June 3, 1988, game, duplicating the feat of two Modesto players in a 1985 contest. Two cycles in the same game has never occurred in the majors or apparently anywhere in the minors except the California League.

The Curtis Report
Curtis Management Group
1000 Waterway Blvd.
Indianapolis, IN 46202
(317) 633-2050
Mark Roesler: President, Curtis Management Group.

Description: The Curtis Licensing Group began as the result of the lawsuit regarding IBM's use of the Charlie Chaplin image (settled out of court). Clients of the Curtis Group include musicians, entertainers, sports figures, and historical figures. The baseball section immediately signed up representatives of the estates of Babe Ruth, Lou Gehrig, Roberto Clemente, Ty Cobb, Mickey Cochrane, Dizzy Dean, Lefty Grove, and others, and became the licensing agent for them. Living baseball clients now include Bob Feller, Whitey Ford, Ralph Kiner, and Eddie Mathews. The 4-page newsletter is a must for promoters, and for those who want to sell images to the public.

Dodgers Dugout
P.O. Box 11
Gothenburg, NE 69138
(308) 537-3335
Tot Holmes: Editor.

Subscription: 10 pages, produced with desktop publishing software, fan newsletter, published irregularly, available for $14.95 (or $19.95 if you also want a copy of the *Dodgers Blue Book*).

Description: Holmes's newsletter is Dodger potpourri—injury report, quotes, feuds, awards, trades, nontrades, obituaries, future Dodgers, ex-Dodgers, road-trip reports, books for sale, testimonials for former Dodgers, draft reports, minor league statistics, Dodger items by guest columnists, and "Tot's Thoughts," a regular feature. This is not a newsletter for the lukewarm Dodger fan. To top off the endeavor, Holmes is also up to date with the doings of other Dodger fanatics and even publishes what could be perceived as competitors' advertisements in his newsletter.

Dodger Blue Book
Annual of *Dodgers Dugout* newsletter
Tot Holmes: Editor.

Description: The 1988 edition offers feature articles on Jackie Robinson, Roy Campanella, Lou Johnson, and the Dodger Fans Hall of Fame. Each edition celebrates anniversaries and gives complete year-by-year statistics for every Dodger. A companion is *Baby Blue*, which provides year-end statistics of the Los Angeles minor league system.

EPSCC Newsletter
Eastern Pennsylvania Sports Collectors Club
P.O. Box 3037
Maple Glen, PA 19002
(215) 643-0910

Subscription: $20 per year for 12 monthly issues.

Description: The hottest memorabilia shows and biggest players in the country congregate in eastern Pennsylvania. One issue bemoans the drying up of pre-1950 memorabilia and foretells the autographed document craze. This letter is on the pulse of a commodities market.

Dan Greenia's Freak Show
819 McLean
Royal Oak, MI 48067
(313) 546-5836
Dan Greenia: Editor.

Subscription: $1.00 per issue.

Description: The 7-page, computer-generated list of interesting statistics amuses and educates the reader. The seer/editor picks four-decade players for the year 2000. In the section on relief pitchers of the 1920s and 1930s, one finds that Firpo Marberry and Johnny Murphy, respectively, are the top twirlers. Other one-time features are the Big Mac team, the Hi Bob squad, and outfielders leading in assists minus errors. A writer could put together several feature articles with the statistical data provided by editor Greenia.

Hardball
P.O. Box 31541
Seattle, WA 98103
Sean Kimball: Editor.

Subscription: This publication of Loose Heads Ink is available to the general public for $20 (10 issues).

Description: The "Newsletter of Northwest Baseball" has regular columnists whose bylines are The Duke and A. J. Looby. While the subtitle suggests that Seattle Mariner baseball is the focal point, happily this is not so. The Winter 1988 issue is devoted to left-handers. In the article "The Left-Handed Road to Success," one discovers that the winning percentage, since 1969, for teams with two lefty starters is .514. For teams with three lefty starters it's .523, and with four it's .552.

The Ivy League Baseball Newsletter
Council of Ivy Group Presidents
70 Washington Rd., Room 22
Princeton, NJ 08540
(609) 452-6426
Jeffery Orleans: Executive Director.

Subscription: Contact the executive director to be put on the mailing list.

Description: Weekly statistics from the Eastern Intercollegiate Baseball League (Ivy League plus Army and Navy) are combined with historical facts that give the readers a perspective of Eastern Collegiate baseball. A recent press release reported that the first televised baseball game took place between Princeton and Columbia on April 8, 1939, at Columbia's Baker Field. Fewer than four hundred television sets were in use at the time.

Japanese Baseball Newsletter
Mizuno Corporation
Osaka Head Office: 29, 6-Chome
Sagisu, Fukushima-ku
Osaka, Japan
Marty Kuehnert: Editor.

Subscription: Write to the Mizuno Corporation explaining why you want to receive this English-language publication.

Description: Typewritten on thin blue

European-size letter paper. The publication leans heavily toward what Americans are doing in the Japanese Baseball Leagues. The information contained in the newsletter has an official tone to it.

MLB Newsletter
Major League Baseball Public Relations
350 Park Ave.
New York, NY 10022
(212) 371-7800
Richard Levin and Jim Small: Editors.

Description: 8 pages, typeset, graphs, charts, Big League quality. Various self explanatory sections are "Stat Facts," "This Date in Baseball History," "Trivial Trivia," "Transactions," "Quotable Quotes," and "This-'n'-That from Around Baseball."

New York Sports
P.O. Box 257
Norwood, NJ 07648
(718) 622-3547
Stephen Hanks: Editor.

Subscription: Bimonthly.

Description: Professional sports news in the New York City metropolitan area.

North American Society for Sport History Newsletter
101 White Building
University Park, PA 16802
(814) 865-2416
Ronald Smith, Editor.

Subscription: Included with $25 membership in the North American Society for Sport History.

Description: The 8-page, magazine-slick newsletter is the program and registration form for the annual convention. Titles of lectures and name of lecturers are given.

Robert Obojski's Big League Newsletter
58 Orchard Farm Rd.
Port Washington, NY 11050
(516) 883-4480
Robert Obojski: Editor.

Subscription: $15 per year or $3 for single issues, published six times annually, 2 to 6 pages, typewritten, photocopied.

Description: Obojski is the author of the book *Bush League,* a comprehensive study of minor league baseball. In the newsletter he confines himself to fan interests: a little bit of history, a few quotes from players and managers he collects at spring training, some gossip about current stars, interviews with old-timers, plus regular reports from the local Getty station, which happens to be frequented by Mets Darryl Strawberry and Doc Gooden; "We're always up to date on what cars the guys are driving."

The Old Judge
P.O. Box 137
Centereach, NY 11720
(516) 981-3286
Lew Lipset: Editor.

Subscription: The 8-page, bimonthly *Newsletter of the Encyclopedia of Baseball Cards and for Baseball and Sports Memorabilia* is available for $8.00 per year.

Description: Lipset, the writer of a definitive three-volume work on the history of baseball cards, acts as the conscience of the hobby by issuing his annual "State of the Hobby" analysis. His comparison of the circulation, subscription, price, and advertising of the baseball card publications is an advertiser's dream (copy research already done). Prices, trends, and nineteenth-century cards are staples.

On the Mark
P.O. Box 133
Washingtonville, NY 10992
(914) 496-5855
Mark Van Overloop: Editor.

Subscription: The 4-page, computer-generated monthly newsletter sells for $27.50.

Description: This newsletter carries in-depth coverage of important most-productive batting seasons and careers in baseball history. The initial issue featured a lead story about questionable Most Valuable Player selections in the 1920s. The editor failed to take into account the voting rules of that period when he lamented that Babe Ruth was not picked in 1926 and 1928,

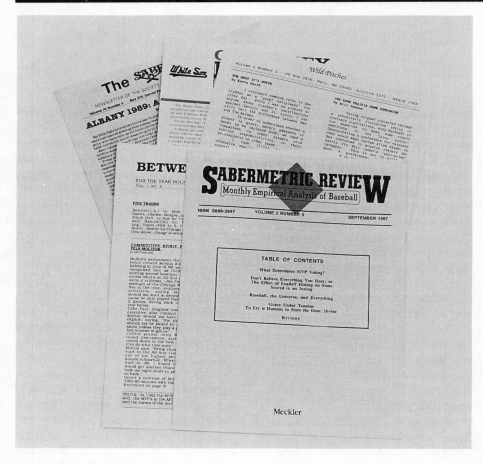

both years when he was ineligible by virtue of being a previous year's winner. Two other articles are old hat (sorry, Harry Walker): Most Dominating Seasons (Lajoie 1901, Cobb 1909, 1911, Hornsby 1921, 1922, and 1924, Musial 1948, etc.) and Top Ten Career Batting Average for the last fifty years. Not the best value in baseball newletters. Look for some improvement.

O.T.R. Cubs Newsletter
1529 E. College St.
Iowa City, IA 52240
(319) 338-2390
Duane Thomas, Editor.

Subscription: Free to friends of the Editor.

Description: A handwritten letter for Cubs fans and discriminating baseball enthusiasts. Interesting compilations propose to answer "Why are games so long today?" Ten straight Wrigley Field games in 1952 (average time, 2:28) and in 1987 (average time, 3:35) are compared. Three proposed reasons: (1) There's more time between innings because of radio and TV

(1952—60 seconds; 1987—140 seconds), adding an extra 22 minutes. (2) There are more throws to first base because of base stealing. (3) There are more pitches by pitchers with poor control, batters taking more pitches, and a changing strike zone. Unique commentary and supporting statistics are presented, including "Wind Effect at Wrigley," "The 3:05 Starting Time Effect," and "Lack of Home Park Advantage in the Cardinals-Cubs Series."

The Overlay
Gamblers' Book Club
P.O. Box 4115
Las Vegas, NV 89127
(800) 634-6243
Howard B. Schwartz: Editor.

Subscription: Free for the asking. Isn't it comforting to know that so many people want to help you lose money?

Description: "Overlay" is a term used mostly around racetracks. It means getting a better price on a winner than figures would indicate. This newsletter, for gamblers only—others would be confused by

the terms—features a baseball-season special review of the year's literature. It's fascinating to learn which baseball books are being used by professional oddsmakers.

Pacific Coast League Potpourri
1244 Brian St.
Placentia, CA 92670
(714) 524-0939/(818) 961-3691
Richard Beverage: Editor.

Subscription: Comes with membership in the Pacific Coast League Historical Society.

Description: 2-page (single-sheet, front and back), typeset, a professional-looking newsletter. In one issue the classified section is sandwiched between a comparison of the 1934 Los Angeles Angels and the 1925 San Francisco Seals and all-time PCL numbers. This is a dandy newsletter for Pacific Coast League aficionados.

Philadelphia Baseball File
1510 Harrison St.
Philadelphia, PA 19124
(215) 533-5776
John Shiffert: Publisher.
Pete DeCoursey: Editor.

Subscription: $20 for five, 12-page issues.

Description: A well-written analysis of baseball, its issues, and the Phillies, in this latest publication out of Philadelphia. "Diamond Gems" is a column of letters to the editor. The March 1989 issue has an interview with Bart Giamatti that was taped during his tenure as National League President.

Pop Flies
P.O. Box 184
Hazelwood, MO 63042
(314) 831-1645
Jimmy Woods: Editor.

Subscription: Included with $10 membership in the St. Louis Browns Fan Club.

Description: 2-page (single-sheet) photocopied newsletter that informs members of informal get-togethers, softball games, Brownie Hall of Fame elections and news, banquets, donations, and books. The club does a little of everything.

Randy's Tiger Fan Club Newsletter
P.O. Box 12748
Research Triangle Park, NC 27709
(919) 832-8871
Randy Aliff: President and Editor.

Subscription: Included with Tiger Fan Club membership.

Description: The newsletter gives intimate details of Detroit Tiger history. One article, "The Search for Power: A Study of Tiger First Basemen Since 1901" details players by nicknames—"Pop," "Sport," "Dutch," "Piano Legs," "Charlie," and "Pinky"—and provides batting averages sprinkled with quotes from Larry Ritter's *Glory of Their Times.* Tiger statistics, "Tiger Tidbits," the "Home Schedule," and "Moments to Remember" keep Bengal fans aware of Detroit happenings.

Right on Schedules
28574 Conejo View Drive
Agoura Hills, CA 91301
(818) 707-2316
Keith Gadbury, Subscriptions.
Jim McConnell: Editor.

Subscription: The typewritten and photocopied 9-page newsletter sells for $12 per year (24 issues).

Description: A newsletter for the schedule-focused collector. A year's subscription to "the hobby's oldest and best sked newsletter" will enable the reader to become almost an expert in this narrowly defined field. The newsletter covers more than baseball, but the editors appear to have a goldmine of baseball advertising memorabilia. One issue featured a checklist of the new Washington Senators' schedule sponsors. Classified ads and auctions are regular features of the newsletter.

Jackie Robinson Foundation Newsletter
80 Eighth Ave.
New York, NY 10011
(212) 675-1511
Shelley Moore: Editor.

Subscription: Free to donors and supporters of the Jackie Robinson Foundation.

Description: 6-page, magazine-slick, typeset, and professionally prepared newsletter follows the business of the foundation, which raises money to fund scholarships for minority students.

The Society for American Baseball Research (SABR) has a dozen or so research committees which produce newsletters that are available to members who participate in the committees' activities. SABR membership costs $30 a year.

SABR Ball Parks Committee Newsletter
244 N. Oxford Drive
San Angelo, TX 76901
(915) 942-0635
Robert F. Bluthardt: Editor.

Description: A wide range of topics is covered in each bimonthly issue. The newsletter acts as a clearing house for ballpark information. Articles on ballpark ceremomies, construction, preservation, destruction, and appreciation from throughout the country are made available.

SABR Biographical Research Newsletter
8220 E. 135th St.
Grandview, MO 64030
(816) 763-1899
Bill Carle: Editor.

Description: This committee gathers birth and death certificates on major league players as well as data on throwing, batting, height, weight, and debut dates. An example is that Chief Bender's birthplace is actually Crow Wing County, Minnesota, though he had claimed he was born in Brainerd.

SABR Bulletin
P.O. Box 470
Garrett Park, MD 20896
(301) 949-7227
Norbert Kraich: Editor.

Description: The Bulletin relays information on the doings of the Society. Vari-

ous sections include "Members in the News," "Bookshelf," and the "Research Exchange," as well as committee and regional reports.

SABR Latin Leagues Newsletter
P.O. Box 2199
West Lafayette, IN 47906
(317) 743-5034
Peter Bjarkman: Editor.

Description: Under the aggressive leadership of Bjarkman, who has located baseball study groups in the Dominican Republic and Puerto Rico, the irregularly published newsletter is steadily growing in size and is on the forefront of Latin baseball statistical and biographical research.

SABR Minor Leagues Newsletter
716 W. 5th St.
Sioux Falls, SD 57104
(605) 338-8006
David Kemp: Editor.

Description: The mouthpiece of the Minor Leagues Committee is currently soliciting names and statistics to publish a third edition of *Minor League Stars.* The committee also works with the staff of the National Association to contribute to their data base of minor league history and statistics.

SABR Negro Leagues Committee Newsletter
1080 Hull
Ypsilanti, MI 48198
(313) 487-5273
Dick Clark, Editor.

Description: Data on Ray Dandridge's career, gathered and presented by members of this committee, helped toward his induction into the Baseball Hall of Fame. The bimonthly newsletter keeps track of former Negro Leaguers and their addresses, reunions, ceremonies, and books. Several on-going projects include gathering of Negro League statistics and collection of oral histories. The committee works with the Baseball Alumni Team (B.A.T.) to provide information on the health and well-being of Negro League veterans.

SABR 19th-Century Committee Newsletter
4518 Wichita Ave.
St. Louis, MO 63110
(314) 535-4215
Robert Tiemann: Editor.

Description: Recently documented data are the features of this bimonthly newsletter. The February issue lists heretofore unpublished winning streaks, twelve games or more, in the 1871–1875 National Association and the 1882–1891 American Association. The committee published the book *19th-Century Stars* and is currently preparing day-by-days and box scores from the Stagno National Association Collection.

SABR Statistical Analysis Newsletter
Division of Business & Economics
Indiana University-Northwest
3400 Broadway
Gary, IN 46408
(219) 980-6646
Donald Coffin: Editor.

Description: In the mid-1970s, this committee consisted of Bill James, Richard Cramer, Pete Palmer, and Everett Cope, who have all done well in carving out careers for themselves on the periphery of baseball. The committee, inactive for the last several years, has started up again under the tutelage of Professor Coffin.

SABR Umpires/Rules Committee Newsletter
950 N. Bonneville Drive
Salt Lake City, UT 84103
(801) 531-9116
Larry Gerlach: Editor.

Description: Gerlach, one of the game's foremost authorities on umpires, is honing his expertise as the chair of this newly formed committee. An initial project is to produce a roster of umpires for all Major League and National Association games.

Seattle Baseball Bulletin
P.O. Box 221
Redmond, WA 98073
(206) 868-8414
Steve Russell: Editor.

Subscription: Contact the editor for the fluctuating price and publication schedule.

Description: The dozen-and-some-page newsletter is not a stylish publication, being typewritten and photocopied. But the information is accurate, concise, and interesting. For example, an analysis of the managerial career of Dick Williams, written in 1986, is remarkably accurate when his performances of '87 and '88 are taken into account.

Shandler Sports Forecaster
P.O. Box 1001
Merrimack, NH 03054
(603) 424-1669
Ron Shandler: Editor.

Subscription: The price of this newsletter is $15 for one year, $27.50 for two years, or $40 for three years. The publication schedule is irregular.

Description: Shandler's *Forecaster* conjures up unlimited possibilities as he uses accepted statistical models and computer simulations to pick the pennant winners and order of finish. It matters little that the forecasts turned out to be only 25 percent correct in 1987—the process of forecasting is the fun of it. Shandler also publishes the *Baseball Forecaster Annual Review,* which includes sabremetric player summaries for all twenty-six teams.

Sports Alert
Phenom Publishing, Inc.
P.O. Box 1651, Grand Central Station
New York, NY 10164-1354
Stephen Hanks: Editor.

Subscription: Free for the asking.

Description: Free newsletters usually have a catch. The purpose of this 4-page Phenom Publication is to sell books and videocassettes.

Sportstar
Sports Museum of New England
1175 Soldiers Field Rd.
Boston, MA 02134
(617) 78-SPORT
Joe Dobrow: Editor.

Subscription: The quarterly publication of the Sports Museum of New England is mailed free to members of the Museum. One may join as an individual member for $25.

Description: The 8-page, glossy newsletter reflects a class operation that is deeply involved in the Boston-area community. A glance through the pages reveals a former players' reunion, news of an internship program, a golf tournament, a fashion show, educational tours, videotape conversion projects, and a week-long series of tributes for Bobby Orr.

Sports Book Digest
Mandell Newsletter Services
1069 Alexander Drive
Rotterdam Junction, NY 12150
(518) 887-2768
Barry Mandell: Editor.

Subscription: 8 pages, 8 issues for $20, published approximately every six weeks.

Description: Reviews tend to be on the soft side, raves you always see on book jackets. Editor Mandell seems to recognize this, however, and is working to fix it. Each issue also includes an interview with the subject or author of one of the books discussed.

Worth mentioning is the "Dusty Bookshelf"—a backlist of older titles that are still in print or have limited copies available. Mandell also offers to help you find the book you want if your local bookstore can't do the job.

Tiger Stripes
P.O. Box 119
Northville, MI 48167
(313) 349-1770
Todd Miller: Editor.

Subscription: Free with membership in the Mayo Smith Society.

Description: This 4-page newsletter advertises memberships, T-shirts, caps, calendars, window decals and lapel pins, and congratulates Sparky on his astute managerial moves. Tiger fact: Anderson, with 17 consecutive winning seasons is closing in on Joe McCarthy's record 21 straight. A regular column entitled "Short Stripes" lets fans know what baby Tigers are doing on the farm.

TransAtlantic Baseball Bulletin
P.O. Box 1013
London, England W2 1DT
(01) 723-9848
Mike Ross and Walt Patterson: Editors.

Subscription: This 12-page, typewritten newsletter for British baseball fans sells for $2.00 per issue.

Description: The newsletter covers the American baseball season for English fans. The enthusiasm must be catching because English leagues are being formed.

Tribal Rhythms
P.O. Box 1574
Medina, OH 44258
Unknown Indian: Editor.

Subscription: $12.00 for six issues, including an end-of-year statistical survey.

Description: Not affiliated with the Cleveland Indians, this 10-page, photocopied marvel of desktop publishing touts itself as the "alternative to the daily sports page." The nameless fan who compiles the newsletter is depicted as drinking beer while watching the Indians on a nine-year-old, fifty-dollar television set. Statistics from Stats, Inc., dominate the publication.

Tribe Talk
Cleveland Indians
Cleveland Stadium
Cleveland, OH 44114
(216) 861-1200

Subscription: Free for the asking.

Description: 4-page glossy, irregularly published newsletter is in the vanguard of baseball-sponsored newsletters. The advantages are that front offices can supply

more and better information about the teams and their activities and that the clubs generally have more money to put into such an enterprise than a mom-and-pop fan effort. But the fan gets left behind as Major League Baseball produces and supports its own fan clubs. One certainly will not see the letter of a malcontent printed in a team-sponsored publication.

Umpire Fact Sheet
P.O. Box 44305
Las Vegas, NV 89116
(702) 435-3151
Unnamed Editor.

Subscription: $12 per year (one issue) is the cost for this umpire dope sheet for baseball betting.

Description: The umpire statistics are extremely detailed: for example, National League Umpire West led all of his colleagues in strikeouts per night game (13.2) while Umpire Engel led in day games with 13.6. The umpire supervisors at the League offices have used such statistics for many years to grade and advise their employees, and they are understandably annoyed that others are gathering the same statistics and using them to bet on games. Using current umpire data for the laying of baseball bets is a questionable proposition,

but the figures are interesting to the average fan.

Unobstructed Views
Tiger Stadium Fan Club
P.O. Box 441426
Detroit, MI 48244-1426
(313) 964-5991
Mike Dutsalt: Editor.

Subscription: The 4-page informational newsletter is included with membership in the Tiger Stadium Fan Club. One may join by requesting to be placed on the mailing list.

Description: A one-issue newsletter aimed at preserving historic Tiger Stadium and preventing a new stadium from being built.

Wild Pitches
P.O. Box 2826
Minneapolis, MN 55402
(612) 574-1275
Jim Rogde: Editor.

Subscription: $10 per year (12 issues). Four pages.

Description: "Not necessarily the official newsletter of the Minnesota Twins." Rogde is a rarity—an editor who lets other columnists express their points of view in his newsletter. In Bill Jensen's article "The

Eden Prairie Dome Companion," the astute observation is made that a reliever's trade value may exceed his value to the team. Jeff Reardon is the case in point; however, the Bruce Sutter, Lee Smith, and Steve Bedrosian examples show that this may be a universal axiom.

The Wishful Thinker
P.O. Box 8006
Long Island City, NY 11101
(718) 784-3201
Marc Tenzer: Editor.

Subscription: Rates are available upon request. A sample copy of the "Newsletter for the Statistical and Fantasy Baseball Player" is available for a self-addressed stamped envelope.

Description: An attempt to relate to Rotisserie League players, the newsletter itself is one of the most attractive and well organized of those that have been reviewed here.

Newsletter editors must be saluted for spending their time and money on a product that has little chance of paying the bills. Several interesting and well-done newsletters have unfortunately succumbed to changing financial scenes or time restraints. Some of my favorites were:

Baseball Trivia Newsletter
   John Grabowski, Editor.
Ballparks Bulletin
   Ray Medeiros, Editor.
Major League Monthly
   Eliot Cohen, Editor.
The Scoreboard News
   Jerry Johnson, Editor.
Sabermetric Review
   Gary Gillete, Editor.
Mac Stats
   Jon McIntyre, Editor.
The Bill James Baseball Abstract Newsletter
   Bill James, Editor.

—LJ

Periodicals

Baseball magazines are more complicated than newsletters in terms of production, technicality, and staff. One man can and usually does produce a newsletter. Magazines require editorial, marketing, and circulation departments.

Major league clubs sometimes toy with the idea of sponsoring their own regular publications. But when a club does not realize immediate success, the project is usually dropped. On the other hand, if the venture is successful, the employee in charge may have to abandon his or her team job to go full-time with the publication. That is what happened with the *Cubs Vine Line.* Few clubs have the foresight to hire a staff specifically to work on publications. Then management cannot comprehend why the public relations assistant fails to produce a publication comparable to *Yankees Magazine* and maintain a paid subscription list of 20,000. Perhaps the time will come when each club realizes it needs its own publications department and professional staff to manage it.

A myriad of annual publications arrive on the newstands in February and March to whet the fans' baseball appetite. They are remarkably similar and reflect the increased attention on memorabilia and trading cards by exhaustive research into the possibilities of rookie candidates. These upbeat magazines reflect the baseball adage "every team is a pennant winner in Spring Training." Maybe that positive position is why fans like baseball so much.

The Majors

Recently an article appeared in *Newsweek* about a sports daily to be published by Frank Deford. The 32–48-page tabloid with color photos would sell for fifty cents a copy and appear six or seven days a week.

Such a newspaper would rely heavily on baseball, since our national pastime lasts nine months a year. Here's a comparison of the leading baseball-oriented publications so the reader can make his/her own judgment as to the viability of each additional sports publication.

The 1989 paid-circulation levels for targeted publications:

Sports Illustrated (SI)	2,975,000
Sport (SP)	932,000
The Sporting News (TSN)	725,000
Inside Sports (IS)	500,000
Baseball Digest (BD)	275,000
Baseball America (BA)	45,000
USA Today (USA)	1,324,000

All of the publications feature photography and advertising. All are available on the newsstands.

The chart shows that a daily sports page with box scores, standings, book reviews, and cartoons would fill a market void. If you really want to be different, run obituaries, which are possibly the most difficult feature to research.

Capsule descriptions of the major sports publications that feature baseball:

Baseball America
P.O. Box 2089
Durham, NC 27702
(800) 845-2726

Published twice a month, *Baseball America* is moving up on *The Sporting News* and has doubled the number of its subscribers in the last eighteen months. It is the best minor league newspaper in the country, taking over that role from *TSN.* The paper has also become the handbook of Rotisserie League participants because of its good coverage of the college and amateur draft, and the rankings of minor league prospects. The paper covers activi-

	SI	SP	TSN	IS	BD	BA	USA
Frequency*	52	12	52	12	12	6	365
Box Scores	no	no	yes	no	no	†	yes
Standings	no	no	yes	no	no	yes	yes
Features	yes	yes	yes	yes	yes	yes	no
Letters	yes	yes	yes	yes	yes	yes	no
Obituaries	yes	no	yes	no	no	no	no
Book Reviews	yes	no	no	no	no	no	no
Cartoons	yes	no	yes	no	no	no	yes
Statistics	no	no	yes	yes	yes	yes	yes

*Number of issues published per year.
†Only box scores of special minor league games.

ties of players, managers, and fans in each minor league and each college conference. It also includes statistics. The publisher, Miles Wolff, is involved in many aspects of our national game, and the advertising in *Baseball America* reflects his varied interests.

Baseball Digest
Century Publishing Company
990 Grove St.
Evanston, IL 60201
(312) 491-6440

The only monthly baseball magazine began in 1942 and has changed little over the years, which is fine with most fans. The bulk of the 7 1/2″ × 5 1/2″ magazine consists of feature articles on players, the history of the game, analysis, and teams. Professional sportswriters contribute the majority of the articles. One outstanding regular feature is "The Fans Speak Out" a section of letters to the editor that fills up to seven pages. Another regular, well-appreciated feature is the "Baseball Leaders of Yesteryear for the Month of June (or July, etc.)." Enjoy reading who was leading the league on August 29, 1929.

Inside Sports
Century Publishing Company
990 Grove Street
Evanston, IL 60201
(312) 491-6440

Published by the same people who produce *Baseball Digest, Inside Sports* is a lighthearted, engaging look at all sports, but one can detect a bias toward baseball. The photos accompanying the articles, as well as the advertisements, consistently feature smiling people. Even Gary Carter is tagging a runner at the plate and smiling. The interviews are especially entertaining.

Sport Magazine
Petersen Publishing Company
8490 Sunset Blvd.
Los Angeles, CA 90069
(213) 854-6870

The salary survey is a special feature of this magazine. Most of the articles are by free-lance writers and topical. It also contains articles on college and professional sports and athletes, plus profiles of stars and articles on trends in sports. A popular and profitable feature is the $1,000 Sport Quiz Challenge. *Sport Magazine* was first published in 1946.

The Sporting News
The Sporting News Publishing Co.
Times Mirror
1212 N. Lindbergh Blvd.
St. Louis, MO 63132
(314) 997-7111

The Sporting News covers professional, collegiate, and amateur sports, primarily baseball, football, basketball, ice hockey, tennis, and golf. Feature articles include

interviews with personalities of the sports. Regular columns are supplemented by statistics and box scores. The paper was first published in 1886. (For additional information, see the *TSN* feature article.)

Sports Illustrated
Time Inc.
1271 Avenue of the Americas
New York, NY 10020
(212) 586-1212
(800) 621-8200

First published in 1954, the bestselling sports weekly has the most outstanding photography this side of the *National Geographic*. Feature articles have recently bordered on investigative reporting. *SI* has the best coverage on special events such as the League Championship Series or World Series. It has special issues with a gigantic annual summary of the year's sports activities (*Mad Magazine* does the same thing, but with a slightly different outcome). The long-time favorite column "Faces in the Crowd" keeps track of outstanding performances by young, nonprofessional athletes. Features are regularly carried on personalities and sports stars, and weekly updates are provided for a variety of sports.

USA Today
Gannett Company, Inc.
P.O. Box 500
Washington, DC 20044
1000 Wilson Blvd.
Arlington, VA 22209
(703) 276-3400

USA Today Sports is a baseball box score and statistics newspaper. The only nationwide daily sports page in America (Frank Deford's publication had not yet debuted at press time for this book) is really one section in a four-part national newspaper. The sports department under baseball editor Hal Bodley displayed a statistical innovativeness that forced many local newspapers to upgrade their baseball statistical coverage. *USA Today* Sports used some new ideas and resurrected a few old ones. The listing of umpires and inning-by-inning accounts of how the runs were scored were features in early issues of the newspaper, but have been discontinued as part of the current efficiency drive by most publications. The cataloging of the "caught stealing" statistic within the box scores was a welcome innovation to veteran box score watchers, as was the daily Top Ten for both leagues. It is obvious that *USA Today* did sports-pages investigation before launching the paper. The newspaper has become the statistical source for many Rotisserie Leagues.

The Minors

Athletic Journal
1719 Howard St.
Evanston, IL 60202
(312) 328-8545
Jay Becker: Editor.

Description: The articles in this monthly journal contain technical information for high school coaches, athletics directors, and trainers for both men's and women's sports.

Baseball Magazine
24, Blvd. Clemenceau
66000 Perpignan
France
Yvon-Marie Bost: Director.

Description: This French baseball publication is produced by Culture et Sport D'Amerique, and is about youth and amateur baseball in France, with regional reporting and photographs. Baseball has arrived in Europe, and its popularity grows steadily.

Baseball Research Journal
Society for American Baseball Research
P.O. Box 470
Garrett Park, MD 20896
(301) 949-7227
Jim Kaplan: Editor.
(413) 586-3394

Subscription: Included with the $30 membership in the Society for American Baseball Research. Single issues are $7.00.

Description: Devoted entirely to baseball research, this annual collection, first edited by SABR founder L. Robert Davids, was a breakthrough publication. Outstanding articles in past issues include "In Search of Bull Durham," "Joe Garagiola: Was He as Bad as He Claims?" "Integration of Baseball After WWII," "Playing Background of Managers," and "The Evangeline League Scandal of 1946." An index published by the Society in 1981 and updated in 1987 increases the journal's usefulness.

Baseball Quarterly Reviews
HOK Enterprises
P.O. Box 9343
Schenectady, NY 12309
(518) 399-7890
Herman Krabbenhoft: Editor and Publisher.

Subscriptions: $15.00 per year; single issues $5.00.

Description: Self-published books and magazines can succeed. Author-publisher Krabbenhoft consistently probes the depths of baseball research: last pitches in the World Series, career statistical leaders year by year, 20 game losers, Warren Spahn versus the Dodgers, leadoff hitters, career doubles hitters. These topics, though hardly original, are still great reading and vastly enjoyable to the serious baseball student.

Chicago Baseball Report
P.O. Box 46074
Chicago, IL 60646
(312) 676-3322
John Dewan: Editor.

Subscription: $19.95 for six issues, $3.75 for a single copy, $4.95 for the end-of-season report.

Description: This six-month publication runs April through August, with an end-of-season report in September and is published in both White Sox and Cubs editions. Dewan and his group of statistics gatherers and analysts provide current, season-to-date statistics and analysis of

team and individual performance. For the less numerically inclined, there is a narrative detailed analysis and a glossary of stat terms, as well as guest commentary. The end-of-season report features in-depth analyses of all players, Cubs or Chisox. An intelligent fan's publication, not frivolous but with a sense of humor.

Chicago Cubs Magazine Scorecard
1060 W. Addison St.
Chicago, IL 60613
(312) 281-5050
Ned Colletti: Managing Editor.
Ed McGregor: Editor.

Description: Wrigley fans have a choice between the single-fold, 25-cent scorecard or the Cadillac model—this magazine scorecard. The magazine version not only gives the standard scorekeeping information but features in-depth articles on such subjects as the history of Chicago ballparks or lifespan of Cubs' general managers.

Chicago Cubs Vine Line
P.O. Box 1159
Skokie, IL 60076
Ned Colletti: Managing Editor.
Ed McGregor: Editor.

Subscription: $17.95 per year (12 issues), single issues $2.50.

Description: The tabloid-size, team-oriented *Vine Line* is a modern success story. Starting with a 75,000-name Diehard Cubs Fans list and backed by the Cubs, the *Vine Line* exceeded 20,000 subscriptions by the end of its second year. It is well written with a blend of nostalgia, memorabilia, player profiles, crossword puzzles, and regular columnists. What ever happened to Jim Brosnan? He writes for the *Vine Line.*

City Sports Magazine
P.O. Box 3693
San Francisco, CA 94119
(415) 788-2611
Jacob Steinman: Editor.

Description: Articles and information
(Cont. p. 164)

The Sporting News

St. Louis was baseball-mad in 1886. The team of honor was the Browns, and the men of the moment were first baseman-manager Charles Comiskey, team owner Chris von der Ahe, and outfielder Curt Welch, whose steal of home in the tenth inning of the final "World Series" game with the Chicago White Stockings had made the Browns champions of the world the previous fall. The paper that would eventually become the "Bible of Baseball," *The Sporting News*, published its first issue on March 17, 1886. It was a five-cent weekly under the visionary leadership of Alfred H. Spink. The new publisher was able to capitalize on the baseball fervor of the St. Louisans, who were still celebrating the winner-take-all World Series victory over the famed White Stockings. Al Spalding, owner of the Chicago team, was so upset with the Browns' victory that he left town hurriedly, forgetting to make travel arrangements for his defeated National League champs.

Fortunately *The Sporting News* was more farsighted than Spalding, as publisher Spink had an eye on his younger brother, Charles C. Spink, who was homesteading in the Dakotas. When Alfred offered Charles a job for fifty dollars per week, Charles abandoned his farming dreams, moved to St. Louis, and stayed around long enough to put his special imprint on his sibling's publication.

TSN broke the Players League story before the 1890 season. From that scoop the paper gained the credibility and subscribers to challenge and surpass the slightly older *Sporting Life*. C. C. Spink made a frontal attack on *Sporting Life* editor F. C. Richter in a *TSN* piece titled "Who's F. C. Richter?" during the paper's early years.

TSN grew during the 1890s and into the twentieth century, while watching the Browns become the Cardinals, the White Stockings become the Cubs, and the ancient and honorable Browns' and White Stockings' names resurface in a brand-new American League.

C. C. Spink died unexpectedly in 1914. His twenty-six-year-old son, J. G. Taylor Spink, took on the reins of editorship and carried the paper to new baseball heights. Taylor, who scored his first World Series game in 1910, turned away from his father's varied sports coverage and devoted the weekly totally to baseball. By 1925 *The Sporting News* was carrying the weekly standings and box scores of eleven minor leagues. The number would eventually grow to twelve.

In the early 1940s, the Bible of Baseball and Spink became embroiled in a serious feud with Commissioner Judge Kenesaw Mountain Landis about who was "Mr. Baseball." Landis decreed himself the title and declared that only the commissioner's office could carry the title "Official" on its publications, thereby stripping the word from the *TSN Baseball Guide*. Landis died in office after having produced two *Official Baseball Guides* during the Second World War, and the "Official" conflict lay dormant for many years.

Veteran *TSN* readers shuddered when nonbaseball news began to appear during World War II. Then in 1946 "The Quarterback," a pull-out section, began publication. "The Quarterback" became "The All-Sports News" after the football season and was issued with the weekly until spring training began each year. In the 1960s other sports began to appear as cover stories. When *TSN* stopped using free-lance writers, it indirectly led to the founding of the Society for American Baseball Research, whose publications carry the work of amateur and free-lance baseball writers.

With the sale of *The Sporting News* to Times Mirror in 1977, the first family of baseball publications went out of business. Along with C. C. Johnson Spink, who had succeeded his father, J. G. Taylor Spink, went much of the personality and insight of the paper. The new management has allowed some of its best writers to slip away. Much of what is left is formula writing, or compilations of excerpts from writers' daily columns, so that the "news" has already been published elsewhere. When Times Mirror announced that *The Sporting News* was considering dropping box scores, baseball fans raised an outcry. *Baseball America* quickly asserted it would pick up major league box scores, but the anticipated battle never took place. *TSN* wisely continued printing the week's boxes.

Although baseball devotees have seen the baseball portion of *The Sporting News* slowly diminish, it is still the most widely read baseball newspaper. —LJ

Vol. I, No. 1—the 1886 debut issue.

for active sports enthusiasts in California.

Giants Magazine
Retail Sales Department
Candlestick Park
San Francisco, CA 94124
(415) 468-3700
Laurence J. Hyman: Publisher and Creative Director.
Duffy Jennings: Editor.

Subscription: $12.00/year (4 issues), single issues $4.00.

Description: Hyman produces imaginative media guides and yearbooks for the Giants. It appears that in the last five years the San Francisco Giants finally got the word that there were Giants before 1958. In one issue the Polo Grounds and George "Highpockets" Kelly are featured. Unusually varied for a team-sponsored publication, one issue contains articles on the physics of a hit, baseball music, sports medicine, great Giants pitchers, rotisserie baseball, an interview with Tito Fuentes, a Chris Berman guest column, and fiction by W. P. Kinsella.

IBA World Baseball
International Baseball Association
Capital Center/251 N. Ilinois St., #975
Indianapolis, IN 46204
(317) 237-5757
David Osinski: Executive Director.

Subscription: $10.00/year (4 issues).

Description: Published in Spanish and English, this slick, 24-page magazine, the official publication of the association, covers international baseball. Cover stories such as "Can USA Dethrone Cuban Pan Am Baseball?" give the reader a sampling of baseball news from around the world, a look at world baseball stars, and tournament schedules.

Indians Game Face Magazine
Cleveland Indians
Cleveland Stadium
Cleveland, OH 44114
(216) 861-1200

Valerie Arcuri: Associate Editor.

Description: Game Face is the scorecard sold at the ballpark. Besides the usual player information, it has articles on the baseball draft, strategy, road trips, and even a continuing baseball fiction story.

Iowa Sports Desk
P.O. Box 1303
Iowa City, IA 52244
(319) 337-9321
James Rice: Editor.

Description: In-depth articles about University of Iowa and national sports.

Journal of Sport History
Northeastern Illinois University/
History Department
5500 St. Louis Ave.
Chicago, IL 60625
(312) 794-2836
Steven Riess: Editor.

Subscription: Included with $25 membership in the North American Society for Sport History. Single issues are $7.50 apiece.

Description: The most scholarly journal in sports research. Articles are always footnoted and carry ponderous titles such as "The Study of the Evolution of Sports in Nineteenth-Century Montreal." The research value of the journal is worthy of its price.

The Minneapolis Review of Baseball
1501 4th St.
Minneapolis, MN 55454
(612) 399-3332
Steve Lehman: Editor-in-Chief/Copublisher.

Subscriptions: published quarterly, $10 per year.

Description: "A Journal of Writing on Baseball" combines scholarly endeavors ("Baseball and the Law") with gonzo journalism ("Judy Aronson's Chicago Fan Diary"). Graphic illustrations by Andy Nelson set the journal a step above the others. While the writing can be uneven at times, this is literature for and by people who are baseball fans as well as writers.

The National Pastime
Society for American Baseball Research
P.O. Box 470
Garrett Park, MD 20896
(301) 949-7227
Bob Tiemann: Editor, (314) 535-4215.

Subscription: is included with $30 membership in SABR. Single issues sell for $8.00 and special pictorial issues are $10.00 each. Published irregularly.

Description: "A Review of Baseball History" offers the reader historical and analytical studies of the game of baseball, written in layman's prose. The premier issue, edited by John Thorn, featured articles by Harold Seymour, David Voigt, Pete Palmer, Lawrence Ritter, G. H. Fleming, Bob Broeg, and others. A sampling of article titles reads, "All the Record Books are Wrong," "Nate Colbert's Unknown RBI Record," "Lee Allen," "Out at Home," "Do Clutch Pitchers Exist?" and "The National Baseball Library."

Articles from *The National Pastime* are

included in the revised *Index of SABR Publications*.

The Oakland Athletics Magazine
Oakland Athletics Baseball Company
Oakland-Alameda County Coliseum
Oakland, CA 94621
(415) 638-4900
A. R. Worthington: Publisher and Editor.
Single copy, $2.50.

Description: The Bay Area is the center of extreme competition among baseball publications, and the fan is the winner. This slick, fat (140 pages plus) magazine has club, stadium, player, and ticket information, plus plenty of topical articles.

SABR Review of Books
Society for American Baseball Research
P.O. Box 470
Garrett Park, MD 20896
(301) 949-7227
Paul Adomites: Editor, (412) 331-2206.

Subscription: is included with $30 membership in the Society for American Baseball Research. Single issues sell for $7.00 each. Published annually since 1986.

Description: "A Forum of Baseball Literary Opinion" fills a need for objective criticism of baseball books. Most baseball books never make the review section in any but the author's hometown newspaper. The *SRB* analyzes and often offers opinions on the quality of the research that went into the book. The reviews, since they are not written by professional reviewers, tend to be airy, descriptive, and fan-oriented.

Spitball Magazine
6224 Collegeview Place
Cincinnati, OH 45224
(513) 541-4296
Mike Shannon: Publisher, Editor, and Cofounder.

Subscription: $12.00 a year for 4 issues.

Description: Baseball's premier literary magazine is ten years old. It is one of the few publications that features baseball poetry, cartoons, and book reviews. The magazine gives the Casey Award for the outstanding baseball book published in the previous year. Past winners include Roger Kahn, Bill James, and John Holway. Even though the magazine's specialty is poetry, W. P. Kinsella, Roger Kahn, and Jim Brosnan are some of the writers who contribute fiction. The Jim Harrison Award (named for the deceased cofounder of *Spitball*) is given for one of two achievements: Lifetime accomplishment in baseball literature or art, or contributions to *Spitball Magazine*, literary or nonliterary.

Sports History
Empire Press
105 Loudoun St., S.W.
Leesburg, VA 22075
(703) 771-9400
J. D. Schulz: Editor.

Subscription: $14.95 for six issues; $2.95 single issue.

Description: This slick production usually has at least one or two baseball articles, but most of them are on events that have been better told elsewhere many times. The number of mistakes that reach print (e.g. Lefty Gomez for Lefty Grove!) can bring a true fan to tears.

Yankees Magazine
Yankee Stadium
Bronx, NY 10451
(212) 579-4495
Gregg Mazzola: Editor-in-Chief.

Subscription: $18 for 12 issues, single copies, $2. Published 12 times a year: every three weeks, March–October, and every six weeks, November–February.

Description: Very slick, with color photography, and well stocked at fifty pages per issue. Minor league reports, rules, and Yankee box scores are some of the regular features, and contributing writers Maury Allen, Mel Allen, Harvey Frommer, Dan Krueckeberg, Rich Marazzi, Paul Mari, Ken Tingley, Leo Trachtenberg, and others add information and spice.   —LJ

So You Want to Be a Baseball Writer?

I just finished writing my one trillionth story on the Baltimore Orioles for spring training 1989. I finished it on an airplane, in a middle seat, between two men who must have weighed a combined 650 pounds. But, computer in my lap, elbows stuck in my ribs (try typing that way), I got it done. And I'm proud to say, it wasn't terrible.

My connecting flight was due to leave in twenty minutes, so I streaked off the plane to send this wonderful piece of work to my office before the first edition, with a 10:15 P.M. deadline. Sending a story via computer from an airport pay phone ranks in degree of difficulty with trying to hit Roger Clemens's ninety-eight-m.p.h. fastball with a Wiffle ball bat—at twilight. But balancing my computer with one hand and dialing with the other, it somehow worked. I sprinted to the gate and made the flight.

I'm sweating, I've got a huge ink stain on my pants, my wife hates me for being away six straight weeks in Florida, I'm exhausted, I'm hungry, I haven't had a day off in forty-five consecutive days, I don't have anything left to write because I've already written it all, and, when I get home, I know there will be a list of errands that is pages long.

And in two days the season starts.

So you want to be a baseball writer?

Happily I tell you that not every day is like this. Honestly I tell you that I do like my job as a baseball writer very much. I've had chances to get out of it, but this is my eighth season and I'm still standing, I still have my enthusiasm, I still love the game. Colleagues at my paper say they don't envy me. One said if his salary was doubled, he wouldn't do my job; one always says, "I am so glad I'm not you." I say it's a great job.

But glamorous, it's not. I have a friend who thinks it's a very glamorous and easy job. He went to college and everything, but he, like others, has absolutely no idea what it takes to be a baseball writer. I asked him once to describe my daily schedule, and he said, "Well, you get to the park about an hour before the game, eat, watch the game, talk to the players afterward, go home, and write your story."

Yeah, that's close.

Here's a normal day.

At home I'm usually up at 6:30 A.M. because my wife gets up early for work. The minute she awakens, my black Labrador, Dunk, goes wild and wants to go out. So I drive my 1981 Celica (glamorous, right?) to the gas station, buy all the local newspapers, let the dog run while I sit in the car and read the papers. I hope and pray some paper (okay, I'm paranoid, I admit it) doesn't have something on the Orioles that I don't. If so, my day is just about ruined.

I do this on every home date of the season; I even read each paper in the same order. (Superstitious? You bet.) I do this rain, snow, or shine, 20 below or 100 degrees above. I sit in the car for an hour; I read each box score, every pitching line, every strikeout. From box scores come your best Sunday-column notes.

I arrive home at 7:30 A.M.; my wife's on her way out the door. I won't see her until 12:30 A.M., when she will be asleep. She's a lawyer. She works very hard. We've been married for five years. No wonder we have no children.

I often go back to sleep at 7:30 A.M. until about 9:30 A.M.; then I do my errands, which seem to take all day. Many times, however, there are work-related calls to make, stories to work on for that night. I leave for the park at 3:30.

I arrive at 4:00. I always go first into manager Frank Robinson's office to check out the lineup, see if anyone is hurt, if any-

thing is new. The game starts in 3 1/2 hours—and three of that is spent finding notes and stories.

I get to the press box at 7 P.M. normally. I eat. I'm the least picky eater of any man alive, but cheeseburger, fries, and crabcakes each night can make you very, very fat. One writer friend gained a cool 35 pounds in his first year on the beat. Me, I weigh the same 140 as I did eight years ago. I'm proud of that.

The game starts at 7:35 P.M., which is when I start writing my Orioles' notes, usually about five hundred words. I have to write them, obviously, as the game is going on. So I spend a lot of time trying to watch the game, my computer, and my scorebook at the same time. I admit, I'm always asking another writer, "How did that play go?"

My notes are sent by 8:30–8:45, when the game is usually in the third, fourth, or fifth inning. Then I have to start to write running for the first edition (running is the account of the first five or so innings). I send that, then start writing the fifth through seventh innings. A completed story must be in the office by 10:15—at the very latest.

Of course, the game is hardly ever over by that time. So I hope and pray that what I wrote stands up. But usually the pitcher seeking his first big league shutout gets knocked out in the ninth or the team that's behind goes ahead and wins. In that case, I have to redo most of my story—and I have five minutes to do it.

If the game ends at 10:30, I have about an hour to get to the clubhouse, talk to the managers and the key players, get back to the press box, and write a whole new story, with quotes.

To reach the clubhouse after a game in Arlington, Texas (where I covered the Rangers for four years), you have to go through the stands. Naturally 25,000 fans are going in one direction and I am going in the other. I learned how to vault seats, railings, and hot dog vendors, but it would still take Jim Thorpe seven minutes to get

from the press box to the clubhouse.

Invariably the player who I need to talk to most is doing a radio show first. Then TV. Then he ices his arm in the trainer's room, which is off limits to the media. By the time he's ready to talk, I'm really running out of time. And if he's someone like Eddie Murray, there's a good chance he won't say anything anyway. And that's the other thing. These players don't understand deadlines, and those who do, don't care about them. They talk when they're ready. I covered a team last year that lost 107 games. Try going into that morgue after every loss and coming up with a new way to ask the basic question, "Hey, you guys really stunk tonight."

Most players on the Orioles are very nice and very cordial and very boring. I take what I have, sprint back up to the press box, and write. I have about forty minutes to get it in the second edition—the big one—at 11:45 P.M.

I've never missed an edition, not even the two times my computer exploded on deadline. It's times like those when you want to hurl it on the field, then jump yourself. When all goes well, I leave the press box by 12:15 A.M., get home by 12:45 A.M., take a while to unwind, then try to go to sleep.

Up at 6:30 A.M. Same routine again.

The road routine is different, of course, since my wife makes very few trips and my dog makes none. I get a chance to sleep in, but when you're so used to getting up at 6:30, sleeping past 9:00 is difficult. On the road, I read the papers, call my office to make sure I didn't miss anything, and work out—mostly basketball at some YMCA or gym. Doing something active on the road is essential. Otherwise you'd lie around until 4 P.M., do some work, eat lunch, then go to the park. There isn't much time for any sightseeing on the road.

I make every Orioles road trip, meaning two trips to thirteen AL cities twice a year. That's a lot of flights, wake-up calls, open suitcases, bellmen who are late, hotel rooms that all look the same.

It gets old. You learn to deal with it.

My first trip as a full-time baseball writer was to New York in April 1982. I was twenty-three. The Rangers' opener against the Yankees was snowed out, so I decided to take care of six weeks worth of dirty laundry from Florida. I sent it—all of it—to the Sheraton Center valet. He returned in the afternoon and presented me with my laundry, underwear folded, socks on hangers.

"That will be one eighty-five," he said.

I gave him a five-dollar bill, "Keep the change," I said.

"That's a hundred eighty-five!" he yelled.

They put it on my room bill.

He was mad that I didn't tip him.

New York is a tough place. Even cab drivers hesitate going to Yankee Stadium, which isn't a nice place to be hanging out at midnight. The only thing scarier is the cab ride from the Stadium to downtown Manhattan. The few New York cabbies who speak our language should be up for Robert DeNiro's part in *Taxi Driver II*. And they are undoubtedly the rudest people in North America.

The only place it's harder to catch a cab after a game is Comiskey Park, home of the White Sox. I've waited two hours there. It's so nice to get to the park at 3:30 P.M., and still be standing outside the stadium at 1:30 A.M. But at least there's nothing to do in Chicago after 1 A.M.

From Chicago it's off to Cleveland and the lovely Bond Court Hotel, easily the worst road hotel at which the Orioles stay. It seems like every time I've been there, there's a construction crew working on the floor above mine at 8 A.M. I got into Cleveland one morning at 3:30 A.M. I went to my room, which looked like a bomb had exploded in it. I returned to the deserted lobby, got a new room, and entered the elevator. So did this other guy. He didn't press any floor buttons. I got out on the twenty-first floor and he followed me.

By now, I'm scared to death. Either he's a killer or he's gay, and I'm neither. I lost him, I thought. I opened my door, turned to pick up my bags, and there he was. "What do you want?" I screamed.

"Just a little company," he said.

I slammed the door and went to bed. The phone rang a couple minutes later. "Can I please come up," he said.

"No!" I yelled.

That was a bad road trip. There are some bad ones during the years and there are some good ones. Me, I can handle the traveling. I can handle players not talking to me and occasionally yelling at me. I can even handle the losing. This is my eighth full year, and I've never covered a team that won more than 77 games in a season. My lifetime winning percentage as a major league beat writer is .409. It's astonishing, I know. But I will manage.   —TK

CHAPTER 10

In the Catbird's Seat

It happened every year, a surer sign than robins or love in the hall that spring had arrived in my Los Angeles high school. While my teachers droned away at math, English, or science, I sat in the back of the classroom, the picture of attention: eyes unblinking, elbow on desk, seeming to rest my head against my hand as I pondered sines, gerunds, or molecules. But behind my fingers was the earplug and masked by my arm was the cord attached to the radio hidden beneath my desk. Around me, other fans mirrored my charade.

There was no way we were going to miss hearing "It's a Beautiful Day for a Ball Game," the tune that opens every Dodger broadcast. The sound of Vin Scully—"And a very good afternoon to you, wherever you may be"—told us that all was right with the world.

Baseball on the radio has an attraction like no other sport. You might listen to a football or basketball game because you want to know the score, but you listen to baseball for the experience. Baseball's voices become celebrities, and the best are honored in the Hall of Fame. The pace of the game encourages the best announcers to paint pictures with words, teach you about the game, or tell great stories. Ask the top sportscasters which sport they prefer working, and most will say baseball because of the freedom it gives to its voices.

There's always something special about spending time on a warm summer evening flipping the dial, looking for a game. The radio puts you in the distant ballpark. Because most of the major league networks include at least one clear-channel station, you can create your own Game of the Day,

Radio and TV

**From crystal set
to satellite dish,
baseball on the air**

or just switch from game to game. Clear-channel stations, those 50,000-watt powerhouses that can be heard across several states, seem designed for the baseball fan. On some nights, East Coast listeners may have their choice of as many as seven or eight games. West Coast listeners don't have as many choices. But even there the

dedicated listener can pick up several games.

Baseball on the radio got a big boost all over the country a few years ago when CBS radio brought back a Game of the Week on Saturdays. The network hires its own announcers, but in the fifth inning it brings in each of the teams' local voices to call the game, giving fans around the country a chance to hear why these announcers are famous in their hometowns.

As radio baseball continues to thrive, baseball on TV takes another step in 1990, with the start of the game's first national cable contract. In 1990, ESPN takes over, broadcasting a game virtually every night of the week.

The radio and TV listings on the following pages are intended to help you find baseball wherever your travels may take you. They are as complete as possible, but beware that changes will take place right up to the last minute. Some minor league teams, in particular, won't know which games will be carried until each season starts.

So use the listings as a guide, but experiment; listening conditions change every night. If you've never heard Jon Miller, you owe it to yourself to seek out the Orioles' network on WBAL or WTOP. Find the Cubs' legendary Harry Caray on WGN or WHO. Or try to find one of the Dodgers' stations in the West and hear Vin Scully at his best. They will bring, to paraphrase the master, a very good baseball evening to you, wherever you may be.   —DK

The incomparable Vin Scully has been a Dodgers' broadcaster since their Brooklyn days and a stalwart on the now departed NBC Game of the Week.

Around the Dial:
The Super Radio Stations

On some nights the radio can be a passport to distant ballparks. Thanks to clear-channel radio, those 50,000-watt AM superstations that can be heard far away after dark, in some parts of the country you can tune in on virtually any baseball game being played. In other parts, you'll be thankful to find one station coming in with a game, even if you need to adjust the antenna every now and then to hold on to it.

You'll have more success bringing in clear-channel signals in the eastern half of the nation, because the cities are closer together. But conditions are different every night. Some nights you'll struggle to pick up anything, and others you'll be amazed by what you hear. Here's what you may find moving up the AM dial:

660—WFAN, New York Mets. Range: Up and down the East Coast. All-sports radio moved here with the Mets in time for the 1989 season. So when the Amazins aren't playing, you can always count on WFAN for sports talk, along with score updates every fifteen minutes. Announcers: Bob Murphy and Gary Cohen.

670—WMAQ, Chicago White Sox. Range: Across the Midwest, sometimes on the East Coast. Their flagship went all-news before the 1988 season, and the Sox changed announcers the next year. John Rooney came in from Minnesota and Wayne Hagin from San Francisco.

680—KNBR, San Francisco Giants. Range: Around the West. Hank Greenwald moved back to the Bay Area after a couple of years with the Yankees. Unfortunately they teamed him with Ron Fairly, who was a good player but has had trouble behind the mike since his days with the California Angels.

700—WLW, Cincinnati Reds. Range: All along the East Coast and across the entire Midwest. This station likes to bill itself as "The Big One," and it features a likeable baseball team of Marty Brennaman and Joe Nuxhall. Brennaman's trademark "And this one belongs to the Reds" closes every Cincinnati win.

720—WGN, Chicago Cubs. Range: Across the Midwest, sometimes to the East Coast. With the Cubs still playing so many day games, you won't get as many chances to try this station. But a few innings of Harry Caray on the radio makes it worth the effort. DeWayne Staats and Dave Nelson are the other announcers.

750—WSB, Atlanta Braves. Range: Throughout the Southeast, into the Northeast. Announcers: Skip Caray, Ernie Johnson, Billy Sample, and Skip Van Wieren. You've heard the same crew on the Superstation TBS, but Caray is more entertaining on Braves radio.

760—WJR, Detroit Tigers. Range: Throughout the Midwest and Northeast, into the Southeast. The veteran team of Ernie Harwell and Paul Caray won't keep you on the edge of your seat, but Harwell deserved his Hall of Fame recognition. His command of the language makes a Tigers game fun.

770—WABC, New York Yankees. Range: All along the East Coast. Once again the Yankees changed crews last year. Jay Johnstone is one voice, and many old Braves fans will be unhappy to hear they brought back John Sterling. But listen in sometime before or after the game for Art Rust, Jr.'s talk show.

820—WBAP, Texas Rangers. Range: Throughout the Southwest, as far west as Arizona. The Rangers have sometimes been known as the Strangers, and their broadcast crew of Mark Holtz and Eric Nadel is unknown outside the region.

830—WCCO, Minnesota Twins. Range: Throughout the Midwest. Veteran Twins announcer Herb Carneal teams with former Yankee voice John Gordon on the Upper Midwest's top sports station.

1020—KDKA, Pittsburgh Pirates. Range: Throughout the East. America's first radio station provides thorough coverage of the Buccos with Lanny Frattare, John Sanders, and Jim Rooker.

1040—WHO, Chicago Cubs. Range: Virtually coast to coast, but strongest in the Midwest. Another chance for Cubs fans is Des Moines' WHO, although you'll have to settle for Harry Caray—Ronald Reagan stopped doing Cubs games here long ago.

1080—WTIC, Boston Red Sox. Range: Throughout the Northeast. This Hartford station is your best chance for the Red Sox and their low-key crew of Ken Coleman and Joe Castiglione. By the way, never tell a New Englander you think Coleman or Red Sox TV voice Ned Martin sounds boring.

1090—WBAL, Baltimore Orioles. Range: Along the East Coast. After several years on weak local stations, the Orioles moved back to 'BAL in 1988. Unfortunately the promos announcing the Orioles were "back where they belong" didn't sound too good during the twenty-one-game losing streak of 1988.

But any chance to hear Jon Miller call a game is worth it, especially now that the Birds are flying high again. Joe Angel is the other voice.

1100—WWWE, Cleveland Indians. Range: Throughout the Northeast and Midwest. Herb Score and Paul Olden are fine, but veteran radio fans missed the Pete Franklin talk show. Franklin, a 3WE mainstay, commanded afternoon drive time on WFAN in New York before leaving in 1989.

1120—KMOX, St. Louis Cardinals. Range: Throughout the East Coast and Midwest, and into the Southwest. "America's Sports Station" brings Jack Buck, Mike Shannon, and the Redbirds to you virtually anywhere on the continent, or so it seems.

1180—WHAM, New York Yankees. Range: Throughout the Northeast. Formerly home for both Mets and Yankees action, this Rochester station dropped the Mets after the 1988 season.

1210—WCAU, Philadelphia Phillies. Range: All along the East Coast. Announcers: Richie Ashburn, Harry Kalas, Andy Musser, and Chris Wheeler. Kalas' voice reminds many of Notre Dame or NFL films, but he's best known at home as the voice of the Phillies.

Stay tuned after the game and hear some of the famous Philadelphia fans rip into their team.

1500—WTOP, Baltimore Orioles. Range: All along the East Coast. The Birds' Washington, D.C., affiliate gives you another chance at Jon Miller, probably the best radio broadcaster around today.

—DK

Baseball on Radio and Television

The following listings are arranged so that if you know where you are, you can tune in to baseball. A few notes: The broadcasters on a team's flagship station will be found all the way around the network. Unless otherwise indicated, stations broadcast all games. Minor league teams are listed in descending order from Triple-A down to Rookie League. See Chapter 13 for starting times and other team information.

ALABAMA

If you're driving through Alabama anytime during the summer, you won't lack for baseball on the radio. Besides the Braves and Cubs, both of the state's minor league teams broadcast all their Southern League games locally. TV choices are more limited, depending mostly on what superstations are available on the cable where you are.

Major Leagues

Braves Radio Network: WAVU, 630, Albertville; WHMA, 1390, Anniston; WKUL-FM, 92.1, Cullman; WAVD, 1400, Decatur; WIJK, 1470, Evergreen; WFPA, 1400, Ft. Payne; WGAD, 1350, Gadsden; WKRG, 710, Mobile; WHHY, 1400, Montgomery; WPID, 1280, Piedmont; WSFF, 1330, Scottsboro; WHBB, 1490, Selma; WFEB, 1340, Sylacauga; WVNA, 1590, Tuscumbia.

Cubs Radio Network: WACV, 1170, Montgomery.

Minor Leagues

Birmingham Barons (Southern League) Radio: WYDE, 850. Announcer: Jeff Lloyd.

Huntsville Stars (Southern League) Radio: WFIX, 1450. Announcer: Steve Carroll.

ALASKA

Don't expect much professional baseball on the radio up here. You might find some games from the semipro Alaska League, assuming that that circuit has solved some of its internal problems. Remember, too, the time difference, which causes East Coast night games to start in early afternoon, and the Saturday Game of the Week to arrive at breakfast time.

Major League

Mariners Radio Network: KRSA, 580, Petersburg.

ARIZONA

Look for all the variety you'd expect from a state that definitely has divided loyalties. You can hear or see much action from the California teams, but remember that the Chicago Cubs have a strong following, too. As for the local Pacific Coast League entries, the broadcast schedules are erratic, much like the interest in the teams. You might have better luck enjoying PCL action on Albuquerque's clear-channel KOB (770). More consistent are the college games, which can be heard whenever they don't conflict with basketball.

Major Leagues

Angels Radio Network: KCKY, 1150, Coolidge; KIKO, 1340, Globe; KFBR, 1340, Nogales; KLPZ, 1380, Parker; KRDS, 1190, Phoenix; KTUC, 1400, Tucson.

Athletics TV Network: KUSK, 7, Prescott.

Cubs Radio Network: KCKY, 1150, Coolidge; KNST, 940, Tucson.

Dodgers Radio Network: KVNA, 690, Flagstaff; KOY, 550, Phoenix; KYCA, 1490, Prescott; KTUC, 1400, Tucson.

Padres TV Network: KUSK, 7, Prescott; KPOL, 40, Tucson; Sun Cable, Yuma. *Radio Network*: KBLU, 560, Yuma; KINO, 1230, Winslow; KNOT, 1450, Prescott; KPGE, 1340, Page.

Minor Leagues

Phoenix Firebirds (Pacific Coast League) Radio: KTAR, 620, number of games, 20. Announcer: Kent Derdivanis.

Tucson Toros (Pacific Coast League) Radio: KTKT, 990. Announcer: Vince Cotroneo. *Spanish Radio*: KXMG, 98.3-FM, Tucson. All home games. Announcer: Francisco Ruiz.

ARKANSAS

Cardinals fans shouldn't have any trouble finding their favorite team in Arkansas. Besides the three TV and 19 radio affiliates in the state, KMOX (1120) beams in strongly from St. Louis. The Redbirds' Double-A affiliate can also be heard in the middle of the state. Eastern Arkansas listeners can hear the Double-A Memphis Chicks on WREC (600), and some of the state gets Kansas City Royals action.

Major Leagues

Astros TV Network: KRZB, 26, Hot Springs.

Cardinals TV Network: KHOG, 29, Fayetteville; KHBS, 40, Ft. Smith; Paragould Cable, Paragould. *Cardinals Radio Network*: KBTA, 1340, Batesville; KSCC-FM, 107.1, Berryville; KHLS-FM, 96.3, Blytheville; KCON, 1230, Conway; KAGH-FM, 104.9, Crossett; KDEW-FM, 96.7, DeWitt; KFPW, 1230, Ft. Smith; KFFA, 1360, Helena; KIXT, 1420, Hot Springs; KBTM, 1230, Jonesboro; KHLT-FM, 94.1, Little Rock; KPCA, 1580, Marked Tree; KOSE, 860, Osceola; KDRS, 1490, Paragould; KCCL, 1460, Paris; KCYN-FM, 103.9, Pocahontas; KSAR-FM, 95.9, Salem; KBRS, 1340, Springfield; KCTT, 1530, Yellville.

Rangers TV Network: KRZB, 26, Hot Springs.

Royals Radio Network: KTOD, 1330, Conway; KQXK, 1590, Springdale.

Minor League

Arkansas Travelers (Texas League) Radio: KEZQ, 1150. All home games. Announcers: Jim Elder, Brady Gadberry.

CALIFORNIA

If you like the local teams, you're set. The Dodgers, Angels, and Padres blanket the southern half of the state, and the Giants and A's have the northern half covered. The Padres (KFMB, 760) and the Giants (KNBR, 680) have the strongest flagship stations. Many Class-A California League teams also broadcast most of their games. It's extremely rare to pick up any out-of-state major league games, although you can get a Triple-A treat on Albuquerque's KOB (770), which carries the Dodgers' top

Graham McNamee was baseball's first radio star, colorfully bringing the World Series to the nation in the 1920s.

minor league affiliate. College baseball is generally limited to campus stations (although Cal's KALX-FM 90.7, and Stanford's KZSU-FM 90.1, cover much of the Bay Area), except in Fresno.

Major Leagues

Angels TV: KTLA, 5, Hollywood; no. of games: 57. Announcers: Bob Starr, Joe Torre. *Cable TV*: Z Channel (pay), no. of games: 35. Announcers: Joel Meyers, Torre. *Angles Radio*: KMPC, 710, Los Angeles. Announcers: Al Conin, Ken Brett. *Radio Network*: KCHJ, 1150, Delano; KXO, 1230, El Centro; KAAT-FM, 107.1, Fresno/Oakhurst; KHSJ, 1310, Hemet; KVOY, 1340, Lancaster/Mojave; KDES, 920, Palm Springs; KPRL, 1230, Paso Robles; KTIP, 1450, Porterville; KRSO, 590, Riverside/San Bernardino; KATY, 1340, San Luis Obispo; KDB, 1490, Santa Barbara; KSMA, 1240, Santa Maria; KCIN, 1590, Victorville. *Spanish Radio*: XPRS, 1090. Announcers: Ulpiano Cos Villa, Ruben Valentin.

Athletics TV: KPIX, 5, San Francisco. Announcers: Monte Moore, Ray Fosse; KICU, 36, San Francisco. Announcers: Moore, Fosse, and John Shrader. *TV Network*: KHSL, 12, Chico; KAIL, 53, Fresno;

KCBA, 35, Salinas. *Athletics Radio*: KSFO 560 AM, San Francisco. Announcers: Bill King, Lon Simmons, Fosse. *Radio Network*: KAHI, 950, Auburn; KCNO, 570, Alturas; KINS, 980, Eureka; KRKC, 1490, King City; KPMO, 1300, Mendocino; KHYV, 970, Modesto; KNRY, 1240, Monterey; KQMS, 1400, Redding; KGNR, 1300, Sacramento; KVML, 1450, Sonora; KUKI, 1400, Ukiah; KOBO, 1450, Yuba City. *Spanish Radio*: KNTA, 1430, all home games. Announcers: Amaury Pi-Gonzalez,

1921: That Wonderful Year

That radio signals can fly through the air is wonderful; that they could get through the smoke-and-soot-laden atmosphere of Pittsburgh in 1921 was truly amazing. Baseball fans among KDKA's few listeners were delighted when, starting with Opening Day, the nation's first commercial radio station began announcing the results of the day's major league baseball games three times each evening. Up-to-the-day results! What would they think of next?

Listeners learned on August 5. Announcer Harold Arlin sat behind the home-plate screen at Forbes Field and reported the game pitch by pitch. In the fourth inning Phillies outfielder Cy Williams smacked radio's first homer to send Pirate pitcher Hal Carlson to the showers, but Pittsburgh rallied with three runs in the bottom of the eighth to give reliever Jimmy Zinn an 8–5 win.

On October 5 in the studio of Newark station WJZ, Tommy Cowan recreated Game One of the Giants-Yankees World Series, using details telephoned to him from the press box. But KDKA still one-upped on everyone. The Pittsburgh station had famed sportswriter Grantland Rice broadcasting live from the Polo Grounds.
—BC

Evelio Mendoza.

Dodgers TV: KTTV, 11, Los Angeles, no. of games: 50. Announcers: Vin Scully, Don Drysdale, Ross Porter. (Note: Although KTTV is not technically a superstation, it is carried on many cable systems in the West. The same is true for the Angels' flagship, KTLA.) *Cable TV*: Z Channel (pay), Santa Monica, no. of games: 35. Announcers: Eddie Doucette, Don Sutton. *Dodgers Radio*: KABC 790, Los Angeles. Announcers: Scully, Drysdale, Porter. *Radio Network*: KPMC, 1560, Bakersfield; KMET, 1490, Banning; KBOV, 1230, Bishop; KJMB, 1450, Blythe; KROP, 1300, Brawley; KHYE-FM, 105.7, Hemet; KAVL, 610, Lancaster; KCMJ, 1140, Palm Springs; KMEN, 1290, San Bernardino; KVEC, 920, San Luis Obispo; KTMS, 1250, Santa Barbara; KUHL, 1440, Santa Maria; KVEN, 1450, Ventura; KHTZ, 1400, Visalia. *Spanish Radio*: KWKW, 1300, Los Angeles. Announcers: Jaime Jarrin, Rene Cardenas. *Spanish Radio Network*: KOXR, 910, Oxnard; KVIM, 970, Palm Springs; KNSE, 1510, Riverside; KSBQ, 1480, Santa Maria; XEGM, 950, Tijuana (Mexico).

Giants TV: KTVU, 2, Oakland, no. of games: 50. Announcers: Hank Greenwald, Ron Fairly, Duane Kuiper. *TV Network*: KMPH, 26, Fresno; KMST, 46, Monterey; KRBK, 31, Sacramento. *Cable TV*: Giantsvision (pay per view), San Francisco, no. of games: 36. Announcers: Joe Morgan, Kuiper. *Giants Radio*: KNBR, 680, San Francisco. Announcers: Greenwald, Fairly. *Radio Network*: KATA, 1340, Arcata/Eureka; KDAC, 1230, Ft. Bragg; KYNO, 1300, Fresno; KFIV, 1360, Modesto; KNZS, 1540, Monterey; KRDG, 1330, Redding; KFYI, 1270, Tulare/Visalia; KIQS, 1560, Willows. *Spanish Radio*: KLOK, 1170. Announcers: Julio Gonzales, Tito Fuentes. *Spanish Radio Network*: KTGE, 1570, Salinas.

Padres TV: KUSI, 51, San Diego, no. of games: 50. Announcers: Jerry Coleman, Rick Monday. *TV Network*: Rogers Cable, Imperial; Cablesystems of the Southwest, El Centro. *Cable TV*: San Diego Cable

Sports Network (pay per view), San Diego, no. of games: 41. Announcers: Bob Chandler, Ted Leitner. *Padres Radio*: KFMB, 760, San Diego. Announcers: Coleman, Monday, Bob Chandler, Ted Leitner. *Radio Network*: KAMP, 1430, El Centro; KNWZ, 1270, Palm Desert; KFBR, 1340, Nogales. *Spanish Radio*: XEXX, 1420. Announcers: Gustavo Lopez, Gustavo Lopez Jr., Mario Thomas, Eduardo Ortega.

Minor Leagues

San Bernardino Spirit (California League) Radio: KCKC, 1350. Announcer: Bob Harvey.

San Jose Giants (California League) Radio: KHTT, 1500, no. of games: Several. Announcers: John Atkinson, Chuck Mallonee.

COLORADO

Until Denver succeeds in its longtime effort to land a major league expansion team, Colorado residents must make do with broadcasts from the Cubs, Royals, and the state's two Triple-A teams.

Major Leagues

Cubs Radio Network: KYBG, 1090. Denver.

Royals TV Network: KWGN, 2, Denver. *Royals Radio Network*: KRYN, 1490, Colorado Springs; KFTM, 1400, Ft. Morgan; KFTM-FM, 101.7, Ft. Morgan; KBZZ, 1400, LaJunta; KLMO, 1060, Longmont; KRYT, 1350, Pueblo.

Minor Leagues

Denver Zephyrs (American Association) Radio: KXKL, 105.1-FM. Announcer: Norm Jones.

Colorado Springs Sky Sox (Pacific Coast League) Radio: KCMN, 1530. Announcer: John DeMott.

CONNECTICUT

For a state with only one professional team, Connecticut does well for broadcast baseball. Besides the clear-channel broadcasts that can be heard around the Northeast, most of the state can also hear games of three major league teams on in-state stations. In fact, Hartford's WTIC (1080) can be heard throughout the Northeast with its Red Sox broadcasts.

Major Leagues

Mets TV Network: WTXX, 20, Waterbury. *Mets Radio Network*: WKHT, 1230, Hartford; WNTY, 990, Southington/Waterbury.

Red Sox TV Network: WVIT, 30, Hartford. *Red Sox Radio Network*: WTIC, 1080, Hartford; WMMW, 1470, Meriden; WNLC, 1510, New London; WLIS, 1420, Old Saybrook; WINY, 1350, Putnam; WILI, 1400, Willimantic.

Yankees TV Network: WTWS, 26, New London. *Yankees Radio Network*: WPOP, 1410, Hartford/New Britain; WREF, 850, Ridgefield/Danbury; WSNG, 610, Torrington; WATR, 1330, Waterbury.

Minor League

New Britain Red Sox (Eastern League) Radio: WCNX, 1150, no. of games: 40. Announcer: Bill Glynn.

DELAWARE

Most of Delaware fits into the Philadelphia market, with Phillies games available on WCAU radio (1210) and WTAF TV (29). Other clear-channel broadcasts can also be heard, particularly the Orioles on WBAL (1090) and WTOP (1500).

Major Leagues

Phillies Radio Network: WDEL, 1150, Wilmington.

Orioles Radio Network: WNRK, 1260, Newark.

FLORIDA

Viewers and listeners in Florida may have more choices than anyone else in the country. Many local stations carry selected major and minor league games, clear-channel stations are within reach, and cable and over-the-air stations televise a variety of games. Some stations in spring training sites carry at least the team's network spring games. Some of this could change, of course, if one of the many groups seeking a major league team for the state is successful. Minor league broadcasts are harder to find.

Major Leagues

Astros TV Network: WCIX, 6, Miami; WAYK, 56, Palm Bay/Orlando; WJTC, 44, Pensacola. *Astros Radio Network*: WFIV, 1080, Kissimmee.

Braves Radio Network: WNUE, 1400, Ft. Walton; WGGG, 1230, Gainesville; WAPE, 690, Jacksonville; WSBB, 1230, New Smyrna Beach; WAUC, 1310, Wauchula.

Brewers TV Network: WFGX, 35, Ft. Walton Beach.

Cardinals TV Network: WFGX, 35, Ft. Walton Beach; WEVU, 26, Ft. Myers; WNFT, 47, Jacksonville; WTMV, 32, Lakeland; WAYK, 56, Palm Bay/Orlando; WPGX, Panama City. *Cardinals Radio Network*: WKUS, 1420, Sanford.

Cubs Radio Network: WTAN, 1340, Clearwater.

Dodgers Radio Network: WAXE, 1370, Vero Beach.

Mets TV Network: WTOG, 44, Tampa/St. Petersburg; WFLX, 29, West Palm Beach. *Mets Radio Network*: WQAM, 560, Miami/Ft. Lauderdale; WNSI, Orlando; WPSL,

How about that, folks! Mel Allen's voice remains one of the game's treasures today.

1590, Port St. Lucie; WSPB, 1450, Sarasota.

Orioles TV Network: WBR, 7, Ft. Myers; WAYK, 56, Palm Bay/Orlando; WAT, 24, Sarasota. *Orioles Radio Network*: WIOD, 610, Miami.

Phillies Radio Network: WIOD, 610, Miami; WTAN, 1340, Clearwater.

Pirates Radio Network: WBRD, 1420, Bradenton.

Rangers TV Network: WAYK, 56, Palm Bay/Orlando; WJTC, 44, Pensacola. *Rangers Radio Network*: WCCF, 1580, Punta Gorda.

Red Sox Radio Network: WIOD, 610, Miami; WSIR, 1490, Winter Haven.

Reds TV Network: WAYK, 56, Palm Bay/Orlando; WJTC, 44, Pensacola; WFTS, 28, Tampa. *Reds Radio Network*: WPLA, 910, Plant City.

Royals Radio Network: KIPC, 1280, Lake Wales; WNSI, 1400, Sanford.

Tigers Radio Network: WONN, 1230, Lakeland.

Twins TV Network: WAYK, 56, Palm Bay/Orlando; WAB, 17, Tallahassee. *Twins Radio Network*: WHOO, 990, Orlando.

White Sox TV Network: WBD, Sarasota. *White Sox Radio Network*: WQSA, 1220, Sarasota.

Yankees TV Network: WCIX, 6, Miami; WFTS, 28, Tampa; WFLX, 29, West Palm Beach. *Yankees Radio Network*: WIOD, 610, Miami; WRBQ, 1380, Tampa/St. Pe-

tersburg; WSBR, 740, Boca Raton/West Palm Beach.

Cable TV: Both SportsChannel Florida and the Sunshine Network carry major league games regularly throughout the summer, picking up the feeds from affiliated cable stations in major league markets.

Minor Leagues

Jacksonville Expos (Southern League) Radio: WAPE, 690. Announcer: Mark Hauser.

Charlotte Rangers, Port Charlotte (Florida State League) Radio: WCCF, 1580, no. of games: 9.

Osceola Astros, Kissimmee (Florida State League) Radio: WMJK, 1220, no. of games: 35.

St. Lucie Mets, Port St. Lucie (Florida State League) Radio: WPFL, 1590, no. of games: 50. Announcer: Randy Lee.

Vero Beach Dodgers (Florida State League) Radio: WAXE, 1370.

Winter Haven Red Sox (Florida State League) Radio: WYXY, 1360, no. of games: All road. Announcer: Steve Tell.

GEORGIA

Despite the slogan "America's Team" and attendance figures that might suggest otherwise, the Atlanta Braves remain Georgia's Team. The superstation status of WTBS means there is no TV network, but

the Braves make up for that by blanketing the Southeast with radio stations. And flagship WSB (750) comes in clearly through the whole state and much of the South. Minor league baseball hasn't made it on the radio, however.

Major League

Braves TV: WTBS, 17, Atlanta, no. of games: 135. Announcers: Ernie Johnson, Skip Caray, Pete Van Wieren, Billy Sample, Don Sutton. *Braves Radio*: WSB, 750, Atlanta. Announcers: Johnson, Caray, Van Wieren, Sample. *Radio Network*: WGPC, 1450, Albany; WGPC-FM, 104.5, Albany; WPUR-FM, 99.7, Americus; WBKZ, 880, Athens; WGAC, 580, Augusta; WMGR, 930, Bainbridge; WBBK, 1260, Blakely; WBBK-FM, 93.5, Blakely; WPPL-FM, 103.9, Blue Ridge; WMOG, 1490, Brunswick; WBTR-FM, 92.1, Carrollton; WBHF, 1450, Cartersville; WCLA, 1470, Claxton; WCLA-FM, 107.1, Claxton; WVMG, 1440, Cochran; WVMG-FM, 96.7, Cochran; WRCG, 1420, Columbus; WBLJ, 1230, Dalton; WDMG, 860, Douglas; WMLT, 1330, Dublin; WWRK, 1400, Elberton; WBHB, 1240, Fitzgerald; WDUN, 550, Gainesville; WKEU, 1450, Griffin; WBTY-FM, 105.5, Homerville; WIFO-FM, 105.5, Jesup; WLAG, 1240, LaGrange; WPEH-FM, 92.1, Louisville; WBBT, 1340, Lyons; WMAZ, 940, Macon; WMVG, 1450, Milledgeville; WMGA, 1130, Moultrie; WCOH, 1400, Newnan; WPGA, 980, Perry; WLAQ, 1410, Rome; WBMQ, 630, Savannah; WWNS, 1240, Statesboro; WJAT, 800, Swainsboro; WTGA, 1590, Thomaston; WTGA-FM, 95.3, Thomaston; WPAX, 1240, Thomasville; WTIF, 1340, Tifton; WVLD, 1450, Valdosta; WRLD, 1490, West Point.

HAWAII

Since the Triple-A Islanders packed up and moved to Colorado Springs after the 1987 season, Hawaii has been without professional baseball of its own. The result is more domination of the market by the University of Hawaii. Some of the West

Coast major league radio networks, however, do reach here.

Major Leagues

Angels Radio Network: KWAI, 1080, Honolulu.

Dodgers Radio Network: KDEO, 940, Honolulu.

Giants Radio Network: KHVH, 990, Honolulu.

Mets Radio Network: KGU, 760, Honolulu.

IDAHO

For several years there was no professional baseball in Idaho. Now the short-season rookie leagues have moved here, providing some broadcasts of games. You won't find much in the way of major league baseball on the air, though. Make do with the networks and superstations.

Major League

Mariners TV Network: K49AZ, 49, Twin Falls. *Mariners Radio Network*: KGEM, 1140, Boise.

Minor Leagues

Boise Hawks (Northwest League) Radio: KIZN, 730. Announcer: Larry Weir.

Idaho Falls Braves (Pioneer League) Radio: KUPI, 980, no. of games: All home. Announcers: John Balginy, James Garschaw.

ILLINOIS

Illinois loyalties have traditionally been divided between the Cubs in the north and the Cards downstate. The White Sox hold their own only on the South Side of Chicago. So as you move between Chicago and St. Louis along I-55, it's no surprise that the Cubs and Cards dominate the radio-TV picture. Mixed in you'll find some minor league action, and of course clear-channel baseball can be heard throughout the state. If you're in northern Illinois, don't forget the Brewers on various Wisconsin

stations, including WTMJ (620) in Milwaukee. And if you're in the Quad Cities area, pick up the minor league games out of Iowa on KSTT (1170).

Major Leagues

Brewers TV Network: WQRF, 39, Rockford.

Cardinals TV Network: WYZZ, 43, Bloomington; TeleCable, Normal; WGEM, 10, Quincy; WQRF, 39, Rockford; WRSP, 55, Springfield. *Cardinals Radio Network*: WRMJ-FM, 102.3, Aledo; WRAJ, 1440, Anna; WJBC, 1230, Bloomington; WKRO, 1490, Cairo; WBYS-FM, 98.3, Canton; WROY, 1460, Carmi; WDWS, 1400, Champaign; WEIC, 1270, Charleston; WITY, 980, Danville; WSOY, 1340, Decatur; WCRA, 1090, Effingham; WCRC-FM, 95.7, Effingham; WGIL, 1400, Galesburg; WGEN, 1500, Geneseo; WEBQ, 1240, Harrisburg; WEBQ-FM, 99.9, Harrisburg; WHPI, 1340, Herrin; WLDS, 1180, Jacksonville; WKEI, 1450, Kewanee; WLUV, 1520, Loves Park; WLPO, 1220, LaSalle;

WTAZ-FM, 102.3, Morton; WMIX, 940, Mount Vernon; WINI, 1420, Murphysboro; WLVN, 740, Olney; WSEI-FM, 92.9, Olney; WKXK-FM, 100.9, Pana; WBBA, 1580, Pittsfield; WTAD, 930, Quincy; WTAY, 1570, Robinson; WTAY-FM, 101.7, Robinson; WKKQ-FM, 96.7, Rushville; WHCO, 1230, Sparta; WTAX, 1240, Springfield; WGFA, 1360, Watseka.

Cubs TV: WGN, 9, Chicago. Announcers: Harry Caray, Steve Stone, DeWayne Staats. *TV Network*: WAND, 17, Decatur; WCEE, 13, Kell; WQAD, 8, Moline; WEEK, 25, Peoria; WGEM, 10, Quincy; WIFR, 23, Rockford. *Cubs Radio*: WGN, 720, Chicago. Announcers: Caray, Staats, Dave Nelson. *Radio Network*: WCIL, 1020, Carbondale; WBZM-FM, 94.3, Chillicothe; WDAN, 1490, Danville; WDZ, 1050, Decatur; WFRL, 1570, Freeport; WINU, 1510, Highland; WJIL, 1550, Jacksonville; WAKO, 910, Lawrenceville; WAKO-FM, 103.1,

Announcers like Garagiola (left) win acclaim; technicians are the unsung heroes.

Lawrenceville; WLBH-FM, 96.9, Mattoon; WMOK, 920, Metropolis; WRAM, 1330, Monmouth; WMOI-FM, 97.7, Monmouth; WCSJ, 1550, Morris; WUEZ-FM, 104.7, Morris; WMLA, 1440, Normal; WPOK, 1080, Pontiac; WGEM, 1440, Quincy; WRTL, 1460, Rantoul; WRHL, 1060, Rochelle; WRHL-FM, 102.3, Rochelle; WKXQ-FM, 96.7, Rushville; WIZZ, 1250, Streator; WRVI-FM, 96.7, Virden; WFRX-FM, 97.7, West Frankfort. *Spanish Radio*: WMXA, 1200, no. of games: 30.

Royals Radio Network: WCAZ, 990, Carthage; WCAZ-FM, 92.1, Carthage.

White Sox TV: WFLD, 32, Chicago, no. of games: 71. Announcers: Gary Thorne, Tom Paciorek. *TV Network*: WQRF, 39, Rockford. *White Sox Cable TV*: SportsChannel (pay), Oak Park, no. of games: 77. Announcers: Thorne, Paciorek. *White Sox Radio*: WMAQ, 670, Chicago. Announcers: John Rooney, Wayne Hagin. *Radio Network*: WRAJ, 1440, Anna; WJTX, 1580, Champaign; WDRW-FM, 102.3, Eldorado; WKAN, 1320, Kankakee; WZOE, 1490, Princeton; WTAY, 1570, Robinson; WYBR-FM, 104.9, Rockford; WCCI-FM, 100.1, Savanna; WSDR, 1240, Sterling; WRVI-FM, 96.7, Virden; WDND-FM, 105.5, Wilmington. *Spanish Radio*: WTAQ, 1300, Chicago, no. of games: all home, 22 road. Announcer: Frank Diaz.

Minor Leagues

Peoria Chiefs (Midwest League) Radio: WTAZ, 102.1-FM, no. of games: 75. Announcer: Norm Ulrich.

Rockford Expos (Midwest League) Radio: WROK, 1440, no. of games: 25. Announcer: Bob Presman.

Springfield Cardinals (Midwest League) Radio: WVEM, 101.9-FM. Announcer: Russ Langer.

INDIANA

Without a major league team of its own, Indiana still has a rooting interest. The northwestern area of the state can follow the Chicago teams, the northeast area the Tigers, and a good deal of the state watches the Reds. Minor league action can be heard in South Bend and Indianapolis, and in southern Indiana from across the river in Louisville (WAVG, 970). Plus all that flat land allows major league signals from Chicago, St. Louis, Detroit, Cincinnati, and Cleveland to be heard in most areas.

Major Leagues

Cardinals TV Network: WEVV, 44, Evansville. *Cardinals Radio Network*: WBIW, 1340, Bedford; WQTY-FM, 93.5, Linton; WUME-FM, 95.3, Paoli; WRAY, 1250, Princeton; WFML-FM, 96.7, Vincennes; WAMW, 1580, Washington.

Cubs TV Network: WFFT, 55, Ft. Wayne; WTTV, 4, Indianapolis; WNDU, 16, South Bend. *Cubs Radio Network*: WHUT, 1470, Anderson; WIFF, 1570, Auburn; WBNL, 1540, Boonville; WBNL-FM, 107.1, Boonville; WEZR, 1450, Ft. Wayne; WKAM, 1460, Goshen; WJNZ-FM, 94.3, Greencastle; WCOE-FM, 96.7, La Porte; WASK, 1450, Lafayette; WBAT, 1400, Marion; WPCO, 1590, Mount Vernon; WYIC, 1110, Noblesville; WNZE-FM, 94.3, Plymouth; WPGW, 1440, Portland; WPGW-FM, 100.9, Portland; WRIN, 1560, Rensselaer; WAXI-FM, 104.9, Rockville; WAMJ, 1580, South Bend; WKUZ-FM, 95.9, Wabash; WRSW, 1480, Warsaw; WRSW-FM, 1480, Warsaw.

Reds TV Network: WPTA, 21, Ft. Wayne; WXIN, 59, Indianapolis. *Reds Radio Network*: WHBU, 1240, Anderson; WRBI-FM, 103.9, Batesville; WBZL, 1130, Brazil/Terre Haute; WSDM-FM, 97.7, Brazil/Terre Haute; WWWY-FM, 104.9, Columbus; WCVL, 1550, Crawfordsville; WNDE, 1260, Indianapolis; WXVW, 1450, Jeffersonville; WORX, 1270, Madison; WLBC, 1340, Muncie; WFPC-FM, 102.3, Petersburg; WKBV, 1490, Richmond; WRCR-FM, 94.3, Rushville; WSVL, 1520, Shelbyville.

White Sox TV Network: WMCC, 23, Marion/Indianapolis. *White Sox Radio Network*: WHBU-FM, 97.7, Alexandria; WIFF, 1570, Auburn; WIBN-FM, 98.3, Earl Park; WEZR, 1450, Ft. Wayne; WXLW, 950, Indianapolis; WSAL, 1230, Logansport; WGOM, 860, Marion; WRIN, 1560, Rensselaer; WAYT, 1510, Wabash.

Minor League

Indianapolis Indians (American Association) Radio: WBCI-FM, 100.9. Announcers: Howard Kellman, Tom Akins. *South Bend White Sox (Midwest League) Radio*: WHME-FM, 103.1. Announcer: Craig Wallin.

IOWA

Signals from a number of major league networks reach at least some part of Iowa. Most of the state can hear the Cubs, and parts are covered by the Cardinals, Royals, and Twins. Triple-A baseball hits the air in Des Moines as well as in western Iowa from across the river in Omaha (KESY, 1420). And several Iowa Midwest League teams broadcast games.

Major Leagues

Brewers TV Network: KLJB, 18, Davenport; KDUB, 40, Dubuque; K39AS, 39, Marshalltown.

Cubs TV Network: KJMH, 26, Burlington; KCRG, 9, Cedar Rapids; KDSM, 17, Des Moines; KTVO, 3, Ottumwa. *Cubs Radio Network*: KLBA, 1370, Albia; KWBG, 1590, Boone; KZBA-FM, 98.3, Boone; KCIM, 1380, Carroll; KCRG, 1600, Cedar Rapids; KCLN, 1390, Clinton; WOC, 1420, Davenport; WHO, 1040, Des Moines; KDTH, 1370, Dubuque; KADR, 1400, Elkader; KEMB-FM, 98.3, Emmetsburg; KOKX-FM, 95.3, Keokuk; KOSG-FM, 92.7, Osage.

Royals TV Network: KOIA, 15, Ottumwa. *Royals Radio Network*: KLEH, 1290, Anamosa; KCOG, 1400, Centerville; KELR-FM, 105.5, Chariton; KCHE, 1440, Cherokee; KCHE-FM, 102.3, Cherokee; KRNT, 1350, Des Moines; KIDA-FM, 92.7, Ida Grove; KXLQ, 1490, Indianola; KLAL-FM, 97.7, Lamoni; KMA, 960, Shenandoah; KMNS, 620, Sioux City.

Twins TV Network: KGAN, 2, Cedar Rapids. *Twins Radio Network*: KDEC, 1240,

Decorah; KWKY, 1150, Des Moines; KILR-FM, 95.9, Estherville; KHBT-FM, 97.7, Humboldt; KGLO, 1300, Mason City; KJJG-FM, 104.9, Spencer.

White Sox Radio Network: KNEI, 1140, Waukon.

Minor Leagues

Iowa Cubs, Des Moines (American Association) Radio: KJJY, 1390. Announcer: Dan Karcher.

Burlington Braves (Midwest League) Radio: KBUR, 1490, no. of games: 30. Announcer: Wayne Coy.

Clinton Giants (Midwest League) Radio: KROS, 1340, no. of games: all home. Announcer: Barry Determann.

Quad-City Angels, Davenport (Midwest League) Radio: KSTT, 1170. Announcer: Mario Impemba.

KANSAS

The Royals radio network blankets the state, but outside of Wichita not much other baseball finds its way in. The Wichita (Double-A) Pilots broadcast every game.

Major League

Cardinals Radio Network: KSSC-FM, 98.3, Pittsburg.

Royals TV Network: WIBW, 13, Topeka; KAKE, 10, Wichita. *Royals Radio Network*: KERE, 1470, Atchison; KKOY, 1460, Chanute; KQSM-FM, 105.5, Chanute; KCLY-FM, 100.9, Clay Center; KGGF, 690, Coffeyville; KQLS-FM, 100.3, Colby; KNCK, 1390, Concordia; KCKS-FM, 95.3, Concordia; KGNO, 1370, Dodge City; KSPG, 1360, El Dorado; KVOE, 1400, Emporia; KOMB-FM, 103.9, Ft. Scott; KIUL, 1240, Garden City; KLOE, 730, Goodland; KVGB, 1590, Great Bend; KAYS, 1400, Hays; KNZA-FM, 103.9, Hiawatha; KHUQ-FM, 106.7, Hugoton; KWBW, 1450, Hutchinson; KIND-FM, 101.7, Independence; KJCK, 1420, Junction City; KANS, 1510, Larned; KANS-FM, 96.7, Larned; KSCB, 1270, Liberal; KSKU-FM, 106.1, Lyons; KMAN, 1350, Manhattan; KNDY-

Baseball's Biggest Deal

Monumental negotiations in late 1988 set the scenario for baseball's TV future through 1993. National broadcasters and cable partners entered contracts beginning in 1990 that will bring baseball $377 million a year in television, cable, and radio. Local broadcasters will formulate or reformulate contracts that will generate another $200 million annually.

For $1.1 billion, CBS got four years of rights to a unified network package of baseball's premier events—the All-Star Game, the League Championship Series, and the World Series, plus twelve regular-season dates. For the first time in the forty-six years baseball has been televised, NBC will not be covering the sport through the first part of the 1990s. Come late 1992, however, NBC and ABC will be back at the negotiating table in what is likely to be a ferocious bid to win back baseball's coveted TV rights.

Major League Baseball's $400-million national cable-television rights arrangement with ESPN packages 175 regular-season dates, more baseball than has ever been distributed nationally. The deal illustrates cable TV's arrival as a significant purveyor of baseball. The ESPN-baseball relationship begins a revolution, but the revolution is not likely to be complete until baseball starts up its own twenty-four-hour-a-day baseball channel, possibly as soon as the middle of the decade.

If and when that happens, the Big Three broadcast networks will still be showcasing Major League Baseball's postseason crown jewels. A bevy of federal regulators will protect the interest of ABC, CBS, and NBC in presenting big-ticket sports events like the World Series as long as the Big Three maintain distribution across more than 90 percent of the U.S. television landscape. —JM

FM, 103.1; Marysville; KNGL, 1540, McPherson; KBBE-FM, 96.7, McPherson; KFNF-FM, 101.1, Oberlin; KLKC, 1540, Parsons; KLKC-FM, 93.5, Parsons; KSEK, 1340, Pittsburg; KWLS, 1290, Pratt; KRSL, 990, Russell; KCAY-FM, 95.9, Russell; KSAL, 1150, Salina; KEZU-FM, 94.5; Scott City; KULY, 1420, Ulysses; KLEO, 1480, Wichita; KSOK, 1280, Winfield.

Minor League

Wichita Pilots (Texas League) Radio: KQAM 1410.

KENTUCKY

At one point, after the Triple-A Louisville Redbirds drew a million fans one year, it seemed Kentucky might get a major league team of its own. But the Redbirds are content in the minors, and no other pro team calls Kentucky home. Cincinnati

Reds games can still be seen and heard in most of the state.

Major Leagues

Cardinals TV Network: Comcast Cable, Paducah. *Cardinals Radio Network*: WCBL, 1290, Benton; WSON, 860, Henderson; WHOP, 1230, Hopkinsville; WYMC, 1430, Mayfield; WMSK, 1550, Morganfield; WSJP, 1130, Murray; WVJS, 1420, Paducah.

Cubs Radio Network: WNGO, 1320, Mayfield.

Reds TV Network: WGRB, 34, Bowling Green; East Kentucky Cable, Hindman; W43AG, 43, Hopkinsville; WTVQ, 36, Lexington; WDKY, 56, Lexington; WDRB, 41, Louisville; Comcast Cable, Paducah. *Reds Radio Network*: WCTT, 680, Corbin; WCYN, 1400, Cynthiana; WFKY, 1490, Frankfort; WUGO-FM, 102.3, Grayson; *(Cont. p. 179)*

Baseball Television 1999:
Through a Glass Brightly

Picture baseball's television landscape in the late 1990s. Behold an incredible shrinking planet. Each year, from April to October, technological advances and marketing momentum drive America's national pastime toward a glowing achievement: the removal of national boundaries, rendering the globe a single baseball state.

The regular season's dizzying abundance of televised baseball (every game accessible) comes to fans' home-entertainment centers (remember when we had TV *sets*?) via cable, pay-per-view, or Direct Broadcast Satellite. For the fan in this country or in any number of others, baseball continues to proliferate. You can literally watch games twenty-four hours a day and store the leftover tapes for winter. Viewers share an ever-greater degree of the costs, a small price for being able to see every pitch of the 1999 season.

The attraction of pay-per-view to baseball executives is that it limits exposure while it maximizes revenues. About 15.3 million homes, 17.1 percent of TV households, have addressable systems now. That number is expected to increase to 51.3 million homes, 52.2 percent of TV homes, by 2001.

Technologies affecting how television covers baseball—addressability and interactivity—have grown in maturity and economic sense during the decade. If a fan wants to follow more than one team in a pennant race at the moment it's happening, he can create windows in his TV monitor and catch the action of all the games simultaneously—assuming he has only one set.

"Put the viewer inside the game," says Charles Milton, senior producer for CBS Sports. That means TV audiences are taking a more active role in sports contests, so active a role that the 1999 viewer, while not actually being able to influence the game, is finally able to play armchair manager.

TV shows more extensive layering of statistical information, and the development of interactive communication between the home and the studio gives the fan a chance to second-guess the manager. If your skipper brings a lefty from the bullpen, you can key in the right-hander of

TV controllers need intense concentration.

your choice. Your home computer, armed with up-to-the-second data from the network feed, analyzes the game situation. While you watch the manager's lefty being shelled, you learn that *your* reliever would (probably) have retired the enemy without incident.

Pinch hitters, defensive substitutions, even infield and outfield overshifts are in your power—at least in so far as knowing the probabilities if the real manager had done it your way.

Home control takes another step as viewers can tap into a control room with a high-speed switcher to pick camera angles on each play or replay. This process, called ACTV, can give you as many as fifteen different views of the same play. "Super slo-mo" and zooming allow you to check if a runner is safe or out, while high resolution lets you count the stitches on the baseball. And umpires thought they had it tough back in 1990!

On the other hand, we may be near the time when the umpiring crew conducts the game from a control booth far beneath the stands, announcing calls simultaneously on the scoreboard and the public-address system. Try arguing with *that*, Earl Weaver!

For the TV viewer, increased use of stereo and more mikes installed in unusual places, such as on players' and managers' uniforms, bring the sounds of the ballpark into his home. And a seven-second delay bleeper lets him sanitize dugout language for the youngsters.

Fact is, the advantages of watching at home so outweigh those of actually going out to the game that crowd noise now has to be electronically augmented. Nevertheless the stands are always packed. With robots.

One more thing. Concessions-à-Go-Go will deliver warm beer and cold hotdogs right to your doorstep.   —JM

WKCB-FM, 107.1, Hindman; WRNZ-FM, 105.1, Lancaster/Danville; WLXG, 1300, Lexington, WVEZ, 790, Louisville; WMDJ, 1440, Martin; WFTM, 1240, Maysville; WFTM-FM, 95.9, Maysville; WMOR, 1330, Morehead; WMOR-FM, 92.1, Morehead; WMST, 1150, Mt. Sterling; WLOC, 1150, Munfordville; WLOC-FM, 102.3, Munfordville; WOMI, 1490, Owensboro; WDHR-FM, 92.1, Pikeville; WCBR, 1110, Richmond; WIDS, 570, Russell Springs; WSFC, 1240, Somerset; WTCW, 920, Whitesburg; WXKQ-FM, 103.9, Whitesburg.

Minor League

Louisville Redbirds (American Association) Radio: WAVG, 970. Announcers: Jim Kelch, Joe Buck.

LOUISIANA

New Orleans remains one of the largest cities in the country without a pro baseball team. Alas, the out-of-town radio and TV pickings are slim, too. In most of the state, content yourself with the Astros, or look for the Braves (WSB, 750) or the Rangers (WBAP, 820) on clear-channel.

Major League

Astros TV Network: WKG, 49, Baton Rouge; WNOL, 38, New Orleans; KMSS, 33, Shreveport. *Astros Radio Network*: WQXY, 910, Baton Rouge; KLCL, 1470, Lake Charles; WWIW, 1450, New Orleans; KFLO, 1300, Shreveport.

Minor League

Shreveport Captains (Texas League) TV: KMSS, 33, no. of games: 22. *Captains Radio*: KEEL, 710. Announcer: Dave Nitz.

MAINE

Despite its out-of-way location and out-of-mind climate, Maine has a lot of baseball fans. Not enough to have kept the state's Triple-A team from moving away, but enough to encourage broadcasts from Bos-

ton and of the University of Maine games. Watch for the Red Sox on the New England Sports Network and Boston's Channel 38, both available on many Maine cable systems.

Major League

Red Sox TV Network: WCSH, 6, Portland; WLBZ, 2, Bangor. *Red Sox Radio Network*: WABI, 910, Bangor; WJTO, 730, Bath; WIDE, 1400, Biddeford; WQDY, 1230, Calais; WQDY-FM, 92.7, Calais; WDME, 1340, Dover/Foxcroft; WDME-FM, 103.1, Dover/Foxcroft; WDEA, 1370, Ellsworth; WKTJ, 1380, Farmington; WKTJ-FM, 99.3, Farmington; WABK-FM, 104.3, Gardiner; WHOU, 1340, Houlton; WHOU-FM, 100.1, Houlton; WXGL, Lewiston; WLKN, 1450, Lincoln; WGUY-FM, 99.3, Lincoln; WSYY, 1240, Millinocket; WKTQ, 1450, Norway; WOXO-FM, 92.7, Norway; WWGT-FM, 97.9, Portland; WKZX, 950, Presque Isle; WMCM-FM, 93.5, Rockland; WRKD, 1340, Rockland; WTVL, 1490, Waterville; WTVL-FM, 98.5, Waterville.

MARYLAND

No one in Maryland can miss the Orioles, not with two of the area's strongest radio stations both carrying all the games (WBAL, 1090; WTOP, 1500). We've already told you about Jon Miller, the game's leading radio man. The Orioles' TV and cable TV networks also blanket the state. Plus Marylanders can also pick up clear-channel radio broadcasts of the Phillies, Mets, and Yankees, among others. The state's two minor league teams have local outlets.

Major Leagues

Orioles TV: WMAR, 2, Baltimore, no. of games: 42. Announcers: Jim Palmer, Brooks Robinson. *TV Network*: WDCA, 20, Washington, D.C.; WMDT, 47, Salisbury. *Cable TV*: Home Team Sports (pay), Washington, D.C., no. of games: 90. Announcers: Mel Proctor, John Lowenstein. *Orioles Radio*: WBAL, 1090, Baltimore. Announc-

ers: Jon Miller, Joe Angel. *Radio Network*: WTOP, 1500, Washington, D.C.; WAMD, 970, Aberdeen; WNAV, 1430, Annapolis; WCEM-FM, 106.3, Cambridge; WTBO, 1450, Cumberland; WFMD, 930, Frederick; WARK, 1490, Hagerstown; WASA, 1330, Havre de Grace; WPTX, 920, Lexington Park; WETT, 1590, Ocean City; WDMV, 540, Pocomoke City; WSBY, 960, Salisbury; WTTR, 1470, Westminster.

Pirates Radio Network: WCBC, 1270, Cumberland.

Minor Leagues

Hagerstown (Eastern League) Radio: WJEJ, 1240. Announcer: Stu Paul.

Frederick Keys (Carolina League) Radio: WZYQ,

MASSACHUSETTS

Most of the state is strongly devoted to the Boston Red Sox, but many Massachusetts listeners can also follow the fortunes of the New York Yankees and Mets. The only minor league baseball left in the state is a short-season New York–Penn League team in Pittsfield, but listeners near Rhode Island can hear the Triple-A Pawtucket Red Sox.

Major Leagues

Mets Radio Network: WBEC, 1420, Pittsfield.

Red Sox TV: WSBK, 38, Boston, no. of games: 78. Announcers: Sean McDonough, Bob Montgomery. *TV Network*: WWLP, 22, Springfield. *Cable TV*: New England Sports Network (pay), Boston, no. of games: 92. Announcers: Ned Martin, Jerry Remy, Tom Larsen. *Red Sox Radio*: WRKO, 680, Boston. Announcers: Ken Coleman, Joe Castiglione. *Radio Network*: WFGL, 960, Fitchburg; WGAW, 1340, Gardner; WHAI, 1240, Greenfield; WHAI-FM, 98.3, Greenfield; WHAV, 1490, Haverhill; WCAP, 980, Lowell; WSRO, 1470, Marlboro; WMRC, 1490, Milford; WNBH, 1340, New Bedford; WNCG, 1450, Newburyport; WNAW, 1230, North Adams; WHMP, 1400, Northampton; WCAT, 700, Orange/Athol; WUPE-FM, 95.5, Pittsfield; WPLM, 1390, Plymouth; WPLM-FM, 99.1, Plymouth; WESO, 970, Southbridge; WQVR-FM, 100.1, Southbridge; WHYN, 560, Springfield; WARE, 1250, Ware; WTAG, 580, Worcester.

Yankees Radio Network: WBRK, 1340, Pittsfield; WIXY, 1600, Springfield/East Longmeadow.

MICHIGAN

The Tigers' radio network stretches across Michigan, and Detroit's powerful WJR (760) beams Hall of Fame announcer Ernie Harwell well past the state line. The proximity to Canada also means the Toronto Blue Jays' broadcasts aren't hard to find. The southern part of the state shouldn't have any problem picking up other major league games, including those of both Chicago teams, as well as the Reds and the Indians.

Major Leagues

Brewers Radio Network: WDBC, 680, Escanaba; WJNR-FM, 101.5, Iron Mountain; WIKB, 1230, Iron River; WIKB-FM, 99.3, Iron River; WJMS, 590, Ironwood; WJPD, 1240, Ishpeming; WJPD-FM, 92.3, Ishpeming.

Cubs Radio Network: WLAV, 1340, Grand Rapids; WJMS, 590, Ironwood; WQSN, 1470, Kalamazoo; WPBK, 1490, Whitehall.

Tigers TV: WDIV, 4, Detroit, no. of games: 45. Announcers: George Kell, Al Kaline. *TV Network*: WWMT, 3, Kalamazoo; WLNS, 6, Lansing/Jackson; WJRT, 12, Flint/Saginaw; WWTV, 9, Cadillac. *Cable TV*: PASS (pay), Ann Arbor, no. of games: 80. Announcers: Larry Osterman, Jim Northrup. *Tigers Radio*: WJR, 760, Detroit. Announcers: Ernie Harwell, Paul Caray. *Radio Network*: WFYC, 1280, Alma; WFYC-FM, Alma; WATZ, 1450, Alpena; WATZ-FM, 93.5, Alpena; WBCK, 930, Battle Creek; WBRN, 1460, Big Rap-

ids; WKJF-FM, 92.9, Cadillac; WMMQ-FM, 92.7, Charlotte; WCBY, 1240, Cheboygan; WYKX-FM, 104.7, Escanaba; WSHN-FM, 100.1, Fremont; WMJZ, 900, Gaylord; WMJZ-FM, 95.3, Gaylord; WCUZ, 1230, Grand Rapids; WCSR, 1340, Hillsdale; WHTC, 1450, Holland; WMKM, 1290, Houghton Lake; WCCY, 1400, Houghton; WION, 1430, Ionia; WKZO, 590, Kalamazoo; WDMJ, 1320, Marquette; WELL, 1260, Marshall; WELL-FM, 104.9, Marshall; WMPX, 1490, Midland; WCEN, 1150, Mt. Pleasant; WCEN-FM, 94.5, Mt. Pleasant; WQKO, 1400, Munising; WQKO-FM, 98.3, Munising; WKBZ, 850, Muskegon; WNBY, 1450, Newberry; WNBY-FM, 93.5, Newberry; WONT-FM, 98.3, Ontonagan; WWPZ, 1340, Petoskey; WSGW, 790, Saginaw; WMIC, 1560, Sandusky; WTGV-FM, 97.7, Sandusky; WSOO, 1230, Sault Ste. Marie; WKZC-FM, 95.9, Scottville; WCSY, 790, South Haven; WCSY-FM, 98.3, South Haven; WSTR, 1230, Sturgis; WSTR-FM, 99.3, Sturgis; WKJC-FM, 103.9, Tawas; WTCM, 580, Traverse City.

MINNESOTA

In most of Minnesota, baseball means the Twins. Even if you can't find a local network affiliate, WCCO (830) covers the state well. Some clear-channel action should be available, at least in the southern part of the state.

Major Leagues

Cubs Radio Network: KVOX, 1280, Moorhead.

Twins TV: WCCO, 4; KITN, 29 (both in Minneapolis), no. of games: 35 (WCCO), 23 (KITN). Announcers: Ted Robinson, Jim Kaat, Dick Bremer. *TV Network*: WDIO, 10, Duluth/Superior; KAAL, 6, Rochester. *Cable TV*: Midwest Sports Channel (pay), Pay Per View; no. of games: 21 (MSC), 46 (PPV). Announcers: Bremer, Harmon Killebrew. *Twins Radio*: WCCO, 830, Minneapolis. Announcers: Herb Carneal, John Gordon. *Radio Network*: KRJB-FM, 106.3, Ada; KATE, 1450, Albert Lea;

KXRA, 1490, Alexandria; KAUS, 1480, Austin; KBUN, 1450, Bemidji; KBMO, 1290, Benson; KSCR-FM, 93.5, Benson; KLIZ, 1380, Brainerd; KROX, 1260, Crookston; KDLM, 1340, Detroit Lakes; KDAL, 610, Duluth; WELY, 1450, Ely; KSUM, 1370, Fairmont; KJJK, 1090, Fergus Falls; KKCQ, 1480, Fosston; KKDQ-FM, 107.1, Fosston; KOZY, 1320, Grand Rapids; WMFG, 1240, Hibbing; WMFG-FM, 106.3, Hibbing; KGHS, 1230, International Falls; KLTF, 960, Little Falls; KEYL, 1400, Long Prairie; KTOE, 1420, Mankato; KMHL, 1400, Marshall; KMGM-FM, 105.5, Montevideo; KNUJ, 860, New Ulm; KOLV-FM, 101.7, Olivia; KFIL, 1060, Preston; KFIL-FM, 103.1, Preston; KROC, 1340, Rochester; KRWB, 1410, Roseau; KMSR-FM, 94.3, Sauk Centre; WJON, 1240, St. Cloud; KTRF, 1230, Thief River Falls; WHLB, 1400, Virginia; KWMB, 1190, Wabasha; KWAD, 920, Wadena; KLLR, 1600, Walker; KLLR-FM, 99.3, Walker; KOWO, 1170, Waseca; KOWO-FM, 92.1, Waseca; KWLM, 1340, Willmar; KDOM, 1580, Windom; KDOM-FM, 94.3, Windom; KWNO, 1230, Winona; KWOA, 730, Worthington.

MISSISSIPPI

Minor league contests are available in Jackson and also near Memphis (WREC, 600). As for the major leagues, try the clear-channel stations for the Braves, Rangers, or Cardinals.

Major Leagues

Astros TV Network: WNTZ, 48, Natchez.

Cardinals Radio Network: WWZQ, 1240, Aberdeen; WCLD, 1490, Cleveland; WTIB-FM, 104.9, Iuka; WNAU, New Albany.

Cubs Radio Network: WCHJ, 1470, Brookhaven; WBKN-FM, 92.1, Brookhaven.

Rangers TV Network: WDBD, 40, Jackson; WNTZ, 48, Natchez.

Minor League

Jackson Mets (Texas League) Radio: WJDX, 620. Announcer: Bill Walberg.

(Cont. p. 182)

A Home Run Call Is Born

A radio play-by-play announcer lives for climactic moments: touchdowns, goals, home runs. But only the baseball announcer has genuine options on how to describe his sport's ultimate event.

Consider the problem. The football announcer simply must yell, "Touchdown!" to conclude his call on the scoring play. In hockey, there are "Score!" and "He shoots, he scores!" and "Goal!" But the choices end there.

Basketball provides the announcer some room for creativity in calling baskets. Marv Albert's "Yes!" enlivens New York Knicks broadcasts. And other announcers have strayed from the standard, "It's good!" by calling "Two!" or "It's down!" or "Swish!" and even "Rip City!" But with over a hundred baskets scored during each broadcast, it doesn't matter how the announcer calls any particular one.

Now consider the baseball announcer. Given the nature of the game, it is expected that he be more lyrical and original than his counterparts in other sports. Compare the time in flight of a baseball traveling four hundred feet with that of a basketball going twenty feet. It is an elongated moment of suspense in which the baseball announcer unfolds the home run story.

Every baseball fan who has cursed out an umpire, studied a boxscore, or been one of those "scoring along at home" thinks he could call the action of a baseball game. And many of you probably could, although the time between pitches would leave you groping and stammering. But how would you call the long ball when your team hits one?

I was faced with that decision in 1979 when, after years of broadcasting hockey, I joined the Texas Rangers' broadcast team. I had several months to prepare for the season, and when that first home run flew out off a Ranger bat, I was going to be ready with my own home run call.

I grew up in New York with Mel Allen's "Going, going . . . gone!" My well-respected predecessor in Texas, the late Dick Risenhoover, cried out "Goodbye, baseball!" And my broadcast partner, Jon Miller, now with the Orioles, would "Tell it goodbye!"

In the early days of broadcasting an announcer could get away with just about anything, no matter how corny it might sound to us now. Can you believe that Pittsburgh's Rosey Rowswell used to shout, "Open the window, Aunt Minnie!" in reference to a lady who lived across the street from the ballpark? And more than one announcer, even recently, has used the call "That's a gone goslin!"

Giants announcer Russ Hodges' home run call, "Tell it bye, bye, baby!" was taken from a popular song. So was the "Up, up, and away!" call used by two of our Canadian colleagues. One of my favorites was made famous by Harry Caray. "It could be. It might be. It is! A home run!" Very dramatic, especially with Harry's theatrical delivery.

All things considered, however, I felt that "Going, going . . . gone!" was the best. Short, to the point, and still providing a dramatic buildup. But it was far from original, and too well known through years of national exposure.

I needed something distinctive. Not too contrived. Unique to me, but still able to get the message across to someone hearing me for the first time. And it had to be a phrase that left a way out, in case the ball somehow stayed in the park after you'd already begun the home run call. I liked the simple cry "That ball is out of here!" But it, too, was overused. The buildup, however, was perfect: "That ball is . . ." You could always finish with "Off the wall!" or "Caught!" if you'd really misjudged it.

Now how to find my own climax to the phrase "That ball is . . ."? I spent agonizing chunks of time pondering the possibilities. Searched the thesaurus for ideas. Asked advice. Did I have sleepless nights? No, let's not get ridiculous.

One day it just came to me. The perfect word. This was it. I checked with a few people to make sure I was not deluding myself. The more I said it out loud, the more I liked it.

The first glorious moment came only after several games of frustration. The Rangers just could not connect in the middle innings, which were my play-by-play innings. Not Buddy Bell. Not Richie Zisk. Not even Al Oliver. Then one Sunday afternoon it finally happened—in Seattle's Kingdome, a large room disguised as a ballpark, a real home run haven. And it almost took me by surprise. Johnny Grubb, a left-handed hitter, slapped a lazy fly ball the opposite way, right down the 316-foot foul line.

"There's a high fly ball down the left-field line." (I expect it to be caught.) "Meyer racing into the corner." (God, he's going back fast.) "He's at the warning track." (I think it has a chance.) "He's at the wall." (He might still catch it.) "He leaps." (This could be it.) "And that ball is . . . *history!* A home run for Johnny Grubb!"

Over the last few years I have refined the delivery somewhat. When Larry Parrish hit one, I usually knew it immediately and just said, "It's history!" And even now and then I'll use another call, just to keep 'em guessing.

"That ball is history!" I hope you like it. And believe me, it sounds better than it reads. Hey, even "Bye, bye, baby!" looks pretty weak on paper.

Think you can come up with something better? Something original? If you do, please send it to me. If I prefer it, then I'll take my call and "Kiss it goodbye!" —EN

MISSOURI

St. Louis' KMOX (1120) has sometimes billed itself as America's sports station. The clear-channel outlet allows Cardinal games with Jack Buck to be heard virtually from coast to coast. The Royals also have a strong network, but without a clear-channel station. And if Missouri listeners tire of the local teams, they should find action from Chicago, Cincinnati, or Minnesota.

Major Leagues

Cardinals TV: KPLR, 11, St. Louis, no. of games: 60. Announcers: Ken Wilson, Al Hrabosky. *TV Network*: KBSI, 23, Cape Girardeau; KOMU, 8, Columbia; TCI Cable, Columbia; K57DR, 57, Joplin; KTVO, 3, Kirksville; Falcon Cable, Sedalia; KDEB, 27, Springfield; TeleCable, Springfield; KQTV, 2, St. Joseph. *Cable TV:* Cencom Cable (pay per view), St. Louis, no. of games: 50. Announcers: Wilson, Hrabosky. *Cardinals Radio*: KMOX, 1120, St. Louis. Announcers: Jack Buck, Mike Shannon. *Radio Network*: KEZS-FM, 102.9,

Cape Girardeau; KLOW-FM, 103.1, Caruthersville; KFRU, 1400, Columbia; KDEX, 1590, Dexter; KOEA, 1500, Doniphan; KDFN-FM, 97.7, Doniphan; KLOZ-FM, 92.7, Eldon; KFMO, 1240, Flat River; KKCA-FM, 97.7, Fulton; KHMO, 1070, Hannibal; KUNQ-FM, 99.3, Houston; KYLS-FM, 92.7, Ironton; KWOS, 1240, Jefferson City; KIRX, 1450, Kirksville; KSAF-FM, 105.5, Knob Noster; KLWT, 1230, Lebanon; KJFM-FM, 101.7, Louisiana; KMEM-FM, 96.7, Memphis; KXEO, 1340, Mexico; KRES-FM, 104.7, Moberly; KKBL-FM, 95.9, Monnett; KLCQ-FM, 106.3, Monroe City; KPWB, 1140, Piedmont; KWOC, 930, Poplar Bluff; KMIS, 1050, Portageville; KCLU-FM, 94.3, Rolla; KSMO, 1340, Salem; KSIS, 1540, Sedalia; KMPL, 1520, Sikeston; KTXR-FM, 101.5; Springfield; KKJO, 1550, St. Joseph; KTUI, 1560, Sullivan; KJPW, 1390, Waynesville; KSPQ, West Plains.

Cubs Radio Network: KAPE, 1550, Cape Girardeau.

Royals TV: WDAF, 4, Kansas City, no. of games: 52. Announcers: Denny Trease,

Paul Splittorff. *TV Network*: KMIZ, 17, Columbia; KSNF, 16, Joplin; KDEB, 27, Springfield. *Royals Radio*: WIBW, 580. Announcers: Denny Matthews, Fred White. (WIBW is in Topeka, Kansas; the Royals are heard in Kansas City on KMBZ, 980.) *Radio Network*: KELE-FM, 100.1, Aurora; KAAN-FM, 95.9, Bethany/Albany; KYOO, 1130, Bolivar; KYOO-FM, 106.3, Bolivar; KOMC, 1220, Branson; KRZK-FM, 106.3, Branson; KMAM, 1530, Butler; KMOE-FM, 92.1, Butler; KZMO, 1420, California; KZMO-FM, 94.3, California; KDMO, 1490, Carthage; KRGK-FM, 104.9, Carthage; KCHI, 1010, Chillicothe; KCHI-FM, 104.1, Chillicothe; KDKD-FM, 95.3, Clinton; KTGR, 1580, Columbia; KESM, 1580, El Dorado Springs; WMBH, 1450, Joplin; KMAL-FM, 92.7, Malden; KMMO, 1300, Marshall; KMMO-FM, 102.9, Marshall; KMRF, 1510, Marshfield; KNIM, 1580, Maryville; KNIM-FM, 95.3, Maryville; KBTN, 1420, Neosho; KNEM, 1240, Nevada; KSWM, 940, Republic; KFEQ, 680, St. Joseph; KDRO, 1490, Sedalia; KWTO, 560, Springfield; KTRX-FM, 93.5, Tarkio; KTTN, 1600, Trenton; KTTN-FM, Trenton; KOKO, 1450, Warrensburg; KAYQ-FM, 97.7, Warsaw.

MONTANA

Until the Pioneer League season gets under way in late June, Montana remains isolated from most of the baseball broadcasting world. But many of the short-season teams air all seventy of their games.

Major League

Twins Radio Network: KGCX, 1480, Sidney.

Minor Leagues

Billings Mustangs (Pioneer League) Ra-

Television cameras perched in an eyrie behind home plate catch an infield play at Yankee Stadium in 1951, when Mel Allen was regaling fans with "White Owl Wallops" and "Ballantine Blasts."

dio: KCTR, 970. Announcer: Glen Hebert.

Butte Copper Kings (Pioneer League) Radio: KBOW, 550. Announcer: Frasier MacDonald.

Great Falls Dodgers (Pioneer League) Radio: KEIN, 1310. Announcer: Gene Black.

Helena Brewers (Pioneer League) Radio: KBLL, 1240, no. of games: All home games.

NEBRASKA

The state that gears up for the College World Series every June doesn't have as much baseball on the air as you might expect. But the Omaha Royals began broadcasting every game in 1988, and the Kansas City Royals radio and TV networks stretch into Nebraska.

Major Leagues

Cubs Radio Network: KKAR, 1180, Omaha.

Royals TV Network: KPTM, 42, Omaha. *Royals Radio Network*: KAUB-FM, 105.5, Auburn; KWBE, 1450, Beatrice; KGMT, 1310, Fairbury; KTNC, 1230, Falls City; KHUB, 1340, Fremont; KMTY-FM, 103.1, Grand Island; KGFW, 1340, Kearney; KRVN, 880, Lexington; KFOR, 1240, Lincoln; KNCY, 1600, Nebraska City; KNCY-FM, 98.1, Nebraska City; KMCX-FM, 106.1, Ogallala; KOIL, 1290, Omaha; KBRX-FM, 102.9, O'Neill; KNLV, 1060, Ord; KNLV-FM, 103.9, Ord; KNEB, 960, Scottsbluff; KRFS, 1600, Superior; KRFS-FM, 103.9, Superior; KAWL, 1370, York.

Minor League

Omaha Royals (American Association) Radio: KKAR, 1180. Announcer: Frank Adkisson.

NEVADA

Walk into a Las Vegas sports book during the season, and you're likely to see any number of baseball games on the screen. In the interest of gambling, the books will pick any game possible off the satellite. Other people will likely need to settle for West Coast action, or for the local minor league club. If you can't find a game anywhere else, check for the Giants on clear channel KNBR (680).

Major Leagues

Angels Radio Network: KLAV, 1230, Las Vegas.

Athletics TV Network: KRLR, 21, Las Vegas; KAME, 21, Reno. *Athletics Radio Network*: KROL, 870, Las Vegas; KONE, 1450, Reno.

Cubs Radio Network: KROL, 870, Las Vegas.

Dodgers Radio Network: KDWN, 720, Las Vegas; KREL, 1280, Las Vegas (Spanish).

Giants TV Network: KAME, 21, Reno. *Giants Radio Network*: KPLY, 1270, Reno/Sparks.

Padres TV Network: KRLR, 21, Las Vegas. *Padres Radio Network*: KROL, 870, Las Vegas.

Minor Leagues

Las Vegas Stars (Pacific Coast League) Radio: KLAV, 1230. Announcers: Dom Valentino, Colin Cowherd.

Reno Silver Sox (California League) Radio: KRCZ, 1340. Announcer: Todd Karli.

NEW HAMPSHIRE

Like the rest of New England, New Hampshire is Red Sox country. Pick up the Sox on any number of stations, or try for Hartford's clear channel WTIC (1080). Since the Eastern League's Nashua team moved, the state has no team of its own.

Major League

Red Sox Radio Network: WMOU, Berlin; WMOU-FM, 103.7, Berlin; WTSV, 1230, Claremont; WKXL, 1450, Concord; WDER, 1320, Derry; WTSN, 1270, Dover; WTSL, 1400, Hanover/Lebanon; WKNE, 1290, Keene; WEMJ, 1490, Laconia; WLTN, 1400, Littleton; WGIR, 610, Manchester.

NEW JERSEY

Somewhere around the middle of the state, New Jersey's baseball fans divide between those who support New York teams and those who root for the Phillies (probably along the lines of the TV signals from those cities). And since, as of this writing, efforts to land a minor league team in the state haven't succeeded, the Yankees, Mets, and Phillies will have to do. All three have clear-channel flagships that cover the state, so all you really need to remember is WABC (770) for the Yankees, WFAN (660) for the Mets, and WCAU (1210) for the Phils.

Major Leagues

Mets Radio Network: WOBM, 1170, Toms River/Lakewood; WTTM, 920, Trenton/Princeton.

Phillies Radio Network: WFPG, 1450, Atlantic City; WCMC, 1230, Wildwood.

NEW MEXICO

Don't expect to pick up much clear-channel baseball on the New Mexico radio dial, although you should be able to hear the Triple-A Albuquerque Dukes anywhere in the state on KOB (770). In the far south of the state you might also find the Double-A El Paso Diablos on KHEY (690).

Major Leagues

Padres TV Network: KNMZ, 2, Santa Fe. *Padres Radio Network*: KZIA, 1580, Albuquerque.

Royals Radio Network: KLMX, 1450, Clayton.

Minor League

Albuquerque Dukes (Pacific Coast League) Radio: KOB, 770. Announcers: Mike Roberts, Jim Lawwill.

NEW YORK

With the move of Mets flagship WFAN onto the clear-channel 660 frequency, New York baseball became more accessible to anyone in the region. The Yankees, on WABC (770), could already be widely heard. The strong signal of Rochester's WHAM (1180) carries some games from each team. Television is another problem, with more and more games going to pay cable. What will happen after the Yankees' 1990 move to the Madison Square Garden Network is anyone's guess. Upstate, you should find plenty of minor league baseball.

Major Leagues

Indians Radio Network: WBUZ, 1570, Fredonia.

Mets TV: WWOR, 9, Secaucus, N.J., no. of games: 75. Announcers: Ralph Kiner, Steve Zabriskie, Tim McCarver. *TV Network*: WUTV, 29, Buffalo; WUHF, 31, Rochester. *Cable TV*: SportsChannel (pay), Woodbury, no. of games: 75. Announcers: Kiner, Fran Healy, Rusty Staub. *Mets Radio*: WFAN, 660, Astoria. Announcers: Bob Murphy, Gary Cohen. *Radio Network*: WPTR, 1540, Albany; WENE, 1430, Binghamton; WFLR, 1570, Dundee; WFLR-FM, 95.9, Dundee; WENY, 1230, Elmira; WCKR-FM, 92.1, Hornell; WHCU, 870, Ithaca; WIZR, 930, Johnstown; WGHQ, 920, Kingston; WLPW-FM, 101.5, Lake Placid/Plattsburgh; WLFH, 1230, Little Falls; WLVL, 1340, Lockport/Buffalo; WALL, 1340, Middletown; WKIP, 1450, Poughkeepsie; WCGR, 1550, Rochester; WKAJ, 900, Saratoga Springs; WCDO, 1490, Sidney; WCDO-FM, 101.1, Sidney; WBAZ-FM. 101.7, Southold; WSPQ, 1330, Springville; WIBX, 950, Utica/Rome. *Spanish Radio*: WJIT, 1480, New York, no. of games: 100. Announcers: Billy Berroa, Armando Talavera, Juan Alicea.

Pirates Radio Network: WGR, 550, Buffalo.

Yankees TV: WPIX, 11, New York, no. of games: 40. Announcers: George Grande, Phil Rizzuto. *TV Network*: WICZ, 40, Bing-hamton; WUHF, 31, Rochester; WUTV, 29, Buffalo. *Cable TV*: Madison Square Garden Network, no. of games: 100. *Yankees Radio*: WABC, 770, New York. Announcers: John Sterling, Jay Johnstone. *Radio Network*: WROW, 590, Albany/Troy; WBTF-FM, 101.7, Attica/Batavia; WNBF, 1290, Binghamton/Endicott; WCLI, 1450, Corning/Elmira; WDNY, 1400, Dansville; WDOE, 1410, Dunkirk; WGVA, 1240, Geneva; WIGS, 1230, Gouvernor; WENT, 1340, Gloversville/Johnstown; WTKO, 1470, Ithaca/Cortland; WKSN, 1340, Jamestown; WKNY, 1490, Kingston; WLVL, 1340, Lockport/Buffalo; WCHN, 970, Norwich; WSLB, 1400, Ogdensburg; WHDL, 1450, Olean; WPDM, 1490, Potsdam; WHAM, 1180, Rochester; WWWD, 1240, Schenectady; WSYR, 570, Syracuse; WRUN, 1150, Utica/Rome; WOTT, 1410, Watertown; WLSV, 790, Wellsville.

Minor Leagues

Buffalo Bisons (American Association) Radio: WGR, 550. Announcers: Pete Weber, John Murphy.

Rochester Red Wings (International League) Radio: WBBF, 950; WGMC-FM, 90.1. Announcers: Jay Colley, Josh Lewin.

Syracuse Chiefs (International League) Radio: WNOR, 1260. Announcer: Dan Hoard.

Albany-Colonie Yankees (Eastern League) Radio: WGNA, 1460. Announcer: Dale McConachie.

Batavia Clippers (New York–Penn League) Radio: WBTA, 1490, no. of games: 29. Announcer: Rich Redantz.

Elmira Pioneers (New York–Penn League) Radio: WEHH, 1590, no. of games: 30. Announcers: Norm Stull, Bob Michaels.

NORTH CAROLINA

The real Durham Bulls aren't the only game on North Carolina radio, where most minor league clubs air at least part of their schedule. The Bulls have even sent two former announcers to the major leagues, Steve LaMar to the Cleveland Indians and Gary Cohen to the New York Mets. The Braves network also covers the state, but beware of the Motor Racing Network, which shares many of the Braves' stations and knocks most Sunday games off the airwaves. Orioles' TV games can be seen in some parts of the state. Clear-channel stations bring in the Braves, Orioles, Phillies, Mets, Yankees, and Reds on most nights.

Major Leagues

Braves Radio Network: WCSL, 1590, Cherryville; WEGO, 1410, Concord; WTIK, 1310, Durham/Raleigh; WLOE, 1490, Eden; WFAI, 1230, Fayetteville; WSSG, 1300, Goldsboro; WHKY, 1290, Hickory; WCBT, 1230, Roanoke Rapids; WCAB, 590, Rutherfordton; WSAT, 1280, Salisbury; WETC, 540, Wendell; WTOB, 1380, Winston-Salem.

Cubs Radio Network: WJTP, 1130, Newland.

Orioles TV Network: WLFL, 22, Raleigh/Durham; WJZY, 46, Charlotte; W47AG, 47, Rocky Mount. *Orioles Radio Network*: WEED, 1390, Rocky Mount; WSOC, 930, Charlotte.

Reds TV Network: WHKY, 14, Charlotte; WNRW, 45, Winston-Salem.

Minor Leagues

Charlotte Knights (Southern League) Radio: WSOC, 930. Announcer: Pat McConnell.

Durham Bulls (Carolina League) Radio: WDNC, 620. Announcer: Rod Meadows.

Kinston Indians (Carolina League) Radio: WFTC, 960. Announcer: Mark Aucutt.

Asheville Tourists (South Atlantic League) Radio: WWNC, 570. Announcers: Walt Childs, Paul Davis.

Greensboro Hornets (South Atlantic League) Radio: WKEW, 1400; WMFR, 1230. Announcer: Bob Licht.

Burlington Indians (Appalachian League) Radio: WBBB, 920. Announcer: Robert Fish.

NORTH DAKOTA

Since the demise of the Northern League, North Dakota has been without live professional baseball. As for the television and radio versions, reach for the Twins network, or try to dial in WCCO (830) out of Minneapolis.

Major League

Twins TV Network: KVRR, 15, Fargo; KFYR, 5, Minot. *Twins Radio Network*: KHOL, 1410, Beulah; KLXX, 1270, Bismarck; KDLR, 1240, Devils Lake; KLTC, 1460, Dickinson; KVOX, 1280, Fargo; KXPO, 1340, Grafton; KNOX, 1310, Grand Forks; KNDC, 1490, Hettinger; KSJB, 600, Jamestown; KQLX-FM, 106.3, Lisbon; KMAV, 1520, Mayville; KMAV-FM, 105.2, Mayville; KPRZ, 1390, Minot; KDDR, 1220, Oakes; KBMW, 1450, Wahpeton; KGCX, 1480, Williston.

OHIO

Baseball is easy to find in Ohio. For the Indians, tune in WWWE (1100) or a network station. For the Reds, WLW (700) covers the state and more. Other major league teams can be heard, including the Tigers, Pirates, Cubs, and White Sox. In both Columbus and Toledo, there are Triple-A games.

A Little Piece of Heaven

A satellite dish is the key to a baseball heaven located in outer space, above the midsection of the United States. There fifteen broadcast satellites hover, receiving addressable digital signals from satellite dishes at the source of the broadcast—in this case, any ballpark that's televising a game—and beaming them back to the programmer, who sticks in his commercials and then offers it to the viewer.

If you own a dish, you are on the baseball breadline right next to the programmer. You choose the game you want, and you get the live feed without commercials.

That also means you can eavesdrop on the broadcasters between innings, when they *really* talk about what's going on. It's also fun listening to the heated, salty exchanges that sometimes occur between the broadcasters in the booth and their director in the broadcast truck.

Ed Bloes, owner of the Voice and Vision Electronics Company in Brewster, New York, sells satellite dishes. He explains (we'll translate) that a dish consists of a parabolic reflector shell (that's the big cone on the outside) made of woven metal, which catches the dispersed signals and focuses them on LNB, low-noise block converter, or LNA, low-noise amplifier (these are two names for the same thing, basically the microphone that extends out

of the cone). The signal is fed to a wire running beneath the ground and into your home. The wire is connected to an IRD, integrated receiver descrambler (your tuner), from which you choose hundreds of available channels. Your dealer also provides a monthly programming guide the size of a restaurant menu.

All baseball games you pick up on your dish are free, with two exceptions. ESPN and SportsChannel New York scramble their signals. To view their programs, you pay a yearly fee ($19.95 for ESPN, around $25 for SportsChannel New York). They assign you an IRD number, sent electronically to the satellite along with their signal. The decoder in your IRD can then descramble it. (If you don't pay your bill, they simply stop transmitting your IRD number.)

A satellite dish is perfect for those who live in areas without cable or where UHF reception is poor. The size of the dish you need depends on the region where you live. Since the signals are strongest over the middle of the country, says Bloes, you would buy a dish eight feet in diameter if you lived in, say, Iowa or Nebraska. On the East or West Coasts, you'd probably need a ten-foot dish; in the South, a twelve-foot dish.

How much do these big boys cost? Bloes says they range from $2,500 to $3,800 for

home models, "but few people buy the cheaper systems." Why? The top-of-the-line models come with a microprocessor which lets you program 150 stations; the lower-priced models require more tinkering with the tuner.

You can purchase a satellite dish most anywhere in the U.S. Check your Yellow Pages under the heading "Satellite Equipment and Systems" for a nearby dealer. Some dealers have a working model on display in their showroom. If you're ready to buy one, ask the dealer to provide you with references from other customers. Be sure you know he can install it as well as sell it.

Before you sign on the dotted line, make sure to check with your local government about your neighborhood's zoning laws. What does land have to do with atmospheric transmissions? Plenty. After all, satellite dishes can be an eyesore. In some areas, the law says you cannot rivet a dish to your roof or plant it in your backyard; you have to install it in a specifically-zoned dish park, which may make it a more expensive proposition. In my neighborhood there are no such laws at present, only neighbors who scowl when I broach the subject. They just don't understand.

—BS

Major Leagues

Indians TV: WUAB, 43, Parma, no. of games: 60. Announcer: Jack Corrigan. *TV Network*: WUPW, 36, Toledo; WKBN, 27, Youngstown; WTTE, 28, Columbus. *Indians Radio*: WWWE, 1100, Cleveland. Announcers: Herb Score, Paul Olden. *Radio Network*: WAKR, 1590, Akron; WBNO, 1520, Bryan; WQCT-FM, 100.9, Bryan; WBCO, 1540, Bucyrus; WQEL-FM, 92.7, Bucyrus; WHBC, 1480, Canton; WDLR, 1550, Delaware; WDOH-FM, 107.1, Delphos; WFOB, 1430, Fostoria; WFOB-FM, 96.7, Fostoria; WJMR-FM, 98.3, Fredericktown; WFRO, 900, Fremont; WFRO-FM, 99.1, Fremont; WMAN, 1400, Mansfield; WBRJ, 910, Marietta; WMRN, 1490, Marion; WLKR, 1510, Norwalk; WLKR-FM, 95.3, Norwalk; WNXT, 1260, Portsmouth; WLEC, 1450, Sandusky; WOHO, 1470, Toledo; WBTC, 1540, Uhrichsville; WQKT-FM, 104.5, Wooster; WBBW, 1240, Youngstown.

Pirates TV Network: WTOV, 9, Steubenville; WKBN, 27, Youngstown. *Pirates Radio Network*: WOHI, 1490, East Liverpool; WFMJ, 1390, Youngstown.

Reds TV: WLWT, 5, Cincinnati, no. of games: 41. Announcers: Thom Brennaman, Johnny Bench. *TV Network*: WTTE, 28, Columbus; WDTN, 2, Dayton; WLIO, 35, Lima; WHIZ, 18, Zanesville. *Reds Radio*: WLW, 700, Cincinnati. Announcers: Marty Brennaman, Joe Nuxhall. *Radio Network*: WATH, 970, Athens; WPKO, 1390, Bellefontaine; WCMJ-FM, 96.7, Cambridge; WKKI-FM, 94.3, Celina; WBEX, 1490, Chillicothe; WCOL, 1230, Columbus; WHIO, 1290, Dayton; WFIN, 1330, Findlay; WYPC-FM, 101.5, Gallipolis; WSRW-FM, 106.7, Hillsboro; WIRO, 1230, Ironton; WKOV, 1330, Jackson/Wellston; WKOV-FM, 96.7, Jackson/Wellston; WLOH, 1320, Lancaster; WIMA, 1150, Lima; WMOA, 1490, Marietta; WMPO, 1390, Middleport/Pomeroy; WMPO-FM, 92.1, Middleport/Pomeroy; WPTW, 1570, Piqua; WPTW-FM, 95.7, Piqua; WPAY-FM, 104.1, Portsmouth; WBLY,

1600, Springfield; WOFR, 1250, Washington Court House; WHIZ, 1240, Zanesville.

Tigers TV Network: WUPW, 36, Toledo.

Minor Leagues

Columbus Clippers (International League) Radio: WBNS, 1460. Announcer: Terry Smith.

Toledo Mud Hens (International League) Radio: WMTR-FM, 95.9. Announcers: Jim Weber, Frank Gilhooley.

Canton-Akron Indians (Eastern League) Radio: WNPQ, 95.9-FM.

OKLAHOMA

A college baseball hotbed, Oklahoma is also home to two minor league teams, as well as network affiliates of the Rangers and Cardinals. Those two teams also have the strongest flagship signals that can be heard in the state.

Major Leagues

Cardinals TV Network: KAUT, 43, Oklahoma City; KOKI, 23, Tulsa. *Cardinals Radio Network*: KWPR, 1270, Claremore; KCRC, 1390, Enid; KOKC, 1490, Guthrie; KBIX, 1490, Muskogee; KNOR, 1400, Norman; WBBZ, 1230, Ponca City; KVIN, 1470, Vinita.

Rangers TV Network: KAUT, 43, Oklahoma City; KGCT, 41, Tulsa. *Rangers Radio Network*: WTAW, 1240, Bryan; WWLS, 640, Norman; KSPI, 780, Stillwater.

Royals TV Network: KGCT, 41, Tulsa. *Royals Radio Network*: KTMC, 1400, McAlester; KGLC, 910, Miami; KTOW, 1340, Tulsa.

Minor Leagues

Oklahoma City 89ers (American Association) Radio: KXY, 1340. Announcer: Brian Barnhart.

Tulsa Drillers (Texas League) Radio: KAKC, 1300. Announcer: Jim Roberts.

OREGON

The state's Triple-A team annually threatens to move out, the state university doesn't field a baseball team, and the closest major league team (Seattle) never wins. But the short-season Eugene Emeralds pack in the fans, and all their games are heard locally.

Major Leagues

Athletics Radio Network: KCMX, 580, Ashland.

Mariners Radio Network: KUIK, 1360, Portland; KVAS, 1230, Astoria.

Minor Leagues

Portland Beavers (Pacific Coast League)

Lost in Space?

There are hundreds of manufacturers producing components for the satellite dish business. Here are a few manufacturers that come recommended (most stores mix and match in suggesting a system):

For complete systems . . .
• Channel Master, Smithfield, NC.
• Weingard, Burlington, IA.
• Parabolics East, Little Rock, ARK (they make a little number called The Perfect 10).

For receivers . . .
• Houston Tracker Systems, Inglewood, CO.
• Chaparral, San Jose, CA.
• R.L. Drake, Miamisburg, OH.

For additional information, check out *Orbit*, published by Commtek Publishing, Des Moines, IA. A technical magazine for the layman, *Orbit* has sections rating equipment, as well as a program guide for satellite-dish owners.   —DK

Radio: KBNP, 1410. Announcers: Mike Parker, John Christensen.

Bend Bucks (Northwest League) Radio: KBND, 1110. Announcer: Bob Hards.

Eugene Emeralds (Northwest League) Radio: KEED, 1600. Announcer: Dave Glass.

Southern Oregon Athletics, Medford (Northwest League) Radio: KMFR, 880. Announcer: Jack Piepgras, Jim Steanek.

PENNSYLVANIA

You'll never have trouble finding Phillies games in the eastern half of the state, or Pirates games in the west. In the middle, check out the minor league teams in Scranton and Harrisburg. If you're still not satisfied, you should be able to find the Orioles, Tigers, Reds, Indians, or either New York team on clear-channel.

Major Leagues

Indians TV Network: WETG, 66, Erie. *Indians Radio Network*: WHDZ, 1260, Erie.

Mets Radio Network: WYOM, Wilkes-Barre.

Orioles TV Network: WPMT, 43, York. *Orioles Radio Network*: WIOO, 1000, Carlisle; WCHA, 800, Chambersburg; WPDC, 1600, Elizabethtown; WHVR, 1280, Hanover; WKBO, 1230, Harrisburg; WLPA, 1490, Lancaster; WLBR, 1270, Lebanon; WSBA, 910, York.

Phillies TV: WTXF, 29, Philadelphia, no. of games: 89. announcers: Richie Ashburn, Harry Kalas, Andy Musser. *TV Network*: WLYH, 15, Lancaster/Lebanon; WBRE, 28, Wilkes-Barre/Scranton. *Cable TV*: PRISM (pay), Philadelphia, no. of games: 40. Announcers: Chris Wheeler, Garry Maddox. *Phillies Radio*: WCAU, 1210. Announcers: Ashburn, Kalas, Musser, Wheeler. *Radio Network*: WAEB, 790, Allentown; WCOJ, 1420, Coatesville; WGET, 1320, Gettysburg; WKBO, 1230, Harrisburg; WAZL, 1490, Hazelton; WLPA, 1490, Lancaster; WLBR, 1270, Lebanon; WBCB, 1490, Levittown; WBPZ,

1230, Lock Haven; WQIN, 1290, Lykens; WPPA, 1360, Pottsville; WEEU, 850, Reading; WYGL, 1240, Selinsgrove; WISL, 1480, Shamokin; WNBT, 1490, Wellsboro; WARM, 590, Wilkes-Barre/Scranton; WRAK, 1400, Williamsport; WCHX-FM, 105.5, Yeagertown; WOYK, 1350, York.

Pirates TV: KDKA, 2, Pittsburgh, no. of games: 50. Announcers: Lanny Frattare, Jim Rooker, John Sanders, Steve Blass. *TV Network*: WWCP, 8, Johnstown; WETG, 66, Erie; WPMT, 43, York. *Pirates Radio*: KDKA, 1020, Pittsburgh. Announcers: Frattare, Rooker, Sanders. *Radio Network*: WVAM, 1430, Altoona; WMBA, 1460, Ambridge; WBFD, 1310, Bedford; WRAX-FM, 100.9, Bedford; WESB, 1490, Bradford; WIOO, 1000, Carlisle; WESA, 940, Charleroi; WCVI, 1340, Connellsville; WFRM, 600, Coudersport; WOWQ-FM, 102.1, DuBois; WPDC, 1600, Elizabethtown; WEYZ, 1450, Erie; WFRA, 1450, Franklin; WEXC-FM, 107.1, Greenville; WHGB, 1400, Harrisburg; WHUN, 1150, Huntingdon; WCCS, 1160, Indiana; WJNL, 850, Johnstown; WCNS, 1480, Latrobe; WAMQ, 1400, Loretto; WMGW, 1490, Meadville; WKST, 1280, New Castle; WKBI, 1400, St. Mary's; WVSC, 990, Somerset; WMAJ, 1450, State College; WTRN, 1340, Tyrone; WMBS, 590, Uniontown; WJPA, 1450, Washington; WANB, 1580, Waynesburg.

If there's a rhubarb in the pea patch, you can bet Red Barber is behind the mike.

Yankees Radio Network: WEEX, 1230, Allenton/Bethlehem/Easton; WARD, 1550, Pittston; WPAM, 1410, Pottsville; WEJL, 630, Scranton/Wilkes-Barre; WWPA, 1340, Williamsport.

Minor Leagues

Scranton/Wilkes-Barre Red Barons (International League) Radio: WICK, 1400. Announcer: Kent Wesling.

Harrisburg Senators (Eastern League) Radio: WHP, 580. Announcers: Dan Kamal, Mark Mattern.

Reading Phillies (Eastern League) Radio: WAGO, 1240. Announcer: Randy Stevens.

RHODE ISLAND

Chances are that most people in Rhode Island want to hear the Red Sox. And then some. For in addition to the parent club, the Pawtucket Red Sox (Pawsox) can also be heard. If you don't like Sox, however, you can try a New York clear-channel station.

Major League

Red Sox TV Network: WLNE, 6, Provi-

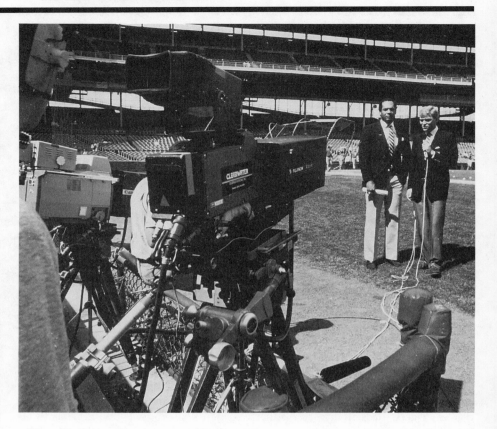

dence/New Bedford. *Red Sox Radio Network*: WKFD, 1370, Wickford; WPRO, 630, Providence; WERI, 1230, Westerly; WWON, 1240, Woonsocket.

Minor League

Pawtucket Red Sox (International League) Radio: WKRI, 1450.

SOUTH CAROLINA

Yes, there is baseball in South Carolina. The Braves' radio network covers the state, and two of the state's minor league teams broadcast games. But even there the influence of football and auto racing is felt. Jim Phillips, the voice of the Greenville Braves, is better known as the voice of Clemson football and as a pit announcer for the Motor Racing Network. You should also have good luck with any number of East Coast clear-channels. Don't forget how far west much of South Carolina is; Cincinnati's WLW (700) should be within reach.

Major League

Braves Radio Network: WPUB-FM, 94.3, Camden; WVOC, 560, Columbia; WSSL, 1440, Greenville; WPJM, 800, Greer; WRIZ-FM, 103.1, Honea Path; WWKT-FM, 98.3, Kingstree; WKDY, 1400, Spartanburg; WBCU, 1460, Union.

Minor Leagues

Greenville Braves (Southern League) Radio: WFBC, 1330. Announcer: Jim Phillips.

Columbia Mets (South Atlantic League) Radio: WODE, 1230. Announcer: Jim Powell.

SOUTH DAKOTA

Summer arrives late in the Upper Midwest, and you have to look hard to find baseball broadcasts. The Twins' TV and radio networks reach into South Dakota, but there's no minor league or college baseball of interest.

Major Leagues

Royals Radio Network: KBFS, 1450, Belle Fourche; KJAM, 1390, Madison; KJAM-FM, 103.1, Madison.

Twins TV Network: KTTW, 17, Sioux Falls. *Twins Radio Network*: KSDN, 930, Aberdeen; KJJQ, 910, Brookings; KIJV, 1340, Huron; KMSD, 1510, Milbank; KGFX, 1060, Pierre; KBWS-FM, 102.9, Sisseton; KSDR, 1480, Watertown; KNAX, 570, Yankton.

TENNESSEE

Baseball at all levels is plentiful on Tennessee radio. Action from three major league teams can be heard on network stations, and minor league games at the Triple-A, Double-A, and rookie levels are available in different parts of the state. For clear-channel action, check first on the Braves (750), Reds (700) or Cardinals (1120).

Major Leagues

Braves Radio Network: WGOW, 1150, Chattanooga; WDXN, 540, Clarksville; WBAC, 1340, Cleveland; WJCW, 910, Johnson City; WLIL, 730, Lenoir City;

The pregame show—a little bit of "inside stuff" and a lot of advertising air time.

WGNS, 1450, Murfreesboro; WAMB, 1160, Nashville; WLIK, 1270, Newport; WLIL-FM, 93.5, West Knoxville.

Cardinals TV Network: WJWT, 16, Jackson; WMKW, 30, Memphis. *Cardinals Radio Network*: WDSG, 1450, Dyersburg; WXIS-FM, 103.9, Erwin; WTJS, 1390, Jackson; WZLT-FM, 99.3, Lexington; WMPS, 1380, Millington; WENK, 1240, Union City.

Reds TV Network: WETO, 39, Bristol/Kingsport/Johnson City; WDSI, 61, Chattanooga; WKCH, 43, Knoxville; KCAY, 30, Nashville. *Reds Radio Network*: WOPI, 1490, Bristol; WKRM, 1340, Columbia/Nashville; WATO, 1290, Oak Ridge.

Minor Leagues

Nashville Sounds (American Association) Radio: WRLT, 1240. Announcer: Bob Jamison.

Chattanooga Lookouts (Southern League) Radio: WDEF, 1370.

Memphis Chicks (Southern League) Radio: WREC, 600. Announcer: Tom Stocker.

Bristol Tigers (Appalachian League) Radio: WFHG, 980, no. of games: 10. Announcer: Mickey Garrett.

TEXAS

The major league radio networks aren't among those things that are "bigger in Texas." Neither the Rangers nor the Astros can match the multistate networks of the Midwest. But both cover good portions of the state, and the Rangers' TV station KTVT is available regionally as a superstation. The Rangers and Astros also both have games on cable's Home Sports Entertainment, a regional pay station.

Major Leagues

Astros TV: KTXH, 20, Houston, no. of games: 77. Announcers: Bill Brown, Larry Dierker, Milo Hamilton. *TV Network*: KCIT, 14, Amarillo; KBVO, 42, Austin; KCIK, 14, El Paso; KETX, 5, Livingston; KPEJ, 24, Odessa; KIDY, 6, San Angelo; KRRT, 35, San Antonio; KLTV, 7, Tyler; KWKT, 44, Waco; KJTL, 18, Wichita Falls. *Cable TV*: Home Sports Entertainment, Houston, no. of games: 79. Announcers: Brown, Hamilton, Bill Worrell. *Astros Radio*: KTRH, 740, Houston. Announcers: Hamilton, Brown, Dierker, Bruce Geitzen. *Radio Network*: KLVI, 560, Beaumont; KIBL, 1490, Beeville; KWHI-FM, 106.3, Brenham; WTAW, 1150, Bryan/College Station; KHLB, 1340, Burnet; KLCR-FM, 102.3, Center; KLEV, 1410, Cleveland; KULM-FM, 98.3, Columbus; KSIX, 1230, Corpus Christi; KIVY-FM, 92.7, Crockett; KQRO, 1600, Cuero; KWMC, 1490, Del Rio; KDNT, 1440, Denton; KURV, 710, Edinburg; KXGC-FM, 96.9, El Campo; KNAP, 910, Fredericksburg; KGID-FM, 101.7, Giddings; KCTI, 140, Gonzalez; KGVL, 1400, Greenville; KRJH, 1520, Hallettsville; KRME, 1460, Hondo; KKNX, 1400, Huntsville; KEBE, 1400, Jacksonville; KWYX-FM, 102.3, Jasper; KERV, 1230, Kerrville; KODK-FM, 92.7, Kingsville; KLAR, 1300, Laredo; KRBA, 1420, Lufkin; KKEE, 1230, Nacogdoches; KBUC,

1310, San Antonio; KOSY-FM, 102.5, Texarkana; KDOK, 1490, Tyler; KNAL, 1410, Victoria; WACO, 1460, Waco; KZEE, 1220, Weatherford; KVLL, 1490, Woodville. *Spanish Radio*: KXYZ, 1320, Houston. Announcers: Orlando Sanchez Diago, Rolando Becerra. *Spanish Radio Network*: KXET, 1250, San Antonio.

Rangers TV: KTVT, 11, Ft. Worth, no. of games: 65. Announcers: Bob Carpenter, Steve Busby. *TV Network*: KCIT, 14, Amarillo; KBVO, 42, Austin; KJTV, 34, Lubbock; KIDY, 6, San Angelo; KJTL, 18, Wichita Falls. *Cable TV*: Home Sports Entertainment, Grand Prairie, no. of games: 60. *Rangers Radio*: WBAP, 820, Ft. Worth. Announcers: Mark Holtz, Eric Nadel. *Radio Network*: KORQ, 1340, Abilene; KVLF, 1240, Alpine; KGNC, 710, Amarillo; KSTA, 1000, Coleman; KSIX, 1230, Corpus Christi; KFYO, 790, Lubbock; KNOW, 1420, Lufkin; KSFA, 860, Nacogdoches; KVOP, 1400, Plainview; KOLE, 1340, Port Arthur; KTEO, 1340, San Angelo; KSST, 1230, Sulphur Springs; KMLA, 1400 AM, 103.9 FM, Texarkana; KTBB, 600, Tyler.

Minor Leagues

El Paso Diablos (Texas League) Radio: KHEY, 690. Announcer: Jon Teicher.
Midland Angels (Texas League) Radio: KCRS, 550. Announcer: Deene Ehlis.
San Antonio Missions (Texas League) Radio: KFHM, 1160. Announcer: Roy Acuff.

UTAH

At one time, after the Triple-A Salt Lake Gulls moved to Calgary, it looked like professional baseball was dead in Utah. But the Pioneer League's Salt Lake Trappers have become a hit at the gate. All seventy games are on radio, too, giving Utah fans something to listen to once the college season ends.

Major League

Dodgers Radio Network: KNKK, 800, Salt Lake City.

Minor League

Salt Lake Trappers (Pioneer League) Radio: KSIN, 570. Announcer: Kurt Wilson.

VERMONT

Vermont's single pro team has changed affiliation several times and ownership once, and it hasn't been on the air. The Red Sox are left to dominate the airwaves, although some in the northern half of the state might identify more with the Expos, who have but one radio affiliate in the state.

Major Leagues

Expos Radio Network: WSNO, 1450, Barre.
Red Sox TV Network: WNNE, 31, White River Junction/Hanover, N.H. *Red Sox Radio Network*: WBFL-FM, 107.1, Bellows Falls; WTSA, 1450, Brattleboro; WJOY, 1230, Burlington; WFAD, 1490, Middlebury; WIDE, 1490, Newport; WSYB, 1380, Rutland; WSTJ, 1340, St. Johnsbury; WDEV, 550, Waterbury.
Yankees Radio Network: WSKI, 1240, Montpelier.

VIRGINIA

Minor league baseball is bigtime on Virginia radio. Virtually every team broadcasts an entire schedule, and the Triple-A Richmond Braves have had as many as three announcers working together. Besides the Orioles, Virginians can tune to clear-channel stations for the Phillies (1210), Braves (750), Pirates (1020), Reds (700), Mets (660), and Yankees (770).

Major Leagues

Braves Radio Network: WLRV, 1380, Lebanon.
Cubs Radio Network: WGH, 1310, Virginia Beach.
Orioles TV Network: WJPR, 21, Lynchburg. (Note: WDCA, 20, in Washington, D.C., also carries most Oriole TV games

Tim McCarver stands in a long line of former players who have become successful announcers.

and is available on cable in much of the state.) *Orioles Radio Network*: WHAP, 1340, Hopewell; WAGE, 1200, Leesburg; WLCC-FM, 106.3, Luray.

Reds Radio Network: WGAT, 1050, Gate City; WSWV, 170, Pennington Gap.

Minor Leagues

Richmond Braves (International League) Radio: WRNL, 910. Announcers: Bob Black, Dan Lovallo.

Tidewater Tides (International League) Radio: WGH, 1310. Announcer: Dave Glass.

Lynchburg Red Sox (Carolina League) Radio: WWOD, 1390. Announcers: Shawn Holiday, John Klobucar.

Prince William Cannons (Carolina League) Radio: WDCT, 1310, no. of games: 100. Announcers: Curt Bloom, Rob Christ.

Salem Buccaneers (Carolina League) Radio: WROV, 1240. Announcer: Dave Newman.

WASHINGTON

For now, the Mariners remain in Seattle,

and fans throughout the Pacific Northwest can enjoy Dave Niehaus' distinctive home run calls. Seattle-Tacoma fans can also hear Pacific Coast League action. And once the Northwest League season starts in June, other broadcasts are available.

Major League

Mariners TV: KSTW, 11, Tacoma, no. of games: 65. Announcers: Dave Niehaus, Rick Rizzs, Joe Simpson. *Mariners Radio:* KIRO, 710, Seattle. Announcers: Dave Niehaus, Rick Rizzs. *Radio Network*: KAYO, 1410, Aberdeen; KLKI, 1340, Anacortes; KPUG, 1170, Bellingham; KULE, 730, Euphrata/Wenatchee; KGY, 1240, Olympia; KONP, 1450, Port Angeles; KQQQ, 1150, Pullman; KMAS, 1030, Shelton; KXLY, 920, Spokane; KVAN, 1550, Vancouver (Canada); KIT, 1280, Yakima.

Minor Leagues

Tacoma Tigers (Pacific Coast League) Radio: KTAC, 850. Annoucer: Bob Robertson.

Everett Giants (Northwest League) Radio: KWYZ, 1230. Announcer: Lee Anders.

Spokane Indians (Northwest League) Radio: KAQQ, 590. Announcer: Rich Waltz.

WEST VIRGINIA

It's a small state, but parts of West Virginia are claimed by three different major league teams as part of their market. As a result, the Reds, Pirates, and Orioles all include West Virginia stations on their networks, although all three can also be heard on clear-channel flagships.

Major Leagues

Indians Radio Network: WHJC, 1360, Matewan.

Orioles Radio Network: WCST, 1010, Berkeley Springs; WKOY, 1240, Bluefield; WEPM, 1340, Martinsburg.

Pirates TV Network: WVAH, 11, Hurricane/Charleston/Huntington. *Pirates Ra-*

dio Network: WWNR, 620, Beckley; WHAR, 1340, Clarksburg; WMMN, 920, Fairmont; WKLP, 1390, Keyser; WAJR, 1440, Morgantown; WETZ, 1330, New Martinsville; WADC, 1050, Parkersburg; WEIR, 1430, Weirton; WKWK, 1400, Wheeling.

Reds TV Network: WVAH, 11, Hurricane/Charleston/Huntington. *Reds Radio Network*: WJLS, 560, Beckley; WCHS, 580, Charleston; WRVC, 930, Huntington; WVOW, 1290, Logan; WVOW-FM, 101.9, Logan; WMON, 1340, Montgomery; WLTP, 1450, Parkersburg; WCEF-FM, 98.3, Ripley; WVRC, 1400, Spencer; WXEE, 1340, Welch; WBTH, 1400, Williamson.

Minor League

Charleston Wheelers (South Atlantic League) Radio: WCHS, 580. Announcers: Don Cook, Don Fliter.

WISCONSIN

The Brewers draw well and are well represented by their networks throughout the state. But many in Wisconsin still consider themselves National League fans, and they follow the Cubs on WGN-TV and the Cubs' radio network. Others in the west follow the Twins.

Major Leagues

Cubs Radio Network: WCWC, 1600, Ripon; WKTS, 950, Sheboygan; WXCO, 1230, Wausau.

Brewers TV: WCGV, 24, Milwaukee, no. of games: 74. Announcers: Jim Paschke, Pete Vuckovich. *TV Network*: WGBA, 26, Green Bay; WLAX, 25, La Crosse; WMSN, 47, Madison; WAOW, 9, Wausau. *Brewers Radio*: WTMJ, 620, Milwaukee. Announcers: Bob Uecker, Pat Hughes. *Radio Network*: WRLO-FM, 105.3, Antigo; WHBY, 1230, Appleton; WATW, 1400, Ashland; WATW-FM, 96.7, Ashland; WBEV, 1430, Beaver Dam; WBEL, 1380, Beloit; WISS, 1090, Berlin; WISS-FM, 102.3, Berlin; WWIS, 1260, Black River Falls; WRDN,

1430, Durand; WRDN-FM, 95.9, Durand; WJJK, 1400, Eau Claire; KFIZ, 1450, Fond du Lac; WNFL, 1440, Green Bay; WRLS-FM, 92.1, Hayward; WCLO, 1230, Janesville; WLIP, 1050, Kenosha; WKTY, 580, La Crosse; WLDY, 1340, Ladysmith; WLDY-FM, 92.7, Ladysmith; WMIR, 1550, Lake Geneva; WIBA, 1310, Madison; WOMT, 1240, Manitowoc; WMAM, 570, Marinette; WDLB, 1450, Marshfield; WRJC, 1270, Mauston; WRJC-FM, 92.1, Mauston; WIGM, 1490, Medford; WIGM-FM, 99.3, Medford; WWMH-FM, 95.9, Minoqua; WEKZ, 1260, Monroe; WEKZ-FM, 93.7, Monroe; WNBK-FM, 93.5, New London; WNBI, 980, Park Falls; WNBI-FM, 98.3, Park Falls; WTOQ, 1590, Platteville; WDDC-FM, 100.1, Portage; WPRE, 980, Prairie du Chien; WPRE-FM, 94.3, Prairie du Chien; WRDB, 1400, Reedsburg; WOBT, 1240, Rhinelander; WJMC, 1240, Rice Lake; WJMC-FM, 96.3, Rice Lake; WRCO, 1450, Richland Center; WRCO-FM, 100.9, Richland Center; WEVR, 1550, River Falls; WEVR-FM, 106.3, River Falls; WTCH, 960, Shawano; WHBL, 1330, Sheboygan; WCOW, 1290, Sparta; WCOW-FM, 97.1, Sparta; WSPO, 1010, Stevens Point; WDOR, 910, Sturgeon Bay; WDOR-FM, 93.9, Sturgeon Bay; WTTN, 1580, Watertown; WMLW-FM, 94.1, Watertown; WSAU, 550, Wausau; WHTL-FM, 102.3, Whitehall; WFHR, 1320, Wisconsin Rapids.

Twins Radio Network: WISM, 1060, Eau Claire.

Minor League

Beloit Brewers (Midwest League) Radio: WBEL, 1380, no. of games: 50. Announcer: Rick West.

WYOMING

If you want to hear baseball, you're in the wrong state. We found only two stations here that belong to one of the major league radio networks, and Wyoming has no pro teams of its own. If you hear baseball (besides national network games) on a Wyoming station, let us know.

Major Leagues

Cubs Radio Network: KTWO, 1030, Casper.

Royals Radio Network: KROE, 930, Sheridan.

CANADA

Both of the country's major league teams broadcast games over far-strung networks. Expos games are also available in French throughout Quebec. And minor league games can be heard in various cities around the country.

Major Leagues

Expos TV: CBMT, 6, Montreal, no. of games: 35. Announcers: Dave Van Horne, Ken Singleton. *French TV*: CBFT, 2, Montreal, no. of games: 35. Announcer: Claude Raymond. *Cable TV*: The Sports Network, Don Mills, Ont., no. of games: 40. Announcers: Jim Hughson, Singleton. *Expos Radio*: CJAD, 800, Montreal. Announcers:

Van Horne, Bobby Winkles. *French Radio*: CKAC, 730, Montreal. Announcers: Jacques Doucet, Rodger Brulotte.

Blue Jays TV: CFTO, 9, Toronto. Announcers: Tony Kubek, Don Chevrier, Fergie Oliver. *Cable TV*: The Sports Network. Announcers: Oliver, Buck Martinez. *Blue Jays Radio*: CJCL, 1430, Toronto. Announcers: Tom Cheek, Jerry Howarth.

Minor Leagues

Calgary Cannons (Pacific Coast League) Radio: CKO, 103.1-FM, no. of games: 87. Announcer: Eric Bishop.

Edmonton Trappers (Pacific Coast League) Radio: COLD, 1070, no. of games: 100. Announcer: Al Coates.

Vancouver Canadians (Pacific Coast League) Radio: CKWX, 1130, no. of games: 63. Announcer: Ron Barrett.

St. Catharines Blue Jays (New York-Penn League) Radio: CKTB, 610, no. of games: 30. Announcer: Doug Hobbs.

Medicine Hat Blue Jays (Pioneer League) Radio: CHAT, 1270.

—DK

Holy Cow! It's Harry's Year!

Since 1978, the Baseball Hall of Fame has given the Ford C. Frick Award to a broadcaster "for major contributions to the game of baseball."

Harry Caray's year came in 1989. Not only did the Cubs' ebullient broadcaster watch his team put together an astounding season, but he also found himself in the Hall of Fame when he received the prestigious Ford C. Frick Award. He could be forgiven if he showed even greater elation than usual as he led the Wrigley Field crowd through its seventh-inning stretch rendition of "Take Me Out to the Ball Game."

Harry started broadcasting baseball in St. Louis with the Cardinals in 1944 and stayed for 25 years. After a season in Oakland, he returned to the Midwest for a 10-year stint with the White Sox before finding a home with the Cubs. After 45 years of baseball, he still brings a little boy's enthusiasm to his sharp-eyed accounts.

At one point, he had a 7,000 consecutive-game streak behind the microphone that even two broken legs in a 1968 auto accident couldn't stop. A stroke finally sidelined him in 1987, as celebrities ranging from Bill Murray to George Will pinch-hit. When he returned on May 19, 1987, the governor of Illinois proclaimed it "Harry Caray Day," and President Ronald Reagan called to welcome him back.

—BC

Talk Radio: The Best of the Call-In Shows, Coast-to-Coast

Caller: "Yo, Art, it's Jerry from Bayside! How's it goin'?"

Host: "Real good, Jerry. What's on your mind?"

Caller: "Well, Art, it's about the Yankees. They gotta do something about Righetti. He's blowin' too many games. They gotta get rid of the guy!"

Host: "Well look, Jerry, I think you have to give Rags a little more time. It's only April, you know."

Caller: "Yeah, I know, but I really think he's shot, Art."

Sound familiar?

If you've ever found yourself glued (or just loosely attached) to the AM radio dial on a clear spring or summer evening when baseball season is in bloom and the blood of America's fans is beginning to boil and churn . . . well, then the above morsel of pseudo conversation is probably music (or at least some kind of rhythmic beat) to your ears.

The sports talk/call-in radio show was not invented just yesterday, mind you. Broadcasting legends such as Don Dunphy, in the 1930s and 1940s, and Bill Mazer, in the 1950s and 1960s, were conducting rap sessions through the airwaves with great popularity long before All-Sports Radio came along. But the proliferation of such programs? And 50,000-watt, clear-channel stations that allow listeners in New York to hear what's happening in St. Louis, Cincinnati, Charlotte, and Boston? And irate or semicrazed callers carrying on night after night after night with irate and semicrazed talk-show hosts?

Welcome to the Wonderful World of Radio Sports. Every major market now has at least one nightly sports talk/call-in show. Many small markets or tiny suburban outposts have their own popular sports gurus

who fill up the night air. The following is a sampling—a personal one, thank you—of ten of the best sports talk shows in the country. We apologize if we've omitted several dozen or so. Our dial is just not wide enough to include them all.

WABC, New York—770 AM, "SportsTalk" with Art Rust, Jr. (Monday–Friday, 9–12 P.M.). The "raconteur and walking sports encyclopedia," Arthur George Rust, Jr., a mainstay at WABC since 1980 (and a fixture on New York radio for thirty-five years), has a classic style all his own. Nobody talks a better game of baseball and boxing, and nobody has a better rapport with his listeners. Unfortunately they moved him from drive time to his present time slot, but loyal callers such as Billy from Brooklyn and Michael from Queens still pay a call each evening. His show is real, hard-core New York and always finds a place for the baseball crazies, whether it's the middle of June or the end of January. Rust is one of the true kingpins of sports talk. WABC is also a 50,000-watt, clear-channel station, and it is not uncommon to be speaking with someone in Florida only to hear him remark, "Yeah, I heard him with Art Rust also last night."

WLW, Cincinnati—700 AM, "SportsTalk" with Bob Trumpy (Monday–Friday, 6–9 P.M.). If you've caught Trumpy's act on television, you know how opinionated and outspoken he can be. Trumpy will spend about 70 percent of his time talking up a storm or chatting (or hollering) with devoted callers. The station is a 50,000-watt clear-channel, and the show can be heard in 30–35 states (late at night during the winter months), and 15–20 states during the summer. A toll-free 800 number

makes it easy for Trumpy fans (and there are many) around the country to trade words with the former Bengals star tight end. A memorable testimony to his talents: he once spent two and a half hours talking a female listener out of a suicide attempt. Whether it's heavy stuff or light fare, Trumpy is always a good listen.

WIP, Philadelphia—610 AM, "The Howard Eskin Show" with Howard Eskin (Monday–Friday, 4–6 P.M.). Eskin represents the best of Philly's version of All-Sports Radio. He's very opinionated, a real name dropper, and can get really annoying at times. But boy, does he know his stuff. The sports director of WTXF-TV as well, and a former talk-show host at WWDB, Eskin is the very model of the Philadelphia sports nut. (We hear he even carries around one of those small, portable sports tickers.) He loves to challenge callers, so you better be ready to back up your opinions. On Tuesdays and Thursdays he does his show from local sports bar/restaurant establishments.

KMOX, St. Louis—1120 AM, "Sports Open Line" with Bob Costas and Dan Dierdorf (day and time varies). This station is the Big Daddy of sports talk. It reaches into 48 states. They've gotten calls from the Bahamas, from Canada, and even a few letters from Iceland. The station employs a number of hosts, including the great Jack Buck, but the best listen is when Costas and Dierdorf get together for their once-a-week gig. These two are loads of fun as they banter back and forth about anything and everything. Their callers are not allowed to stay on too long, so you get a chance to really hear these two guys go at it. Toll-free 800 lines make this a real national talk show, especially during baseball season. There is probably no better baseball radio station in the country, and no better baseball schmoozer than Costas.

WFAN, New York—1050 AM, "Mike and the Mad Dog," with Mike Francesa and Christopher Russo (Monday–Friday, 3 PM to 7 PM). America's first all sports radio station, WFAN has a diverse choice of sports talk; from "The Cole Man and the Soul Man" (featuring Ed Coleman and Dave Sims), to the lunchtime chats at Mickey Mantle's restaurant with Bill Mazer and his amazing memory, to the nonstop baseball orgies with Howie Rose. The best item on the menu, however, is the one served up by Russo and Francesa. These two gents are just plain good—they're knowledgeable, interesting, well-prepared and handle their listeners with the proper amount of restraint. Francesa (who has long served as a college sports consultant for CBS Sports) is the real star here, even though he has a voice made for newspapers. The show falls short on some of the other goodies at WFAN when it comes to baseball (Rose, Mazer and late-nighter Jody McDonald are the best listen there), but the dynamic duo of Russo and Francesa make for one of sports' best all around radio shows.

WTAE, Pittsburgh—1250 AM, "Myron Cope on Sports" with Myron Cope (Monday–Friday, 6–7 P.M.). A longtime legend in the Steel City, Myron Cope (who has hosted his own show on WTAE since 1973 and also serves as an analyst for Steelers' broadcasts) represents all that is good about sports along and around the Three Rivers. Sparking the airwaves with his tough, gritty persona, Cope combines a fine interviewing technique (no-nonsense) with lots of good shtick, an occasional mock rage to keep things lively, and a tremendous amount of respect for his loyal listeners in western Pennsylvania. A former sportswriter (for the *Pittsburgh*

Post-Gazette and the *Saturday Evening Post*), he likes to book guests himself. And he's a man who likes diversity.

WLUP, Chicago—1000 AM, "Coppock on Sports" with Chet Coppock (Monday–Friday, 7–10 P.M., Saturday, 6–8 P.M.). The flamboyant and excitable Mr. Coppock, who has created a strong sports presence for the "hip" Loop station after coming over from WMAQ last year (after they canned sports talk), is one of the most prolific talk-show hosts in the country. One avid listener swears that Coppock has had 10–15 guests on in one night, shuttling them in and out for 5–15-minute bombardments of insightful questions and Windy City criticisms. A former sportscaster at WMAQ-TV before moving over to radio in 1981, Coppock is always breaking stories, constantly trying to beat the boys at giant WGN for hot scoops. Too bad his signal doesn't carry all over.

XTRA, San Diego—600 AM, "SportsNite" with Lee Hamilton (Monday–Friday, 6–9 P.M.). There aren't enough words to accurately describe Lee "The Hacksaw" Hamilton. He's arrogant, fast-paced, encyclopedic in his knowledge of sports, industrious, entertaining, etc. Heard from the Baja to the Great Northwest, the station is 100,000-watt clear-channel. This former Phoenix radio legend (he arrived in San Diego two years ago) is conversant in everything from baseball to bocci, and he includes a little of everything in his show: interviews (live and taped), features, previews, the works. Unfortunately his listeners lag way behind him.

WDHA, Boston—850 AM, "Anything Goes" with Eddie Andelman (Monday–Friday, 6–7 P.M.). One of the more intriguing characters in radio sports, Eddie Andelman throws a little of everything into the chowder: humor, intelligence, cleverness, and a certain naïveté not often shared by the hard-core Boston media troops. He loves to talk about gambling, rarely is seen

in the press box, and thinks less of Wade Boggs's batting skills than anyone east of Margo Adams. On Sunday nights he is joined by Mark Witkin and Jim McCarthy for a show called "Sports Huddle" (6–9 P.M.) but Andelman is best left by himself. Like his guests (whom he prefers live in the studio), Andelman rarely phones it in—he's always prepared and ready to entertain. The show can be heard in eastern Massachusetts, southern New Hampshire, and Rhode Island, but it does not ride on as powerful a signal as the other shows on this list. Pity, because during baseball season there is little better radio to be offered than listening to Eddie lament (or praise) the haunted Sox.

"Costas Coast to Coast"—Hosted by Bob Costas (Sundays, 9–12 P.M. Eastern, tape-delayed whenever necessary), nationally syndicated on over 200 stations. Perhaps the best that sports talk has to offer. No callers, no shilling guests. Just Bob Costas sitting in Runyon's (a popular New York sports hangout that usually serves as the site of the program) or some other sports outpost around the country with the likes of Tommy Lasorda, Ted Williams, or some other giant in the sports world. Costas has a knack for keeping the listener enthralled by simple conversation; he never asks a dull question and rarely lets a guest get away without first drawing a few beads of sweat. His first love is baseball—and it shows.

—BH

Art Rust, Jr., "raconteur and encyclopedia."

CHAPTER 11

Going by the Book

Y ou can have a complete baseball library for approximately what it costs to buy a franchise in the American League. Of course you'll never find time to read your whole collection, and when you *do* have some reading time, you won't know where to begin. There's got to be a better way to spend fewer of your hard-earned dollars and get more out of it.

There is.

It's possible to build a well-balanced, informative, entertaining baseball library for $250. You won't have everything. Not even Hugh Hefner has *everything!* But what you will have is enough baseball to keep you happily reading away for the next decade. And you'll have money left over to go to as many games as you want. And buy hotdogs too.

Together the books on this list form a basic source for those who want to increase their enjoyment and understanding of baseball. It also forms a good basic collection for small public and college libraries. Oh, sure, a baseball writer probably won't make a living using only these sources, but that's not the intention of this list. The selections described here are intended to give the best value in information and enjoyment for the money.

You could pig out on Roger Angell or Tom Boswell and spend hours in erudite rumination contemplating your navel and the vagaries of left-handed pitchers, but never find Wahoo Sam Crawford's 1908 triples total. On the other hand, the Figure Filberts can collect *Total Baseball, The Baseball Encyclopedia, The Elias Baseball Analyst,* and *The Sporting News Record Book* yet never understand Boston's love-hate affair with Ted Williams, chuckle at

Baseball Between the Covers

Best, worst, and most unusual—plus hot tips for aspiring writers

the Daffiness Boys, or try to translate Stengelese.

The books listed here provide history, statistics, information, and literature about the national pastime. Better yet they're easily and painlessly acquired; selected titles and their prices are listed in the 1989 edition of *Books in Print.* Not on the shelf? Don't worry, most large-chain bookstores will (grudgingly) order anything listed in *Books in Print* for you, and a smaller, personal-touch bookstore will be glad to do so. When both hardcover and paperback are available, the less expensive softcover version is listed.

No, we didn't list *The Whole Baseball Catalogue.* You already bought that.

Here we go . . .

The Poor Fan's Guide to Baseball Books

Baseball America's 1990 Directory. Durham, NC: American Sports Publishing Inc., 1989. Paper, $7.95 (ISBN 0-671-65615-7). The sportswriter, researcher, columnist, community organizer, and super fan can have a ball with the *Baseball Directory.* Complete major and minor

league front-office information as well as schedules make this the book for entrepreneurs who wish to become acquainted with the business of baseball. Recent editions include addresses and phone numbers for Latin and winter ball, college baseball, high school, summer, and youth baseball programs.

Baseball—The Early Years, Harold Seymour. New York: Oxford University Press, 1960. Paperback, $11.95 (ISBN 0-19-505912-3). Professor Seymour taught high school history for twenty years while he researched his magnum opus, "The History of Major League Baseball to 1893." When he took his idea of a study of baseball for a doctoral dissertation to the Cornell University history department in the 1950s, most universities would have sneered at baseball as a serious academic subject. Happily Cornell was more enlightened. The careful researcher finished his Ph.D. in 1956 with the best documented, most detailed baseball history ever written. His dissertation, still available from University Microfilms, was rewritten for public consumption (i.e., so you and I can understand it) and published by Oxford University Press. Seymour ends *The Early Years* with the advent of the American League. It has recently been reissued by the same publisher. Incidentally Professor Seymour was a batboy at Ebbets Field in the early 1920s, founder of the Drew University baseball team, and still the holder of the Drew single-season batting-average record.

Baseball—The Golden Years, Harold Seymour. New York: Oxford University Press, 1971. Paperback, $11.95 (ISBN 0-19-

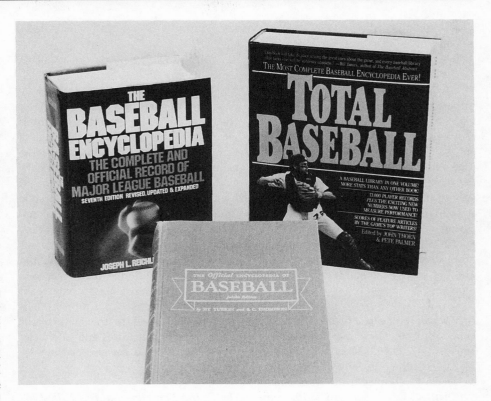

505913-1). Part Two of Professor Seymour's proposed baseball trilogy is an easier read than his first because it was written from the git-go for the general baseball public. Here he follows baseball from 1903 through the 1920s. Serious baseball fans will make Part Three of his trilogy a bestseller when and if it's completed.

The Baseball Reader: Favorites from Fireside Books of Baseball, Charles Einstein, ed. New York: McGraw-Hill, 1986. Paper, $4.95 (ISBN 0-07-019532-3). Einstein's classic collection compiled from his earlier anthologies, *The Baseball Reader* is close to a source book of baseball literature. Some of the classics you'll want to read over and over are Don Hoak's "The Day I Batted Against Castro," Heywood Hale Broun's "The Ruth Is Mighty and Shall Prevail," Al Stump's "Ty Cobb's Wild Ten-Month Fight to Live," and the greatest single-game piece—John Updike's "1960: Hub Fans Bid Kid Adieu." This book has almost all that you could want in an anthology. Who would know about James Whyte Davis of the Knickerbocker Base Ball Club requesting that he be buried in his baseball uniform if not for Charles Einstein?

The Bill James Historical Baseball Abstract, Bill James. New York: Random House, 1988. Paper, $15.95 (ISBN 0-394-75805-6, originally published by Villard Books). James, the king of controversial baseball-stat analysis (his *Abstracts* might be called *The King James Version*), here ventures into baseball history with his usual hey-look-what-I-found good humor. To be true to his legions of friends and enemies, he includes a detailed annotated statistical look at two hundred top players in the closing section, but the real fun comes earlier, in his whimsical, yet provocative dissection of baseball history. Where else can you find such nuggets as decade-by-decade discussions of the best minor league team, fastest player, heaviest player, ugliest player, most agreeable super-

star, best movie yet to be made, and best unknown player? Special features include the first woman official scorer, suicides, and men banned or informally blacklisted.

The Complete Baseball Record Book, Craig Carter. St. Louis: The Sporting News, 1989. Paper, $12.95 (ISBN 0-89204-266-4). If you want to talk baseball, you had better know your stuff. Who made the most errors in the history of the game? Who played in the first major league night game in Philadelphia? Who holds the Milwaukee Braves' record for the most sacrifice hits? While the baseball crank memorizes such questions (along with the answers) and waits for a convenient moment to spring baseball minutiae on unsuspecting bystanders, the rest of us are content to look it up in *The Complete Baseball Record Book*.

Under Carter's guidance, the publication has taken on a new look, with an easy-to-use four-part index divided into Regular Season, Championship Series, World Series, and All-Star Games sections. Use this book to settle arguments. Better yet, buy the book for your best friend and avoid arguments altogether.

The three generations of baseball encyclopedia: Turkin-Thompson (1951), "Big Mac" (1969), and Total Baseball *(1989).*

Eight Men Out, Eliot Asinof. New York: Henry Holt and Company, 1987. Paper, $8.95 (ISBN 0-8050-0346-0). You already know who-done-it, but this is an intriguing how-done-it and why-done-it. Follow the powerful Chicago White Sox from the first "Fix" meeting at the Ansonia Hotel in New York through the Soiled Series to the Chicago courtroom and on to the Baseball Commissioner's Office. Nonjudgmental (which is more than can be said for most readers), the book uses only original source material: newspapers, court records, or firsthand accounts. The 1963 classic has been reprinted twice in the last eight years and is valuable to the researcher and fun for the casually interested fan.

The No-Hit Hall of Fame: No-Hitters of the Twentieth Century, Rich Coberly. Newport Beach, California: Triple Play Publications, 1985. Paper, $13.95 (ISBN 0-934289-00-X). This delightful book is simply conceived, simply crafted, and a fine addition to anybody's library. Coberly gathered the actual news stories and box scores of twentieth-century no-hit games, rewrote them when necessary, and placed one game account and box score on each page, thus making it perfect reading material for a five-minute interlude. You can open to any page and find a complete story at your fingertips. If controversy existed during or after the game, as in Ernie Koob's tainted no-hitter, Coberly adds an explanatory paragraph. Don't argue about who did what in a no-hitter; go to the source.

The Official Price Guide to Baseball Cards, James Beckett. New York: Ballantine Books, 1987. Paper, $4.95 (ISBN 0-317-56724-1). Author Dr. James Beckett, who received a Ph.D. in statistics from Southern Methodist University in 1975, combines collectors' information and the history of card collecting with an inventory checklist to produce an extremely useful publication. Over 100,000 market values covering Topps, Donruss, Fleer, Bowman, Kellogg, Hostess, and Sportflics cards are listed.

Only the Ball Was White: A History of Legendary Black Players and All-Black Professional Teams, Robert Peterson. New York: McGraw-Hill, 1984. Paper, $9.95 (ISBN 0-07-049599-8). The original work in 1970 was a breakthrough from the curtain of silence that enveloped the twentieth-century black major leagues. The 1893 *Plessy vs. Ferguson* "separate but equal" doctrine successfully rendered the Negro Leagues invisible until Peterson published this book aimed at a white audience. Although it's fostered many additional publications about the players and their teams, it remains the only major study that contains league standings and player rosters.

Sport Americana Baseball Address List, No. 4, Dennis Eckes and Jack Smalling. Lakewood, Ohio: Edgewater Book Company, 1986. $9.95 (ISBN 0-937424-30-7). Sometimes ideas come along that are so

good one wonders why they were never tried before. *The Baseball Address List* is like that. In this case the Baseball Hall of Fame and the Society for American Baseball Research laid the groundwork by working diligently to find former major league players. But few could have foretold the thriving autograph, card, and memorabilia business that exists today. Writers, autograph seekers, and baseball historians use this slim volume that lists the last known address of former major leaguers. Sometimes the given address is only a contact person, such as a cousin or brother, who screens access to the players, but many valuable signatures and interviews have been obtained because of this pioneering effort.

The Sports Encyclopedia: Baseball, 1988 Edition, David S. Neft and Richard M. Cohen. New York: St. Martin's Press, 1988. Paper, $15.95 (ISBN 0-312-01828-2). Why do you need another book of statistics if you already have *Total Baseball* and "Big Mac"? Because unlike the others, this one is arranged by year with each team's roster, including batting and pitching stats. If you want to see how all the NL second basemen compared in hitting triples in 1926, or if you want to compare the Red Sox' whole 1948 team with the Indians of that year, or just follow your favorite team year by year, this is the way to go. Brief summaries lead into each season and there are cumulative record sections. The only disappointment: it starts with the 1901 season.

Take Me Out to the Ball Park, Lowell Reidenbaugh and Craig Carter. St. Louis: The Sporting News, rev. ed., 1987. Paper, $17.95. Reidenbaugh and Carter, two editors for the Bible of Baseball, used the popular 1948 ballpark drawings by *Boston Globe* cartoonist-sportswriter Gene Mack and current updates by free-lance artist Amadee plus photos and historical content to produce a first-class baseball book—both enjoyable and a top-notch reference

source. Mack and Amadee both have a nice knack for presenting a clear view of the field surrounded by historical vignettes—Stan Hack dying at third in the 1935 World Series or the 251-foot left-field distance that spawned "Moon Shots" at the L.A. Coliseum. For fun or information, *Take Me Out to the Ball Park* is a must buy that won't spend much time on the bookshelf.

Total Baseball, John Thorn and Pete Palmer, eds. New York: Warner Books, 1989. $49.95 (ISBN 0-446-51389-X). The most recent of encyclopedic histories is also the most complete. Some of the new stats are a little intimidating, but the old ones are there for reassurance. Never-before-listed features include a coaches roster, an extensive baseball bibliography, in-depth chronology of rule changes, register of City Series games, "phantom" players, and a history of baseball statistics as an introduction to Part Two, the stats. The All-Star and Postseason Play section is satisfactory for most reference work. As the third generation of baseball encyclopedias—the first included books of the 1920–1968 period; second was the computerized *Baseball Encyclopedia* by the Macmillan Publishing Company—*Total Baseball* ushers in the New Age of Baseball Information. Pat Kelly, photo librarian at the Baseball Hall of Fame, says, "We'd be lost without it!"

The Unforgettable Season, G. H. Fleming. New York: Simon & Schuster (Fireside Sports Classic), 1989 (reissue of 1981 edition from Holt, Rinehart & Winston). $7.95 (ISBN 0-671-67660-1). Fleming uses newspaper accounts of the 1908 National League season (that is, the season of the Merkle Blunder and the pennant that was "stolen" from New York and John McGraw) to produce a graphic portrayal of baseball, New York, and the pre–World War I era. As the author writes in his preface, the players lived in a vivid era. The rich rode in horse-drawn carriages. The

The *Spitball* Survey

Spitball is a literary baseball magazine published by Mike Shannon in Cincinnati, Ohio. He recently sent a questionnaire to sixteen baseball authors, requesting their lists of favorite baseball books. The full text of the survey and responses is printed in the Summer 1989 issue. In the following excerpts, only the choices that were mentioned more than once are listed, unless otherwise noted.

Favorite Book

The Baseball Encyclopedia.
Babe.
The Bill James Historical Baseball Abstract.
The Glory of Their Times.

Most Ingenious/Original Baseball Book

The Bill James Historical Baseball Abstract.
The Universal Baseball Association.

Baseball Book with Best Cover/Dust Jacket

Each author picked a different book. The selections ranged chronologically from *The Krank: His Language and What It Means* (1888) to *Baseball Anecdotes* (1989).

Funniest Baseball Book

Ball Four was the runaway choice.

Best Book for Converting Pagans to Baseball

The Celebrant wins out with two votes. (Do these guys read the same books?)

Most Underrated/Unknown (But Great) Book

The Imperfect Diamond by Lee Lowenfish and Tony Lupien drew two votes, which made it a winner. In the interest of undiscovered treasures, here are the one-vote choices:
Ballpark Figures: The Blue Jays and the Business of Baseball by Larry Milson.
Baseball by Robert Smith.
Baseball by the Rules by Glen Waggoner, Kathleen Maloney, and Hugh Howard.
Baseball from the Newspapers, 1845–1891 by Preston Orem.
Baseball, I Gave You All the Best Years of My Life by Kevin Kerrane and Richard Grossinger.
Coming Back with the Spitball (1914) by James Hopper.
Great Baseball Feats, Facts, and Firsts by David Nemec.
The High Hard One by Kirby Higbe and Martin Quigley.
High and Inside: The Complete Guide to Baseball Slang by Joseph McBride.
The Hot Stove League by Lee Allen.
My Baseball Diary by James T. Farrell.
My Life in Baseball: The True Record by Ty Cobb and Al Stump.
The Thrill of the Grass by Donald Honig.
The Life That Ruth Built by Marshall Smelser.

Best Baseball Picture Book

The Ultimate Baseball Book was the top choice, though three separate Donald Honig books were each mentioned once.

Best Baseball Novel

The Celebrant.
Shoeless Joe.
The Universal Baseball Association.
The Year the Yankees Lost the Pennant.
You Know Me, Al.

Baseball Book with the Best Title

Why Time Begins on Opening Day.
The Boys of Summer.

Most Disappointing Baseball Book

Oh, Baby, I Love It!
Strikeout.

Best Topic Nobody's Done a Baseball Book On

Baseball Mortality.
Baseball and Alcoholism.
The American Association (of 1882–1891).
Baseball's Front Offices.
Marvin Miller Biography.

Respondents' Suggestions for Topics for Survey

Sustained Excellence Award.
Baseball Book with Worst Title.
Best Book on a Single Historical Baseball Topic.
Baseball Book Treasured as a Boy.
Best Encyclopedia.
Best Juvenile Baseball Book.
Book That Exhausts a Subject. —LJ

poor bought goods from door-to-door vendors whose horse-drawn carts waited in the hot, stinking, narrow streets. In 1908, America's baseball fans smelled life: poor sanitation, open-air markets, and rotting animal carcasses. John McGraw and the New York Giants went to their graves feeling that the pennant had been wrongfully denied them by a gutless front office and league president who required the Giants to replay a game that they had rightfully won—according to the practices of the times. A tragic postscript shows how the feelings from the 1908 race festered with then National League President Harry Pulliam. Heckled by New York fans in every NL city, he took his own life in 1909.

Voices of the Game: The First Full-Scale Overview of Baseball Broadcasting, 1921 to the Present, Curt Smith. Notre Dame, Indiana: Diamond Communications, 1987. $22.95. (ISBN 0-912083-21-2). " . . . it was the BROADCASTERS—more than the players, managers or even the glorious ball parks—that set one's sense of fancy rippling and proselytized, as the most fervent newspaper never could, the ethos and characters of the game," says Curt Smith. He relates tales of Graham McNamee, Mel Allen, Red Barber, Ernie Harwell, Bob Prince, and Russ Hodges. Smith lets the stories tell themselves instead of trying to stick to a preconceived chronology. Harwell explains why so many broadcasters came from the South. "We came from a storytelling background. We learned early on how to tell a tale." Although Smith tackles the subject of the intrusion of television and corporate America into the announcer's booth—remember when baseball's image was changed by the firing of Dizzy Dean and Mel Allen almost simultaneously?—the future of baseball as a tube sport is not really addressed. The author's purpose is to relive the great days of the game through the eyes and ears of those who brought it to us on the radio.

That totals $237.70 spent so far, not counting tax. You've got $12.30 left over. Go buy some baseball cards . . .   —LJ

B.O.L.O.

The books listed in *The Poor Fan's Guide* certainly do not exhaust all the worthwhile baseball reading out there; they don't even get the possibilities breathing hard. In fact, we may not have included your personal, all-time, absolute, without-a-doubt, forever-and-ever favorite. Hey, we're not even chagrined. Tastes vary. (That's what makes horse races and horses' asses.) Here's a B.O.L.O. Best Nonfiction Books Addendum made up of our favorites and the preferences of a few hundred of our closest and dearest friends. If you don't see a book you think belongs here, feel free to write it in the margin. We don't care.

Our choices are arranged alphabetically in categories for easy reference. Many are currently out of print (hence, no prices or publishers are listed), but if you frequent used bookstores, flea markets, or just go to the library, you can find 'em.

Oh, in case you don't know, "B.O.L.O." is cop talk for "*Be On the LookOut.*" We just thought we'd interject a note of excitement. Ten-four.

Statistics and Records

The Baseball Encyclopedia by Macmillan Publishing Company, with various editors, notably Joe Reichler. Called "Big Mac" by its legion of followers because of its comfortable familiarity, the book is still one of the best browsing books of all time. While some claim that the 1969 version is the best, others prefer the updated statistics and complete player career totals that each revision offers. Additions such as the trade register have proven to be useful.

The Bill James Baseball Abstracts by Bill James. Published annually in 1982–1988 and privately printed in 1977–1981. You don't have to be a stat nut to enjoy James's witty and astute essays. And you don't have to be an MIT grad to understand his "sabermetric" approach to baseball.

The Elias Baseball Analyst by Seymour Siwoff, the Hirdt brothers, et al. Published annually since 1985, this is where you get *all* the numbers. You wanna know how well some left-handed hitter with a hitch in his swing and athlete's foot did in night games after day games against a right-handed pitcher with acne? It's probably in here.

Great Baseball Feats, Facts, and Firsts by David Nemec. A baseball "Book of Lists," trivia, records, and (as it says) firsts, all rolled into one entertaining whole.

The Hidden Game of Baseball by John Thorn and Pete Palmer. Statistics stretched across the seasons are the "only tangible and imperishable remains of games played yesterday or a hundred yesterdays ago." Controversial but highly readable, the book uses numerous "new" stats to rank players from the past and present. (Yeah, Babe Ruth. Who else?) You also get a neato history of stats and stuff like who does and doesn't belong in the Hall of Fame.

The Sporting News Baseball Guides and *The Sporting News Baseball Registers* by the Sporting News, published annually since the early 1940s. You may have grown up with the *Guides* (major and minor league stats from the year before) and *Registers* (lifetime records for active players). They're still just as much fun to browse through.

History

American Baseball (3 vols.) by David Q. Voigt. Harold Seymour has more detail, but Voigt is more inclusive and an easier read. Many prefer Voigt's one-volume *Baseball: An Illustrated History*.

The American League: An Illustrated History and *The National League: An Illustrated History* by Donald Honig. Solid histories by a veteran baseball writer.

Baseball by Robert Smith. A good one-volume history.

Baseball as I Have Known It by Fred Lieb. One of the greats of baseball journalism recalls the highs and lows he witnessed during his 1911–1975 career.

Baseball from the Newspaper Accounts, 1845–1891 (11 vols.) by Preston Orem. Compiled entirely from newspaper accounts and features, the volumes (one hardback volume covers 1845–1881 and ten loose-leaf supplements cover 1882–1891) give the reader information that he could only glean otherwise by risking his eyes for months at a public library microfilm reader.

Baseball's Great Experiment: Jackie Robinson and His Legacy by Jules Tygiel. Not a Robinson bio, this tells the whole story of baseball's desegregation on both the major and minor league levels.

The Boys of Summer by Roger Kahn. If this merely relived 1952, its appeal would be limited. Instead, by following the Dodgers' postbaseball lives, Kahn's book becomes a timeless study of humanity.

Daguerreotypes by The Sporting News. Good fun tracing the career stats (including minor league) of just about everybody who was anybody in baseball history.

Even the Browns by William B. Mead.

While focusing on the St. Louis Browns, Mead gives a picture of World War II baseball, a time when *even the Browns* could win.

Judge Landis and Twenty-five Years of Baseball by J. G. Taylor Spink. Both an excellent bio of the judge and a thorough history of his times (1920–1945). Read it; then *you* pick the category.

Putnam Team Histories. From 1946 to 1955, G. P. Putnam published this grand series of team histories by writers like Fred Lieb, Lee Allen, and Frank Graham. Alas! Only sixteen of them (the one entitled *Connie Mack* is also the history of the Philadelphia Athletics).

The Ultimate Baseball Book, Daniel Okrent and Harris Lewine, eds. The terrific photos sold the book, but the buoyant text and sidebars make it a volume to be treasured.

Biography

The Babe: A Life in Pictures by Lawrence Ritter and Mark Rucker. You think you've seen all the pictures of the Babe? Not until you've seen this. And don't skip over Ritter's text.

Babe: The Legend Comes to Life by Robert Creamer. Creamer's treatment of Ruth as a human being who sometimes rose to divine performances gets most (but not all) votes as the top portrayal of the Bambino.

Ball Four by Jim Bouton with Len Shechter. Written while Bouton inhabited the bullpens of the Seattle Pilots and Houston Astros, this is an exposé of the adolescent male ego. Some prefer the updated *Ball Four Plus Five*, which includes the author's unsuccessful comeback bid in 1978. This is more than just a "kiss-and-tell" tome, as Bouton's sense of the absurd makes this a joy to read unless you hap-

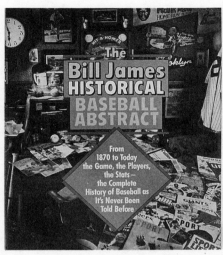

Bill James created a huge audience for sabermetrics with his annual Baseball Abstract; *in this book he casts a cold eye on the whole of baseball's past.*

pened to be one of his former teammates.

Ban Johnson, Czar of Baseball by Eugene Murdock. An excellent and scholarly account of the man who started the American League and was arguably the most important man in baseball in 1901–1920.

Baseball Between the Lines and *Baseball When the Grass Was Real* by Donald Honig. Oral history, not Orel Hershiser, and the successors to *The Glory of Their Times*. *Real* is about players from the 1920s and '30s; *Lines* is about the '40s and '50s. Although these books are now out of print, the impecunious reader may acquire both—plus selections from two other Honig titles—in the paperback *Donald Honig Reader,* issued at $12.95 by Simon & Schuster's Fireside divison.

Catcher in the Wry by Bob Uecker (with Mickey Herskowitz). In the great tradition of funny catchers—well, anyway, in the great tradition of Joe Garagiola—this is a look at the light side of baseball. Uecker, we keep hearing, wasn't as bad a player as

he says. Who cares? He's *funny*!

A False Spring by Pat Jordan. Baseball, like life, starts in spring, flourishes in summer, celebrates its victories in fall, and lies dormant in winter, waiting to begin again. Jordan's book is about his failed baseball career—the spring that had no summer—and why. His penetrating stare at his own shortcomings makes this one of the best books about baseball and about growing up.

The Glory of Their Times by Lawrence S. Ritter. Not only the yardstick used to measure other oral histories, this is many fans' choice as the best baseball book ever written. More than twenty-five stars of the early part of the century tell just the way it was. Edd Roush, Sam Crawford, Al Bridwell, and the rest come alive through Ritter's inspired editing of their tape-recorded memories.

My Greatest Day in Baseball as told to John C. Carmichael. Published in 1945, this was a staple of high school libraries for years. It still makes exciting reading.

The High Hard One by Kirby Higbe and Martin Quigley. Good autobio of the Hig and his times.

The Life That Ruth Built by Marshall Smelser. If Creamer didn't tell you everything you wanted to know about the Babe, Smelser will. It's a minority report, but some discerning people prefer this one.

The Long Season and *Pennant Race* by Jim Brosnan. When *The Long Season* came out, there was (1) general amazement that a baseball player could be literate, and (2) general shock that one would actually tell the truth about their off-field lives. Number 2 has been done to death since, but not any better because of number 1.

Nice Guys Finish Last by Leo Durocher

with Ed Linn. In fifty years of baseball, Durocher learned everything except when to keep his lip buttoned. He was never at a loss for words or opinions, but while those were vices in baseball, they're virtues in authorship.

Stengel—His Life and Times by Robert Creamer. The author treats Casey as a human being instead of the genius-clown you've seen elsewhere.

Ty Cobb by Charles Alexander. Mayhap a trifle academic for some, but you get a warts-and-all, well-balanced picture of the perhaps unbalanced star.

The Umpire Strikes Back by Ron Luciano. The author is a lot funnier—in fact, very funny—in print than he was as an umpire.

Veeck As in Wreck by Bill Veeck. Either you love Veeck or you're a club owner. Innovative to a fault, he had a torrid love affair with baseball fans that kept him on every owner's list (and not the one for parties). Forget the midget and the scoreboard; his worst sin was honesty.

Anthologies and Collections

The Armchair Books of Baseball (2 vols.),

A respectable starter baseball library.

John Thorn, ed. Good choices, good reading, good anthologies.

The Fireside Books of Baseball (4 vols.), Charles Einstein, ed. Even if you get *The Baseball Reader*—check that—especially if you get the *Reader* listed in *The Poor Fan's Guide*, you'll want all of these legendary anthologies.

The Summer Game; *Five Seasons*; *Late Innings*; and *Season Ticket* by Roger Angell. The essays of the *New Yorker*'s baseball writer are collected every half dozen years or so and reinforce the widely held view that Angell is the best diamond writer around.

The Hot Stove League by Lee Allen. The late Hall of Fame historian wrote always with style, wit, and unquestioned authority. It's hard to pick his best work, but this wide-ranging work may be it.

How Life Imitates the World Series and *Why Time Begins on Opening Day* by Thomas Boswell. Are those who say Boswell writes like an angel making a pun on Roger? Actually Boswell writes like Boswell (no, not Samuel Johnson's—the *Washington Post*'s!), and these treasures from his columns are plenty good enough to stand alongside Angell's.

Insiders' Baseball, Bob Davids, ed. Various writings by members of the Society for American Baseball Research. Davids, of course, is the organization's founder and spiritual leader.

Miscellaneous

The Ballparks by George Kalinsky and Bill Shannon. A decade old, but still a useful work on the subject.

Baseball Is a Funny Game by Joe Garagiola. It seems like this collection of droll stories has been around forever. Well, it's been thirty years, and it's still worth some chuckles.

A Century of Baseball Lore by John Thorn. The author combines humorous yarns with oddball incidents to present one hundred years of anecdotal baseball.

Dollar Sign on the Muscle by Kevin Kerrane. Subtitled *The World of Baseball Scouting*, this is a fascinating look at characters and situations in a side of the game that's left out of other books.

Green Cathedrals by Phil Lowry. A reference work on ballparks: all those ever used in the majors, the Negro Leagues, and selected minor leagues.

The Imperfect Diamond by Lee Lowenfish and Tony Lupien. The history of players struggling against all odds, dastardly machinations, and evil potentates is

chronicled in this best history of player unionization and the reserve clause fight.

The Men in Blue by Larry R. Gerlach. Enough of players, managers, and owners! Let's hear what the men who run the game on the field have to say. A different and worthwhile perspective.

The Old Ball Game by Tristram Coffin. The mythology of baseball related to that of the nation in an often overlooked classic.

Voices from the Great Black Baseball Leagues by John Holway. A "Glory of Their Times" of black baseball by the leading authority and Hall of Fame tub thumper. Eighteen players and one owner are interviewed.   —LJ

Baseball Fiction

Truth is stranger than fiction, or at least it damned better be if the fiction hopes to get published.

In his essay "Why Is It So Hard to Write a Good Baseball Novel?" Luke Salisbury concludes it's because such novels "compete with the game's history." The point has been made by others and is essentially one of those homilies we all accept without asking for the pink slip. After all, we reason, who'd believe Bobby Thomson's home run, Johnny Vander Meer's second no-hitter, or the sixth game of the 1986 World Series if they were plopped down in a novel?

The real world of the sports page (an oxymoron?) is filled with incredible, wondrous, and ridiculous events that come out of nowhere to grab us by the short hairs of our emotions. A journeyman player like Dale Long pumps out homers in eight straight games and we buy it. We have to. It happened. But if a journeyman *character* named Dale Long suddenly became a

slugger-par-excellence, we'd put down the book and check Channel 2.

Fiction must be believable (at least at the moment we read it) and baseball isn't (even at the moment we live it). Writers hoist the believability quotient in a novel or short story by laying a foundation of cause-and-effect so that when the impossible happens we know where it came from. It's like the classic whodunit: we need to be shown that the revealed miscreant couldadunit and wouldadunit.

How could you lay a foundation for Bobo Holloman's no-hitter? Or Billy Buck's bobble? And if you could foreshadow such events, they wouldn't be so wonderful or tragic.

All well and true, but baseball's implausibility doesn't really keep anyone from writing a great baseball novel. After all, is baseball any more unlikely than war? Or love? Or adolescence? Suppose Mark Twain had thrown up his hands and said, "I better deep six this Huckleberry kid

'cause real growing up is even more incredible."

When reading a baseball novel—or any novel—our willing suspension of disbelief, shock of recognition, and all that other stuff are dependent on the writer's ability to create authentic, entertaining characters who endure provocative, credible situations in an interesting, reliable world. To put it another way, we have to recognize something of ourselves in the people, see our real or imagined concerns in the plots, and live it all in a place we've been.

Salisbury suggests three ways to write a baseball novel: create a fictitious story in a real setting, create a fictitious story in a fictitious setting, or put a fictional character in a real setting. As an example of the first, he trots out *The Natural*'s Roy Hobbs, star of a fictitious pennant race in a real National League. The second possibility, which Salisbury calls "The *Alice in Wonderland* approach," is represented by W. P. Kinsella's *Shoeless Joe* and his possessed Iowa farmer in his Wonderland cornfield. The third way to do it is seen in Eric Greenberg's *The Celebrant*, with its fictitious jeweler-fan hobnobbing with a real Christy Mathewson during such actual events as the 1908, Merkle Boner pennant race. Salisbury favors the last way.

Without taking sides, we'll say that some very good writers have written some very good novels and stories by using all three ways. During the first quarter of the twentieth century, baseball reporters such as Ring Lardner (*You Know Me, Al*), Heywood Hale Broun (*The Sun Field*), and Gerald Beaumont (*Hearts and the Diamond*) turned to writing baseball stories designed for adult readers. In the 1930s and '40s, superb writers such as Thomas Wolfe (*You Can't Go Home Again*) and James T. Farrell (*Danny O'Neill* and *My Baseball Diary*) wrote novels that contained baseball passages. Short stories by such diverse writers as Robert Penn Warren ("Goodwell Comes Back"), James Thurber ("You Could Look It Up"), and Damon Runyon ("Baseball Hattie") were aimed at the mass readership of *The Saturday Evening Post* and *Collier's*.

In the grip of post–Charles Van Doren realism, Eliot Asinof (*Man on Spikes*), Martin Quigley (*Today's Game*), and Charles Einstein (*The Only Game in Town*) gave us players who used profanity, exercised poor judgment, and displayed serious character flaws. (Gee! just like you and me!) Bernard Malamud (*The Natural*) and Mark Harris's Henry Wiggen Trilogy (*The Southpaw*, *Bang the Drum Slowly*, and *A Ticket for a Seamstitch*) deal with themes broader and deeper than winning ballgames.

The insecurity of the 1980s (how long till *you* get mugged?) has led to sensitive, nostalgic novels set in an earlier, less threatening era. Eric Greenberg (*The Celebrant*), W. P. Kinsella (*Shoeless Joe*, and *The Iowa Baseball Confederacy*), and Harry Stein (*Hoopla*) have chosen the 1900s to 1920s as the settings for their works.

The following selected list of adult baseball fiction represents, we think, some of the best and most insightful baseball stories ever written. More important, they can stand up and be counted as excellent fiction—and baseball be damned.

The Bingo Long Traveling All-Stars and Motor Kings (1973) by William Brashler. Episodic novel affectionately portraying the adventures of a black All-Star team touring the 1930s South.

The Celebrant (1983) by Eric Rolfe Greenberg. An excellent portrait of pre-1920s baseball as well as a depiction of America's loss of innocence through the eyes of a hero-worshiping fan.

The Cheat (1984) by Pat Jordan. If you think all baseball writers are unscrupulous misanthropes looking to stick it to our heroes, you'll love the way this novel's reporter goes after a scandal.

The Curious Case of Sidd Finch (1987) by George Plimpton. A Tibetan pitcher with a 168-m.p.h. fastball? We're in fantasyland here, but if you can smile at baseball, you can chuckle through this.

The Dixie Association (1984) by Donald

Robert Coover's
The Universal Baseball Association, J. Henry Waugh, Prop.

In this unique baseball novel, J. Henry Waugh is the founder, president, press secretary, sportswriter, historian, and proprietor of the Universal Baseball Association, a baseball board game. Although he can't control his own fate, he controls all facets of life in the Association by throwing dice. At first, he plays the game straight, but slowly, like any fan, he begins to develop favorite players. He openly roots for the phenom pitcher Damon Rutherford, the son of all-time UBA great and Hall of Fame inductee Brock Rutherford. The proprietor's identification with Damon Rutherford is underlined when Waugh seduces a woman at a bar by telling her that he is Damon Rutherford, who has just pitched a perfect game.

But Waugh's game can go awry the same as life.

In the game, dice throws of 1-1-1 or 6-6-6 trigger Waugh's Chart of Extraordinary Occurrences, where almost anything can happen: fistfights, suspensions, fixed games, and injuries. Through an extraordinary set of rolls, Damon Rutherford is killed by a pitch. A grief-stricken Waugh investigates the dastardly pitcher who threw the fatal fastball and discovers a consistent pattern of evil behavior. The proprietor begins to manipulate the game in order to thwart the sinister hurler. Finally, in an act of desperation, he maneuvers the dice to kill the pitcher who had killed Damon Rutherford. With the game out of control, Waugh attempts to go back and change the history of the Association to cover up his crime, but if history is manipulated, is it still history? Fantasy blends with reality until he no longer knows the difference.

The Universal Baseball Association is perhaps too intellectual for some tastes. Yet we can all identify with Waugh's fan mentality, his desire to control his fate, and his anguish as his game/life tumbles from his grip.
                                         —LJ

Hays. Cartoonish and predictable, this story of a paroled bank robber and his team of outcasts nevertheless has some moments of high humor, especially if you didn't vote for Reagan or Bush.

The Great American Novel (1973) by Philip Roth. Critics skewered this when it was first published, but it's been making a comeback. The tongue-in-cheek story of the Patriot League, a since-forgotten aggregation of castoffs, has-beens, and 4-F's.

Hoopla (1983) by Harry Stein. A novelized version of the Black Sox scandal as related by an old-time sportswriter and Buck Weaver.

Man on Spikes (1955) by Eliot Asinof. Follows a ball player's career from the beginning through the final pitch.

The Natural (1952) by Bernard Malamud. Much darker than the movie, but that just makes for an interesting comparison. This Roy Hobbs is the victim of his own immature lusts. Malamud incorporated every scintilla of the Great American Baseball Myth to create this wonderful allegory.

The Only Game in Town (1954) by Charles Einstein. After paying his dues and then some in the minors, a former major leaguer gets a crack at managing in the Bigs.

The Red-Headed Outfield, and Other Baseball Stories (1915) by Zane Grey. Eleven baseball tales by a classic storyteller who once roamed outfields himself.

Score by Innings (1919) by Charles E. Van Loan. The author was the most popular sports fiction writer of the early twentieth century. Here are ten baseball tales showing why.

Shoeless Joe (1982) by W. P. Kinsella. The source for the movie *Field of Dreams*, this allegorical fantasy about an Iowa farmer obsessed with Joe Jackson is a love-it-or-hate-it kind of book.

She's on First (1987) by Barbara Gregorich. This story of the first female major leaguer and the obstacles and prejudices she faces is *not* just for women readers.

The Southpaw (1953); *Bang the Drum Slowly* (1956); *A Ticket for a Seamstitch* (1957), and *It Looked Like Forever* (1979) by Mark Harris. The first three make up a trilogy about the career of pitcher Henry Wiggen, told by the star hurler himself. In *It Looked Like Forever*, Wiggen copes with life after baseball. Read them in order.

Strike Three You're Dead (1984) by R. D. Rosen. Probably the best baseball murder mystery. An aging outfielder seeks his roommate's killer.

Today's Game (1965) by Martin Quigley. Fictionalized account of a day in the life of a big league manager.

The Universal Baseball Association, J. Henry Waugh, Prop. (1968) by Robert Coover. See sidebar.

The Year the Yankees Lost the Pennant (1954) by Douglass Wallop. *Damn Yankees* without the songs and dances still makes an enjoyable switch on the Faust story. Of course, it had more bite when the Yankees were The Yankees.

You Know Me, Al: A Busher's Letters (1916) by Ring Lardner. These amusing stories disguised as letters from a White Sox pitcher by a great American writer can tell you more about baseball-think before World War I than a pile of histories. —LJ

Juvenile Fiction

You won't find many (if any) examples of juvenile baseball fiction at Ye Olde Bookseller's. Mostly they're sold to school libraries. That doesn't mean they don't get read. Walk into almost any high school or junior high school library in the country and you'll see the kids have been at the baseball fiction. The pages are dog-eared and the cards in back are filled with names.

But since they're ordered by teacher-librarians, you can bet your Perfect Attendance Award that the books are going to have an *uplifting, wholesome message*. In the first half of the twentieth century, all the high quality kids' baseball novels hammered themes like the sportsman's code of behavior, good citizenship, fairness, competition, and fitting into society. When the social climate of the 1960s–1980s changed the way people lived, it changed the way authors write. Today's juvies are hipper and subtler. You can't expect a kid weaned on "Miami Vice" (whether on TV or in his neighborhood) to freak out over whether a white bread like Frank Merriwell will win the Big Game for Yale. Today's authors depict credibly flawed dudes doing their baseball thing in more sordid settings, but they still come down on the side of the Good Guys.

Formula Writing

The earliest writers of baseball fiction—Zane Grey, Gilbert Patten, Edward Stratemeyer, Ralph Henry Barbour, and Harold Sherman—used the juvenile baseball book to examine the set of safe, conventional ideas concerning personal morality and public success that were prominent during their lifetimes. Honor, integrity, sacrifice, and honesty combined with fair play, sportsmanship, competitiveness, and loyalty as the proper virtues for the young readers who would one day become the Good Citizens and Leaders of Our Country.

Code of Behavior

The Sportsman's Code of Behavior meant playing in pain, being modest about successes, and having great loyalty to the team. Lord knows what Mickey Mantle read growing up in Oklahoma, but in the 1950s and '60s, he embodied the heroes of an earlier generation's reading. He played in pain. He played with blood seeping through bandages and through his uniform because the team needed him to win. Yankee manager Ralph Houk asked, "But Mick, can you play?" Mantle's answer was always, "I'll give it a try."

In *Strike Three* (1949), Chip Hilton, Clair Bee's extraordinary triple-threat athlete, recovers from a football injury that forced him to sit out the basketball season. His catching ability is called into question by the team's pitcher, who also represents the clique of Bad Guys from the Other Side of Town. Hilton, after securing pitching instruction from a former big league hurler, takes to the mound to save his teammates from a season of losses. The team wins game after game until the state championship, when Hilton is not allowed to pitch back-to-back games. He convinces his coach and teammates to give former pitcher Nick Trullo—the sour southpaw whose truculent temper, involvement in a high school betting ring, and propensity to throw beanballs led to his quitting the team—another chance. Trullo experiences difficulty pitching because his shoes are too tight. Hilton the Hero trades cleats with his former antagonist, now his hearty supporter, and bears the misery of tight shoes himself. Of course, Hilton knocks in the only run in a pinch-hitting role and saves the game with one relief pitch—his patented blooper—in the bottom of the ninth, all with shoes suited for a Geisha.

The Outsider

One of the earliest features in juvenile sports fiction is the notion of successful integration into a peer group. The Outsider may be a newcomer to a town split by years of dissension, a person who is re-

markably different, or a first-year player, but he always experiences the same situations as the juvenile reader is likely to experience in life.

Zane Grey's Chase Alloway in *The Shortstop* (1909) is an Outsider because he was born with a crooked eye that causes women to turn away and men to ridicule him. In this novel about discrimination, his crooked-eyed pitching creates a sensation as he befuddles the popular local team. The game is called a forfeit in favor of the locals because Alloway throws a "crooked ball." A riot ensues and Alloway beats it out of town. The crooked-eyed hero is shunted from town to town, playing some ball here and there. Finally he arrives in Findlay, Ohio, where people are more liberal and accept Chase, who stars for the hometeam. A benefactor pays for an operation to correct his crooked eye. Alloway becomes handsome and idolized, but he soon learns his manners are unacceptable for high society functions. Church groups harass him for leading young boys to the playing field instead of the praying field. Alloway retreats into insecurity and spends more and more time with the village hunchback, the team's batboy, until the daughter of a local minister befriends him and facilitates his social salvation. They marry, adopt the hunchbacked boy, and live—what else?—happily ever after.

Sacrifice and Good Citizenship

Harold Sherman in *Hit by Pitcher* uses his characters as though he were writing Greek tragedy. Wally, the best hitter on the team, wants to be captain, but his teammates choose Eagle, the all-around Good Guy. Like Achilles sulking in his tent, Wally intentionally goes into a hitting slump to prove the team needs him. In a fistfight Wally injures Eagle's throwing arm. The disability shows up in the first Big Game, when Eagle can't handle his center-field throwing duties. When Good Guy Eagle refuses to disclose the real

Baseball's Greatest All-Star Team

The greatest possible collection of baseball talent won't be found at any summer's All-Star Game nor in the hallowed Hall at Cooperstown. No indeed. Baseball's greatest All-Star team can be found at your local library wearing dust jackets instead of pinstripes.

Player	Pos.	Book
Frank Merriwell	P	Frank Merriwell Series
Jocko Klein	C	*The Keystone Kids*
Biggie Cohen	1B	Chip Hilton Series
Bobby Russell	2B	*The Keystone Kids*
Babe Raglan	3B	*The Seventh Babe*
Linda Sunshine	SS	*She's on First*
Joe Matson	LF	The Baseball Joe Series
Joe Hardy	CF	*The Year the Yankees Lost the Pennant*
Roy Hobbs	RF	*The Natural*
Kid Who Batted 1.000	DH	*The Kid Who Batted 1.000*

Subs		
Sidd Finch	P	*The Curious Case of Sidd Finch*
Gil Gamesh	P	*The Great American Novel*
Henry Wiggen	P	*The Southpaw*
Lefty Locke	P/Manager	The Big League Series
Chip Hilton	P/OF	Chip Hilton Series
Jack Keefe	P	*You Know Me, Al*
Damon Rutherford	P	*The Universal Baseball Association*
Bruce Pearson	C	*Bang the Drum Slowly*
Brick Owens	C	The Big League Series
Hog Durham	1B	*The Dixie Association*
Spike Russell	INF	*The Keystone Kids*
Buck Weaver	INF	*Hoopla*
Roy Tucker	OF	*The Kid from Tomkinsville*
Joe Jackson	OF	*Shoeless Joe*
Harvey Blissberg	OF	*Strike Three You're Dead*
Rhubarb	OWNER	*Rhubarb* —LJ

reason for his injured wing, a chastened Wally comes out of his slump and assists Eagle in a double-play catch and throw that is the greatest play anyone has ever seen. With his newly discovered humility, Wally is elected captain for the next season. He is about to set the school record for consecutive base hits when Eagle misses a sign and Wally's sacrifice bunt becomes a fielder's choice. Wally loses his temper and lashes out at the downcast Eagle. In the next game Wally is beaned and spends the rest of the book trying to regain his confidence. In the second Big Game, Eagle takes a pitch in the head (no batting helmets in those days) to allow Wally to get to the plate. Wally gets his at bat, his big hit, and his confidence.

Societal Issues and Changes

We can follow society's changes through its fiction. The setting for early juvenile fiction was often private schools or prestigious colleges. Athletes often belonged to the highest social classes. At Yale Frank Merriwell frequently sipped afternoon tea with budding socialites. The Bad Guys usually came from the Other Side of Town. In real life few kids from the wrong side made it to high school, so they were unlikely to read the books.

After World War I, as more kids from lower social classes attended high school, the restrictive school boy environment in juvenile fiction was replaced by more democratic, middle-class settings like high schools and state universities. Baseball itself was dominated by the professional game and the major leagues became a typical setting.

Gilbert Patten wrote the Merriwell stories using the pseudonym Burt L. Standish. In the Big League series, he created Phil Hazelton, who played professionally under the name Lefty Locke. As the embodiment of the American Dream, Lefty started in the minors (*Lefty O' the Bush*) in 1914 and ended with his own team (*Lefty Locke, Owner*) in 1925. Along the way Lefty saved games and eventually baseball while surviving game rigging, poisoning, drugging, kidnapping, and being run down by an automobile.

The most successful author of juvenile sports novels, John R. Tunis, set his baseball books in Brooklyn. In his *Keystone Kids*, brothers Spike and Bobby Russell join the Dodgers as a shortstop–second base combination. After a dazzling half season, Spike is named manager to instill some spirit into the lifeless team. Sparks

fly with the arrival of Jocko Klein, a rookie catcher. He becomes the target of anti-Semitic bench jockeying. His team mistakes his passive resistance for cowardice. Spike's brother Bobby falls in with the Jew-baiting clique as some of the teammates try to chase Jocko Klein off the team. Jocko fights back and cements his place as a member of the Dodgers.

Author Tunis defines teamwork by showing how each member of the team was descended from people who settled America and came together to better their families. He further explains the reasons why the country is at war (1943) and the dangers of valuing one's self-interest over the common good. Of course, any post-1947 reader can't help but transpose Jocko Klein and Jackie Robinson.

Part of preparation for life is the loss of innocence. By the mid-1920s, adults began to play roles other than father, uncle, and coach. Grown-ups became villains. The schoolboy-battling-adult-oppressors theme continued through Clair Bee's Chip Hilton series.

Chip, left fatherless due to an industrial accident, not only protects his gray-eyed mom, who works nights as a telephone operator, but solves the town's problem of spoiled goods in the pottery kiln. Hilton beats up bullies, outwits scheming hustlers, catches criminals with prison records, and sets good-boys-gone-bad back on the road to good citizenship and success, while attending school, working six days a week, and winning championships nearly every season of every year in baseball, basketball, and football.

Win One for the Gipper

Victory over seemingly impossible odds is a standard plot and helps instill the uniquely American idea that anyone can succeed if he or she only tries hard enough. This attitude is perhaps the greatest contribution by juvenile sports literature to the youth of American society.

In Harold Sherman's *Batter Up*, Pete

Dailey, a World War I veteran, suffers from mustard gas poisoning but coaches the Traverse City American Legion team to the finals of the American Legion tournament, where they face the powerful Chicago team in Yankee Stadium while Babe Ruth and New York Mayor Jimmy Walker sit watching in the stands. The road to the championship is paved with gang feuds, stolen money, a swell-headed pitcher, last-minute heroics, and a disastrous train wreck. Then the team learns their coach is dying and their star pitcher has an injured arm. The boys visit the coach in the hospital. He gives them a pep talk about two soldiers dying in battle and appoints a captain to lead them to New York City to play in the championships. Word of the coach's death inspires the team to an eight-run rally to win the title.

Today's Flawed Heroes

The modern-day version of the Big Game ending is not very attractive to fans of older juvenile literature. In Robert Lipsyte's book *Jock and Jill*, hero athlete Jack Ryder prepares for the championship game to be played in Yankee Stadium by taking cortisone shots and popping greenies to keep his arm strong and his energy level up. He becomes involved with Jillian, a young lady undergoing psychiatric treatment. In the course of their adventures they meet Hector, a former gang leader who has developed a social conscience. Hector is arrested just before the big game at Yankee Stadium, and Jack and Jillian seize the stadium during the game to protest. Jillian is sent away for more psychiatric treatment and Jack is reunited with his cheerleader girlfriend Kristie.

Today's kids don't know any Frank Merriwells or Chip Hiltons, and they have little faith in eight-run rallies. But they still need guidance in growing up; lessons in behavior, citizenship, and fitting in with society; and inspiration to strive against the odds—all of which go down better wrapped in a good baseball story. —LJ

So You Want to Write a Baseball Book

Assume that you have spent three years reading microfilm about the Syracuse Stars in the Onondaga County Public Library. You think that you have a pretty nifty piece of research that would make a fine book. The Stars were a one-year franchise in the National League in 1879, but you have found that they were also an outstanding team from 1876 through 1879, frequently competing with and defeating the best nines in the country, including the Boston Red Stockings. You want to write a book about the Star Base Ball Club of Syracuse. So what do you do first?

Determine the Market

There's not much use in writing something that interests no one but yourself. Who will want to read your book about the Syracuse Stars? Will they want it enough to buy it, tell their friends about it, and give it as a Christmas gift? This is important because it will determine your choice of publishers. For your book Syracuse is an obvious market, as are aficionados of nineteenth-century baseball.

Of course you'll give away a few copies, but remember writing is your livelihood, or could be if you're successful in this, your first attempt. The more copies you give away, the fewer will be bought. Regardless, don't rely too heavily on friends to buy the book. You don't have *that* many.

A lesser market will be the local historical society and local bookstores, but that's limited. What to do next?

With a limited market you must decide if you want to continue with the working title *The Syracuse Stars* or to expand the title and marketplace. For example, *The Stars in the National League* or *Nineteenth-Century Baseball in Upstate New York*, or *Baseball in the Early Years*. Don't limit yourself by a restrictive title.

You decide to go ahead with the project. You've already spent three years reading blurry microfilm in poor lighting; you owe it to your failing eyesight to continue with the book. After all, the Syracuse Star book will bring to the baseball book-buying public a subject that probably never came to mind when discoursing on nineteenth-century baseball. No other book that you know of has ever been published on the Stars. The study will fit nicely into that historical void that covers the 1879 National League season.

Why Not Hire an Agent?

Good idea! Where do you find one? What should you look for in an agent? Why do you need one? Talk to other authors. Find books that are similar to yours and contact the authors. Ask any of your friends who have written books about their agents. You should get to know other authors because the literary agents know each other and the publishers know each other. Check out a bunch of agents at once, and select the best for your needs.

The most sought-after quality in an agent is trustworthiness. Secondly, hope that the agent knows something about the subject of your expertise. It's important that your agent-to-be personally knows the editors at the publishing houses. You should get along with your agent. If the agent isn't the sort of person you can call to express your latest brilliant idea, he or she may not be the agent for you. And third, if the agent charges a fee to read your manuscript, chuck him (or her).

The more successful you are, the more you'll need an agent to sell your manuscripts and your ideas to publishers. A good agent frees up time for the writer to write. The agent knows the publishing end of the book business and can help with financial planning and taxes. Let your agent sell your book on the Syracuse Stars.

Select a Publisher

Your agent wants a sample of your published work. If one publisher paid you for writing something, maybe the next publisher will do the same. You explain that this is your first book and you do not have published samples to show. The agent needs at the very minimum one chapter of your book.

You and the agent agree that major publishing houses will not be interested. Don't waste your time or the publisher's by sending hopeless proposals. Your agent, who is most likely used to dealing with major publishers and is looking for a best-seller, decides that specialty or university presses are the most likely candidates to publish *The Stars in the National League.* You pick some likely candidates out of *Literary Market Place* and your agent tries to find out something about the selected publishing houses.

Learn the names of the people who will be making the decision on your manuscript. A package sent to a specific person has a much better chance of being read. Find a list of titles that the company has published in the last five years to get an idea what kind of books they are interested in publishing. Try publishing houses that you know have produced baseball books in the past.

If the publisher doesn't pursue the marketing of your newly printed book, you can kiss good-bye any chance to collect royalties. It's your publisher's responsibility to market your book. Talk about marketing possibilities and the publisher's ideas for promotion. A publisher without promotional ideas is unlikely to do a good job selling your book to the public.

If the publisher is convinced that the project will be profitable, he'll usually offer an advance. Get as much in advance as possible because many factors can enter the picture to restrict your chance of making money on royalties. Suppose a plant closing in Syracuse leaves hundreds of unemployed baseball fans and book buyers without the means to support your endeavors. Or suppose a blockbuster *Pictorial History of the Amazing Salt City Stars* comes from left field to destroy your chances. How'd you like to hear, "Sorry, kid, we didn't make a dime off your book.

Smaller Publishers That Specialize in Baseball Books

Algonquin Books of Chapel Hill
Box 2225
Chapel Hill, NC 27515
(919) 933-2113

Meckler Press
Ferry Lane West
Westport, CT 06880
(203) 226-6967

McFarland Press NC
P.O. Box 611
Jefferson, NC 28640
(919) 246-5560

North Atlantic Books
2320 Blake St.
Berkeley, CA 94704
(415) 540-7934

Greenwood Press
P.O. Box 5007

Westport, CT 06881
(203) 226-3571

Taylor Publishing
1550 W. Mockingbird Lane
Dallas, TX 75235
(214) 637-2800

Diamond Communications
P.O. Box 88
South Bend, IN 46624
(219) 287-5006

Redefinition Press
700 N. Fairfax St.
Alexandria, VA 22314
(703) 739-2110

Do not forget university presses. Good sources for publishers' addresses are *Books in Print, Writers' Market,* and *Literary Market Place.* —LJ

Can you imagine two Syracuse Stars books in one year? Tough break, kid." Get the money up front.

Sending the Manuscript

Be sure your best work is displayed in your proposal and manuscript. It's the most important calling card you have. The editor's opinion of you will be based on his perception of your work. The proposal can be typed single space, but the manuscript must be double spaced. Always make a photocopy of whatever you send in the mail. Send it by registered mail and ask for a postal receipt. You might as well make sure that the publisher receives it. If you are sending your work to several publishers at once, let them know.

Rejection

Don't become discouraged. As a budding writer you must realize that rejection is part of the business. It may seem that people in the publishing business don't want you to succeed, but the publisher will spend thousands of dollars to make you a published author—if he thinks he can make thousands of dollars back. Hang in there!

After many rejection slips, you and your agent may decide to part company. But *The Stars in the National League* is still your book. You can publish the book on your own, as explained on the facing page . . . —LJ

Do-It-Yourself Publishing

An author can make more money by handling the writing, text design, layout, cover design, choice of type style, choice of printer, editing, proofreading, and marketing. (And for this afternoon Signore Da Vinci will paint a portrait of his neighbor Lisa.) The self-publisher must be willing to bear the entire cost of the operation. Be aware of the $1,000 that it is likely to cost you to print five hundred copies. If you truly want to be a writer, this might be considered investing in your future. The Syracuse Star book will be your open door to the writing profession. The next time your agent asks for a sample of your work, he won't go home empty-handed.

Writing, editing, and proofreading are just as necessary to a good book as choosing a good printer and designer. Don't take shortcuts. You want a book that you can be proud of. Don't publish, don't go to the printer if you haven't done the very best that you can do. There's no worse feeling than to be stuck with 450 books that you're embarrassed to give away. If you can do your own reading, writing, and proofing, you still need a printer.

Ask around, attend local book fairs, meet the area's authors. The book printing business is the same whether one has *The Stars in the National League* or *The Vikings in Oklahoma, Part 2*. Many times a printer can save you scads of money by typesetting directly from a floppy disk. If you have the capacity to put your book on disk, then do so and find a printer who can work with you. Ask questions, find a printer who fills your needs.

Some printers offer design, layout, and copy pasteup. They will *never* be the sole proofreaders of your galley proofs. You must find someone to proofread. It is not a good idea for you to be the only proofreader since you know more about the Stars than any living person and you see the intent of each sentence. Let someone else decide if that intent is communicated properly.

Only if you're experienced at designing book layout should you do your book. The same goes for the design of the cover. Whether or not the public buys your book on impulse depends largely on its attractiveness. If you are not knowledgeable in design, hire someone who designs covers for a living. Photos must be handled differently from text. Once again it is best to hire a professional unless you really know what you're doing. To end the confusion, you have decided on AG Press, a small Manhattan, Kansas, firm that prints many farm and university publications as well as some academic journals. The owner likes baseball and has published several baseball books in the past. Also the printing house offers the services of text design, layout of photos, copy pasteup, and cover design. In your phone conversation you were able to agree on a typeface, paper weight, publication size, and copy deadline. You rush home to copy your disks and mail them off the next day.

What is taking so long? Be patient—the printer wants to do a good job too. As the writer/editor you must be ready to proof when the printer is ready.

The book is out. *The Stars in the National League* looks like a winner. It has a perfect binding, sixty-four pages, with ten photographs in the middle of the book. The printer mails you all 500 copies and an invoice. What do you do next?

Unfortunately the easy part is over. The printer did most of the work in producing your book. Now you must sell it. Go back to the market strategy that you first had to consider before you even wrote the book. It is now time to implement your theories.

Since you self-published it, the book probably lacks the national interest necessary to get bookstore chains to pick it up. Besides, with 500 copies you don't have enough to send out and risk returns with a major chain. Independent bookstores are your best bet. That means you must visit 100 stores if you are to sell your book in 100 places.

No money for promotion means that no one is going to know about your book. There are marketing firms who specialize in self-published books. They advertise a large number of books in their catalog; they will add your volume to the catalog or carry a flyer about *The Stars in the National League* for a fee.

Self-marketing is similar to self-publishing—you must ask around. Who uses marketing firms? Where are books like mine sold? What about advertising?

Find out the return rate for the advertising dollar. One percent of the readership is considered normal. For example, if 100,000 people see the flyer about *The Stars*, only 1,000 can be expected to respond if the readership is normal. Costs for advertising can quickly get out of hand. For a topic such as the Syracuse Stars, it would make sense to go to local historical societies in the cities of every team in the book. Show Rochester and Buffalo that their teams are an integral part of Syracuse baseball history. Don't overlook public libraries or special interest groups such as the Society for American Baseball Research. Are there newsletters that will carry an announcement of your book for little or no cost?

Do what you can to sell *The Stars* book, relish the self-importance of authorship, and prepare your next blockbuster, *Baseball Camps of the Northeast.*   —LJ

Ten Great Ideas for Baseball Books Not Yet Written

Here are some terrific untapped subjects which you can have perfectly free. Of course, when you're rich and famous you might send a small, four-figure check by way of saying thanks.

Who Was Who Once Upon a Time: Rosters of the Early Non-League Years, 1850–1885. The rosters of the 1850–1868 amateur era are available in the *New York Clipper* and local newspapers. An enterprising researcher could in a short time produce an amazing number of rosters.

Baseball: The Inside Inside Story. General managers, public relations, and major league front-office staff tell their own story of what really happens behind the scenes in organized ball. Gossip books, when they are controversial and well written, sell. Why should players get to dish all the dirt?

I Think That I Shall Never See a Poem As Lovely As .333: Baseball Poets and Their Poetry. From the mighty Casey's famous K/through *Sporting Life*'s witty rhymes/ poets have always found their way/to lines that scan 'bout baseball's times./*Spitball* and *Minneapolis Review of Baseball*/ should both get great big gold awards/for daring to print just about all/of the top diamond verses by modern bards.

The Bushers of Their Times: Oral History of the Minor Leagues. Former players from the Golden Age of the minor leagues (1946–1955) are still alive, and many still inhabit the same localities where they hung up their spikes. Someone should get their stories on a tape recorder.

Separate but Equal Fastballs: Black Baseball 1900–1919. Despite some excellent recent works on later years, this period still needs its Seymour history.

Blandball: Walter Johnson, His Life and Times. So what if baseball's greatest speed king was an early-to-bed, early-to-rise farmboy? He was as great a pitcher as is ever likely to come along, and his career brought him into contact with enough col- orful characters to liven up every page.

This Curve Is Brought to You by . . .: Baseball and Its Advertising. Signs on outfield walls, endorsements, today's TV! Great stories and what a pictorial!

Definitely Out: Baseball Mortality. Grab this account of the often strange, sometimes gruesome ends of former players before Geraldo does. F'rinstance, did you know Jack Powell's last words were "Watch this" as he tried to swallow a steak whole in order to win a bet? Yep, as horrified restaurant patrons watched, he choked to death.

Marvelous Marvin: Biography of Marvin Miller. Dare you write the life story of the most influential man in baseball since Branch Rickey? Would the public buy it? He is still alive. On second thought, perhaps *he* should write an autobiography.

100 Great Ideas for Baseball Books Not Yet Written. We'll buy it.   —LJ

The Perfect Title

Okay, I've written a baseball book and I'm sure everybody, or at least some people besides my friends, will buy it, if only I can think of a spiffy title. *What I Know About Baseball* wouldn't make it even if I gave away free thimbles.

Here's what *not* to do.

1. Don't be too clever. God knows how many clerks put Ron Luciano's *Fall of the Roman Umpire* in the ancient history section.

2. Don't be too honest. *History of the Piedmont League 1920–1955* (Chrisman) certainly exemplifies truth in packaging, but I defy you to name ten people *you know* who want to read about the Piedmont League. Five!

3. Don't start with "Baseball." There are by my count ninety-three books in print with "Baseball" leading off the title. Dropping my book into that crowd would be like sending a horse's hindquarters to Congress. It could be years before anyone noticed.

4. Don't leave "Baseball" out of the ti- tle. A lot of people thought Roger Angell's *Five Seasons* was about farming.

5. Don't say "Greatest." Nobody believes it anymore. I think there are more "Greatest" 's than "Baseball" 's. Any day now somebody will write *The Greatest Mundane Commonplaces*.

Anyway, I've decided on a name for my book: *Lincoln's Mother's Doctor's Dog's Fireplug Book of Unlimited Baseball and Diet Plan.*

Next, I need a complimentary foreword from a famous baseball personality. Does anybody here know Margo Adams's address?   —BC

CHAPTER 12

The Game Above the Title

Recently we conducted a poll to pick the best baseball movie of all time. It was an unofficial poll and not very scientific. We called a couple of people who watch both baseball games and movies and asked them what baseball movies they thought were the best and why. None of the people we called were named Siskel or Ebert. Nevertheless some of the answers jarred us.

Like "None."

Come on, purist. Even if they're all awful, isn't one less so?

Or, "*The Winning Team.*" Why? "Because I'm a Republican."

Or, "*Damn Yankees*" Why? "Gwen Verdon is sexy as hell."

Or, "*Pride of the Yankees*. Because it was really sad about Lou Gehrig."

Or, "World Series highlight films 'cause they're almost believable."

The most useful answer was actually a question. "Do you mean the best baseball in a movie or the best movie with baseball?"

We put our poll on hold and sat down to define our terms.

If all we were looking for was the best baseball in a movie, then a highlight film would make a good choice. Pick a well-played World Series that's decently photographed and you've got it. Or if we insisted on a *movie* movie with a plot and everything, we could name any one of several made in the 1940s and '50s that used actual game footage to fill in between the acted scenes. For example, in *It Happens Every Spring* they used footage from the 1945 World Series.

Okay, bad example. The '45 Series was played with a sloppiness that would make a biker gang's skin crawl. But there are plen-

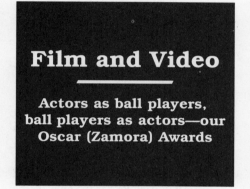

Film and Video

Actors as ball players, ball players as actors—our Oscar (Zamora) Awards

ty of examples of good baseball spliced into some of those old movies. Sometimes the uniforms on the real footage don't match the uniforms on the actors in their scenes, but wotthehell. If you want realism, watch a newsreel.

Scratch "the best baseball in a movie."

"The best movie with baseball in it" isn't quite right either. For example, there are baseball scenes in *A Soldier's Story*. We distinctly remember Larry Riley hitting a home run. But *A Soldier's Story* is a mystery about racial prejudice set in the World War II Army. It's hardly a "baseball movie."

We have to draw a line somewhere or we'll be including every movie that has a baseball scene, regardless of how really "basebally" the picture was. In *Battleground* (1949), a tough war movie about the Battle of Bastogne, Ricardo Montalban tosses a baseball around Belgium. There's a quick scene in Woody Allen's *Radio Days* (1987) in which a blind man plays baseball. Were there baseball scenes in *Gone with the Wind*? Frankly, we don't give a damn. *GWTW* is no more a "baseball movie" than *Miracle on 34th Street* is the Miracle of

Coogan's Bluff. For that matter, Clint Eastwood's *Coogan's Bluff* (1968) is no baseball flick either.

We decided a baseball movie contains characters who purport to be baseball players and who spend a significant portion of the film playing, talking about, or, at the very least, dressed to play baseball. The baseball can be on a major, minor, or Little League level. It can be treated in a dramatic, tragic, or comedic way. The movie does *not* have to be *about* baseball (as we already pointed out elsewhere, baseball movies are almost never about baseball), but baseball does have to play an important part in the story line.

So what we were really looking for was the best baseball-movie *movie*. And we should judge it by normal movie-going, sit-in-the-balcony-and-scarf-up-popcorn criteria. Did we get involved? Did we care what happened? When "it" happened, did we get the emotional charge that a good movie can deliver? If the film was true to our real-life baseball experience, that's a bonus.

In our rating of the movie's success, we decided against holding it to strict conformity with arcane baseball knowledge so long as the contours were true. In other words, the average fan and movie-goer might not know when the Yankees started wearing pinstripes, but he'd cry foul if they got four outs in an inning.

Back to the telephone. With great care and pardonable pride, we explained our new-found criteria to our callees.

"None."

"*The Winning Team* because I'm a Republican."

"*Damn Yankees* because Gwen Verdon is sexy as hell."

Damn!

Scratch the whole poll.

Partly in frustration and partly in recognition of the money we could save on our telephone bill, we decided to embark on a revolutionary course: ignore the poll and express our own opinion. Right away we were miles ahead of just about any politician you can name.

Of course, there are risks.

What if you don't agree with our choices? Well, that's easy enough. You're wrong.

Ah, but what if you know all about some baseball movie we've never seen? That's a little harder. We'll readily admit we've never seen either *Elmer the Great* (1933) or *Alibi Ike* (1935), two Joe E. Brown comedies with baseball backgrounds. Old-timers say these films were funny, and we'll be sure to watch them if they ever make it to our "Late Show." There may be a couple of later baseball flicks we've missed, but their reputations are such that none of them are likely to make anyone's ten-best list except the producer's mother's.

And finally we risk letting personal prejudices creep into our evaluations. True. And Gwen Verdon *is* sexy as hell!

In ascending order:

The Absolute Best Baseball Movies

10. *Casey at the Bat* (1946) isn't a whole movie but a nine-minute segment from the full-length Disney cartoon feature *Make Mine Music*. It has the usual Disney excesses: a song that adds nothing but noise to the soundtrack, a player who gets his bat caught in his handlebar mustache, and characters drawn so maddeningly cute you want to vomit.

    Nevertheless the good outweighs the bad. Jerry Colonna's narration of the Thayer poem has a carbonated fizz yet is stilted enough to fit with the nineteenth-century setting. We've heard better actors deliver the poem since, but this is the one we remem-

ber. No one has ever better intoned "with cru-el vi-o-lence his bat upon the plate." Casey, drawn as all chest and bluster, is such a narcissistic load of smugness that you don't mind his inevitable K. Best of all, the feature keeps faith with the original Thayer ending, although you're never sure that Mickey Mouse isn't going to pinch-hit at the last second and save the day.

    (If you want to see how far they *might* have gone wrong, just watch *Casey Bats Again,* Disney's 1954 sequel.)

9. *Major League* (1989) with Tom Berenger, Charlie Sheen, and Corbin Bernsen. This will never be our favorite baseball movie. The characters are about as deep as the Mets outfield against Rafael Belliard. Some of the incidents don't work and a lot of the lines are idiotic.

    On the other hand, most of the actors look like they could actually go a few innings, and that certainly helps suspend disbelief.

    The film's heaviest cross is its inevitable comparison with *Bull Durham*. Look on the good side. Had it not been for *Bull*'s success, they'd have never made this one.

8. *Long Gone* (1987) with William L. Peterson, Virginia Madsen, Dermot Mulroney, and Larry Riley. This made-for-cable *Son of Bull Durham* carries the same cross as *Major League*. Still, until the plot takes a fatal turn for the tried and trite, it serves an amusing, raunchy retrospective of life among the losers in a Florida bush league, circa 1957.

    You may choke when Peterson rushes onto the field to relieve in the Big Game and blazes his fastball past the batter after nary a warmup, but most of the baseball action has an authentic veneer nearly as gritty as the dust on the Tampico Stogies' podunk diamond. And it was nice to see him

win the Big One with his head rather than his bat.

7. *Field of Dreams* (1989) with Kevin Costner, James Earl Jones, and Burt Lancaster. This surprise moneymaker has a lot of good things to offer. Costner, as always, is convincing without being showy. James Earl Jones can grab us anytime he lowers his head five degrees and stares out from under those eyebrows. And you certainly can't gripe about a movie that treats baseball with a reverence usually accorded pieces of the true cross.

    We *could* complain that they spend a lot more time talking about baseball than practicing it, but our sex life has inured us to such inequities. Talk is okay, but, as more than one reviewer has noted, the talk isn't really about baseball; it's about the *idea* of baseball. Or to be precise, about Hollywood's idea of the idea of baseball.

    Maybe we just can't take much whimsy in our crabby old age. If we knew a guy who hears a voice telling him to build a ballpark in the middle of his cornfield, we'd advocate heavy sedation and keep him away from sharp instruments.

6. *Bang the Drum Slowly* (1973) with Robert De Niro, Michael Moriarty, and Vincent Gardenia. De Niro and Moriarty were unknowns when this was made but not afterward. De Niro is convincing as a journeyman catcher who wants to play one last season even though he's dying of Hodgkin's disease. Reportedly he spent a couple of weeks with the Cincinnati Reds learning to catch like a pro. The most believable aspect is that De Niro's catcher is no saintly phenom but a tobacco-chawing hick with marginal skills. Healthy, this guy would be one of the last you'd take to lunch, but dying, we learn to see him as a fellow human being with whom we share an inevitable mortality. Moriarty comes across well as the team's ace pitcher

who befriends him.

The characters and their relationship make this worth a lot more than just a good cry. It's filled with compassion and hope, and—dare we say it?—you'll feel like a better person for having watched it.

You may think you've seen this movie before. Bette Davis made it *sans* baseball a couple of times in the 1930s. If you remember it in football togs, you're thinking of *Brian's Song,* and this is better.

5. *Damn Yankees* (1958) with Tab Hunter, Gwen Verdon, and Ray Walston. Okay, this is song-and-dance instead of baseball, but it's fun, fun, fun. In one

of the better variations on the Faust story, the devil transforms a fat and fortyish Washington fan into young Joe Hardy, superstar, so the Senators can wrest the pennant from the Yankees. If you're fat and fortyish, don't pretend you haven't dreamed of the same thing happening to you. But there's a catch—the price is Joe's soul. And the kicker is that Ray Walston's devil is really a Yankees fan.

The screen version of the hit Broadway musical (based on Douglass Wallop's novel *The Year the Yankees Lost the Pennant*) kept Gwen Verdon as the temptress, which was a major plus. Tab Hunter as Hardy seems out of his

element dancing and singing. Or acting. But when things lag, Walston is usually good for a chuckle.

Songs include "Heart" (as in "You've Gotta Have . . ."), "Shoeless Joe from Hannibal, Mo.," and "Whatever Lola Wants."

4. *Eight Men Out* (1988) with Jon Cusack and Charlie Sheen. Despite lapses like Collins' batting right-handed and Kerr's aforementioned strikeout binge, this movie really tries hard to tell its story accurately. It looks like

Don't they look like real ball players? That's part of the appeal of Bull Durham, *the most true-to-baseball movie ever.*

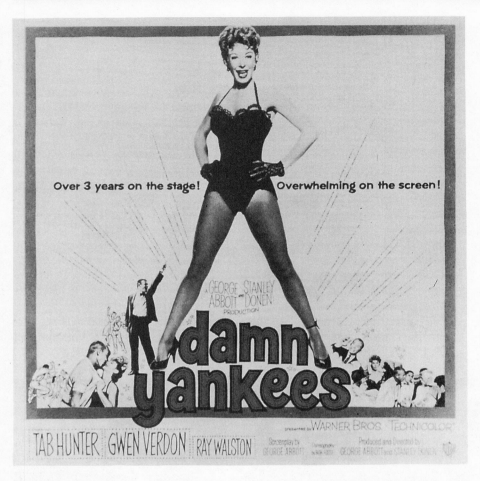

Gwen Verdon played the vamp to Tab Hunter in Damn Yankees; *Olivia de Havilland was sweetness and light alongside Joe E. Brown's eponymous role in* Alibi Ike.

1919 and you even get some understanding of why the Black Sox decided to go in the tank. You can also appreciate how really fouled up things got, with no one quite sure who was going to throw which game when. You'd probably have to watch it twice and take notes before you could describe half the ins and outs and degrees of culpability.

The problem is focus, not by the camera, but on the actors. The movie tries to show us everybody and ends up not showing us enough about anybody. Just whom are we supposed to empathize with here? The players, the owner, gamblers, sportswriters—all come front and center at one time or another, but none of them ever take center stage so we can have some perspective. Shoeless Joe Jackson was the most famous player and the one who was asked to "Say it ain't so," but he was never at the center of the conspiracy and is properly portrayed as a sullen sort who spends most of the movie staring at a hotel room wall. Pitcher Eddie Cicotte seems to be the key until he virtually disappears after confessing. In the last reel we see mostly Buck Weaver, but up until then he was mostly a face in the crowd. The gamblers are on screen as much as anyone. Surely we're not expected to view events from their side?

What you finally have is a movie like one of those European cathedrals, erected with devout reverence and completely covered from steps to steeple with marvelously artful carvings. It's impressive, but a little cold. And darned if we can remember the details.

3. *The Bad News Bears* (1975) with Walter Matthau, Tatum O'Neal, and Vic Morrow. When this Little League tale was released, all you heard was comment about the four-letter vocabularies of the kids. To a generation used to Wally and the Beaver, it came as a

shock to hear adolescents talking like real adolescents. Apparently most adults had forgotten how it really was when they were young—how you practiced for days in your room before you dared unleash a forbidden word on your peers lest you get it wrong. Or how once you'd crossed the threshhold into foul-mouthdom, it got easier daily until you could nonchalantly sprinkle every sentence with words describing acts the likes of which you still weren't certain how to commit. And can you ever forget that awful day when you slipped in front of your mother? You tried to swagger it through while your face turned the shade of Pete Rose's cap.

Anyway, *Bad News* was good enough to spawn two sequels that were so bad as to end the succession. Matthau, who was smart enough to appear only in the original, is perfect as the beer-guzzling manager. The secret of Matthau's comedy is he never goes for a cheap laugh. Every moment is played with absolute sincerity. Put the same role in the hands of some actors and you'd get mugging, smirking, and eye rolling. By the second reel it wouldn't be funny anymore. Matthau doesn't play to you; he lets you come to him, get to know him, even like him, much against your better judgment. So when something funny happens—and it happens a lot in this picture—you're right there with him, sharing the moment, but still outside so you can laugh about it.

Tatum O'Neal plays a girl pitcher. The character is a year too old to be playing Little League, so when she pitches for the Bears, they're really cheating. But by the time she gets to the mound, you're so charmed, you think of it as "adjusting to a higher competitive level."

2. *The Natural* (1984) with Robert Redford, Robert Duvall, Glenn Close, Kim Basinger, Wilford Brimley, and Rich-

There were those who complained that the movie wasn't faithful to Malamud's somber book; others expressed relief.

ard Farnsworth. Baseball has never been better photographed. You could watch this story of a gifted athlete making a middle-aged (in baseball terms) comeback just for the gorgeous cinematography. The only thing that compares is the first time you looked down at a major league diamond.

If you want a good story and superb acting, you'll find them here too. The all-star cast is great up and down the batting order, with Redford batting clean-up and going four-for-four. Despite a meticulous veneer of truth, the plot is more allegory than factual, so you can forgive such mythological elements as Redford's unbreakable bat.

There are some who'll tell you they prefer Bernard Malamud's book, to which this holds a nodding acquaintance. It probably depends on whether you see the glass half empty or half

full. The movie makes it half full. No cynics need apply.

1. *Bull Durham* (1988), with Kevin Costner and Susan Sarandon. Comparing this with *any* other baseball movie—at least on a reality level—is like comparing the Chicago Cubs with the Three Bears. The bear trio ask a couple of questions, but we already know the answers. The Cubbies are an endless source of revelation, heartbreak, and ecstasy. Most baseball movies are painful to view one time. There are so many true baseball moments in *Bull Durham* that we doubt if there are ten fans who rent the video and then play it only once.

Five of our favorite things:

a. The Bulls don't win the pennant. In fact, Crash Davis and Nuke Laloosh, our protagonists, aren't even with the club at the end of the season.

b. Robert Wuhl's chatter from the dugout is completely incomprehensible, and sounds just like all the real chatter we've ever heard.

c. A conference on the mound gets sidetracked by a discussion of a suitable present for a teammate who is to wed. It's a set piece but carried off nicely so you don't see it coming.

d. The player marries a pretty young thing who's shared her bed with practically the whole league, and his teammates agree not to tell him. And they don't. A less true movie would have had someone blurt out the truth, followed by a big fight scene with stuntmen flying through windows. You know the bit.

e. The games have ground outs and fly outs and hits that aren't homers.

Bull Durham may not be quite a great movie, but it is definitely a great baseball movie. We can only hope that the wave of pale imitations it's spawned, like *Long Gone* and *Major League*, were inspired by its truth rather than its box office success.

Well, it never hurts to hope . . . —BC

The Five Worst Baseball Movies

Some of the worst movies ever made have taken the name of baseball in vain. Old-timers say *Somewhere in Georgia*, a 1916 brutality starring Ty Cobb, set some sort of standard for stinking up the silver screen. But because it had the good sense to be silent, you probably won't ever get the chance to change channels away from it, even on the latest of "Late Shows."

Warnings against *Somewhere in Georgia* or Ruth's *Babe Comes Home* are as practical as cautions about runaway stage coaches. On the other hand there are some really awful movies that can turn up on TV. They should have warning labels from the Surgeon General. You absolutely *must* avoid them if you ever hope to be able to look a baseball in the eye again.

In descending order of lousiness:

5. *The Babe Ruth Story* (1948) with William Bendix, Claire Trevor, and Charles Bickford. When this one was on the "Late Show" thirteen years after its release, it probably set a lot of fans rooting for Roger Maris. As a movie for people who never heard of Babe Ruth, it's barely ordinary. Fans expecting historical accuracy will cringe—often. Bendix plays a milk-swigging Babe who swings a bat like Grandpa attacking a *piñata*.

The movie has it both ways and both ways are wrong. It's so respectful of Ruth that you wonder why he didn't win more Nobel Prizes than home run titles, but Bendix plays him as a bumpkin who probably couldn't count past three outs. Reportedly Ruth okayed the script. Why not? It makes him out like Mother Teresa in pinstripes. But who okayed the casting? And did you know the Babe became a successful pitcher when a waitress told him to stop sticking out his tongue before throwing his curve? It's a good thing she never dished up advice to Michael Jordan.

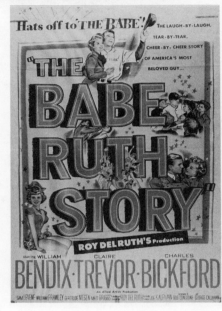

4. *Safe at Home* (1962) with Mickey Mantle, Roger Maris, and William Frawley is strictly for eight-year-olds, but find an eight-year-old today who doesn't think Mickey and Roger are a mouse and a rabbit. This blatant attempt to capitalize on the Maris-Mantle homer feats of 1961 grounds out. Roger and Mickey play themselves and both lose. If you find this exercise in hero merchandising listed in your *TV Guide*, unplug your television to be sure you'll be safe at home.

3. *The Kid from Cleveland* (1949) with George Brent, the Cleveland Indians, and Russ Tamblyn. Lou Boudreau said, "I would like to buy every print of the film and burn it." Bill Veeck and other involved Indians have made public apologies for this piece of celluloid, but they got off easy. A few strokes with a cat-o'-nine-tails would have been more like it.

Tamblyn, billed as "Rusty," plays a

delinquent befriended by the 1948 champion Indians. Had the Tribe played as badly as they acted, they'd have finished behind the Browns. And you probably thought no movie with George Brent could be all bad!

2. *The Slugger's Wife* (1985) with Michael O'Keefe, Rebecca De Mornay, Martin Ritt, and Randy Quaid. This unfunny Neil Simon bomb does for baseball what Lizzie Borden did for axes. Where's *The Odd Couple* when we really need it?

Simon presents a picture of baseball here that makes you understand why Phillies fans boo. O'Keefe plays a bullying, conceited jerk of a ball player who makes you want to root for the visiting team. O'Keefe's slugger is such a major league boor, you can't believe De Mornay would ever become his keeper, much less his wife. And if you can't even buy the title, where can you go with the plot?

If you catch it on cable, there's some nudity, but don't get your hopes up. By the time the skin comes on, you'll be too impotent with rage to enjoy it.

1. *Stealing Home* (1988) with Mark Harmon, Jodie Foster, Blair Brown, Jonathan Silverman, Harold Ramis. This is the kind of movie about which they used to say, "It wasn't released; it escaped." Actually it's the prototype. If you paid to watch this in a theater, it should be called *Stealing Money*. Charitably it's a pointless, plodding drama made all the more confusing by flashbacks—even the flashbacks have flashbacks—enlivened only by Harmon's incredible ability to portray tedium apathetically. It's something about Harmon at age thirty-four deciding to pick up a baseball career he quit for no good reason fourteen years earlier because he's entrusted with the ashes of Foster, his one-time baby-sitter. If that doesn't make sense to you, join the club. Oh, at both the beginning and the end he steals home. See, that's where they got the title. Clev-*er*!

The one good laugh in this dog is unintentional. The I've-got-a-secret expression on Harmon's face as he scatters Foster's ashes to the wind is priceless. Only God and Harmon know what emotion he was trying to convey. Would he had been scattering ashes of the film!

Still, you learn something new every day. When we took this back to our video parlor (along with a written request that the tape be degaussed), the girl behind the counter assured us that some of her customers said it was "real good." Who does she rent to? Rain Man? —BC

Why Is It So Hard to Make a Good Baseball Movie?

Whether you watch your baseball movies at a theater, on your VCR, or at two in the morning on the "Late Show," you always sense something is missing. It's never quite real enough. Well, in truth, most of what you're likely to see on the "Late Show" isn't real at all, but at that time of the night, what is?

Reel baseball still hasn't quite got the feel of real baseball, though Hollywood is coming a lot closer, with movies such as *Eight Men Out, Bull Durham,* and *Major League.*

Near the end of *Eight Men Out,* Buck Weaver explains why he loves playing: "Sometimes, when you're feelin' right, there's a groove there, an' the bat just eases into it an' meets that ball. When the bat meets that ball an' you can just feel that ball give, an' you know it's gonna go a long way—*damn!* if you don't feel like you're gonna live forever!"

Weaver is telling us the tragedy of the Black Sox was not that the men who threw the World Series went to jail (which they didn't) or had their names blackened (which they did), but that their actions cost them the right to *play*—the right to feel so good. You can almost see *Author's Message* flashing above his head. But that groove, that give in the ball, that live-forever feeling is not vicariously translatable. If you've never felt it yourself, Weaver's

words don't mean much.

Stan Musial once said that his greatest thrill in baseball was pulling on his Cardinals' uniform. Others have said the same thing. To put it another way, just *being* a ball player is greater than being a good ball player. Most movies don't tell us that. Worse, they don't *show* us that! Even "good" baseball movies tend to exalt something other than baseball.

Most baseball movies are made by people who don't particularly like baseball. They might go on an obligatory pilgrimage to Chavez Ravine on a Thursday night and root for the Dodgers because it's a place to be seen, or a place to make a deal, or the thing to do. They're in a box seat for reasons other than the game. They'll be out of there by the eighth inning no matter what the score.

So when they make a baseball movie, they're scared Williams-shiftless that there's no audience out there that can understand or appreciate baseball. How could the audience know something they don't? So they make their flick about something other than baseball. Baseball is only the scaffolding on which to erect their moralistic tale of man triumphing over physical affliction (*The Stratton Story*), mental illness (*Fear Strikes Out*), prejudice (*The Jackie Robinson Story*), natural law (*It Happens Every Spring*), or even the

devil (*Damn Yankees*). Maybe someday we'll see a movie about a baseball-loving producer triumphing over corporate mentality and making a real baseball movie.

The good news, of course, is that in recent years baseball movies have been getting better. You'll find more love of baseball (and more baseball) in one reel of *Bull Durham* than you can get from all the baseball movies made in the 1950s put together. *Eight Men Out* has its moments. So does *The Natural. Field of Dreams* may not be to every fan's taste, but it fairly drips with love of baseball.

It's not hard to find a half dozen movies with major league characters and plots. They're only bush league when they pretend those actors are playing baseball. In a baseball movie we have to insist that the baseball portrayed (or discussed) will not be at such variance with our own knowledge and experience that our teeth are set on edge and we miss the next six plot points.

Curiously the better the movie, the more any slip-ups offend.

For example, in *Eight Men Out* Eddie Collins steps up to bat. Any real baseball fan is immediately jarred by the firm chin on the actor portraying Collins. As we all know, the real Eddie's face made a beeline from his lower lip to his collar. But we let that one go. A look-alike actor (if one exists) probably couldn't hit a curve. So we watch Eddie take a last chomp on his gum and then affix it to the button atop his cap. Great! Just what the real Collins always did! But then—oh, no! He takes a right-handed batting stance!

The gaffe is all the more unforgivable because the film has tried so hard to be historically accurate up to then. We can watch a clunker like *The Babe Ruth Story* (if someone ties us down) and merely sneer at inaccuracies piled on anachronisms. Who cares? But if we're to continue believing in *Eight Men Out,* Eddie Collins should bat left-handed. The more "real" the movie, the more it needs to be true to the reality we already know. —BC

If We Were Running the Show . . .

It's not our job to create fascinating characters or intricate plots, but we have a couple of simple tips for moviemakers on how they can improve their next epics:

1. *Cut down on the strikeouts.* No, we're not addressing Pete Incaviglia. This is for scriptwriters who think the only way to show a pitcher is effective is to have him strike out every batter in sight. Not even Nolan Ryan does that. Dickie Kerr, one of the "Clean Sox" in *Eight Men Out*, must have fanned a half dozen Reds in a row to show he was honest. In point of fact, Dickie struck out a total of 6 in 19 World Series innings.

   One reason moviemakers like strikeouts is they figure a swinging third strike is instantaneously understood by the audience. Hey, give the ticket buyers a break! Most of them can decipher the meaning of a groundout if they see one. And for those who can't, superimpose a scorecard with a big "GO 6–3" on it.

   The real appeal of a strikeout to any director is that it's so cheap: a stationary camera and three actors. He can shoot ten strikeouts in the time it takes to set up one groundout. Pay the two dollars! When there was a real-live pop-up in *Bull Durham*, we cheered.

2. *Use more TV-like shots.* Most, or at least some, of the real baseball we watch is on television. We get lots of close-ups of pitchers, but when the ball is hit to somebody, the camera doesn't usually zoom in on his tonsils. TV directors know enough to stay back a little so we can see the play in some context. Okay, maybe that context is only an expanse of plastic grass surrounding Ozzie Smith, but we can appreciate the plays he makes only when we see how far he goes to make them.

   Another problem is depth of shot. Set up a TV camera in center field and the pitcher seems to be practically standing on home plate. That's misleading, but we've seen it so often that we're used to it. Film distorts in the other direction, making the pitcher seem a good April's hike away from the batter. And *that* we're not used to seeing.

3. *All big games are not won in the last of the ninth.* Ever since Casey went to bat, the bottom of the ninth has been *the* critical moment in any baseball fiction. By now it's such a cliché that the lights on movie scoreboards work only for the ninth inning. Fellas! have your hero hit his grand slam in the fifth, then cut to the locker room celebration. We'll understand.

4. *Cut down on the time frame.* It used to be, any serious baseball flick had to start with the hero's boyhood, then go through the minors and a couple of major league seasons before we got to the good stuff. Today the most common movie time frame is the season. Nobody wants to believe a single game in June can mean anything.

   How about a movie built around real time? It worked for *High Noon*, didn't it? In a movie using real time, we see the first pitch behind the opening credits and the last out behind the crawl. Of course, we don't want a three-hour movie, so rain it out in the sixth.

5. *Fire the stock characters.* Not all managers are chubby dunderheads. Not all umpires are bulky sourpusses. Not all rookies from Nebraska are naive. Not all sportswriters are slimy misanthropes. Not all owners are money-grubbing connivers.

   Some are, but we've seen too many stereotypes. How about a slimy, money-grubbing rookie from Nebraska who's a dunderheaded sourpuss?

   We have little faith that moviemakers will take our tips to heart, but that won't stop us from seeing the next baseball flick (which is probably what they're counting on). After all, bad, boring, banal baseball is still better than no baseball at all.   —BC

A typical levitation by the Wizard of Oz.

Oscar, Shmoscar! Can He Hit .270? Actors as Ball Players

Can Burt Lancaster bunt? Can Ronald Reagan throw a curve? Can Gary Cooper hit to left?

These are all questions Hollywood directors faced while managing an all-star line-up of actors through more than a dozen baseball movies in the 1940s and '50s. Of course they weren't *critical* questions in an era when successful screen at bats were more apt to produce sniffles than singles. Young, virile athlete (along with plucky wife/girlfriend) bats against overwhelming obstacle—alcoholism, mental illness, double vision, missing limb, or terminal disease. Action sequences were secondary to meaningful stares. Close-ups and fast cuts hid the fact that actors rarely made contact at the plate. Just so long as they

connected at the box office!

Not anymore. Today's leads must be solid .270 hitters if they expect to win audiences by donning a uniform. The same fans who go to the theater on Saturday night watched a game on TV that afternoon. They know what major leaguers look like.

"My only goal when I first stepped to the plate was to not completely embarrass myself in front of all those people," says Corbin Bernsen, who put aside his "L.A. Law" briefcase to act like a third baseman in *Major League*. "The first time up, I drilled a line drive to the warning track," he laughs. "I was so much in awe I forgot to run."

To keep his team of Bernsen, Charlie

Sheen, and Tom Berenger from making such baserunning mistakes, *Major League* director David Ward had ex-Dodger Steve Yeager lead the cast through weeks of batting and fielding practice. "Today's audiences are so sophisticated that you can't fake athletic ability," Ward says. "There's so much confusion in football and basketball scenes that actors don't have to be decent athletes. But baseball is mostly isolated action. An actor can mimic body language, but he has to catch the ball. You can't be filmed throwing off the wrong foot."

Ward's casting sessions often began in his office and concluded outside in a game of catch. "We'd throw the ball around because I didn't want to find out in the dailies that we had a last-place club."

Ward had one of Hollywood's top prospects in Charlie Sheen, making his second big league appearance after his rookie baptism in *Eight Men Out*. A graduate of four glorious summers in the Mickey Owen Baseball School, Sheen can deliver an eighty-five m.p.h. fastball. "In school I could pitch and turn the double play, but I was a lifetime .214 hitter—the kind of guy you'd pinch-hit for with the game on the line," Sheen says modestly. But he's often found on weekends practicing his swing in Malibu batting cages. If they ever make *The Willie Keeler Story*, he'll be ready.

Other actors who are top draft choices when casting baseball movies: Kevin Kline, Jeff Bridges, Kurt Russell, Billy Crystal, Bill Murray, Mark Harmon, and Kevin Costner. "I'd sign Costner tomorrow if he quit acting," says Pete Brock, baseball adviser on *Bull Durham*. "Kevin can hit from both sides of the plate with power. You believe the guy in close-ups."

That's something that Gary Cooper (as Lou Gehrig in *The Pride of the Yankees*) never had to worry about. "Cooper was terrific," says Ward. "But I don't remember seeing a close-up of him really striking the ball. You'd see an extreme close-up of his face followed by the crack of the bat. Next, you'd see a wide shot of the ball going somewhere. But did Cooper really stroke it?"

Michael Moriarty in *Bang the Drum Slowly* gets high marks from Ward: "He seemed to really be able to throw strikes." Brock praises Robert Redford in *The Natural*: "It wasn't so much the famous power swing but the way Redford threw the ball in the field. The toughest thing is throwing. Anybody can pick up a bat and look average."

Tom Selleck can pick up a bat and look awesome. "I'd give up everything to play one season and do well," says the devout Detroit Tigers fan. A scuffed baseball is proudly displayed in his office as a memento of the day he took batting practice with his heroes and blasted two into the stands.

"What a feeling that was! I mean, there were guys in the outfield who watched the ball take off and did a double take when they realized who was at bat. They said, 'I didn't think actors could hit.' I wish I had *that* moment on film!"   —SS

From Gold Gloves to Silver Screens: Ball Players as Actors

Back in 1912 New York Giants lefthander Rube Marquard won 19 straight games. Before the next season rolled around, Marquard starred in a movie, appropriately called *19 Straight*. Although that was probably the first example of a movie producer attempting to translate a ball player's success on the field into bucks at the box office, it was far from the last.

Ty Cobb went before the camera and got lost *Somewhere in Georgia* three years later. Babe Ruth made a couple of forgettable films in the 1920s. In the 1930s Lou Gehrig imitated a cowboy and the Dean brothers imitated themselves. Ruth encored as Ruth in *The Pride of the Yankees*. The whole Cleveland Indians' 1948 championship team trooped on screen in *The Kid from Cleveland*, and Jackie Robinson played himself in *The Jackie Robinson Story*. Roger Maris and Mickey Mantle went to bat in *Safe at Home* in 1962. Tommy Lasorda has cameoed a couple of times. In fact, the list of cameos perpetrated on film and TV by Dodgers alone would fill a few lineup cards.

These days real live baseball players are almost exclusively seen in cameos or as doubles for actors playing players. Movies cost too much today to make one just to draw the kind of audience that will pay to see a bubble-gum card talk.

It's documented that no baseball player–actor has as yet been nominated for an Oscar.

Football players have done better in getting their names up in lights. Ex–Florida State halfback Burt Reynolds has done fairly well, they say. Such ex-NFL grid stars as Jim Brown, O. J. Simpson, Alex Karras, Dick Butkus, Bubba Smith, Crazylegs Hirsch, Joe Namath, and Fred Dryer have all been cast in "straight" roles (i.e., as a character other than an athlete).

There are a couple of theories as to why football stars seem to do better at moviemaking than baseballers. One holds that a football star is more likely to be a "hunk" (e.g., Namath, Simpson, Brown, Dryer) or a "type" (e.g., Smith, Butkus, Karras, or lesser-knowns such as Lyle Alzado and Tim Rossovich). The average baseball star looks like anybody else in street clothes. Another theory is that football careers are shorter, allowing the neophyte actor an earlier entry into films. Similarly the football season is shorter, making gridders more available for acting roles.

Our favorite theory holds that football is a game more dependent on unleashed emotion than baseball. A football player is at his best when he is nearly "out of control." Baseballers, on the other hand, are worthless if they let emotion dictate their play. Therefore a gridder is psychologically more able to open his emotional baggage for a camera. All of which sounds like Bo Jackson should be signed for a remake of *Dr. Jekyll and Mr. Hyde*.

Regardless of the reason, if you see an ex-jock in a movie, he probably emotes when the director yells, "Lights, camera, hut-one!"

But baseball players are not totally offers as actors. It's just that the ones who've made it as thespians were never household names as athletes.

Going way back, Turkey Mike Donlin spent nearly two decades in Hollywood after leaving the majors. Though never a major screen star, his handsome Irish profile and flamboyant personality kept him working in silents. But how many movie fans knew they were watching an outfielder with a .333 lifetime batting average?

At six-five, ex-Cubs first baseman Chuck Connors was made for the big screen, but his greatest success came on the small screen as TV's "Rifleman" in the late 1950s. Far deadlier with his gimmicky gun than he'd been with a Louisville slugger, his Nielsen rating outshone his .232 lifetime B.A. Of course, Connors, who's been a regular feature player since Lucas McCain ran out of ammunition, is as much an ex-player in basketball as in baseball, having played 53 games for the Boston Celtics in the late 1940s.

Kurt Russell rates as a top movie star today, but he never got out of the minors on the ballfield.

The ex–major leaguers with the best résumés today are two who've found steady work on television.

John Berardino was a good-field, no-hit infielder for the St. Louis Browns and Cleveland Indians in the 1940s. He was featured in *The Kid from Cleveland* and

Turkey Mike Donlin was bitten by the showbiz bug early on, quitting baseball at the height of his career to mount the vaudeville boards; Hollywood came later.

may have been the only one in that disaster to come out ahead. After a series of film walk-ons in the 1950s, he walked into soap opera success as Dr. Steve Hardy, the main muckety-muck of the long-running "General Hospital." Considering GH's five-a-week schedule, Berardino, who's still dispensing a soapy mixture of medicine and fatherly advice, probably holds the record for appearances before a camera by an ex-jock.

Bob Uecker parlayed a self-proclaimed ineptitude as a catcher and a flaky reputation into a career that's gone from after-dinner speaker, through broadcaster and a series of commercials, finally to stardom as the harried foil for TV's "Mr. Belvedere." Actually Ueke was never quite as bad a player as his comedy routine would lead you to believe. He spent six seasons in the majors and hit better than his 190-pound weight by ten glorious points. He was only a backup backstop, but in the annals of baseball's actors Mr. Uecker belongs "in the front *roooow*."   —BC

Let's Make a Movie About That Pitcher What's-His-Name

If Martin Scorsese ever makes a movie about the life of Babe Ruth (*Raging Babe*?), with Robert De Niro as the Bambino, we'll be first in line for a ticket. The gritty kind of psyche probe Scorsese did on boxer Jake LaMotta would blow every other baseball bio film out of the water. Of course, most of the existing bio pics have eggshell hulls.

So far, the successful baseball biographical movies have all been about ball players who were stricken with some catastrophic physical, mental, or societal disaster. Sort of a disease-of-the-season. No one has made a decent movie about a ball player just because he was an interesting person. You could write terrific books about Babe Ruth (and several have), but *The Babe Ruth Story* (1947) wasn't a decent movie and had as much to do with the real Babe Ruth as with Babe the Blue Ox. And when are we going to see a movie about catcher/linguist/spy Moe Berg?

There are a few bio movies that work on the level they aspire to:

1. *The Stratton Story* (1949) with James Stewart, June Allyson, Frank Morgan, and Bill Williams. Stewart plays former White Sox pitcher Monty Stratton, who lost his leg in a hunting accident, then made a comeback of sorts in Texas. The film stretches Stratton's big league success a bit and strums every sentimental string, but the Stewart-Allyson chemistry works. The climax, with Stewart/Stratton pitching against an all-star team, could make Rocky envious. Douglas Morrow received an Oscar for best original story.

2. *It's Good to Be Alive* (1974) with Paul Winfield, Ruby Dee, and Louis Gossett, Jr. This made-for-TV movie tells the story of Roy Campanella's life after he became a quadraplegic in a 1958 auto accident.

What could have been a syrupy disaster is carried by Winfield's luminous performance as Campy. Conveying the whole emotional range with only his face and voice, Winfield keeps our sympathy without slipping into maudlin traps. Dee is more than the typical movie wife and Gossett is fine as a tough therapist.

3. *Fear Strikes Out* (1957) with Anthony Perkins, Karl Malden, and Norma Moore. Fortunately this was made before *Psycho*, or no one on the Red Sox would have showered with Anthony Perkins around. Perkins doesn't resemble Jim Piersall in physique or persona, but his acting carries him. The film, based on Piersall's book, centers around the ball player's famous breakdown as a Bosox rookie in 1952, its causes, and his subsequent recovery. Karl Malden is very good as Piersall's pushy papa.

4. *A Winner Never Quits* (1986) with Keith Carradine, Mare Winningham, and Dennis Weaver. If it hadn't really happened, no one would believe a story about a one-armed outfielder making the majors. Sure, it was the Browns, and, yes, it was a war year. Nevertheless . . . given the one-in-a-billion circumstance of the plot, most of this made-for-TV movie works. Carradine's understated performance as Pete Gray keeps it from becoming cloying.

5. *The Pride of the Yankees* (1942) with Gary Cooper, Teresa Wright, Babe Ruth, Walter Brennan, and Dan Duryea. Because this is the one that all other baseball bio pics are rated against, you could be disappointed if you watch it today. The long buildup in which Gehrig goes from street youth to diamond star is of interest mainly to fanatical Yankees fans. Teresa Wright creates the generic movie baseball-wife,

Jackie Robinson played himself in the 1950 film, The Jackie Robinson Story; *starring with him as his wife, Ruth, was Ruby Dee.*

and Babe Ruth plays himself with total conviction, but you keep wondering about Cooper. The actor resembled the ball player facially, and both were laconic. But Coop was long, lean, and western while Lou was stocky and from New Yawk. The right-handed Cooper was a bit awkward as the left-handed-hitting first baseman (though Gehrig himself was no gazelle). But we wish someone could give us a definitive answer on one thing: Some sources say Coop struggled manfully to bat lefty; others insist they turned the film over so he played for the *seeknaY kroY weN.*

Once Cooper-Gehrig contracts the disease that eventually kills him, the movie is a solid tear-jerker. When he tells the crowd he's the luckiest man on the face of the earth, your reaction will be just as dewy as were those in Yankee Stadium that day.

6. *The Jackie Robinson Story* (1950) with Jackie Robinson and Ruby Dee. This is better than you might think, and Robinson is surprisingly effective as himself. The story is familiar to any veteran baseball fan and no new insights are delivered, but it should be seen by youngsters—and any oldsters who've forgotten.

7. *The Pride of St. Louis* (1952) with Dan Dailey, Joanne Dru, and Richard Crenna. This sentimentalized, sanitized version of the life of Dizzy Dean contains most of the anecdotes you've read elsewhere, and Dailey makes a good stab at being the Cardinals pitcher, but you'll have to close one eye and half your head to believe a moment of it. Incidentally, don't confuse this with Jimmy Stewart's 1957 bio pic of Lindbergh, *The Spirit of St. Louis.* On second thought, if you're renting a videotape, *do* confuse them; the Stewart picture is a lot better.

8. *Don't Look Back* (1981) with Louis Gossett, Jr., Beverly Todd, Ossie Davis. As far as Gossett is concerned, you'd have to go a long way to find a better actor to portray Satchel Paige. Unfortunately you could probably find a more involving script on just about any walk around the block. The plot of this made-for-TV film follows Paige from his early reformatory days, through his years as a black star denied access to the majors by prejudice, to his final entry into the majors as a forty-three-year-old "rookie." It's all very sincere and as pat as Nixon's wife.

9. *One in a Million: The Ron LeFlore Story* (1978) with LeVar Burton, Madge Sinclair, Paul Benjamin, and Billy Martin (yes). In case you've forgotten, LeFlore made it out of the violence and drugs of a Detroit ghetto all the way to the majors. This made-for-TV film tells an inspiring story, even if it's not done with a whole lot of inspiration.

10. *The Winning Team* (1952) with Ronald Reagan, Doris Day, and Frank Lovejoy. This highy fictionalized biography of pitcher Grover Alexander is actually pretty dreadful. Wife Day maneuvers hubby Reagan to his greatest pitching just as skillfully as she landed a four-engine jet in that other movie. The real Mrs. Alexander was technical adviser, and you can almost hear her saying, "And then I inspired Alex to go out and win twenty games."

You get the idea that someone decided Alex's strikeout of Lazzeri in the 1926 World Series would make a helluva climactic scene and then called in the second string to write the rest of the movie. This isn't vintage Reagan, but how often can you see an ex-President (then a future President, playing the role of a player named after another President) throwing the *last* ball of the season?   —BC

Baseball for Laughs

Movies like *The Bad News Bears* and *Bull Durham* are doubly funny if you're a baseball fan, but they're first-rate comedies even if you have only a nodding acquaintance with the game. Back around the time of the Korean War, Hollywood tried to wring humor out of baseball (not to mention some dollars) with several films that seemed to be designed for the non–baseball fan.

At a distance, it looks like they wanted to fit some of the screwball comedies of the *Topper* ilk into a baseball mold. Pennants were not won by hitting, pitching, and fielding; they came by way of divine intervention or suspension of natural law. Since most of them make the rounds on the TV "Late Show," you might want to catch one of them some night. Or you might want to catch the flu.

The first of these was *It Happens Every Spring* (1949) with Ray Milland, Jean Peters, and Paul Douglas. To our thinking, this was both the best and the worst of the genre. Ray Milland is a college chemistry professor who invents a potion that repulses wood. Since Milland is a baseball fan, he immediately sees the possibilities. Bats are made of wood! By rubbing his potion on baseballs, he becomes a great strikeout pitcher. Milland is properly earnest and awkward as the professor-cum-pitcher, but Paul Douglas as his grizzled catcher steals every scene he's in.

When we saw this back in '49, we laughed every time Milland's pitch did its dipsy-do away from a frustrated batter's swing. It *is* a great sight gag and we were young and callow. Only years later when we watched it on TV did it suddenly occur to us—*Hey! he's cheating!* If Joe Niekro can get the boot for a nail file and Gaylord Perry could be kept out of the Hall of Fame for spit, why are we laughing at this guy

who's winning with a substance that is not only illegal but probably shouldn't be dumped near drinking water? What'll they do for a sequel? Cork a bat?

What they did was eschew science and go with God. Well, by 1951, everybody was worried about nuclear attack, so scientists weren't very popular.

Angels in the Outfield, with Paul Douglas, Janet Leigh, and Keenan Wynn, tried to convince us that God would always look out for the good folks. Douglas apparently retired after his season with Milland and was hired to manage the Pittsburgh Pirates. The first time we see him, he's no longer the jovial nice guy Milland pitched to. Instead he's become misanthropic and foul-mouthed (within strict 1950s limits). Small wonder, as just about everybody knows, the Pittsburgh Pirates of the early 1950s would have finished last in the Sally League. A nun tells Douglas that he needs to change his ways to start winning. Any port in a storm. Douglas does an instant Dale Carnegie, and the team, playing under the smoke of Andrew Carnegie's steel mills, begins tearing up the league.

It seems like a miracle. Seems, hell! It *is*! Sure enough, one day an orphan notices an angel of the non-California variety playing behind each Pirate. The rest of the reels deal with Douglas's efforts to stay out of the booby hatch.

Only fair as entertainment, the movie drew pretty well in Pittsburgh and surrounding areas, probably because fans could see Forbes Field without having also to watch the real Pirates, who were about as much fun as a root-canal dig.

The same year, Milland made a comeback with another movie that took a non-scientific approach. In this one the faith was nondenominational.

Rhubarb, with Ray Milland, Jan Ster-

ling, and Gene Lockhart, had its good moments. Based on a story by H. Allen Smith, the title character is a cat that inherits a baseball team and then leads it to a pennant as its mascot.

The humans are okay, but the cat takes acting honors. If you've ever been owned by a cat (that's the way it works: own a dog, be owned by a cat), you know that they lead the league in arrogant stupidity. How the director ever got this animal to move or meow on cue ranks with Hitchcock's trick of convincing all those birds to fly in formation. We tried to teach our cat to roll over once, but he wouldn't come down off the curtain rods long enough to even twitch.

Movies starring animals were big in the 1940s and '50s, but cats never caught on. Otherwise we might have been treated to *Rhubarb, Come Home* or *Rutabaga, Son of Rhubarb*.

The Kid from Left Field (1953) with Dan Dailey, Anne Bancroft, and Lloyd Bridges, was a little closer to reality, but not much. Dan Dailey, who was Dizzy Dean the season before, is reduced to a peanut vendor this year. There's some nonsense about his batboy son breaking the hometeam's slump by passing on sage tips to the players. The insights really come from Dailey, but it's the kid who gets named as the team's manager. Not even Steinbrenner has tried that one.

The Kid Etc. is one of those modestly pleasant 1950s comedies that filled Saturday night before it was time to go park. Probably its only real claim to fame is that somebody remembered it (God knows why!) in 1979, when they were looking for a vehicle for Gary Coleman. The remake-for-TV is so sugary it could rot your teeth before the first commercial.

Kill the Umpire (1950), with William Bendix and Una Merkel, wasn't a gimmick comedy. No gimmick, not much comedy. Still, if you're going to see only one William Bendix baseball movie, make it this

Hollywood version of an ump's training, life, and love of the game rather than *The Babe Ruth Story. Umpire* doesn't have Babe's laughs, but those it does produce are mostly intentional.

The Great American Pastime (1956), with Tom Ewell, Anne Francis, and Ann Miller, is the tame ancestor of *The Bad News Bears.* Ewell plays a suburban lawyer who becomes a Little League manager. We always thought Ewell was wasted in most of his movies. Except for *The Seven Year Itch*, he wasn't given anything very funny to do, but his lumpy face that never seemed to be on straight could make us laugh. In this one he tries to convince his losing team that trying their best is more important than winning, while the parents teach them the opposite. The film never pushes very hard and lacks bite, but its point is made up until an out-of-left-field happy ending.

Take Me Out to the Ball Game (1949) sounds like a music cue, and in this case it is. Gene Kelly, Frank Sinatra, and Jules Munshin are a turn-of-the-century double-play combination joining Esther Williams' traveling baseball team. The producers didn't ever tinker with their chance for box office success, so you'll see more song-and-dance than hit-and-run. There are also a couple of obligatory paddles in the pool by Williams, which give you a chance to go to the kitchen for a sandwich.

The Bingo Long Traveling All-Stars and Motor Kings (1976), with Billy Dee Williams, James Earl Jones, and Richard Pryor is nearly a great movie. This comedy-adventure about a black baseball team barnstorming the South in the 1930s has so many good moments, you really want it to work. And though the whole never quite adds up to the sum of its parts, the results are still satisfying.

Curiously the film has been criticized by some ex-Negro Leaguers for putting too much emphasis on the clowning black teams often had to resort to if they hoped to draw crowds. Mayhaps they're overly protective of an image that too few white fans know about anyway. This isn't a documentary, but if it leads a white audience to learn about Josh Gibson, Buck Leonard, Judy Johnson, and the hundreds of other stars who were kept out of the majors by the color of their skins, all to the good.

All to the bad are two dreadful sequels to the excellent *Bad News Bears—The Bad News Bears in Breaking Training* (1977) and *The Bad News Bears Go to Japan* (1978). The only real argument is over which one is worse. Lost are wit, compassion, and humor; added is a smart-alecky cutesiness that makes you worry about what these kids are going to grow up to be. The best we could hope for is TV weathermen.

If most of what passes for baseball comedy in the movies is junk, don't worry. Most westerns, thrillers, love stories, or what-have-you are junk too. Just pray your local channel shows *Citizen Kane* or *Dr. Zhivago* once in a while. Or you can usually find an old Abbott and Costello. If you're really lucky, they'll do "Who's on First?"

Now, *that's* funny!   —BC

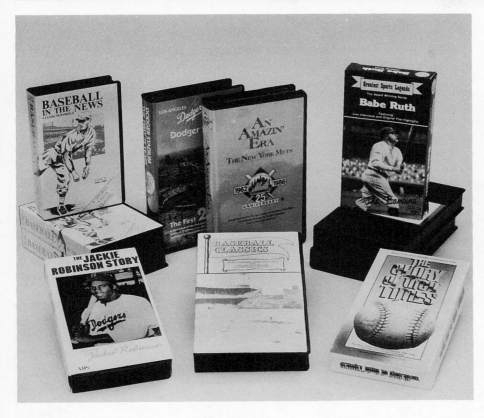

Baseball on Video

The popularity of baseball on video is understandable. Who wouldn't want Babe Ruth as a guest in his home? And you don't even have to feed him! Or you can watch your favorite team's highlight film and see mostly wins—even if you're a Mariners fan. On a more practical note, you or your kids can improve playing techniques by hearing and seeing how the stars do it.

You can check your local supplier for rentals of the following, or you can purchase most of them through such businesses as Sports Books etc., Sports Bookshelf, Rare Sportsfilms, Major League Baseball Properties, or, for some, the teams themselves.

Biographical

Greatest Sports Legends (30 mins. each)

Hank Aaron	*Lou Gehrig*
Johnny Bench	*Mickey Mantle*
Roberto Clemente	*Willie Mays*
Joe DiMaggio	*Stan Musial*

Brooks Robinson	*Pete Rose*
Frank Robinson	*Babe Ruth*
Jackie Robinson	*Ted Williams*

Doubleheaders (45 mins. each)

Mickey Mantle/Willie Mays
Jackie Robinson/Roberto Clemente
Babe Ruth/Joe DiMaggio
Ted Williams/Pete Rose

Baseball Legends (Old newsreels—15 mins. each)

Babe Ruth
Lou Gehrig
Connie Mack

Eleanor and Lou Gehrig Story: A Love Affair (96 mins.) Starring Edward Herrmann and Blythe Danner.
Jackie Robinson Story (77 mins.) Starring Robinson himself.
My Dad, the Babe
Ozzie: The Movie (45 mins.) Ozzie

Baseball videos have proliferated in recent years; these are some of the better ones.

Smith highlights.
Pride of the Yankees (127 min.) Gary Cooper as Lou Gehrig.
Roberto Clemente: A Touch of Royalty (30 mins.)
Golden Greats of Baseball (45 mins.) Highlights of baseball's all-time greats.
Golden Greats of Baseball, Pitchers (45 mins.) Highlights of baseball's all-time great pitchers.

Highlights

Nearly all major league teams offer highlight videos yearly. Also available are season highlight videos from the television show *This Week in Baseball*, narrated by Mel Allen. Among the other highlight videos on the market are:
Doubleheaders (60 mins.) 30 minutes of *This Year in Baseball (1986)* and 30 minutes of 1986 season highlights for individual teams.
All-Star Games, 1962–88 (30 mins. each)
World Series, 1943–83 (30 mins. each)
World Series, 1984–89 (60 mins. each)
The All-Star Game from Ruth to Mays, 1936–56 and *The 1956 All-Star Game* (40 mins.)
20 Years of World Series Thrills: 1938–58 (40 mins.)
75 Years of World Series Memories (30 min.) Prod. 1979.
M.V.P.: World Series Edition (60 mins.) Prod. 1979.
October Spotlight: World Series Heroes (30 mins.) Prod. 1980.
Once in a Lifetime: World Series Heroes (30 mins.) Prod. 1981.
Great World Series Heroes: The Men Who Made It Happen (30 mins.) Prod. 1982.
World Series Unsung Heroes (30 mins.) Prod. 1983.
Two Best World Series Ever (58 mins.) 1975 and 1978.

Instructional

Art of Hitting .300 (50 mins.) Charlie Lau's classic book.

Baseball Bunch—Johnny Bench: Fielding (60 mins.) With Ozzie Smith, Graig Nettles and Gary Carter.

Baseball Bunch—Johnny Bench: Hitting (60 mins.) With Lou Pinella, Jim Rice and Ted Williams.

Baseball Bunch—Johnny Bench: Pitching (60 mins.) With Dan Quisenberry, Tom Seaver and Tug McGraw.

Baseball with Rod Carew (60 mins.) Baseball Masters Series:

Pitching (25 mins.) Jerry Koosman.

Conditioning & Baserunning (40 mins.) Jerry Kindall and Al Kaline.

Fielding (40 mins.) George Kell and Frank Quilici on infield play; Al Kaline on outfield.

Hitting (25 mins.) With Al Kaline and George Kell.

Baseball Our Way (90 Mins.) With Eric Davis, Wally Joyner, and Tommy Lasorda.

Baseball Skills and Drills with Dr. Bragg Stockton Six videos on fundamentals.

Baseball the Pete Rose Way (60 mins.)

Baseball the Right Way (30 mins. each) Three videos on fielding, hitting and pitching fundamentals by Mets coaches.

Baseball the Yankee Way (45 mins.) Mantle, Maris, Ford, Howard, Richardson, Downing; filmed after 1964 season.

Dick Howser's Baseball Workout Series Two 60 min. videos.

Dodgers Way to Play Baseball (90 mins.) Narrated by Vin Scully.

George Brett's Secrets of Baseball (25 mins.) Guide to hitting.

Going, Going, Gone! Powerhitting Tips by Reggie Jackson (30 mins.)

Hitting with Harry "The Hat" Walker

How to Play Better Baseball (47 mins.) Mike Schmidt hosts.

Infield Techniques & Catching with Bud Middaugh (45 mins.) Techniques and drills by U. of Michigan head coach.

Little League's Official How-to-Play

Baseball by Video (70 mins.)

Mickey Mantle's Baseball Tips for Kids of All Ages (70 mins.)

Pete Rose on Winning Baseball, Claude Osteen on Pitching and Sonny Ruberto on Catching (55 mins.)

Pitching Absolutes Tom House on pitching grips, conditioning, and theory.

Pitching Mechanics: Problem Recognition & Solutions Sequel to House's *Absolutes*.

Pitching with Bud Middaugh (45 mins.)

Techniques and drills from the U. of Michigan coach.

Play Ball with Mickey Mantle Mick, Gary Carter and Tom Seaver present inside tips for kids.

Sports Clinic: Baseball (80 mins.) Instruction by Dick Williams.

Steve Garvey's Hitting System

Teaching Kids Baseball with Jerry Kindall (75 mins.) U. of Arizona coach on teaching youngsters beginning baseball.

Teaching the Mechanics of the Major

Most Memorable Baseball Scene
in a Movie Having Nothing to Do with Baseball

Blake Edwards' 1962 thriller *Experiment in Terror* builds up a pretty good head of scream with its plot about a cold-blooded killer who's terrorizing a bank clerk into helping him with a robbery. Ross Martin is properly scary as the killer and Lee Remick is beautifully scared as the clerk. FBI agent Glenn Ford is staunch enough to pass muster for J. Edgar Hoover or even Efrem Zimbalist, Jr.

The climax comes at Candlestick Park. As a night game with the Dodgers ends, the FBI closes in on Martin, but at first he uses the exiting crowd to escape. Finally they corner him on the pitcher's mound,

where the rubber offers nary a bit of concealment. Martin is breathing hard as G-men come out of both dugouts. More Feds advance from the outfield. There's even a police helicopter coming down fast from where you'd expect to see pop flies and swirling retributional dust around the trapped killer. You think Stu Miller had problems on that mound!

And then a shot rings out and Martin falls spread-eagle on the mound.

Unless you're really caught up in an eye-for-an-eye, you've gotta wonder about the tactics. Remember, the Feds are lined up cheek-to-jowl around Martin along all four

basepaths. He couldn't get a grounder through, much less himself. But any G-man who squeezes a trigger has one skinny killer and a lot of hefty FBI men in front of him. And this is in Candlestick Park where the winds have been known to turn home runs into second-base popouts and ball players into missiles. If those Candlestick winds catch the bullet, it's bye-bye, good guy.

Fortunately in the last reel of a movie all happiness is ever-after, all hits are home runs, and all G-men shoot straight. Even in Candlestick Park.   —BC

League Swing Based on actual mechanics of top major league hitters.

Winner's Edge: Baseball With Don Kessinger.

Team Histories

Amazin' Era: New York Mets 25 Years (71 mins.)

Battlin' Bucs: The First 100 Years of the Pittsburgh Pirates (60 mins.)

Centennial: Over 100 Years of Philadelphia Phillies Baseball (60 mins.)

Chicago & the Cubs: A Lifelong Love Affair (60 mins.)

Chicago White Sox: A Visual History (60 mins.)

Detroit Tigers: The Movie (86 mins.)

Diamond in the Emerald City: 10 Years of Seattle Mariners Baseball (59 mins.)

Forever Fenway: 75 Years of Red Sox Baseball (60 mins.)

Giants History: The Tale of Two Cities (60 mins.)

Los Angeles Dodgers Stadium: 25th An-

niversary (60 mins.)

Mission Impossible: The First Decade (60 mins.) Toronto Blue Jays.

New York Yankees: The Movie (100 mins.)

Oakland A's: All-Star Almanac (25 mins.) A's in All-Star Games.

Reds: The Official History of the Cincinnati Reds (60 mins.)

St. Louis Cardinals: The Movie—109 Years of the Cardinals (90 mins.)

Silver Odyssey: 25 Years of Houston Astros Baseball (60 mins.)

Then & Now: The Minnesota Twins' Silver Anniversary (1961–1985) (27 mins.)

Miscellaneous

Andre Dawson: He's a Hero (60 mins.) Dawson's 1987 MVP season.

Ball Talk: Baseball's Voices of Summer (50 mins.) Larry King hosts Mel Allen, Red Barber, Jack Brickhouse, Jack Buck, Curt Gowdy, and Ernie Harwell as they reminisce, along with rare archival footage.

Baseball Fun & Games (60 mins.) Bloopers hosted by Joe Garagiola.

Baseball Funnies: A Hilarious Look at Baseball (30 mins.)

Baseball Funny Side Up (45 mins.) Hosted by Tug McGraw.

Baseball in the News (60 mins. each) Three videos containing old newsreels: 1951–55, 1956–60, 1961–67.

Boys of Summer (90 mins.) Based on Roger Kahn's best-seller.

Collecting Baseball Cards for Fun and Profit (30 mins.)

Glory of Their Times (60 mins.) From Lawrence Ritter's book.

Greatest Comeback Ever (58 mins.) Yankees' 1978 season.

History of Baseball: Greatest Moments from Baseball's Past (120 mins.)

Pinstripe Power: Story of the 1961 Yankees (49 mins.)

Reel Moments—Baseball (40 mins.) Historic highlights.

10 Greatest Moments in Yankees History (30 mins.)   —BC

Ewing: The Man and His Dream
A Short Film in the Nostalgic Spirit

*O*pening credits: Doak Ewing / Rare Sportsfilms, FL / 1534 Lakeview Drive, #210 / Darien, IL 60559 / (312) 910–1858.

Opening montage: The 1947 Boston Braves, the 1948 World Series, the '55 Washington Senators, the '56 All-Star Game, the World Champion Milwaukee Braves of 1957—all in color.

Scene 1, 1961: Most kids growing up on an Ohio farm might feel deprived to be without a television set for relaxation when the day's chores are done. Not Doak Ewing. His family has its own "bonanza," a 16mm movie projector. They spend their evenings at home watching movies. The youngster's favorite is an eight-minute highlight film of the 1948 World Series. *Voice-Over—Ewing*: "I bet I watched that thing a hundred times. I had it memorized." *Close-Up*: Young Ewing stares at film while sorting through his large cache of baseball cards. How will he combine his collecting mania with his passion for film?

Dissolve to 1978: While working for the Class-A Greenwood Braves in South Carolina, Ewing acquires a copy of the 1976 World Series highlights. *Zoom In*: He places it on a shelf alongside his '48 Series film.

Fade In—1979: Now in sales for the Atlanta Braves, Ewing discovers the team has a library of films dating back to the 1940s. As a matter of fact, the 1947 Boston Braves were the first team to do a color baseball film. When the team moved, color was continued in all but the first Milwaukee Braves promotional film. *Crowd Scene*: Ewing and nine or ten other enthusiasts run films on a rented projector and talk baseball. Several in the group express the wish to own these films on videotape. *Close-Up*: Ewing rubs his chin and thinks

about that a while. *Voice-Over—Ewing*: "Hmmmmm."

Dissolve to First Problem: Finding old films is a job for a detective. *Cut to infinitely detailed scene*: Ewing queries other collectors, libraries, and even haunts garage sales and flea markets. *Voice-Over—Ewing*: "By 1983, I'd collected nearly two-thirds of the World Series highlight films from 1943 to the present."

Dissolve to Second Problem: Simply acquiring a piece of rare film is only the beginning. There are rights and legalities. An error here could dash Ewing's dream and land him in a lawsuit. *Cut to long, involved scene*: Ewing contacts a Washington, D.C., copyright lawyer. He learns how to get copyright permission and how to do a copyright search to find if a piece of film has ever been copyrighted and if copyright has expired.

Dissolve to Third Problem: Color films fade. Although those few old films shot in I.B. Technicolor still retain much of their original brilliance, by the mid-1950s almost everything was shot in Eastmancolor, a "faster" film. After five or ten years, Eastmancolor films fade to a reddish hue. *Cut to short, colorful scene*: Ewing discovers an Atlanta firm has a state-of-the-art process called the Da Vinci Color Corrector. Armed with this, an operator can adjust the color on a faded film while it's being copied onto videotape, enhancing even such details as a player's socks. The color in the video will be more "correct" than the original, long-faded film. Moreover, the process can remove shadows, scratches, and dirt.

Dissolve to Fourth Problem: When film is transferred to videotape, a degree of resolution is lost. Some of the original film's clarity becomes fuzzy. *Cut to sharply defined scene*: By making the half-inch vid-

eotape copies he will sell from a one-inch master tape (instead of the more common three-quarter inch), Ewing is able to greatly improve his product's quality. The image will be sharper with more detail.

Music—Theme from Chariots of Fire: It's 1985 and Ewing offers his first two videos for sale by mail: A 1947 Boston Braves promotional film and the filmed highlights of the 1956 All-Star Game played at Griffith Stadium. Each runs 40 minutes. *Voice-Over—Ewing*: "My goals were to put out a quality collector's item and to simply break even."

Music—Theme from Jaws: In the following year, Ewing's catalogue shows only four or five more titles. His personal collection is, of course, much larger—400 to 500 films.

Music—Theme from Rocky: But in 1987 his business increases dramatically. Among the videos available from Rare Sportsfilms: Milwaukee Braves 1954, 1955, 1956, and 1957; Boston Red Sox 1954, 1955, 1956, and 1957; the 1955 Washington Senators, the 1956 Kansas City Athletics, the 1956 New York Yankees, and in black and white an old weekly TV show from 1955–56 called *Baseball News*. He's even begun to dabble in 1950s pro football and pro basketball films.

Fade to Ewing—Voice-Over: "Right now, of course, my regular job as an account executive with the Chicago White Sox, the Rare Sportsfilms sideline, and my collecting of sports movies doesn't leave me much time for watching my films. But, when I retire . . ."

Long Shot: Doak Ewing surrounded by hundreds of old baseball films—obviously a very happy man.

Fade Out.

Closing Credits: BC

CHAPTER 13

Less Than a Business, More Than a Game

One Durham Bulls fan likes to tell the story of his trip to Australia. No sooner had he gotten off the plane than he spotted a T-shirt with the familiar bull jumping through a D. He was amazed. The Bulls were everywhere!

And that was in the PBD (pre–*Bull Durham*) days. The real Bulls had something of an international following even before the movie about a fictional herd. After the movie, of course, Bulls souvenirs became an even hotter item. Almost every one of Durham's 100,000 residents got at least one call from out of town asking for a Bulls cap, T-shirt, or jacket.

The Bulls themselves sold many items directly through the mail or through a newly opened store at a local mall. The Toledo Mud Hens did similar business after Jamie Farr wore Mud Hen caps on the TV show "M*A*S*H."

Major league and major college souvenirs have never been hard to find. Sporting goods stores nationwide stock a good selection of caps, T-shirts, and jackets. But to get most minor league items, you'll need to contact the team directly. Almost any club will sell you souvenirs through the mail, and many are equipped to charge orders to a major credit card.

The range of souvenirs available varies from club to club. Expect to find at least pennants, caps, and T-shirts. Some clubs will also have jackets, sweatshirts, seat cushions, key chains, even old uniforms. Generally the teams with fancier logos will have a better variety available, and most Triple-A and Double-A clubs will have more than Class A teams.

Of course there are many more things you might like to know about a ball club

League and Team Offices

Mascots and munchies and names and numbers: A, AA, AAA, aaah!

than just how to get its trinkets. You may need to know who's in charge of publicity, or, for that matter, who's in charge overall. You may very well want to know what it's going to cost you to get into a game and when the game starts. Or something really basic: How do you get there?

In the listings that follow we've tried to give you an idea of what to expect in professional baseball. We've listed addresses and phone numbers, directions on how to get to the ballparks, ticket prices, and game times. We've also told you whether a team's souvenirs are sold anywhere in town other than at the ballpark.

Keep in mind that this information

changes frequently. Use the listings as a guide, but call or write ahead to keep from being disappointed. —DK

Major Leagues

Commissioner's Office, National League Office, and American League Office, 350 Park Ave., New York, NY 10022

National League

ATLANTA BRAVES
P.O. Box 4064, Atlanta, GA 30302. (404) 522-7734.

Atlanta–Fulton County Stadium (grass; seats 52,003): off I-75/85 just south of intersection with I-20 in Atlanta.

President: Stan Kasten. General Manager: Bobby Cox.

Public Relations Director: Jim Schultz.

Tickets: $4.00–9.50 (children $1.00); for information call (404) 577-9600.

Souvenirs: at stadium, or from Braves Clubhouse Collection, PO Box 4066, Atlanta, GA 30302.

Game Times: 7:40 (weeknights), 7:10 (Saturdays), 2:10 (Sundays).

CHICAGO CUBS
1060 West Addison St., Chicago, IL 60613. (312) 281-5050.

Wrigley Field (grass; seats 38,143): at Clark and Addison Sts. on the North Side of Chicago.

President: Donald Grenesko. Executive Vice President, Baseball Operations: Jim Frey.

Media Relations Director: Ned Colletti.

Tickets: $5.00–11.50 (children $3.50), available at stadium and TicketMaster; for information call (312) 878-CUBS; to

In a historic scene, Babe Ruth signs his first pro contract as Jack Dunn (left) and Ned Hanlon of Baltimore stand by.

charge call (312) 559-1212 or (800) 548-4000.

Souvenirs: at stadium.

Game Times: 1:05, 6:35 (April, September), 7:05 (other nights).

CINCINNATI REDS
Riverfront Stadium, Cincinnati, OH 45202.
(513) 421-4510.

Riverfront Stadium (artificial turf; seats 52,392): on the Ohio River east of I-71 and I-75 in downtown Cincinnati.

President: Marge Schott. General Manager: Murray Cook.

Vice President, Publicity: Jim Ferguson.

Tickets: $3.50–8.50, available at stadium, Reds gift shop, and TicketMaster; for information call (513) 421-REDS or (800) 525-5900.

Souvenirs: Available at Reds Gift Shop in the Hyatt Regency Hotel, Fifth and Elm Sts., in downtown Cincinnati; call (513) 651-7200.

Game Times: 7:35 (weeknights), 7:05 (Saturdays), 2:15 (Sundays).

HOUSTON ASTROS
P.O. Box 288, Houston, TX 77001.
(713) 799-9500.

Astrodome (artificial turf; seats 45,000): just north of the South Loop Freeway (I-610), southwest of downtown Houston.

Chairman of the Board: Dr. John McMullen. General Manager: Bill Wood.

Public Relations Director: Rob Matwick.

Tickets: $4.00–10.00 (children $1.00); for information call (713) 799-9555.

Souvenirs: at stadium.

Game Times: 1:35, 7:35.

LOS ANGELES DODGERS
1000 Elysian Park Ave., Los Angeles, CA 90012.
(213) 224-1500.

Dodger Stadium (grass; seats 56,000): off the Pasadena Freeway (Calif. 110) and the Golden State Freeway (I-5) just north of downtown Los Angeles.

President: Peter O'Malley. Executive Vice President, Player Personnel: Fred Claire.

Publicity Director: Mike Williams.

Tickets: $4.00–8.00 (children $2.00), available at stadium, TicketMaster and Ticketron; for information call (213) 224-1400; to charge call (213) 410-1062 or (714) 634-1300.

Souvenirs: to order call (800) 762-1770.

Game Times: 7:05 (weeknights, April, May; all Saturday nights); 7:35 (weeknights, rest of year); 1:05 Sunday.

MONTREAL EXPOS
P.O. Box 500, Station M, Montreal, Que. H1V 3P2.
(514) 253-8282.

Olympic Stadium (artificial turf; seats 59,123): at Sherbrooke St., Pie IX Blvd., Pierre de Coubertin Ave. and Viau St. in the city's east end, at Pie IX and Viau Metro stations.

Chairman of the Board: Charles Bronfman. Vice President, Player Personnel: David Dombrowski.

Publicists: Richard Griffin, Monique Giroux.

Tickets: $11.00–18.50.

Souvenirs: available at Expos Boutique in the stadium, at Place Ville-Marie, and in the Fairview Shopping Centre.

Game Times: 1:35, 7:35.

NEW YORK METS
126th St. and Roosevelt Ave., Flushing, NY 11368.
(718) 507-METS.

Shea Stadium (grass; seats 55,300): in Flushing, Queens, off the Grand Central Parkway north of the Long Island Expressway (I-495), near LaGuardia Airport; take the IRT Flushing line # 7.

President: Fred Wilpon. General Manager: Frank Cashen.

Public Relations Director: Jay Horwitz.

Tickets: $6.00–11.50 (senior citizen discount); for information call (718) 507-TIXX.

Souvenirs: at stadium.

Game Times: 7:35 (weeknights), 7:05 (Saturday), 1:35 (Sunday).

PHILADELPHIA PHILLIES

P.O. Box 7575, Philadelphia, PA 19101. (215) 463-6000.

Veterans Stadium (artificial turf; seats 64,538): on Broad St. in South Philadelphia, just south of the approach to the Walt Whitman Bridge and west of I-95.

President: Bill Giles. General Manager: Lee Thomas.

Vice President, Public Relations: Larry Shenk.

Tickets: $4.00–9.00 (children $1.00); for information call (215) 463-1000.

Souvenirs: at stadium.

Game Times: 7:35 (weeknights), 7:05 (Saturday), 1:35 (Sunday).

PITTSBURGH PIRATES

P.O. Box 7000, Pittsburgh, PA 15212. (412) 323-5000.

Three Rivers Stadium (artificial turf; seats 58,437): on the north bank of the Ohio River, at the intersection of the Allegheny and Monongahela Rivers, next to the Ft. Duquesne Bridge (I-278).

President: Carl Barger. General Manager: Larry Doughty.

Media Relations Director: Jim Lachimia.

Tickets: $4.00–10.50 (children $2.00), available at stadium, Kaufmann's Department Stores, National Record Marts, Oasis Stores, and Pirates' Club House Stores; for information call (412) 321-BUCS or (800) BUY-BUCS; to charge call (412) 323-1919 or (800)366-1212.

Souvenirs: available at Pirates' Club House, located at the Westin William Penn Hotel and Allegheny Center.

Game Times: 7:05 (weeknights April, May, September, all Saturday nights), 7:35 (other weeknights), 1:35 (Sunday).

ST. LOUIS CARDINALS

250 Stadium Plaza, St. Louis, MO 63102. (314) 421-4040.

Busch Stadium (artificial turf; seats 53,138): in downtown St. Louis at 7th and Walnut Sts., north of I-64 and west of I-70.

President: August Busch, Jr. General Manager: Dal Maxvill.

Public Relations Director: Kip Ingle.

Tickets: $4.00–10.50; for information call (314) 421-3060; to charge call (314) 421-2400.

Souvenirs: at stadium.

Game Times: 7:35 (weeknights), 7:05 (Saturday), 1:15 (Sunday).

SAN DIEGO PADRES

P.O. Box 2000, San Diego, CA 92120. (619) 283-7294.

Jack Murphy San Diego Stadium (grass; seats 58,396): off I-8 east of I-805 and west of I-15 north of downtown San Diego.

Chairwoman of the Board: Joan Kroc. Vice President, Baseball Operations: Jack McKeon.

Media Relations Director: Bill Beck.

Tickets: $4.00–9.50, for information call (619) 283-4494.

Souvenirs: at stadium.

Game Times: 1:05, 7:05.

SAN FRANCISCO GIANTS

San Francisco, CA 94124. (415) 468-3700.

Candlestick Park (grass; seats 58,000): off the Bayshore Freeway (U.S. 101) on Candlestick Point south of downtown San Francisco.

Chairman: Bob Lurie. General Manager: Al Rosen.

Media Relations Director: Matt Fischer.

Tickets: $2.50–10.00, available at stadium, Giants Dugout Stores, Ticketron, and BASS/TicketMaster; for information call (415) 467-8000; to charge call (415) 392-SHOW, (408) 247-SHOW, (209) 486-SHOW, (916) 489-SHOW, and (707) 224-SHOW.

Souvenirs: available at Giants Dugout Stores at 170 Grant Ave. in San Francisco, Serramonte Center in Daly City, Valley Fair Mall in Santa Clara, and Stanford Shopping Mall in Palo Alto.

Game Times: 7:05 (Monday), 7:35 (other nights), 1:05 (weekends).

American League

BALTIMORE ORIOLES

Memorial Stadium Baltimore, MD 21218. (301) 243-9800.

Memorial Stadium (grass; seats 54,076): on 33rd St. north of downtown Baltimore.

President: Larry Lucchino. Vice President, Baseball Operations: Roland Hemond.

Public Relations Director: Rick Vaughn.

Tickets: $4.75–9.50 ($2.50 children/senior citizens); available at stadium, Hechts, and Standard Drug; call (301) 243-9800 or (202) 296-BIRD; to charge call (301) 481-6000 or (800) 448-9009.

Souvenirs: Available at stadium or at Orioles stores in Washington, D.C. and Lanham, Md.

Game Times: 1:35 (Sundays), 8:05 (Fridays), 7:35 (most others).

BOSTON RED SOX

4 Yawkey Way Boston, MA 02215. (617) 267-9440.

Fenway Park (grass; seats 33,589): South of I-90, west of downtown Boston.

General Manager: Lou Gorman.

Vice President, Public Relations: Dick Bresciani.

Tickets: $6.00–16.00; for information call (617) 267-8661; for charge call (617) 267-1700.

Souvenirs: available at park.

Game Times: 7:35 (weeknights), 1:05 (Saturday, Sunday).

CALIFORNIA ANGELS

2000 State College Blvd., Anaheim, CA 92806.

(714) 937-6700.

Anaheim Stadium (grass; seats 65,158): at the intersection of Katella Ave. and State College Blvd., between the Santa Ana Freeway (I-5) and the 57 Freeway, just north of the Garden Grove Freeway (Calif. 22).

President: Gene Autry. General Manager: Mike Port.

Public Relations Director: Tim Mead.

Tickets: $3.00–9.00 ($1.00 children); available at stadium, Ticketron, or Teletron (714) 634-1300, (213) 410-1062.

Souvenirs: available at stadium.

Game Times: 7:05 Monday through Saturday (April); 7:35 Monday through Saturday (rest of year); 1:05 Sunday.

CHICAGO WHITE SOX

324 W. 35th St., Chicago, IL 60616.
(312) 924-1000.

Comiskey Park (grass; seats 44,087): on 35th St., just off the Dan Ryan Expressway (I-90/94) on the South Side of Chicago.

Chairman: Jerry Reinsdorf. General Manager: Larry Himes.

Vice President, Public Relations: Chuck Adams.

Tickets: $4.00–8.50, available at stadium and TicketMaster; to charge call (312) 559-1212.

Souvenirs: at stadium.

Game Times: 7:30 (weeknights), 1:30 (Sundays).

CLEVELAND INDIANS

Boudreau Blvd., Cleveland, OH 44114.
(216) 861-1200.

Municipal Stadium (grass; seats 74,208): on Lake Erie, north of the Cleveland Municipal Shoreway (U.S. 6/20) and I-90.

Chairman of the Board: Richard Jacobs. President: Hank Peters.

Media Relations Director: Rick Minch.

Tickets: $4.00–9.50 ($3.00 children); for information call (216) 861-1200 or TicketMaster at (216) 241-5555 or (800) 248-8888.

Souvenirs: at stadium.

Game Times: 7:35 (weeknights), 7:05 (Saturday nights), 1:35 (day games).

DETROIT TIGERS

Tiger Stadium Detroit, MI 48216.
(313) 962-4000.

Tiger Stadium (grass; seats 52,806): at Michigan and Trumbull Aves., near the intersection of I-75 and the John C. Lodge Freeway (Mich. 10).

President: Jim Campbell. General Manager: Bill Lajoie.

Public Relations Director: Dan Ewald.

Tickets: $4.00–10.50; for information call (313) 962-4000.

Souvenirs: at stadium.

Game Times: 7:35 (Monday through Saturday), 1:35 (Sunday).

KANSAS CITY ROYALS

P.O. Box 419969, Kansas City, MO 64141.
(816) 921-2200.

Royals Stadium (artificial turf; seats 40,625): in the Harry S. Truman Sports Complex, off I-70 at the intersection with I-435.

Chairman of the Board: Ewing Kauffman. General Manager: John Schuerholz.

Vice President, Public Relations: Dean Vogelaar.

Tickets: $3.00–10.00; for information call (816) 921-8000; to charge call (816) 921-4400 or (800) 422-1969.

Souvenirs: at stadium.

Game Times: 7:35 (weeknights), 7:05 (Saturday), 1:35 (Sunday).

MILWAUKEE BREWERS

201 S. 46th St. Milwaukee, WI 53214.
(414) 933-4114.

County Stadium (grass; seats 53,192): at I-94 and the Stadium Freeway (U.S. 41), west of downtown Milwaukee.

President: Bud Selig. General Manager: Harry Dalton.

Publicity Director: Tom Skibosh.

Tickets: $4.00–12.00; for information call (414) 933-1818; to charge call (414) 933-9000.

Souvenirs: at stadium.

Game Times: 1:30, 7:30.

MINNESOTA TWINS

501 Chicago Ave. South, Minneapolis, MN 55415.
(612) 375-1366.

Metrodome (artificial turf; seats 55,244): at 6th St. and Chicago Ave., off I-35W, east of downtown Minneapolis.

Owner: Carl Pohlad. General Manager: Andy MacPhail.

Media Relations Director: Tom Mee.

Tickets: $3.00–11.00; for information call (612) 375-1366.

Souvenirs: at stadium.

Game Times: 1:15, 7:05.

NEW YORK YANKEES

Yankee Stadium, Bronx, NY 10451.
(212) 293-4300.

Yankee Stadium (grass; seats 57,545): just off the Major Deegan Expressway at 161st St. and River Ave. in the South Bronx; take the IND 6th Avenue line D or CC local, or the IRT Lexington Avenue line #4 Woodlawn.

Principal Owner: George Steinbrenner. General Manager: Bob Quinn.

Public Relations Director: Arthur Richman.

Tickets: $4.50–12.00 (senior citizens $1.00), available at stadium or TicketMaster; for information call (212) 293-6000; to charge call (212) 307-7171, (914) 965-2700, (516) 888-9000, or (201) 507-8900.

Souvenirs: at stadium.

Game Times: 1:30, 7:30.

OAKLAND ATHLETICS

Oakland–Alameda County Coliseum, Oakland, CA 94621.
(415) 638-4900.

Oakland–Alameda County Coliseum (grass; seats 50,219): at Hegenberger Road off I-880 south of downtown Oakland.

Owner: Walter Haas. Vice President, Baseball Operations: Sandy Alderson.

Baseball Information Director: Jay Alves.

The Best of the Wurst, and Other Big-League Eats

Blue skies, green grass, a warm sunny Saturday afternoon in the bleachers, and major league baseball. Can life get any better? Well, only if you share the day with the right company—a hot dog, something cold to sip on, and a bag of peanuts in the shell. Baseball and baseball food—they kind of go together like a ballpark and real-live green grass.

At least that's what I think. And I'm just your average everyday peanut-shucking bleacherite . . . well, with a twist, actually. You see, in the summer of 1985, I fulfilled every baseball fan's dream. Me and my Toyota visited every single major league baseball park. It took us fifty-one days and 12,000 miles, and besides a little summer-long indigestion from living on hot dogs and peanuts, the final result was *Dodger Dogs to Fenway Franks*—the story of my journey. I've found that no matter where you go or what you eat, no matter if you visit the most luxurious luxury box that any California ballpark has to offer, the best things to eat at any ballgame are the same as they were when The Babe was still swatting homers.

Oh sure, it's fun to experiment. It's neat to munch on Milwaukee County Stadium's entire line of sausages. And I wouldn't

miss a cruise through Comiskey's food fair for anything. Liquor lounges in Anaheim are interesting, even if it's for just checking out the clientele. And with stuff like sushi, shrimp, salad bars, crabcakes, and oysters in the half shell floating around the majors, gourmet menus are almost as prevalent as plastic grass. But if you really want to catch baseball at its best, just do what your dad did when he went to the ballyard. And I guess what his dad and *his* dad before him did too: Find the bleachers on a hot sunny day. Bring along a stash of peanuts, hit the dog stand on your way to the seat, yell "Hey beer!" when the suds vendor strolls by, put your feet up, smile in the sunshine, and tell yourself "Life just don't get no better than this."

Major League Baseball's "Best of" Menu

Twenty-six baseball parks, twenty-six menus; these are the best:
- Best "under-stand" wiener—Milwaukee County Stadium.
- Best "in-stand" wiener– Detroit Tiger Stadium.
- Best peanuts—Seattle Kingdome.
- Best assortment of beer—Three Rivers Stadium.
- Best assortment of food—Comiskey Park.
- Best line of sausages—Oakland Coliseum

Best in the specialty department:
- Barbecue sandwich—Kansas City Royals Stadium.
- Knish—Yankee Stadium, Shea Stadium.
- Crabcakes—Baltimore Memorial Stadium.

Best-Eating Baseball Park in the World

Tie—Milwaukee County Stadium and Comiskey Park.   —BW

Tickets: $3.50–10.00; available at stadium and BASS ticket centers; for information call (415) 638-4900; to charge call (415) 762-BASS, (408) 998-BASS, (707) 762-BASS, or (916) 923-BASS.

Souvenirs: at stadium.

Game Times: 7:05 (nights except Friday), 7:35 (Friday), 1:05 (day).

SEATTLE MARINERS
P.O. Box 4100, Seattle, WA 98104.

(206) 628-3555.

Kingdome (artificial turf; seats 59,348): just west of I-5 in downtown Seattle.

Chairman of the Board: Jeff Smulyan. Vice President, Baseball Operations: Woody Woodward.

Public Relations Director: Dave Aust.

Tickets: $3.50–9.50, available at stadium and TicketMaster; for information call (206) 628-3555; to charge call (206) 628-0888 or 272-6817.

Souvenirs: at stadium.

Game Times: 1:35, 7:05.

TEXAS RANGERS
P.O. Box 1111, Arlington, TX 76010. (817) 273-5222.

Arlington Stadium (grass; seats 43,508): south of I-30 in Arlington.

President: Mike Stone. General Manager: Tom Grieve.

Media Relations Director: John Blake.

Tickets: $4.00–10.00 (children $2.00), available at stadium and Rainbow Ticket-Master; for information call (817) 273-5000.

Souvenirs: at stadium.

Game Times: 2:05, 7:35.

TORONTO BLUE JAYS
300 The Esplanade West, Suite 3200, Toronto, Ont. M5V 3B3.
(416) 595-5541.

SkyDome (artificial turf; seats 53,000):

southwest of the CN Tower and north of the Esplanade between John and Peter Sts.

Chairman: N.E. Hardy. Executive Vice President, Baseball: Pat Gillick.

Public Relations Director: Howard Starkman.

Tickets: $4.00–15.00; for information call (416) 595-5541.

Souvenirs: at stadium.

Game Times: 1:35, 7:35.   —DK

Triple-A Alliance

Sit in the stands in Buffalo or Louisville, and you'll soon have your image of the minor leagues ruined. No longer does the American Association seem ready to jump up in classification and become a third major league, but it remains the most "major" of the minor leagues. Both Buffalo and Louisville have drawn more than one million fans in a season, and Denver is one of baseball's prime expansion candidates.

Adding 25,000 seats would make Buffalo's Pilot Field ready for the big leagues. Indianapolis's Bush Stadium hosted the 1987 Pan American Games baseball and then served as a main location for the movie *Eight Men Out*. The Association's 1988 near merger with the International League did nothing to hurt either league. Even before the Alliance, Richmond and Columbus had two of the nicest minor league ballparks anywhere. And the 1989 move from Maine to Scranton/Wilkes-Barre brought another new stadium into the IL.

The Triple-A level also provides the fan with some well-known names. As minor league baseball has become a bigger business, major league organizations have become more willing to sign higher-priced veterans to help their top affiliates. So along with the hot prospects, expect to see

more than a few former big leaguers. Unfortunately some Triple-A teams end up with more fill-in veterans than up-and-coming prospects. So much for player development.

American Association

BUFFALO BISONS
Pittsburgh Pirates
P.O. Box 450, Buffalo, NY 14205.
(716) 846-2000.

Pilot Field (seats 19,500): At Washington and Swan Sts. in downtown Buffalo.

President: Bob Rich, Jr. General Manager: Mike Billoni.

Public Relations Director: Mike Buczkowski.

Tickets: $3.00–7.00; call (800) 382-8080 to order.

Souvenirs: available at stadium or call (716) 846-2222.

Game Times: 7:05, 1:05 (Wednesday), 2:05 (Sunday).

DENVER ZEPHYRS
Milwaukee Brewers
2850 W. 20th St., Denver, CO 80211.
(303) 433-8645.

Mile High Stadium (seats 76,000): off I-25 at Exit 210-B west of downtown Denver.

President and General Manager: Robert Howsam, Jr.

Public Relations Director: Doug Ward.

Tickets: $4.50–7.50, available at stadium and TicketMaster.

Souvenirs: Sports Fan, on Federal St. in Denver.

Game Times: 12:35, 7:00

INDIANAPOLIS INDIANS
Montreal Expos
1501 W. 16th St., Indianapolis, IN 46202.
(317) 632-5371.

Bush Stadium (seats 12,500): on 16th St. west of downtown Indianapolis.

President and General Manager: Max Schumacher.

Publicity Director: Cal Burleson.

Tickets: $3.50–6.00 ($2.50 children).

Souvenirs: at stadium and at Gallayns stores.

Game Times: 7:30, 2:00 (Sundays).

IOWA CUBS
Chicago Cubs
2nd and Riverside Drive, Des Moines, IA 50309.
(515) 243-6111.

Sec Taylor Stadium (seats 7,600): south of I-235, west of the Des Moines River.

President: Ken Grandquist. General Manager: Sam Bernabe.

Public Relations: Todd Weber.

Tickets: $2.50–5.00 ($1.00 children).

Souvenirs: at stadium.

Game Times: 7:00 (April, May), 7:30 (rest of year), 6:00 (Sundays).

LOUISVILLE REDBIRDS
St. Louis Cardinals
P.O. Box 36407, Louisville, KY 40233.
(502) 367-9121.

Cardinal Stadium (seats 33,500): on the Kentucky State Fairgrounds, next to Freedom Hall.

General Manager: Dale Owens.

Publicity Manager: Ed Peak.

Tickets: $3.00–4.00 ($1.50 children, senior citizens).

Mr. Peanut's relief pitcher is prettier.

Souvenirs: at stadium.
Game Times: 7:15, 6:00 (Sundays).

NASHVILLE SOUNDS
Cincinnati Reds
P.O. Box 23290, Nashville, TN 37202.
(615) 242-4371.

Herschel Greer Stadium (seats 18,000):
Wedgewood exit off I-65, south of I-40.

President and General Manager: Larry
Schmittou.

Publicity Director: Jim Ballweg.

Tickets: $3.00–5.50 ($2.00 children).

Souvenirs: at stadium or through
Sportservice (615-242-4629).

Game Times: 7:35.

OKLAHOMA CITY 89ERS
Texas Rangers
P.O. Box 75089, Oklahoma City, OK
73147.
(405) 946-8989.

All-Sports Stadium (seats 12,000): on
the Oklahoma fairgrounds, just north of
I-40 and west of downtown.

President: Patty Cox-Hampton. General
Manager: Jim Weigel.

Media Coordinator: Kathy Walker.

Tickets: $3.00–5.00.

Souvenirs: at stadium.

Game Times: 2:00, 7:15.

OMAHA ROYALS
Kansas City Royals
P.O. Box 3665, Omaha, NE 68103.
(402) 734-2550.

Rosenblatt Municipal Stadium (seats
15,000): just south of I-80 on the east side
of town, next to the Henry Doorly Zoo.

President: Gus Cherry. General Manager: Bill Gorman.

Media Relations: John Kramer.

Tickets: $3.50–5.50 ($2.00 children, senior citizens).

Souvenirs: at stadium.

Game Times: 7:05 (weekdays), 2:05
(weekends April-May), 6:05 (other weekends). *(Cont. p. 237.)*

Here Comes Mr. Peanut

They call me Mr. Peanut," drawls Max Herring, a large, outgoing man with an ever present smile and an endless supply of bad jokes. "When baseball people see me and see the briefcase, they know what's coming. They may not know my name, but they know my product."

Herring can easily be spotted at baseball's annual Winter Meetings. He's the guy who's constantly pulling little bags of peanuts out of his brown briefcase and tossing them to the minor league executives he meets.

Not just any peanuts, mind you. Houston's peanuts, salted in the shell, fresh from the factory in tiny Dublin, North Carolina. As Max will tell you, Houston's peanuts and baseball are a perfect match.

Herring first attended the Winter Meetings in Nashville in '83. Jim Mills, then president of the Class A Carolina League, introduced Herring to scores of club presidents and general managers.

His sales pitch was, and is, simple: "The real competitive edge I have is, I'm the representative of the factory. We are the roaster of peanuts. When someone places an order with me, they get 'em direct from the processor. There's no middleman, no peanuts sitting around a warehouse getting stale."

Herring lined up twenty teams to sell Houston's nuts during the '84 season. Today, about forty minor league clubs, from San Jose to Buffalo, sell the 2½-ounce bags of peanuts at prices ranging from 50 cents to $1. He's also in twenty to twenty-five college football stadiums, two NBA arenas, and he follows the NASCAR auto-racing circuit. "Have peanut, will travel," Mr. Peanut says.

If you'd like to buy a case of Houston's peanuts directly from Max, write to P.O. Box 1353, Cary, NC, 27512. Or call (800) 441-3393. Prices may vary according to the size of the latest peanut crop, which likely is determined by how much rain has fallen on the Piedmont region of North Carolina during the previous six months. —JS

The Changing Face of Minor League Promotions

Once upon a time, in the not too distant past, minor league baseball was known for its crazy promotions. There was Tropical Pet Night in Greensboro, North Carolina, where first prize was a boa constrictor and fans prayed they didn't have the winning ticket. Some clubs staged mud-wrestling contests on a tarpaulin spread over home plate. There were innumerable cash scrambles, in which beered-up contestants raced around the infield picking up dollar bills and stuffing them in their drawers.

The list could go on and on.

Today things are a lot more conventional. Jim Paul, president of the El Paso Diablos, will tell you, "There are no original ideas anymore."

Paul is partly to blame. He runs an annual seminar for minor league executives, where promotional ideas are exchanged and dissected. Everybody who's anybody attends, and, as a result, if you go to Elizabethton, Tennessee, in June and

Eugene, Oregon, in August, you might run across the same promotion.

Seat-cushion night. Beach towel night. Cap night. Every giveaway treasure smothered with the sponsors' logos, of course. A few promotions aim at a little fun. The Albuquerque Dukes still hold their Funny Nose and Glasses Night, the Savannah Cardinals toss paper-airplane-throwing contests, and many clubs toodle through Kazoo Nights or stretch bellies with ice cream-eating contests, or dispense old clunkers on Used Car Night. But the really wild promotions are few and far between.

These days, a postgame Beach Boys concert is considered state-of-the-art promotion. The Buffalo Bisons host regular Friday-night tent parties under the scoreboard beyond center field at Pilot Field, featuring bands and ethnic food.

"Nowadays, the modern operator is not interested in goofy things," harrumphs Bob Beban, general manager of the Eu-

gene Emeralds. "We're out of the business schools rather than the playgrounds. We'd rather spend our time selling tickets.

"Minor league baseball has changed."

And Eddie Gaedel need not apply.

Here are a few examples of the old-time religion:

Saturday Night Doubleheaders, Ray Winder Field, Little Rock, Arkansas—"We do fun things," says Bill Valentine, general manager of the Arkansas Travelers. "The old Bill Veeck type of things."

Veeck, the old fox, would love Valentine's style. Because beer can't be sold on Sundays in Little Rock, the Travelers schedule Saturday-night twin bills. On a given Saturday, you might find any number of things happening on the field between games: stuntmen blowing themselves up, Frisbee-catching dogs, Dixieland bands, you name it. "You know what fans like more than anything?" Valentine asks. "The old egg-tossing contests. We do the simple things, the things they did twenty-five years ago. And the fans really have a good time."

Noah Night, Charleston, West Virginia—The Charleston Wheelers had suffered through nine consecutive rainouts. When the rainstorms cleared, general manager Dennis Bastien had a brainstorm. He promoted the Wheelers' May 20, 1989, game against the Columbia Mets as "Noah Night."

"Anybody who came dressed as any kind of ark animal and came two by two, we let in free," Bastien explained. "And anybody who came dressed as Noah, we let in free. And anyone who brought along a toy boat, we let in for one dollar. We had a couple hundred crazies come out with horns on. One guy wore a rhinoceros nose. Some came in with antlers they got off their father's gun rack. And of course it rained. In the fourth inning, it rained."

Giant Banana Split, Nashville, Tennes-

"Hit the Bull Durham sign and win $50!" That was the tobacco company's promotion in professional ballparks all across the country, and the campaign was, well, a hit.

see—Back in 1982, the Nashville Sounds decided to liven up a midsummer double-header by constructing a huge banana split between games. Strips of aluminum guttering were connected and placed on top of sawhorses, so the guttering extended 360 feet around the bases. Wax paper was placed inside, and 700 gallons of ice cream were dumped in. Then ballgirls topped the ice cream with bananas, chocolate syrup, and cherries. And 3,000 people who had bought ice cream in the concession stands at Herschel Greer Stadium during the first game were allowed to bring their plastic spoons down to the field to eat the rapidly melting concoction.

"It went well, until we realized we had to play a second game and we had to get all that syrup up," said Larry Schmittou, the Sounds' president and general manager. "There were a lot of sticky balls thrown out of that game."

Martinez Night, El Paso, Texas—This was a case of a general manager not doing his homework. Before one game back in 1974, the El Paso Diablos announced they'd let anyone named Martinez in free. "It didn't work," Paul said. "It turns out, the most popular name around here is Lopez."

Greased Pig Contest, Gastonia, North Carolina—Here's another legendary promotion from the rollicking summer of '74. Gastonia Rangers' general manager Dave Fendrick purchased a pig, greased it with Crisco, and let it loose in the outfield between games of a doubleheader. About thirty kids were brought out of the stands, eager for the chase. In less than a minute, one kid had a secure grip on the pig. So much for the promotion.

"But the better pig chase occurred after the event," said Fendrick, who now works for the Texas Rangers. "The pig got loose under the grandstand. We could not catch this pig. Finally we trapped him in one of the stalls in the women's bathroom. Needless to say, that was the last greased-pig contest I ever had."   —JS

International League

COLUMBUS CLIPPERS
New York Yankees
1155 W. Mound St., Columbus, OH 43223.
(614) 462-5250.
  Cooper Stadium (seats 15,000): west of downtown on I-70.
  President: Richard Smith. General Manager: George Sisler, Jr.
  Media Relations: Jeff Buettner.
  Tickets: $2.50–4.00 ($1.00 children, senior citizens).
  Souvenirs: at stadium.
  Game Times: 7:30 (Monday–Saturday), 2:00 (April Sundays), 6:00 (other Sundays).

PAWTUCKET RED SOX
Boston Red Sox
P.O. Box 2365, Pawtucket, RI 02861.
(401) 724-7300.
  McCoy Stadium (seats 6,010): off I-95 in Pawtucket.
  President: Michael Tamburro. General Manager: Lou Schwechheimer.
  Public Relations Director: Bill Wanless.
  Tickets: $3.00–4.00 ($2.00 children, senior citizens).
  Souvenirs: at stadium.
  Game Times: 7:00 (Monday–Saturday), 1:00 (Sunday).

RICHMOND BRAVES
Atlanta Braves
P.O. Box 6667, Richmond, VA 23230.
(804) 359-4444.
  The Diamond (seats 12,000): just west of I-95 at the Boulevard exit north of downtown.
  President: Stan Kasten. General Manager: Bruce Baldwin.
  Public Relations Director: Scott Torok.
  Tickets: $3.00–5.00 ($2.00 children, senior citizens).
  Souvenirs: at stadium.
  Game Times: 7:00 (Monday–Saturday), 2:00 (Sunday).

ROCHESTER RED WINGS
Baltimore Orioles
500 Norton St., Rochester, NY 14621.
(716) 467-3000.
  Silver Stadium (seats 12,503): South of Rte. 104 between Seneca and Clinton Ave.
  President: Fred Strauss. General Manager: Bob Goughan.
  Public Relations Director: Kevin Greene.
  Tickets: $3.50–7.00 ($3.00 children, senior citizens).
  Souvenirs: at stadium, at Sugar Creek stores, and at Merle Harmon Fan Fare in the Marketplace Mall.
  Game Times: 7:05 (Monday–Thursday), 7:35 (Friday–Saturday), 2:05 (Sunday).

SCRANTON/WILKES-BARRE RED BARONS
Philadelphia Phillies
P.O. Box 3449, Scranton, PA 18505.
(717) 969-2255.
  Lackawanna County Multi-Purpose Stadium (seats 10,004): I-81 at Montage Mountain Road exit.
  President: Paul Taramelli. General Manager: Bill Terlecky.
  Tickets: $3.00–5.00.
  Souvenirs: at stadium.
  Game Times: 7:00 (Monday–Saturday), 6:00 (Sunday).

SYRACUSE CHIEFS
Toronto Blue Jays
MacArthur Stadium, Syracuse, NY 13208.
(315) 474-7833.
  MacArthur Stadium (seats 10,500): just off Rtes. 81 and 690.
  President: Donald Waful. General Manager: Tex Simone.
  Public Relations: John Simone.
  Tickets: $3.00–4.50 ($1.50 children).
  Souvenirs: available at stadium and at The Complete Athlete store in the Shopping Town mall.
  Game Times: 7:30 (Monday–Saturday), 6:00 (Sunday).

TIDEWATER TIDES
New York Mets
P.O. Box 12111, Norfolk, VA 23502.
(804) 461-5600.

Met Park (seats 6,162): at Military Hwy. and Northampton Blvd., just off I-64.

President: Richard Davis. General Manager: Dave Rosenfield.

Tickets: $3.00–4.00 ($2.00 children, senior citizens, active military).

Souvenirs: at stadium.

Game Times: 7:00 (Monday–Saturday through mid-June), 1:30 (Sundays through mid-June), 7:30 (Monday–Saturday rest of year), 6:00 (Sunday rest of year).

TOLEDO MUD HENS
Detroit Tigers
P.O. Box 6212, Toledo, OH 43614.
(419) 893-9483.

Ned Skeldon Stadium (seats 10,025): in Maumee near Exit 4 on the Ohio Turnpike.

General Manager: Gene Cook.

Tickets: $2.50–4.00.

Souvenirs: at stadium and at Seven S. L. Forman Enterprises stores around Toledo.

Game Times: 7:00, 2:00 (Sunday in April, May), 6:00 (Sunday rest of year).

Pacific Coast League

About all most people know about the PCL is that batting averages and ERAs soar in the high-altitude ballparks. Older fans remember the glory days of the league, when franchises in Los Angeles and San Francisco made it the West Coast's major league. Now the PCL doesn't get the publicity of the other two Triple-A leagues, and the great distances will probably always keep it out of interleague play.

But the Pacific Coast League has big cities and modern stadiums of its own. The lights of Las Vegas, the food of the desert Southwest, and the beauty of the Pacific Northwest make the PCL the best league

to travel to see, even though it moved out of Hawaii after 1987. Half of the PCL cities have a major league team in at least one sport, and besides that Tucson has spring training and Tacoma shares a metropolitan area with Seattle. That can hurt attendance, although Albuquerque, Calgary, and Las Vegas are perennially among the tops in the minors.

ALBUQUERQUE DUKES
Los Angeles Dodgers
P.O. Box 26267, Albuquerque, NM 87125.
(505) 243-1791.

Albuquerque Sports Stadium (seats 10,510): Just east of I-25 at Stadium Blvd.

President and General Manager: Pat McKernan.

Publicity Director: David Sheriff.

Tickets: $3.00–4.00 ($2.50 students, senior citizens; $1.00 children), available at stadium and at TicketMaster at Smith's.

Souvenirs: at stadium.

Game Times: 7:00 (Monday–Saturday), 1:00 (Sunday)

CALGARY CANNONS
Seattle Mariners
P.O. Box 3690, Station B, Calgary, Alta., T2M 4M4.
(403) 284-1111.

Foothills Stadium (seats 7,500): 24 Avenue and Crowchild Trail NW.

President: Russ Parker. General Manager: Bill Cragg.

Public Relations Director: Mark Stephen.

Tickets: $4.50 ($3.50 children).

Souvenirs: at stadium.

Game Times: 7:05, 1:35.

COLORADO SPRINGS SKY SOX
Cleveland Indians
4385 Tutt Ave., Colorado Springs, CO 80922.
(719) 597-1449.

Sky Sox Stadium (seats 6,130): on Tutt Ave. near Barnes Rd.

President and General Manager: Fred Whitacre.

Tickets: $3.00–4.50 ($2.00 children), at stadium and at Gart Brothers, Dave Cooke, and Long's Drugs.

Souvenirs: at stadium and at Sears, Gart Brothers, Dave Cooke, and Merle Harmon Fan Fare.

Game Times: 7:05 (Monday–Friday first half of season, Monday–Saturday second half), 1:35 (Sunday, holiday, first half Saturday).

EDMONTON TRAPPERS
California Angels
10233 96th Ave., Edmonton, Alta. T5K 0A5.
(403) 429-2934.

John Ducey Park (seats 5,000): 102 St. and 96 Ave.

President and General Manager: Mel Kowalchuk.

Public Relations Director: Dennis Henke.

Tickets: $5.50–6.00 ($3.50 children, senior citizens), at stadium and BASS outlets.

Souvenirs: at stadium.

Game Times: 7:05 (Monday–Saturday), 2:05 (Sunday).

LAS VEGAS STARS
San Diego Padres
850 Las Vegas Blvd. N., Las Vegas, NV 89101.
(702) 386-7200.

Cashman Field (seats 9,370): on Las Vegas Blvd. north of downtown.

President and General Manager: Larry Koentopp.

Public Relations Director: Bob Blum.

Tickets: $3.50–4.50 ($1.50 children, $2.00 military, senior citizens, students), at stadium and Ticketron.

Souvenirs: at stadium.

Game Times: 7:05 (Monday–Saturday), 1:05 (Sunday).

PHOENIX FIREBIRDS
San Francisco Giants

Minor League Baseball and Beer

The lines at the beer stands are shorter. The beer is colder. It's certainly cheaper and more plentiful. And there's no better feeling than to stretch out in the bleachers at a minor league baseball game, with a program in your lap and a beer in your right hand. Especially if it's dusk, when the heat of the day is beginning to lift and a gentle breeze is blowing to right field.

Ever since the 1880s, when wily old Chris Von Der Ahe bought the St. Louis Browns in order to secure the right to sell beer at Sportsman's Park, major league baseball and beer have enjoyed a special relationship. But despite Augie Busch's laps-around-the-field-at-Busch-Stadium folksiness, the environment for beer lovers at major league ballparks has become downright hostile. Aside from high prices—$3 or more is not uncommon for a *small* cup—casual drinkers are confronted by warm, flat beer, guilt trips from frequent antidrinking announcements, and the infamous no-beer sections.

"At a major league ballpark, they take your money, herd you to your seat, herd you back out again, and hope you might buy some food or a beer," says Jim Paul, president of the El Paso Diablos and the czar of an annual minor league promotions seminar that attracts executives from across the country. "In minor league baseball, the attitude is, it's great to have you here, we hope you enjoy the game . . . beer lends itself to an atmosphere like that."

At major league games, obnoxious drunks are inevitably given free rein to slosh beer over their neighbors. "Beer drinking is not a problem for the 22 million people who attended minor league games last year," Paul says. "When somebody's had one too many, the vendors are going to tell the general manager, and he'll take care of the problem."

"I don't buy the premise that you've gotta have a beer to have a good time," says Dave Chase, general manager of the Durham, North Carolina–based Baseball Concessions Inc., which operates concessions for several minor league clubs. "But it can be a positive part of the atmosphere at the ballpark."

Aside from the aesthetic factors, beer is essential to the profitablity of minor league teams. Beer sales range from 30 to 50 percent of a club's gross income from concessions.

In most cases, clubs that cannot sell beer wither and die. In Gastonia, North Carolina, in the heart of the Bible Belt, the local Class-A team in the South Atlantic League finally was granted a beer license in 1989. Attendance immediately increased threefold.

San Bernardino, California, is the home of one of the most successful minor league teams in the country. The San Bernardino Spirit drew more than 150,000 mostly beer-drinking fans in 1988. Ten miles down the road, the Riverside Red Wave, who won the California League championship, drew a meager 60,000. Riverside has been unable to secure a beer license from the state of California.

"If they don't get it, they'll go under," says Larry Schmittou, president and general manager of the Triple-A Nashville Sounds. "It'll double their per-capita."

A collective shudder ran through the world of minor league baseball in 1985, when the Class-A Madison (Wisconsin) Muskies were canceled by their liability insurance carrier. The insurance company was afraid of alcohol-related claims. The Muskies stopped selling beer for weeks, as crowds and profits plummeted. Ultimately the National Association of Professional Baseball Leagues, minor league baseball's governing body, set up a special group-insurance plan to which any minor league club can subscribe.

As the end of the century approaches, minor league baseball is riding a wave of popularity unseen since the golden age of the 1940s and '50s. Clubs that used to change hands for $1 and assumption of debts are now selling for millions.

And the fashionable thing to do is to promote a family atmosphere. Beer nights are no longer welcome.

"What brought us to the decision was that eighteen- to twenty-year-olds were coming out here to get drunk," Paul says. "They didn't care about baseball. Our attendance was beginning to drop because people didn't want to be at a baseball stadium with a crowd like that. So we junked the ten-cent beer night for a ten-cent hot dog night. It's a family thing, and that's increased attendance."

Schmittou, a Southern gentleman who used to be the baseball coach at Vanderbilt, was ahead of the trend. "I've never used beer nights, and I never will. It is successful in some cities, but if I had to do it, I'd get out of the game."

Schmittou is no prohibitionist. His clubs sell 16-ounce beers for $1.75 and 24-ounce cups for $2.50—slightly higher than the prices in most minor league cities. And don't tell him no-alcohol seating solves anything.

"I don't think nondrinking sections work. I've proved they don't work," he asserts. "When I started the team in Huntsville, they wouldn't give me a permit to sell beer unless we had a nondrinking section. Well, we sold 1,700 season tickets, and do you know how many we sold in the nondrinking section? Two. We can never sell that section out unless no other seats are available. In Nashville, we have a 220-seat section set off. Nobody sits in it."

So, fellow beer lovers, it looks like our rights are secure. Now truck on down to your nearest minor league park and stake out a seat in the bleachers. The beer vendor will be along shortly.   —JS

5999 E. Van Buren St., Phoenix, AZ 85008.

(602) 275-0500.

Phoenix Municipal Stadium (seats 7,983): north of I-10 east of downtown, near Sky Harbor Airport.

President: Martin Stone. General Manager: Greg Corns.

Public Relations Director: Craig Pletenik.

Tickets: $3.00–5.00 ($2.00 children, senior citizens), at stadium and Dillard's Ticket Outlets.

Souvenirs: at stadium and at Olé Stadium store at Tower Plaza Mall.

Game Times: 7:05 (Monday–Saturday), 6:05 (Sunday)

PORTLAND BEAVERS
Minnesota Twins
P.O. Box 1659, Portland, OR 97207.
(503): 223-2837.

Civic Stadium (seats 26,500): off I-5 on Morrison, 1 block south of Burnside.

President: Joe Buzas. General Manager: Mark Helminiak.

Public Relations Director: John Christensen.

Tickets: $4.00–6.00 ($2.00 children).

Souvenirs: at stadium.

Game Times: 7:15 (Monday–Saturday), 1:30 (Sunday).

TACOMA TIGERS
Oakland Athletics
P.O. Box 11087, Tacoma, WA 98411.
(206) 752-7707.

Cheney Stadium (seats 8,002): just off I-5 on Highway 16.

President and General Manager: Stan Naccarato.

Public Relations Director: Steve Spry.

Tickets: $3.00–5.00.

Souvenirs: at stadium.

Game Times: 7:35 (Monday–Saturday), 2:00 (Sunday, holiday).

TUCSON TOROS
Houston Astros
P.O. Box 27045, Tucson, AZ 85726.
(602) 325-2621.

Hi Corbett Field (seats 9,500): in Randolph Park east of town on Broadway.

President: Richard Holtzman. General Manager: Monty Hoppel.

Tickets: $3.00–5.00 ($2.00 children, senior citizens, military).

Souvenirs: at stadium.

Game Times: 7:00 (Monday–Saturday), 6:00 (Sunday).

VANCOUVER CANADIANS
Chicago White Sox
4601 Ontario St., Vancouver, BC V5V 3H4.

(604) 872-5232.

Nat Bailey Stadium (seats 6,500): on Ontario St. near 41st.

President: John Winter. General Manager: Brent Imlach.

Tickets: $5.00–6.00 ($3.00 children, senior citizens), at stadium and TicketMaster.

Souvenirs: at stadium.

Game Times: 7:05 (Monday–Saturday), 1:30 (Sunday).

Double-A

Eastern League

The Eastern League spent much of the 1980s as a league of contradictions. On the one hand, major league teams hated the EL's early-season weather, which could include snow in places like Vermont and Glens Falls. On the other, teams in the Northeast loved the idea of having a Double-A affiliate so close to home. Some EL ballparks were rundown and others weren't even suited for baseball, but distances were shorter and travel much easier than in the other two Double-A leagues. Eastern League teams rarely did well at the gate, yet because so many wealthy Northeasterners wanted a piece of the minor league baseball boom, EL franchises were among the most valuable in the business.

Well, you get the picture. By the end of the decade, the Eastern League had expanded its boundaries westward to Canton, Ohio, and London, Ontario. This would no longer be the nice little compact league. But neither would the facilities lag behind the rest of baseball. The addition of Albany and Harrisburg gave the EL a pair of vibrant cities and fancy stadiums. Other cities, including Reading, upgraded their facilities.

The Eastern League still gives people from the large metro areas of the Northeast a chance to experience minor league baseball. Albany and New Britain are easy

Some Minor League Records

• *Most Games, Career* (All Minor Leagues), George Whiteman, 1905–29: 3,282.

• *Most Runs Scored, Career* (All Minor Leagues), Spencer Harris, 1921–48: 2,287.

• *Most Runs Scored, Season,* Tony Lazzeri, Salt Lake City, Pacific Coast League, 1925: 202.

• *Most Hits, Season,* Paul Strand, Salt Lake City, PCL, 1923: 325.

• *Most Doubles, Season,* Lyman Lamb, Tulsa, Western League, 1924: 100.

• *Most Home Runs, Season,* Joe Bauman, Roswell Longhorn League, 1954: 72.

• *Runs Batted In, Season,* Bob Crues, Amarillo West Texas–New Mexico League, 1948: 254.

• *Stolen Bases, Season* (Since 1900), Vince Coleman, Macon South Atlantic League, 1983: 145.

• *Highest Batting Average, Career* (Minimum ten years, All Minor Leagues), Ike Boone: .370.

drives from New York and Boston, and Reading and Harrisburg make good day trips from Philadelphia. Fans from Baltimore or Washington don't need to stay overnight to see the Orioles' Double-A club in Hagerstown. And Indians fans can head an hour down I-77 to Canton. The league that struggled during the 1970s and was the butt of many jokes in the early 1980s is now alive and well.

ALBANY-COLONIE YANKEES
New York Yankees
Albany-Shaker Road, Albany, NY 12211.
(518) 869-9236.
Heritage Park (seats 5,700): at Exit 4 off I-87, on Albany-Shaker Rd.
President: Paul Keating. General Manager: Ralph Acampora.
Vice President, Public Relations: Rip Rowan.
Tickets: $3.75–4.75.
Souvenirs: at stadium.
Game Times: 7:05 (Monday–Friday all year, Saturday July–August), 2:05 (weekends April–June), 5:05 (Sunday rest of year).

CANTON-AKRON INDIANS
Cleveland Indians
Canton, OH 44707.
(216) 456-5100.
Thurman Munson Memorial Stadium (seats 5,600): at Exit 103 off I-77.
President: Mike Agganis. General Manager: Sam Polizzi.
Public Relations Director: Geoffrey Belzer.
Tickets: $3.50–4.50, at stadium and at Ticketron outlets.
Souvenirs: at stadium.
Game Times: 7:05 (Monday–Saturday), 1:05 (Sunday).

HAGERSTOWN SUNS
Baltimore Orioles
P.O. Box 230, Hagerstown, MD 21741.
(301) 791-6266.
Municipal Stadium (seats 6,000): at Memorial Blvd. and Cannon Ave.

President: Peter Kirk. General Manager: Bob Miller.
Tickets: $4.00–5.00 ($2.00 children, senior citizens, military), at stadium and at Pro Image in the Fredericktown Mall.
Souvenirs: at stadium.
Game Times: 7:35, 2:35 (Sunday April–May).

HARRISBURG SENATORS
Pittsburgh Pirates
P.O. Box 15757, Harrisburg, PA 17105.
(717) 231-4444.
Riverside Stadium (seats 5,000): on City Island, just south of downtown Harrisburg.
President: Scott Carter. General Manager: Rick Redd.
Public Relations Director: Mark Mattern.
Tickets: $3.00–5.50 ($1.50 children, senior citizens), at stadium, and at club office on 2nd St., and the Ticket Place in Strawberry Square.
Souvenirs: at stadium, at Shenk Athletic, and Mr. T's Sportswear.
Game Times: 7:05 (Monday–Saturday), 2:05 (Sunday).

LONDON TIGERS
Detroit Tigers
89 Wharncliffe Rd. N., London, Ont. N6H 2A7.
(519) 645-2255.
Labatt Park (seats 6,000): on Queens Ave. near Wellington Rd. N.
President: Dan Ross. General Manager: Bob Gilson.
Public Relations Director: Steve Howe.
Tickets: $4.00–6.50 ($3.00 children, senior citizens).
Souvenirs: at stadium and club office.
Game Times: 7:00 (weeknights), 1:30 (weekends).

NEW BRITAIN RED SOX
Boston Red Sox
P.O. Box 1718, New Britain, CT 06050.
(203) 224-8383.
Beehive Field (seats 4,000): at Willow-brook Park Complex.
President: Hilary Buzas. General Manager: Gerry Berthiaume.
Tickets: $3.50–4.50 ($1.50 children, $2.00 senior citizens).
Souvenirs: at stadium.
Game Times: 7:15 (Monday–Saturday), 2:00 (Sunday).

READING PHILLIES
Philadelphia Phillies.
P.O. Box 15050, Reading, PA 19612.
(215) 375-8469.
Reading Municipal Stadium (seats 7,500): off Pennsylvania Rte. 61.
President: Craig Stein. General Manager: Chuck Domino.
Public Relations Director: Jan Steven Marcus.
Tickets: $3.50–4.50 ($1.50 children, senior citizens).
Souvenirs: at stadium.
Game Times: 7:05 (Monday–Saturday), 1:35 (Sunday).

WILLIAMSPORT BILLS
Seattle Mariners
P.O. Box 474, Williamsport, PA 17703.
(717) 321-1210.
Bowman Field (seats 3,500): on W. 4th St. near Maynard St.
President: Stuart Revo. General Manager: Rich Kluczyk.
Tickets: $2.75–4.50 ($2.25 children, senior citizens).
Souvenirs: at stadium.
Game Times: 7:05 (Monday–Saturday), 2:05 (Sunday).

Southern League

Think for a moment about the most time you've ever spent on a bus. Then think about the players in the Southern League, which stretches from Orlando and Jacksonville in the south and east to Memphis in the north and west. "It's not too bad overnight," said one SL veteran. "The problem is when you wake up in the morning, and you've still got five or six hours to go." Not every SL trip is so long, but the ride from Orlando to Memphis is almost 800 miles.

But forget about the bus rides for a minute. Unless you plan on playing in the league, you don't need to take them. And if you want to see a league as a fan, the SL isn't a bad place to go. Modern stadiums in Birmingham, Huntsville, Greenville, and Charlotte are among the nicest in minor league baseball. Few people wanted to see the Birmingham Barons abandon beautiful old Rickwood Field, but no one complained about brand-new Hoover Metropolitan Stadium. The Memphis park isn't new, but it's been kept up very well and is a fun place to watch a game. Birmingham, Memphis, Huntsville, and Greenville also compete each year for the league's top attendance total, and all prove that baseball interest is alive and well in the Southeast.

BIRMINGHAM BARONS
Chicago White Sox
P.O. Box 360007, Birmingham, AL 35236.
(205) 988-3200.

Hoover Metropolitan Stadium (seats 10,000): at Hwy. 150 off I-459 in Hoover, south of Birmingham.

President: Jack Levin. General Manager: Art Clarkson.

Public Relations Director: Rusty Radwin.

Tickets: $3.00–4.00 ($2.00 children).

Souvenirs: at stadium.

Game Times: 7:30, 2:00 (Sunday April–May).

CHARLOTTE KNIGHTS
Chicago Cubs
2280 Deerfield Dr., Fort Mill, SC 29715.
(704) 332-3746 or (803) 548-8051.

Multipurpose Stadium (seats 10,000): on I-77 in York County, S.C., 3 miles south of the North Carolina border.

President: Roman Gabriel. General Manager: Bill Lavelle.

Public Relations Director: Tanya Whipple.

Tickets: $3.00–5.00 ($1.00 children, senior citizens).

Souvenirs: at stadium, Belks stores, TC Sports stores, and Kerr Drug Stores.

Game Times: 7:30 (Monday–Saturday), 5:00 (Sunday).

CHATTANOOGA LOOKOUTS
Cincinnati Reds
P.O. Box 11002, Chattanooga, TN 37401.
(615) 267-2208

Engel Stadium (seats 8,000): at 4th St. exit on I-124.

President: Richard Holtzman. General Manager: Bill Lee.

Tickets: $2.75–4.75 ($1.75 children).

Souvenirs: at stadium.

Game Times: 7:00 (Monday–Saturday), 2:00 (Sunday).

COLUMBUS MUDCATS
Houston Astros
P.O. Box 2425, Columbus, GA 31902.
(404) 324-3594.

Golden Park (seats 6,000): at Hwy. 280 and U.S. 27.

President: Steve Bryant. General Manager: Joe Kremer.

Tickets: $2.50–4.00 ($1.50 children, senior citizens, military).

Souvenirs: at stadium.

Game Times: 7:35, 2:05 (Sunday April–May).

GREENVILLE BRAVES
Atlanta Braves
P.O. Box 16683, Greenville, SC 29606.
(803) 299-3456.

Greenville Municipal Stadium (seats 7,023): two miles east of I-85 at Mauldin Road.

President: Stan Kasten. General Manager: Steve DeSalvo.

Public Relations Director: Jeff Phillips.

Tickets: $3.00–5.00 ($2.00 children).

Souvenirs: at stadium and Pantry stores.

Game Times: 7:15, 2:15 (Sunday).

HUNTSVILLE STARS
Oakland Athletics
P.O. Box 14099, Huntsville, AL 35815.
(205) 882-2562.

Joe W. Davis Stadium (seats 10,250): south of Hwy. 20 on Memorial Parkway.

President: Larry Schmittou. General Manager: Bill MacKay.

Tickets: $3.00–5.00.

Souvenirs: at stadium, and at Merle Harmon Fan Fare in Madison Square Mall.

Game Times: 7:35, 2:05 (Sunday April–May).

JACKSONVILLE EXPOS
Montreal Expos
P.O. Box 4756, Jacksonville, FL 32201.
(904) 358-2846.

Wolfson Park (seats 8,200): next to the Gator Bowl.

President: Peter Bavasi, Sr. General Manager: Peter Bavasi, Jr.

Tickets: $3.00–5.00.

Souvenirs: at stadium.

Game Times: 7:35, 2:35 (some Sundays).

KNOXVILLE BLUE JAYS
Toronto Blue Jays
633 Jessamine St., Knoxville, TN 37917.
(615) 525-3809.

Bill Meyer Stadium (seats 8,000): at 5th Ave. and Jessamine St., south of I-40.

President: Paul Beeston. General Manager: Gary McCune.

Tickets: $3.50–4.50 ($2.50 children).

Souvenirs: at stadium.

Game Times: 7:30 (Monday–Saturday), 2:00 (Sunday).

MEMPHIS CHICKS
Kansas City Royals
800 Home Run Lane, Memphis, TN 38104.
(901) 272-1687.

Tim McCarver Stadium (seats 10,000): in the state fairgrounds, next to the Liberty Bowl and the Mid-South Coliseum.

General Manager: Pete Rizzo.

(Cont. p. 244.)

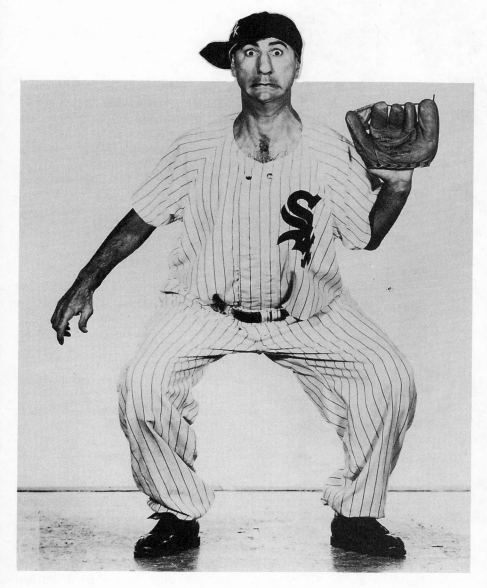

The venerable Clown Prince of Baseball.

The Great Baseball Entertainers and Mascots

1. *The Famous Chicken.* Hatched in 1974 as a mascot for a San Diego radio station, the Chicken remains a rare bird. Ted Giannoulas performs a variety of wing-flapping routines at approximately 125 baseball games a year. The act has been popular for a long time, yet, the Chicken still has the ability to pack a minor league park—even on traditionally slow Monday and Tuesday nights. The Famous Chicken's rates range from $1,500 a night for a performance at a single-A park to $2,500 for a Triple-A site. He is not available for private parties. Contact Jane Bernard at The Famous Chicken, 3675 Ruffin Rd. #220, San Diego, CA, 92123, phone (619) 278-1987.

2. *Max Patkin, the Clown Prince of Baseball.* Has Max really been around forever, or does it only seem that way? Minor league fans have been digging his crazy act since 1946, but Max finally received national attention because of his cameo role in the 1987 film *Bull Durham.* The producers wanted to fit in a couple of scenes in which Max dies on the field during a game and his historic ashes are sprinkled on the pitcher's mound at historic Durham Athletic Park. But, no bull, the scene died on the cutting-room floor. In any event, Max's career is alive and well, and his rates have gone up to around $1,200 a night, but he's still a bargain. Private parties? You can try. Contact The Clown Prince of Baseball at 2000 Valley Forge Circle #837, King of Prussia, PA, 19406, phone (215) 783-5933.

3. *The Miami Maniac.* Keep an eye on the guy in the furry green costume. The Maniac has a creative act, full of improvisation and mimicry. John Routh got his start as Cocky, the Gamecock mascot, as a student at the University of South Carolina in the early eighties. His allegiance was swayed by a full-time job offer from the University of Miami, where he appears at all basketball and baseball games. He's also the official mascot of the College World Series. All that contract labor limits him to about 25 appearances a year at minor league baseball games. But the Maniac's contract with Miami expires soon, and he's hoping to be able to increase his national exposure. He's worth every penny of the $1,500–2,000 appearance fee. The Maniac is available for parties and charity functions, although he does most of this type of work in South Florida. The Miami Maniac, 6200 S.W. 57th Drive, Miami, FL, 33143, phone (305) 666-0230.

4a and 4b. *The Philly Phanatic and Fredbird* are probably the best-known and least-reviled mascots for major league teams. The Phanatic has a more raucous routine and performs more regularly outside of his home base (10–15 minor league dates a year). At around $2,500 a pop, he's also more expensive. Contact Chris Legault care of the Philadelphia Phillies, P.O. Box 7575, Philadelphia, PA, 19101, phone (215) 463-6000. The Cardinals bill Fredbird as "the premier mascot in the Mid-

west." With more than 200 charity and team-related bookings a year in the St. Louis area, Fredbird only makes about a half dozen appearances at minor league parks—most of which are home to Cardinals' farm teams. But if you live nearby and the schedule works out, he'll liven up your party for between $275 and $550. Contact John Kendall care of the St. Louis Cardinals, 250 Stadium Place, St. Louis, MO, 63102, phone (314) 421-4040.

5. *Captain Dynamite*. At seventy-three, Captain Dynamite, a.k.a. Patrick "Midnight" O'Brien, has his sights set on becoming the oldest stuntman in history. With luck, Captain Dynamite will make it to seventy-five, breaking the record set by Karl Wallenda, who fell off a tightrope at seventy-four. The Captain's act is pretty simple, really. He constructs a makeshift

paper coffin behind second base, then climbs in and lies down, wearing only a crash helmet for protection. He pushes an unseen button and BOOM!, the coffin disintegrates and the Captain flies through the air and lands on his keister. The Captain has been traveling the circuit blowing himself up since 1953. He performs at a number of festivals and functions, as well as at about two dozen minor league games a year. There's a Lady Dynamite (no relation) running around out there now, but insist on the original. Contact Captain Dynamite care of Midnight O'Brien, 9215 East Avenue P, Houston, TX, 77012, phone (713) 928-6035.   —JS

The 1950s had the Man in the Gray Flannel Suit; the 1980s got the Man in the Green Furry Suit.

Public Relations Director: Ted Tornow.

Tickets: $2.75–4.00 ($2.25 students, senior citizens, military), at stadium and TicketMaster outlets.

Souvenirs: at stadium and Pro Image stores.

Game Times: 7:15 (Monday–Saturday), 2:00 (Sunday).

ORLANDO TWINS
Minnesota Twins
P.O. Box 5645, Orlando, FL 32855.
(407) 849-6348.

Tinker Field (seats 6,000): next to the Citrus Bowl on Tampa Ave. South.

General Manager: Jamie Lowe.

Public Relations Director: Shereen Samonds.

Tickets: $3.00–5.00.

Souvenirs: at stadium, and at Maison Blanche stores.

Game Times: 7:05 (Monday–Saturday), 5:00 (Sunday).

Texas League

Seldom does one game so define a league's image as a game of April 30, 1983, defined the Texas League. That day at El Paso's Dudley Field, the host Diablos routed Beaumont, 35–21. And when people think of the Texas League, that's exactly the image that sticks in the mind. Pitchers shouldn't even be sent to this league. Just stand a pitching machine out on the mound. Better yet, set the ball on a tee. That might be just as challenging to the hitters.

In reality not every Texas League ballpark is a hitters' paradise. Even in El Paso, teams don't need 35 runs to win every game. But the short fences and hard infields of the TL's Western Division have given the league this reputation, and fans question any batting accomplishment.

El Paso has another reputation in minor league baseball, though. Club president Jim Paul is one of the minor leagues' leading promoters. A game at the Dudley Dome is a unique experience, with cheering from the public address announcer and cheerleaders dancing on the dugout roofs. Each fall, Paul and the Diablos run a marketing seminar which annually draws executives from the top minor league clubs. Arkansas's Bill Valentine, a former major league umpire, has also been a successful promoter. Valentine believes in getting fans to the ballpark any way possible, so be on the lookout for free tickets to almost every game. The Travelers also have more doubleheaders than any other minor league team; they play two on Saturday and rest on Sunday. As in the Southern League, the Texas League teams travel great distances to games. But a heavy division schedule limits the mileage, and several teams now fly on most road trips.

ARKANSAS TRAVELERS
St. Louis Cardinals
P.O. Box 5599, Little Rock, AR 72215.
(501) 664-1555.
Ray Winder Field (seats 5,975): off I-630 at War Memorial Park.
President: Bert Parke. General Manager: Bill Valentine.
Tickets: $3.00–4.00 ($1.00 children).
Souvenirs: at stadium.
Game Times: 7:30 (Monday–Friday), 6:30 (Saturday doubleheaders).

EL PASO DIABLOS
Milwaukee Brewers
P.O. Box 9337, El Paso, TX 79984.
(915) 544-1950.
New field (seats 10,000); NE El Paso, N-S Freeway close to Transmountain Drive.
President: Jim Paul. General Manager: Rick Parr.
Tickets: $3.50–4.50 ($2.50 children, senior citizens).
Souvenirs: at stadium.
Game Times: 7:00 (April–May), 7:30 (rest of year).

JACKSON METS
New York Mets
P.O. Box 4209, Jackson, MS 39296.
(601) 981-4664.

Smith-Wills Stadium (seats 5,200): East of I-55 at Lakeland Dr.
President: Con Maloney. General Manager: Bill Blackwell.
Tickets: $3.50–4.50 ($2.50 students, senior citizens).
Souvenirs: at stadium.
Game Times: 7:00 (Monday–Saturday), 2:00 (Sunday April–May), 6:00 (Sunday rest of year).

MIDLAND ANGELS
California Angels
P.O. Box 12, Midland, TX 79702.
(915) 683-4251.
Angel Stadium (seats 3,800): at the intersection of Lamesa Rd. and Loop 250.
President: Richard Holtzman. General Manager: Bill Davidson.
Tickets: $3.00–4.00 ($2.00 children, senior citizens), at stadium, and at the Odessa Chamber of Commerce.
Souvenirs: at stadium.
Game Times: 7:00 (Monday–Saturday), 6:00 (Sunday).

SAN ANTONIO MISSIONS
Los Angeles Dodgers
P.O. Box 28268, San Antonio, TX 78228.
(512) 434-9311.
V. J. Keefe Memorial Stadium (seats 3,500): at 36th and Culebra in northwest San Antonio.
President: Dave Elmore. General Manager: Burl Yarbrough.
Public Relations Director: Jim Wehmeier.
Tickets: $3.00–7.00 ($2.00 children), at stadium and local military bases, USAA and Southwest Research.
Souvenirs: at stadium.
Game Times: 7:05, 2:05 (first-half Sunday).

SHREVEPORT CAPTAINS
San Francisco Giants
P.O. Box 3448, Shreveport, LA 71133.
(318) 636-5555.
Fair Grounds Field (seats 5,400): on the Louisiana State Fairgrounds at I-20

and Hearne Avenue.
President: Taylor Moore. General Manager: Jon Long.
Tickets: $3.00–10.00 ($2.00 children).
Souvenirs: at stadium.
Game Times: 7:05 (April–May), 7:35 (rest of year).

TULSA DRILLERS
Texas Rangers
P.O. Box 4448, Tulsa, OK 74159.
(918) 744-5901.
Tulsa County Stadium (seats 8,350): on Yale Ave. at the Tulsa State Fairgrounds, south of I-244, north of I-44.
President: Went Hubbard. General Manager: Joe Preseren.
Media Relations Director: Brian Carroll.
Tickets: $3.00–5.00.
Souvenirs: at stadium.
Game Times: 7:35 (Monday–Saturday), 2:05 (Sunday April–May), 6:05 (Sunday rest of year).

WICHITA WRANGLERS
San Diego Padres
P.O. Box 1420, Wichita, KS 67201.
(316) 267-3372.
Lawrence-Dumont Stadium (seats 7,488): West of I-135 on Kellogg Ave. at Sycamore.
President: Bob Rich, Jr. General Manager: Steve Shaad.
Tickets: $3.00–5.00 ($1.00 children, senior citizens).
Souvenirs: at stadium.
Game Times: 7:15 (Monday–Saturday), 2:15 (Sunday).

Class A

California League

There was a time when the California League would have been better known as the Central California League. Conceding the state's metropolitan areas to major league baseball, the Cal League concentrated on cities like Lodi, Visalia, and Stockton. Not that there's anything wrong with any of those towns, but they don't exactly conjure up the visions of California held by most of the country. No bright lights, no movie stars, not many flakes. There was always a team in San Jose, but the independent Bees had more headlines than fans. And there were a few attempts at settling in Southern California, none of them great successes.

Then came San Bernardino. When the former Lodi franchise settled there in 1987 after a troubled season in Ventura, it helped change the face of Cal League baseball. The Spirit quickly became the league's attendance leader, despite being only 1 1/2 hours from Dodger Stadium. A strong Southern Division developed with Riverside, Palm Springs, and Bakersfield. Other teams around the league tried to replicate the San Bernardino atmosphere. And other cities thought about building ballparks to create their own Spirit.

The Cal League still hasn't found a solution to its other major problem—geography. The league has trouble finding working agreements for all of its teams, because not many teams from the East are looking for a West Coast Class A affiliate. The Giants love having a team just down the road in San Jose, the Dodgers are happy developing fans two hours up the road in Bakersfield, but the Orioles would rather have their players close to home in Frederick. If California League president Joe Gagliardi finds an answer to that problem, Cal League expansion won't be very far behind.

BAKERSFIELD DODGERS
Los Angeles Dodgers
P.O. Box 10031, Bakersfield, CA 93389.
(805) 322-1363.

Sam Lynn Ball Park (seats 3,000): on Chester Ave., north of California Ave.

President: Lowell Patton. General Manager: Rick Smith.

Tickets: $2.50–3.50 ($2.00 senior citizens, military; $1.50 children).

Souvenirs: at stadium.

Game Times: 7:30 (April), 7:45 (May),

8:00 (rest of the year).

MODESTO A'S
Oakland Athletics
P.O. Box 2437, Modesto, CA 95351.
(209) 529-7368.

Thurman Field (seats 2,500): on Neece Drive near Tuolomne Blvd.-B St. exit on Hwy. 99.

President: Burton Boltuch. General Manager: Dan Kiser.

Tickets: $3.00–4.00 ($1.50 children, senior citizens).

Souvenirs: at stadium.

Game Times: 7:30, 2:00 (Sunday April–May).

PALM SPRINGS ANGELS
California Angels
P.O. Box 1742, Palm Springs, CA 92263.
(619) 325-4487.

Angels Stadium (seats 5,185): on Baristo Road, one block east of Sunrise Way.

President: Bruce Corwin. General Manager: Marshall Stone.

Tickets: $3.00–3.50 ($1.50 children, $2.50 senior citizens).

Souvenirs: at stadium.

Game Times: 7:30.

RENO SILVER SOX
Independent
P.O. Box 11363, Reno, NV 89510.
(702) 825-0678.

Moana Stadium (seats 4,500): on Moana Lane, west of U.S. 395.

President: Jerry Leider. General Manager: Jack Patton.

Tickets: $3.00–4.00 ($2.00 children).

Souvenirs: at stadium.

Game Times: 7:00 (Monday–Saturday), 1:00 (Sunday).

RIVERSIDE RED WAVE
San Diego Padres
P.O. Box 5487, Riverside, CA 92517.
(714) 682-8880.

Riverside Sports Center (seats 3,500): on Blaine Ave., north of the 60 Freeway.

President: Bobby Brett. General Manager: Leanne Pagliai.

Tickets: $2.50–4.50.

Souvenirs: at stadium.

Game Times: 7:05, 1:05 (Sunday April–May).

SALINAS SPURS
Co-op
P.O. Box 4370, Salinas, CA 93912.
(408) 422-3812.

Salinas Municipal Stadium (seats 3,540): on Maryal, north of Laurel.

President: Joe Buzas. General Manager: John Christensen.

Tickets: $2.50–3.50 ($1.50 children, senior citizens).

Souvenirs: at stadium.

Game Times: 6:30 (Monday–Saturday April–May), 7:00 (Monday–Saturday rest of year), 1:30 (Sunday).

SAN BERNARDINO SPIRIT
Seattle Mariners
P.O. Box 30160, San Bernardino, CA 92143.
(714) 881-1836.

Fiscalini Field (seats 3,000): on Highland Ave. off I-215 in north San Bernardino.

President: Henry Stickney. General Manager: Bill Shanahan.

Tickets: $2.00–3.00 ($1.00 children).

Souvenirs: at stadium.

Game Times: 7:05 (Monday–Saturday), 1:05 (Sunday April–June), 6:05 (Sunday rest of year).

SAN JOSE GIANTS
San Francisco Giants
P.O. Box 21727, San Jose, CA 95151.
(408) 297-1435.

San Jose Municipal Stadium (seats 5,200): at S. 10th and E. Alma Sts.

President: Richard Beahrs. General Manager: Harry Steve.

Tickets: $3.00–4.00 ($1.00 children, senior citizens), at stadium and BASS ticket outlets.

Souvenirs: at stadium, Giant Dugout Stores, and The Sports Fan in San Jose.

Game Times: 7:15 (weekdays), 5:00 (Saturday, second-half Sunday), 2:00 (first-half Sunday).

STOCKTON PORTS
Milwaukee Brewers
Sutter and Alpine, Stockton, CA 95204.
(209) 944-5943.

Billy Hebert Field (seats 3,500): on Alpine east of I-5 and west of Hwy. 99.

Chairman of the Board: Geoffrey Cowan. General Manager: Don Miller.

Tickets: $3.00–4.00 ($1.50 children, senior citizens).

Souvenirs: at stadium.

Game Times: 7:30 (Monday–Saturday), 1:00 (first-half Sunday), 6:00 (second-half Sunday).

VISALIA OAKS
Minnesota Twins
P.O. Box 48, Visalia, CA 93279.
(209) 625-0480.

Recreation Park (seats 2,000): On Giddings Ave., north of Hwy. 198.

President: Stanley Simpson. General Manager: Bruce Bucz.

Tickets: $2.50–4.50 ($1.50 students).

Souvenirs: at stadium.

Game Times: 7:35.

Carolina League

The world discovered the Carolina League in 1988, when Hollywood released *Bull Durham*. Carolina League fans had only discovered it a few years earlier. In the 1970s, when even the original Durham Bulls went out of business, the CL was at one point reduced to four teams. The Bulls returned in 1980, and soon after that the CL became the strongest of the Class A leagues.

Even before the movie, Durham had more success than all but a few minor league teams on any level. Hagerstown did so well in the CL that the Suns' owners went out and bought a Double-A team to put there. A struggling franchise in Alexandria, Va., became a strong one when

nearby Prince William County built a new stadium. By the end of the 1980s, cities as far north as Delaware were lining up to get into the CL.

Arguments will continue about whether the California or Carolina League is the strongest Class A league on the field, but both can be considered "fast" A leagues. The Carolina League was helped in the early 1980s by a run of strong teams in Peninsula, where the Philadelphia Phillies sent first Julio Franco and then Juan Samuel, and in Lynchburg, where the New York Mets sent stars Darryl Strawberry, Dwight Gooden, and Gregg Jefferies. Both those organizations have left the CL, but improvements in the Braves and Indians organizations have kept the league strong.

DURHAM BULLS
Atlanta Braves
P.O. Box 507, Durham, NC 27702.
(919) 688-8211.

Durham Athletic Park (seats 5,000): at Morris and Corporation Sts., just north of the downtown Durham loop.

President: Miles Wolff. General Manager: Rob Dlugozima.

Tickets: $3.00–4.50 ($2.00 children, senior citizens), available at stadium and at Ballpark Corner in Northgate Mall, and at Extra Innings in Greystone Village in north Raleigh.

Souvenirs: at stadium and Ballpark Corner at Northgate Mall.

Game Times: 7:30, 2:30 (Sunday April–May).

FREDERICK KEYS
Baltimore Orioles
P.O. Box 3169, Frederick, MD 21701.
(301) 662-0013.

McCurdy Field (seats 3,500): on Jefferson St., north of I-70.

General Manager: Keith Lupton.

Tickets: $3.00–4.50 ($1.50 children, senior citizens, military).

Souvenirs: at stadium.

(Cont. p. 248.)

Why "Bush League?"

The terms "bush league" and "farm team" have grown beyond the realm of baseball into common usage, but their origins remain cloudy.

The *Dickson Baseball Dictionary* cites a New York *Herald Tribune* article in 1898 for the first use of the phrase "*farm team*." Back then Cincinnati owner John Brush was using his secret network of minor league teams to draft players indiscriminately, against the spirit of the National Agreement that governed baseball. The practice became known as syndicate baseball or Brushism, and it gave farm systems a bad name until the 1920s, when Branch Rickey rehabilitated the idea over the protests of Commissioner Landis and others. Whether these early affiliates became known as farm teams due to their location (out in farm country) or function (a place to raise players before bringing them to market) is not known.

"Bush" first emerged around 1905 as a synonym for minor league, apparently derived from the undeveloped condition of minor league towns. Throughout the English-speaking world, the bush is considered wild and untamed, but it took baseball to add the pitiable connotation now associated with things bush. It remains to be seen whether the current presidential administration can further redefine the term. —EJC

Game Times: 7:30, 2:00 (Sunday April–May).

KINSTON INDIANS
Cleveland Indians
P.O. Box 3542, Kinston, NC 28502.
(919) 527-9111 or 527-5651.
Grainger Stadium (seats 4,100): on Grainger Ave., just north of Hwy. 11 and east of U.S. 70 Business.
Chairman of the Board: Stuart Revo. General Manager: North Johnson.
Tickets: $2.50–3.50 ($1.50 children, senior citizens).
Souvenirs: at stadium.
Game Times: 7:00, 3:00 (Sunday April–May).

LYNCHBURG RED SOX
Boston Red Sox
P.O. Box 10213, Lynchburg, VA 24506.
(804) 528-1144.
City Stadium (seats 4,200): just north of U.S. 29 at the City Stadium or Lynchburg College exit.
President: Calvin Fallwell. General Manager: Paul Sunwall.
Tickets: $3.00–3.50 ($2.00 students, senior citizens).
Souvenirs: at stadium.
Game Times: 7:00, 5:00 (Sunday April–May).

PENINSULA PILOTS
Co-op
P.O. Box 9194, Hampton, VA 23670.
(804) 244-2255.
War Memorial Stadium (seats 4,330): on Pembroke Ave., near the Powhatan exit off I-664.
General Manager: James Rhoades.
Tickets: $3.00–5.00 ($2.00 children, senior citizens, military).
Souvenirs: at stadium.
Game Times: 7:00 (Monday–Saturday), 2:00 (Sunday).

PRINCE WILLIAM CANNONS
New York Yankees
P.O. Box 2148, Woodbridge, VA 22193.

(703) 590-2311.
Prince William County Stadium (seats 6,000): on Davis Ford Road, 5 miles west of I-95.
President: Jack Tracz. General Manager: Jeff Mercer.
Public Relations Director: Karis Kercher.
Tickets: $3.00–4.50 ($2.00 children, senior citizens).
Souvenirs: at stadium.
Game Times: 7:30 (Monday–Saturday), 2:00 (Sunday).

SALEM BUCCANEERS
Pittsburgh Pirates
P.O. Box 842, Salem, VA 24153.
(703) 389-3333.
Municipal Field (seats 5,000): on Florida St. near downtown Salem.
President: Kelvin Bowles. General Manager: Sam Lazzaro.
Tickets: $2.50–3.50 ($1.50 children, senior citizens).
Souvenirs: at stadium.
Game Times: 7:00, 2:00 (Sunday April–May).

WINSTON-SALEM SPIRITS
Chicago Cubs
P.O. Box 4488, Winston-Salem, NC 27115.
(919) 722-5333.
Ernie Shore Field (seats 4,280): just west of U.S. 52, north of I-40 on 30th St. next to Groves Stadium.
Chairman of the Board: Peter Shipman. General Manager: William Blemings.
Tickets: $3.00–4.00 ($2.00 students, $1.50 senior citizens).
Souvenirs: at stadium.
Game Times: 7:00, 2:00 (Sunday April–May).

Florida State League

By some measures, the Florida State League is the most successful of baseball's Class A leagues. The league has fourteen teams, tied with the Midwest League for

the most in the minors. Other organizations stand in line waiting to get in. The facilities, most of which are also used for major league spring training, are the best around. The fields are in good condition, there's plenty of room for extra practice and the locker rooms are spacious and luxurious for Class A players. About the only thing missing from the FSL is fans.

While spring training can attract capacity crowds to ballparks in small towns, many FSL games are played before intimate gatherings. Communities like Kissimmee, Winter Haven, and Lakeland come alive during spring training. When the big leaguers leave, they revert to being sleepy towns. Other FSL teams, including Miami, Dunedin, and Clearwater, suffer from the minor-league-team-in-a-big-league-town syndrome. Fans in those big cities figure they have more important things to do than watch Class A baseball. They'll show up when Florida gets its expansion team.

A few FSL teams have learned how to break the mold. Vero Beach has continually drawn well, despite having one of the smallest populations in pro ball. Port Charlotte has also drawn better than expected. And St. Petersburg, despite its major league size, has supported the FSL Cardinals. The biggest question about the FSL, as it continues its expansion, is what effect a major league expansion team will have on the league. Will there be fewer fans, or will interest in baseball expand?

BASEBALL CITY ROYALS
Kansas City Royals
P.O. Box 800, Orlando, FL 32802.
(813) 424-7130 or (800) 826-1939 (out of state), (800) 367-2249 (Florida).
Baseball City Stadium (seats 7,000): on I-4 south of Orlando, at the intersection of U.S. 27 near Haines City.
President: Dick Howard. General Manager: Karl Rogozenski.
Public Relations Director: Dan Pearson.
Tickets: $3.00. *(Cont. p. 251.)*

The Best Food in the Minors

Pilot Field, Buffalo, New York—They still play minor league baseball in Buffalo, but there's nothing minor league about the food at beautiful Pilot Field (capacity 19,500, expandable to 40,000). Bob Rich's Buffalo Bisons played before 1,147,514 fans in 1988, a new minor league record. Since the team that year was mediocre, it's safe to assume many patrons kept coming back to sample the delicious charbroiled hotdogs ($1.50, foot-longs $2.25), made by Adrian's Meats of Buffalo. Adrian's also supplies the Bisons with Polish sausages, which are charbroiled and sold in buns smothered with peppers and onions ($2.25). The open-air food court on the main concourse features everything from ice cream (Rich's, of course) to barbecue to beef on weck (a local favorite, sliced roast beef on salty kaiser rolls). And, of course, no visit to Buffalo would be complete without an order of spicy chicken wings ($4.95 for 16). You can find them in Pettibone's Grill, the stylish restaurant on the first base side.

Cardinal Stadium, Louisville, Kentucky—The previous minor league attendance champ, Louisville still features the food-court concept that was copied by Buffalo. A wide variety of foods are available at a number of stands. Try one (or both) of the chicken sandwiches (barbecued $2.25, fried $2).

Herschel Greer Stadium, Nashville, Tennessee—Larry Schmittou wrought a revolution in minor league food service in the late seventies, when he introduced home-cooked pizza and began serving ice cream in miniature plastic souvenir batting helmets. Both ideas quickly spread throughout the industry, and their popularity even forced most major league concessionaires to begin offering them (at grossly inflated prices, to be sure). In Nashville, where Schmittou remains the

Sounds' president and general manager, you can pick one of five kinds of ice cream-in-a-helmet for $1.25, and the pizza costs $1.50 a slice. Schmittou says he sells one slice of pizza (cheese, pepperoni, or sausage) for every two people that enter the park. "That's very misleading, though," he says softly. "Very few people buy just one slice of our pizza." Schmittou also recommends the Southern-style barbecue sandwiches ($2.25), stuffed with barbecue cooked by Byron's of Nashville.

New Ballpark, El Paso, Texas—The Diablos, who invented ballpark nachos in 1974, abandoned sixty-five-year-old Dudley Field last year and plan to open 1990 in an as-yet-unnamed new stadium. But they're bringing all their signature food items with them. You still can sample the Diablo Burrito Hotdog ($1.25), a jalapeno-and-cheese-stuffed hot dog wrapped in a tortilla and smothered with cheese. Don't miss the sensational Mesilla Valley Mesquite Smoked Chicken, smoked in El Paso and grilled right at the ballpark. We're not talking wings or thighs here, folks. For $2.39, you get a quarter of a chicken.

Angel Stadium, Midland, Texas—Bring a healthy appetite with you when you come to a Midland Angels game. Then try the Jumburrito ($3.75). It's a foot-long tortilla wrapped around chunks of beef smothered with cheese, peppers, and onions. "One is probably the equivalent of eating three hot dogs," says Bill Davidson, general manager of the Angels. "You better get here early to have one. They always sell out." Angel Stadium also sells 64-oz. pitchers of beer for $8. You keep the pitcher, and refills are $5.

V. J. Keefe Stadium, San Antonio, Texas—The newly renamed San Antonio Missions specialize in a couple of regional delights. The most popular item is beef fajitas, which sell for $2. But general man-

ager Burl Yarbrough recommends the "Catcher's Mitt," a pita filled with spicy ground beef, sausage, onions, and spices ($2, hot sauce optional).

Durham Athletic Park, Durham, North Carolina—Before *Bull Durham*, the Durham Bulls made a name for themselves among minor league operators for their efficient and innovative concessions. Along the colorful, jam-packed walkways of historic Durham Athletic Park, you'll find stands selling home-cut french fries, steak sandwiches, and traditional ballpark fare (beer, hot dogs, and slices of pizza are still $1). The longest lines (and the best food) can be found at the Flying Burrito stand, which specializes in—you guessed it—the Flying Burrito (beef, beans, cheese, sour cream, etc., $3). There's also the Bull City Burrito (Polish sausage, beans, cheese, sour cream, and sauerkraut, $3). Be sure to ask for the hot sauce, and buy plenty of beer. The stand is operated by the Flying Burrito Restaurant in nearby Chapel Hill, which features the best Mexican food this side of El Paso.

Grainger Stadium, Kinston, North Carolina—Another great old Southern ballpark, Grainger Stadium is the home of the Carolina League's Kinston Indians. The concession stand at the red-brick park features a fried shrimp plate, with french fries and cole slaw ($3.50). General manager North Johnson recommends the barbecued chicken dinners, cooked on a big gas grill. A two-piece dinner is $2.50, and a three-piece dinner sells for $3.50. Both dinners include fries and slaw. If you're still hungry after the game, head for the Barbecue Lodge for some family-style, all-you-can-eat barbecue, barbecued and fried chicken, hush puppies, and delicious Brunswick stew.

The Diamond, Richmond, Virginia—You want greasy food when you go to a ball

game? Here's the ultimate. A calorie-packed corn dog $1.50, deep-fried to perfection. Take one, then skip lunch for the rest of the week. For a real taste treat, try a minced pork barbecue and a fresh limeade at Bill's Barbecue across from the park before or after the game.

Golden Park, Columbus, Georgia—When Columbus's Southern League team changed its name from the Astros to the Mudcats (named after a local variety of catfish) for the 1989 season, the club changed its concessions as well. Along with hot dogs and popcorn, the Mudcats offer "Muddy Fingers," (fried catfish fingers, $1.75 for six, $2 served in a souvenir helmet). There's homemade ice cream in flavors called "Mudcats" (vanilla, raspberry, and dark chocolate, which approximates the team colors) and "Muddy" (dark chocolate with gummy fish—sort of like gummy bears, but shaped like fish—embedded in it). The ice cream sells for $1 in a cone, and $1.25 in those all-important souvenir helmets. Like most teams in South Carolina and Georgia, the Mudcats sell that old Southern favorite, boiled peanuts ($2 for a ten-ounce bag). They taste a lot better than they look.

Meinen Field, Peoria, Illinois—Economic prosperity eluded Peoria during the eighties. So why are the Peoria Chiefs one of the top-drawing Class-A teams in the country? Some say it's the affiliation with the Chicago Cubs. But those who know better say it's the terrific boneless butterfly-pork chop sandwiches ($3.50) they sell at Meinen Field. Smothered in barbecue sauce, they melt in your mouth.

Lanphier Park, Springfield, Illinois—There's not much to Lanphier Park. It's a roofless aluminum structure, tucked off the main drag in Lincoln's hometown. But old Abe would have loved the charcoal-broiled steak sandwiches ($3).

Pohlman Field, Beloit, Wisconsin—At most ballparks in the upper Midwest, you'll find charcoal-grilled bratwurst on the menu. We chose to highlight Pohlman

Field because of the classic scene behind the counters as the all-volunteer concessions staff serves up the food and gabs with the customers. Buy your brat ($1.50) and an Old Style beer in the beer garden down the right-field line, sit down at one of the picnic tables, and relax. But watch out for foul balls!

Memorial Stadium, Boise, Idaho—When the Boise Hawks opened Memorial Stadium in 1989, they pulled out all the stops, establishing a concessions operation virtually unparalleled in variety of fare. The short-season Class-A club printed a two-page menu which includes combo burritos ($2.75), jumbo tacos ($1.75), charcoal-grilled Polish sausages ($2.25), spicy chorizo dogs ($2.25), hamburgers ($2.00), and hot dogs ($1.25). The more conservative fans might go to the Pizza Hut window and order a Personal Pan Pizza ($3). But you really should try one of the specialties: Super Nachos (a mountain of chips layered with beans, cheese, beef, tomatoes, olives, sour cream, green onions, and jalapenos, $5.50) or the ubiquitous Ball Park Baker (an Idaho potato split and filled with butter, beef, cheese, sour cream, and scallions, $2.75). For dessert there's Haagen-Dasz ice cream ($2.25), root beer floats ($2.00), and frozen Snickers bars (75 cents).

Derks Field, Salt Lake City—Salt Lake may be major league in basketball, but in baseball it's the home of the wildly successful Trappers (remember the 29-game

Derks Field, home of the veggie plate.

winning streak of 1987?) of the rookie-level Pioneer League. The brand of ball doesn't seem to matter to the fans, who turn out 6,000 strong each night. General manager Dave Baggott is particularly proud of the gourmet stuffed potatoes ($2.50), giant snow cones ($1.25), and, get ready, the vegetable platter. For $2, you get a plate full of carrots, celery, broccoli, and ranch dressing. "We are a health-conscious community in Salt Lake," Baggott says. "When people bring their kids out to a ball game, they don't want 'em filling up on junk food." But Dave, a *veggie plate?* "It sounds kind of bland," he admits, a bit defensively, "but dip 'em in the ranch sauce and it tastes quite nice."

Ray Winder Field, Little Rock, Arkansas—Don't tell Bill Valentine he ought to be selling any vegetable plates. The general manager of the Arkansas Travelers is an old-fashioned guy. "My theory is, I can't make a hamburger as good as Wendy's, I can't do roast beef as good as Arby's, and I can't do pizza as good as Pizza Hut," says Valentine, a former American League umpire. "But we can say we sell the best hot dog in town." The all-meat, locally made hot dogs, resplendent in a fresh-baked butter-batter bun, sell for $1. "We go for what a ballpark should sell," says Valentine, whose approach seems to work. The Travs annually are among the minor league attendance leaders.   —JS

Souvenirs: at stadium.

Game Times: 7:05.

CHARLOTTE RANGERS

Texas Rangers

P.O. Box 3609, Port Charlotte, FL 33949.

(813) 625-9500.

Charlotte County Stadium (seats 6,026): on El Jobean Road (S.R. 776), west of U.S. 41, north of Port Charlotte.

General Manager: Ted Guthrie.

Tickets: $2.75–3.75.

Souvenirs: at stadium.

Game Times: 7:00 (Monday–Saturday), 6:00 (Sunday).

CLEARWATER PHILLIES

Philadelphia Phillies

P.O. Box 10336, Clearwater, FL 34617.

(813) 441-8638.

Jack Russell Stadium (seats 5,106): at Seminole St. and Greenwood St.—use Drew St. off U.S. 19.

President: Bill Gargano. General Manager: Tom Mashek.

Tickets: $2.50–3.50 ($1.50 children, $1.00 senior citizens).

Souvenirs: at stadium.

Game Times: 7:00, 2:00 (Sunday April–May).

DUNEDIN BLUE JAYS

Toronto Blue Jays

P.O. Box 957, Dunedin, FL 34697.

(813) 733-9302.

Grant Field (seats 3,417): on Douglas Ave., one block east of Alt. U.S. 19.

General Manager: Ken Carson.

Tickets: $2.00–3.00 ($1.00 children, senior citizens).

Souvenirs: at stadium.

Game Times: 7:00 (Monday–Saturday), 6:00 (Sunday).

FORT LAUDERDALE YANKEES

New York Yankees

5301 NW 12th St., Fort Lauderdale, FL 33309.

(305) 776-1921.

Yankee Stadium (seats 7,211): just east

of I-95 on Commercial Blvd.

Chairman of the Board: Jim Ogle. General Manager: Mark Zettelmeyer.

Tickets: $2.50–3.50.

Souvenirs: at stadium.

Game Times: 7:00 (Monday–Saturday), 2:00 (Sunday).

LAKELAND TIGERS

Detroit Tigers

P.O. Box 2785, Lakeland, FL 33806.

(813) 686-1133.

Joker Marchant Stadium (seats 7,500): on Lakeland Hills Blvd., north of downtown and south of I-4.

President: Frank Decker. General Manager: Ronald Myers.

Public Relations Director: Lisa Limper.

Tickets: $2.00–3.00 ($1.50 children, senior citizens).

Souvenirs: at stadium.

Game Times: 7:00 (Monday–Saturday), 6:00 (Sunday).

MIAMI MIRACLE

Independent

7875 N.W. 12th St., Miami, FL 33126.

(305) 220-7040.

Florida International University Park (seats 2,000): at Tamiami Trail exit off Florida's Turnpike.

Managing General Partner: Stuart Revo. General Manager: Bruce Bielenberg.

Tickets: $4.00 ($2.00 children, senior citizens).

Souvenirs: at stadium.

Game Times: 7:30 (Monday–Saturday), 1:35 (Sunday).

OSCEOLA ASTROS

Houston Astros

P.O. Box 2229, Kissimmee, FL 32742.

(407) 933-5500.

Osceola County Stadium (seats 5,100): on U.S. 92 at Osceola Blvd., near Florida's Turnpike Exit 65.

President: Bill Wood. General Manager: Pat O'Conner.

Tickets: $2.25–3.00 ($1.50 children, senior citizens), at stadium, and at the Club-

house and Sports Capital in Kissimmee.

Souvenirs: at stadium and Sports Capital.

Game Times: 7:00 (Monday–Saturday), 6:00 (Sunday).

ST. LUCIE METS

New York Mets

P.O. Box 8808, Port St. Lucie, FL 34985.

(407) 340-0440.

St. Lucie County Sports Complex (seats 7,347): just east of I-95, west of downtown Port St. Lucie.

Vice President: Joe McShane. General Manager: Scott Brown.

Tickets: $3.00–4.00.

Souvenirs: at stadium and at Fanfare stores around South Florida.

Game Times: 7:00 (Monday–Saturday), 2:00 (Sunday).

ST. PETERSBURG CARDINALS

St. Louis Cardinals

P.O. Box 12557, St. Petersburg, FL 33733.

(813) 822-3384.

Al Lang Stadium (seats 7,004): on 2nd Ave. SE, next to the Bayfront Center in downtown St. Petersburg.

President and General Manager: Jack Tracz.

Tickets: $3.00–4.00 ($2.00 students, senior citizens).

Souvenirs: at stadium and at St. Petersburg Cardinals shop at 770 Pasadena Ave. S.

Game Times: 7:30.

SARASOTA WHITE SOX

Chicago White Sox

P.O. Box 9, Sarasota, FL 34230.

(813) 954-SOXX.

Ed Smith Stadium (seats 7,500): at 12th St. and Tuttle Ave., east of downtown Sarasota.

General Manager: Debbie Aitchison-Brooks.

Tickets: $3.50–4.50 ($2.50 children, senior citizens), at stadium and at Ticket-Master.

Souvenirs: at stadium.

Game Times: 7:00 (Monday–Saturday), 2:00 (Sunday April–June), 6:00 (Sunday rest of year).

VERO BEACH DODGERS

Los Angeles Dodgers

P.O. Box 2887, Vero Beach, FL 32961.

(407) 569-4900.

Holman Stadium (seats 6,500): two blocks north of S.R. 60, 3 miles west of U.S. 1.

President: Peter O'Malley. General Manager: Tom Simmons.

Tickets: $3.00 ($2.00 children, senior citizens).

Souvenirs: at stadium.

Game Times: 7:00, 1:30 (Sunday April–May).

WEST PALM BEACH EXPOS

Montreal Expos

P.O. Box 3566, West Palm Beach, FL 33402.

(407) 684-6801.

West Palm Beach Municipal Stadium (seats 4,392): just east of I-95 at Palm Beach Lakes Blvd.

Director: Kevin McHale. General Manager: Robert Rabenecker.

Tickets: $2.50–3.50 ($2.00 children, senior citizens).

Souvenirs: at stadium.

Game Times: 7:05.

WINTER HAVEN RED SOX

Boston Red Sox

Winter Haven, FL 33880.

(813) 293-3900.

Chain O'Lakes Park (seats 5,000): just east of Rte. 17 on Cypress Gardens Blvd.

General Manager: Dick Radatz, Jr.

Tickets: $2.50 ($2.00 senior citizens; $1.25 children).

Souvenirs: at stadium.

Game Times: 7:00.

Midwest League

In 1988 a few Chicago White Sox players traveled through South Bend. They were surprised to find that the locker room for the Sox' low Class A affiliate was much nicer and larger than the White Sox' major league clubhouse at Comiskey Park. With luxury boxes and a full-service restaurant, South Bend is part of the new Midwest League. No longer is this a league of small-time, community-run ball clubs playing in old-time parks. Now the ballparks are fancy and attendance is high, and owners make big profits. Besides South Bend, the new Midwest League includes Rockford, Madison, Peoria, Quad City, and Springfield.

Peoria, a dying franchise until it was bought by local celebrity and businessman Pete Vonachen, became one of the minor leagues' true success stories. The Chiefs annually draw 200,000 fans, among the most in Class A. Meinen Field isn't the palace that South Bend has at Coveleski Stadium, but it comes alive when the Chiefs play. Springfield's Lanphier Park has a similar feel. And though attendance has fallen off since the glory years in Madison, fans there keep alive the "Let's Go Fish" cheer.

If you'd prefer to see the old Midwest League, community-operated franchises still thrive in Appleton, Clinton, Burlington, Beloit, and Cedar Rapids. The stands may not be full, but this is minor league baseball the way it used to be. The only difference is that these players come from major league organizations, and they don't stick around long enough to become local heroes.

In fact, although some in the Midwest League will dispute it, this is a low Class A league, closer to the South Atlantic League than to the California or Carolina. That means you'll find more young players, fewer veterans and more errors. It's not bad baseball, just less experienced players.

APPLETON FOXES

Kansas City Royals

P.O. Box 464, Appleton, WI 54912.

(414) 733-4152.

Goodland Field (seats 4,300): off College Ave. exit on Hwy. 41.

President: Milt Drier. General Manager: Larry Dawson.

Tickets: $2.00 ($1.00 senior citizens, students; $.50 children).

Souvenirs: at stadium.

Game Times: 6:00 (April–May 15), 7:00 (rest of year).

BELOIT BREWERS

Milwaukee Brewers

P.O. Box 855, Beloit, WI 53511.

(608) 362-2272.

Telfer Park (seats 3,800): On Skyline Dr., just off I-90.

President: Tim Monahan. General Manager: David Tarrolly.

Tickets: $2.50–3.00 ($2.00 senior citizens, $1.50 students).

Souvenirs: at stadium.

Game Times: 7:05, 5:05 (Sunday).

BURLINGTON BRAVES

Atlanta Braves

P.O. Box 824, Burlington, IA 52601.

(319) 754-5705.

Community Field (seats 3,500): 1 block east of Hwy. 61.

President: David Walker. General Manager: Paul Marshall.

Tickets: $2.00–3.00 ($1.00 students).

Souvenirs: at stadium.

Game Times: 7:00, 2:00 (Saturday–Sunday April–May).

CEDAR RAPIDS REDS

Cincinnati Reds

P.O. Box 2001, Cedar Rapids, IA 52406.

(319) 363-3887.

Veterans Memorial Stadium (seats 6,000): south of Hwy. 151 at 15th St. SW.

President: Bob Nance. General Manager: Don Buchheister.

Tickets: $2.50–3.00 ($1.50 children).

Souvenirs: at stadium.

Game Times: 7:00 (Monday–Saturday), 5:00 (Sunday).

CLINTON GIANTS
San Francisco Giants
P.O. Box 789, Clinton, IA 52732.
(319) 242-0727.

Riverview Stadium (seats 3,600): at 6th Ave. North and 1st St., at the Mississippi River Bridge.

President: Bill Gardner. General Manager: Kevin Temperly.

Tickets: $2.00–3.00 ($1.00 children, senior citizens).

Souvenirs: at stadium.

Game Times: 7:05 (Monday–Saturday), 2:30 (Sunday April–May), 5:00 (Sunday rest of year).

KENOSHA TWINS
Minnesota Twins
P.O. Box 661, Kenosha, WI 53141.
(414) 657-7997.

Simmons Field (seats 3,500): on Sheridan Road., off Hwy. 50.

President and General Manager: Robert Lee.

Tickets: $2.50–3.50 ($2.00 children, senior citizens).

Souvenirs: at stadium.

Game Times: 7:05 (Monday–Saturday), 2:00 (Sunday).

MADISON MUSKIES
Oakland Athletics
P.O. Box 882, Madison, WI 53701.
(608) 241-0010.

Warner Park (seats 3,923): at Sherman Ave. and Wisc. 30.

President Charles Barnhill. General Manager: Don DuChateau.

Tickets: $3.75–5.50 ($2.50 children, senior citizens).

Souvenirs: at stadium.

Game Times: 7:00 (Monday–Saturday), 2:00 (Sunday).

PEORIA CHIEFS
Chicago Cubs
1524 W. Nebraska Ave., Peoria, IL 61604.
(309) 688-1622.

Meinen Field (seats 5,000): at University exit off I-74.

General Partner: Clar Krusinski. General Manager: John Butler.

Tickets: $2.75–3.75 ($1.75 children, senior citizens).

Souvenirs: at stadium.

Game Times: 7:00, 2:00 (Sunday April–May).

QUAD CITY ANGELS
California Angels
P.O. Box 3496, Davenport, IA 52808.
(319) 324-2032.

John O'Donnell Stadium (seats 5,000): on U.S. 61 at the Mississippi River.

President: Richard Holtzman. General Manager: Mike Feder.

Tickets: $3.00–4.00 ($2.00 children).

Souvenirs: at stadium and at J. C. Penney's.

Game Times: 7:00 (Monday–Thursday), 7:30 (Friday–Saturday), 6:00 (Sunday).

Home of the Pittsfield Mets.

ROCKFORD EXPOS
Montreal Expos
P.O. Box 6748, Rockford, IL 61125.
(815) 964-5400.

Marinelli Field (seats 4,200): at 15th Ave. off Hwy. 2.

President: Bill McKee. General Manager: Bill Larsen.

Tickets: $2.50–5.00.

Souvenirs: at stadium and at Sports Warehouse on South Main St.

Game Times: 7:00 (Monday–Saturday), 6:00 (Monday–Thursday April–May), 2:00 (Sunday).

SOUTH BEND WHITE SOX
Chicago White Sox
P.O. Box 4218, South Bend, IN 46634.
(219) 284-9988.

Rare Feats in the Minors

• July 19, 1911: In a Pacific Coast League game, Walter Carlisle of Vernon executed an unassisted triple play. Wonder of wonders, Carlisle was the Vernon centerfielder! He made an "unbelievable" shoestring catch. The baserunners were both heading home as Carlisle somersaulted into second base and then trotted over to step on first.

• On August 13, 1913, Harry Hedgpeth of Petersburg in the Virginia League shut out Richmond, 1–0, on one hit (a scratch single in the fourth) in the opener of a doubleheader. Determined to get it right, he went to the mound for the second game. He did: a 10–0 no-hitter!

• The no-hitter Ron Necciai hurled for Bristol against Welch in the Appalachian League on May 13, 1952, was secondary to the fact that he struck out 27 batters in nine innings. A quick count and you're going to say that's as many as possible. Wrong! A strikeout victim reached first on a passed ball and another batter grounded out. Still, it was a fair night's work.

• In 1919, Joe Wilhoit in the Western League hit safely in 69 consecutive games. During the streak, he knocked out 151 hits in 299 at bats for a batting average of .505.

• Those looking for the greatest single minor league season are directed to the 1948 record of Roy Sanner of Houma in the Evangeline League. In 23 trips to the mound, the lefty won 21 and lost two, setting league records with a .903 percentage and 251 strikeouts. Pretty good, huh? But when he *wasn't* pitching, Sanner played the outfield and led the league in batting (.386), homers (34), and RBI (126), a triple crown! We assume he had a strong shot at league MVP that year.   —BC

Coveleski Stadium (seats 5,000): at Western and Taylor in downtown South Bend.
General Manager: John Baxter.
Tickets: $3.00–5.00.
Souvenirs: at stadium.
Game Times: 7:00, 2:00 (Sunday April–June).

SPRINGFIELD CARDINALS
St. Louis Cardinals
P.O. Box 3004, Springfield, IL 62708.
(217) 525-6570.
Lanphier Park (seats 5,000): on Grand Ave. in northeast Springfield.
President: August Busch, Jr. VP/General Manager: Lee Landers.
Tickets: $2.50–3.50.
Souvenirs: at stadium.
Game Times: 7:00, 1:15 (Sunday April–May).

WATERLOO DIAMONDS
Co-op
P.O. Box 611, Waterloo, IA 50704.
(319) 233-8146.
Municipal Stadium (seats 5,500): at Park Rd. exit on Hwy. 20.
President: Dan Yates. General Manager: James Peterson.
Tickets: $2.00–3.50.
Souvenirs: at stadium.
Game Times: 7:00, 1:30 (Saturday April–May), 3:00 (Sunday).

WAUSAU TIMBERS
Seattle Mariners
P.O. Box 1704, Wausau, WI 54402.
(715) 845-4900.
Athletic Park (seats 2,500): at Wausau Ave. and Third St.
President: Dale Cochard. General Manager: Jack Roeder.
Tickets: $2.50–3.50 ($1.50 students, senior citizens; $1.25 children).
Souvenirs: at stadium.
Game Times: 7:00, 1:30 (Saturday April–May, Sunday).

South Atlantic League

Some people in baseball own a team. A few own more than one, and one or two have virtually put together a full farm system. But few control a league the way that John Moss does the South Atlantic League. Moss, the league president, has kept the Sally League alive through the tough times, and he's always ready to add new cities. Even one Charleston wasn't enough for Moss. He found another one. And there's no doubt the league belongs to the former mayor of Kings Mountain, N.C. His colleagues may look down on some of his cities, or on the quality of play in his league, but Moss always has cities and major league organizations interested.

One of the reasons they're interested, of course, is that they don't need to send experienced stars to be competitive. The South Atlantic League certainly has the lowest level of play of any of the Class A leagues. But an SAL game can be entertaining, especially in one of the league's more successful cities.

The return of baseball to Watt Powell Park in Charleston, W.Va., proved a great success. Greensboro has dominated the league attendance race, but Augusta has also drawn well since entering the league. Asheville's picturesque McCormick Field was featured in the movie *Bull Durham*. And Spartanburg's Duncan Park includes box seats from New York's Polo Grounds, complete with "NY" in the metalwork.

ASHEVILLE TOURISTS
Houston Astros
P.O. Box 1556, Asheville, NC 28802.
(704) 258-0428.
McCormick Field (seats 3,500): on Charlotte St. south of I-240.
President: Peter Kern. General Manager: Ron McKee.
Tickets: $3.00–4.00 ($2.00 students, $1.50 children, senior citizens).
Souvenirs: at stadium.
Game Times: 7:00 (Monday–Saturday), 2:00 (Sunday).

AUGUSTA PIRATES
Pittsburgh Pirates
P.O. Box 3746-Hill Station, Augusta, GA 30904.
(404) 736-7889.
Heaton Stadium (seats 4,000): Milledge Road at Lake Olmstead.
President: Len Monheimer. General Manager: Chris Scheuler.
Tickets: $2.75–4.50 ($2.25 children, senior citizens, military).
Souvenirs: at stadium.
Game Times: 7:30, 2:30 (Sunday April–June).

CHARLESTON (S.C.) RAINBOWS
San Diego Padres
P.O. Box 2840, Charleston, SC 29403.
(803) 723-7241.
College Park (seats 4,300): At Exit 219-A off I-26.
President: Stuart Revo. General Manager: Kevin Carpenter.
Tickets: $3.50–4.50 ($2.00 children), available at stadium and SCAT outlets.
Souvenirs: at stadium.
Game Times: 7:00, 2:00 (Sunday April–May).

CHARLESTON (W.VA.) WHEELERS
Chicago Cubs
P.O. Box 2669, Charleston, WV 25304.
(304) 925-8222.
Watt Powell Park (seats 6,500): on MacCorkle Ave., across the 35th St. Bridge from I-77.
President/General Manager: Dennis Bastien.
Tickets: $3.00–4.00.
Souvenirs: at stadium.
Game Times: 7:30 (Monday–Saturday), 2:00 (Sunday).

COLUMBIA METS
New York Mets
P.O. Box 7845, Columbia, SC 29202.
(803) 256-4110.
Capital City Park (seats 4,000): on South Assembly St. near the University of South Carolina football stadium.

President: Richard Holzman. General Manager: Skip Weisman.
Tickets: $3.00–4.00.
Souvenirs: at stadium and J.B. White's.
Game Times: 7:00 (Monday–Saturday), 2:00 (Sunday).

FAYETTEVILLE GENERALS
Detroit Tigers
P.O. Box 64939, Fayetteville, NC 28306.
(919) 424-6500.
J. P. Riddle Stadium (seats 3,000): on Legion Road, south of Owen Drive.
President: Charles Padgett. General Manager: Matt Perry.
Tickets: $3.00–4.00 ($2.00 children, students, senior citizens, military).
Souvenirs: at stadium.
Game Times: 7:15 (Monday–Saturday), 5:00 (Sunday).

GASTONIA RANGERS
Texas Rangers
P.O. Box 309, Gastonia, NC 28053.
(704) 867-3721.
Sims Legion Field (seats 4,600): just south of I-85 at the Lincolnton-Dallas exit.
President: Roman Gabriel (yes, the one-time quarterback of the Rams and Eagles). General Manager: Harold Green.
Tickets: $3.00–4.00 ($1.00 children, senior citizens).
Souvenirs: at stadium.
Game Times: 7:00 (Monday–Saturday), 3:00 (Sunday).

GREENSBORO HORNETS
Cincinnati Reds
P.O. Box 22093, Greensboro, NC 27420.
(919) 275-1641.
World War Memorial Stadium (seats 7,500): on Yanceyville St. at Lindsay St.
President: Steve Bryant. General Manager: John Dittrich.
Tickets: $3.00–4.00 ($2.00 children, senior citizens).
Souvenirs: at stadium.
Game Times: 7:30 (Monday–Saturday),

2:00 (Sunday).

MYRTLE BEACH BLUE JAYS
Toronto Blue Jays
P.O. Box 1110, Myrtle Beach, SC 29578.
(803) 626-1987.
Coastal Carolina Stadium (seats 7,500): on Hwy. 501 at the Coastal Carolina College campus in Conway.
President: Winston Blenckstone. General Manager: Dan Rajkowski.
Tickets: $2.50–4.25 ($1.50 children, senior citizens), at stadium and at 809 Main St. office in Myrtle Beach.
Souvenirs: at stadium and at 809 Main St. office in Myrtle Beach.
Game Times: 7:30, 2:30 (First-half Sunday).

SAVANNAH CARDINALS
St. Louis Cardinals
P.O. Box 3783, Savannah, GA 31414.
(912) 351-9150.
Grayson Stadium (seats 7,500): on Victory Drive, east of downtown Savannah.
President: Fred Kuhlman. General Manager: Jim Bayens.
Public Relations Director: Mike Finocchairo.
Tickets: $2.50–4.00 ($1.50 student, senior citizens; $2.00 military).
Souvenirs: at stadium.
Game Times: 7:15 (Monday–Saturday), 2:00 (Sunday).

SPARTANBURG PHILLIES
Philadelphia Phillies
P.O. Box 1721, Spartanburg, SC 29304.
(803) 585-6279.
Duncan Park (seats 3,900): Duncan Park Drive at South Converse St.
President: Brad Shover. General Manager: Jeffrey Kurkis.
Tickets: $2.00–4.00 ($1.00 students, senior citizens).
Souvenirs: at stadium.
Game Times: 7:30 (Monday–Saturday), 4:00 (Sunday).

(Cont. p. 258.)

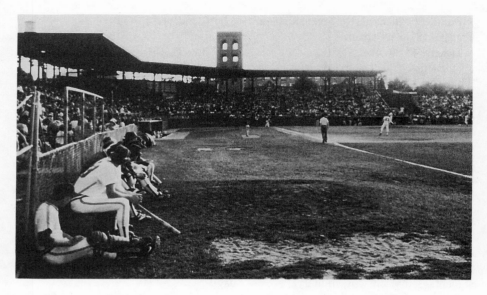

Durham Athletic Park, not surprisingly one of this writer's favorite ballparks.

My Favorite Ballparks

Picking the ten best minor league ballparks, at least for someone who loves the minors as I do, is like choosing the best ten bites out of all the pies in the bakery. Sure, some parks are better than others; lemon meringue is better than rhubarb. And, yes, some of those new pre-fab aluminum stadiums lack the character of the older ballparks, just like plain apple can taste bland after Dutch apple. But just as a pie-lover can always find something lip-smacking, I taste something special in every minor league baseball facility. And to paraphrase Will Rogers, I've never met a minor league park I didn't like.

What some call small, I call cozy. Their "cramped" is my "intimate." If minor league players are less competent and their fans less sophisticated, that's more than offset by enthusiasm and spontaneity. Even the largest and newest minor league parks like Louisville's 33,500-seat Redbird Stadium or the mint Buffalo Pilot Field still retain the charm and personality that make minor league baseball special.

Naming the ten best parks sounds like I've seen them all. No way. There are some 150 minor league parks in use, plus others

that once hosted long-gone baseball teams. I confess, I've never been to Chattanooga's Engel Stadium, one of the old WPA parks, but I know I'd love it. Joe Engel packed 20,000 fans into the 8,500-seat facility once during the Depression when he gave away a house. Even though I've only seen photos, it's one of my favorites. I'd love Riverview Stadium in Clinton, Iowa, too. It sits on the bank of the Mississippi, and you can see barges push cargo up the river as you relax and watch a game. Just to say you've been to the Athletic Park in Medicine Hat, Alberta, for a Pioneer League game would be fun. And someday I want to go to Harrisburg, Pa., where the ballpark is on an island in the middle of the Susquehanna River.

For some ballparks, the setting makes the stadium. In Vancouver, B.C., Nat Bailey Stadium sits in the middle of beautiful Victoria Park. At Salt Lake City in July, you can be in Derks Field to watch the Trappers play while snow-capped mountains tower beyond the third base grandstand.

Alumni Coliseum is on the campus of Montana Tech in Butte, Montana. Despite its pretentious name, the Coliseum is a

small, 2,000-seat, metal ballpark with a big football grandstand in deep left field. The brown hills and mountains that make up that part of the Big Sky country surround the park. One night while I sat at a game, the sun set so purple and magnificent I forgot the baseball show for God's. Then, almost as if not to be outdone, a huge white moon came in over the eastern mountains to shine on that little patch of emerald grass, shaming the manmade lights on poles. If I could stop time, it would be that evening in Butte, Montana.

There are so many special things about each ballpark. In little Pulaski, Virginia, Calfee Park holds only 1,200, but it has a massive stone entrance more befitting a Dickensean prison than a baseball park. In Burlington, N.C., the grandstand may be the most efficient, compact design I've ever seen; a friend accurately describes it as a "sweet little ballpark." I'm not that fond of some of the spring training facilities in Florida, but Winter Haven, where the Red Sox train, has wonderful Chain O'Lakes Park. The winding walk up to the main grandstand's red seats beneath an overhanging roof gives it a real minor league park feel.

Even the names of some minor league parks are great. In New Britain, Conn., there's Beehive Field, and in Calgary, the park's called Foothills Stadium. Richmond, Va., has simply named its fine new park "The Diamond," and Duffy Fairgrounds has a ring in Watertown, N.Y. The old parks that no longer house minor league baseball had some tremendous names. Was there ever a prettier name than Raleigh, N.C.'s, Devereaux Meadow? And in Palatka, Fla., the Azalea Bowl was home to the Palatka Azaleas.

In the late 1950s, the rule makers standardized things by deciding all parks should be 330 down the lines and 400 feet in center field. Fortunately the rule was not retroactive, and even today minor league outfield dimensions often make for a more interesting game than their bland big league counterparts. My favorite ballpark dimensions were in Pennington Gap, Va., which had a team in the Appalachian League from 1937 to 1940. Down the lines to left field and right field, the distance was a staggering 640 feet, but the distance to straight-away center field was a mindboggling 1,050 feet. Compare this to the old park in Welch, W.Va., where the foul lines were a respectable 375 and 390 feet, but center field was only 310 feet. Even in more recent years there have been some unique minor league field dimensions. For three years in the mid-seventies, Sacramento played in Hughes Stadium, a football bowl, where the left-field foul line may have reached all of 235 feet. In 1977 Charleston, W. Va., playing in the International League, decided to remove an interior fence, and the left-field line became 410 feet and center field was a distant 525 feet.

What really makes a minor league ballpark are the memories and feelings it evokes for the individual. For me, three stadiums are special.

If you had the good fortune to grow up in a minor league town, the park where you first followed baseball will always be special to you. Greensboro, N.C.'s Memorial Stadium is my childhood park. When it was built in 1927, the city had grand plans. It was to be a large oval for baseball, football, and track. However, for starters only half of the stadium was erected, and to this day, the "J" shape of the stadium is all that has ever been finished. Because of that, the playing field is slightly off center, but some of the best hours of my youth were spent stretched out in the third-base grandstand with a snow cone, trying to yell something obnoxious enough to get the nearby third baseman to throw an obscene gesture my way.

I started running baseball clubs in Savannah, Ga., and quickly came to love every inch of old Grayson Stadium. For three years I spent every waking moment in that stadium, as I tried to figure ways to entice people out to the ball game. Grayson sits in a large city park filled with huge oaks and Spanish moss. In truth, the dark red-brick grandstand, another WPA project of the late 1930s, is not that attractive. The two concrete bleachers, one down the right-field line and the other in left field, were built in 1925 for a football stadium. Because of this, the left-field line is only 296 feet, and home plate is less than thirty feet from the grandstand. That the rule book says it should be at least sixty is ignored in Savannah, where close-by fans can helpfully point out batters' failures without straining their delicate throats.

The third park that has special meaning for me is Durham Athletic Park, home of the Durham Bulls and the setting for the movie *Bull Durham*. I've been president of the club for the last ten years. Wedged into part of a city block in downtown Durham, this site has hosted baseball since 1926, with the current grandstand having been built in 1939. Originally outfielders had to run up banks in left and center field to catch long fly balls and the warehouse in right field was the wall. An interior fence has ended some of those eccentricities, but there's still a short right-field porch—only 305 feet down the line and 330 feet to the power alley. There's almost no foul territory and fans are right on top of the action. It may be as intimate a minor league park as there is in baseball.

Much of the special fun in following the minors is watching rising stars, of course, but you can also find enjoyment in seeing the different parks. Nearly every minor league park is unique, and every fan has one or two that he likes best.

Ten to see:

Buffalo, NY. Pilot Field. One of the newest and grandest of all minor league parks, this 19,500-seat stadium remains intimate. And with its downtown setting, Pilot Field has the feel of some of the old major league parks. It will be expanded to 40,000 if Buffalo gets big league ball.

Asheville, NC. McCormick Field. Built in 1924—the oldest existing ballpark in the minor leagues—this ramshackle, wooden park has had several noticeable additions slapped on. It's not glamorous, but set in the mountains with a short right-field porch, it is a great place to watch a game. Considering the transient nature of minor league rosters, you can't find a better team nickname than Asheville's Tourists.

Louisville, KY. Cardinal Stadium. One of the few stadiums in the country to combine football and baseball effectively, this 33,500-seat park enabled Louisville to become the first city in minor league history to draw over one million fans in a season. The area under the grandstand is one of the liveliest concession areas in all of sports.

Pioneer League. Yes, the whole league. To travel from beautiful Derks Field in Salt Lake City, across Idaho, to the Big Sky country of Montana, while watching baseball games along the way is perhaps the perfect way to spend a couple of summer weeks. The weather is cool, and the parks are interesting. How can you top Cobb Field in Billings, Alumni Coliseum in Butte, or Legion Field in Great Falls?

Durham, NC. Durham Athletic Park. Sure, I'm prejudiced, but it's still one of the great old minor league parks. Set in a difficult-to-find warehouse district with no parking, the stadium makes you part of the game. Durham has had a team named the Bulls since 1902. The smoking bull in right field, erected for the movie, is a fun individual attraction.

Oneonta, NY. Damaschke Field. Only about twenty miles from Cooperstown, N.Y., this old grandstand has the feel of baseball a century ago without a musty, museumlike quality. Mountains rise above the outfield fence to watch the first-year players of the New York-Penn League truly hustle.

Birmingham, AL. Hoover Stadium. Another of the good new ballparks being con-

structed around the minor leagues, Hoover was finished in 1988 and seats 10,000. It's first-rate in every category. While in Birmingham, also try to see Richwood Field, the site of Birmingham baseball since 1914 and home of the Barons until Hoover was built. It's a great old stadium. Shed a tear that its time has passed.

Albuquerque, N.M. Sports Stadium. Completed in the early 1970s, this park still can be considered one of the better new stadiums. A great setting! It remains unique, with cars allowed to park on the bluff overlooking the outfield and enjoy drive-in baseball.

Eugene, Ore. Civic Stadium. This old, wood park in the shape of a "J" seats 6,000, but the fans in this college town make this ballpark fun. The Emeralds play in the short-season Northwest League with games beginning in mid-June.

Laredo, Texas. West Martin Field. Okay, this isn't the greatest park in baseball. It's one of the new aluminum pre-fab grandstands. But the box seats may have the widest aisles in all of baseball. And more important, the Owls of the Two Laredos play a third of their home games in this park. It's a chance to see the Mexican League play in the U.S. with some of the great former major league names that usually show up in the Mexican League. Great fans who love their beer are another attraction.   —MW

SUMTER BRAVES
Atlanta Braves
P.O. Box 2878, Sumter, SC 29151.
(803) 773-9932.
    Riley Park (seats 4,000): just north of Broad St. (U.S. 521) on Church St.
    President: Stan Kasten. General Manager: Ed Holtz.
    Tickets: $2.50–3.50 ($2.00 senior citizens, military; $1.50 children).
    Souvenirs: at stadium.
    Game Times: 7:00.

New York-Penn League

Maybe you don't remember much about the New York-Penn League. You don't know that it was once known as the PONY League, for Pennsylvania, Ontario, and New York. (And since Hamilton, Ontario, joined the circuit in 1988, the PONY name could be revived.) You certainly couldn't identify McNamara and Stedler, for whom the two NY-P divisions are named. You didn't realize it was the setting for Roger Kahn's *Good Enough to Dream*, the story of the 1983 Utica Blue Sox. You can't identify it as one of baseball's two "short-season Class A leagues," a wordy classification that puts it between rookie ball and the rest of Class A. You don't know that baseball sends many of its college-level draft picks here each June for a 78-game initiation into pro ball.

What you should know about the New York-Penn League is that it's the best place to catch a baseball game during a trip to the Hall of Fame in Cooperstown. Either Oneonta, to the south, or Utica, to the north, is an easy drive from Cooperstown after a day at the Hall of Fame. Catch a game in Oneonta, and think about John Elway playing there in his only year of pro baseball. Go to Utica, and think about Roger Kahn storming around with the ragtag Blue Sox. Or get another taste of the NY-P League. Head east to Pittsfield and find a beautiful former Double-A ballpark that has only one fault—the sun sets directly in

center field. When Wahconah Park was built, there were no lights and sunset meant the game was over; now the sun must go down before the game goes on. If that's not enough history for you, check out Elmira, where professional baseball has been played for more than one hundred years, including fifty at Dunn Field.

AUBURN ASTROS
Houston Astros
P.O. Box 651, Auburn, NY 13021.
(315) 255-2489.
    Falcon Park (seats 3,000): on Division St., one mile north of the Arterial Highway (Rtes. 5 and 20).
    President: Charles Savage. General Manager: Bob Neal.
    Tickets: $2.00–3.00 ($1.50 children, senior citizens).
    Game Times: 7:30 (Monday–Saturday), 6:00 (Sunday).

BATAVIA CLIPPERS
Philadelphia Phillies
P.O. Box 802, Batavia, NY 14021.
(716) 343-7531.
    Dwyer Stadium (seats 3,000): at Main and Denio Sts.
    President: Edward Dwyer. General Manager: Brad Rogers.
    Tickets: $2.00–10.00 ($1.50 students, senior citizens).
    Game Times: 7:05.

ELMIRA PIONEERS
Boston Red Sox
P.O. Box 238, Elmira, NY 14902.
(607) 734-1811.
    Dunn Field (seats 5,100): at Maple Ave. and Luce St.
    President and General Manager: Clyde Smoll.
    Tickets: $2.50–4.00 ($1.75 children, senior citizens).
    Game Times: 7:00.

ERIE ORIOLES
Baltimore Orioles
P.O. Box 488, Erie, PA 16512.

(814) 453-3900.

Ainsworth Field (seats 3,200): on 21st St., east of Greengarden.

President: William McKee. General Manager: Bob Shreve.

Tickets: $2.50–4.00 ($2.00 children, senior citizens).

Game Times: 7:00 (Monday–Saturday), 6:00 (Sunday).

GENEVA CUBS
Chicago Cubs
P.O. Box 402, Geneva, NY 14456.
(315) 789-2827.

McDonough Park (seats 2,200): at Lyceum St. and Nursery Ave.

President: Paul Velte. General Manager: Ken Shepard.

Tickets: $2.00–3.00 ($1.50 children, senior citizens).

Game Times: 7:30.

HAMILTON REDBIRDS
St. Louis Cardinals
P.O. Box 1200, Station A, Hamilton, Ont. L8N 4B4.
(416) 549-5100.

Bernie Arbour Stadium (seats 3,200): on Mohawk Road, east of Mud St.

President: Jack Tracz. General Manager: Jack Liotta.

Tickets: $4.00–5.00 ($3.00 children, senior citizens).

Game Times: 7:30 (Monday–Saturday), 6:30 (Sunday).

JAMESTOWN EXPOS
Montreal Expos
P.O. Box 338, Jamestown, NY 14701.
(716) 665-4092.

College Stadium (seats 3,328): on Falconer St., 2 miles west of Rte. 17-Southern Tier Expressway.

General Manager: Tom O'Reilly.

Tickets: $1.50–3.50 ($1.00 children, senior citizens).

Game Times: 7:00 (Monday–Saturday), 6:00 (Sunday).

NIAGARA FALLS RAPIDS
Detroit Tigers
1201 Hyde Park Blvd., Niagara Falls, NY 14305.
(716) 298-5400.

Sal Maglie Stadium (seats 4,000): on Rte. 62 off the Robert Moses Parkway.

President: Bob Rich, Jr. General Manager: Tom Prohaska.

Tickets: $2.00–3.00 ($1.50 children, senior citizens).

Game Times: 7:05.

ONEONTA YANKEES
New York Yankees
95 River St., Oneonta, NY 13820.
(607) 432-6326.

Damaschke Field (seats 3,200): at Exit 14 on I-88.

President and General Manager: Sam Nader.

Tickets: Call for information.

Game Times: 7:15 (Monday–Saturday), 6:00 (Sunday).

PITTSFIELD METS
New York Mets
P.O. Box 328, Pittsfield, MA 01202.
(413) 499-6387.

Wahconah Park (seats 5,200): on Wahconah St., west of Rte. 7 North.

President: Michael Casey. General Manager: Adam Froelich.

Tickets: $2.00–2.75.

Game Times: 7:00 (Monday–Saturday), 3:00 (Sunday).

ST. CATHARINES BLUE JAYS
Toronto Blue Jays
P.O. Box 1088, St. Catharines, Ont. L2R 3B0.
(416) 641-5297.

Community Park (seats 2,000): on Merritt St. at Seymour.

Director: Bob Nicholson. General Manager: Steve Stunt.

Tickets: $3.75–4.00 ($3.25 children, senior citizens).

Game Times: 7:00 (Monday–Saturday), 1:30 (Sunday).

UTICA BLUE SOX
Chicago White Sox
P.O. Box 751, Utica, NY 13503.
(315) 738-0999.

Murnane Field (seats 5,000): on Sunset Ave. near Burrstone.

General Partner: Bob Fowler. General Manager: Joanne Gerace.

Tickets: $2.50–6.00.

Game Times: 7:00.

WATERTOWN INDIANS
Cleveland Indians
P.O. Box 802, Watertown, NY 13601.
(315) 788-8747.

Duffy Fairgrounds (seats 4,300): at Exit 46 on I-81.

President: Michael Schell. General Manager: Tom Van Schaack.

Tickets: $2.00–4.00 ($1.50 children, senior citizens, military).

Game Times: 7:00 (Monday–Saturday), 6:00 (Sunday).

WELLAND PIRATES
Pittsburgh Pirates
P.O. Box 594, Welland, Ont., L3B 5R3.
(416) 735-7634.

Welland Sports Complex (seats 2,500): Hwy. 406 at Quaker Rd., next to the Regional Exhibition Grounds.

General Manager: Bill Kuehn.

Tickets: $4.00–5.50 ($3.00 children, senior citizens).

Game Times: 7:00 (Monday–Saturday), 1:30 or 6:00 (Sunday).

Northwest League

If left to the Seattle Mariners, professional baseball might be dead in the Pacific Northwest. Not so in the Northwest League, not even in the Seattle metro area. While the Mariners struggle in the Kingdome, right up the road the NWL Everett Giants pack their small ballpark virtually every night. Owners Bob and Margaret Bavasi decided to give up law practices and run their own team. Now they can be

found running the snack stand and re-
minding fans that Everett is the only place
in the area to see "Real Baseball" on "Real
Grass." Bob's father Buzzie, who once ran
the Dodgers, Angels, and Padres, would be
proud. His brother Bill, the current Angels
farm director, isn't as happy when his
Bend affiliate loses to Bob's Giants.

And Everett isn't even the NWL's most
successful franchise. That honor belongs
to Eugene, where the Emeralds have
thrived despite local economic problems.
Eugene is a former Triple-A town, as is
NWL member Spokane, the Ems' annual
challenger for the league's attendance
crown. Both cities have had great success
as short-season sites after failing at the
higher level.

BELLINGHAM MARINERS
Seattle Mariners
1500 Orleans St., Bellingham, WA
98226.
(206) 671-6347.
Joe Martin Field (seats 1,500): on Orle-
ans St., two blocks west of the Lakeway
Drive exit on I-5.
President: Rook Van Halm. General
Manager: Bob Lagana.
Tickets: $3.00 ($2.00 students and se-
nior citizens, $1.00 children under 12).
Game Times: 7:00 (Monday–Saturday),
2:00 (Sunday).

BEND BUCKS
California Angels
P.O. Box 6603, Bend, OR 97708.
(503) 382-8011.
Vince Genna Stadium (seats 3,000): on
Roosevelt, one block east of Hwy. 97 in
southern Bend.
President: Mary Cain. General Manager:
Bob Hards.
Tickets: $3.00–4.00 ($1.50 children).
Game Times: 7:00 (Monday–Saturday),
6:00 (Sunday).

BOISE HAWKS
Independent
1109 Main St., Suite C, Boise, ID 83702.

(208) 34H-AWKS.
Memorial Stadium (seats 3,000): at the
Western Idaho Fairgrounds, Glenwood at
Chinden.
President: Bill Pereira. General Manag-
er: Fred Kuenzi.
Tickets: $3.00–4.50.
Game Times: 7:00 (Monday–Saturday),
1:00 or 6:00 (Sunday).

EUGENE EMERALDS
Kansas City Royals
P.O. Box 5566, Eugene, OR 97405.
(503) 342-5367.
Civic Stadium (seats 6,400): on Willam-
ette St., south of downtown Eugene off
Pearl St.
President and General Manager: Bob
Beban.
Public Relations Director: Rian For-
strom.
Tickets: $3.00–4.50.
Game Times: 7:00 (Monday–Saturday),
6:00 (Sunday).

EVERETT GIANTS
San Francisco Giants
P.O. Box 1346, Everett, WA 98206.
(206) 258-3673.
Everett Memorial Stadium (seats
1,800): at corner of 39th and Broadway.
General Manager: Mark Pajak.
Information Director: Charlie Poier.
Tickets: $3.75–4.75 ($2.75 children).
Game Times: 7:00 (Monday–Saturday),
2:00 (Sunday).

SALEM DODGERS
Los Angeles Dodgers
P.O. Box 17641, Salem, OR 97305.
(503) 371-7121.
Chemeketa Field (seats 2,500): At Che-
meketa Community College, on Lancaster
Drive.
President: Dave Elmore. General Man-
ager: Steve Ford.
Tickets: $3.00–4.00 ($2.00 children).
Game Times: 7:00 (Monday–Saturday),
6:00 (Sunday).

SOUTHERN OREGON ATHLETICS
Oakland Athletics
P.O. Box 1457, Medford, OR 97501.
(503) 770-5364.
Miles Field (seats 2,900): on South Pa-
cific Highway south of Medford.
President and General Manager: Fred
Herrman.
Tickets: $2.50–4.00 ($2.00 children, se-
nior citizens).
Game Times: 7:00.

SPOKANE INDIANS
San Diego Padres
P.O. Box 4758, Spokane, WA 99202.
(509) 535-2922.
Indians Stadium (seats 10,000): in In-
terstate Fairgrounds Park.
President: Bobby Brett. General Manag-
er: Tom Leip.
Public Relations Director: Janice Ful-
ton.
Tickets: $3.00–4.50 ($2.00 children, se-
nior citizens, military).
Game Times: 7:00 (Monday–Saturday),
6:00 (Sunday).

Appalachian League

Walk into most Appalachian League parks,
and you'll quickly realize you've reached
the entry level of professional baseball.
Most of the players are barely old enough
to shave. The umpires look like they might
be some of the players' older brothers.
Some of the ballparks even double as high
school fields. Take away the hand-me-
down major league uniforms, and you
could be at an American Legion game. But
even as the walks and errors pile up, stick
around for a while.

Ball players have to start somewhere,
and many of the best played in the Appy
League. Darryl Strawberry tore up this
league in 1981. Gregg Jefferies was here a
few years later. Every year there are a few
number one draft choices. As for atmosphere, head to Burlington if you want
crowds. The Indians pack them in nightly.
The other parks are less likely to be full,

but some of them are still interesting. Check out Wytheville. The sloped warning track in center field, the municipal swimming pool off the right-field line, and the city jail behind first base make Withers Field unique among pro baseball parks.

BLUEFIELD ORIOLES
Baltimore Orioles
P.O. Box 356, Bluefield, WV 24701.
(304) 325-1326.
Bowen Field (seats 3,000): just off Rte. 460 at Westgate.
President and General Manager: George Fanning.
Tickets: Call for information.
Game Times: 7:30 (Monday–Saturday), 6:00 (Sunday).

BRISTOL TIGERS
Detroit Tigers
P.O. Box 1434, Bristol, VA 24203.
(703) 466-8310.
DeVault Memorial Stadium (seats 1,200): on Euclid Ave., off I-381.
President: Boyce Cox. General Manager: Bob Childress.
Tickets: $1.00–2.00.
Game Times: 7:30.

BURLINGTON INDIANS
Cleveland Indians
P.O. Box 1143, Burlington, NC 27216.
(919) 222-0223.
Burlington Athletic Stadium (seats 3,500): on Graham St., near Beaumont St.
President: Miles Wolff. General Manager: John Browne.
Tickets: $3.00–4.00 ($2.00 children, senior citizens).
Game Times: 7:15.

ELIZABETHTON TWINS
Minnesota Twins
P.O. Box 6040, Elizabethton, TN 37644.
(615) 543-3551.
Joe O'Brien Field (seats 1,500): on Holly Lane, one block off Hwy. 321.

Complex Baseball

As the 1980s closed, complex baseball was the game's biggest player-development trend. Virtually every club fielded at least one team in either the Arizona League or one of the Gulf Coast League's divisions. The advantage to the teams is that spring training complexes offer good facilities, and little time is wasted on travel. Besides, there's no local owner and no fans to please with a winning team. While the leagues don't attempt to draw fans, the games are open and usually are free. That's the good part. The bad part is they're played in the middle of the afternoon in Florida and Arizona heat. Most of the players are either low-round draft picks out of high school, or players signed from Latin America. Each year, however, a few number one draft picks begin their careers here.

The teams and sites often change, so check the local newspapers or call the league offices (Gulf Coast—[813] 966-6407; Arizona—[602] 483-8224) for schedules.   —DK

President and General Manager: Carmon Dugger.
Tickets: $2.25 ($1.25 children).
Game Times: 7:30.

JOHNSON CITY CARDINALS
St. Louis Cardinals
P.O. Box 568, Johnson City, TN 37601.
(615) 926-7109.
Howard Johnson Field (seats 2,753): on Legion St.
President: Al Ferguson, Jr. General Manager: Lonnie Lowe.
Tickets: Information unavailable.
Game Times: 7:00 (Monday–Saturday), 2:00 (Sunday).

KINGSPORT METS
New York Mets
P.O. Box 3522, Kingsport, TN 37664.
(615) 245-1973.
J. Fred Johnson Stadium (seats 8,000): at Dobyns Bennett High School on Fort Henry Dr.
President and General Manager: Dottie Elsea.
Tickets: $2.25 ($1.25 students).
Game Times: 7:00 (Monday–Saturday), 7:30 (Sunday).

MARTINSVILLE PHILLIES
Philadelphia Phillies
P.O. Box 3614, Martinsville, VA 24115.
(703) 666-2000.
English Field (seats 3,200): on Commonwealth Rd., east of Hwy. 220.
President and Director of Operations: Tim Cahill.
Tickets: $3.00–3.75 ($2.00 children, senior citizens).
Game Times: 7:30.

PRINCETON PIRATES
Pittsburgh Pirates
Municipal Building, Princeton, WV 24740.
(304) 425-9546.
Hunnicutt Field (seats 1,500): at downtown exit on U.S. 460.
President: James Thompson. General Manager: Frances Christie.
Tickets: $2.50 ($1.00 children; $2.00 senior citizens).
Game Times: 7:30.

PULASKI BRAVES
Atlanta Braves
P.O. Box 814, Pulaski, VA 24301.
(703) 980-8200.
Calfee Park (seats 2,000): at intersection of 5th, Pierce, and Calfee Sts.

President: Don Bowman. General Manager: Mike Dixon.

Tickets: $2.00–3.00 ($1.50 children, senior citizens).

Game Times: 7:00.

WYTHEVILLE CUBS
Chicago Cubs
P.O. Box 972, Wytheville, VA 24382.
(703) 228-3183.

Withers Field (seats 1,700): at Monroe and 4th Sts.

President: Trent Crewe. General Manager: Kenny Sayers.

Tickets: Information unavailable.

Game Times: 7:30 (Monday–Saturday), 6:00 (Sunday).

Pioneer League

In 1984 the Triple-A Salt Lake Gulls drew 167,000 fans. In 1988 the Pioneer League's Salt Lake Trappers attracted 176,000 in half as many dates. So who said rookie league ball has to be smalltime? The Trappers have also attracted national attention, especially after they set a minor league record in 1987 by winning 29 straight games. Salt Lake is an especially attractive story because the Trappers are independent of any major league organization. They sign players overlooked in the draft, then proceed to beat teams stocked with drafted players.

The Trappers remain the headliner, but the Pioneer League also fields successful franchises in Billings, Great Falls, and Idaho Falls. The league's only problem is its location, and the distances between cities that cause major league farm directors to cringe. In the late 1980s, problems attracting major league affiliates were so severe that at one point it looked as though the Pioneer League might even fold. Since then, the league has stabilized, and the addition of Salt Lake has given it one of baseball's strongest franchises.

BILLINGS MUSTANGS
Cincinnati Reds

P.O. Box 1553, Billings, MT 59103.
(406) 252-1241.

Cobb Field (seats 4,500): at 9th and 27th Sts.

President and General Manager: Robert Wilson.

Tickets: $2.50 ($1.50 students, $1.00 children).

Game Times: 7:30, 1:30 (some Sundays).

BUTTE COPPER KINGS
Texas Rangers
P.O. Box 186, Butte, MT 59703.
(406) 723-8206.

Alumni Coliseum (seats 1,800): at Montana Tech, on Park St.

President: Miles Wolff. General Manager: Chris Kemple.

Tickets: $3.50–4.00 ($2.00 children, senior citizens, military).

Game Times: 7:00.

GREAT FALLS DODGERS
Los Angeles Dodgers
P.O. Box 1621, Great Falls, MT 59403.
(406) 452-5311.

Legion Park (seats 4,000): at 26th St. and River Rd.

President: Howard Gaare. General Manager: Ray Klesh.

Tickets: $3.00–3.50 ($2.00 children).

Game Times: 7:00 (Monday–Saturday), 2:00 (Sunday).

HELENA BREWERS
Milwaukee Brewers
P.O. Box 4606, Helena, MT 59604.
(406) 449-7616.

Kindrick Legion Field (seats 2,000): at Warren and Memorial Sts.

President: Ron Romaneski. General Manager: Steven Warshaw.

Tickets: $3.00–4.00 ($2.00 students, senior citizens).

Game Times: 7:05.

IDAHO FALLS BRAVES
Atlanta Braves
P.O. Box 2183, Idaho Falls, ID 83403.

(208) 522-8363.

McDermott Field (seats 3,800): at Mound Ave. and Elva St.

President: Dave Elmore. General Manager: Rai Henniger.

Tickets: $3.00 ($2.00 children).

Game Times: 7:00 (Monday–Saturday), 2:00 (Sunday).

MEDICINE HAT BLUE JAYS
Toronto Blue Jays
P.O. Box 465, Medicine Hat, Alta. T1A 0A5.
(403) 526-0404.

Athletic Park (seats 2,800): at Medicine Hat Athletic Complex on 2nd St.

President: Bill Yuill. General Manager: Scott Jamieson.

Tickets: $4.00 ($2.50 children, senior citizens).

Game Times: 7:00.

POCATELLO GIANTS
San Francisco Giants
P.O. Box 4668, Pocatello, ID 83205.
(208) 238-1200

Halliwell Park (seats 2,580): at 1100 W. Alameda Rd.

General Manager: Martin Cusack.

Tickets: $2.50–4.00.

Game Times: 7:00 (Monday–Saturday), 3:00 (Sunday).

SALT LAKE TRAPPERS
Independent
1325 S. Main #102, Salt Lake City, UT 84115.
(801) 484-9900.

Derks Field (seats 10,200): 4 blocks east of I-15 at 13th South exit.

President: Jack Donovan. General Manager: Dave Baggott.

Tickets: $4.00–5.00 ($2.50 children, senior citizens).

Game Times: 7:00 (Monday–Saturday), 1:30 (Sunday).

goes to Mississippi State, where every game is a party behind the left-field fence. Ron Polk's Bulldogs are the talk of the state.

Both Texas and Texas A & M have beautiful ballparks, but don't walk up to the box office on game day and expect to find a ticket. The big games can be sold out weeks ahead of time, as can the Southwest Conference tournament. Arizona and Arizona State create the most interest when they meet, although the Sun Devils promote heavily and can draw big crowds any time. Hawaii also regularly packs the stands, despite local TV coverage of almost every game. As a result, the Rainbows can bring in the best in college baseball opponents every year.

The college game is so strong in the South and West that even NCAA Division II and NAIA teams can play good baseball and attract attention.

You can catch an occasional college game on ESPN and see tomorrow's stars today. Or you can wait until June and go to Omaha.

College Baseball and Other Events

College baseball shot up in popularity during the 1980s, but the growth was uneven.

While new stadiums were built and more people than ever attended games in the South and West, the game remained virtually the same in the Northeast. And while the NCAA tournament expanded to forty-eight teams, with the entire College World Series televised nationally, the CWS itself became more of a regional event. In 1988 four of the eight teams entered were from California, two more from Florida and one from Arizona. Only Wichita State kept it from being an eight-team Sun Belt party.

The colleges in the South and Southwest play a stronger brand of baseball, and emotions run higher. The crowds follow,

and some schools have averaged more fans for baseball than for basketball. In the college baseball hotbeds, you can expect coverage of the teams in the papers and on TV and radio. The promotions are as imaginative as with any professional team.

Among the college strongholds, a few stand out.

The show Ron Fraser puts on at the University of Miami (Fla.) was revolutionary in college baseball. Before Fraser, no one thought college baseball could make money. But Miami gave him no choice. He had to make money to keep the program alive, and he became the game's master promoter. Now there are Fraser imitators around the country, but none match the master. Miami's Mark Light Stadium doesn't have a Left Field Lounge, however. That honor

In Case You Missed It . . .

For most of the year, Omaha is a quiet little town. People get excited about University of Nebraska football, but the home games are an hour away in Lincoln. The stockyards are at work filling America's supermarkets and restaurants, but few people who don't work there know or care.

For two weeks in June, though, Omaha comes alive. Rosenblatt Stadium fills up every night, tailgate parties filling the surrounding parking lots. The civic clubs get to work. And the College World Series brings national attention to Nebraska's biggest city. The CWS isn't on the scale of a major football bowl game or the NCAA Final Four. At least not yet. But the length of the event (nine days), the number of teams (eight) and the double-elimination format give the CWS a feeling all its own.

It's become one of the events that true baseball fans should sample.

Most baseball fans have, at one time or another, planned a trip to visit a big league ballpark or two outside their hometowns. Some companies even offer group tours to major league parks. But check the schedule more carefully, and you might be able to include an interesting non–major league event on your calendar. Every year there are special baseball happenings all over the country.

The college baseball year begins in late January for teams in Florida, Arizona, and California. The Caribbean Series brings winter league champions together somewhere in Latin America each February. But for most baseball fans the first signs of a new season come at the earliest major league spring training workouts in mid-February. With the growth of spring training tourism, even these workouts can get crowded. The real fun for fans starts with the exhibition season, around the first of March. Plan early because spring training games now often sell out.

For smaller crowds and games that mean more to the participants, find a college tournament. Many in-season events are played in March and April, some in Florida not far from spring training sites. Minneapolis also invites teams to the Metrodome, and New Orleans hosts the Busch Classic at the Superdome. California has two major week-long tourneys, the Best in the West at Fresno and the traditional Riverside Baseball Invitational in Riverside.

It's harder to plan for postseason events. Many conference tournaments, as well as the NCAA regionals, aren't set until a few weeks before the event begins. A few conferences have had success with constant sites, and the Big Eight Tourney in Oklahoma City and the Atlantic Coast Tournament in Greenville, S.C., are worth consideration.

Besides the College World Series in Omaha, there are other national college tournaments worth noting. The NAIA World Series has found a home in Lewis-ton, Idaho, and the Junior College World Series is played each year at Grand Junction, Colo. The NCAA Division II and Division III events have moved more frequently, although they've been played in Montgomery, Ala., and Bristol, Conn., respectively, in recent years. All the college championships are played in late May or early June.

Starting in June and continuing through July, many of the minor leagues have all-star games. Formats and sites vary from year to year and league to league. Attendance also varies. Of particular interest is the Triple-A All-Star Game, played in July the day after the major league game.

Later in July, the Hall of Fame induction ceremonies and the Hall of Fame Game are held in Cooperstown, N.Y. Plan early; Cooperstown and Doubleday Field are both very small.

Starting in August, be on the lookout for amateur tournaments, both national and international. The best-known include the National Baseball Congress World Series, a 32-team double-elimination event in Wichita, Kans.; the Little League World Series in Williamsport, Pa.; and the American Legion World Series, which is held at a different site each year. The NBC series is especially interesting, with games going on virtually around the clock. Some teams that compete there include former pro players; others, though true town teams, include future pros on summer break from their college teams.

Minor league playoffs shouldn't be overlooked. Formats vary, but most leagues have some sort of semifinal, followed by a best-of-five final series in early September. The Triple-A Alliance series matches the champions of the International League and American Association. None of the minor league playoffs come with the fanfare or interest involved in college playoffs, let alone in the major league championship series or World Series.

While the major league playoffs are going on in October, other baseball is being played. Major league organizations send some of their top minor league prospects to Florida and Arizona for instructional league experience. All games are played during the day, no admission is charged, and rules vary from league to league, but some of baseball's future stars are always present.

The baseball year ends for most fans and players with the World Series, but baseball executives have another event on the calendar. The annual Winter Meetings are held the first week of December, usually at a warm-weather site. Every year someone complains that no trades are being made at the Winter Meetings anymore—until there's a big trade. The meetings themselves aren't much of a spectacle, unless you thrill at seeing managers, general managers, and owners standing around hotel lobbies and bars. But don't think that everyone wearing a suit and tie is a major league executive; most of the well-dressed are simply seeking minor league front-office jobs.

—DK

CHAPTER 14

A World Serious

Baseball will have no real Olympic tradition until the 1992 Games in Spain are in the books. Up to now baseball and the Olympics have been casual acquaintances, exhibition and demonstration partners. The two crossed paths for the first time during the 1912 Olympics in Stockholm, Sweden. A United States team clobbered a Swedish squad 13–3, and then baseball and the Olympics went their separate ways until the 1936 Berlin Games, when two United States teams put on an exhibition before 125,000 bewildered Germans.

World War II canceled the 1940 Olympics (and a lot of other, more important things), wiping out a promising nine-team baseball tournament in the process, and baseball didn't return to the Games until 1952 in Helsinki, where the U.S. soccer coach organized a pickup team of American Olympians to play the Finland national squad. The U.S. slaughtered the Finns 19–1 before 4,000 fans confused by baseball's slight resemblance to pesapallo, Finland's national game.

In Melbourne four years later, 100,000 turned out to watch a pickup group of U.S. servicemen beat an equally hastily organized Australian outfit, 11–5. Another eight years passed before University of Southern California coach Rod Dedeaux, at the invitation of the Japanese, led an American team to Tokyo for two demonstration games.

Baseball and the Olympics parted after the 1964 Tokyo Games and didn't meet again until the Los Angeles Games twenty years later. The 1984 L.A. Games set in motion a course of events that eventually led to baseball's inclusion as the twenty-

Baseball Abroad

The Russians are coming! The Japanese are coming! And the Cubans, the Italians, the . . .

fifth Summer Olympic sport. The eight-team tournament won by Japan attracted huge crowds to Dodger Stadium to watch future major leaguers Mark McGwire, Will Clark, Barry Larkin, Oddibe McDowell, Cory Snyder, and B. J. Surhoff. The event's success accomplished the improbable: it elevated amateur baseball's status in the eyes of the International Olympic Committee. Two years later the IOC granted baseball full medal status.

In Seoul in 1988, the U.S. names changed to Jim Abbott, Ty Griffin, Tino Martinez, and Robin Ventura, the crowds were much smaller, and the U.S. brought home the gold medal in another eight-team "demonstration" tournament that, as in Los Angeles, did not include Cuba. It's a good bet that Cuba, virtually unbeatable during the 1980s, will not let politics interfere with its desire to claim the gold in the 1992 Olympic baseball competition, the first to be declared official. The U.S., as defending champions, and Spain, as the host country, will fill two more slots in what looks at this writing to be another eight-team field. The countries most likely to complete the list include Japan, Chinese

Taipei, South Korea, Puerto Rico, The Netherlands, Italy, Australia, or Guam. If the Cubans show up at Barcelona, the United States amateurs, defending Olympic champions of America's national pastime, will assume an unaccustomed role of underdogs.

Below is a world tour of baseball programs with "grades" on an ascending scale of 1 to 10.   —JE

United States

Professional Grade: 10
Amateur Grade: 7.5

More than 25 million men, women, and children participate in organized baseball and softball in the U.S., the country that gave birth to baseball. The extensive U.S. professional network of major league baseball and its minor league affiliates, added to the thousands of college, high school, semipro, summer, youth, and softball teams, is unmatched anywhere in the world. Japan, with more than 20 million participants, comes closest to the U.S. in its liking for baseball.

Contacts:
Major League Baseball
Office of the Commissioner
350 Park Ave., 17th Floor
New York, NY 10022
Telephone: (212) 371-7800

National Association of Professional
   Baseball Leagues
P.O. Box "A"
St. Petersburg, FL 33731
Telephone: (813) 822-6937

United States Baseball Federation
2160 Greenwood Ave.
Trenton, NJ 08609
Telephone: (609) 586-2381

As one might expect, United States amateur baseball has fared well against the rest of the world in major international competitions, with one overwhelming exception. The numbers show that in the major tournaments from 1976 to 1989, ten countries are looking for their first win over Team U.S.A. That first victory will be particularly sweet for The Netherlands and Australia. The Netherlands has lost eight straight and Australia six in a row to the Americans.

Team U.S.A. has pummeled Nicaragua, Puerto Rico, and South Korea. Chinese Taipei hangs fairly tough against the U.S., and Japan has a slight edge on the Americans. Canada and Italy have been surprisingly tough. The U.S. is only 11–6 combined against those two nations.

Then there's Cuba.

Cuba accounts for one-third of the U.S. team's losses in the past thirteen years. The U.S. has beaten Cuba only once in fifteen tries. (Throw in the Pan American Games, considered a regional tournament, and the U.S. is 2–17 against Cuba, since 1976.) Take away Cuba, and the U.S. is 99–30 against the rest of the world, a winning percentage of .767. So what accounts for its dismal record vs. the Cubans?

The usual U.S. explanation is that the Cuban team is actually professional. It plays together, stays together year after year, and its members are taken care of by the Cuban government. All of that is true, but the flip side to that broken record is that the U.S. professional leagues weaken the rest of the competition by signing top prospects from other countries. Amateur baseball is holding fast to the no-professional rule, despite the examples set by basketball, tennis, etc. The Dominican Republic, Puerto Rico and Venezuela continually lose top amateur players to U.S. pro-

fessional leagues. Other countries are affected to a lesser extent, but affected nonetheless. Under current amateur baseball rules, once a player signs a professional contract, he is off the national team forever.

For example, prior to the 1988 Olympics, Spain's top pitching prospect signed a U.S. pro contract and was lost to the national team. The U.S. defeated Spain at Seoul, 28–0. Spain is not happy about any of this.

While the U.S. points out the reasons for Cuba's dominance, the rest of the world complains about the Americans' practice of "stealing" players.

All that aside, in recent years the U.S.-Cuba rivalry has resulted in some of the best ball games of the century, amateur or professional. In the title game of the 1981 Intercontinental Cup in Edmonton, Canada, Cuba scored twice in the top of the ninth to tie the score, but the U.S. won the game and the championship in the tenth. At the 1987 Pan Am Games in Indianapolis, Ty Griffin beat the Cubans in a preliminary game with a nationally televised two-run homer in the bottom of the ninth. Those have been the only U.S. tournament victories over Cuba in the past dozen years.

But Team U.S.A. has had Cuba on the ropes many times. Cuba had to come from behind three times, the last time in the eighth, to pull out a 13–9 title victory in the 1987 Pan Am Games. At the 1988 World Championships in Italy, Cuba's Lourdes Gurriel blasted a three-run homer in the ninth to tie the U.S., and Alejo O'Reilly followed with a game-winning shot over the center-field fence. In the title contest of that tournament, Gurriel again tied the score with a ninth-inning blast. Cuba won the championship in the same inning on three singles.

The U.S. won the 1988 Olympic demonstration games in Seoul, but Cuba did not attend. The rivalry will come to a boil in 1992 in Barcelona, when they play for medals, bragging rights, and national

pride in the land that launched Christopher Columbus.

U.S. Senior Amateur Team vs. World,
1976–1989
(World Championships, Intercontinental
Cups, and Olympics)

Opponent	U.S. Wins	U.S. Losses	Pct.
Netherlands	8	0	1.000
Australia	6	0	1.000
Dominican Republic	5	0	1.000
Colombia	4	0	1.000
Venezuela	3	0	1.000
Netherlands Antilles	2	0	1.000
Aruba	2	0	1.000
Belgium	2	0	1.000
Mexico	2	0	1.000
Spain	1	0	1.000
Nicaragua	10	1	.909
Panama	5	1	.833
Puerto Rico	8	2	.800
South Korea	13	3	.812
Italy	5	2	.714
Taiwan	9	6	.600
Canada	6	4	.600
Japan	8	10	.444
Cuba	1	14	.066
Totals	100	43	.699

Japan

Professional Grade: 9
Amateur Grade: 7.5

An American, or Americans, introduced baseball to Japan in the 1870s. Barnstorming visits by major league teams increased the sport's popularity during the early twentieth century, and by the 1930s, baseball in Japan was second only to *sumo* wrestling. World War II caused the breakup of the Japanese professional leagues, but they reorganized after the war. In 1950 Japanese pro ball formed into two six-team leagues, the Pacific and Central, which remain today. Baseball in Japan now has far outdistanced *sumo* as the country's national pastime.

Professional

Pacific League	*Central League*
Daiei Hawks	Chunichi Dragons
Kintetsu Buffaloes	Hanshin Tigers
Lotte Orions	Hiroshima Toyo Carp
Nippon Ham Fighters	Yakult Swallows
Orix Braves	Yokohama Taiyo Whales
Seibu Lions	Yomiuri Giants

The Japanese professionals play a 130-game season from April to October. The two division winners meet in the Japan Baseball Championship Series in the fall. The Japanese do not play extra innings, and they make up all postponed games at the end of the regular season. Teams have been known to play as many as seventeen postseason makeup games.

The Japanese consider their level of baseball every bit as good and maybe even better than the U.S. major leagues. The pay is good and facilities are excellent. Generally, Japanese players are opposed to even the thought of playing baseball in America. Such an action is considered shameful by native Japanese.

Masanori Murakami, born in Otsuki, pitched for the San Francisco Giants in 1964–65, compiling a 5–1 record in 54 games. His decision to play in the U.S. was very unpopular in Japan, and he soon gave in to public opinion and returned to his country.

Each team is allowed two non-Japanese players on its main roster at any one time. Americans make up the majority of that quota, with the remainder coming from Taiwan.

Among the Americans who have played or are playing in Japan: Matty Alou, George Altman, Tony Bernazard, Clete Boyer, Don Buford, Warren Cromartie, Willie Davis, Doug DeCinces, Larry Doby, Mike Easler, Bill Gullickson, Bob Horner, Frank Howard, Dave Johnson, Clarence "Deacon" Jones, Leron Lee, Johnny Lo-

The honorable Festus Perera, Sri Lankan Minister of Fisheries, biting at a hook.

gan, Bill Madlock, Carlos May, Felix Millan, Don Newcombe, Ben Oglivie, Joe Pepitone, Reggie Smith, Dick Stuart, Willie Upshaw, Roy White, and Don Zimmer.

The Japanese look to the Americans to supply home run power. Former major leaguer Randy Bass won two Triple Crowns and hit .337 during a six-year stay in Japan, but his tale shows why it is difficult for Americans to make the adjustment to the Japanese way of life, and vice versa. Bass, a journeyman major leaguer in the U.S., won the Japanese Triple Crown in 1985 and again in 1986, putting up numbers like 54 HRs, 134 RBIs, and a .350 batting average (1985), and 47 HRs, 109 RBIs,

and .389 in 1986. In 1987 he "slumped" to 37 HRs, 79 RBIs, and .320.

On June 27 of the 1988 season, Bass told his team, the Hanshin Tigers, that he had to return to San Francisco because doctors had discovered a brain tumor in his eight-year-old son. The Tigers, floundering in last place, released Bass. In Japan it is generally believed that a man's work comes before his family.

In July of that year, Hanshin Tigers' chief executive officer Shingo Furuya visited Bass in San Francisco, where he tried

Japan's pitchers feature curves and control, but fastballs are on the rise.

For seventy years the Japanese have held a national high school tournament. After local eliminations involving about 4,000 schools, the fifty finalists travel to Osaka, Japan's second-largest city, for a ten-day, nationally televised final tournament that packs Koshien Stadium.

Japan's national amateur team is one of the top three in the world, along with Cuba and the U.S. Japan won the 1984 Olympic demonstration games in Los Angeles, defeating a U.S. team that sent sixteen players into professional baseball.

Japan finished fourth at the 1988 World Amateur Championships in Italy and second to the U.S. at the 1988 Olympic demonstration games in Seoul. Pitcher Takehiro Ishii was 3–0 in Italy and 2–1 in Seoul. First baseman Terushi Nakajima hit .364 at the World Championships and .476 in Seoul.

Contacts:
Japan Professional Baseball Office
Imperial Tower, 7F, 1-1-1
Uchisaiwai-cho, Chiyoda
Tokyo 100, Japan
Telephone: 81-3-502-0022

Pacific League Office
Asahi Bldg, 9F, 6-6-7
Ginza, Chuo-ku
Tokyo 104, Japan
Telephone: 81-3-573-1551

Central League Office
Asahi Bldg., 5F, 6-6-7
Ginza, Chuo-ku
Tokyo 104, Japan
Telephone: 81-3-572-1673

Japan Amateur Baseball Association
Palaceside Bldg.
1-1-1 Hitotsubashi
Chiyoda-ku
Tokyo 100, Japan
Telephone: 81-3-201-0707

unsuccessfully to convince Bass to leave his son and play ball for the Tigers. Upon his return to Japan, Furuya committed suicide by jumping out of an eighth-floor hotel window.

The Japanese call foreign players *gaijin* and prefer to admire native stars like Shigeo Nagashima and Hiromitsu Ochiai. Nagashima, who retired in 1974, was the most popular player ever in Japan. The Yomiuri Giants third baseman won six batting crowns, two home run titles, five MVP awards, and, along with teammate Sadaharu Oh, the all-time Japanese home run leader, led the Giants to nine straight championships from 1965 through 1973.

Ochiai is the top Japanese slugger of today. He won Triple Crowns in 1982, 1985, and 1986, as well as two other batting titles.

Sadaharu Oh is undoubtedly the Japa-

nese player most well known to Americans. Oh hit 868 home runs, 113 more than Hank Aaron and 154 more than Babe Ruth. He averaged one homer every 10.65 times at bat, compared to one every 11.76 for Ruth and one every 16.37 for Aaron.

Oh was born in Japan, but is a citizen of Taiwan, which helps to explain why he never reached the popularity attained by Nagashima. Oh was actually a *gaijin* to many Japanese fans.

About 20 million people of all ages play some form of baseball in Japan. About half that number play "rubber baseball," a youth game that is the Japanese substitute for tee ball. Nine million men and women play softball, and about 830,000 play regular amateur league baseball.

Each city and town in Japan has its own stadium, and there are more than 16,000 baseball stadiums in the country.

Cuba

Professional: None
Amateur Grade: 9

Cuban university students introduced baseball to Cuba in 1866 upon returning from the United States. Baseball became such a favorite among Cuban youth that the Spanish colonial rulers banned it, fearing the money collected from the traditional "passing of the hat" would be used to support opponents of the Spanish government.

After Cuban independence was gained, baseball flourished on the island and in the neighboring countries of the Caribbean. In 1914 the National League of Amateur Baseball of Cuba was formed and regional leagues sprang up all over the island. Cuba contributed great stars like Tony Oliva, Tony Perez, Luis Tiant, Orestes "Minnie" Minoso, Tony Taylor, and Adolfo Luque to U.S. baseball until the 1959 Cuban Revolution cut off the pipeline to the major leagues. After Castro took control, Cuba discontinued its professional leagues, booted out the Havana Sugar Kings (a Cincinnati farm team), and opted out of the Caribbean World Series.

Today in Cuba more than 1,300,000 play baseball at the local, municipal, provincial, and national levels, making it by far the island's most popular sport.

For most of the year, Cuban players are free to represent their home cities and regions in various leagues and tournaments. But when the summer comes and it's time for international competition, Cuba's best players are assembled to form national teams at three age levels: 13–15, 16–18, and 18 and above. National teams also play exhibition games in other countries and serve as host teams when other countries' teams visit Cuba.

The Cuban senior national team changes little from year to year, unlike the U.S. team which changes coaches and almost all of its players every year. Of course, the biggest U.S.-Cuba difference is

that most U.S. players move on to professional baseball, barring them from further representing their country.

Cuba's national team is the world's best amateur squad, based on its record in major world tournaments. It has won the last fourteen World Championships in which it has played. (It did not compete in 1974, 1975, and 1982.) Cuba has claimed the last four Intercontinental Cups and the last five Pan American Games titles. Its record in world competitions since 1976 is 112–11, an astounding .910 percentage. Although Cuba did not play in the 1984 and 1988 Olympics, it is expected to show up at Barcelona in 1992.

In the years since Castro, the names of Cuban players have not been familiar to most U.S. baseball fans, but Cuba's roster is filled with men who could be major league stars. A look at its top hitters at the 1988 World Championships reveals one aspect of Cuba's dominance of international amateur baseball:

Cuban Batters'
1988 World Championship Statistics
(11 Games)

Name	AB	H	Ave	HR	RBI
Lourdes Gurriel	26	13	.500	3	9
Antonio Pacheco	42	21	.500	1	8
Pedro Rodriguez	26	13	.500	4	10
Luis Casanova	43	18	.419	7	20
Luis Ulacia	37	14	.378	1	5
Omar Linares	47	17	.362	6	15
Victor Mesa	40	14	.350	1	15

Despite its overwhelming record, the Cuban team is not universally admired by most of the amateur baseball world. Its flashy and aggressive style of play is meant to intimidate opponents and even umpires. Occasionally the entire Cuban team, including coaches and bench players, will protest ball and strike calls by encircling the home plate umpire, a tactic that should result in ejections left and right.

(Cont. p. 270.)

Caribbean World Series

This February tournament brings together the winter league champions of Venezuela, Puerto Rico, Mexico, and the Dominican Republic in a double round-robin format. It has been played since 1949, with a nine-year layoff in the 1960s and a one-year hiatus in 1981.

Financial difficulties and decreasing attendance threaten to halt the Caribbean Classic. Lack of participation in the winter leagues by Puerto Rican, Dominican, and, to a lesser extent, Venezuelan major league baseball stars has led to apathy among Latin baseball fans, who now are packing the amateur ballparks.

At this writing, Maracaibo, Venezuela, is the scheduled site of the 1990 Caribbean event. Miami and Tucson have expressed interest in hosting the series, but Caribbean baseball officials thus far have rejected the offers of the U.S. cities, arguing that the tournament should be played in one of the participating countries.

Cuba once was a regular in the Caribbean Series, but it pulled out of the event after the Castro Revolution. Cuba was invited but declined to participate in the 1989 series at Mazatlan, Mexico, and they again were invited to play in 1990.

Of the thirty-one Caribbean championships played in 1949–1989, Puerto Rico has won nine, Cuba seven (out of twelve attempts), the Dominican Republic six, Venezuela six, Mexico two, and Panama one.

Contact:
Caribbean Baseball Confederation
171-A, C.P. 83190
Hermosillo, Sonora, Mexico
Telephone: 621-4-35-62 or 621-4-86-20

For reasons unexplained, Cuba gets away with such antics.

Contact:
To contact Cuban baseball officials, the best bet is to call the International Baseball Association: (317) 237-5757.

Cuban Federation of Amateur Baseball
Calle 13, No. 601, Esq. C
Zona Postal 4, Vedado
Havana, Cuba

Puerto Rico

Professional Grade: 8
Amateur Grade: 7

Baseball was established in Puerto Rico long before the U.S. Marines landed there in the early 1900s. The U.S. presence influenced the development and popularity of Puerto Rican baseball, but, as is the case throughout the Caribbean basin, much of the impetus came from Cuba. The Puerto Rican professional leagues, bolstered by black Americans barred from the U.S. major leagues, remained strong throughout the 1930s and into the 1940s, until Jackie Robinson broke the major league color barrier in 1947 and cleared the way for blacks and dark-skinned Latinos to play in the States.

As blacks and Puerto Ricans signed on with big league clubs, Puerto Rico and other Caribbean baseball countries turned to a winter league season to attract those same players. The winter leagues flourished in the 1950s and 1960s, but began to decline in the 1970s, mainly due to economic factors and less participation by native players.

The six participating cities in the Puerto Rican winter league are San Juan, Santurce, Mayaguez, Ponce, Arecibo, and Caguas. Each team is allowed to import eight players. The teams play a 60-game schedule from October 20 to January 23, and the top four finishers meet in a round-robin playoff to determine a champion. The Puerto Rican champion goes on to play in the annual Caribbean World Series.

Puerto Rico has contributed many great players to the major leagues. At the top of the list is Hall of Famer Roberto Clemente, who died in a plane crash in 1972 while attempting to deliver medical supplies to earthquake-torn Managua, Nicaragua. Other past and present Puerto Rican players include Orlando Cepeda, Vic Power, Willie Hernandez, Bobby Bonilla, Jose Oquendo, Candy Maldonado, Ivan Calderon, Dicky Thon, Benito Santiago, Roberto Alomar, and Jose Lind.

With close to 60,000 registered players and more than 100,000 including sandlot ball, Puerto Rico is one of the world's best amateur baseball countries. Its national team is ranked just slightly below the United States and Japan, and is on the rise heading into the 1990s. Puerto Rico placed third at the 1988 Olympics and is 42–49 in nine world tournaments since 1976. As the eighties waned, Puerto Rico moved past South Korea for the distinction of being among the world's top five amateur baseball nations.

First baseman Efraim Garcia posted a .409 batting average at the 1988 World Championships in Italy, and Jorge Robles hit .379 in Italy and .350 at the Seoul Olympics. Outfielder Angel Morales, a .379 hitter at the World Championships, is another good stick.

The island hosted the 1989 Intercontinental Cup, one of the Big Three events on the world amateur baseball schedule. Puerto Rican amateur baseball has surpassed professional baseball in attendance and fan interest throughout the island. Natives say that is because most of Puerto Rico's best professionals play in the States and ignore the island's winter leagues. At the amateur level, every city and town has a ballclub, which creates local and regional interest lacking at the professional level.

Contacts:
Puerto Rican League
Apartado 1852
Hato Rey, PR 00919

Telephone: (809) 765-6285

Puerto Rico Amateur Baseball
    Federation
Apartado 41058
Minillas Station
Santurce, Puerto Rico 00940
Telephone: (809) 722-3340

Venezuela

Professional Grade: 8.5
Amateur Grade: 6.5

Baseball in Venezuela goes back to 1895, when a group of Venezuelan students returned from study in the U.S. and Europe, and started the sport in Caracas. In 1927, the year Babe Ruth hit 60 home runs for the Yankees, the Venezuelan Federation of Amateur Baseball was formed. Today baseball is the country's national sport.

The professional six-team Venezuelan League includes Caracas, Zulia, Laguaira, Aragua, Lara, and Magallanes. The teams play a 60-game, October–February schedule culminating in a four-team, two-tiered, best-of-seven series. The champion goes on to the Caribbean World Series, won in 1989 by Zulia. Every team except Caracas may import seven players. Caracas is limited to six imports because of its relative strength.

Shortstops Luis Aparicio (a Hall of Famer), Chico Carrasquel, and Dave Concepcion are among the best-known Venezuelans who have played major league ball. Others are all-time Venezuelan League base hit leader Vic Davalillo, Cesar Tovar, Andres Galarraga, Bo Diaz, Ozzie Guillen, Tony Armas, and Luis Salazar.

More than 200,000 play amateur league baseball in Venezuela, and approximately 3 million Venezuelans play baseball in some form. Despite its reputation as a strong baseball country, the Venezuelan national team entered only four world-level tournaments from 1976 through 1988 and compiled a 22–23 record. It did not play in the 1988 World Championships, 1988 Olympics, or 1989 Intercontinental Cup. At the 1987 Pan American Games, considered a regional tournament, Venezuela was 1–6.

Undoubtedly, Venezuela, along with the Dominican Republic, could be more of a factor on the international amateur circuit. Lack of money and poor organization hurt the baseball programs of each country. The Dominicans and Puerto Ricans can rightly blame the signing of their top amateurs to professional contracts. Venezuela suffers much less from that standpoint. A concentrated effort backed by sufficient money could push Venezuela and the Dominican Republic to the front line of international amateur baseball.

Venezuela's top amateurs are little known outside the country in recent years because of its lack of major tournament experience. Venezuela's last major world tournament was the 1986 World Championships in The Netherlands. At the 1987 Pan Am Games, catcher Miguel Castaneda hit .428 and first baseman Evencio Chacon hit .360.

Contacts:
Venezuelan Winter League
Avenida Sorbona
Edif. Marta, 2do piso, No. 25
Colinas de Bello Monte
Caracas, Venezuela
Telephone: 58-2-751-2079 or 58-2-766-6897

Venezuelan Amateur Baseball
    Federation
Animas a Platanal
Edificio las Marias, Piso 4-401
Avenida Urdaneta
Caracas, Venezuela
Telephone: 58-2-563-5865

Dominican Republic

Professional Grade: 8
Amateur Grade: 6

Cubans fleeing the Cuban Revolution of

Omar Linares is one of the finest players in the world. Scouts say he could start for most major league clubs now.

the 1890s brought baseball to the Dominican Republic, and the Dominicans identified closely with Cuban baseball for more than half a century. In the late 1950s and early 1960s, Dominicans like Juan Marichal, Manny Mota, Rico Carty, and the Alou brothers (Felipe, Mateo [Matty], and Jesus) broke into the big leagues, and the focus on the island shifted to the U.S.

Professional

DOMINICAN LEAGUE
La Romana Azucareros
San Pedro de Marcoris Estrellas
Santo Domingo Licey
Santo Domingo Escogido
Santiago Aguilas

San Cristobal Caimanes

The Dominican season runs 60 games from October to January, culminating in a four-team round-robin playoff. The Dominican champion moves on to the Caribbean World Series. Each team is limited to six foreign players.

The Dominican League has the same problem as Puerto Rico, and to a lesser extent, Venezuela, in that the country's top stars play in the U.S. major leagues for big money and no longer want to play or are discouraged by U.S. team owners from playing in the winter leagues. With few exceptions, Dominicans like Tony Pena, Pedro Guerrero, Juan Samuel, Alfredo Griffin, Rafael Ramirez, Julio Franco, Tony Fernandez, George Bell, and Jose DeLeon take the winter off. Dominicans who have not reached the star category still compete in their native land, and many young U.S. major and minor league players use the Caribbean to improve their skills, impress their bosses, and get a jump on spring training.

Officially more than 100,000 play organized ball at various age levels, but unofficially many more thousands of Dominican youngsters play with guava-limb bats, rubber balls, and homemade gloves. The Dominican amateur program has suffered because of the emphasis (some would say overemphasis) on signing its players to professional contracts. Los Angeles Dodgers scout and Dominican native Ralph Avila says, "Everyone wants to sign, sign, sign these players . . . but if our amateur programs don't start receiving outside funds pretty soon . . . there won't be any amateur programs left."

More than half of the major league baseball clubs have established scouting camps in the Dominican Republic, and it is estimated that there are more than 1,000 "bird dogs," or part-time scouts, in the country. The town of San Pedro de Marcoris has become a buzzword for budding baseball talent, especially infielders, having produced Tony Fernandez, Julio Franco, Alfredo Griffin, Mariano Duncan, Ra-

fael Ramirez, Manny Lee, Juan Samuel, as well as Pedro Guerrero, George Bell, and Joaquin Andujar.

Once a Dominican player turns seventeen he may be signed to a professional contract. For that reason, and because of the lack of money going into the country's amateur program, the Dominican Republic will continue to flounder at the amateur level, even though the island possesses top talent.

The Dominican Republic has competed in just five international tournaments, compiling a record of 16–24, and it has not fielded a team at a major international tournament for several years.

Contacts:
Dominican League
Apartado 1246
Santo Domingo
Dominican Republic
Telephone: (809) 567-6371

Dominican Republic Amateur Baseball
    Federation
Centro Olimpico, Juan Pablo Duarte
Santo Domingo
Dominican Republic
Telephone: (809) 566-9515 or
    (809) 556-3722

Mexico

Professional Grade: 8
Amateur Grade: 5.5

American railroad workers introduced baseball to Mexico in the 1880s. A Mexican semipro league formed in the 1920s, followed a decade later by professional leagues. Black players from the U.S. and Latin America fueled Mexican baseball in the 1940s. In 1946 Mexican businessman and baseball franchise owner Jorge Pasquel signed major league players Sal Maglie, Mickey Owen, Max Lanier, and others, leading to agreements between the U.S. and Mexican professional leagues on player movement between those two countries.

Baseball Lingo— Spanish

English	Spanish
1. Shortstop	Torpedero
2. Stolen base	Base robada
3. Balk	Lanzamiento ilegal
4. Home run	Cuadrangular
5. Inning	Entrada
6. Run	Carrera
7. Pitcher	Lanzador
8. Walk	Base por bolas
9. Wild pitch	Lanzamiento malo
10. Hit by pitch	Golpeado por lanzamiento

(Source: Baseball Federation of Spain)

There are two Mexican professional leagues, divided into summer and winter play. Unlike most Latin American countries where winter play predominates, the summer league is the more important in Mexico.

Mexican League (Summer)

South Division	*North Division*
Aguascalientes Railroadmen	Monterrey Sultans
Campeche Pirates	Saltillo Sarape Makers
Leon Braves	San Luis Potosi Cactus Men
Mexico City Reds	Monterrey Industrials
Mexico City Tigers	Owls of the Two Laredos
Tabasco Cattlemen	Monclova Steelers
Yucatan Lions	Union Laguna Cotton Pickers

These teams play a 132-game regular season followed by a playoff among the top

A Filipino team of 1924; baseball arrived with the Spanish-American War.

four teams in each division. The two playoff winners meet in a best-of-seven series for the league championship.

Each team is allowed to import three players. Most Mexican clubs have partial working agreements with major league teams. U.S. players are generally absent from Mexico in the first two or three weeks of the season because they are finishing spring training in the States.

Willie Aikens has had more impact in Mexico than any other U.S. player. Aikens, who played for California, Kansas City, and Toronto from 1977 through 1985, made $6,000 a month in 1988—at that time the highest salary in the Mexican League. The league's highest-paid native player in 1988, first baseman Andres Mora, received $2,000 a month.

Pitchers Fernando Valenzuela and Ted Higuera have found success north of the border, but not many Mexicans have made it to the major leagues. This is generally attributed to the grueling bus rides and hot weather endured by Mexican League players. Another consideration is that big league clubs have to pay the Mexican League teams relatively high prices to sign players. It is said by major league scouts that "you can sign four Dominicans for the price of one Mexican."

Mexican Pacific League (Winter)

South Division	North Division
Los Mochis	Mexicali
Mazatlan	Ciudad Obregon
Navojoa	Hermosillo
Culiacan	Guaymas

The Mexican winter league season runs from October to January and is followed by a playoff to determine the league champion. The winner goes on to the Caribbean World Series. Mexico last won the Caribbean title in 1985.

At least 200,000 play organized amateur baseball in Mexico, and an estimated million participate in some form of the sport, including sandlot baseball and softball. In terms of total participants, Mexico trails only the United States, Japan, and possibly Cuba. Mexico holds local and regional championships at all age levels.

Mexico's national team has played in only four international tournaments since 1976 and has done poorly. Its combined record of 8–31 in those tournaments might surprise those who think of Mexico as a strong baseball country. The raw talent is there, but Mexico, like many other Latin nations, cannot afford to pour money into its amateur program. Mexico fin-

Schedule

1990

Central American Games baseball competition: January 5–14, Tegucigalpa, Honduras.

First IBA World All-Star Game: August 22, Atlanta–Fulton County Stadium.

IBA AAA World Youth Championships (16–18 years): August 25–September 5, Cuba.

European Youth Championships: July, Antwerp, Belgium.

Goodwill Games baseball competition: July 26–31, Seattle.

IBA XXXI World Championships: August 4–19, Edmonton, Canada.

Central American and Caribbean Games baseball competition: August, Guatemala City, Guatemala.

1991

IBA X Intercontinental Cup: July, Barcelona and Pamplona, Spain.

IBA AAA World Youth Championships (16–18 years), August, Brandon, Canada.

Asian Baseball Federation Championships: July 27–August 4, Beijing, People's Republic of China.

XI Pan American Games, August 3–18, Havana, Cuba.

European Championships: Summer, Rome, Italy.

1992

Summer Olympics: July 25–August 9, Barcelona, Spain.

ished 2–6 at its last major tournament, the 1987 Intercontinental Cup in Cuba.

Amado Muriel Tarin hit .348 and Adan Ontiveros Andujo batted .323 in the 1987 Cup, but Mexican amateur players are not well known internationally because of the country's nonparticipation in the top events.

Contacts:
Mexican Summer League
Angel Pola No. 16
Col. Periodista
C.P. 11220 Mexico D.F.
Telephone: 905-557-10-07 or 905-557-14-08

Mexican Pacific League
Pesqueira No. 613-B Sur
Navojoa, Sonora
Mexico
Telephone: 642-2-31-00 or 642-2-14-38

Mexican Amateur Baseball Federation
Plaza de la Republica 51
4to. Piso, Col. Tabacalera
C.P. 06030
Mexico 1 D.F., Mexico
Telephone: 52-5-546-1890

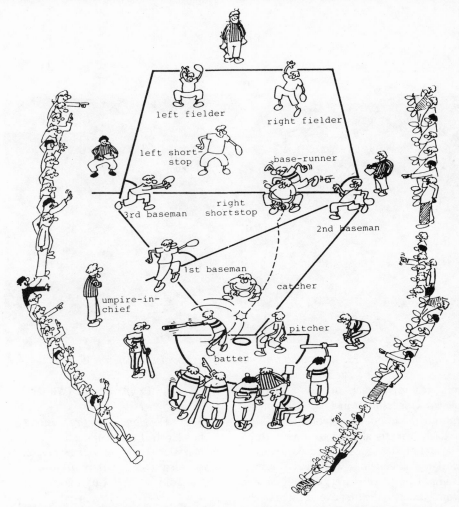

About the time of World War I, Lauri Pihkala adapted parts of American baseball to the old Finnish game of King Ball and created, by 1921, the Finns' national pastime of pesapallo. Note the location of the pitcher, who simply serves the ball up in the air.

Nicaragua

Professional: None (see below)
Amateur Grade: 5.5

Baseball arrived in Nicaragua during the early part of the twentieth century. One story goes that the first team was founded in 1905 by Carter Donaldson, then U.S. consul to Nicaragua. The U.S. Marines later occupied the country for almost twenty years and further popularized the sport. Baseball is the number one sport in Nicaragua, whereas soccer is tops throughout the rest of Central America.

Professional baseball was played in Nicaragua beginning in the 1940s, but today its socialist government does not admit to such a capitalist concept. As in Cuba, Nicaragua's best baseball players are paid and housed much better than the majority of

the population, and are exempt from military service.

The civil war in Nicaragua precludes an estimate on the number of baseball players in the country. Most young men are wearing a different kind of uniform. Nicaraguan President Daniel Ortega says that "all men and boys who live in Nicaragua play baseball," but until the war ends, the country only has limited time and money to spend on baseball. The existing teams serve to boost the morale of the Sandinista government and its backers.

Nicaragua's government subsidizes all ten of the country's major league teams. For obvious reasons, no Americans are playing in Nicaragua. The most well known of the five Nicaraguan players who have made it to the U.S. major leagues is

pitcher Dennis Martinez.

The war also clouds any judgment about the current level of Nicaraguan amateur baseball. At the 1988 World Championships in Italy, Nicaragua was 5–6, good for seventh place out of twelve teams. In ten world tournaments since 1976, Nicaragua is 36–54. Pitcher Felix Moya posted a 3–1 record at the World Championships, and Ariel Delgado hit .341 with 2 home runs in the same tournament. When the war ends, the country will try to rebuild its amateur baseball program quickly as a means to restore its pride and reputation. The Cubans are always on call to help the Nicaraguan baseball program, and in turn the Nicaraguans are assisting with the Soviet Union's attempts to get a baseball program off the ground.

Contact:
Nicaraguan Amateur Baseball
Federation
Apartado Postal 303
Managua, Nicaragua
Telephone: 505-2-22295

Canada

Professional Grade: 10 (Canada is home to
the Montreal Expos, Toronto Blue Jays, and
eight minor league franchises.)
Amateur Grade: 6.5

Baseball in Canada did not begin in 1969
with the expansion Montreal Expos.
Records of Canadian baseball go back to at
least 1877, and some Canadians even claim
that the first baseball game, ever, was
played in the Ontario town of Beachville in
1838.

The original Canadian Amateur Baseball
Association was formed in 1893. Canada's
national team first took the field at the
1967 Pan American Games in Winnipeg,
and the Canadian National Youth Team
was formed in 1978.

At the professional level, Canada boasts
the Expos and Blue Jays, plus the following
minor league franchises:

Pacific Coast League, Class AAA
Calgary Cannons, Alberta
Edmonton Trappers, Alberta
Vancouver Canadians, British
Columbia

Eastern League, Class AA
London Tigers, Ontario

New York-Penn League, Class A
Hamilton Redbirds, Ontario
St. Catherines Blue Jays, Ontario
Welland Pirates, Ontario

Pioneer League, Rookie
Medicine Hat Blue Jays, Alberta

Ferguson Jenkins of Chatham, Ontario,
is among the most well known and successful of more than 150 Canadians who

have made the major leagues. Here are
some others:
Reggie Cleveland (Swift Current,
Saskatchewan)
Rob Ducey (Cambridge, Ontario)
Russ Ford (Brandon, Manitoba)
Dick Fowler (Toronto)
Jack Graney (St. Thomas, Ontario)
John Hiller (Toronto)
Tip O'Neill (London, Ontario)
Ron Piche (Verdun, Quebec)
Terry Puhl (Melville, Saskatchewan)
Claude Raymond (St. Jean, Quebec)
George Selkirk (Huntsville, Ontario)
Pete Ward (Montreal)

More than 250,000 people play organized baseball in Canada. Its national team
is a step below the top amateur baseball
powers, but is making up ground quickly.
Much of the credit for that goes to the
Canadian National Baseball Institute in
Vancouver, where the country's top prospects go to learn baseball from Canada's
best coaches. The Canadians have surpassed the level of Italy and The Netherlands, and are a threat to crack the top
three at future international tournaments.

Canada is 36–53 in eleven major international tournaments since 1976. It has
defeated the U.S. four times in ten tries.
Third baseman Greg Roth and first baseman Greg Duce both hit .359 at the 1988
World Amateur Championships, and Duce
pounded the ball at a .538 clip in the Seoul
Olympics.

Edmonton will host the 1990 World
Championships on August 4–19, and
Brandon, Manitoba, will be the site of the
AAA World Youth Championships for six-
teen- to eighteen-year-olds in August
1991. Trois Rivieres, Quebec, hosted the
1989 AAA Youth tournament.

Almost one hundred Canadian players
are now attending U.S. colleges and universities on baseball scholarships. Bob
Prentice, the head of Canadian scouting
for the Toronto Blue Jays, says that in
1980 virtually no Canadians played col-

lege-level baseball in the U.S.

Contacts:
Major League Baseball
Office of the Commissioner
350 Park Ave., 17th Floor
New York, NY 10022
Telephone: 212-371-7800

National Association of Professional
Baseball Leagues
P.O. Box "A"
St. Petersburg, FL 33731
Telephone: 813-822-6937

Canadian Federation of Amateur Base-
ball
1600 James Naismith Dr., 7th Floor
Gloucester, Ontario
K1B 5N4 Canada
Telephone: 613-745-9315

South Korea

Professional Grade: 8.5
Amateur Grade: 6.5

U.S. missionary P. L. Gillet is credited with
introducing baseball to Korea in 1905. The
first Korean Baseball Championship was
played in 1929. The Korea Amateur Baseball Association, formed in 1946, is the
founding member of the Baseball Federation of Asia, established in 1954. Today
there are more than 30,000 registered
players from youth through senior levels,
and South Korea has a six-team professional league that began in 1982.

Long one of the top five amateur baseball nations, South Korea is slipping. In
fifteen world tournaments since 1976, it
has a fine 84–56 mark, winning the 1982
World Championships and the 1977 Intercontinental Cup. South Korea also has
won or shared five Asian Baseball Championships since 1963. But it finished in
eighth place among twelve teams at the
1988 World Championships and in fourth
place among the eight teams at the 1988
Olympics in Seoul.

Taek-Jae Kwon hit .417 at the 1988

World Championships and .300 at the 1988 Olympics. Pitcher Kwang-Woo Lee had a combined 3–1 record in the same two events.

The Seoul Olympic baseball competition was poorly attended. Korean baseball officials blamed the empty seats on the Koreans' lack of faith in a relatively poor 1988 Korean baseball team. International Baseball Association officials say the Korean Olympic Baseball Committee did a poor job of promoting the tournament within the country. In any case, the sparse attendance led to the 1989 International Olympic Committee decision to limit the 1992 Olympic baseball tournament to eight teams instead of the twelve hoped for by the IBA. At this writing, the IBA is still lobbying for a twelve-team baseball tournament.

Contact:
Korea Amateur Baseball Association
No. 19 Mookyo-Dong
Choon-ku
Seoul, South Korea
Telephone: 82-2-777-7891

Taiwan

Professional: None
Amateur Grade: 7

The history of baseball in Chinese Taipei is forever linked to the Little League World Series in Williamsport, Pennsylvania. A Taiwanese team won the Little League Series for the first time in 1969, beginning a run on American youth baseball titles. From 1969 through 1988, Taiwan won the Little League World Series thirteen times.

The Chinese Taipei Amateur Baseball Association was formed in 1949. Today baseball encompasses players from youth to senior levels.

Chinese Taipei's national team, regarded as one of the top five in the world, is 62–47 in twelve world tournaments since 1976 but has yet to win a major international event. It finished third in the 1988 World Amateur Championships, but faltered at the 1988 Olympic demonstration games, losing all three of its contests. Some of its top players are signed by the Japanese professional leagues, thus weakening the country's national team. One of Chinese Taipei's best players is Tsung-Chiu Lin, who hit .371 with 3 home runs at the 1988 World Championships in Italy, and .385 at the 1988 Olympics in Seoul.

There is talk among Chinese Taipei baseball officials about starting a professional league in the country, but as of this writing it has not come about.

Contact:
Chinese Taipei Baseball Association
53 Jen Ai Road
Section 3
Taipei, Taiwan
Republic of China
Telephone: 886-2-771-3849

The Netherlands

Professional: None
Amateur Grade: 5

Baseball, or "honkbal" in Dutch, was introduced to The Netherlands in 1910 by a Mr. J. C. G. Grasse upon his return from the United States. Grasse established the Dutch Baseball Federation in 1912. The Netherlands reached the 100-team plateau in 1954, and today there are more than 13,000 youth and adult players on 200 clubs. The Netherlands' high schools and universities do not have baseball programs, or any other sport programs, for that matter. To play organized baseball or another organized sport in The Netherlands, one must join a club.

The Netherlands and Italy have been the only serious contenders for the European Championships, but neither is much of a threat to whip top-level amateur baseball countries like Cuba, the U.S., and Japan. The Netherlands has won thirteen European baseball titles to Italy's five since the tournament's inception in 1954. However, Italy has fared better than The Netherlands in world competition, with a 27–49 mark in eight tournaments since 1976 compared with The Netherlands' 21–62 mark in nine events during the same span.

Starting in the 1960s, American college coaches such as the University of Miami's Ron Fraser have guided the Dutch national team, and in the early 1980s many Americans began traveling to The Netherlands to play with or coach club teams. The American influence evident in the Dutch style of play has led to moderate interest from major league scouts. Pitcher Bert Blyleven was born April 6, 1951, in Zeist, The Netherlands, but grew up in the U.S. Bill Groot is one of the country's best modern-day players. Groot hit .326 at the 1988 World Championships in Italy and .333 at the Seoul Olympic demonstration games.

Each year The Netherlands is the site of Europe's best baseball tournaments. Haarlem Baseball Week, an invitational event held in odd-numbered years, attracts 60,000 spectators and strong international competition. In even-numbered years the focus shifts to Rotterdam for the World Port Tournament.

Contact:
Royal Dutch Baseball and Softball Association
P.O. Box 60
2080 Santpoort-Zuid
The Netherlands
Telephone: 31-23-390244

Italy

Professional: None
Amateur Grade: 5

Private clubs began playing baseball in Italy in 1919, and competition between club teams began in 1945. After the formation of the Italian Baseball Federation in 1950, Italy was the catalyst in the founding of the European Baseball Federation in 1953. Today close to 100,000 Italians play organized baseball.

Italy and The Netherlands are the strongest teams in Europe, but they represent

the third tier of world amateur baseball. At the top level are Cuba, the U.S., Japan, Chinese Taipei, and Puerto Rico. The next group includes South Korea, Canada, Venezuela, and the Dominican Republic. Then come Italy and The Netherlands along with Nicaragua, Australia, Panama, and Mexico. The Netherlands and Italy battle each year to qualify as the European representative for world tournaments, but neither is yet a threat to win those events.

Americans can play in Italy, but each Italian local team is limited to a pair of foreign players.

The Italian national team consists entirely of resident citizens of Italy. Giuseppi Carelli hit .389 in the 1988 World Championships. Catcher Roberto Bianchi hit only .235 in the same tournament but is regarded as an excellent receiver and perhaps the best player in Italy.

In 1978 and again in 1988, the Italians hosted the Amateur World Championships.

For the 1988 Championships, which were played in eleven northern cities, Italy spent approximately $20 million to build and upgrade baseball stadiums and facilities. Because of that effort, Italy now is regarded as the center for European baseball.

Italian amateur baseball federation president Aldo Notari is a leading candidate to replace current International Baseball Association President Robert E. Smith of Greenville, Illinois, who is expected to step down as IBA leader when his four-year term expires in 1992.

Contact:
Italian Baseball and Softball Association
Viale Tiziano 70
Rome 00196
Italy
Telephone: 39-6-36858297

(Cont. p. 278.)

South Korea faced Australia in the 1988 Olympic Games; both teams are likely participants in the Barcelona Games of 1992.

Baseball Lingo— Italian

	English	Italian
1.	Home run	Fouricampo
2.	Pitcher	Lanciatore
3.	Caught stealing	Colto rubando
4.	Shortstop	Interbase
5.	Hit	Battute valide
6.	Inning	Riprese
7.	Run	Punti
8.	Stolen base	Basi rubate
9.	Run batted in	Punti battuti a casa
10.	Wild pitch	Lanci pazzi

(Source: Italian Baseball Federation)

Australia

Professional: None
Amateur Grade: 5

It is said that American gold miners played an early form of baseball in Victoria in 1856 and 1857, but there is no mention of team play until 1879, when the first Australian baseball club, St. Kilda of Melbourne, began to arrange games with sailors from visiting ships and with American business groups in Australia. A. G. Spalding of the U.S. brought a touring team to southern Australia in 1888, inspiring the creation two years later of the Victorian Baseball League.

An Australian barnstorming team toured the U.S. in 1897, but illness and injury decimated the squad, which went broke and had to rely on relatives and friends in Australia to send money for their return trip. Australia formed its amateur baseball federation in 1934, but things didn't really get moving until the 1960s with the arrival of U.S. college coaches.

Australia thus far has contributed two players to the major leagues. Second baseman Joe Quinn from Sydney collected 1,797 hits from 1884 through 1901. Shortstop Craig Shipley batted .194 for the Los Angeles Dodgers in 1986 and 1987.

Australia has about 100,000 registered baseball players at all age levels. In comparison, more than 500,000 Australians play cricket. The national team is 11–36 in six world amateur tournaments. It once had difficulty qualifying for major world events because it belonged to the Baseball Federation of Asia, which meant it had to qualify against the likes of Japan, Chinese Taipei, and South Korea. Now, as a member of the Oceania Baseball Confederation, Australia's only real challenger is Guam.

At the 1988 Seoul Olympics, Australia defeated Canada, lost to South Korea 2–1 in ten innings, and stayed close to the U.S. for seven innings before the Americans rallied for a 12–2 victory. Shortstop Matthew Sheldon-Collins hit .333 and played errorless defense.

Australian baseball has a built-in handicap in that the distances are so great to the other Oceania island countries, and within Australia itself. Huge travel costs are incurred in the course of staging national and regional tournaments. Unless increased popularity attracts more sponsors, travel costs will continue to hinder the sport's development in Australia.

Many Americans are attracted to Australian baseball because the level of play is lower than in the States, and the climate provides for year-round play. Australians prefer to stock their local teams with natives, but will accept American players. As with all other countries, the national team may contain only resident citizens.

Contacts:

To inquire about playing in Australia, call or write to the International Baseball Association.

Canadian amateur baseball, with a tradition dating to 1893, is poised to make a dramatic advance in the 1990s.

Australian Baseball Federation
2a Barkly Ave.
Armadale 3143
Australia
Telephone: 61-3-500-9815 or 61-3-500-9666

Panama

Professional: None
Amateur Grade: 5

Rod Carew and Hector Lopez have brought some fame to Panamanian baseball. Carew, born in the Canal Zone, piled up 3,053 hits in a nineteen-year career with the Minnesota Twins and California Angels. Lopez, a native of Colon and the first Panamanian to play in the majors, collected 1,251 hits with the Kansas City Athletics and New York Yankees during the 1950s and '60s.

Panama used to have a professional league and at one time participated in the Caribbean World Series. The Carta Vieja team won the Caribbean Classic in 1950, and Panama hosted the tournament in

1952, 1956, and 1960.

Panama's national amateur team is 14–34 in five major international tournaments since 1976, a percentage that places it between The Netherlands and Colombia. Baseball, with about 16,000 registered players, takes a back seat to soccer in Panama, just as it does in every Central American country except Nicaragua.

Contact:
Panama Baseball Federation
Estadio Juan D. Arosemena
Apartado 9664, Zona 4
Panama City, Panama
Telephone: 507-25-3381

Colombia

Professional: None
Amateur Grade: 4.5

The northern coastal city of Cartagena is the hub of Colombian baseball. Colombian brothers Ibrahim and Gonzalo Zuniga Angel share the credit for bringing baseball there around the turn of the century. Interestingly enough, records show that a Colombian, Luis "Jud" Castro, played for the Philadelphia Athletics in 1902. Only Cuba, among the Latin and Caribbean countries, cracked the major leagues at an earlier date. Castro hit .245 in 143 at bats with 1 home run in his only big league season.

Besides Cartagena, baseball also is played in Barranquilla, Santa Marta, and a few other cities on the northern coast. It is seldom seen inland. An estimated 15,000 play organized baseball in Colombia.

Colombia, with a respectable 16–28 record in four world tournaments since 1976, is a full grade behind its baseball-crazy neighbor, Venezuela. In Colombia soccer, bicycling, and tennis are all far more popular than baseball. The thriving drug business and its related problems have taken a toll on Colombian baseball, just as they have affected many other aspects of Colombian life. For example, Colombia once had a professional winter league that attracted many U.S. players, but when the players began to fear for their safety and stopped going to Colombia, the league disbanded.

Contact:
Colombia Amateur Baseball Federation
Edificio Banco del Comercio
Piso 7
2253 Cartagena de Indias
Cartagena, Colombia
Telephone: 57-53-642626 or 57-53-644968

Guam

Professional: None
Amateur Grade: 4.5

United States military personnel stationed on Guam during World War I introduced baseball to the island. The sport slowly gained in popularity and now includes more than 2,000 registered players of all ages. In 1974 the Guam Major League, the most popular of three amateur leagues on the island, began operations with six teams, the same number it has today. The GML teams are a mixture of natives and U.S. military forces stationed on Guam. A majority of the league's games are broadcast on radio. League games are played in 2,500-seat Paseo Stadium, completed in 1982 at a cost of more than $1 million. As many as 4,300 fans have jammed the facility for a championship final contest.

Guam and Australia are the only serious contenders for the Baseball Confederation of Oceania title, which might mean a berth in the 1992 Olympics. The other members of the confederation are New Zealand, American Samoa, the Northern Marianas, the Marshall Islands, Micronesia, and Palau. If amateur baseball officials decide that Oceania must compete with the Asian teams for 1992 Olympic berths, the chances are good that neither Australia nor Guam will qualify. Australia will be a slight favorite over Guam if Oceania is allowed to hold its own qualifications.

Guam has yet to compete in a major international tournament; thus its players are virtually unknown outside of Oceania. Pitcher-infielder Patrick Sablan and power hitter Ken Benavente starred in 1989. Some of the league's best players come from Guam's U.S. military base, but the national team members must be natives.

Contact:
Guam Baseball Federation
P.O. Box 1617
Agana, Guam 96910
Telephone: 671-477-9125

Netherlands Antilles

Professional: None
Amateur Grade: 4

Standard Oil played a role in bringing baseball to the Netherlands Antilles during World War II. The presence of 9,000 Standard employees producing oil for the war effort, plus the influx of immigrants from Cuba, Venezuela, Puerto Rico, and the Dominican Republic, resulted in baseball. The Netherlands Antilles Amateur Baseball Federation was formed in the 1960s, and today about 5,000 play organized ball throughout the island chain.

In three international tournaments, the Netherlands Antilles is 7–25, including a 1–10 effort at the 1988 World Championships in Italy. The country does not have the manpower or baseball tradition to challenge the better baseball nations, although it will continue to qualify for a major tournament now and then.

Rafael Josefa of Aruba, part of the Netherlands Antilles until 1986, is regarded as the best hitter in Netherlands Antilles baseball history. Josefa, now forty years old, averaged one home run every 11.6 times at bat during a sixteen-year career with Curaçao. The current team does not have a true star, but Arthur Mari hit .308 with 4 doubles at the 1988 World Championships. Josefa, well past his prime, hit .250 at the same tournament.

Contact:
Netherlands Antilles Baseball Federation
Saint Rosa 62
P.O. Box 488
Curaçao, Netherlands Antilles
Telephone: 599-9-672-280

Belgium and Spain

Professional: None
Amateur Grade: 3.5

At this level the rankings for international amateur baseball become utterly subjective. Other countries that could be ranked alongside Spain and Belgium are Brazil, Ecuador, the Philippines, and possibly Honduras and El Salvador. Belgium gets a top-twenty nod because of its participation in the 1978 and 1986 World Championships, and Spain because it played in the 1988 World Championships and will be the host country for the 1992 Olympics.

Both Spain and Belgium have been plastered in World Championship competition. Belgium is 1–20 in two tournaments, its lone victory a 4–1 decision in 1986 over the Netherlands Antilles in The Netherlands. During that same tournament, Belgium took it on the chin by scores of 16–0,

Baseball Lingo— French

English	French
1. Balk	Feinte illégale
2. Grand slam	Grand quatre
3. Hit and run	Court-et-frappe
4. Knuckle ball	Balle papillon
5. Pinch hitter	Frappeur d'urgence
6. Spit ball	Balle mouillée
7. Home run	Coup de circuit
8. Inning	Manche
9. Walk	But sur balles
10. Squeeze play	Risque-tout

(Source: French Baseball and Softball Federation)

13–1, 26–2, 17–0, 21–3 and 19–0. In the same vein, Spain went 0–11 at the 1988 World Championships in Italy, losing by scores of 28–0, 10–0, 17–1, 15–0, 16–3, 17–0, and 20–2. These massacres point clearly to the steep decline in quality that occurs at the tail end of this top-twenty list.

Spain and Belgium cannot really be considered serious baseball countries, although each has dabbled in baseball and will continue to field teams. Belgium's baseball history goes back to 1923 and Spain's to 1920, but they are minor histories, much like the history of United States rugby or field hockey. Belgium actually won the European baseball championships in 1967, but only because Italy and The Netherlands did not play that year. Since 1970 Belgium and Spain have battled it out for third place behind the Dutch and the Italians, although West Germany and Sweden occasionally sneak in to win the third spot.

The fledgling Soviet Union now is part of the European baseball scene, which may mean that Spain and Belgium, The Netherlands and Italy, and the rest of the European baseball community must upgrade their programs or get used to finishing behind the U.S.S.R. The Soviets will not waste any time in taking over the third position in European baseball and then will set their sights on The Netherlands and Italy for the top spot.

Contacts:
Belgium Baseball and Softball Federation
Post Bus 13
Antwerp 2000
Belgium
Telephone: 32-3-325-4910

Baseball and Softball Federation of Spain
Coslada 10, 4o izqda
Madrid 28028
Spain
Telephone: 34-1-245-2844

The Soviet Union

Listen closely: in the vast expanse of Eurasia known as the Soviet Union, you will hear the most American of sounds—the smack of *miuch* against *lovooshkah*. In Moscow, in Leningrad, in Minsk, comrades don *shlems* and grip their *beetahs*.

Of course I'm talking about baseball. *Miuch* is ball, *lovooshkah* means glove, *shlem* is helmet, and *beetah* is bat. The U.S.S.R. intends to use them to qualify for the 1992 Olympic baseball tournament, maybe even to win the gold medal.

Stand with any Soviet baseball official for five minutes and he will probably say, "We win the Olympic gold medal in hockey after playing only few years. Same with basketball. Gold medal. We can do same in baseball."

American baseball men snort and fume and respond this way: "Sure, you did it in those sports, but baseball is different, totally different. It takes more finesse, strategy, talent, smarts. You can't learn baseball in such a short time. It takes years just to understand the balk rule, for crying out loud! Try turning a 3–6–3 double play, try snapping off a split-fingered fastball over the outside corner at the knees. Hell, by 1992 we'll still be fooling you with the hidden-ball trick."

Plainly the Soviet ambition of instant baseball mastery rankles many in the U.S. baseball community, which, naturally, is doing everything it can to make sure the Soviets achieve their goal. In 1986, when Olympic baseball sparked the Soviets' interest, U.S. baseball people began falling all over themselves trying to help them. As T. M. Shine wrote in the April 3, 1988, edition of *Tropic*, the Sunday magazine of the *Miami Herald*, "We have been our usual flattered selves, responding with idiotic generosity and goodwill. We have turned over our dungarees, our Coca-Cola Classic, our Ford Falcons, our pop music. We gave them Billy Joel. They can have Billy Joel. But *baseball?*"

To the fledgling Soviet baseball program, the U.S. has contributed balls, bats, gloves, uniforms, caps, jocks, books, charts, diagrams, videos, chewing tobacco, and time. Lots of time.

In February 1988 the International Baseball Association arranged a deluxe U.S. baseball tour for Soviet coaches Alexander Ardatov and Guela Chikhradze. The pair visited Dodgertown in Vero Beach, chummed with Alan Trammell of the Tigers and the Twins' Steve Lombardozzi, took a road trip with Florida Southern University, practiced with Georgia Southern, and got the royal treatment at the U.S. Baseball Federation complex in Millington, Tennessee. Ardatov absorbed everything, soaked up baseball like a bone-dry sponge. Chikhradze recorded everything, filled notebooks like Tolstoy reincarnated as a baseball freak. They returned to the motherland with 100 years worth of baseball knowledge and half a ton of baseball hardware and software, all donated by grinning Americans.

The U.S. is not alone in its desire to help the Soviets master the grand old game. Cuba, Japan, Nicaragua, and other, less talented baseball nations routinely fork over instructional material and exchange coaching visits with the U.S.S.R.

Baseball Lingo—
Russian

English	Russian
1. Ball	Miuch
2. Glove	Lovooshkah
3. Bat	Beetah
4. Mask	Mahskah
5. Chest protector	Nahgroodnick
6. Base	Bahsah
7. Home	Dom
8. Pitcher's rubber	Plasteenah pitcherah
9. Pitching machine	Pitcher-avtomat
10. Helmet	Shlem

(Source: International Baseball Association)

Which brings us to the question that begs to be asked: Would it be so terrible if the Soviets achieve parity with, or God help us, superiority to U.S. baseball?

During the Dodgertown stay of Ardatov and Chikhradze in the spring of '88, Soviet baseball was new and innocent and inept. Witnesses recall the atmosphere of hope inspired by blue skies and soft days full of promise common to all spring camps, but with the uncommon addition of the Dodgers working out with the Japanese Chunichi Dragons and—look over there—two Soviet *baseball* coaches! Nice moments followed one after another, as almost everyone, even some of the journalists, tried extra hard to believe that baseball could lead to better things, globally speaking. (Strategic arms, you say? You must be talking about relief pitchers.) Fed up with summits and superpower nonsense, the Dodgertown crowd gladly turned to baseball for solutions it will never be able to deliver.

But lest anyone worry that the Soviets really can win the gold at Barcelona, here

The crack of the beetah, *the flight of the* miuch, *the smack in the* lovooshkah—*ah, now that's talkin'* beisbol! *Above, the visiting Czechs play the Soviets at Tbilisi, Georgia, in October 1987.*

are a few scores from a series of exhibition games between the Soviet national team and U.S. colleges in 1989:

Navy 20, U.S.S.R. 1

George Washington 21, U.S.S.R. 1

Virginia Commonwealth 16, U.S.S.R. 2

It's clear that long days lie ahead for Soviet baseball. Its first official test will come at the 1990 Goodwill Games this July in Seattle, where the U.S.S.R. undoubtedly will endure more poundings.

But U.S. baseball might as well get used to the idea that one day, perhaps as early as the year 2000, Alexander Ardatov could step up on the victory platform and accept an Olympic medal, maybe even a gold medal. He might even thank the U.S. for its role in the success of the Soviet baseball program.

Would that be such a terrible thing?

CHAPTER 15

Magnates Made Easy

In the cold, dark winter of 1979–1980, a group of outwardly sane, seemingly mature adults came together in a now-defunct restaurant in Manhattan named La Rotisserie Française. Their mission: to eat snails and make history. They were united in the passionate conviction that they could do for fun what the likes of Fred Claire and Frank Cashen do for a living. And do it better.

Run a big league baseball club? No problem. All it takes is an abiding love of baseball, quick wits, the willingness to pore over box scores with the dedication of a medieval scholar, a smidgen of luck—and about $75 million, the going price of a major league team. Oh. *That.*

There it might have all ended had not a lone, heroic soul among them refused to relinquish his dream. Undaunted by their temporary inability to meet the financial prerequisite for major league ownership, Daniel Okrent answered the group's dejected looks with a simple question: "Why don't we invent our own game?" And so they did.

The Rotisserie League concept is simple. Each "owner" acquires a team of 23 real, live major league players at a draft auction (9 pitchers, 5 outfielders, 6 infielders, 2 catchers, 1 utility/designated hitter). There are 10 owners in a league using National League players, 12 when American Leaguers are employed. Each team has a total budget of $260 to spend in buying its players (or 260 "units" if a league does not wish to play for cash). The money goes into a pot that is divided among the winners at the end of the season. The pennant winner is the team whose players produce the best numbers over the course of the season in eight statistical categories—four

Rotisserie Leagues and Stat Services

Caveat emptor and other fantasy league realities

offensive and four pitching—that are commonly used to measure baseball performance. For example, in a 10-team Rotisserie League, the team with the most home runs gets 10 points, the team with second most gets 9 points, and so on. A team's total points determines its place in the standings.

The most important day of the year for a Rotisserie League owner is draft auction day. Imagine a long table, around which are seated ten or twelve people, each surrounded by a small mountain of notes and baseball record books. "Orel Hershiser—one dollar," somebody says. "Ten dollars," somebody else raises the bid. Your team needs an ace starting pitcher, and they don't come any better than Orel. "Fifteen dollars," you say. And so it goes, each owner calculating how many dollars/units he has left, how many more players he needs, what pitchers are left in the free-agent pool, quickly rethinking his original strategy and hastily scribbling "Plan B" on a notepad. "Twenty-seven dollars," the owner next to you says. What to do? You had only planned to spend $25 on Orel. Go

higher and you might not get the power hitter you need. "Twenty-eight dollars," a quivering voice says. Who was that? It's not until the auctioneer has said, "Going, going . . ." that you recognize the last bidder. It was you.

That's only the beginning. The "Third League" has everything that the other two leagues have: trades, free-agent signings, long-term contracts, minor league farm systems, September roster expansion. Only more so. Whereas an American or National League GM might swing one or two deals a year, a Rotisserie League team owner aflush with pennant fever can easily make twice that many in a single week.

What drives Rotisserie League baseball? Easy. It's the impulse that causes an eight-year-old boy to memorize every line on the back of a baseball card . . . it's the conviction held by every bleacher bum worth his dog and brew that he knows more about baseball than those idiots in the front office . . . and in the end, it's the chance to put your money where your mouth is. You build a team with just the blend of power, speed, and pitching that you like. *You* scout the free-agent market for good buys. *You* wheel and deal, matching wits and wiliness with your fellow owners. And *you* dump overpriced bums to make way for hungry young rookies.

Given America's long-standing love affair with baseball, it's no surprise that Rotisserie League Baseball has become a nationwide craze. According to *USA Today* and *The Sporting News*, upwards of a million people play, and the number is growing. A far cry from your playing catch with Dad and buying your first pack of baseball cards? Not at all. Matter of fact, that's where it all began.   —GW

Stat Services and Fantasy Leagues

A large part of the game's appeal is the way it enables the average fan to suffer the trials and tribulations of a real general manager or principal owner. Anyone who has played the game and overpaid for an unproductive superstar begins to develop respect for George Steinbrenner.

Recent estimates say 500,000 to a million people are torturing themselves each summer by owning fictitious teams of lazy millionaires. That figure seems low, especially if you talk to the harried personnel in the publicity departments of the twenty-six major league teams. They've been brought to their knees by a flood of phone calls from fantasy-team owners seeking details about a particular player's injury or why he didn't appear in the lineup the previous day.

Over at the classified ad department of *The Sporting News*, Caroline Phillips reports that she and her staff had their brains reduced to mush during spring training last year by a mob of entrepreneurs seeking advertising space for their fantasy statistic services, leagues, computer software, tip sheets, and newsletters aimed at this booming market.

"I'd say from 1988 to 1989, we saw a 40 percent increase in the number of ad requests we received," Phillips says, echoing a figure cited by her counterparts at *Baseball America*, a weekly newspaper revered by fantasy owners. "We had more new people than ever before. You'll see even more next year."

The popularity of fantasy baseball has also sparked a tremendous thirst for information about major league players and their teams. Data base services now provide the owners of personal computers with access to up-to-the-minute game accounts, box scores, injury reports, and sta-

To record daily stats, someone scores the plays onto a laptop computer, then transmits the data to a computer at Major League Baseball's N. Y. headquarters.•

tistics. The benefits to the casual fan are also tremendous. Even if you don't play fantasy baseball, you can follow your favorite major league teams more closely than ever before.

The intent of this section is to provide you with a handy reference catalog of goods and services designed for everyone, from the most rabid fantasy leaguer to the Little League, high school, or college baseball coach who wants to keep stats for his team more efficiently. Prices quoted may have changed by the time you read this.

—JR

Statistics Services

Generally stat services provide weekly standings reports in two ways: (1) If you have a personal computer (IBM-compatible or Macintosh are the most common hardware) and a modem, some will send you a software program that enables you to plug into their data bases, download your stats, and print them out each week. (2) Other services print the stats and mail or fax them to you.

Athough the standard fantasy scoring format ranks teams according to eight statistical categories (batting average, home runs, RBIs, stolen bases, wins, saves, earned run average, and walks plus hits divided by innings pitched), some services can tabulate twelve or more stats, usually for an additional fee.

ARISTO-STAT SPORTS
7706 Feliciana
Spring, TX 77379
(713) 370-5898
Weekly reports by mail with standard 8-category format. Yearly fee: $55 per team.

BAR-B-QUE STATS
P.O. Box 1165
Piscataway, NJ 08854
(718) 336-2171
Weekly reports by fax or mail with choice of 8 to 12 categories. Yearly fee: $55 per team. Newsletter (5 issues annually), $5. Rules/general questions welcome during the season.

BUSH LEAGUE SERVICES
P.O. Box 28097
Dept. 18
St. Louis, MO 63119
(314) 962-4490
Weekly reports by mail with choice of 19 stat categories. Yearly fee: $15 per team. Modem service with 19-category league-management program (IBM-compatible), $79. Strategy newsletter, yearly subscription: $24.95.

CENTER FIELD SOFTWARE
P.O. Box 52014
Durham, NC 27717
(919) 361-5851
Reports by modem or mail with selection of 23 categories. Yearly fee: $300 per league for newcomers, $125 per league after renewal of service. Monthly newsletter available for $10 per year.

COMPU-STAT SPORTS
P.O. Box 1264
Solana Beach, CA 92075
(800) 456-3698
One of the larger services with a full-time staff and over 100 client leagues. Reports by modem or mail with choice of up to 12 stat categories and monthly newsletter. Yearly fee: $40 per team.

FASTATS
1650 West Chester Pike BE3
West Chester, PA 19382
(800) 631-6111

Reports by fax or mail with flexible stat formats. Yearly fee: $37 per team.

HEATH RESEARCH
3841 Croonenbergh Way
Virginia Beach, VA 23452
(804) 498-8197
One of the top services with over 172 client leagues. Reports by modem, mail, or fax ($3 per week). Standard 8 categories only. Yearly fee: $60 per team.

MENDOZA-LINE STATS
P.O. Box 83251
Los Angeles, CA 90083
(213) 305-8875
Yearly fee: $38 per team.

NORTH SHORE SOFTWARE
280 Lafayette St.
P.O. Box 792
New York, NY 10012
(212) 941-6924
Reports by modem, fax, or mail with flexible stat formats. Yearly base fee: $25 per team. Additional charges for customized formats.

ON THE BALL STATSERVICE
P.O. Box 39700
Cincinnati, OH 45239
(513) 742-0761
Weekly reports by mail with standard 8 categories. Yearly fee: $34.95 per team.

ROTISSERIE LEAGUE STATS
211 West 92nd St., Box 9
New York, NY 10025
(212) 496-8098
The stat service founded and run by the fellows who invented the game. Weekly reports by fax or mail. Standard 8 categories with choice of traditional 23-player rosters or new 40-player "Ultra" format. Yearly fee: $675 per league.

ROTI-STATS
11770 Warner Ave., Suite 225
Fountain Valley, CA 92708
(714) 668-0158

One of the larger, more established services with over 198 client leagues. Reports by fax, modem, or mail. Choice of up to 20 categories. Yearly fee: $50 per team.

SAC PROGRAMS
P.O. Box 458
Flint, MI 48501
(313) 767-0749
Reports by mail with flexible stat formats. Yearly fee: $35 per team.

SPORTS PROGRAMMING
P.O. Box 172
Moline, IL 61265
(309) 797-8230/(309) 792-9452
Reports by mail in standard 8-category format. National League players only. Yearly fee: $40 per team.

STATKEEPERS
122 South Main
Woodstock, VA 22664
(703) 459-2793
Flexible format. Yearly fee: $35 per team for first 8 teams, $30 for each additional team.

STATMAN
P.O. Box 18162
Baltimore, MD 21220-0262

Flexible format. Yearly fee: $350 per league.

THINKING MAN'S BASEBALL
Dept. 45
2832 Shady Ave.,
Pittsburgh, PA 15217
(412) 521-6033
Reports by modem, fax, diskette, or mail with flexible format. Yearly fee: $45 per team.

USA TODAY SPORTS CENTER
(800) 722-2846
The newspaper with the sports section that has won the hearts of fantasy leaguers everywhere will supply your league's stats by modem for a fee of $60 per team. You tap in to their data base; they give you your stats. They don't come any more reliable.

WORD PROCESSORS
8807 Halford Way
Louisville, KY 40299
(502) 491-9305
Weekly reports by modem or mail plus free strategy or rules advice from proprietor Warren R. Donaldson, the official statkeeper for Vanderbilt University's football team. A small, but competent service. Seasonal fee: $35 per team.   —JR

Leagues

These are fantasy baseball's answer to those gab hotlines for singles. If you can't scrape up enough warm bodies to form a league of your own, they will place you in one of theirs. You'll get a list of your fellow owners, their addresses, and phone numbers. If you want to exchange pictures, that's up to you. Be aware, however, that your new comrades may reside in such far-flung outposts as Pistol Thicket, Louisiana, or Hypothermia, Alaska, so expect to incur ghastly phone bills when you want to talk trades.

Another drawback is that while some services will arrange a player draft by conference call (another added expense), others use a mail-in arrangement whereby you must rate all available players at each position in the order in which you want them. You will be given the first pick for at least one position, but the rest of the way it's strictly luck of the draw. This takes the challenge out of drafting a team. There are few tests of mettle greater than a live draft where you must go to the mat with stubborn rivals for the rights to Spike Owen.

DIAMOND FANTASY
P.O. Box 732
Glastonbury, CT 06033
(203) 568-1814
Option of mail, live, or phone drafts. Can assign you to a league during the season. Fee: $90–$160.

ELITE BASEBALL LEAGUE
101 Overpeck Ave.
Ridgefield Park, NJ 07660
(201) 641-4780
Traditional format and mail draft. Entry fee: $80.

J & J COMPUTER SPORTS
P.O. Box 98
East Northport, NY 11731
(516) 754-2221

One of the top services, with over 130 leagues. Draft in person or by mail. Entry fee: $195 plus franchise fee of $16.95 or $19.95 according to placement in beginner or advanced play league.

MAJOR LEAGUE FANTASY BASEBALL
P.O. Box 230184, Gravesend
Brooklyn, NY 11223
(718) 336-4149
Offers 18-team leagues and choice of 12 stat categories.   —JR

Full-Service Companies

The following services process stats for private leagues or place stray owners in their own leagues:

BIG LEAGUE FANTASY, INC.
1617 South Pacific Coast Highway, Suite F
Redondo Beach, CA 90277
(213) 316-1120
Weekly stats by modem or mail for $50 per team. Entry fee to their own leagues is $95. League-management software programs available from $49.95 to $99.95.

GENERAL MANAGER BASEBALL LEAGUE
P.O. Box 19757
San Diego, CA 92119
(619) 465-2255
Weekly reports by mail (fax/modem possible for 1990) in 10 stat category format for private leagues. Yearly fee, $45 per team. Placement in 10-category standard-format leagues with mail drafts, $95.

SANDLOT BASEBALL LEAGUE
P.O. Box 55
Collingswood, NJ 08108
(800) 535-0123/ (609) 854-7739
Standard format with mail draft. Entry fee, $85. Weekly stats for private leagues, $25 per team.

SUPER FAN BASEBALL, INC.
3208 North Tucson Blvd.
Tucson, AZ 85716.
(602) 882-2226
Offers 8-team leagues with 12-stat-category format and mail draft. Entry fee/biweekly stat reports for private leagues: $95.

WALTER MITTY SPORTS
425 Kirkwood Cove
Burr Ridge, IL 60521
(312) 850-7230/ (800) 443-5913
Entering its eighth year. Offers a selection of 18 stat categories, free WATS, and fax service. Will organize draft-by-mail leagues. Yearly fee for either service, $75 per team with unlimited transactions; $50 per team with additional fee per transaction.   —JR

Variation Leagues

Over the years the original Rotisserie baseball game has spawned a number of variations. One of the most common is a head-to-head format by which teams are scheduled to play week-long "games" against one another. Each Monday an owner fills out a lineup card and phones it in to the service. The stats of the nine players he lists that week are then matched against the lineup of a designated opponent. His team is awarded points for each statistical category it wins during that week and a bonus for winning a majority of the categories. Teams are ranked according to their overall point totals.

Advocates of this format say it offers more challenge and involvement than the traditional fantasy game. By requiring them each week to select nine players from their roster who match up best with an opponent, they must think like a field manager as well as a front-office executive.

The only game to play for aspiring Steinbrenners.

ARMCHAIR SPORTS GROUP
P.O. Box 8294
Longview, TX 75607
(214) 236-4795
Head-to-head format with mail or phone drafts. Entry fee, $110. Will also process stats for private leagues using same format for $100 per team.

BASEBALL FAN-TASTIC
Dept. 25
P.O. Box 698
North Bellmore, NY 11710
(516) 781-9030
Weekly head-to-head format. Entry fees $20–$30 with $5 report-processing charge.

BILL JAMES FANTASY BASEBALL
7250 North Cicero Ave.
Lincolnwood, IL 60646-9911
(800) 637-8287
The Sultan of Stat has invented his own version of fantasy baseball, and the complex scoring system will surely enthrall lawyers and physicists. But don't panic— any owner can calculate his team's progress from box scores. For a $75 entry fee you can play in a separate league or take on the Master himself. He'll even make fun of your team in a newsletter. Unlike most leagues, you can enter this one at any time during the season and make player transactions on any day of the week. That's a very nice luxury.

NUTMEG LEAGUE
P.O. Box 2631
Waterbury, CT 06723
(203) 393-3142
Head-to-head format. Fee: $85 per season.

PLAY-BY-PLAY BASEBALL, INC.
P.O. Box 27
Bend, OR 97709
(800) 678-7117
Computer-simulated games based on weekly lineups. Stat reports sent in the form of a detailed box score. Fee: $80–$95 per year.

SUN SPORTS
P.O. Box 199
Cheltenham, PA 19012
(215) 725-7700
Head-to-head format uses all official major league stat categories. Entry fee, $130 with additional charge for conference-call draft ($39) or computer draft ($13).

USA TODAY SPORTS CENTER
(800) 722-2846
If you subscribe to their computer data base service, you can play a head-to-head game with a funky twist. Each week you select your lineup by computer from a pool of players provided by the service. If your opponent also chooses one of your players, you both get him. Your roster changes every week, and you get the results on your PC. Fee, $4.95 per hour.   —JR

Sports Data Bases

Any fantasy leaguer can tell you that playing the game inevitably causes obsessive-compulsive behavior in even the most stable personalities. Each morning you seek box scores with the determination of a salmon fighting its way upstream to spawn. Each evening you do virtually anything to find out how your players are doing, even it means watching the Atlanta Braves on cable.

Thanks to personal computers, the mental health of thousands of fantasy leaguers is being saved. If you have access to a PC and a modem, these services can

give you up-to-the minute scores, game reports, box scores, stats, and even betting lines on all sports virtually around the clock. Ideal for all fans, especially during the heat of a pennant race.

COMPUSERVE
5000 Arlington Centre Blvd.
P.O. Box 20212
Columbus, OH 43220
Offers modem connection with AP sports wire for up-to-the-minute box scores, game accounts, and breaking stories. Compatible with many brands of personal computer. One-time membership fee: $39.95. Additional charges, according to usage, are $6–$12.50 per hour.

COMPUTER SPORTS WORLD
1005 Elm St.,
Boulder City, NV 89005
(702) 294-0191
Provides fantasy-league management software and modem access to official major league statistics as well as over 5,000 files of sports information, updates of games in progress, betting lines, and injury reports. Subscriber's fee: $29.95 with access charge of $0.30–$0.96 per minute.

PROJECT SCORESHEET
P.O. Box 12009
Lansing, MI 48901-2009
(517) 394-3070
Like SABR, Project Scoresheet is a not-for-profit, member-based organization that is dedicated to providing more and better baseball information. Members score all major league games each season on a play-by-play basis; these scoresheets are used to compile a comprehensive data base. The fantasy league player (as well as other fans or researchers) with an IBM-compatible or Macintosh computer may purchase data for teams and leagues from 1984 to date, including pitch-by-pitch scoring for 98 percent of the games played.

Teams are available for $25 per season; whole leagues are available at $250 per season.

The Stats Inc. logo.

SPORTSTICKER
Harborside Financial Center
600 Plaza Two
Jersey City, NJ 07311
(201) 309-1200
Their PC Plus software offers 24-hour modem access to stats, updated scores, and complete coverage of all sports events and breaking stories. Widely used by the media in the U.S., Canada, and Europe. Fees set according to use.

STATS INC.
7250 North Cicero
Lincolnwood, IL 60646
(312) 676-3322
These guys cover every major league game play-by-play, pitch-by-pitch, including where and how hard every ball is hit. Over 30, often incredibly detailed—even customized—reports are available on paper or computer disk, or through modem link, including how well every player hit when he was behind in the count, how effective each pitcher was on three, four, or five days rest, and much more. Major league clubs such as the Yankees and White Sox use the STATS Inc. daily reports to scout opponents or belittle players at salary arbitration hearings. Ain't nothing like the real thing, baby. Report prices vary.

USA TODAY SPORTS CENTER
(800) 722-2846
Modem access to official major and minor league stats, box scores, game reports, and feature stories. You'll be able to get the paper hours before it reaches the newsstands. Fee: $4.95 per hour plus phone charges.

HOWE SPORTS DATA INTERNATIONAL
401 D St.,
Boston, MA 02210
(617) 269-0304
Compiles complete, official statistics for all minor league baseball teams during the season and makes them available by mail only. Fees are $50–$350 per year according to the number of league, team, or single-game reports requested.   —JR

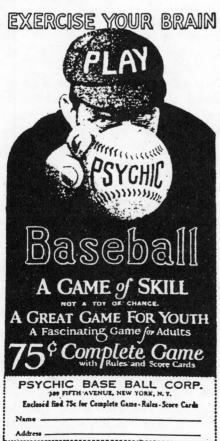

How about psychic leagues, with connections not electronic but telepathic?

Computer Software

The new wave of software products can help you manage your own fantasy league, rate players, plan a strategy for draft day, or keep complete, accurate stats for your Little League team. New items arrive on the shelves of your local computer store all the time, and magazines such as *Personal Computing* or *PC* often spotlight the latest developments in the field. Here's a sampler of what's out there:

CENTER FIELD SOFTWARE
P.O. Box 52014
Durham, NC 27717
(919) 361-5851
IBM- or Macintosh-compatible league-management software for $110 allows you to tap into their stat data base and print out your league's weekly stat reports.

FANTASY BASEBALL
2838 Precise Lane
Henderson, NV 89014
(800) 999-9891
IBM-compatible fantasy-league management disk for $24.95. Instructions on how to work it, $19.95.

ISMS
2442 Brussels Court
Reston, VA 22091
(800) 937-7828
IBM-compatible stat software for softball or baseball coaches, $35–$55, according to detail capability.

JACOBSEN SOFTWARE DESIGNS
1590 East 43rd Ave., Eugene, OR 97405
(503) 343-8030
Stat software for baseball coaches. Capable of tabulating 22 pitching and 23 batting-and-fielding categories. Not designed for fantasy league management. Apple II-compatible, $49.95; Commodore 64/128-compatible, $39.95; IBM-compatible will be available for 1990.

PLAYER PROJECTIONS, INC.
18 Euston St., Brookline, MA 02146
(617) 731-2631
Computer program disk to help you prepare for your league's draft. Calculates the dollar value of each player based on past and expected performance. Not a cure for the ills of the world, but knowing how much is too much to pay for Darryl Strawberry can save your season. Easily adapted to your league's stat format, number of teams, etc. American or National League player disk, $24.95; both for $44.95. State your format.

POTATO LEAGUE SPORTS
Dept. BA
4569 Mission Gorge Place, #6
San Diego, CA 92120
(619) 282-8186
Computer program allows you to practice drafting and anticipate what your rivals will bid on any particular player. Program assigns values to each player based on past performance and will play the role of up to 16 rivals. Price: $89.95.

RJL SYSTEMS
106 New Haven Ave.
Milford, CT 06460
(203) 878-0376
IBM-compatible stat program for baseball/softball coaches, $69.

SPORTS STATS, INC.
320 Brookes Drive, Suite 231
Hazelwood, MO 63042
(800) 227-8287
Basic scorebook program allows coaches to tabulate team stats and organize a schedule and roster. Complete stats package can analyze pitching performances according to type of pitch thrown, its location, and how often it was hit into the upper deck. Program prices start at $49.95.

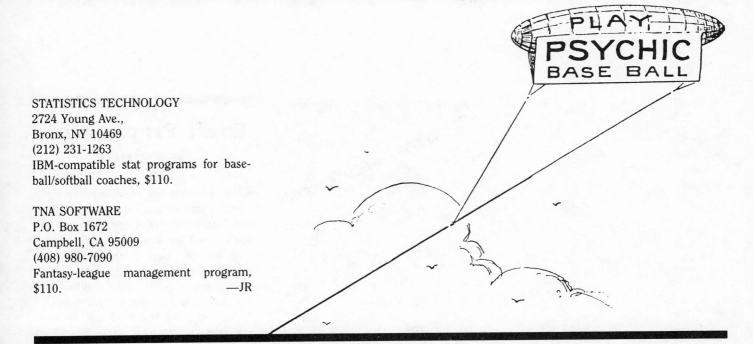

STATISTICS TECHNOLOGY
2724 Young Ave.,
Bronx, NY 10469
(212) 231-1263
IBM-compatible stat programs for baseball/softball coaches, $110.

TNA SOFTWARE
P.O. Box 1672
Campbell, CA 95009
(408) 980-7090
Fantasy-league management program, $110.   —JR

Some Words of Wisdom
on Shopping for a Fantasy League Stat Service

It's anyone's guess as to exactly how many fantasy-baseball services there are out there. We found over seventy, but it is well worth knowing that new companies appear virtually overnight while others succumb to incompetence and disappear just as quickly.

"The market is very competitive right now," says Jerry Heath, who runs Heath Research, one of the largest and best-known fantasy-league stat services. "It's also in a state of flux. Running a fantasy-league stat service looks so easy to some people that they think they can buy a computer, get the necessary software, and sign up a bunch of leagues as customers. A lot of them get in over their heads because they don't realize the work that's involved. It's time-consuming and costly. I've heard stories about services that have gone under in the middle of the season and left their customers holding the bag."

If you and your friends have formed a league and are looking for a service to compile your statistics and standings reports, you can avoid a lot of dissatisfaction and heartache by following a few guidelines.

1. Shop around and compare services. An effort was made in compiling this chapter to note the most-established, reliable companies and exclude the fly-by-night outfits. But it still pays to call or write and ask for samples of their work as well as the names and addresses of customers who can provide an appraisal of the service.

2. Don't be seduced by low prices. As with many things, you get what you pay for. There are reliable, inexpensive services out there, but what you want is one that gets reports to you on time each week with consistency. You also want a service that has the capability to correct player-transaction or scoring errors. Such a service is generally more costly to employ, but the expense is worth it.

3. Make sure the service will be there when you call with a question or a complaint during the season. Life is aggravating enough without having to leave messages on an answering machine for a week while you wait for your calls to be returned. Ask about the size of the company's staff, how many customers it has, and how often the phones are manned.

4. Watch out for hidden fees. Some services will charge you 55 cents or so each time you make a trade or place a player on the disabled list. If there's a streak of Trader Jack McKeon in you, you'll wind up paying a fortune in added expenses by the end of the season.

5. Watch out for hucksters. Some services offer cash prizes to league champions or chances to win a trip to Yucca Flats, Nevada, or some other exotic locale. Several years ago one such service in Florida went out of business after the proprietor began accepting fee payments by credit card without having arranged for a bank to process them. Customers who paid by check, cash, or money order were left in the lurch.

—JR

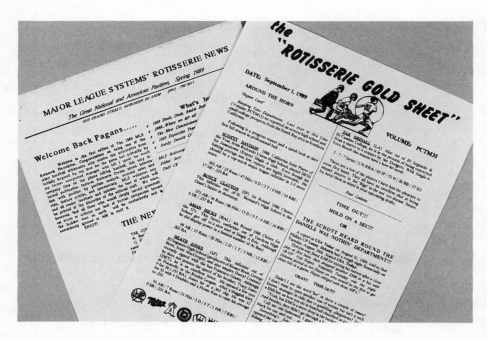

Fantasy League Newsletters

Most fantasy leaguers rely on local newspapers, the *USA Today* sports section, *Baseball America,* and *The Sporting News* to keep them informed about trade rumors, hot minor league prospects, injury updates, and other vital matters. These newsletters also offer the same kinds of information. You'll ask yourself if they are truly reliable sources. Your initial answer may be no, but once you've taken as gospel *Baseball America*'s word that Matt Williams is going to be the next Mike Schmidt and suffered for it, you'll be more inclined to give these guys a look.

FANTASY BASEBALL WEEKLY
c/o TV Sports Inc.
P.O. Box 48
Rockville Centre, NY 11571.
Costs $2.95 per copy. Nicely done on glossy stock, produced weekly from May to October, monthly from November to March, by a professional staff headed by *KO Magazine*'s Steve Farhood. *KO* is a boxing magazine, by the way. No word yet on what Mike Tyson will go for.

ROTISSERIE GOLD SHEET
P.O. Box 7000-793
Redondo Beach, CA 90277
(213) 540-6469
A biweekly newsletter published by Big League Fantasy, Inc., a full-service fantasy baseball operation founded by Los Angeles radio sports reporter Tony Hernandez. Likely to provide real inside dope. Yearly subscription, $49.

THE ROTISSERIAN
P.O. Box 155
Scarborough, NY 10510
A 6- to 8-page monthly with emphasis on current minor league statistics and prospects to watch. Yearly subscription, $30.

THE WISHFUL THINKER
P.O. Box 8006-D
Long Island City, NY 11101
(718) 784-3201
Produced by the guys at Bar-B-Que Stats. Five issues per year for $5 if you use their stat service, $14.95 if you don't.   —JR

Draft Preparation Services

One of the maxims of fantasy-league life is that teams are made or broken on draft day. Draft a roster of overpriced bums, and you'll spend the summer trying to trade your way into next year's pennant race instead of fighting for the flag now, so many owners spend weeks scouting and evaluating players prior to their drafts.

Everyone from respected baseball writers to the cop on the corner has an opinion about who is on the verge of a career season and who the biggest bargains will be. Try your bookstore in April for the Waggoner, Pathon, Welch, or Golenbock guides. If they can't help you make up your mind, the self-appointed experts listed below will be happy to send you their player ratings, statistical evaluations, and predictions—for a modest price, of course.

BEST STATS
P.O. Box 27241
Santa Ana, CA 92120
Nearly 1,000 players evaluated for $14.95. A 3-year scouting report included for total price of $22.95.

DRAFT-RITE STATS
P.O. Box 500
Paramount, CA 90723
Players ranked by position for $8.95.

LAKE PUBLISHING
P.O. Box 12432
Columbia, SC 29201
Players ranked according to strength in traditional fantasy-league stat categories, $6.75.

MAJOR LEAGUE SYSTEMS
Suite 3C
1015 Grand St.,
Hoboken, NJ 07030
(201) 792-5011
Players ranked according to dollar value,
$14.95.

RELIABLE ROTISSERIE
P.O. Box 340
Thomaston, CT 06787
(800) 288-8464
American League players rated according
to performance over the previous 2 seasons plus lists of minor leaguers to watch.
A whopping 70-plus pages. How reliable? It
will cost you $12.95 to find out.

WOZAP
P.O. Box 1958
East Hanover, NJ 07936
For $8.95 you get tips on drafting strategy,
a statistical analysis of player performance
in the first and second half of their previous seasons, and value rankings determined by the "exclusive WOZAP-7 rating
system." Looks like fantasy baseball has
caught on in outer space.   —JR

The Sorrow and the Pity:
The Making of the Rolfe Reds Media Guide

Mark Twain once noted that "Everything human is pathetic. The secret source
of humor itself is not joy but sorrow."

Sweet Jesus, was he ever right! I know
because I am human, my fantasy baseball
team, the Rolfe Reds, is pathetic, and the
sorrow caused by years of drafting wretch-
ed players and making bonehead trades is
indeed a source of humor—mostly bitter.
But it serves to fill the annual *Rolfe Reds
Media Guide*.

Writing a media guide about your fantasy team is a fun way to flaunt your success
or, if your team is like mine, vent emotions that can lead to lithium dependence.
My initial inspiration was a line in *The
New York Yankees Media Guide*: "Every
young man searching for his own place in
today's world would be well advised to
heed the advice and example of sportsman,
business executive and civic leader,
George M. Steinbrenner."

As a Yankee fan tormented by Steinbrenner's endless stream of ugly deeds, I
couldn't help laughing myself into deliri-
um. A week later I presented my fellow
owners in the Justice League of America
with a bombastic, twenty-page chronicle
of my ineptitude. It contained player bios
and, of course, an owner's profile that advised young men searching for their place
in today's world to heed my example.
There was also a bio of Red Rolfe, the

team's manager and namesake. Red, my
father's second cousin, played third base
on the great Yankee teams of the 1930s.
Rolfe died in 1969, but I figured my dead
Reds deserved a dead manager, so the
guide happily announced, "Red's back!"

The reaction to the first guide was so
positive that it is now an annual endeavor
that consumes my first few weeks after
draft day. I've added an all-time roster,
team records, and nasty profiles of my
rivals. (Envy is not pretty.) A "Reds Team
Awards" section lists the recipients of the
One Man to a Pair of Pants Out There MVP
Trophy, the Verne Ruhle Rag Arm Award,
the Miguel Dilone Tit-on-a-Boar Hog
Award, and several other dubious-achieve-
ment trophies named after the most woefully inept of my Reds of yesteryear. The
format is intentionally ragged. Pictures
are laid out on paper with tape and then
Xeroxed. The shabbiness of the finished
product reflects the quality of the team.

Over the past six years, *The Rolfe Reds
Media Guide* has taken on a modest life of
its own. Requests for copies now come
from friends, coworkers, and, occasionally, people so far outside of my league's circle that I can't believe they've heard about
it. This is flattering, but now I worry more
about satisfying the expectations of the
guide's readers. Luckily, true to Twain's
words, my team is a reliable source of

material. So is my job as a reporter for
Sports Illustrated for Kids.

It isn't easy to present sports to children
as a wholesome activity while drug abuse,
greed, and stupidity run rampant in pro,
college, and amateur athletics. Deplorable
conduct has disqualified so many star athletes as story subjects that our list of worthy role models has been reduced to a
handful of utility infielders, a backup goal-
ie, and several members of the PGA Senior
Tour. This sad state of affairs spawned *The
1989 Rolfe Reds Media Guide for Kids* with
its beer ads aimed at Little Leaguers and
tips from a particular Reds pitcher, who
shall remain anonymous, on how to throw
scuffballs. "A Child's Garden of Sports
Terms" gives kids who want to learn to
talk sports the definitions of substance
abuse, bimbo, bookie, paternity suit, and
other germane words and phrases.

To my relief, *The Reds Media Guide for
Kids* went over well although my wife was
horrified and my boss at *SI For Kids* said,
"You are one sick puppy." I can only reply
that I am merely a reflection of society in
general.

Also, one of my fellow owners remarked
that he just can't imagine what *The Rolfe
Reds Media Guide* would be like if my team
was winning. "I don't think it would be
half as entertaining," he said. I agree, but I
still dream about finding out.   —JR

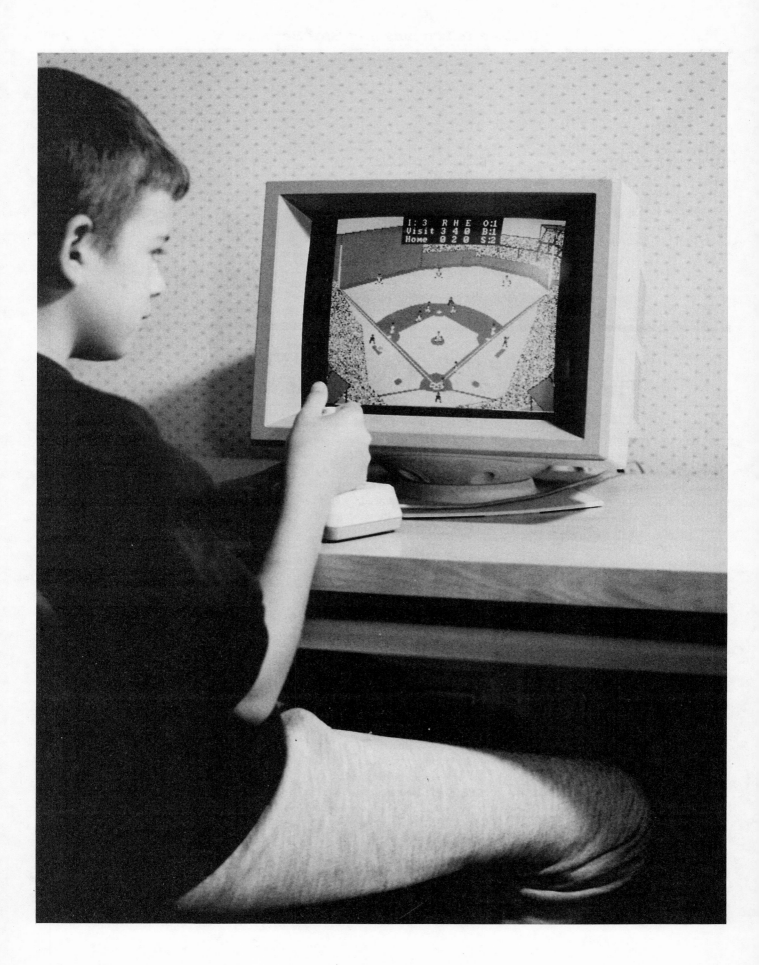

CHAPTER 16

The Search for Real Life

Table Games and Software

Dice and spinners, joysticks and cards—a journey into the twi-night zone

Quit that whizzing up there!"

I was hooked. There I was, lying upstairs on my bed at three A.M., completely impervious to the outside world and all its "real" hassles. Brant Alyea, my cleanup hitter, was up. Ted Sizemore took a few steps off second. It may have been the wee hours, but in my fantasies it was the bottom of the ninth with the score tied 2–2. My team, whom I called the Mets, was in the sixth game of the playoffs.

"Leave me alone, Dad," I implored. "Just a few more minutes. The game's almost over." Who cared about school the next day? This was important.

With a flick of my left index finger, the spinner was set in motion, and the sound of the metal spinner hitting the protective plastic could be heard throughout the house. I waited for the result: "Ten." Strikeout. Extra innings.

Cadaco's All-Star Baseball, the inexpensive granddaddy of all the simulations, was my introduction to the joys of fantasy baseball. I was only eleven at the time, and I hadn't yet seen more mature, modern versions like APBA or Strat-O-Matic. As I grew up in a small rural town in upstate New York in the early seventies, it was hard to obtain anything better, but at that point my beloved All-Star was all I needed.

For about two years, I kept records for the six teams in my "league." I'd selected five teams at random and put all my favorites on my Mets roster. In this game, offensive records were kept on round cardboard disks. I would match the number on which the spinner landed to the result listed on the game board, a gorgeous re-creation of Chicago's Wrigley Field.

How I loved those days! I introduced the joys of simulated baseball to a handful of friends, and soon we all had our own teams, happily "whizzing" away in my basement through the dead of winter.

With maturity came a sense of discontent. As we advanced into our high school years, we realized the game's shortcomings. Too many random numbers. No pitching statistics. All-Star, despite its historical importance to me, was suddenly too simple.

We pooled our money and sent away for a Strat-O-Matic game from an ad in a pulp baseball magazine. We used the Strat-O-Matic board and player cards almost daily for the next two years. It was around my junior year in high school when my adolescent baseball fantasies came to an end, replaced mainly by the discovery of adolescent fantasies of another kind. That's a story for another book, however.

College followed, then marriage and a career, which led to a miraculous and wonderful thing: free time! A chance to pursue baseball simulations once again. But my old card cronies had found new lives of their own. I had to find a suitable solitaire simulation.

Frankly televised baseball has always turned me off. I prefer interacting with the game. Something keeps driving me back to the days of my youth, when it was just me and my Cadaco spinners and looseleafs, my own team, my own records, and my own business.

Games were one thing, but the laborious recordkeeping of my youth was something else. I didn't have *that much* free time! That's where the computerized baseball simulations have been a blessing for me. Now, with the press of a button, the records are kept for me. No more endless hours of tabulations. No more changing calculator batteries. Now I need only insert the floppy disk, and I'm instantly commissioner of my own league. If it weren't for computerized simulations, I probably wouldn't be able to take part in anything other than TV games or going out to the ballpark. I'm too busy for board games, too cheap for Rotisserie, and too demanding for anything less complicated. Computer baseball fits me like a good fielder's glove.

There are others I know who have their favorite board-game simulations, who insist the computerized versions don't come close to capturing the realism of the game; it reminds me of those who prefer their old LPs to those "newfangled" compact discs. To me, it's a clear case of apples and oranges.

As someone who has played both types of simulations over the years, I can say there isn't that much difference between the two. Most players who fancy the strategy simulations keep cumulative records for their teams, and with the use of a computer those tabulations are often done with no more than a simple keyboard command.

Board games, on the other hand, tend to be much more detailed statistically; restrictions on memory force some computer game manufacturers to cut corners in certain areas. Even many of the best computer strategy simulations leave important data out, most typically batting against left- and right-handed pitching; one game keeps fantastic records but does not tabulate runs scored, for some reason.

On the following pages, table game fan Jack Kavanagh and I will rate the current state of the art in board games and computer games. Which is better? It's really all a matter of taste. —RS

Table Game Reviews

A first-time buyer will find among the descriptions to follow some game characteristics that will please him more than others. We are inclined to stress APBA and Strat-O-Matic because they have pleased the most gamers the longest. Also, because even if we designated some other game as "better," it might go out of business as so many have. Without the company to issue new data, the satisfied game player will be unable to play added seasons.

Prices represent suggested retail price. You might find better deals at discount toy and department stores. Expect to pay postage and handling on mail orders. Most game manufacturers have brochures they will send to you before they try to make the sale.

APBA MAJOR LEAGUE PLAYERS BASE-BALL
APBA Game Company, Inc.
1001-11B Millersville Road
P. O. Box 4547
Lancaster, PA 17604
(800) 334-APBA, ext. 11B
Availability: Mail order, or very limited retail distribution.
Suggested price: Basic game, $32.95 (includes 520 player cards); Master game, $29.50 (add $21.95 for player cards).

As the orginal dice and chart game, bolstered by persistent efforts by its adherents to define and defend it, APBA leads the list. The Basic game is simply tops for speedy play and for satisfying most entry-level players, many of whom will remain contented for a lifetime. The Master game is an attempt to catch up to the more finely tuned and sophisticated games of the day, but frankly there are better options out there for the more demanding table gamer. Because both Basic and Master APBA use the same individual player cards, the increased scope is carried on the game boards. Although effective they are unwieldy to handle.

Stick to the Basic game, which is played with two dice, individual player cards, and eight game boards, which are alternated according to base runner circumstances (half the time the bases-empty board is used). Batters perform credibly, but pitchers are less satisfactory due to being judgmentally graded. Defensively teams are ranked by composite fielding ratings according to three grades. This expands each chart to three columns, each reflecting (to sometimes insignificant degrees) the ability of the team in the field to limit the batter and runners.

APBA provides a wide range of teams; not only are each year's 26 major league teams provided, but full seasons from the past and historic teams are available.

The game is constructed with Pennsylvania Dutch sturdiness and the business-like procedures of this Lancaster, Pennsylvania, company are a blessing in an era of mail-order capriciousness. The customer-

players are linked via the *APBA Journal*. It's biased but reassures true believers, the devout followers of Richard J. Seitz. In his seventies, Seitz still stands by imperiously, asserting the superiority of APBA to the many schisms which followed his parting of the table-gaming Red Sea.

STRAT-O-MATIC
Strat-O-Matic Game Co., Inc.
46 Railroad Plaza, Glen Head, NY 11545
(800) 645-3455
(516) 671-6566 in New York State
Availability: Retail stores or by mail.
Price: $34.50, deluxe; $15.00, smaller set

Strat-O-Matic first appeared in 1961 and has improved its game steadily, in some ways spectacularly. Designer Hal Richman has combined game inventiveness with business acumen to place his game first in sales and first in the hearts of more table gamers than any other.

The game's most admired feature is its absence of boards or charts requiring separate consultation on every play. Each batter and each pitcher has an individual card, printed front and back, with outcomes on them.

Although the original game, now called the Basic version satisfied beginners (and still does), Strat-O-Matic developed the Advanced version to satsify more sophisticated tastes. Both forms use three dice, but they are read differently according to the level of play. The individual cards are used at both levels—the Basic Version on one side and Advanced on the other.

Strat-O-Matic pioneered righty-lefty concepts based on actual performances, not a standard assumption of how this affects all batters and pitchers. Add to this a finely tuned defensive process (with outfielder throwing included) and a realistic base-running and stealing system, and you have a game to delight baseball strategists. Also, the game's complexities, while easy to master, are optional. You are not commanded by a pontificating designer to ac-

(Cont. p. 296.)

The World of Table Baseball

It began for me the summer Artie Marggraf broke his leg. It was 1932 and most of us were twelve-year-olds, hanging out on the Marggraf stoop. (In Brooklyn brownstone houses don't have porches.) Someone told us about a way to play baseball with dice, and six or seven of us made up teams and started a league.

It didn't take long to realize our heroes didn't play on Artie's stoop the way they did on big league diamonds. When we made up our teams, it didn't matter who got Babe Ruth. Rabbit Maranville, whose glove would get him to the Hall of Fame, was the home run king. I sold Hack Wilson for a nickel to a boy who had moved to Brooklyn from Chicago, and the Cubs' star wasn't worth it.

I've long forgotten whatever the game was we played that summer. There were thousands of such games, frustrating their players with unrealistic outcomes.

The undisputed Father of Table Baseball was Francis C. Sebring, whose board game, Parlour Baseball, was described in an 1866 issue of Frank Leslie's *Illustrated Newspaper*. (It was patented no. 74154 in 1868.) Parlour Baseball was a mechanical game, in which one player sent a coin plateward by a spring mechanism while another

swung a swiveled bat. The coin, when struck, would end up in a slot, designated an out or a hit. This was a simple beginning, and it was followed by many mechanical games which tried to imitate actual play with miniature bats and balls.

Thousands of other baseball games were marketed over the next half century, usually with a famous player's name associated. Baseball games played with dice, cards, or spinners became a staple of a growing toy and game market. And although they usually produced final scores in line with those of real games, none could provide a way for the players to perform as they did in real life.

That challenge was finally met by Clifford A. Van Beek of Green Bay, Wisconsin. Although he applied for a patent in 1923 (and it was issued, no. 1,536,639, on May 5, 1925), Van Beek didn't get his National Pastime onto the market until 1931, using star players with 1930 stats. Although it was advertised in the 1931 issues of *Baseball Magazine*, it succumbed to the Great Depression and disappeared after that one year.

National Pastime was APBA, unmistakably—or at least its pioneering forebear. It had the same eight different base occu-

pancy situations for its charts. But it remained an unknown and unacknowledged ancestral game, with Van Beek the forgotten founding father of real-life table baseball games, until the card collecting craze began to stir in the early 1970s. Then nonpicture cards with names like Babe Ruth, Rogers Hornsby, and George Sisler turned up. They looked like APBA cards, but on the back they said "National Pastime."

The game was returned to the market as APBA in 1951, by J. Richard Seitz of Lancaster, Pennsylvania, who significantly improved it by grading pitchers and adding defensive adjustments.

Between the demise of National Pastime and its second coming, another real-life game reached the market in 1941. This was a totally different concept from Van Beek's coded cards. It used individual player disks with different-size spaces on the rim. A spinner would stop (often maddeningly "on the line") to tell you what the player had done. A wider space for Babe Ruth's home runs assured that he would hit the most. It was—and still is—called All-Star Baseball. Designed by Ethan Allen, a thirteen-season big leaguer from the 1920s and '30s with a lifetime .300 batting average, the game was a juvenile treat, fun to play, and just what we should have had on Marggraf's stoop. Alas, it was only half of a real-life reconstruction; pitchers had no effect whatsoever. Still, All-Star Baseball links the prehistoric era of games with no real-life characteristics to the whole spectrum of sophisticated dice-and-chart games.

Hard on APBA's heels came the other still dominant giant of the table baseball game market, Strat-O-Matic. Like two legendary western gunfighters, APBA and Strat-O-Matic have survived in a field where they are constantly being challenged by the latest claimant to the title of "best game." Year after year new games toss their dice. Some last, perennially marginal; most fade away—although not before acquiring some loyal followers in their first years.   —JK

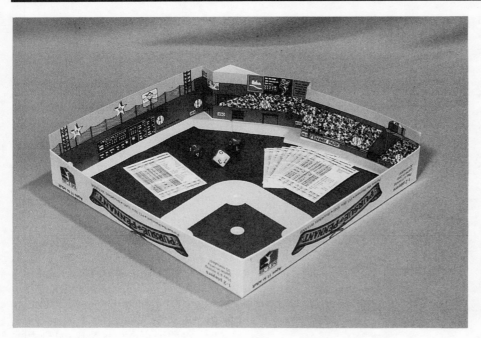

Pursue the Pennant pursues APBA and Strat-O.

cept the full scale. The one game can be played either Basic or Advanced.

This is a customer-friendly company with a newsletter and a good reputation in all aspects of the table gaming field. Once mail order only, the company has dealt with the shelf-life problem of selling the game retail by including in the box a redeemable coupon for player cards for the latest season.

PURSUE THE PENNANT
Pursue the Pennant
P.O. Box 38364-A
Greensboro, NC 27438
(800) 288-4PTP
Availability: Retail stores or mail.
Price: Deluxe (complete) game, $44.95, Super Star version (same game, but with only 108 various players from the 1980s, rated on their best-season performance) $24.95 (add $20 for cards from the latest season).

Mike Cieslinski has designed a game with fast-action card concepts, righty-lefty matchups . . . the full range of strategy possiblilities. It provides 729 players for its 26 teams, not 520 as does its main competition, which uses 20-man rosters (with additional players available for an added cost). And unlike APBA and Strat-O, PTP

offers charts in addition to the cards. Unfortunately, the charts slow the action. Another drawback, particularly for those with limited hobby time, is the requirement for added dice rolls with the advances of baserunners on hits and outs.

The game uses 3 ten-sided dice, read sequentially (and patriotically) in red, white, and blue to provide 999 possibilities. The individual player cards are color-coded, with printing on both sides, and can also accommodate adding the player's baseball card. There are even replica playing fields: results on fly balls are different at Fenway Park from those at Yankee Stadium.

STATIS PRO
The Avalon Hill Game Company
4517 Hartford Road
Baltimore, MD 21214
(800) 638-9292
Availability: Retail stores or mail order.
Price: $39.00 for complete game including all current player cards (new season cards, $14.00) $22.00 for Great Team game including player cards for 10 teams of the past (Great Team cards available separately for $10.00).

A skilled table game designer, Jim Barnes, launched Statis Pro early in the game-prolific 1970s. His inspiration was to use fast-action cards instead of dice as the

game's activator. The cards are divided into ranges for batters and pitchers, and a random-number process refers the player to one or the other, shifting the influence so the game is not dominated by hitting or pitching.

The game incorporates assessments of individual skills, such as error propensity in fielding, base running and throwing, and has a token rule for righty-lefty pitching. There's a basic and advanced level of play. The current game tells you how to rate players of the past or do your own ratings in the future.

Like Pursue the Pennant, Statis Pro requires extra actions to advance baserunners. However, in two-handed play, this can be a feature that involves the player in the field.

When Avalon Hill, a major war strategy game company, bought out Statis Pro Baseball, it was assumed that its superior graphic design and Madison Avenue advertising would move the game to the top seller slot. However, Statis Pro lags behind and, ironically, it seems its fast-action cards are holding it back. Imagine how play would fall off in Las Vegas casinos if, at the crap tables, the high rollers were asked to flip over cards instead of imparting their personal touch to throwing the dice. Handling the dice is a powerful value baseball table gamers seem reluctant to give up.

ALL-STAR BASEBALL
Cadaco, Inc.
200 Fifth Ave.
New York, NY 10010
(212) 675-5678
Availability: Toy stores and other retail outlets.
Price: $12.95.

Ethan Allen's simplistic spinner game continues to find shelf space in retail outlets. Its updated version, with assorted star players, is identical to those of past generations, only now pictures have been added to the once empty-center disks. This creates, for consumers, yet another collectible. It also has doubled the price of the game without adding anything but a cosmetic touch.

Over the years the game has added, nearly annually, disks for players while maintaining all-time star groupings. All can be used interchangeably and, for an astute game owner, one man's disk can be another man's version—if their stats are similar.

Pitchers, of course, have no influence on outcomes and their disks represent only their batting propensities—half the dubious value this once had, since the advent of the designated hitter.

Still, All-Star Baseball is a great rainy day time passer. It requires minimal strategy knowledge from two small boys or is a fine father-and-son experience—if Dad can get the kid away from his computer console.

BIG LEAGUE MANAGER
Big League Game Company
321 East Superior St.
Duluth, MN 55802
(218) 722-1275
Availability: Mail order only.
Price: $39.95 (complete game with latest year teams). Write for catalog first.

A pioneer in the field, Don Henricksen designed Big League Manager while waiting for his World War II service time to end. It has earned chevrons for reenlistments ever since, as evidenced by the succession of activators with which the game is played.

Originally a spinner was used to start the action. Subsequently fast-action cards were introduced, as well as a pair of ten-sided dice and a random-number book based on the linear readings they can produce. Now, you can use a combination of cards and dice. (The varied forms of this game are a result of encounters with the baseball players' union, which caused BLM to abandon individualized player cards for coded data printed in booklet form, and now roster sheets.)

Through it all, BLM has provided its

Spinning Jose

Making your own player batter disks for spinner games is an easy proposition up to a point. The spaces on the disk for hits and outs are all determined by percentages. For example, if a batter strikes out in 10 percent of his total at bats, 10 percent of his disk space should be strikeouts. (Remember, total at bats includes bases on balls, hits-by-pitch, sacrifices, and sacrifice flies, as well as official at bats, figures available to most fans in various record books.)

Dividing a circle into 100 equal parts might be a little tough for most of us who barely survived high school math, but we can simply divide the circle into 360 degrees with a protractor and then multiply the percentage (use the decimal) by 360 to get the number of degrees to devote to home runs, doubles, triples, etc. Don't try to guess fractions of degrees; round them

off; the lines between the sections will more than make up the difference.

For example, see Jose Canseco's 1988 record (his 40–40 season), below.

So far, so good. Problems develop in the fine-tuning. Canseco went through 1988 without a triple, but do you want to leave three-base hits off his disk completely? Surely he always had the *capability* of hitting a triple. And how many of his singles could have advanced runners two bases? How many doubles would have scored a runner from first? What percentage of his outs were long flies, pop outs, ground outs? And how many might have been turned into double plays had there been runners on base?

Unless you have access to more detailed stats than most fans, you're going to have to guess.

—BC

Type of Stat		Actual Stats	/	Tot. ABs*		Percent of ABs	×	360		No. of Degrees
1B	=	111	/	705	=	.157	×	360	=	57
2B	=	34	/	705	=	.048	×	360	=	17
3B	=	0	/	705	=	.000	×	360	=	0
HR	=	42	/	705	=	.060	×	360	=	21
BB	=	78	/	705	=	.111	×	360	=	40
SO	=	128	/	705	=	.182	×	360	=	65
HBP	=	10	/	705	=	.014	×	360	=	5

*Total ABs (AB + HBP + SH + SF) = 705.

owners with an intriguing, if intricate, tracking procedure to obtain play results, with both batters and pitchers influencing the outcomes. Objectivity is sought, even though it leads the player through more steps than many players care to follow. You must roll the dice to discover whether a batter has walked or struck out; if neither, you roll again to find if he's made a hit or an out. Finally, on a base hit, you use the spinner to find out whether he has singled, doubled, tripled, or homered.

BLM has long been a top choice for those who care more about losing themselves in a thoughtfully constructed game than toting up wins and losses and crowning champions in their own league.

NEGAMCO BASEBALL
Big League Game Company
321 East Superior St.
Duluth, MN 55802
(218) 722-1275
Availability: Mail order only.

Price: $9.95 (including current rosters; for previous seasons, inquire).

A somewhat juvenile version of Big League Manager, this Don Henricksen game sacrifices subtleties for the sake of a more quickly played game. Like the original BLM, it still comes with a spinner, but fast-action cards have been added. There are fewer possibilities to deal with, but those are divided into variations for seven classes of graded pitchers, who are in turn divided according to pitching characteristics, not by win-loss or ERA reputation so one pitcher will register K's and walks profusely, while another will be a crafty curver who gets ground-ball DPs.

Like its big brother, Negamco now uses roster sheets updated annually. Why is the game called of all things, Negamco? Because prior to merging with Big League Game Company, Negamco was headquartered in Nemadji, a small town near Duluth—thus the NEmadji GAMe COmpany.

EXTRA INNINGS
ATC Company
321 East Superior St.
Duluth, MN 55802
(218) 722-1275
Availability: Mail order only.
Cost: $14.95 (including current rosters; inquire for previous seasons).

Extra Innings plays in only twenty minutes the way its designer, Jack Kavanagh (yeah, the same guy), plays it. Charts are taken from a book and tacked at eye level on a blackboard. Dice are rolled in a glass jar (baby food), and the play of the game is jotted into a scorebook. There are no player cards to turn; teams are on roster sheets. Three-colored dice, for linear reading, provide 216 assignments for action. Baserunner movement and the tracks of batted balls can easily be memorized because the first die number corresponds to standard position scoring symbols (i.e., 1 = pitcher, 6 = shortstop); double numbers are outfielders.

There are two rolls. Events which are

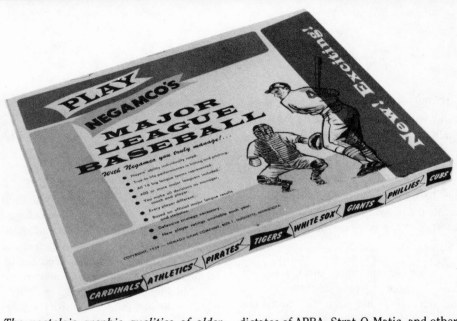

The nostalgic graphic qualities of older table games make them top collectibles.

not factors in determining batting averages, such as walks and hit batsmen, are assigned to the first roll. Hits and outs occur only on the second roll to assure obtaining clearly defined averages. Pitchers are rated on ERA to raise or lower the batter's average and power.

The game comes with 26 current-season major league rosters, plus a Top 400 players on a "best season" basis, a pool that provides eight 25-man rosters. There are Hall of Fame members, career-rated, and dozens of great teams of the past.

EI, which shows how to rate players from any stats, is intended for those who like to tinker and shape their own games. For example, the book that comes with it describes later-designed improvements for double-play and error assignments. It is not for the timid gamer.

BASEBALL MANAGER
Valgames
565 Avenue A, #101
Uniondale, NY 11553
(516) 538-3247
Availability: Mail order.
Price: $15.95 (dice not included).
Baseball Manager is a neat, perceptive game, inexpensively and intelligently intended to satisfy those looking for the titillation of divorcing themselves from the

dictates of APBA, Strat-O-Matic, and other doctrinaire games. At least, run off for the weekend with John Swistak's game. It's a two-dice affair, but the rolls are interpreted with the aid of a Power Chart to widen the probability ranges. There is a "normalization process" to convert players from different eras to a competitive and comparable standard. The instructions tell you how to rate players.

You get latest-season player data, plus 5 earlier seasons of full major league rosters and 22 Great Teams of the past. And you get Swistak's observations in the text of Baseball Manager, which definitely will appeal to those who have moved beyond the vicarious thrill of "managing real players."

SHER-CO GRAND SLAM BASEBALL
Sherco Games Inc.
P. O. Box 524 - 1
Malaga, NJ 08328
(800) 255-8989, ext. 3109
(609) 728-4071
Availability: Mail order.
Price: $22.95 (includes rosters; no individual player cards).

The pure game designer in Steve LeShay got the upper hand in 1968, when he developed his table baseball game. The result is a fun-to-play, uniquely visualized entertainment that sacrifices accuracy and takes an hour to play. It's a novel, change-of-pace game to interweave with games that play at a faster rate.

Antique Baseball Table Games

The title "Father of Baseball" has been bestowed variously upon Abner Doubleday, Alexander Cartwright, Henry Chadwick, and Harry Wright, and all but the first have a reasonable claim to the honor. But for readers of this chapter of *The Whole Baseball Catalogue*, the burning question is: Who is the Father of Baseball Table Games and Software?

As Jack Kavanagh wrote earlier, the answer appears to be one Francis C. Sebring, pitcher for the Empire Base Ball Club of New York (and bowler for the Manhattan Cricket Club) in the mid-1860s. At some time around the conclusion of the Civil War, this enterprising resident of Hoboken, New Jersey, designed a mechanical table game; sporting papers of 1867 carried ads for his "Parlor Base-Ball" and the December 8, 1866, issue of *Leslie's* carried a woodcut of parents and young'uns playing the game (the woodcut is shown on page 295 of this book).

No examples of "Parlor Base-Ball" survive, but from the patent application and drawing of February 4, 1868, we see that a spring propelled a coin ("one of the thick nickel coins of the denomination of 'one cent,' issued by the United States Government in and about the year 1860") from pitcher to batter, and another spring activated a bat that propelled the coin into one or another of the cavities in the field. A modern pinball game is not very much different.

According to the article in *Leslie's*, the idea of making a toy version of the nascent national pastime occurred to Sebring while riding a ferry across from Hoboken to New York to visit an ailing teammate. But was his brainchild the first baseball game? There is another game with a prior patent: the "Base-Ball Table" patented by William Buckley of New York on August 20, 1867, which like Sebring's game operates on the pin-ball principle. And like Sebring's game, it too has no remaining example; the earliest surviving baseball table game is a card game from 1869: "Base Ball: The New Parlor Game." (An enterprising antiquarian might reconstruct both games from their schematic drawings and play them today.) And there are hints—requiring further research—that the McLoughlin Brothers Game Company of New York City may have issued a chromo-lithographic game as early as 1856. But until hard evidence to the contrary turns up, Francis C. Sebring will retain the title: Father of Baseball Table Games (and Software).

Sebring's name was not attached to his game. He was not a famous player, and baseball was still an amateur game, only beginning to produce national heroes. But in the remaining years of the nineteenth century, game manufacturers learned that invoking a star's name—on either the game packaging or its components—made for greater sales. Today's games endorsed by Pete Rose, Reggie Jackson, Orel Hershiser, et al., descend in a straight line from "Zimmer's Base Ball Game, by Zimmer the Catcher, Cleveland" (1893) and the Tom Barker and Fan Craze card games of the teens.

Did Sebring understand that the real game of baseball is similar in concept to the ancient Indian game of Parcheesi, in which a player (or marker) leaves home and makes his way back—stopping at each of three bases—to tally success? No; that's just art imitating life, the essence of creation for painters, poets, and gamemakers alike.

—JT

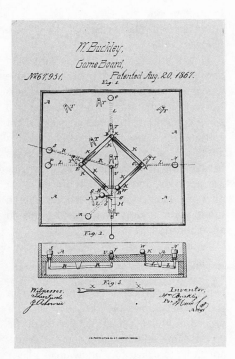

Was this "Base-Ball Table" the pioneer?

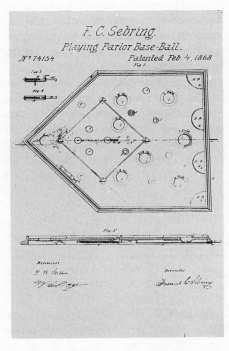

Or did Sebring's game come first?

The game is played with a pair of dice on a simulated baseball field divided into grid squares. Through multiple rolls of the dice, you track the batted ball, and have it fielded and thrown while the runner moves along the base path. The configurations of ballparks—including such bygones as Ebbetts Field and the Polo Grounds—are as important as your choices of where to position your players.

Sher-Co provides its rating formulas so you can convert any stats—past or future—into playing data. Yet for convenience you can buy groups of famous teams of the past for $4.95 a unit.

ABC BASEBALL
Valgames
565 Avenue A, #101
Uniondale, NY 11553
(516) 538-3247
   Availability: Mail order.
   Price: $20.

   This intricate game is not as easy to play as A-B-C, although patient adherence to clearly explained procedures will bring about satisfactory results. What won't be satisfied is a gamer's wish for quickly resolved outcomes. A game played with five dice and multiple rolls ensures the gamer's lengthy participation.

ABC's uniqueness stems from the different results you get with different "counts on the batter." If the pitcher is two strikes and no balls ahead in the count, he will have the advantage over the hitter. Let him be 3 and 0, and the batter can take a toehold.

The game provides the full range of strategy options and nuances, such as righty-lefty batting and pitching influences and a factor for defensive plays. It has all the potential to become "the game" for those who are constantly looking for something more sophisticated in table baseball. ABC comes with the latest season major league results on individual player cards, 22 to a team. Past seasons can be ordered.

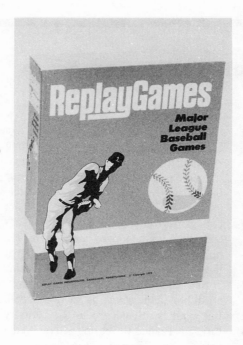

REPLAY
Replay Games Inc.
100 Park Ave.
Carmichaels, PA 15320
(412) 966-5884
   Availability: Mail order.
   Price: $40.

   This well-designed, satisfying game first appeared in 1973 and ushered in table baseball's modern era, and designers Norm Roth and John Brodak have added some fine-tuning touches in subsequent editions. It's a two-dice game but produces amply diversified outcomes by interactions between the batter and pitcher cards. They are accurate, too, although the logic of pitching changes can be questioned due to too broad a grading system and too rigid an application.

Replay rates high in those strategy particulars which appeal to the more advanced table gamers; the righty-lefty component, formerly less influential than in some other games has recently been improved. A plus is the attractiveness of the boxed game and its components. Teams are fully stocked on individual player cards, with rosters of 30 players for recent

seasons and old-time campaigns. Once you're familiar with the limited use of a chart book, the game rolls along at a comfortable 20-minute pace.

At $30 a year, the sets for previous seasons (23 of them) are expensive compared to other games, but then again, you are getting all the teams for each year, not a single team for $5.00 or so.

WINNING INNING
S.T.G.
2311 Humbolt Avenue South
Minneapolis, MN 55405
   Availability: Mail order.
   Price: $14.95 (includes latest-season rosters, with over 700 players).

   This is a second-generation game based on the old Solitaire Tabletop Baseball Game and uses the same roster sets. It's one of the fastest-playing, full-strategy games; albeit without the righty-lefty factor. There are no individual playing cards, but a simple way of using colored dice as activators produces a diversity of accurate outcomes. The game uses a prejudged fatigue and form factor to enhance a simplistic pitcher-grading system.

WI also comes with an ingenious fea-

Come On, Four!

A baseball dice game from the nineteenth century called Game of Baseball (clever name!) was marketed by McLoughlin Brothers of New York, starting in 1888. The rules provide some interesting comments on baseball as it was played then. For example, rolling a 7—the most likely number in any two-dice roll—produced a passed ball, a fairly uncommon play today but very prevalent in the last century. On the other hand, home runs were rolled with fours, meaning a batter would homer on average every twelfth at bat—a rate that would make any modern slugger green with envy.   —BC

ture, the Simulated Seasons Plan, which permits forecasting complete-season results and year-long batting and pitching records from a small sample of actually played games. (SSP can be applied in other tabletop baseball games, too.)

Winning Inning is definitely a novel, clever entry that, unlike the competition, doesn't claim to be the "best game of all" and is priced as modestly as its pretensions.

CLUBHOUSE BASEBALL
Clubhouse Games, Inc.
P.O. Box 7438
Buffalo Grove, IL 60089
Availability: Mail order.
Price: $35.96.

For those who enjoy complex board games, here's one with more successive steps to trace than there are performance clauses tacked onto a star player's contract. There's no beginners' version of Clubhouse Baseball, you jump right in with a very advanced game. It's barely on the cusp of 20 minutes playing time but shouldn't be played in a hurry just to complete a lot of games for statistical toting up.

This is a highly rewarding game for those who don't mind sequential steps that can trip up the unwary. All strategy moves are here, with counteractions provided. The activator is three dice. After rolling them, you arrange them in numerical order. Assume they now read 3–4–6. The two lowest are "3–4" and take you to both a batter's card and pitcher's card, where they achieve a new numerical identity. The "6" comes into use to learn the results of defensive plays. The first two create a series of actions, the third adds direction. Events come together on the playing field chart, fine tuned further with suffix letters added to some numerical readings.

Batters and pitchers, rated on individual cards, interact as righty-lefty performers with outcomes that vary with base-occupancy situations. You not only have to flip to the correct chart among eight, but a

runner who steals second before the ball is hit, for example, moves the interpretation to another base-situation chart for possibly a different outcome.

All is explained thoroughly (thank God!), if laboriously, in a voluminous instruction book. Little has escaped the anticipation of the designer. Each team, rated on the latest season's stats, has 24 player cards. Even the dimensions of all major league ballparks are replicated on cards for their effect on the games.

This is a fine game for detached table gamers who can hold their breath while the action unfolds.

ASG BASEBALL
4070 West St.
P.O. Box F
Cambria, CA 93428
(805) 927-5439
Availability: Mail order.
Price: $35 (includes 26 teams of primary players; add $10 for 50 borderline players and $20 for Old-Timers).

Table game design has reached a point where designers are essentially reinventing the wheel and putting more spokes into it. These strengthen the wheel and make it look more interesting—but do not turn it in new directions.

Designers George Gerney and Gerry Klug have brought the pitcher-batter confrontation to a new level with ASG Baseball. A delicate balance is obtained without seriously impeding the flow of the game. The batter and pitcher cards subtly interface so that, for example, a free-swinging slugger will do better against a fastball pitcher than against a knuckleballer. ASG also fine-tunes fielding results so that an adroit first baseman who can dig throws out of the dirt can cut down on his infielders' throwing errors.

ASG's enhancements will excite table gamers who appreciate fine tuning. It might fall flat with the romancer who wants his home run hero's drives to always clear the fence and not be snatched back sometimes by a high-leaping outfielder.

Do It Yourself

If you ever thought of creating your own dice baseball game, the first thing you should know is the odds of throwing particular numbers. This is dependent on how many combinations there are that will total that number. For example, with two dice you're twice as likely to roll a 3 as a 2 because there are two ways to roll a 3 (1 and 2 or 2 and 1) but only one way to roll a 2 (1 and 1). However, since there are 36 possible combinations, the odds of rolling a 2 are 35 to 1. That means if you make a 2 equal a home run, you'll see two homers a game on average (both sides). If you made 7 your home run number (5 to 1), you'd have games that were real slugfests with a dozen or more homers common.

Here are the combinations and odds for two dice:

No. Combinations	Odds
2 = 1 & 1	35 to 1
3 = 1 & 2, 2 & 1	17 to 1
4 = 1 & 3, 3 & 1, 2 & 2	11 to 1
5 = 1 & 4, 4 & 1, 2 & 3, 3 & 2	8 to 1
6 = 1 & 5, 5 & 1, 2 & 4, 4 & 2, 3 & 3	31 to 5
7 = 1 & 6, 6 & 1, 2 & 5, 5 & 2, 3 & 4, 4 & 3	5 to 1
8 = 2 & 6, 6 & 2, 3 & 5, 5 & 3, 4 & 4	31 to 5
9 = 3 & 6, 6 & 3, 4 & 5, 5 & 4	8 to 1
10 = 4 & 5, 5 & 4, 5 & 5	11 to 1
11 = 5 & 6, 6 & 5	17 to 1
12 = 6 & 6	35 to 1

One way to increase the number possibilities is to use different-color dice, always reading one number first. This will give you 36 possible numbers between 11 and 66, with the odds on each number the same (35 to 1). In other words, you are no more likely to roll a 4–3 than a 1–1. With that in mind, you'd want to make several numbers represent common plays like strikeouts.

If you go to three dice, the number of combinations jumps to 216, but the odds of throwing a 3 or 18 are 215 to 1. —BC

STARTING LINEUP—TALKING
BASEBALL
Parker Brothers
Beverly, MA 01915
(508) 927-7600

Availability: Toy & department stores.
Price: $79.95 (includes three teams).

This game is a link between the traditional dice and chart games and the realm of floppy disks, computer terminals and console screens. SLTB is played electronically and staged in a replica of a baseball stadium. Batter and pitcher controls are placed at either end, behind home plate for the hitter and in back of centerfield for the pitcher. It's powered with four size C batteries, and you could fit it inside a Nike box for Kareem Abdul-Jabbar's shoes, making it as portable as any game.

SLTB uses a broadcast announcer to describe the action. There is nothing to look up. The gamer controls the strategy choices and the results are made automatically from the game's 250,000 possible outcomes. The game tells you the outcomes audibly and keeps a running line score, inning by inning. It's a pitch-by-pitch progression that requires about an hour to play nine innings.

The game's focus is more on the batter. He can swing for power, sacrificing his average. Because the player can't alter the correlation with new stats, the game doesn't profess to be fine tuned in this department. The player has a wide range of strategies. "Lefty-righty" factors are built into the game, making substitutions practical choices. Steals can be attempted (runners are rated) and pitchouts called. Batters can sacrifice and the infield played shallow against the bunt—which automatically increases the batter's chances of singling through a drawn-in infield. There may be a wild pitch, passed ball, or pick-off.

SLTB can be played solitaire or by two opponents. The solo player has the choice of controlling the pitching selections or making the batter responses. Whichever role he selects, the game will counter as a programmed opponent, playing at one of four levels of complexity. The highest provides a good challenge to a college-level student, yet the game can be a great gift for a twelve-year-old. It is, obviously, very appropriate for father and son matchups.

With only three teams available with the game, interest would wane soon after Christmas morning. However, all major league teams (based on 1988 performances) can be added. Three or four teams are on each cartridge, which sells for $25. One division of a league costs $50, the full league (four cartridges) $100; both leagues, $200.   —JK

Eulogy to Games Departed

Once the opportunity to replicate real-life results with a table game had been demonstrated by APBA and Strat-O-Matic, more and more gamers began to invent their own versions of dice-and-chart games, stressing those aspects of established games that were important to them. All probably had early optimism that their game was destined to become the best game on the market.

But in most cases the inventor's talent for design was not matched with appropriate marketing techniques. Lack of capital also condemned many fledgling games to brief lives. And some were simply bad ideas.

They were all part of an evolutionary process. Table games now come to market with the genes of many ancestors. Rest in peace, Gil Hodges' Pennant Fever, Great Pennant Races, Time Travel, and others gone before their time or whose time never came.

One of those most fondly remembered here is a game from Ashburn Industries of Massachusetts called Longball. A pioneer in seeking to increase the readings attainable with conventional six-sided dice, Longball used eight-sided dice to generate random numbers from 00 to 77. The game had pitching grades and divided results between a pitcher's card and a batter's.

In 1983 Ashburn Industries put its marketing heart into an effort to carve its place in the small industry of table baseball and managed to stay long enough to establish a toehold. But once a table game is gone, it's truly gone. Like automobiles which have gone off the market, parts become difficult to find and, for a real-life game with unrevealed codes, extension by buying newly updated seasonal data is impossible.

As a game, Longball had a few problems, too niggling to cite now that it is only a curiosity value to inquisitive table gamers who might find the game in flea markets. If you happen to come across it, be sure to check the box for those odd-shaped dice and the individual playing cards.   —JK

Read All About It

Perhaps one of the most significant contributions to table baseball came in 1967, when brothers Ron and Len Gaydos started the *APBA Journal*. The publication has since changed hands. Although APBA includes a brochure about the publication with its game, it's not subsidized by APBA (which does, however, keep a watchful eye on it for heresy or ecumenical attitudes toward other games). The *APBA Journal* provided a link among table gamers who had thought they were aberrantly playing a kid's game. We're not crazy after all, it told us. Or, at least, we can all be crazy together.   —JK

Separating the Men's Games from the Boys'

Any attempt to rate the various table games will founder on the notion that "the best" can be decided by formula. The "best game" for each individual gamer is the one which best meets his expectations. Different table gamers have different needs to be gratified.

Depending on what you're looking for, here are the factors to consider while you're shopping around.

Accuracy. Although very close approximations of actual major league stats can be programmed into a game, that accuracy may not be realized until the gamer puts his team(s) through a schedule of the same major league length—154 or 162 games. More importantly, if the game is based on a "righty-lefty" factor, each batter must hit against the same mix of pitching as he did in real life. For a table game to be minimally accurate, after twenty-five or thirty games, the players should have sorted themselves out into the stars, the run-of-the-mill, and those at the bottom rank.

Playability. While accuracy is measurable, playability involves a great many subjective assessments. Individual table gamers may be more comfortable with two dice, rather than three, or with unfamiliar shapes and sizes of activators. Then again, they may take tactile pleasure from individual player cards.

Ease of memorization, or handy reference, probably explains the perennial popularity of APBA and Strat-O-Matic. After a dozen or so games with APBA, the interpretation of most of its two-dice codes becomes clear by repetition. With Strat-O-Matic printing the outcomes on the individual player cards, the gamer doesn't have to memorize as much. However, the auxiliary actions—stolen bases, sacrifices, etc.—lead the game player off to other interpretative sources, which can become labyrinthian.

Obviously games will play more rapidly—although not necessarily logically—the fewer times the flow of action is interrupted to refer to additional charts or to make further dice rolls. We've suggested twenty minutes as the standard length because most dice and chart games stress that time length.

Realism. Various games achieve degrees of realism differently. The use of a game board, with a colorful ball field on it, can help focus imaginations. Other games assume a ballpark and the diamond action are visualized in the gamer's imagination. If it's vivid enough, only the scorebook is needed to track the movement of baserunners and note the scoring of runs.

Flow of the Game. Plays begin, proceed and end in a logical progression in real play. How the action which follows the ball being hit is integrated into the rules of a game impacts the way different table baseball games are played. A table game must be a static series of steps and should, at least, take place sequentially. How stolen bases, hit-and-run, sacrifice bunts, and other strategies are handled differs greatly from one game to another and impact the flow of the game and what the gamer views as "realism."

Batter vs. Pitcher. The confrontation between batter and pitcher is resolved differently by different table baseball games. Some, like All-Star Baseball, avoid the conflict by ignoring the pitcher's individual characteristics. Some games slow their flow by requiring each batter to be rerated when pitchers are changed.

Designers have puzzled over where to place the emphasis equitably. Starting with Statis Pro, some games cope with this with "fast action cards" which alternatively assign control of the outcome to a pitcher's individual card or the batter's. This speeds the action, appears to be impartial, but leaves any connection to realism strictly to the luck of the draw.

Strat-O-Matic is the top-selling baseball table game.

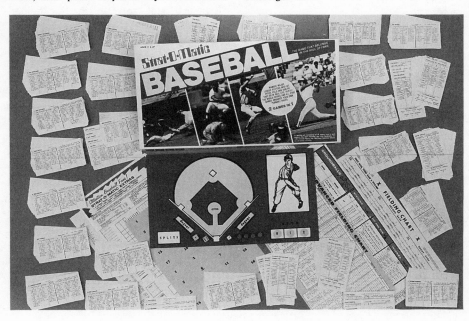

Righty-Lefty. Much actual baseball managerial strategy is based on off-setting an opponent's strength by using a left-handed pitcher to oppose left-handed batters and vice versa with righties. This characteristic is accepted by some games as indispensable and ignored by others. It's essentially a matter of sophistication. The basic APBA game ignores it and the APBA Master Game makes it a feature. Some games offer a generalized assumption of the way all batters are advantaged or not by the side from which the pitcher throws. Strat-O-Matic makes its ratings on actual player-by-player experience against right- and left-handed pitchers.

Diversified Scores. In trying to bring about final scores that reflect the average number of runs scored in actual play, there is a danger of far too many games ending with average scores rather than the great variety of final tallies which created the average. Games which hew too closely to the myopic viewpoints of mathematicians tend to produce mostly 4–3 and 5–4 results. This makes for more interesting, and intense, competitions, but in real-life baseball, the lopsided shutout win, the high-scoring barrage by both teams, or the low-scoring pitching duel are more characteristic.

Defense, the Stepchild of Stats. To some table games and their players an out is an out. To others directional instructions are important. Surely this is one of the finer points of realism. How putouts are made and at which position has a major effect on the outcome of a game—whether base runners move up on a ball hit behind them or are forced out. The movement of base runners is a preliminary to scoring them, and they can advance in ways other than on a base hit.

Perhaps game designers haven't known the percentages. They are not detailed in official statistics as are batting averages and earned run averages.

Freak Plays. Want to have the game interrupted while the players chase a stray dog off the field or to apply ground rules

covering rare plays? To some gamers such innovations add realistic touches, while others resent such breaks in the action. Variety is not necessarily the spice of every table gamer's life.

Licensing Fees. In the early 1970s the Major League Baseball Players Association claimed its members "owned their records," and that before a table game company could use actual statistics, they had to be licensed by the MLBPA. APBA and Strat-O-Matic accepted this contention, but most new games then were offered by designer-marketers with limited capital who could not afford to pay the license fee ($5,000). Although the players won a class-action suit against the Big League Game Company of Duluth, Minnesota, the subsequent agreement arrived at

required the game company to pay royalties only if the individual player stats appear on personalized cards (as they do in APBA and Strat-O-Matic).

Consequently some games offer coded data on roster sheets. Others provide the process to convert anyone's stats to data for the game. Some provide the data in booklets, contending that when bound— as in baseball guides and annual yearbooks—this separates the data from a player's claim to exclusivity. Some companies merchandise their license as an "endorsement," implying the game has been judged superior by the MLBPA when all it signifies is that the players will appear on cards, and that often the customer is paying extra for that privilege.   —JK

Strategy vs. Arcade

With board games everything is fantasy. When the card says that Kevin McReynolds hit a double, you put your marker on second base. When McReynolds hits a double in most computer games, you get to see the ball skip down the left-field line, or hit the wall and end up in the fielder's glove.

While traditionalists tend to stick with stalwarts such as APBA or Strat-O-Matic, those with computers tend to gravitate toward the wealth of more visually satisfying, statistically oriented games that have flooded the marketplace during the past several years. It only makes sense that as personal computer sales have grown, so has the popularity of computer baseball.

The world of computer baseball simulations is divided between the strategy games and the joystick-driven, arcade-style games.

Strategy. These games put players directly in the manager's chair. With this kind of software, players pick lineups, choose pitching rotations, and set defenses. Then the manager sits back and

watches his team perform, and makes changes where necessary, just like in the big leagues. He can visit the mound and make pitching changes, pinch-hit, call for steals, etc. In most cases he can't call the pitches, though. Too much time. Instead the computer shows you the result of the particular at bat.

Most of the games listed here include some sort of recordkeeping functions, so that managers may draft players and start their own leagues. It's very much like Rotisserie baseball, except that stats are based on past seasons instead of the present. While most games take about twenty-five minutes to complete, most also have a quick-game function for those who need results for an entire league for a whole season. The computer flashing faster than the eye can see will give you the box score result of a game in three to five minutes.

These games can be player vs. player or player vs. computer. Results on most are very realistic. Because of the random numbers of computers, no two contests will ever be exactly alike.

Joystick. Those who stand in arcades and pump endless streams of quarters into video games are who these simulations are intended for; strategy players will no doubt want to stay away. Those who treasure Micro League or Earl Weaver Baseball will find joystick games insipid, while joystick players usually find the strategy games boring or too complicated. It's like comparing the "MacNeil-Lehrer News-hour" to MTV.

In joystick games, managers try to hit the pitch, and they use the joystick to position fielders, run, catch, and throw. There are two varieties. The basic arcade-style game relies entirely on the skill of the player/manager. (Don't expect as sophisticated a game as you'll find in an arcade, though; home computers simply don't have that kind of memory.) A newer generation of games claim to be statistically based, meaning that players will perform according to their actual real-life tendencies. Don't ask me how, or whether this really works (sometimes it seems like just a marketing ploy; the manager's skill with the joystick is still the prime mover). Those companies that have licensing agreements with the Major League Baseball Players Association or with specific players will use actual big league players' names and stats. Those that don't will make up names for players and assign them particular talents (for example, a slugging first baseman, a speedy second baseman, etc.). The time it takes to play a joystick game depends largely on the skill of the players. (A double no-hitter can go by pretty quickly.) But twenty minutes is a good average number.

Baseball computer gaming is proving to be quite popular, and there's never been a better time to get involved. With increased competition, and more software chains popping up all over the country, many software manufacturers have lowered prices. So warm up the VDT, turn off the printer, and play ball! Keep the beer away from the disk drive, though.   —RS

Computer Game Reviews

This portion of the chapter will look at the two different kinds of computer baseball games: strategy games, and joystick-driven, "arcade"-style games. The computer format available—generally Apple, Commodore, or IBM-compatible (noted as "IBM")—will let you know how powerful a machine you'll need to run the programs. The prices given are the manufacturers' suggested list price; however, heavy discounting will enable you to pay considerably less. The cost of the basic software for the strategy games generally includes player rosters for at least one recent season. (Because of the number and variety of add-ons available, we've described them separately in the game reviews.) We've also included a few games no longer manufactured, but still available in stores. Replacement parts, after all, are not a problem with software, and the manufacturers are still around to answer questions.

APBA MAJOR LEAGUE PLAYERS BASEBALL
McGraw-Hill Educational Resources
11 West 19th St.
New York, NY 10011
(800) 843-8855
Availability: Selected software stores or mail order.
Formats: IBM, Apple.
Simulation style: Strategy.
Price: $59.95.
This enjoyable simulation is the computerized version of APBA, the card and dice game that has been played in thousands of bedrooms and dens for the past two decades. Like the board game, players perform exactly as they would in real life. All batters are rated for average, power, and speed and are categorized against both left- and right-handed pitchers. Pitchers

Bases Loaded by Jaleco.

are also rated for the platoon differential and for stamina and strikeout/walk tendencies. If you enjoy APBA but desire the simulation in a faster, more comprehensive format, this is the right choice for you. But hard-disk users, beware: the copy-protection scheme for this game makes it imperative that you have two floppy-disk drives.

APBA was one of the first companies to expand their product line to include a computer simulation, but at press time this game was in a state of flux. The most recent publisher, Random House Software, was acquired by McGraw-Hill Educational Resources, but the new owners insist that the game will remain on the market. In fact, a new version is being prepared for the spring of 1990.

Aimed at serious strategists, APBA features a results-only format. In other words, you'll see no colorful playing field re-creation, as you do in many of the newer computer simulations. Managers pick lineups and starting pitchers, and results from each play are offered on the screen after the computer determines the outcome. That speeds up game play dramatically. Line scores and the capability to print out box scores are included, making this a good system for those who wish to re-create whole seasons. It comes complete with rosters for an entire recent MLB season.

Also available are three volumes of old-timer disks ($19.95), which contain statistical data for most Hall of Fame players, plus many other former stars. Individual season disks ($19.95) are also available.

Those interested in APBA are advised that the programs offered in Statis Pro and Pure Stat are very similar, despite the price differences. There is, however, a feature in software capabilities that makes APBA unique. The company recently added a peripheral disk ($19.95) that allows managers from across the country to play statistically based seasons via modem. This alone could make APBA the most popular simulation in the country.

BASES LOADED (I & II)
Jaleco USA Inc.
5617 West Howard St.
Niles, IL 60648
(312) 647-7077
Availability: Most toy and department stores.
Format: Nintendo.
Simulation style: Joystick.
Price: $49.95.

Nintendo is the most popular home-arcade system in history, and this simulation is one of the most popular cartridges available—if you can find it.

This easy-to-play, colorful game is statistically based to a minor extent. Managers can choose from 30 players on each roster (18 offensive players and 12 pitchers), each rated on pitching and hitting ability. Twelve teams are included, but it's really up to the player's arcade ability to succeed in this simulation.

While the game is easy to understand and play, batting against the computer's pitcher is extremely hard. Younger players will enjoy it much more in the two-player mode. The new features added to Bases Loaded II include enhanced graphics, an umpire's "voice" to call out the count, and music as annoying as that at the ballpark. But that's verisimilitude for you—kids who have previewed it seem to love it.

The main difference between Bases Loaded, R.B.I. Baseball, and even the Sega titles is in graphics. Most games employ a similar style of play, so it's really up to a manager's taste in graphics when deciding where to plunk his or her fifty bucks.

The Nintendo-style game must be played on a Nintendo Home Entertainment System (much like the old Atari and Intellivision systems); that'll run you another $100.

BIGGS COMPUTER BASEBALL
TGIS
6047 N. Marmora
Chicago, IL 60646
(312) 631-1917
Availability: Mail order.

Format: IBM.
Simulation style: Strategy.
Price: $29.95.

Looking for wild color graphics? The national anthem before the game? The sound of fans cheering after a home run? You won't find them in the Biggs Computer Baseball simulation. What you will find, however, is hard-hitting, statistically based baseball at an attractive price.

All you'll see is a brown and green "board" with players' names where their positions would normally be. When a ball is "hit," the name of the batter automatically advances to the base. TGIS has opted to cut down on the fancy graphics in order to present a more serious game which should appeal to those wishing to play full seasons of their favorite MLB teams. As with most simulations, managers select lineups, set up starting rotations, and generally call the shots during each game. But there is no playing field, no stadium, no music. You name the play, and—*bang!*—the results pop onto the screen. The game features one of the most impressive box score printouts yet devised (which even goes so far as to include game-winning hits), and a data base that can keep track of accumulated stats. Games may be played against another manager, against the computer, or all-computer games may be played.

Fielders are rated on fielding percentage for up to four different positions. Hitters are rated for power, average, and strikeout/walk tendencies, but not for platoon differentials. Pitchers are rated for ERA and other major stats like K/BB's, but not for stamina or platoon differentials.

Older players will likely enjoy this game because of its detailed descriptions of famous teams of the past, available on historical disks ($9.95). Teams from the 1986, '87, and '88 seasons are also available at the same price.

While the graphics are the blandest on the market, this game more than makes up for it in statistical accuracy and ease of play.

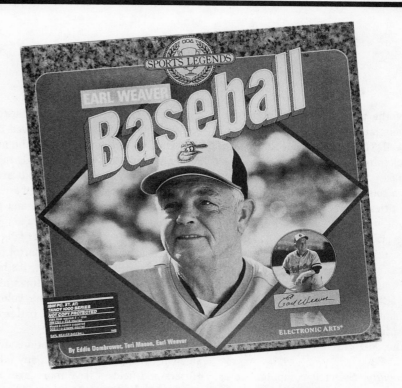

CHAMPIONSHIP BASEBALL
Solid Gold Software
Distributed by Mediagenic
3885 Bohannon Drive
Menlo Park, CA 94025
(415) 329-0500

Availability: Most software stores.

Format: Commodore 64, IBM, Apple, Amiga.

Simulation style: Joystick.

Price: $14.95.

Another popular software title that's undergone a surprising price decrease, Championship Baseball is a certified hit in the software stores, with more than 100,000 units sold. Created by Darrin Massena, Scott Orr, and Mark Madland, it features some of the most unusual split-screen graphics on the market; this has led to its standing as an industry leader.

With a batter at the plate, the split screen offers a view of the entire field on the left and a batter's-eye view of the pitching mound on the right. When the ball is hit, the graphic immediately switches to a full-screen view of the field as seen from the upper deck in right field. Unlike other arcade-style games, dugouts, coaches' boxes, and umpires are fully depicted on the playing field.

Managers control every aspect of this game, including drafting a new lineup or roster. Each player has been rated for hitting, fielding, running, and pitching ability (not based on actual major leaguers). Pitchers are rated on three separate skill levels; all other players have four.

After rosters are selected, a batting order is chosen, and managers are then ready to play either against another player or against the computer. A batting practice function allows managers to get in a few fungoes before the game. Also, rosters may be entered against other teams in a four-division, twenty-four-team league, enabling an entire season of games to be played.

This game is an easy one to understand, though it takes several plays to master it.

(Cont. p. 308.)

Batter Up, Prices Down

What a difference a year can make. After the completion of the 1988 Major League season, the manufacturers of computer baseball simulations saw the marketplace become softer than it had in years. The result? Lower prices and improved products, both factors that help make becoming a computer manager easier than ever.

On the joystick front, stagnant sales have prompted even the best of the games to undergo some surprisingly steep price cuts. Accolade's Hardball!, which is one of the better arcade games on the market, now features a low list price of $14.95, a fraction of the title's original cost. Mediagenic's Championship Baseball, another popular title, also lowered its list to $14.95. These two titles, like most arcade-style games, are available at even more attractive discounts at retail.

With strategy games, many older titles have fallen by the wayside because of flagging sales. Once popular simulations such as The World's Greatest Baseball Game and Radio Baseball are no longer in production. Another title, Software Simulations' Pure-Stat Baseball, has recently cut its list price from $39.95 to $19.95.

Other titles, though still popular, have gone through some improvements, with, if any, only a modest price increase.

Electronic Arts' new Earl Weaver Baseball Version 1.5 boasts improved statistical data, a better view of the pitcher and batter, and more colorful graphics. Micro League Baseball II takes the features of MLB I, soups up the graphics, and adds attractive features such as player injuries, rain delays, umpire arguments and a quick-play function.

The result of all these changes? There are fewer new titles on the market, but it's less expensive to get started, and the strategy titles are reaching new heights of realism. Another important factor is the advent of software chains that are becoming increasingly popular in shopping centers and malls. While discounting was unheard of only a few years ago, most in-print titles are now available at discounts of 10 to 20 percent regularly.

If this keeps up—and all indications are that it will—computer baseball may soon threaten the real version of the Grand Old Game. After all, in this kind of baseball, computer players can't hold out for a better deal—only the manager can. —RS

Many of the unique functions, however, offer enough of a reason to try to learn to play it well. The ability to slide under tags, dive back into bases, and throw a knuckleball make the software entertaining. There's a touch of realism here that most arcade titles don't even begin to approach.

However, as in all other arcade games, this one neither generates nor compiles statistics.

COMPUTER STATIS PRO BASEBALL
The Avalon Hill Game Company
4517 Harford Road
Baltimore, MD 21214
(301) 254-5300
Availability: Selected computer stores or mail order.
Format: Apple, Commodore 64.
Simulation style: Strategy.
Price: $35.

This simulation, which seemingly had disappeared from the market, is still available in some outlets and through the manufacturer. It's based on the Statis Pro board game, which until recently had been known as Sports Illustrated Statis Pro. Those familiar with the card and dice variation will feel right at home.

While it takes a bit longer to play than other simulations, Statis Pro offers strategists a host of options. All managerial strategies, including hitting, fielding, stealing bases, and pitching, are available. Major league season disks are available separately ($19.95). Although easy to play and reliable, it lags behind many of the newer games in statistical accuracy and graphics.

EARL WEAVER BASEBALL 1.5
Electronic Arts
1820 Gateway Drive
San Mateo, CA 94404
(415) 571-7171
Availability: Most software stores.
Format: IBM.
Simulation style: Strategy.
Price: $39.95.

Strategy fans of Earl Weaver Baseball freaked out when it was announced that the game was being pulled from the market. How could this be? This highly rated, imaginative game was the only software of its kind and ranked as one of the bestselling simulations of all time, in any format.

Thankfully experienced Weaver fans are now wiping their brows in relief. Not only is this game still on the market, it's been improved. The new version features more accurate statistics, a new, more colorful look, and better control of the batter and pitcher.

There are more strategy options available with this game than with any other. Hitters and fielders have more than fifty ratings, and pitchers have an additional thirty. Besides, the game employs a unique "Ask Earl" feature. In any given situation, managers may press a computer key and obtain "advice" on how to position fielders, hold runners, and other factors.

Other enjoyable features include a radar gun that measures pitch velocity, an instant replay (including slow motion), wind conditions, umpire arguments, and a feature that allows managers to choose from thirty-two different ballpark configurations.

The visuals are highlighted by a split-screen view that shows the pitcher and hitter on the right and the entire playing field on the left. Besides setting lineups, changing pitchers, and the usual game strategy decisions, managers choose who warms up in the bullpen.

Also included is a "General Manager" function that allows managers to trade players or draft entirely new teams. The game also compiles all statistics so managers may keep track of an entire season's worth of games. Box scores may also be printed after each contest.

The game is now available only for IBM format because of increased memory demands, but the new product shows the improvements were well worth the effort. The most unusual aspect of this game is

that players can actually "see" the computer-generated image of Weaver, sitting in the dugout and thinking about what decisions he is about to make. When operating in the player vs. computer mode, Weaver takes the role of the opposing team manager.

This simulation offers full box scores, cumulative recordkeeping, and optional team and Commissioner's disks ($19.95), which allow players to draft their own teams.

An industry leader for more than five years, it's so well programmed that it is by far the bestselling sports software, continually challenging the usually more popular fantasy simulations like Dungeons & Dragons for the top spot on the bestseller lists. If you've got an IBM PC or clone, give this game a tryout—and we defy you to keep your finger off the "Ask Earl" button.

FULL COUNT COMPUTER BASEBALL
Lance Haffner Games
P.O. Box 100594
Nashville, TN 37210
(615) 242-2617
Availability: Mail order and through selected software outlets.
Formats: Commodore 64/128, IBM, Apple, Atari ST.
Simulation style: Strategy.
Price: $39.99.

This strategy simulation features a complete roster of 1989 MLB teams, plus (the best feature!) 52 great teams of the past, giving it one of the largest on-disk roster menus of any game currently available. Another difference is that rosters consist of 17 offensive players and 12 pitchers, whereas other games usually offer more limited rosters. Managers can either use the team rosters or create their own teams through trading or holding a draft.

As with most other strategy games, managers make all decisions for their teams. This game also takes into account ballpark effects (usually an extra with other formats) and platooning abilities. The batters are rated on all the usual stats, including their averages versus left- and right-handed pitchers. A stats compiler automatically records player and team statistics, and a box score may be obtained at the finish of each contest. An option is the Standings & League Leaders disk ($14.99), which allows players to keep track of the top players in their leagues in newspaper style. Additional team disks are also available.

Overall, this game has so many unique variations that one must consider it for purchase. While not overly fancy in graphics, it has a host of statistical features not available on other formats, making it a worthwile choice for ultra-serious strategists.

HardBall! may be had at bargain prices because of the advent of HardBall II.

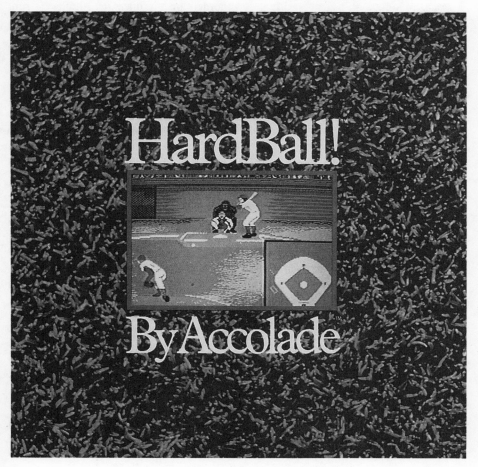

HARDBALL! and HARDBALL II
Accolade
550 South Winchester Blvd.
San Jose, CA 95128
(800) 245-7744
Availability: Most software stores or mail order.
Formats: IBM, Apple, Atari ST, Amiga.
Simulation style: Joystick.
Price: $14.95 for HardBall!; $39.95 for HardBall II for the IBM and $44.95 for the Amiga.

The Software Publishers Association once proclaimed this "the bestselling computer baseball game of all time," and more than 400,000 units of software have already been sold. It's not hard to see why. Designed by veteran arcade genius Bob Whitehead, this is one of the most realistic joystick games available today.

It offers a degree of playability that is challenging but not overly complicated, and graphics that are more realistic than most joystick games. Managers may choose between two teams and select batting orders from statistically based lineups (not based on real MLB players). Complete control over pitching, hitting, fielding, and running is achieved with the joystick. Players may play against each other or against the computer, which is extremely hard to defeat. Hurlers have four different pitch variations: fastball, knuckler, slider, and curveball. Hitters may swing low, high, inside, outside, or level by manipulating the joystick.

A real delight in this game is that fielders make accurate throws to bases. Players even dive and make difficult plays, and computer-generated ballpark noise reacts in kind. HardBall! was recently reduced in price, and it is a superior purchase for joystick game fans of all ages. It's addictive and charming, and features one of the funkiest musical soundtracks of any game available, and that includes the strategy titles. HardBall II provides more realistic animated gameplay and advanced statistical data.

INTELLIVISION MAJOR LEAGUE BASE-
    BALL
Mattel Electronics
Hawthorne, CA 90520
(213) 978-5150
Availability: Out of print but still available in some toy stores.
Formats: Intellivision, Sears Tele-Games.
Simulation style: Joystick.
Price: $19.95.

Intellivision was Mattel's attempt to compete with Atari in the fledgling video-game market eleven years ago. Intellivision and Atari are now looked upon as relics of the past, both having been long supplanted by the higher-memory antics of Nintendo and Sega.

Major League Baseball, however, is remembered as about the only enjoyable

Because of its club-finance feature, Pete Rose Pennant Fever is the only game Marge Schott could have played to prepare for negotiations with Kal Daniels.

game the Intellivision system ever had. It featured a simple green playing field with no crowd or outfield fence, frog-like fielders, and a computer-generated umpire who croaked "You're out!" as each play was made. The game was simple, but it was easy and fun to play, considering the clumsy Intellivision disk controllers.

Although Mattel has long abandoned Intellivision, the game hardware is still being manufactured and distributed. It was being offered at bargain-basement prices through the Toys R Us chain as of mid-1989. This cartridge (of which there are thousands still floating around out there) is also available at prices as low as $1.99.

Those who love the designated hitter will likely fall in love with this one. It's offense all the way, making 30–17 final scores common even after the game has been fully mastered. It's not realistic, but it can be entertaining.

MAJOR LEAGUE
LJN Toys
1107 Broadway
New York, NY 10010
(212) 243-6565
Availability: Most toy and department stores.
Format: Nintendo.

Simulation style: Joystick.
Price: $49.95.

This simulation, which has been licensed by the Major League Baseball Players Association, uses real player names and statistics on its rosters (though not real team names—that would have required a separate license from Major League Baseball), an appealing feature for younger players who wish to live out the heroics of their favorite stars.

As with most of the arcade-derived titles, managers pitch, hit, run, and field for all players. All player moves are made with the joystick. Runs are tabulated on a between-innings line score. Among the more notable features are several views of the colorful field, and having balls and strikes displayed on the playing field at all times. This game is moderately easy to master, making it appropriate for family play.

MICRO LEAGUE BASEBALL (MLB 1)
Micro League Sports Association
2201 Drummond Plaza
Newark, DE 19711-5711
(302) 368-9990
Availability: Most software stores or mail order.
Formats: Commodore 64, Apple, IBM, Atari ST (the latter two are going out of

print, while each of the former two is being offered in a $24.95 package that includes the General Manager's disk).
Simulation style: Strategy.
Price: $39.95.

This game does an excellent job of putting players in the manager's seat in a major league dugout. Now six years old, Micro League is probably the most famous of the computer-strategy simulations and continues to gain in popularity while others released at about the same time have gone out of print.

The realism of game play, even in this smaller-memory "original" MLB version, borders on the uncanny. All players run, hit, field, and pitch as they would in real life (the game is statistically based). Managers can choose from 25 great teams of the past, such as the 1927 Yankees or 1973 Oakland A's, or select one of the optional season disks available ($19.95 each). Another option is the season-franchise disks ($29.95 each), which highlight the 10 greatest seasons for a particular club.

Another plus for Micro League is the computerized recordkeeping, which is possible with the optional Box Score/Stat Compiler Disk ($24.95). This enables computer owners with printers to accumulate a whole season's worth of stats and print out box scores. The General Manager/Owner's Disk ($39.95) enables managers to hold Rotisserie-style drafts and select their players from the team disks.

Game play can pit two managers against each other, player vs. computer, or computer vs. computer, a real plus if accumulating a season's worth of stats. For those who opt to manage their teams, nine offensive and defensive strategies are available, complete with pitch selections. The game "board" features a colorful depiction of a major league ballpark, complete with the National Anthem and "Take Me Out to the Ball Game" during the seventh-inning stretch.

Overall, this game offers the best aspects of Strat-O-Matic–style game play, without the endless hours of recordkeeping. Not a simpleminded joystick action game, it's recommended for serious, knowledgeable baseball fans only.

MICRO LEAGUE BASEBALL (MLB II)
Micro League Sports Association
2201 Drummond Plaza
Newark, DE 19711-5711
(800) PLAYBAL
Availability: Most software stores or mail order.
Formats: IBM, Atari ST, Macintosh (1M RAM).
Simulation style: Strategy.
Price: $49.95 for IBM and Atari ST; $59.95 for Macintosh.

This recently released update of Micro League's MLB I has all the features of the company's previous game, plus a wide range of enhanced features and graphics. The original Micro League game is a quality product, but if you own a higher-memory computer, this is surely the version to choose. The General Manager and Stat Compiler disks are included in the MLB II package.

The most startling update on this game is the graphics. On the older format all the players looked similar to frogs in baseball uniforms. These players are really built, as if they had spent the off-season working out on a computer-chip Nautilus. The pluses don't end there; also included are stadium factors, pitcher-stamina factors, bullpen warm-up ratings (which tell you if a reliever is warm or lets you take the chance of bringing him in before he's ready), expanded fielding ratings, and a built-in box score function.

Another feature added is the "Quick Game" function, which enables managers to play a complete computer-managed game in just a few minutes. This is an invaluable asset for those who wish to create an entire 162-game season, and a real

plus for those who don't have the time to sit through the usual fifteen-minute version. Not to degrade the original MLB I game, but if that was a Cadillac, this is a Rolls-Royce. The attention to detail in both the graphics and game play is first-rate. Even rain delays, umpire arguments (and ejections; imagine being tossed out of your own game!), and player injuries are all figured in, giving this simulation many of the spatial, quirky realities that make actual major league baseball such a hoot. (By the way, ejected managers can only watch from the clubhouse as the computer takes over running the team.)

If your computer has the memory, spend the extra money for MLB II. No joysticks to be found here, just keyboard-driven realism. Luckily the only thing MLB II leaves out are the parking fees and high-priced concessions.

PETE ROSE PENNANT FEVER
Gamestar/Distributed by Mediagenic
3885 Bohannon Drive
Menlo Park, CA 94025
(415) 329-0500
Availability: Most software stores.
Formats: IBM, Apple, Commodore 64.
Simulation style: Strategy/Joystick.
Price: $34.95 for Commodore; $44.95 for the others.

Exceptionally realistic graphics and exciting game play are two of the hallmarks of Pete Rose Pennant Fever, a game as gritty as the man himself. Even those who don't enjoy baseball simulations owe it to themselves to at least see this game being played on the IBM version. The sight of the three-tiered simulated Riverfront Stadium is worth the price of admission all by itself.

Managers may use simple keyboard commands or a joystick to play this game. Eight different views of the colorful field follow the action, and all umpire calls are computer-generated. A whopping 23 different pitch variations from a combination of button and joystick moves (most joysticks have only eight functions) are avail-

Baseball's Future

The next generation of big leaguers will be products of the computerized-game age. What skills are being sharpened in the arcades?

Finger Dexterity—Despite weak arms, the joystick-trained generation will be able to throw split-fingered fastballs, screwballs, and curves far beyond the capabilities of today's hurlers.

Fearless Fielding—If they learn to catch, they'll crash bravely into any fence, expecting only funny music.

Oblivious Play—After surviving blips, whirrs, dings, and buzzes, they'll never be upset by such dugout calls as "Your mother's a bleep!"   —BC

able to managers, and players can control sliding into bases as well. One or two players can participate. Managers may draft rookies and purchase free agents. One humorous aspect to this simulation is that managers also have to control club finances, which surely qualifies this as a product of our times.

While it's probably too statistically oriented for joystick mavens and too whimsical for hardcore strategists, Pennant Fever is worth owning just to hear the hilarious umpire calls and watch the players slide into bases—the same way "Charlie Hustle" used to do it himself.

PURE-STAT BASEBALL
Software Simulations
959 Main St.
Stratford, CT 06497
(203) 377-4339
Availability: Most software stores or mail order.
Formats: Commodore 64, IBM, Apple.
Simulation style: Strategy.
Price: $19.95.

With this simulation, the name tells you what you get. Players familiar with Avalon

Hill's excellent "NBA" game will likely fall in love with this baseball game; it's one of the better strategy simulations on the market.

The graphics are a bit on the bland side—your choice of Yankee, Dodger, or Royal Stadiums, viewed from the upper deck in left or right fields (depending on which side the batter hits from)—but managers have a host of offensive and defensive options from which to choose, including the ability to attempt to hit behind baserunners, call for squeeze bunts, order steals, and even have runners try for extra bases.

Pure-Stat provides batting statistics against both left- and right-handed pitchers. Batters are also rated for walk and strikeout tendencies, power, and bunting and sacrificing abilities. Running speed and base stealing abilities are also taken into account. All players are rated on fielding percentage, range and throwing ability. Pitchers are rated for strikeout, walk, and home run tendencies. A "tiring factor" is also assigned to each pitcher, measuring his stamina as the game goes on.

For the money (the list price was recently lowered from $39.95), it's an excellent value. Box score and cumulative statistic keeping are included on the game disk, so that even low-memory computer owners can begin playing entire seasons right away without having to purchase extra disks. Even more impressive is the quick-play function, which allows managers to set lineups and play a complete contest in under four minutes. Included on the team disk are every team from the 1985 season and eight classic teams of the past.

On the down side, mastering the stat-initializing process takes quite a bit of time, and most of the software we tested was balky. Graphics are among the slowest in the market on plays such as a ball hit to the outfield, but this is not a big problem. Pure-Stat offers a complete statistical program in one inexpensive package.

Additional season and stadium disks are available ($19.95), as well as team disks for the 1986, '87, '88, and '89 seasons. Also available is the "Create Your Own Team" disk ($24.95), which allows managers to invent their own players and give them statistical histories.

REGGIE JACKSON BASEBALL/GREAT
   BASEBALL
Tonka
6000 Clearwater Drive
Minnetonka, MN 55343
(612) 936-3300
   Availability: Most toy and department stores.
   Format: Sega.
   Simulation style: Joystick.
   Price: $49.99.
The famous former Athletic, Oriole, Yankee, and Angel has lent his name and face to this joystick simulation, which resembles another Sega game called Great Baseball, but which has several new features and a different mode of play. It's played on the Sega Home Entertainment System, which runs about $150.

This game offers four different views of the field and they shift when the ball is hit. Managers may control pitching and hitting with their joystick, which also is used to throw the ball from base to base. The cartridge may be used as either a one- or a two-player game. Since it is a simple product, it will likely be enjoyed by younger players.

There isn't much of a difference, however, in this and the company's Great Baseball, which is still available at the same price. Game play is essentially the same, but Sega, a Japanese company, has included in Great Baseball some of the most humorous between-innings graphics we've seen in any format. If a pitcher gets pounded, you see his image on the stadium's big screen, stomping frantically on his glove. If a team has a big offensive inning, you see a player happily slurping away at a can of cola. Granted these moments aren't important to game play, but they add a small touch of welcome humor.

R.B.I. BASEBALL
Tengen
P.O. Box 361110
Milpitas, CA 95035
(408) 435-2650
   Availability: Most toy and department stores.
   Format: Nintendo.
   Simulation style: Joystick.
   Price: $49.95.
This game, licensed by the Major League Players Association, is based on the popular R.B.I. Baseball game that can be seen crowded with youngsters at penny arcades all over the country. Each manager can select one of 10 teams with players' statistics of 8 actual and 2 All-Star teams. Players meld their arcade ability with the statistics to achieve the plays.

Although it features real player names, R.B.I. Baseball is actually quite lighthearted, and the player images are short and squat. Hitting, either in the two-player mode or against the computer, is much easier in this game than in other joystick simulations.

Pitching, too, is easy to master, making R.B.I. a good choice. One fault with many of the arcade games over the years was that it took dozens of plays to master even one aspect of the game, but with R.B.I., managers will be able to sit down and get comfortable almost at once.

THE SLUGGER
Mastertronic
711 West 17th St.
Costa Mesa, CA 92627
(714) 631-1001
   Availability: Most toy and department stores.
   Format: Commodore 64.
   Simulation style: Joystick.
   Price: $9.99.
This simple, easy-to-use software would be a good bet for younger baseball fans, but it doesn't offer much for statistics buffs. It's much more whimsical than it is serious.

One thing The Slugger does feature,

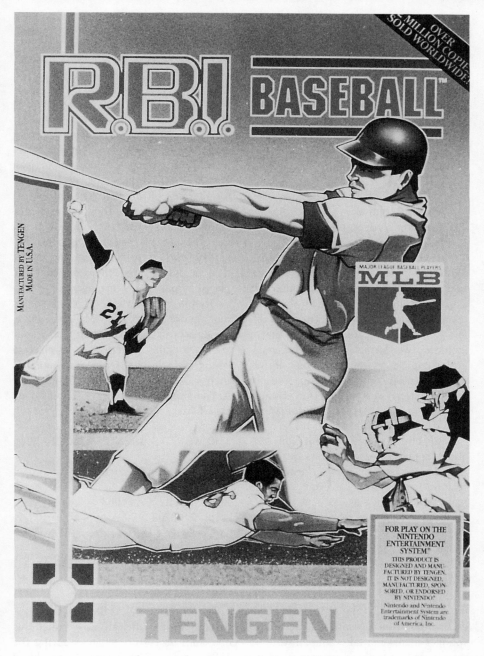

MANUFACTURED BY TENGEN
MADE IN U.S.A.

R.B.I. BASEBALL™

OVER A MILLION COPIES SOLD WORLDWIDE

MAJOR LEAGUE BASEBALL PLAYERS
MLB

FOR PLAY ON THE NINTENDO ENTERTAINMENT SYSTEM®
THIS PRODUCT IS DESIGNED AND MANUFACTURED BY TENGEN. IT IS NOT DESIGNED, MANUFACTURED, SPONSORED, OR ENDORSED BY NINTENDO® Nintendo and Nintendo Entertainment System are trademarks of Nintendo of America, Inc.

TENGEN

SPORTING NEWS BASEBALL
Epyx Computer Software
P.O. Box 8020
600 Galveston Drive
Redwood City, CA 94063
(415) 368-3200

Availability: Most software stores, mail order.

Format: Commodore, IBM, Apple.

Simulation style: Joystick/Strategy.

Price: $39.95.

This game replaced The World's Greatest Baseball Game on Epyx's roster of baseball simulations in 1988. There isn't anything else quite like it on the market today. Sporting News (licensed by the weekly publication of the same name) is a statistically driven game combined with a joystick game; the results obtained when batting are intended to simulate those of real life. For instance, even though the manager is actually manning the joystick for his player, a Felix Fermin won't hit with the same kind of power as a Darryl Strawberry, and so on.

The game is activated by using the joystick, or, in the case of the all-computer variation, by using a single-letter keyboard command. A pregame blackboard allows managers to choose the computer or another manager as the opponent—or a game in which the computer plays itself in a purely stat-driven format, with managers having no control over the visual outcome. Managers may also create their own teams by using the "Build Your Own Team" option at the beginning of team and player selection.

Managers may choose lineups from more than 150 past baseball greats, or choose from players of 26 teams, statistically based on the 1987 season. Batters are rated on all stats, including walks and strikeout tendencies. Pitchers are rated on ERA, strikeout/walk tendencies, and fatigue. Fielders are rated on fielding percentage.

Managers have a number of strategic options. When using the joystick, they can deploy various baserunning options, in-

however, is the most comical "players" we've seen. These little, bandy-legged guys run out to the field in unison, resembling the Keystone Cops more than the Kansas City Royals. Also, several cheerleaders take the field to hail the arrival of the home-team, but when was the last time anybody saw a cheerleading squad at a baseball game?

Managers have complete control over pitching, hitting, and fielding, as they do in most other joystick games. Batting is unique, however, in that a side view of the

pitched ball comes in on a large screen above the field. Hitting the ball is quite easy, but fielding will take several hours to master. Also included is a self-demonstration mode for instructions.

The Slugger, while its graphics are sorely lacking in comparison to other games on the market, still is a worthwhile purchase for young children. Adults, however, may not enjoy the silly tone of the product as much as the small fry.

cluding steals. They control all pitch selections, and can reposition fielders and change their lineups at any time.

A final line score and game-highlights screen (winning and losing pitchers, home run hitters, etc.) pops up on the screen automatically after each game. But, unlike other simulations, this game will not provide accumulated stats or box scores, so those interested in keeping track of their teams will have to get out the pencils and notebooks. It also takes quite a bit of time to master, particularly the hitting and fielding.

Serious fans who are into managing will probably want to pass on this one, but it seems perfect for arcade players looking for something a bit more realistic. The three-dimensional playing field graphics are among the best on the market.

SPORTS SPECTACULAR
Keypunch Software
1221 Pioneer Building
St. Paul, MN 55101
(612) 292-1490
Availability: Most software stores.
Formats: Commodore 64, Apple, IBM.
Simulation style: Joystick.
Price: $7.99.
It's a bit unfair to call this a baseball simulation, since also included on the same disk are golf, football, and bowling games. As is the case with most budget software, you get what you pay for—an ultra-simple, easy-to-play game. One drawback to the software is that it is a two-player game only, so single players will probably want to pass it up. As in other games, managers hit, pitch, and field for themselves. The game is not statistically based.

Also this simulation includes a playing field that is not three-dimensional, and, as the price may suggest, the graphics are on the exceptionally primitive side. This software, however, is discounted for prices as low as $3.99, so it might not be the worst investment a younger gaming fan could make.

STEVE GARVEY VS. JOSE CANSECO IN GRAND SLAM BASEBALL
Cosmi
431 N. Figeroa St.
Wilmington, CA 90744
(213) 835-9687
Availability: Most software stores.
Formats: Commodore 64, IBM, Apple.
Simulation style: Joystick.
Price: $14.95.
This joystick simulation offers high-resolution graphics and, of course, the images of Steve Garvey and Jose Canseco as they hit cleanup for the statistically based teams included on the disk. The game differs from many on the market in that it includes two formats: a regular nine-inning contest, as well as a home run-hitting game where only round-trippers score points. Cleverly designed by Don Gault, it has a playing field that scrolls automatically to where the ball has been hit.

While hurling, eight different pitch variations are possible, and hitters can swing high, low, or level. Players perform in correlation to statistical data (not based on real major league players) which appears on the disk. Managers may substitute players, and there is a function which allows league play by grading and utilizing players that have been stored in memory.

Also included is a pamphlet extolling the virtues of Garvey and Canseco, and offering career statistics and other facts about each player. This game, though geared for younger managers, takes quite a while to master, but once that's accomplished it's quite entertaining and exciting considering its budget price.

STREET SPORTS BASEBALL
Epyx Computer Products
600 Galveston Drive
Redwood City, CA 94063
(415) 368-3200
Availability: Most software stores.
Formats: Commodore 64, IBM, Apple.
Simulation style: Joystick.
Price: $19.95.
They could have called this one Stick-

ball. In this joystick simulation, managers pick their teams from among "the hottest players on the block." The diamond isn't a diamond at all—it's a neighborhood street littered with garbage-can lids and old tires. Each of the 16 available players are rated for pitching, hitting, and fielding. Players also have to be able to jump over tree stumps, leap over bushes, and watch out for other hazards such as puddles and passing cars. A split-screen view of the field is offered, and the game may be played by one or two managers.

Overall, this entertaining software offers much more than the usual baseball game, as fielders can end up on their faces if they aren't careful. It's very easy to play, so youngsters will likely enjoy it as much as their elders. Those wishing for a major league simulation, however, should look elsewhere.

THE WORLD'S GREATEST BASEBALL GAME
Epyx Computer Products
600 Galveston Drive
Redwood City, CA 94063
(415) 368-3200
Availability: Out of print; still available in some software outlets.
Formats: Commodore 64, IBM, Apple.
Simulation style: Strategy/Joystick.
Price: $19.95.
The World's Greatest Baseball Game apparently wasn't, after all. Epyx pulled this one from its roster of games during the 1988 season, right before it introduced Sporting News Baseball to unsuspecting strategists.

Like Sporting News, this game offered statistically based rosters which then could be played in an arcade-style game, or used for a computerized no-player game. Included were 75 World Series winners and All-Star teams, classic players, and rosters from the 1984 and 1985 seasons. Managers could also create their own teams by utilizing these rosters. The software also included trading functions and trivia questions. Where available, this disk can be had at almost giveaway prices. Those who wish to play season by season updates will have to look to other titles, as no further season disks are available.

Here are other games you might want to consider:

OREL HERSHISER'S STRIKE ZONE
18001 Melbourne House
Irvine, CA 92714
(714) 833-8710
Availability: Some software stores, mail order.
Formats: IBM, Commodore 64.
Simulation style: Joystick.
Price: $39.99, IBM; $29.99, Commodore 64.

PROCHALLENGE BASEBALL
JBE
869 Yonge St.
Toronto, Ontario
Canada M4W 2H2
(416) 961-6233
Availability: Some software stores, mail order.
Format: IBM.
Simulation style: Strategy.
Price: $39.95.

All 26 major league teams. For 0, 1, or 2 players. Eighteen defensive player formations, 20 offensive strategy options, 10 different views of field, and help screens. A special feature allows users to alter the game speed to optimize visual synchronization with speed of computer being used.

STAR-LEAGUE BASEBALL
Gamestar/Distributed by Mediagenic
3885 Bohannon Drive
Menlo Park, CA 94025
(415) 329-0500
Availability: Most software stores.
Format: Commodore 64.
Simulation style: Joystick.
Price: $9.95.

Packaged with another game called On Field Football.

—RS

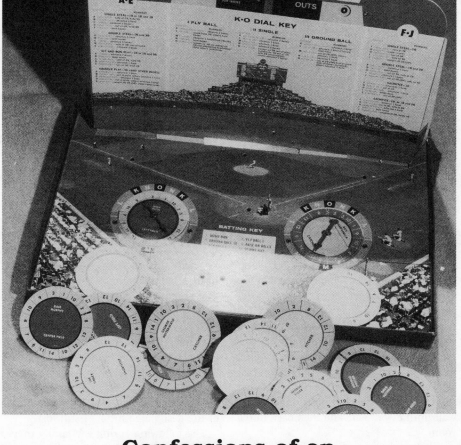

Confessions of an Ethan Allen Dropout

Yesterday I learned I'm on the mailing list for the company that sells all those "Now You Can Be a Big League Manager" baseball games. My postman left me a choice of reading my electric bill, an important message from my congressman, or the company's tabloid advertising newspaper. I started thumbing through their ads and got so involved I forgot to watch "Bingo for Big Bucks" on Channel 4.

There's a lot more than baseball games available these days. I can be an NFL quarterback, or an NBA coach, or a Mohawk in the French and Indian War. I can refight the Battle of Verdun or run my "own megabucks corporation in the economic jungle of Big Business." I can even save Mankind from the Invasion of the Aireaters.

All these games promise "realistic action," but I'm no judge. I wouldn't know a real Aireater from one of those cheap imitation Aireaters from Taiwan you buy at Earnest Ernie's Discounts.

All these games seem to involve dice, but I'm sure they're very realistic dice. Still, I guess they just don't make games the way they used to.

When I was nine, my best friend Billy had an Ethan Allen Baseball Game. It had little cardboard disks representing, I understood, real baseball players. I don't remember how I knew *Claude Passeau–Pitcher* or *Lonnie Frey–Second Base* were real players—maybe Billy told me so—but one of the cards was named *Joe DiMaggio–Outfield*, and I'd heard of him. For some reason I imagined he was a redhead.

Each disk had printed on it, in addition to a player's name and position, about a dozen or so numbered sections circling its edge. The idea was to put the disk on a spinner and then look at a chart to see what the player had done. Some numbers were hits, some were outs, and they were all in different-size sections depending on how good the player was. I remember 1 was a home run and 10 was a strike out. When Billy and I divvied up sides, we each tried to get players with big 1's and little 10's.

Other than liking 1's and hating 10's, we had different sets of values. He was going to be a movie star; I planned to be a pilot. He read the Hardy Boys; I read *Terry and the Pirates*. When he fell off our school fire escape and got a neat little scar on his forehead, he worried that it would ruin his good looks. I envied his scar because scars made people look tough. My only scar was on the back of my head, earned when I walked in front of Chuckie Thomason just as he was throwing half a brick into a big mud puddle. To look tough, I'd have to wait until I went bald and then back into a room.

Billy's favorite game disk was *Phil Cavarretta–First Base*, only he pronounced it "car-a-VETT-a". I explained the *v* came first and made it "cav-a-RETT-a," but Billy said Phil didn't hit as well that way.

I liked another first baseman—Nick Etten. He had a good 1 section, and his name sounded like he had lots of scars.

The sections on the disks had been mathematically computed to represent what the real players had done in real major league baseball games. A player who had actually hit a high number of doubles would have a big 11 section. If you played long enough, he'd get more doubles than

players with little 11's. If he really hit a lot of long fly outs, his disk had a big 8.

We learned about the mathematic accuracy of the sections only after we'd been playing for weeks because we got into an argument and had to read the directions. However, since neither Billy nor I knew anything about major league baseball, Ethan Allen could have saved himself all that arithmetic and just guessed.

Most days, of course, we played real baseball in our brick-paved schoolyard. We only turned to Ethan Allen baseball when it rained or when one of our gang had to "go with his mother"—an occupational hazard common to nine-year-olds—so that we couldn't get a full three players on each side.

The Ethan Allen game made no provision for pitching, so for Billy and me the best pitchers were the ones with the best batting disks. Once, after I'd lost a couple of games, I made *Bill Nicholson–Outfield* my starting pitcher. Despite my invention of the designated hitter, I still lost.

The following spring my family moved to another part of the state and way out in the country. I lost track of Billy; maybe I just haven't seen the right movies.

With no gang around, I listened to the radio most of the time, and one day I discovered the Cleveland Indians. This was back in the days when they used to win sometimes. I became a loyal fan. But in between baseball broadcasts there wasn't a whole lot to do. My father suggested I take up a hobby like mowing the grass, but I decided to make my own Ethan Allen baseball game with the players I was learning about through the cogent descriptions of Jimmy Dudley and Jack Graney, the

Cleveland announcers.

I built a spinner out of a block of wood, a roofing nail, and a cardboard arrow. Then I spent a week cutting out little paper disks for all the players Dudley and Graney told me about. I had to estimate their 1's and 10's and other numbers because I didn't have complete statistics.

Besides, the season was still going on.

Besides, I didn't know how to do the math.

That summer I played a whole Ethan Allen season and kept careful records. Sure enough, my Indians won my pennant. Better still, my new favorite player—Cleveland third baseman Ken Keltner—led my league in home runs, runs batted in, and batting. He also went 10–2 as a pitcher.

By the next summer I'd made a friend on the next hill. His family had a television set. I never played another Ethan Allen season, but for years I kept the spiral notebook with that one season's records. From time to time I'd look at it and remember Dale Mitchell, Walt Judnich, and Allie Clark.

When my son was old enough, I found a dusty Ethan Allen game in a toy store and bought it for his birthday. He thanked me and asked where it plugged in. I told him about the spinner and the mathematical correctness of the sections and about my one Ethan Allen season.

He said he thought that was nice and took the game to his room. But that Sunday when I asked him if he wanted to play, he said he'd lost all the disks and besides he was right in the middle of a "Hogan's Heroes" rerun.

They don't make kids like they used to either.   —BC

CHAPTER 17

Finding Your Position

Winning a job in the front office of a baseball team requires many of the same qualities a player needs to make it on the ball field. Just to gain an entry-level position with a major league or even a minor league club takes hustle, determination, timing, and a will to succeed. The money may not match the salary of even a poorly paid major league player, but for those with a love of the game, a job in baseball offers unique rewards —excitement, contact with headline-grabbing athletes and personalities, and the pleasure of being part of the great American pastime. After all, where else can you find a job that frequently requires you to go to a ballpark?

There is no sure-fire way to get a job in baseball, but many of today's baseball executives came up through the system by a prescribed route. Using a combination of research, resourcefulness, and a willingness to start at the bottom, these executives broke into major and minor league team management and found the career of their dreams. Here's a classic example; it just might work for you.

Ever since high school, Dave Dombrowski dreamed of running a major league ball club. He was fascinated with how big league teams were put together, how trades were made, how minor leaguers were developed. Fifteen years later he's living out his fantasy—and that of many baseball fans—as general manager of the Montreal Expos.

Dombrowski, thirty-three, started his trip to the top while still in college. A business administration student at Western Michigan University, he wrote a term paper entitled "The Man in the Middle" about

---

Jobs in Baseball

Is this any way for a grown man (or woman) to make a living?

---

being a major league general manager. His premise was "travel, night baseball, and the Basic Agreement [the series of collective bargaining pacts initiated in 1968] had changed the general manager's role." To test his hypothesis he sent a questionnaire to major league GMs, asking how their jobs had changed.

Roland Hemond, then of the Chicago White Sox and now general manager of the Baltimore Orioles, was particularly intrigued by Dombrowski's survey.

"Roland was very helpful," recalls Dombrowski, who grew up in the southern suburbs of Chicago. "I even got to meet with him. The questionnaire helped me get to know a lot of baseball people."

Hemond advised Dombrowski that baseball's annual Winter Meeting was the best place for job seekers to meet front-office people and find out about job openings. So later that year, in December, Dombrowski scraped together the funds for airfare and lodging to attend the 1977 Winter Meeting in Honolulu.

As it turned out, Dombrowski did meet a lot of baseball people, and there were jobs to be filled—including that of administra-

tive assistant for player development with the White Sox. Hemond remembered Dombrowski and they talked about the job. Hemond offered him the position at a salary of $7,000, effective immediately.

Back in Chicago, Dombrowski discussed the offer with his parents. His mother suggested he graduate from school and "get a nice job with an accounting firm." His father okayed accepting the job on two conditions: (1) that Dave did not lose money on the proposition and (2) that Dave would complete his college credits.

"My dad and I totaled up my living expenses and found I would need $8,000 to break even," Dombrowski explains, "so I asked for $1,000 more and got it. And I finished my education with correspondence courses."

Even so, Dombrowski's baseball education was just beginning. After handling all kinds of tasks as an administrative aide ("I learned a lot typing up player-evaluation forms"), Dombrowski was promoted to assistant director of player development in April 1978. By November 1980 he was assistant general manager. He figured his future was secure with the White Sox.

Five years later Roland Hemond was fired. Months after that so was Dombrowski. But the Expos were quick to recognize his talents and hired him as their minor league director in December 1986. He was promoted to assistant GM in August 1987 and GM the following July. Based on experience, Dombrowski and other baseball executives offer job seekers the following advice.

1. *Get a good education.* Dombrowski strongly suggests taking business courses and says it helps to know how to type.

Jeff Reeser, twenty-nine-year-old marketing director for the Class A Peoria (Illinois) Chiefs, says a sports administration degree makes a bigger impression today than it did ten years ago. "The market for jobs has become very competitive," explains Reeser. "The sports administration degree gives you an edge."

"The best thing about sports administration programs is the summer internship requirements," says Bob Richmond, copartner of Baseball Opportunities, Inc., a minor league baseball consulting firm. "It gives students the chance to find out if working in sports is really the right career for them." In fact, Richmond says some of the most productive internships are those that help students decide which phases of sports administration to avoid (see Chapter 5, The Lefty Groves of Academe).

Most minor league employees, like minor league players, hope to make it to the big leagues. The Kansas City Royals' assistant to the general manager Dean Taylor began his baseball career in 1974 as an intern in the Northwest League. The internship was a requirement for his graduate degree in sports administration from Ohio University, one of the pioneer programs in the field.

"Like any other business, the formal education you get can only go so far," Taylor says. "You really need hands-on experience." Minor league officials agree that internships are the most important element of sports administration programs. They offer prospective employees a chance to build their résumés. Through internships clubs can offer an opportunity to someone they couldn't afford to hire under

You can't tell the players without a scorecard, and you can't sell the scorecards if you don't love the game.

normal circumstances, possibly discovering a good worker who could be offered a regular position after graduation.

2. *Develop a well-rounded knowledge of baseball as a game and a business.* Though he's always been involved in on-the-field matters, Dombrowski admits that most baseball jobs are not in the areas of player personnel and development. Baseball, whether in the majors or the minors, is a business, he says, and many others in the game agree with him.

"The thing we look for in a young person is whether he or she can sell," says Richmond, who helps minor league clients staff their front offices. "Working in baseball begins and ends with selling. If you can understand what sells program ads, radio spots, ballpark signs, or whatever, then there's a place for you in baseball."

Jeff Reeser says game promotions are important in Peoria. "My job is to put bodies in the park," he says. "We own our concession stands, so if we attract fans, they'll spend some money. There are all kinds of ways to fill the park—giveaways or special nights for local businesses are two of many—and you have to understand what works and what doesn't."

In the minors Reeser also says to be ready for anything. "I've helped roll out the tarp during a rain delay more than once," he says, laughing.

3. *Get your "foot in the door" at a young age.* "You can't support a family on the entry-level salaries," Dombrowski explains. "It's best to look for a baseball job right out of school."

Entry-level salaries for front-office minor league employees average about $700 to $800 a month, according to Bob Sparks, director of information for the National Association of Professional Baseball Leagues, which oversees the minor leagues. In some smaller markets it may be even less, say $500 a month. (Commissions or additional benefits, such as housing allowances, may be offered as performance incentives.)

Once you're established, Class A and AA general managers and other top executives stand to make $12,000 to $18,000 a year. GMs at the Triple-A level, depending on their experience, earn $20,000 or more.

Also, the long hours make it tough on a marriage or family life. "I work from 9 A.M. to 11 P.M. almost every day during the season," says Reeser. "That doesn't leave much time for a social life. But the way I look at it, I see 5,000 people at the park every night."

Getting your foot in the door is, of course, a most critical matter. Reeser says baseball is "the good old boy system at its

Major League Jobs

The minors are where most everyone gets his or her start. But the big leagues are where everyone wants to end up.

Just what are the chances of working for a major league club in the front office? According to Alexander & Associates, a Washington consulting firm retained by the commissioner's office, there were 1,854 front-office positions in 1989 versus 1,495 such jobs in 1988. As clubs generate more business—the general trend among major league teams—there should be even more people added to staffs.

Alexander & Associates also reports increased jobs for minorities and women.

There were 273 minority members, or 15 percent of the 1,854 positions, in the major league work force in 1989. That sharply contrasts with 1988, when there were 142 (9 percent) of 1,495 positions held by blacks, Hispanics, and Asians. The 1989 figures show 163 were black, 88 Hispanic, and 22 Asian.

Data compiled in 1984 show minority group members comprised only 2 percent of the clubs' front-office employment base.

As for women, they hold 700 positions in 1989 as compared to 564 in 1988.

—RC

finest." He's living proof, since his boss at the Peoria Chiefs was his fraternity brother in college.

But there are other ways to get to know baseball people. The Winter Meeting (see below) is one alternative. Another is writing a "request-for-advice letter," in which you seek information about how to get a job in baseball rather than applying for any job that team may have available.

"It helps us relax if you let us know you're looking for a job but realize few are available and what you want is advice," says one major league executive. It's easy to say no to job applicants if no jobs are available, explains this exec, but much more difficult to turn down someone asking for a bit of advice.

"Many executives may not give a well-thought-out answer," Reeser adds, "but enough of us will to make the original inquiry worthwhile."

Such a letter should be concise, no more than a page. It should focus on asking for advice (don't be afraid to request other people to write, too) and state how you will follow up the letter. It's important

to make it convenient for the executive to give the advice, either by phone or letter. Also, send a résumé with the letter, just in case the club may be interested in hiring.

Once you do get to know some baseball people, then use them as references. It is quite helpful when a team executive can call someone in baseball about you.

Bob Sparks says one common mistake aspiring baseball employees make is to write letters in the spring, as the baseball season is about to begin. "Most clubs are thinking about filling job openings in August through October, when their seasons are just ending. That's because a lot of important groundwork in baseball is done in the off-season."

4. *Attend the Winter Meeting.* Dave Dombrowski says that anyone sincerely interested in baseball jobs should attend this annual gathering of front-office personnel. "But don't forget, people have other things to do there besides simply hiring employees," he warns. Some major league and most minor league hiring for front-office

work, as well as broadcast jobs, takes place at the Winter Meeting, where teams have the opportunity to meet with a wide variety of applicants, and job seekers can find representatives from every team.

First find out where and when the meeting will be held. (It's almost always in December. In midsummer the commissioner's office will know exact details.) You'll want to make hotel reservations as soon as possible, since staying at the same hotel as the baseball people is a good way to mingle.

The National Association of Professional Baseball Leagues (mailing address: 201 Bayshore Drive, P.O. Drawer A, St. Petersburg, FL 33731) does conduct an Employment Opportunities Program at the meeting each year. It was started in 1973 by Bill Woods, currently the Houston Astros' general manager. It's now coordinated by Bob Sparks. The program office in the main hotel will post available jobs and hold a seminar in which team employees make short presentations on their job openings. Interested job seekers—there are generally about 400 to 500 at the meeting applying for approximately 50 positions—are asked to submit a résumé for each opening. The clubs review the résumés and choose up to a dozen names for interviews at the meetings. It's a good idea to follow up any submission with the team.

"If you haven't heard from someone and it's getting toward the end of the meeting, don't be afraid to check in with the club," says Dombrowski.

Sparks suggests good grooming is important at the Winter Meeting. "A neat personal appearance says something about yourself," he says.

In contrast Steve Warshaw says the Winter Meeting is "basically a free-for-all" and "you have to be an animal" pursuing people for jobs. Warshaw, a team sports marketing manager with the International Management Group (IMG), says his experience at the 1988 Winter Meeting in Atlanta was one he won't forget.

"The hotel was crawling with baseball celebrities," he recalls. "You had to do your homework to find out who everybody was. And you couldn't be afraid to go right up to people and say hello. I rode the elevators and slept maybe two or three hours a night."

Warshaw notes that the law of survival of the fittest is always at work at the meeting. "In the seminar with team representatives discussing job openings, there were job applicants with suits that cost as much as one month's salary," he recalls. "The competition for jobs was intense—it was sort of 'interviewing Darwinism.' "

Warshaw, thirty, had extensive management experience in the Continental Basketball Association before attending the meeting. He eventually landed the general manager's job of the Class A Helena (Montana) Brewers. He worked the job for six months, then moved to IMG when a friend in the business called about the opportunity. Warshaw noted the competition at the meetings is fierce and the pressure tremendous.

"It was the most stressful week I ever spent," says James Jessel, who got his job as an account executive with the Hamilton (Ontario) Redbirds at the 1988 meetings. While working in sales with the San Diego Sockers of the Major Indoor Soccer League, Jessel launched a major letter-writing campaign. He received form letters in response, most of which urged him to continue his search at the Winter Meeting. He saved his money, quit his job, and flew to Atlanta, that year's site for the meeting, with a stack of résumés.

At the meeting Jessel attended the business seminars sponsored by the National Association and put his résumés in the teams' envelopes. While other hopefuls were in their rooms waiting for phone calls, Jessel prowled the lobby of the headquarters hotel, introducing himself to officials, identified by badges, and putting a résumé in their hands personally. "You have to try to do something to separate yourself from the crowd when they're going through a couple hundred résumés,"

Jessel says. "You've got to hustle."

About a dozen teams liked Jessel's résumé sufficiently to call him for an interview. Jessel says that he kept noticing many of the same applicants' names appearing on interview lists, indicating that something on those particular résumés—in Jessel's case, professional sports sales experience—separated them from the crowd.

In interviews teams asked him what he could bring to their operation that they didn't already have, including specific ideas for promotions and sales activities. They also asked about his experience and inquired into his personal background, including questions on his drinking habits and drug use, if any. Many questions were aimed at determining his personal integrity, a key element in any minor league operation, where virtually every employee handles cash. (If your good name has been tarnished in the baseball world, don't expect to keep it quiet. Cronyism gets the word through the network in a couple of weeks.) The teams also tended to emphasize the negative aspects of the job, to make sure that they're getting someone who loves baseball and won't balk at the often outrageous hours required. Jessel recalls, "The three words I heard most often were *pay your dues*."

After six days Jessel hadn't gotten any job offers. He delayed his scheduled flight departure for a day and received four offers, the lowest a $600-per-month-plus-commission deal. He chose a job with Hamilton because, as a native of Toronto, he wanted to be close to home. A lot of fellow aspirants just went home disappointed.

5. *Be persistent but not a pain.* "Follow up if you say you will," Dave Dombrowski explains, "but don't pester someone with all kinds of phone calls." Dombrowski adds that it's important not to quit too soon when looking for a baseball job. In all likelihood it will take a while to find your field of dreams.

Regardless of how you find your job, whether you really want a career in baseball is a separate question. The hours are long, and the pay probably less than you can make in almost any other field. "If someone wants to waste one, two, three years and have some fun, that's okay," according to Joe Vellano, a partner in several minor league teams. "I love baseball, but I made my money in the sewer pipe business." He compares the lure of baseball to a narcotic or the moth's fatal attraction to a flame, adding, "I hope nobody gets burned."

In addition to using the National Association program, Bob Sparks suggests that anyone dreaming of a baseball career arrange an interview with a minor league team in his or her area, preferably on a game day. Aside from making a potentially helpful contact, the visit will offer the flavor of working in the minors. "Do a day in the life of the club," Sparks urges. "Then go to sleep, and see if you wake up with the same dream."   —RC

Just one big happy family.

Major Opportunities in the Minors: One Fan's Story

Gary Rigley, vice president for baseball operations of the St. Petersburg Cardinals, started at the very bottom of the baseball business. He was a fan.

After graduating from Boston College with a degree in political science and vague plans about going to law school, Rigley was attending an Albany-Colonie Yankee game in the spring of 1985 when the public-address announcer invited interested fans to call the team office regarding an opening in the telephone sales department. Rigley wasn't busy and figured he might as well check it out.

Following a phone call and interview, the Yankees put him to work selling tickets, program ads, and promotional events to sponsors. Rigley did well enough to be hired back for the following season as the team's director of sales. When Albany management purchased the Class A St. Petersburg franchise, Rigley moved to Florida to join that operation.

Now Rigley is on the hiring end of the baseball business. He says that his club evaluates its needs each fall for the upcoming season. They review résumés that they've received during the year and contact the best prospects, hoping to schedule interviews at the annual Winter Meeting, where the applicant pool swells. Successful candidates can expect to start their jobs in early January.

The first rule in the minor leagues is financial survival. Rigley confirms the observation of Bob Richmond of Baseball Opportunities, Inc., that selling ability is crucial in any entry-level position.

"Everyone must sell," he says. Expect to hawk everything from ads in the program to hot dogs at the concession stand.

Applicants should show at least an interest in sales, if not sales experience. Expertise in a specific field is nice, but minor league teams, especially at the lower classifications, just aren't specialized enough to use entry-level help that knows only public relations or statistics.

To fit the utility role, Rigley favors versatile applicants. "In one day you can be writing copy for the program, then working the concession stand, rolling out the tarp, and doing cleanup of the park." Since sixteen-hour days are the norm during the season, Rigley looks for applicants who present themselves as "hardworking, successful in some way, go-getters." Most of all, applicants must demonstrate enthusiasm. "You can't work in baseball without a love for the game."   —RC

No Minor Money

Minor league baseball hit a home run in the 1980s. Attendance was up 50 percent, and values of team franchises increased five-, ten-, and even twentyfold.

Two cases in point:

- The Louisville Cardinals, the Triple-A farm club of St. Louis, routinely attracted more than 1 million fans each year, even outdrawing some major league clubs.
- Robert Rich, Jr., who paid $900,000 for the Triple-A Buffalo franchise in 1986, reportedly turned down an $8 million offer for the club two years later.

According to Bob Richmond, whose consulting firm matches club buyers and sellers, the increased value of minor league teams parallels major league success.

"People are looking for wholesome entertainment these days," Richmond says. "Baseball provides it. And communities are realizing the value—financial and otherwise—of having a team in town. Plus, at the minor league level it's cheaper to take the family out to a game than to the movies."

If you're interested in owning a team, get the checkbook ready. Most teams are controlled by one to four owners, with very few opportunities to buy limited shares of a club.

Richmond says that Rookie League and "Short-A" franchises range in price from $200,000 to $500,000; Single-A teams run $750,000 to $1 million; Double-A outfits cost $2 million to $3 million, and Triple-A clubs are $3.5 million and up. "Of course, the specific price will vary according to a market's demographics, history, travel costs, and stadium situation," he explains. "Ten or twelve years ago, minor league ballparks around the country were falling apart. Today, with renewed interest in the game, ballparks have been upgraded tremendously."

Minor league clubs affiliated with major league teams are provided with players and coaches, as well as money for equipment. That helps most minor league owners turn a 5 to 10 percent net profit each season. Some of the more successful clubs may bring profits of up to 20 percent.

You could probably do better with growth stocks or land speculation. But because you bought this book, for you it wouldn't have the same excitement.

"I guess there is glamor to owning the teams," says Richmond. "One owner, a successful real estate developer, once told me that as a developer he was actually disliked by some people. But as the town's minor league owner, he said, 'Everybody says hello to me at the park.' " —EJC

The Economics of Baseball

Since baseball is first and foremost a business, it will help a job seeker if he or she understands the economics of running a ball club. The figures below represent a typical budget for a Single-A ball club, one affiliated with a major league team that, under terms of the Player Development Contract, picks up the bushers' salaries.

—EJC

Revenues

General Admissions/Game Day (34 dates, $4 per ticket)	$ 37,600
Season Tickets	22,905
Park Buyouts (3 dates at $800 per)	2,400
Advertising (includes program ads and ballpark signs)	33,445
Concessions	69,010
Total Revenues	**$165,360**

Expenses

General Manager's Salary	$ 18,000
Taxes	1,425
Team Travel/Lodging	29,500
Insurance	2,500
Repairs/Maintenance	2,500
Advertising	5,000
Concessions	38,476
Utilities	1,500
Licenses	6,000
Freight/Postage	500
Supplies	10,000
Rent	7,000
Janitors	2,275
Commissions	5,000
Miscellaneous	1,000
Total Expenses	**$130,676**

Revenues	$165,360
Expenses	130,676
Net	**$34,684**

Owning Your Own Affiliates

Most major league teams are content to leave the headaches of running upper-level farm clubs to entrepreneurs and let them try to squeeze a few dollars out of the deal. But the Atlanta Braves own six of their eight minor league affiliates, including their Triple-A and Double-A teams.

"We own so that we can have total control over our entire baseball picture," says Bruce Baldwin, the Richmond Braves' general manager, who worked his way up the Atlanta chain through chain stops at Pulaski, Savannah, and Greenville. That total control includes greater freedom in personnel decisions and the choice of a manager—two frequent sources of friction between the parent club and affiliate. It also ensures more influence over the quality of facilities.

Chip Moore, Atlanta's assistant controller, ranks facilities first on his list of advantages of outright ownership. "You can't always go to a PDC operator [a parent club under the Player Development Contract] and say, 'We want better facilities— or else.' Or else what? We'd go to another PDC operator and find the same problems." The Richmond Braves play in the Diamond, a $9 million facility opened in 1985, built with public and private funds in six months on the site of the R-Braves' previous home. Unlike Buffalo's Pilot Field, which was constructed with an eye to major league expansion, Baldwin says Richmond's park "was built to be the temple of minor league ball."

The Braves' organization considers minor league profits "a top-ranked goal, but we don't sacrifice player-development goals for the sake of money," according to Moore. Although the Braves don't turn a profit on their minor league holdings, Moore says minor league cash flow during the season is helpful. Instead of simply paying money out to affiliates for player

salaries and other PDC requirements, Atlanta enjoys some offsetting revenue.

"Profits are not as big a factor for this team," Richmond's Baldwin agrees, "but it's a matter of pride for me to show the best P & L [profit and loss] statement possible. But don't get me wrong—we'd love to make money." The opening of the Diamond lifted attendance from below 200,000 to 379,000 in 1985; the club has drawn in the mid-300,000s ever since.

Baldwin's sole complaint in running the Richmond club has less to do with the Braves than with the nature of absentee ownership. "A local owner would be more cognizant of our immediate needs," he says. For example, Baldwin tried for weeks to get a new tarp. "I can see we need one, the fans can see we need one, but some-

body in Atlanta can't see that." Such problems may be exacerbated by the size of the Braves' parent company, Turner Broadcasting System. But Baldwin is quick to add, "I have the best of both worlds. I work for a major league club, and I don't have a local owner looking over my shoulder."

Buyers have made overtures about purchasing the Richmond franchise and the community's role in building the Diamond indicates potential for a local ownership group. However, Baldwin doubts that the R-Braves' current market value, about $7 million, offers a great temptation to the Atlanta ownership. "With the money that Turner rolls over, I'm not sure $7 million means that much to them."   —EJC

Raising crops down on the farm.

Ticket Taker Talks Technique

Every Holyoke Millers player hopes to make the major leagues someday, and the team's head ticket taker has the same aspiration.

"My dream is to be a big league ticket taker," admits Bill Kane of 38 Kane Road.

Kane, a science teacher at Holyoke High School in the off-season, is in his rookie year as a Mackenzie Field ticket taker. He says he has worked hard to improve his ticket-tearing skills to get a chance to rip in the big leagues.

"I can rip from either side," said the six-foot, 160-pounder, who claims only one thing has prevented him from making the jump to the majors.

"I have no experience with turnstiles whatsoever, and I think that's what's holding me back," he said.

Millers' general manager Tom Kayser thinks the rookie has plenty of potential. "He's got the style and he's got the personality, but he's a little weak in ticket-tearing

speed," Kayser noted. "His hand-eye coordination is off."

While Kane dreams of ripping in the majors, he doesn't have stars in his eyes.

"If I'm not there by the time I'm thirty, I'll have to reassess my future," said Kane, who will turn thirty in October. "I'm not getting any younger. When you get to be thirty, you have to realize you may never tear a ticket in the bigs."

Tearing tickets isn't easy, but Kane has it down to a science. One of the trickiest ticket tears is a multiple ticket rip.

"We just call it 'multiple' in the business," said Kane.

The only thing trickier than a multiple ticket rip is a double multiple rip. A double multiple rip is ripping two stacks of two or more tickets at once.

But there's more to being a ticket taker than ripping. After ripping the ticket in half, a ticket taker must make sure he gives the rain check back to the fan and places the other half in the ticket box. Ear-

There are no truly routine jobs in baseball; every endeavor has its rulebook and refinements known only to its initiates.

ly in the season Kane often became confused and gave the wrong half back to the fan.

Kane said he practices his ticket tearing by "tearing up the *Transcript* at home, but only after I read it."

Part of the job is being pleasant to incoming fans. Kane said he greets the fans with one of two phrases as he rips their tickets—"Enjoy the game" or "Don't kick the dirt."

Kane said he has wanted to be a minor league ticket taker since he attended a game at the now-demolished Pynchon Park in Springfield as a boy.

"I idolized the ticket taker there," said Kane. "He was incredibly fast and sure-handed. And he was tall."

Kane got his chance at ripping professional tickets after a one-year stint tearing for Holyoke Trade High School basketball games in 1976.

Kane's father, Ed, is also a ticket taker at Miller games. Ed has been shipped to the back gate while Bill rips at the busier Beech Street entrance. "They've decided to go with youth," said Kane.

Kane thinks ticket tearing just may run in the family's blood.

"My two-year-old son Chris tears up a lot of stuff at home," said Kane. "He might have what it takes."

Ticket takers have to stay relaxed during a game.

"I do stretching exercises because I don't want to run the risk of pulling a finger," he said.

Kane has managed to avoid injury so far this season, but admits he shares every ticket taker's fear—hangnails.

If Kane doesn't get his shot in the big leagues, he could settle for ripping tickets at movie theaters. But it wouldn't be the same.

"This is the American pastime," he said.   —BD

Women in Baseball

The baseball business is, as Peoria Chiefs' executive Jeff Reeser points out, a "good old boy system," but for the past fifteen years, women have begun to gain a significant place in it too. Actually women played baseball at Vassar College in 1866—scarcely twenty years after the game's inception by Alexander Cartwright's Knickerbocker Base Ball Club. Since then, women's involvement in the game has largely been marked by novelty and not by ability, but that situation is changing.

For women trying to break into baseball, part of the problem is conquering a past storied with either glamor or controversy. In 1931 seventeen-year-old Jackie Mitchell signed a contract with the Class AA Chattanooga Lookouts, making her baseball's first professional female player. Mitchell—a five-eight lefthander with only high school and semipro playing ex-

perience—made her first Lookouts appearance in an exhibition game against the mighty New York Yankees and struck out Babe Ruth and Lou Gehrig back to back. Ironically, only a few days later baseball commissioner Judge Kenesaw Mountain Landis voided Mitchell's contract on the grounds that "life in baseball is too strenuous for women." In 1952 organized baseball passed a rule barring women from signing professional baseball contracts with major league teams. That rule still stands today.

In the mid-1940s, however, a twist of fate made women welcome on baseball diamonds. When World War II threatened to cancel the big league season, Cubs' owner Philip K. Wrigley developed a women's professional league to keep the ballparks open and the fans titillated. They proved to be a big drawing card. At its peak in 1948, the All-American Girls Professional Base-

ball League attracted one million spectators; former major leaguers Jimmie Foxx, Johnny Rawlings, and Max Carey were even brought in as team managers and beauty specialist Helena Rubinstein trained the players in areas of personal conduct and grooming. In 1954, after eleven years of play, the league folded, a victim of the rise of television and the lack of funding.

Twenty years later, women—very young women—would play baseball again, this time with their male counterparts. After scores of lawsuits and demonstrations, the Little League Congressional Charter was finally altered in 1974 to include girls. Representatives today estimate that 7,000 girls play Little League ball each

It was not so long ago that women were regarded as mere novelty acts in baseball, like the Peterboro, NY, club of 1869.

season, an average of one girl per league; however, 2.5 million children play Little League overall, so only 28 of every 10,000 players are girls. Figures for the older Babe Ruth division show far fewer women pursuing baseball: fewer than 1,000 girls among over 450,000 players. Both Little League and Babe Ruth Baseball oversee separate national baseball programs.

After Al Campanis created a furor with his comment about minorities in 1987, baseball has endeavored to open its doors to blacks and Hispanics and bring them into the front office. Women, too, have benefited, but not in all areas of the game.

While there are three women owners in major league baseball, to date there are no women working in player development or general scouting departments in positions of power. And while the public relations directors of both the American and National League are female, along with a half dozen other women working in team media-relations posts, upper-level management jobs in baseball for women have been limited to the sales or marketing areas. There is one female director of stadium operations (Monique Lacas of the Montreal Expos), one female general counsel (Beth Benes of the San Diego Padres), and even one league vice president (Phyllis Collins of the National League). There are currently only two women certified as player-agents by the Major League Players Association: Cynthia Key represents her husband, Toronto pitcher Jimmy Key, while Miami lawyer Kim Strasos handles negotiations for Boston reliever Rob Murphy. These numbers increase only slightly in the minor leagues.

"The vast majority of women in baseball are somebody's secretary or administrative assistant," complains Stephanie Vardavas, a ten-year veteran of major league baseball who most recently served as assistant counsel to the commissioner's office. "There are no women on the general manager track in the major leagues. But there are twenty-six secretaries of GMs a lot of

women with the technical knowledge of what it takes to be a GM because they've been doing the nuts-and-bolts work for the men they work for.

"Any business organized around a sport played only by men will have male traditions," Vardavas adds. "Women can only accommodate themselves to that if they want to be in baseball. Baseball is a male institution and will always be one, but it doesn't have to be a sexist institution."

Baseball's battle of the sexes has moved into the courts. In June 1986 former Atlanta Braves media relations director Robin Monsky was barred from traveling with her team and banned from the team clubhouse by manager Chuck Tanner. Monsky, in turn, filed a discrimination complaint with the Equal Employment Opportunity Commission. One of the first women to hold a publicity job for a big league team, Monsky was hired in February 1985, demoted in June 1986, and fired shortly after the New Year in 1987. She was reportedly

fired after Tanner complained to team officials that too many negative statistics had appeared in the Braves' daily news releases. In June 1987 Monsky sued the team in Atlanta federal court, alleging sex discrimination and two other federal violations. A year later she filed a separate slander suit against Tanner in U.S. District Court in Pittsburgh. The outcomes of these suits are still pending, and Monsky remains in Atlanta waiting for her case to come to trial.

On another legal front, in March 1988 seventeen-year-old Julie Croteau filed suit in Alexandria (Virginia) federal court against school officials at Osbourn High School, claiming that she was cut from the varsity baseball team because she was a girl. The U.S. district judge ultimately ruled against Croteau, saying "There is no constitutional right to play ball." Croteau has since continued her fight to play baseball, and—after a stab at semipro ball in the Virginia Baseball League—she became

the first woman ever to play collegiate baseball.

For those women willing to forge past the obvious problems of gender, there are opportunities for work in a fast-paced, constantly growing field. National League vice president Phyllis Collins estimates that the league receives almost as many job applications from females as males, but, she says, "The applications from women are mainly for marketing and public relations positions."

"But you can't just walk off the street and get a job in baseball," cautions Karen Paul, vice president and general manager for the Class AA El Paso Diablos, who sixteen years ago came into the organization as a part-time bookkeeper. "You really need a master's degree in sports administration today. Then you'd serve an internship with one of the teams and that would get your foot in the door. We use a lot of interns here, and now a few are even minor league general managers. The major leagues will hire women as secretaries, not as assistant GMs."

"When you do get your foot in the door, do everything to learn and know baseball operations," advises Leanne Pagliai, vice president and general manager of the Class A Riverside Red Wave. A former salesperson for IBM, Pagliai broke into the game while dating a player. Her subsequent involvement in team functions led to a job as the club's sales manager and five years later resulted in a GM post. She now has part ownership of the Red Wave, an affiliate of the San Diego Padres. "Take on extra responsibility, don't be afraid to take on a dirty job. In baseball, as long as you love the product and prove your credibility, people don't care what you are, man or woman." —SK

The joy of playing ball is not available exclusively to men, any more than the right to earn a living in a front office. Will we ever see a woman play in the major leagues? Surely. Shirley who? Never mind.

Profiles—Women in Baseball

The Owners: Joan Kroc, Marge Schott and Jean Yawkey

As the most visible women in baseball, by virtue of their positions as majority team owners, Joan Kroc, Marge Schott and Jean Yawkey are also the most examined and judged women in the sport. Despite the bond they share as female owners, they are extremely different personalities with varying interests in the teams they control. Jean Yawkey assumed control of the Boston Red Sox upon her husband's death in 1977. Tom Yawkey, president of the Red Sox since 1933, was the sole owner of the team for forty-four seasons, longer than anyone in baseball history. While Mrs. Yawkey is chairwoman of the board of directors, majority owner, and general partner of the Red Sox, most of the day-to-day tasks of running the ball club are handled by other team officers. Mrs. Yawkey does, however, attend virtually every home game, seated in her Fenway Park rooftop box, and she is the first woman ever elected to serve on the board of the National Baseball Hall of Fame and Museum.

While Mrs. Yawkey has been directly involved in baseball since her marriage in 1944, Joan Kroc has had relatively few years of experience in the field. When her late husband Ray—the McDonald's hamburger magnate—informed her that he had bought the San Diego Padres in 1974, Mrs. Kroc's response was "What on earth is that, a monastery?" Ten years later, when the Padres won the National League pennant, Mrs. Kroc had her own Padres uniform and was even thrown into the pool by reliever Goose Gossage at the team victory party. Kroc has made the Padres into a family experience: on Opening Night in 1985, her daughter Linda sang the national anthem, and today Linda is married to player-agent Jerry Kapstein, who represents several of the Padres. Mrs. Kroc has devoted much of her time to philanthropic and activist pursuits: AIDS research, alcohol rehabilitation, aid for the homeless, and animal rights; and in 1988 she gave $1 million to the Democratic Party, the party's largest single donation ever. She has also recently donated $18 million to build a hospice in San Diego. While she remains on the sidelines for the most part, Mrs. Kroc has, at times, taken a personal stance on team personnel matters. In 1985, for example, after second baseman Alan Wiggins returned to drug rehabilitation, she decreed he would never again play for the team.

Unlike her female counterparts, Marge Schott takes an active role in the running of her ball club. A sixth-generation resident of Cincinnati, she joined the Reds' organization as a limited partner in 1981 because of her love for baseball and civic pride. She became the team's general partner in December of 1984 and took over the club as president and chief executive officer in July 1985. While she has been criticized for some unusual and unorthodox practices—her dog, Schottzie, at one time had a full-page biography in the team media guide—Mrs. Schott has stabilized the Reds' fiscal matters (if at the expense of some long-term employees). During spring training in 1989, she became personally involved in contract negotiations, talking directly to All-Star player Eric Davis when he'd reached a deadlock in salary discussions with the team general manager.

The League Executive: Phyllis Collins

When league officials scoured the nation in the winter of 1989 for a successor to then-National League president A. Bartlett

Giamatti, they didn't have to venture far to find one of the names that made the search committee's short list. Phyllis Collins—the NL vice president and the highest-ranking woman in baseball—was considered a serious candidate for the NL presidency, surprising much of the general public unfamiliar with her work and background. Despite Collins's relatively low profile ("I don't like attention very much. I'm very comfortable being in the background. I'm much too reticent for a high-visibility post," she says), Giamatti found her immensely qualified for the job. "She's a genuine vice president who assists me in everything I do," he said in the summer of 1988. "If I'm not here, she has all the powers I do."

Bill White was eventually selected for the post, and today Collins remains the number two chief administrative officer of the league. The fifty-eight-year-old Collins began her baseball career in 1968 as an executive secretary for the Atlanta Braves. She started working with the NL staff in 1978 as an administrative assistant to the president. That year, at the Winter Meeting, she was hired as league secretary. In 1986 she was promoted to vice president. As such her duties range from overseeing the day-to-day administration of the NL office, acting as league liaison to legal counsel and the Player Relations Committee, supervising legal counsel and the Player Relations Committee, supervising arrangements for World Series and All-Star games, and other responsibilities.

Collins downplays her role as a leader in the field and in fact generally sidesteps commenting on the issue of women in the game. "I'm pleased that you see more women in high-level baseball jobs and that they all seem to be doing a good job," the vice president says. "I'm sure more mid-level and upper-level management jobs in baseball will open for women in the future." She does note, however, that six of the nine employees in her office are female, which may be more than just a coincidence.

Marge Schott introduces the new manager of the Cincinnati Reds to David Letterman.

The Umpire: Pam Postema

Pam Postema is not the first woman umpire in baseball, and, no doubt, she will not be the last. Her predecessors had marginal success. In 1972 Bernice Gera lasted just seven innings; after an argument at second base during the first game of a New York–Penn League Class A doubleheader, Gera left the park in tears. Christine Wrenn worked four seasons as an umpire in the Northwest and Midwest Class A leagues before leaving baseball for a better-paying job in 1979. Now in her thirteenth season, Postema has spent the last two springs under the watchful eye of the National League, which has twice invited her to umpire at spring training. Working her seventh season at the Triple-A level, Postema continues to hope that she will soon earn a promotion to the big leagues.

In her first spring training tryout, in 1988, Postema was scrutinized by the national media, and, throughout her career, she has paid her dues. Her collarbone was once broken by a high fastball a catcher couldn't handle and she has had a toe bro-

ken by a foul tip. Postema has been spat on, sworn at, booed, and insulted by fans, and propositioned by players. She has had several now legendary run-ins with managers. For instance, in 1986 she ejected Larry Bowa from three games when he managed the Las Vegas Stars of the Pacific Coast League. And Houston Astros' pitcher Bob Knepper caused a stir in 1988 when he said, in reference to Postema, that women should not be umpires because God created them to be feminine. Still, she has persevered.

"I want to make it as an umpire, not as a woman," the thirty-four-year-old Postema says. "I think I've been judged pretty much as an umpire so far. I really haven't had any resistance. They've always moved me up when I was ready."

Postema grew up on a farm in Willard, Ohio. Her high school didn't have organized sports for girls, so she played games with her brothers and even joined a women's fast-pitch softball team. After graduating in 1972, she worked several odd jobs and contemplated enrolling at the University of Florida. Then she heard about the Al Somers Umpiring School. Although Somers had once vowed, "There'll never be a woman student in my school; it's just not a job for a woman," she was accepted. When she finished seventeenth in a class of 130 in 1977, she earned a spot in the Gulf Coast Rookie League; she has since done stints in the Florida State (Class A) and Texas (Double-A) leagues, as well as the Triple-A Pacific Coast League and American Association. In 1988 Postema worked as a crew chief for the first time. The same year she was behind the plate for the Triple-A All-Star Game and did the same for a winter league All-Star Game in Venezuela. In the off-season, she drives a UPS delivery truck in Phoenix.

Postema soft-pedals her landmark, albeit lonely, position: "I've always been the only woman umpire at all levels of the minor leagues. I was always one of a kind. But I don't want to be a cause. I umpire because I love the game." In 1989, however, Postema had some company; Theresa Cox, a graduate of the Harry Wendelstedt School for Umpires, began her umpiring career with an assignment in the Arizona Rookie League.

The League Founder: Darlene Mehrer

As an avid Chicago Cubs fan, Darlene Mehrer could hardly pass up the opportunity to attend former Cubs catcher Randy Hundley's fantasy baseball camp. So after three years of scrimping, plus a bank loan, the Glenview, Illinois, free-lance editor finally scraped up the $2,400 she needed and headed off to Mesa, Arizona, for the week-long camp in 1987. When she returned home, her interest in baseball was as keen as ever. "I played baseball for the first time in my life and I was hooked," Mehrer says. "I came home and looked for a league, but there wasn't one. So I advertised for other women, started my own league, and it grew from there." And so began the American Women's Baseball Association, the country's only active women's baseball league.

In 1989, the league's second year, forty-five Illinois women of all ages played baseball each Saturday morning at Elm Park in Glenview. While the pitcher's mound was only fifty feet from home plate and the bases were eighty feet apart, the game was definitely hardball.

Mehrer, hoping her league is the beginning of a movement to include women in the national pastime, has some hard words for baseball's establishment. "Women's contribution to baseball is mostly ignored," says the forty-six-year-old catcher. "Major league baseball doesn't take women seriously. Women love the game too. But baseball focuses all its advertising and public relations on the male fan. Little girls fantasize about playing baseball just like little boys. Why shouldn't the opportunity be there for us too?"

Mehrer invited former baseball commissioner Peter Ueberroth and league presidents Bart Giamatti and Bobby Brown to her league's first game in July 1988. But major league baseball has been less than enthusiastic with its support of Mehrer's effort. "I wrote to them to request funding," Mehrer says. "They said they prefer to fund youth leagues." Currently the AWBA is funded on its own—players buy their own uniforms and fund-raisers cover other costs—although the league is looking for sponsors. Mehrer also publishes a monthly newsletter called *BaseWoman*, devoted solely to news and features about women in baseball. —SK

Pam Postema can bellow with any ump.

CHAPTER 18

Talkin' Baseball

See, Morrie, this kid pitches on a Podunk Little League team and nobody likes him 'cause he's poor or an orphan or like that. Maybe we can get that kid from *E.T.* or maybe Dustin Hoffman can still play young. So the kid tries to impress all the other kids by saying he could get this superstar to come to the team banquet at the end of the season if he wanted to. I dunno *what* superstar! Whoever's big this year.

"Okay, so none of the other little creeps believe him, an' the kid gets backed into a corner until he finally says he'll *get* the superstar. Of course he don't know this ball player from Adam, see. He's just braggin'. The twist is, he even bets this ball bat his mother has. Did I say he was an orphan? Well, halfway. But the only thing his mother has to remember his father, who was some big hero in a war, is his old ball bat. Or maybe a glove. How 'bout Ellen Burstyn for the mother and Robert Redford in a flashback as the father?

"So the kid hitchhikes to New York, meeting all kinds of interesting characters along the way. Great cameos! Gielgud! Nicholson! Maybe even Reagan. The kid sneaks into the locker room after a game. They're gonna throw him out, but then the superstar says, 'Wait a minute.' It turns out—how's this for a twist?—the superstar knew his ol' man. In fact, the kid's father was the one that *made* the ball player a superstar—taught him to throw a curve or hit to right or something. So the superstar promises to come to the kids' Little League banquet. Tom Cruise for the superstar?

"The kid goes back to Podunk all smiles. He even hits a home run to win the cham-

Speakers and Appearances

Say, Orel, if you're not doing anything tonight . . .

pionship an' he's a big hero 'cause he's got this superstar coming. But what he don't know is the owner of the team—a real Scrooge type, maybe Robert Vaughn—never liked the kid's ol' man back when he was playing for the team. So he orders the superstar to stay away from Podunk. If he don't, Scrooge threatens he'll send him to Columbus or something.

"Well, there's the kid at the banquet all disappointed an' Burstyn's cryin' an' he's about to hand over the ball bat or glove or whatever it was he bet. An' everybody's calling him names—not real bad ones, though; we want a G rating.

"But—now get this, Morrie—at the same time, the superstar's baseball team is

on a road trip and just happens to be flying over Podunk. That's when the superstar hears he's just been elected the Most Valuable Player. Get it? He's too *big* for Columbus! So the superstar *bails out* of the plane and lands at the banquet! Did I mention the banquet was outdoors? An' we fade out on the kid with his arms around the superstar's neck, sayin' 'I knew you'd come! Baseball's the greatest game ever!'

"So whaddya think, Morrie? Maybe another *Batman*?"

That's the way it's done in the movies. Now for the real world . . .

Athletes, particularly baseball players, have been celebrities since the first fan clapped Abner Doubleday on the back and asked him to speak to the Cooperstown Kiwanis. Ball players are four-star All-American heroes, idolized for their on-the-field accomplishments by children and adults alike.

More than ever, today's public clamors for a chance to get closer to the athletes, to see them in the flesh, and hear their words of wisdom. But at the same time, it's harder to reach them than it was in good old days. They're busy with their careers and families; they make few public appearances and demand top dollars for lectures and endorsements.

This chapter will help you cut through the red tape and get to a ball player as quickly and as cheaply as possible. The majority of athletes have agents whose job it is to handle speaking engagements and endorsements. In the following sections, you'll get a better understanding about how to contact your favorites, what types of appearances they like to make, what it will cost, and what you'll get for your money.
                                                    —BC

Top Baseball Agents

Sports agents serve two primary functions: they negotiate team contracts and handle a player's off-the-field business. For their trouble, they get anywhere from 10 to 20 percent of all financial transactions. Some agents also get an annual guaranteed payment from each client.

The sports agent profession has become more popular in recent years—though not with fans or media. Some players have sought representation from "agent" lawyers and Certified Public Accountants, who can give them more individual and specialized attention. Today for every ten rookie baseball players, there seem to be just as many new agents eager to represent them.

Below is a list of the top agents, based on the number of high-profile, high-salaried players and the total number of players,

Mike Schmidt is one of the bright stars on the speakers' circuit, as he was in the uniform of the Philadelphia Phillies.

according to the Major League Players Association. Tom Reich and Dick Moss are considered the two biggest agents, with as many as 150 major and minor players in their stables. The rest are listed in alphabetical order.

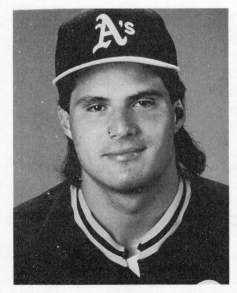

From the top, Jose Canseco, Kirby Puckett, Roger Clemens—disciples of Cicero.

TOM REICH
Tom Reich/International Management Group
300 E. 56th St., 6E
New York, NY 10022
212-838-0308
    Clients include: Jack Clark, Andres Galarraga, Rick Honeycutt, Candy Maldonado, Jeffrey Leonard, Dave Parker, Floyd Youmans, Claudell Washington.

DICK MOSS
17857 Porto Marino Way
Pacific Palisades, CA 90272
213-454-9991
    Clients include: Andy Van Slyke, Brett Butler, Andre Dawson, Jack Morris, Larry Parrish, Nolan Ryan.

JIM BRONNER
Speakers of Sport
666 Dundee Rd., Suite 704
Northbrook, IL 60062
312-291-0603
    Clients include: Rick Reuschel, Dan Quisenberry, Gary Gaetti, Mel Hall.

RICHMAN BRY
Bry & Associates
7701 Forsyth, Suite 700
St. Louis, MO 63105
314-862-5580
    Clients include: Hubie Brooks, Scott Fletcher, Rickey Henderson, Mookie Wilson.

ROBERT FRALEY/KIRK WOOD
Fraley and Associates
390 N. Orange Ave.
1 DuPont Center, Suite 2600
Orlando, FL 32801
407-425-1800
    Clients include: Glenn Davis, Orel Hershiser.

DENNIS GILBERT
Beverly Hills Sports Council
9665 Wilshire Blvd., Suite 420
Beverly Hills, CA 90212
213-858-1935

    Clients include: Jose Canseco, Tim Leary, Bret Saberhagen, Bobby Bonilla.

WILLIAM HAYES
Hamilton Projects
617 Vine St., Suite 1307
Cincinnati, OH 45202
513-421-9611
    Clients include: Jim Abbott, Johnny Bench, Pete Rose.

HENDRICKS BROTHERS
Randall A./Alan B. Hendricks
Hendricks Sports Management
400 Randal Way, Suite 106
Spring, TX 77388
713-350-7000
    Clients include: Roger Clemens, Mike Scott, Greg Swindell.

ARTHUR C. KAMINSKY
Athletes and Artists, Inc.
421 Seventh Ave., Suite 1410
New York, NY 10001
212-695-0300
    Clients include: Chris Berman, Gayle Gardner, Al Michaels.

JERRY KAPSTEIN
P.O. Box 1356
La Jolla, CA 92038
619-454-8569
    Clients include: Don Baylor, Carlton Fisk, Steve Sax, Mike Marshall, Carney Lansford.

ED KEATING
Keating Management Agency, Inc.
747 Statler Office Tower
Cleveland, OH 44115
216-621-2021
    Clients include: Dale Berra, Buddy Bell, Dennis Eckersley.

JIM KRIVACS
Dynamic Sports Management
2431 Estancia Blvd., A-1
Clearwater, FL 34621
813-791-7559
and

RAY SCHULTE
214 E. 84th St.
New York, NY 10028
212-772-8605
   Clients include: Howard Johnson, Don Mattingly, Harold Reynolds.

ALAN MEERSAND
Professional Sports Management
330 Washington St., Suite 612
Marina Del Rey, CA 90292
213-306-3400
   Clients include: Lenny Dykstra, Kevin Mitchell, Jesse Orosco.

MATT MEROLA
Mattgo Enterprises
185 E. 85th St., 18G
New York, NY 10028
212-427-4444
   Clients include: Gary Carter; for commercial use only: Nolan Ryan, Reggie Jackson, Tom Seaver.

JACK SANDS
Sports Advisors Group
1 Exeter Plaza
Boston, MA 02116
617-262-5535
   Clients include: Harold Baines, Dwight Evans, Ozzie Smith.

RON SHAPIRO
Ron Shapiro/Brooks Robinson
Robinson and Associates
2330 W. Joppa Rd., Suite 155
Lutherville, MD 21903
301-583-5888
   Clients include: Kirby Puckett, Cal Ripken, Jr., Storm Davis, Mark Gubicza, Danny Jackson.

JIM TURNER
Sports Management Group
222 S. Central, Suite 1008
St. Louis, MO 63105
314-862-5560
   Clients include: Joe Carter, Gerald Perry, Pat Tabler, Ryne Sandberg.

Speakers' Bureaus

Tommy Lasorda is the great guru of sports speech makers. He loves to address a crowd, especially during a meal—although his much-publicized diet caused a sharp drop in rubber chicken stock. If the Dodgers have a night game, the Dodger manager may speak at a breakfast and luncheon beforehand. Of course, listening to Lasorda pontificate for an hour may cost from $12,500 to $15,000. Other baseball celebrities charge anywhere from $2,000 to $15,000, plus travel and expenses for a two-hour appearance. The price tag often depends on the amount of time and travel involved. When Carl Yastrzemski played for the Red Sox, he made complimentary speeches in Boston but charged a fee for gigs outside the city. If you want the athlete to hobnob with guests or sign autographs, the price goes up.

A cheaper alternative is to request a videotape of a speech ($2,000).

Sports celebrities are usually asked to expound on teamwork, motivation, and success. Some players like talking before crowds more than others. Many young players, unused to public speaking, would prefer getting rabies shots. Lasorda, Willie Mays, Jim Palmer, and Johnny Bench enjoy speaking. Active players don't do the speech circuit as often as well-known retired players. Most active players favor signing autographs or mingling with a crowd for a couple of hours.

It's best to try to book a speaking appearance at least three months in advance. The most popular orators give as many as seventy speeches during the off-season. Lasorda's busiest period begins in late October and runs through January. Most active players are busiest right after the World Series because they don't usually accept engagements during the season. Retired players are often more available for speaking engagements than active players.

Speakers' bureaus seldom handle a ball player exclusively. Instead, the companies act as brokers between the player's agent and the public. In some cases, you might do just as well to contact the agent directly. However, the advantage in using one of the speakers' bureaus is that they often have an established relationship with agents and athletes, making it easier to book the appearance.

Below is a list of speakers' bureaus:

Burns Sports Celebrity Service Inc.
230 North Michigan, Room 2020
Chicago, IL 60601
312-236-2377
Contact: Nova Lanktree, Vice President.

Celebrity Speakers
1042 Second St., Suite 3
Santa Monica, CA 90403
818-887-5066 or 888-9242
Contact: Bruce Merrin.

Harry Walker
1 Penn Plaza, Suite 2400
New York, NY 10119
212-563-0700
Contact: Don Walker, President.

The Professional Speakers Exchange
1000 North Rand Rd., Suite 214
Wauconda, IL 60084
312-526-5995
Contact: William E. Robinson.

Promotional Sports Stars
130 El Camino Dr.
Beverly Hills, CA 90212
213-273-8807
Contact: Marc Reede, President.

Sports Marketing Services
3330 Dundee Rd., Suite S-5
Northbrook, IL 60062
312-291-0095
Jack Tompkins, Executive VP.
The company has fifty corporate clients and will book athletes for those clients' events.

Washington Speakers Bureau, Inc.
310 S. Henry St.
Old Town, Alexandria, VA 22314
703-684-0555
Contact: Bernie Swain, Partner.

Sample Speeches

Retired players are some of the most popular speech makers. Below are two excerpts from speeches. One was given by that popular pitchman Dodger manager Tommy Lasorda shortly after the Dodgers clinched the 1988 World Series. The second excerpt is a motivational speech given by Johnny Bench.

LASORDA: I come to you today as the happiest man in the world. What a difference to come out and speak after you've been crowned the World Champions of baseball. The last couple of years it was difficult to come out and speak, believe me. It got so bad last year that we got a call from Judge Bork. He wanted to speak to someone who was worse off than he was.

It got so bad last year that when the season was over, after I said goodbye to all of my players, I sat in my office all alone, very dejected and depressed, feeling very sorry for myself because I thought we were going to go to spring training and really win in 1987. But unfortunately we had so many injuries we weren't able to do it. So as my coaches came in and said goodbye to me, I said something to them I probably shouldn't have said. I said, "Right now, the way I feel, I feel like killing myself." And

my third base coach said, "Hey, Tommy, don't do it. Don't let the players drive you to that. Have you ever heard of this organization, Suicide Anonymous?"

I said, "No. I've heard of Cocaine Anonymous and Alcoholics Anonymous but never Suicide Anonymous."

He said, "It's a new organization—here's the number."

So when he left, I thought, why not? I need a word of encouragement. I need someone to say something nice to me. I need someone to build up my confidence. So I called them. And the guy that answered put me on hold. When he came back and I told him what happened to my team, he said, "Buddy, after listening to your story, I think you're doing the right thing . . . "

. . . Some of the things my players have done to me: Steve Sax, one of the finest young men you'll ever meet in your life. Outstanding player, but sometimes some of the things he does are not too good. I've been trying to get him to hit the ball up the middle. So he came to me one day. He said, "Skip, now I've got this hitting theory down straight. When I walk up to the plate, 80 percent of the time I try to hit up the middle, the other 20 percent I try to go to right, and the other 20 percent I try to go to left."

Now, Kenny Landreaux, my center fielder, who we call "The General" (and it isn't because of his brains), was standing right behind me, and I said, "Did you hear what he said, Kenny?" And Kenny said, "Yeah, I heard that. Man, that's the damnedest hitting theory I've ever heard."

Now, I don't know if Kenny ever graduated, but he went to Arizona State. To give you an idea about Kenny, my office in Vero Beach for spring training looks right out on this big table where the players come in off the field and start eating. They have a big pot of soup there, and Kenny was getting some out of the pot so I hollered, "Hey Kenny, what's the soup?" And he said, "Of the day."

BENCH: Sparky Anderson was the Reds manager during the seventies and he has a great deal to do with creating a winning environment. We were a good club when Sparky came in 1970, but he created a productive environment and a winning attitude. He involved others on the team in handling problems and situations that came up. He talked to people about the type of job they were doing, what was right about it, was wrong about it, all with the idea of getting them to do their very best.

At the same time the management went out and got good people who would fit into the club. Sparky always said that to be a great manager you have to have great people, and he's right. In your daily life that can mean being the right person to help others achieve success.

Pardon My Blooper

As great a ball player as Lou Gehrig was, he never seized the public's fancy the way Babe Ruth did. While the Babe made hundreds of thousands of dollars from public appearances, exhibitions, and endorsements, Larrupin' Lou hardly made a cent. He simply lacked Ruth's charisma—but then again, didn't everyone?

On one of the few occasions that Gehrig picked up an endorsement, he fumbled it. Once, he was signed to go on radio to plug a breakfast cereal called Huskies.

"To what do you owe your strength and condition?" the announcer asked.

"Wheaties," Gehrig replied.

The mortified Gehrig refused to accept any money for the commercial, but the company insisted. Huskies had gained more publicity from Gehrig's boner than the cereal could ever have achieved if the commercial had gone smoothly.

—from *A Century of Baseball Lore* by John Thorn

CHAPTER 19

Let's Get Together

Baseball fans like to congregate. They find comfort in talking with fanatics who not only know that Grover Cleveland Alexander struck out Tony Lazzeri with the bases loaded in the seventh game of the 1926 World Series but that he did it in the seventh inning, not the ninth. Mention it to a fanatic and he'll remind *you* that the final out came on a failed steal attempt, as second baseman Rogers Hornsby took a peg from catcher Bob O'Farrell to tag—yes—Babe Ruth. Tell it to a "normal" person and you get a blank stare. This chapter lists associations of like-minded people.

There are four sections of associations: professional baseball; amateur leagues; fan clubs and research societies; and media. The professional baseball section covers groups affiliated with organized baseball. Associations of amateur leagues include peewee to adult baseball leagues. The portion on fan clubs and research societies lists organizations to join for fun or to study and improve one's understanding of the national pastime. The final section, on media associations, is comprised of groups of people who observe, analyze, and report on baseball.

Most of these associations are not expensive to join, and they all offer benefits to anyone interested in baseball.

Professional Baseball

Major League Baseball
Office of the Commissioner
350 Park Ave.
New York, NY 10022
(212) 371-7800
  Contact: Richard Levin, Director of Public Relations.
  Purpose: The Office of the Commission-

Associations and Organizations

Baseball nuts of the world, unite! Or at least mingle

er was established in 1920 by the National League, American League, and National Association of Professional Baseball Leagues to administrate Organized Baseball. The News Department publishes a newsletter, *MLB Newsletter*.

American League of Professional Baseball Clubs
350 Park Ave.
New York, NY 10022
(212) 371-7600
  Contact: Phyllis K. Merhige, Director of Public Relations.
  Activity: The American League, founded in 1901 by Ban Johnson as a rival major league to the National League, currently operates major league baseball in Anaheim, Baltimore, Boston, Chicago, Cleveland, Dallas–Fort Worth, Detroit, Kansas City, Milwaukee, Minneapolis–St.Paul, New York City, Oakland, Seattle, and Toronto. The American League publishes the *Red Book*.

National League of Professional Baseball Clubs
350 Park Ave.
New York, NY 10022

(212) 371-7300
  Contact: Katy Feeney, Director of Media Relations.
  Activity: The National League, organized in 1876, operates major league baseball in Atlanta, Chicago, Cincinnati, Los Angeles, San Diego, San Francisco, Philadelphia, Pittsburgh, St. Louis, Houston, New York City, and Montreal. The National League's publication is the *Green Book*.

Association of Professional Baseball Players of America
12062 Valley View St., Suite 211
Garden Grove, CA 92645
(714) 892-9900
  Contact: Chuck Stevens, Secretary-Treasurer.
  Purpose: The Association cares for sick and indigent baseball players, umpires, and trainers, and is endorsed by organized baseball.

Association of Professional Baseball Physicians (APBP)
606 24th Ave. South, Suite 701
Minneapolis, MN 55454
(612) 339-8976
  Contact: Dr. Harvey O'Phelan, Chairman.
  Activity: The Association aims to provide the best possible medical care to players. The group also conducts seminars on drug abuse.

Baseball Alumni Team (BAT)
350 Park Ave.
New York, NY 10022
(212) 371-7800
  Contact: Frank Slocum, Executive Director.
  Purpose: BAT aids indigent ball players

and is located in the Commissioner's Office.

Baseball Blue Book, Inc.
7225 30th Ave. North
P.O. Box 40847
St. Petersburg, FL 33743
(813) 381-5147 or (813) 345-3545
  Contact: Larry Halstead, President.
  Activity: The National Association publishes *Minor League Digest, Major League Year & Notebook*, and *The Blue Book*, a complete directory of Organized Baseball.

Baseball Chapel, Inc.
P.O. Box 20,000	P.O. Box 300
Liberty University	Bloomingdale, NJ
Lynchburg, Va	07483
24502	
	(201) 838-8111
(804)582-2102	(201) 838-7070

  Contact: Dave Swanson, Executive Director.
  Activity: Founded in 1973, the organization brings church services to the professional baseball locker room. Bible studies and wives' chapel are two additional responsibilities. President Bobby Richardson is the baseball coach at Liberty University.

Baseball Hall of Fame Committee on Baseball Veterans
P.O. Box 590
Cooperstown, NY 13326
(607) 547-9988
  Contact: Charles Segar, Chairman.
  Activity: The Committee elects to the Baseball Hall of Fame players, managers, executives, umpires, and Negro League players who have been retired for twenty-three years or more.

Baseball Network, Inc.
3013 Fountain View Drive, Suite 100
Houston, TX 77057
(713) 953-0040
  Contact: Ben Moore, Executive Director.

  Purpose: In 1987 the Network began assisting in the affirmative-action process in major league baseball.

Baseball Writers' Association of America
36 Brookfield Rd.
Fort Salonga, NY 11768
(516) 757-0562
  Contact: Jack Lang, Executive Secretary.
  Activity: The BBWAA, founded in 1908, has a chapter in each major league city. Membership is restricted to sportswriters on direct assignment to major league baseball.

Major League Baseball Players Alumni (MLBPA)
500 South Florida Ave., Suite 600
Lakeland, FL 33801
(813) 858-3886
  Contact: Nelson Briles, Executive Director.
  Activity: The group sponsors golf tournaments for charity with former major league baseball players. The MLBPA also works with former players on drug or alcohol rehabilitation and keeps current address and biographical files.

Major League Baseball Players Association
805 Third Ave.
New York, NY 10022
(212) 826-0808

  Contact: Donald M. Fehr, Executive Director.
  Purpose: The union, founded in 1966, represents the interests of major league baseball players.

Major League Baseball Properties (MLBP)
350 Park Ave.
New York, NY 10022
(212) 371-7800
  Contact: Edwin Durso, Chairman.
  Activity: The MLBP is the licensing branch of the Commissioner's Office. Manufacturers and suppliers apply to this organization for the right to use Major League Baseball logos.

Major League Scouting Bureau
23712 Birtcher Drive, Suite A
El Toro, CA 92630
(714) 458-7600
  Contact: Donald F. Pries, Director.
  Purpose: The Bureau provides written reports on amateur players. The Bureau is intended to augment, not replace, the scouting department of each major league club.

Major League Umpires Association
One Logan Square, Suite 1004
Philadelphia, PA 19102
(215) 568-7368
  Contact: James Evans, President.
  Purpose: The Association represents the interests of umpires in major league baseball and seeks to improve their working conditions. The group further desires to aid in the constructive improvement of major league baseball.

Major League Baseball Umpire Development
201 Bayshore	P.O. Box A
Drive S.E.	St. Petersburg, FL
St. Petersburg, FL	33701
33701	
(813) 823-1286	(813) 823-3729

  Contact: Edwin W. Lawrence, Executive Director.
  Purpose: The organization provides an

annual evaluation course for persons interested in becoming professional baseball umpires. Recommendations are made to the minor leagues by this group.

National Association of Professional
Baseball Leagues
P.O. Box A
St. Petersburg, FL 33731
201 Bayshore Drive S.E.
St. Petersburg, FL 33701
(813) 822-6937
  Contact: Sal Artiaga, President.
  Activity: The National Association administrates the minor leagues, maintains records, and publishes the *Orange Book*.

National Baseball Hall of Fame and
Museum
National Baseball Library
P.O. Box 590
Cooperstown, NY 13326
(607) 547-9988
  Contact: Howard Talbot, Director.
  Purpose: The Hall of Fame displays memorabilia depicting the history of our national game. Plaques honoring its members are displayed in the Hall of Fame Gallery. The National Baseball Library houses the world's largest collection of baseball reference materials, photographs, and audiovisual resources. The Hall of Fame Club publishes a newsletter sent to all members.

Player Relations Committee
350 Park Ave.
New York, NY 10022
(212) 371-2211
  Contact: Barry Rona, Executive Director.
  Purpose: The Committee is composed of the owners of major league baseball clubs and is used for disseminating baseball information.

Phoenix Communications Group
Major League Baseball Productions
(MLBP)
1212 Avenue of the Americas
New York, NY 10036

(212) 921-8100
  Contact: Joseph L. Podesta, Chairman.
  Activity: MLBP is the commercial arm of Major League Baseball. The group produces films for sale to the public. The TV pregame show "This Week in Baseball" is filmed by the staff.

Pro Athletes Outreach
72 E. Sunset
P.O. Box 1044
Issaquah, WA 98027
(206) 392-6300
  Contact: Norm Evans, C.E.O. and Board Chairman.
  Activity: Professional athletes from football, baseball, hockey, and other sports seek to provide nondenominational, Christian training to professional athletes and their spouses.

Professional Baseball Athletic Trainers
Society (PBATS)
P.O. Box 386
Atlanta, GA 30361
(404) 522-7630
  Contact: David Pursley, Secretary-Treasurer.
  Purpose: The Society was organized to improve the image of major league baseball trainers by developing a continuing education program for athletic trainers at all levels of professional baseball.

Amateur Leagues

All American Amateur Baseball Association
340 Walker Drive
Zanesville, OH 43701
(614) 453-7349
  Contact: Tom J. Checkush, Executive Director.
  Activity: The group consists of leagues and associations that emphasize sports for sports' sake. It bars commercial elements within the association and compiles statistics from annual tournaments.

Cooperstown: The Right Wrong Place

Way back in 1905, baseball appointed the Mills Commission to determine the game's origin. Was it a native American game, as most fans wanted it to be? Or was it descended from crude English games, as some historians feared? After three years of not working very hard, Chairman A. G. Mills, a former NL president, announced to partisan cheers that the national pastime had indeed been created on these shores. His evidence was the testimony of one Abner Graves, who distinctly remembered a day in April of 1839 when his friend Abner Doubleday invented the whole thing in a field at Cooperstown, N.Y.

A mere 27 years later, among the possessions of Graves was discovered an old baseball—undersized, misshapen and homemade—that might have been the very ball Doubleday had used.

Cooperstown resident Stephen C. Clark purchased the baseball and began exhibiting it. As public interest grew, Clark and associate Alexander Cleland obtained the backing of NL President Ford Frick in establishing a National Baseball Museum. Contributions and memorabilia poured in. On June 12, 1939, the National Baseball Hall of Fame and Museum was officially dedicated.

Does it really matter that General Doubleday never mentioned his great invention? Or that historians have found numerous examples of the existence of baseball long before Graves said the General thought it up? No.   —BC

American Amateur Baseball Congress (AABC)
P.O. Box 467
118 Redfield Plaza
Marshall, MI 49068
(616) 781-2002
Contact: Joseph R. Cooper, President.
Activity: The AABC promotes and conducts competition leading to a national Amateur World Series for teams in seven age divisions: Stan Musial (unlimited age), Connie Mack (18 and under), Mickey Mantle (16 and under), Sandy Koufax (14 and under), Pee Wee Reese (12 and under), Willie Mays (10 and under), and Minor Willie Mays (8 and under).

American Legion Baseball
700 N. Pennsylvania St.
P.O. Box 1055
Indianapolis, IN 46204
(317) 635-8411
Contact: Jim Quinlan, Program Director.
Activities: The American Legion stimulates baseball activity in local communities, conducts coaching clinics, maintains

Post-season play in the AABC is intense and high quality.

a library, sponsors competitions, and compiles statistics.

Babe Ruth Baseball
1770 Brunswick Ave.
P.O. Box 5000
Trenton, NJ 08638
(609) 695-1434
Contact: Ronald Tellefsen, President.
Activity: The group supervises state and local baseball actvity for youths 6–18 years of age. It sponsors conferences, workshops, and four annual World Series. The group's official publication is called *Bullpen* and circulates to 28,000 supporters.

Collegiate Summer Baseball Association
3723 Hermes Drive
Cincinnati, OH 45247
(513) 385-8831
Contact: Jim Kindt, Commissioner.
Purpose: The Association, founded in 1984 to administrate the division of Pony Baseball called Thorobred, provides a su-

pervised national baseball program for amateur players 19–22 years old.

Little League Baseball
P.O. Box 3485
Williamsport, PA 17701
(717) 326-1921
Contact: Luke L. LaPorta, Chairman of the Board.
Activity: Little League organizes baseball programs in every state, many countries, and U.S. territorial possessions, and offers clinics for managers, coaches, and umpires. It also maintains a museum and sponsors an international World Series.

George Khoury Association of Baseball Leagues
5400 Meramec Bottom Rd.
St. Louis, MO 63128
(314) 849-8900
Activity: The Association consists of 60,000 leagues organized by local fraternal, church, service, or community organizations and believes in the motto "Good citizens can be built on baseball diamonds much better than in back alleys."

National Amateur Baseball Federation, Inc.
12406 Keynote Lane
Bowie, MD 29715
(301) 262-0770
Contact: Charles M. Blackburn.
Purpose: The Federation, which conducts five Annual National Tournaments, is the oldest sandlot organization in America, operating continuously since 1914.

National Association of Intercollegiate Athletics (NAIA)
1221 Baltimore
Kansas City, MO 64105
(816) 842-5050
Contact: Jefferson Farris, Exec. Dir.
Activity: The Association organizes and administrates intercollegiate athletics at the national level. The group forms committees, gathers statistics, gives awards, and operates a film library.

National Association of Leagues, Umpires and Scorers
P.O. Box 1420
Wichita, KS 67201
(316) 267-7333
Purpose: The Association is sponsored by the National Baseball Congress to provide continuity for teams, leagues, tournaments, umpires, and scorers.

National Athletic Trainers Association
1001 E. Fourth St.
P.O. Box 1865
Greenville, NC 27858
(919) 752-1725
Contact: Otho Davis, Executive Director.
Activity: The Association organizes trainers at both the amateur and professional levels of baseball. It also compiles statistics, conducts research, and maintains biographical files and an archive.

National Baseball Congress
300 S. Sycamore
Wichita, KS 67213
P.O. Box 1420
Wichita, KS 67201
(316) 267-3372
Contact: Dian Overaker, Director of Administration.
Activity: The Congress is a nationwide organization that conducts a series of district and state tournaments to qualify teams for the NBC World Series in Wichita, Kansas. The NBC also sponsors the National Association of Umpires, the National Association of Leagues, the National Association of Scorers, and the Hap Dumont Youth Leagues.

National Christian College Athletic Association (NCCAA)
P.O. Box 80454
Chattanooga, TN 37411
(615) 899-7980
Contact: E. C. Haskell, Exec. Director.
Activity: The Association provides national competition for the Christian college movement.

National Collegiate Athletic Association (NCAA)
Nall Avenue at 63rd St.
Mission, KS 66201
(913) 384-3220
Contact: Richard Schultz, Executive Director.
Purpose: The NCAA administrates intercollegiate athletics.
Member schools are provided with services in the statistical, publishing, and film-production areas.

National Federation of State High School Associations
1724 Plaza Circle
P.O. Box 20626
Kansas City, MO 64195
(816) 464-5400
Contact: Brice Durbin, Executive Director.
Purpose: The Federation protects and supervises high school interstate athletic, musical and speech contests and coordinates the activities of state associations. The group also sponsors TARGET, an alcohol and drug abuse program for high schools.

National Junior College Athletic Association (NJCAA)
P.O. Box 7305
Colorado Springs, CO 80933
(303) 590-9788
Contact: George E. Killian, Executive Director.
Purpose: The Association promotes junior college athletics on intersectional and national levels. The group sponsors an intercollegiate insurance program, compiles statistics, and maintains a film library.

PONY Baseball, Inc.
P.O. Box 225
Washington, PA 15301
(412) 225-1060
Contact: Abraham Key, Administrative Director.
Activity: PONY, which stands for Protect Our Nation's Youth, sponsors summertime baseball programs for players ages 7–21. The group publishes a newspaper called *Pony Baseball*.

Press Associations and Statisticians

AP Photo
50 Rockefeller Plaza
New York, NY 10020
(212) 621-1908
Contact: George Mikulec, Deputy News Photo Editor.

Associated Press (AP)
50 Rockefeller Plaza
New York, NY 10020
(212) 621-1630
Contact: Darrell Christian, Sports Editor.

Canadian Press
36 King St. East
Toronto, Ontario
Canada M5C 2L9
(416) 364-0321
Contact: Scott White, Sports Editor.

Elias Sports Bureau
500 Fifth Ave.
New York, NY 10110
(212) 869-1530
Contact: Seymour Siwoff, General Manager.
Activity: The Bureau provides official statistics for the American and National Leagues.

Howe Sportsdata
401 "D" St.
Boston, MA 02210
(617) 269-0304
Contact: John Montague.

West Coast Office
P.O. Box 5061
San Mateo, CA 94402
(415) 345-2907
Contact: William Weiss.
Purpose: The Howe group provides official statistics for all minor leagues.

Newspaper Enterprise Association (NEA)
United Feature Syndicate
200 Park Ave.
New York, NY 10166
(212) 692-3700
Contact: Howard Siner.

Perea Talarico
Angel Pola #16
Col Peridodista
CP 11220 Mexico, D.F.
Contact: Ana Luisa.
Purpose: Provides official statistics for the Mexican League.

Sports Newssatellite (SNS)
250 Harbor Plaza Drive
P.O. Box 10210
Stamford, CT 06904
(203) 965-6789
Contact: Jim Scott, Director.
Activity: SNS is part of the Phoenix Communications Group.

Sports Press Service
1133 Broadway
New York, NY 10010
(212) 242-4887
(212) 807-7100
Contact: Bill Shannon, Managing Editor.

Sportsticker, Inc.
Harborside Financial Center
600 Plaza Two
Jersey City, NJ 07311
(201) 309-1300
Contact: Joe Carnicelli, Managing Editor.
Purpose: Sportsticker provides twenty-four-hour sports scores and information updates to PC owners.

United Press International (UPI)
5 Penn Plaza
New York, NY 10001
(212) 560-1120
Contact: Fred McMane, Sports Editor.

UPI Photo
5 Penn Plaza
New York, NY 10001
(212) 560-1171
Contact: Larry DeSantis, Managing Editor.   —LJ

Associations

AAU-U.S.A. Junior Olympics
3400 W. 86th St.
Indianapolis, IN 46268
(317) 872-2900
Contact: Janice L. Lyon, Co-Administrator.
Activity: The AAU-U.S.A. Junior Olympics is sponsored by the Amateur Athletic Union of the United States. Its goal is to establish, develop, and implement a comprehensive youth sports program for athletes, 8–18. The AAU maintains a library, biographical archives, and a Hall of Fame.

American Athletic Trainers Association and Certification Board (AATAC)
660 W. Duarte Rd.
Arcadia, CA 91006
(818) 445-1978
Contact: Joe S. Bordland, Board Chairman.
Activity: The board qualifies and certifies individuals as athletic trainers and establishes minimum standards for the care and prevention of athletic injuries.

American Baseball Coaches Association
P.O. Box 3545
Omaha, NE 68103
(402) 733-0374
Contact: Jerry A. Miles, Executive Director.
Activity: The association encourages a deeper sense of responsibility among coaches for the conduct, maintenance, and development of the game of baseball in accordance with the highest tradition of interscholastic competition. The group correlates baseball with educational objectives and creates a representative body throughout the United States, thereby

promoting a rapport between coaches at all levels of baseball. The association publishes a newspaper called *Collegiate Baseball.*

American Sports Education Institute (ASEI)
200 Castlewood Drive
North Palm Beach, FL 33408
(305) 842-3600
Contact: Anthony Kucera, Executive Director.
Activity: The institute promotes amateur sports and physical education throughout the United States.

Associated Sports Fans (ASF)
1501 Lee Highway, Suite 205
Arlington, VA 22209
(703) 243-9101
Contact: Chris Burke, Exec. Dir.
Purpose: The ASF has formulated a Fans' Bill of Rights that includes the right to fair prices, reasonable access to tickets to sporting events, the right to organize fans, and the right to present fans' opinions before decision-making bodies.

Dick Littlefield Club
801 Public Ledger Bldg.
Philadelphia, PA 19106
(215) 922-4949
Contact: Lawrence H. Wentz, Pres.
Activity: The club honors great ball players of the past who are not in the Baseball Hall of Fame. Honorees include Red Schoendienst, Richie Ashburn, Enos Slaughter, Jim Bunning, Nellie Fox, Gil Hodges, and Roger Maris. Slaughter and Schoendienst have subsequently been named to the Hall.

Don Mossi Society
(513) 556-0627
Contact: Doug Bureman.
Activity: The society began when members of the Cincinnati Reds scouting department (Marge Schott, "all they [scouts] ever do is watch baseball games") met one

(Cont. p. 342.)

You Hear It All the Time

Two strangers meet for the first time at a dull party and discover a common interest in baseball. After mutually trashing their local ball club's manager and assuring each other that there's still hope for a pennant this year, one of them casually drops a remark indicating his baseball knowledge goes deeper than this morning's sports page—something like, "Doe's OBA is down 10 points from his career norm" or "Red Sox fans still haven't forgiven Harry Frazee."

That's the cue for the other fan to inquire, "Are you a member of SABR?"

If the answer is no, it's time for the commercial.

"Well, friend," says the SABR-ite, "the initials stand for Society for American Baseball Research, a group formed on August 10, 1971, in the library of the Baseball Hall of Fame by longtime baseball researcher Bob Davids and fifteen others."

The noninitiate looks skeptical. "Sixteen guys isn't much."

"In less than twenty years, the Society has grown to more than 6,000 members. And not just guys; there are many women members."

"But what do they do?"

"Do? Well, the first objective of the Society is to foster the study of baseball as a significant social and athletic institution. Members research whatever historical or statistical areas interest them. Then they have the opportunity to share their findings through presentations at the national convention or regional meetings or in one of the Society's publications."

"Gee, I dunno. Do you have to research something? I'm pretty busy."

"Not every member does research," explains the SABR-ite. "Many join to have access to the presentations and publications. Or just to meet others with the same interest in baseball. It's amazing what you

can learn. A recent *Research Journal* had articles on Bob Gibson in 1968, a study of how jet lag affects pennant races, a discussion of nineteenth-century baseball writing, an account of a Latin American All-Star game, and more than a dozen other articles. Fascinating stuff you won't see in national magazines that have to cater to fans who can't spell Canseco.

"Did you know that one member assembled the 1871–1875 National Association box scores? He found that Levi Meyerle won the first batting title with a .496 average and lost his third base position. His .654 fielding average just may have had something to do with sending him out to right field in 1872."

"What was that about a convention?" asks the noninitiate.

"A great chance to talk baseball till it's running out your ears! Every summer SABR holds a three-day convention, usually in a city with a major league team so a game can be part of the fun. There've been conventions in Chicago, Washington, Los Angeles, Milwaukee, Albany . . ."

"Wait a minute. There's no major league team in Albany."

"No, but in 1989 the Eastern League All-Star Game was held there, and of course part of that convention was a trip to the Hall of Fame in Cooperstown. Another high point of every convention is the Player Panel, where former big leaguers get up there and you can ask them questions. Sparky Anderson enthralled the 1982 convention attendees with tales of his days as mentor to the Big Red Machine. Ted 'Double Duty' Radcliff explained his nickname as the result of having pitched one game of a doubleheader and caught the other. Milt Pappas spoke of his brush with immortality—one out in the ninth with a perfect game on the line. Former players such as Gene Benson, Chico Carrasquel, Sam

Chapman, Tim Harkness, Joe Hauser, Johnny Klippstein, Tony Lupien, Dave Malarcher, Rich Nye, Nelson Potter, Marv Rottblatt, and Spec Shea have shared their stories and answered questions.

"Oh, and speaking of questions, there's the darndest baseball trivia contest you ever saw."

The noninitiate smiles. "At the office they're always trying to stump me. I do okay."

"Yeah? Try these brain teasers:

"1. In 1933 the St. Louis Cardinals had two future Hall of Fame pitchers. One never won a game prior to his thirtieth birthday and the other never won a game after his thirtieth. Who are they?

"2. Five foreign-born hurlers have won at least 240 games in the major leagues. Can you name them?

"3. Name the outfielder who performed the only unassisted triple play in the high minors."

The noninitiate stops smiling. "Nobody knows that stuff."

"Some SABR members do. The champ is Ron Liebman, a senior statistician for the New York Housing Authority. Ron and his three teammates won the trivia contest in 1974, 1982, 1984, 1987, 1988, or five of the seven years that the contest has been held. Jamie Selko, with U.S. Army Intelligence in Berlin, flies in every year to match wits with Liebman. Selko's team won in 1985 and 1986."

"Do *you* know the answers?"

"Sure," says the SABR-ite modestly.

"1. Dazzy Vance and Dizzy Dean.

"2. Tony Mullane (Ireland), Ferguson Jenkins (Canada), Jim McCormick (Scotland), Bert Blyleven (the Netherlands), and Juan Marichal (Dominican Republic).

"3. Walter Carlyle, 1911, with Vernon in the Pacific Coast League.

"Yeah, the conventions are great. Bill Borst, the St. Louis Browns' Fan Club founder, said, 'We are baseball junkies. Each year we go to the convention to shoot up.' And then through the year there are also smaller, regional conventions and meetings.

"Say, did I tell you about the SABR publications?"

The noninitiate shakes his head. A small rattle is heard, but it may have been only the ice in his drink.

"That's one of the ways the Society disseminates research information. There's the annual *Baseball Research Journal*; a magazine, *The National Pastime*; *The SABR Review of Books,* and special publications like *Nineteenth Century Stars*, *The Federal League*, and *Minor League Stars*.

"When SABR published career statistics of forgotten minor league greats in the 1978 issue of *Minor League Stars*, the baseball community took notice of the Society. Minor league standouts Bunny Brief, Paul Easterling, Ox Eckardt, Joe Hauser, Oyster Joe Martina, Lou Novikoff, Frank Shellenback, Jigger Statz, Paul Strand, and Bill Thomas have long been known to front-office personnel but were little appreciated beyond that enclave. SABR now boasts of a sizable membership among those in organized ball. The late Commissioner, A. Bartlett Giamatti, was a SABR member."

The noninitiate uncrosses his eyes. "It sounds outstanding, but . . ."

"The Society recognizes the outstanding efforts of its members by a series of awards," continues the SABR-ite. "The Annual Banquet has become the Awards Banquet. The Bob Davids Award, named for the founder, honors a member who reflects the ingenuity, integrity, and self-sacrifice of the founder in areas of administrative responsibility, original research, information exchange, or voluntary efforts in the best interests of baseball. The SABR Salute recognizes the baseball research efforts of senior members, including work they may have performed prior to the establishment of the Society. The recent SABR-Macmillan Award, presented by the Macmillan Publishing Company, has been given to both members and nonmembers who have produced or published outstanding baseball research within the past twelve months."

The noninitiate holds up his hand. "Terrific, but what I want to know is . . ."

"What *I* want to know," interrupts the party host, "is will you two continue this outside? Everyone's gone home. My wife and I want to go to bed." He hands them their coats.

"Probably a hockey fan," the SABR-ite remarks on the way to the door. "Now what was it you wanted to know, friend? Nap Lajoie's 1910 batting average?"

"No. Just tell me how to become a member."

"Easy. I'll give you the address, or you can just look it up on page 343 of *The Whole Baseball Catalogue.*"   —LJ & BC

January 11 in mutual need for a baseball fix. Discovering that former major league pitcher Don Mossi had been born on that particular day, they phoned him and found the conversation reassuring in a baseball sense. Subsequent years and calls turned into gigantic Don Mossi birthday parties, with thousands in downtown Cincinnati and Mossi in his California home waiting by the telephone. Recently the birthday events have toned down.

Franchise of Americans Needing Sports (FANS)
2160 Yorkshire Rd.
Sacramento, CA 95815
(916) 927-5296
Contact: Michael Ross, Executive Director.
Activity: FANS, founded in 1981, represents the interests of sports fans and consumers. The group sponsors legislation designed to enhance consumer rights.

International Baseball Association
Pan American Plaza, Suite 490
201 S. Capitol Ave.
Indianapolis, IN 46225
(317) 237-5757
Contact: David Osinski, Executive Director.
Activity: The association promotes amateur baseball throughout the world and seeks to have baseball recognized as an official Olympic sport. It publishes a quarterly magazine in Spanish and English, called *International Baseball Association.*

Jackie Robinson Foundation
80-90 Eighth Ave.
New York, NY 10011
(212) 675-1511
Contact: Betty Adams, President.
Activity: The foundation was established to develop the leadership and achievement potential of minority and urban youth. It bestows the Robbie Award for Humanitarianism and publishes a newsletter about the society's activities.

National Baseball Fan Association (NBFA)
P.O. Box 4192
Mt. Laurel, NJ 08054
(609) 235-4192
Contact: Robert E. Godfrey, President.
Purpose: The NBFA was founded to promote, protect, and preserve baseball as a sport, not as part of the entertainment industry. Through member surveys, the Association functions as the fans' representative in the Commissioner's Office.

National Collegiate Baseball Writers Association
Arizona State University
Sports Information Dept.
University Activity Center
Tempe, AZ 85287
(602) 965-6592
Contact: Mark Brand, Sec.-Treasurer.
Purpose: The Association seeks to upgrade and improve media coverage of intercollegiate baseball. It bestows the annual Wilbur E. Snypp Award.

National High School Athletic Coaches Association
P.O. Box 1808
Ocala, FL 32678
(904) 622-3660
Contact: Carey McDonald, Exec. Dir.
Purpose: The Association was formed to give greater national prestige and professional status to high school coaching and to promote cooperation among coaches, school administrators, the press, game officials, and the public. The office sponsors a National Awards Program to recognize outstanding high school athletic directors, coaches, and players.

National Operating Committee on Standards for Athletic Equipment (NOCSAE)
11724 Plaza Circle
P.O. Box 20626
Kansas City, MO 64195
(816) 464-5470
Contact: Glen Meredith, Executive Director.

Activity: The Committee is concerned with the safety of sports equipment. It conducts research on head and neck injuries, and sets standards for baseball, football, and hockey helmet specifications.

National Semi-Professional Baseball Association
P.O. Box 29965
Atlanta, GA 30359
(404) 296-0800
Contact: Lt. Col. McDonald Valentine, Executive Director.
Purpose: The Association is concerned with the longevity of our national pastime. The group works to improve the skills and advance the baseball careers of individual members. It sponsors the Fastest Kid on the Bases Contest, open to kids, ages 8–30.

North American Society for Sport History (NASSH)
101 White Bldg.
Penn State University
University Park, PA 16802
(814) 865-2416
Contact: Ronald Smith, Secretary-Treasurer.
Purpose: The Society was founded in 1972 to promote, stimulate, and encourage study, research, and writing of the history of sport. A secondary aim is to support and cooperate with local, national, and international organizations having the same purposes. The not-for-profit group offers membership to qualified individuals and publishes *The Journal of Sport History*, annual proceedings, and a newsletter.

Pacific Coast League Historical Society
1244 Brian St.
Placentia, CA 92670
(714) 524-0939
Contact: Dick Beverage, Founder.
Activity: The society hosts reunions of PCL players and fans. The 1988 reunion brought out over 100 interested participants, including many former players and an umpire as well as relatives of all-time

PCL greats. The society trades memorabilia and information. It may sponsor a fantasy camp in the near future. Beverage edits the society newsletter called *Pacific Coast League Potpourri*.

Society for American Baseball Research (SABR)
P.O. Box 470
Garrett Park, MD 20896
(301) 949-7227
Contact: Norbert Kraich, Executive Director.
Purpose: The society publishes baseball research by its members in annual journals, facilitates the dissemination of data, and safeguards the proprietary interests of its members. Some of the publications are *The Baseball Journal*, *The National Pastime*, *SABR Review of Books*, and the *SABR Bulletin*.

Sporting Goods Manufacturers Association (SGMA)
200 Castlewood Drive
North Palm Beach, FL 33408
(305) 842-4100
Contact: Howard J. Bruns, President.
Activity: Members are manufacturers of athletic equipment and sporting goods. The Association compiles statistics and operates an international trade library.

Sports Foundation
Lake Center Plaza Bldg.
1699 Wall St.
Mt. Prospect, IL 60056
(312) 439-4000
Contact: Thomas Fitzgerald, Executive Officer.
Activity: The foundation is chartered "to expand sports markets for the common business interests of every segment of the sporting goods industry." It provides financial and promotional assistance to newer and smaller segments of the industry and supplements the work of existing organizations. The group presents the awards to recognize excellence in the area of park and recreational management and

community achievement in work with the handicapped.

United States Baseball Federation (USBF)
2160 Greenwood Ave.
Trenton, NJ 08609
(609) 586-2381

Contact: Richard W. Case, Executive Director.

Purpose: The federation is, by an act of Congress, the national governing body for all of amateur baseball in the United States. The USBF is dedicated to developing fans and players, nationally and internationally, to providing nonduplicating services to its members, and to protecting the rights of amateur athletes. USBF publishes a newspaper entitled *USA Baseball News.*

United States Stickball League (USSBL)
P.O. Box 363
East Rockaway, NY 11518
(516) 764-6307

Contact: Ronald B. Babineau, President.

Activity: The goal is to establish stickball leagues and sponsor stickball competitions. The group has a speakers' bureau and Hall of Fame, compiles statistics, and bestows awards. There is a telephone hot line for stickball score playbacks.   —LJ

How to Start a Fan Club

So you admire the St. Louis Cardinals. Their hitting, pitching, and defensive prowess are so extraordinary that you want to show your appreciation by starting a fan club.

Where do you start?

First off, you need to contact prospective members or have them contact you. Obviously there's no such thing as a secret fan club. At least no one ever let us in on such a secret.

No doubt you'll start with your friends. Talk it up. They'll have other friends, so you have a nucleus. Perhaps you can convince a local sportswriter to mention your group in his column. Don't count on that, of course; you're not big news yet. You may also try a local radio talk show, particularly one that concentrates on sports. Classified ads may help. And when you go to the ballpark, carry a sign declaring your group's undying support for the team. You'll be surprised how many people will come up and ask you about joining.

According to Bill Borst, who formed the St. Louis Browns fan club because he wanted to retire Rick Ferrell's jersey, "You have to keep your name in the papers. If the press likes you, they will advertise for nothing. You constantly want new blood to join your organization because old members get tired after a while. You have to be conscious of public relations. Never turn down an interview."

Eventually you're going to have your first meeting. Depending on how many members you've recruited, you can hold it in someone's living room or a conference room at a member's place of business. You may even have to rent a hall. You might contact the team's P.R. department about a meeting room, but you'll have better luck with them once you have a club in being, rather than a club in planning.

Before that first organizational meeting, you've got a lot of work to do.

For one thing, you can't even begin to organize a team fan club unless you are sanctioned by an existing team. Their blessing means that the team logo can be attached to newsletters, T-shirts, or any assorted items that can best publicize your fraternity. You'll want that sanction either before or right after your first meeting. Either way, talk to the team as soon as you can. There is usually someone in the front office assigned to handle and coordinate fan clubs.

But let's say you are forming a Jose Canseco fan club. Do you need the Oakland A's permission? No, because most major league teams will not get involved with such fan clubs. And there's a good reason.

"It's an administrative nightmare to sanction fan clubs for ball players," says Patty Cerrano, fan club coordinator for the New York Mets. "Players are traded all the time. For example, let's say we had sanctioned a Wally Backman [recently traded to the Minnesota Twins] fan club. We can't say to club members, 'Good luck, go to Minnesota.' By not getting involved in those fan clubs, we are not open to lawsuits."

Naturally, you'll want a democratic fan club (at least we hope so), but you'll still have to choose some officers. It would be embarrassing to show up at that first meeting and discover that no one is willing to serve. A little pre-meeting canvassing can help you avoid standing up there and pleading for someone who's willing to be the secretary. On the other hand, if all of the important positions are held by you and your nearest buddies, the other members may get the idea that they're being used.

Another thing you should do before that first organizational meeting is give some thought to your newsletter. There's no rule that says you *must* have a newsletter, but it's hard to hold a group together without one. Someone will have to serve as editor, and that can be a lot of work for a volunteer. Even if your membership is bursting with would-be writers anxious to express themselves in your newsletter, somebody will have to be responsible for weeding through their efforts, correcting grammar, spelling, and punctuation. And having them all typed up. This can be wearying, especially with those submissions that come in handwritten by chickens on toilet tissue. And you can bet your bippy there will be times when no submissions come in, and it will be up to your editor to fill those empty pages. You certainly can't

assign somebody to be your editor or else! so there better be someone willing to step forward before you even bring it up.

You'll have to set some policy on how often your newsletter will come out and how many pages it will be. And how will it be produced? By photocopy? Computer printout? Commercially printed? Remember, we're talking time and money here.

Speaking of money, you'll be amazed at how much you'll spend in postage. A nice thick newsletter can cost you a dollar or more per member every mailing. On the bright side, when you get up to 200 members (actually 200 pieces per mailing), you can purchase a bulk mailing permit for $50 at the post office. A permit will cut your per-unit cost to a fraction, although you'll be mailing third class.

Starting a fan club will cost you more in time than money, but the money can be considerable. But don't expect to *make* money off your favorite player or team. Fan clubs are nonprofit. Annual dues are used to finance newsletters, mailings, banquets, and trips.

"I spent $2,000 just to put an ad in the *Giants Magazine*," says Ken Castle, president of the Giants Booster Club.

And how do the founders expect to get their money back considering that these clubs are nonprofit? The solution can be anywhere from pocketing the yearly dues to soliciting sponsors who will advertise in the monthly newsletter. But club leaders like Castle don't expect to break even for at least one year.

"I knew going in that I might not get my money back," he says. "In our case, the bottom line is to put fans in the seats. In order to attract these fans you have to throw dinners, organize trips, and somehow be able to meet the ball players as well."

There are big-city organizations, however, like the Junior and Lady Mets fan clubs, who feel that investing a lot of money in advertising is not necessary. Said Patty Cerrano, "New York is a big city, and all you need is word of mouth to get recruits."

Jim Powers, president of the Blohards, a Red Sox fan club, says, "Club members are diehard fans. We don't care about the money we spend. All we want to do is talk about the positives and negatives about our teams, past and present."

Dollar figures or the number of members you have do not determine the success or failure of a fan club, even if you're Ken Castle trying to attract fans to Candlestick Park. It's the enthusiasm that will make it everlasting.

"We had a meeting that featured Hank Greenwald [the Giants announcer]," says Castle. "The members came out and ate food and met a man they had heard on the radio. It was a very entertaining evening. If you can keep it on that level, where there's no moaning or bitching, the fan club will be a success regardless of the numbers."

—BL

Fan Clubs

Atlanta Braves

Atlanta Braves 400 Club
P.O. Box 7689
Atlanta, GA 30309
(404) 498-0347
Person to contact: Wayne Coleman.
Cost to join: $12 a year.

Any Braves' fan can gain sustenance and mingle with the 300 club members at the monthly luncheons which are frequently attended by current players like Dale Murphy and Gerald Perry. That's not all. You have the pleasure (or misfortune) of traveling to National League cities to watch the Braves play.

Baltimore Orioles

The Fantastic Fan Club
Memorial Stadium
Baltimore, MD 21218
(301) 243-9800
Cost to join: $10 per year.

Baltimore fans will love this. You'll receive one general-admission ticket to eight Oriole games, plus a coupon with which you can purchase eight more tickets at 15 percent off. There's more. An annual baseball clinic is held during the month of May at Memorial Stadium, featuring current Oriole stars giving baseball advice.

Club members will also be picked by lottery to participate in a bullpen party at the end of the year.

Boston Red Sox

The Blohards
U.S.A. Weekend
535 Madison Ave.
New York, NY 10022
(212) 715-2106
Person to contact: Jim Powers.
Cost to join: $10.00 per year or $100.00 for lifetime membership.

As the calling card says, "*B*enevolent *L*oyal *O*rder of the *H*onorable *A*ncient *R*ed

Sox *Diehard Sufferers* of New York."

All right, so some New York Red Soxers winced when Bucky Dent hit that three-run home run to help the Yankees win the Eastern Division in 1978. And others suffered cardiac arrest when Bill Buckner couldn't handle a ground ball to force a seventh game in the 1986 World Series against the Mets. But the Blohards forgive and forget by holding two luncheons a year and going to Fenway Park every opening day. The Red Sox players and coaches return the appreciation by attending the luncheons and also by going to Fenway on opening day.

The Pawtucket Red Sox Hot Stove League Fan Club
P.O. Box 2365
Pawtucket, RI 02861
(401) 724-7300
Person to contact: Bill Wanleff.
Cost to join: $5.00 per year.

Besides the juicy tidbits on the Red Sox in the monthly newsletter, there's a big hot stove league party held during the month of January, where the 2,000 members mingle with the players and talk baseball.

Bradenton Pirates

The Bradenton Pirates Booster Club
P.O. Box 10213
Bradenton, FL 34282
(813) 792-4131
Person to contact: Jack Stuhltrager.
Cost to join: $5.00 per year.

For $5.00 you can see the Bradenton Pirates play in the Gulf Coast League for free and dine with the Pirates at banquets held in January and February. Monthly newsletters are included in this package.

California Angels

Angels Booster Club
P.O. Box 3820
Anaheim, CA 92803
(714) 522-8190

Person to contact: Lorraine Campanozzi.
Cost to join: $15.00 for the first member of the family, $10.00 for each additional family member, $8.00 for out-of-state people.

There's volunteer work involved here. Club members hand out free promotional gifts during Angel games. In return they'll get a free admission to these same games, as well as parking accommodations.

But there's leisure time too. Besides the annual luncheons and picnics, club members travel around the American League to watch the Angels play.

The Wally Joyner and Jack Howell
Fan Club
Anaheim Stadium
2000 State College Blvd.
Anaheim, CA 92806
(714) 937-6700
Person to contact: Marisa Zubas.
Cost to join: $5.00 per year.

The $5.00 fee will get you the following:

- A membership card.
- Four newsletters a year.
- A baseball cap.
- Autographed pictures of both players.

Chicago Cubs

Die-Hard Cubs Fan Club
P.O. Box 522
Prospect Heights, IL 60070
(312) 541-3370 or 887-7780
Cost to join: $9.00 per year.

Would you believe that there are 90,000 diehard members in this fraternity, which includes George Will and Bryant Gumbel? Believe it! So how can one benefit with this crowd? Well, you are going to receive the usual package: a discount subscription to *Vine Line*, the Cubs' magazine, and a diploma proving your loyalty to the Cubs. But there's got to be more, right? The grand prize is the annual convention, which is held in January at the Hyatt Regency Hotel. You can mingle with cur-

rent and former players and tell them how much you love being a Cubs fan.

Emil Verban Memorial Society
4406 Franklin St.
Kensington, MD 20895
(202) 371-6934
(301) 493-8424
Contact: Bruce Ladd, President.

Cubs fans are different and this society is the proof. In 1975 a group of Washingtonians met to form a Chicago Cubs fan club. Deciding they could relate to Emil Verban, a competent but unheralded Cubs infielder of the 1940s, they named their club the Emil Verban Memorial Society. Former President Ronald Reagan is a member, as is columnist George Will. Emil Verban himself was hesitant about joining but became member number seven, which matched his uniform number. Members are nominated and must be residents of the Washington metropolitan area. The Society meets for lunch every two years. In the words of the founder, "We have a hell of an extravaganza." Luncheon guests have included the 1969 Cubs, Dallas Green, the 1945 Cubs, and Emil Verban.

Chicago White Sox

ChiSox Fan Club
Comiskey Park
324 W. 35th St.
Chicago, IL 60616
(312) 924-1000
Person to contact: Sharon Sreniawski.
Cost to join: $10.00 per year.

For $10.00 you'll receive a membership card, two gift certificates to a baseball game, a ChiSox patch, and a set of baseball cards.

Cincinnati Reds

The Todd Squad
P.O. Box 1516
Newport, KY 41071
(513) 752-3932

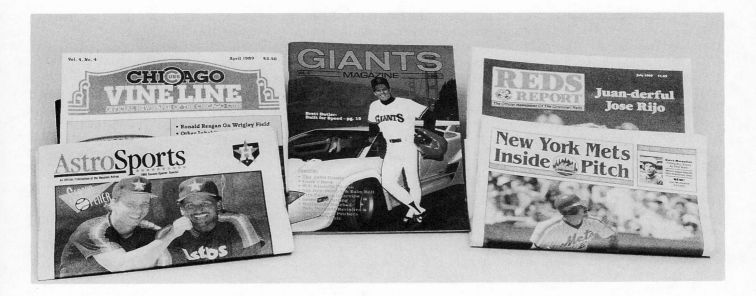

Person to contact: Kim Benzinger.
Cost to join: $15.00 per year.

This club is named after Todd Benzinger, Kim's husband, who patrols first base for the Cincinnati Reds. Members will receive the Todd Squad T-shirt, with the first baseman's name and number 25 on the back, a membership card, an autographed picture, and juicy tidbits on Todd and the Big Red Machine in the monthly newsletter. Occasional parties will also take place with Todd in attendance from time to time.

Cleveland Indians

Wahoo Club
Cleveland Indians
Cleveland Stadium
Cleveland, OH 44114
(216) 861-1200

The Wahoo Club, unlike most fan clubs, is sponsored by the major league team. For a $20 annual fee, Wahoo Club members may attend luncheons with players and visiting baseball officials. A Little Indians Fan Club is sponsored by Kenny Kings. Related but not connected is the *Tribe Talk* newsletter of upcoming Indians activities.

Columbus Clippers

The Clippers Booster Club
P.O. Box 18283
Columbus, OH 43218
(614) 983-3214
Person to contact: Martha Martin.
Cost to join: $7.50 per year or $5.00 for children, 14 years or younger, and senior citizens.

This fraternity has a good time in supporting the Columbus Clippers, the Triple-A affiliate of the New York Yankees. They throw a barbecue once a year for the players and their wives, as well as putting together a "Meet the Players" dinner right before Opening Day. The boosters also donate $5 to cystic fibrosis whenever a Clipper hits a home run.

Detroit Tigers

The Tiger Stadium Fan Club
P.O. Box 441426
Detroit, MI 48244-1426
(313) 964-5991
Person to contact: Frank Rashid.
Cost to join: Varies.

Having fun isn't what this group is all about. They're trying to keep baseball tra-

Fan-club publications can have wider appeal.

dition in Detroit. Why? There's talk of tearing down seventy-eight-year-old Tiger Stadium and moving the Bengals to a suburb of Michigan. How are they protesting? They circle the stadium and hold hands and express their anger. This protest, however, is not only heard in Detroit. The fraternity travels to AL cities and distributes the newsletter *Unobstructed Views*, which gives reasons why this noble relic should not be in baseball heaven.

Mayo Smith Society
P.O. Box 119
Northville, MI 48167
(703) 525-0243
Contact: Dave Raglin, Publicist.

A national organization of Tigers fans named after the manager of the 1968 World Championship Detroit Tigers, the Society sponsors an annual spring training trip to Lakeland, Florida, and publishes a newsletter called *Tiger Stripes*. The Society was founded in Washington, D.C., in 1983 by congressional aide Dale Petrosky, who met with Tiger fans at breakfast to discuss the situation in Detroit.

Edmonton Trappers

The Junior Trappers Fan Club
10233-96th Ave.
Edmonton, Alberta T5K 0A5
(403) 429-2934
Person to contact: Dennis Henke.
Cost to join: Go to any Petro-Canada Station, fill out the application, and you're a member.

It's like Christmas time during the summer for kids 14 and younger. They will have free admission to every Saturday home game, various discounts at the souvenir shop, and a chance to be a bat boy for a game. Semi-monthly newsletters will keep them abreast on the Angels' minor league team.

Houston Astros

Astros Orbiters' Booster Club
P.O. Box 540402
Houston, TX 77254-0402
(713) 688-3523
Person to contact: Connie Clark.
Cost to join: $15.00 for new members; $12.50 for renewals.

Members will receive a monthly newsletter and a golf shirt with the Orbiters' logo attached. There are also some fringe benefits. You can vote for the Astros' hitter and pitcher of the month during the baseball season and honor him at various luncheons.

Kansas City Royals

The Royal Lancers
P.O. Box 419969
Kansas City, MO 64141
(816) 921-2200
Person to contact: Chris Muehlbach.
Cost to join: None; application for membership required.

This is a support group that's making sure baseball remains in Kansas City. Can you blame them? They've already lost the A's to Oakland. Membership is limited, but there is an incentive to be in this fraterni-ty. Help sell season tickets during spring training and you'll get a chance to go on a road trip with George Brett and company, as well as additional trips with club members during the year. That's provided, of course, you reach a certain quota in ticket sales. Annual picnics and dinners are included.

Los Angeles Dodgers

Go-Go Dodgers Fan Club
3332 N. Stallo
Rosemead, CA 91770
(213) 283-2444
Person to contact: Vern Chesterton.
Cost to join: $20.00 per year.

Named after Maury Wills for his running ability, this club supports the Dodgers by going to 30 games a year, including trips to San Diego and San Francisco. Club members are charitable too. They take 50 underprivileged kids to a Dodger game when it's giveaway night at the stadium.

Milwaukee Brewers

The Brewer Pepsi Fan Club
Milwaukee County Stadium
Milwaukee, WI 53214
(414) 933-4114
Person to contact: The ticket office for an application.
Cost to join: $9.95 per year.

God bless the child who's 16 or younger. He'll receive 6 tickets to 6 Milwaukee Brewers games, a one-year subscription to *What's Brewing Magazine*, a membership card, and a Pepsi baseball cap. Could he ask for more?

Minnesota Twins

The Dan Gladden Fan Club
P.O. Box 390191
Mountain View, CA 94039
Cost: $12.00 per year.

This is organized by Gladden's mother, Joyce Russo, and it's more than just paying $12.00 to be part of her society; you must be a law-abiding citizen, which means:
• No disorderly conduct.
• No illegal drugs or substances in your possession.
• No public drunkenness.

If you can follow those simple rules, you can participate in the two tailgate parties each year at the Metrodome and win baseball memorabilia by entering various contests.

New York Mets

The Junior Mets Fan Club
Shea Stadium
Roosevelt Ave. and 126th St.
Flushing, NY 11368
(718) 565-4320
Person to contact: Patty Cerrano.
Cost to join: $5.00 plus two proofs of purchase from Farmland Dairy, the sponsor.

This is a package for kids, 14 or younger, which contains the following:
• A baseball card collectors' album with eight baseball cards inside.
• Discount coupons for two Met games.
• An invitation to an instructional clinic at Shea Stadium.

The Lady Mets Fan Club
Shea Stadium
Roosevelt Ave. and 126th St.
Flushing, NY 11368
(718) 565-4320
Person to contact: Patty Cerrano.
Cost to join: $3.00 a year to be put on the mailing list.

This women's group gets together during the year to have barbecues before and during games at Shea Stadium's picnic area. The food, by the way, is catered by Rusty's (Staub) Restaurant. There is also one trip to a National League city to watch Mets baseball.

New York Yankees

The Yankee Haters Club
P.O. Box 521
Henrietta, NY 14467

(716) 787-1704
Person to contact: Cliff Cabriolla.
Cost to join: $10.00 per year.

Why do they hate the Bronx Bombers? George Steinbrenner, of course. And they will express their feelings at an American and minor league ballpark near you. Monthly newsletters will also keep tabs on the Bronx Zoo.

Philadelphia Phillies

The Phan Clan—An Exclusive Phillies Society
P.O. Box 7575
Philadelphia, PA 19101
Cost to join: $25.

Pay this fee and you're a lifetime member with good benefits: A lifetime membership card, membership certificate, Phan Clan lapel pin, window decal, Phillies Yearbook (for year joined only), box seat ticket voucher (for year joined only), six-month subscription to the *Phillies Report*, discount on publications, discount on selected Phillies games, and the *Phan Clan Newsletter*. The best benefit of all is being on the "priority list" for tickets if the Phillies are involved in postseason play.

Richmond Braves

The Richmond Braves Booster Club
P.O. Box 6667
Richmond, VA 23230
(804) 233-4891
Person to contact: George Beadles.
Cost to join: $5.00 per year.

For the twenty-fourth consecutive year, the players will mingle with this fraternity at banquets during the season.

Rochester Red Wings

The Rochester Heavy Hitters Fan Club
500 Norton St.
Rochester, NY 14621
(716) 467-3000
Person to contact: Kevin Green.
Cost to join: Free.

This is for you CEOs out there. Call the P.R. department and help find ways to generate money for the Rochester Red Wings, who have monetary problems because of a recent renovation project. In return, members will go on the road with the Red Wings to places like Syracuse and Virginia. Club members will also be treated to lunches and dinners at various haunts.

St. Louis Browns

St. Louis Browns Fan Club
P.O. Box 184
Hazelwood, MO 63042
(314) 997-5907
Persons to contact: Bill Borst, Founder; or Jimmy Woods, President.
Cost to join: $10 per year.

This club began on October 4, l984, the fortieth anniversary of the Browns' victory over the Cardinals in the first game of the 1944 World Series. The fraternity has flourished in five years by publishing three books on the Browns: the two-part compendium *The Brown Stockings* and *Ables to Zoldak*— all written by club members and edited by Bill Borst.

Borst has also kept the Browns' memory alive by building a Hall of Fame in Maryville College, where most of the players are or will be enshrined.

In a recent escapade, thirty-five members trucked to Kansas City to entice the Baltimore Orioles to return to their native city. Orioles' Public Relations Director Bob Brown participated and declined the invitation to play the rest of the schedule in St. Louis. Members contented themselves with placing Browns caps on their heads in a solemn reCAPturing ceremony.

St. Louis Cardinals

The Stan Musial Society of Washington D.C.
901 31st St. N.W.
Washington DC 20007
(202) 333-7400

Five Reasons . . .

Fans love the Yankees: (a) 22 World Championships; (b) 32 pennants; (c) Yankee Stadium; (d) pinstripes; (e) Babe, Lou, Joe, Mickey, Yogi, etc.

Fans hate the Yankees: (a) 22 World Championships; (b) 32 pennants; (c) Yankee Stadium; (d) pinstripes; (e) George.

—BC

Persons to contact: Vic Gold and Frank Mankiewicz, Founders.
Cost to join: Free.

The society was founded "to put down the Emil Verban Society" and to support the St. Louis Cardinals in their annual race to the pennant, especially in contests versus the Chicago Cubs. Bylaws require that a meeting be held every once in a while, if at all.

The St. Louis Baseball Cardinal Fan Club
10555 East Dartmouth Ave., Suite 250
Aurora, CO 80014
(303) 337-1400
Person to contact: Jeff Laskey.
Cost to join: $10 a season for the cost of newsletters.

It's very simple: If you are a Cardinal fan, you can meet Laskey and the gang every two weeks at various watering holes to watch the Red Birds play.

Stan the Man shows his admirers the swing that launched 3,630 hits.

San Diego Padres

The San Diego Hot Stove League
P.O. Box 477
San Diego, CA 92104
(619) 449-4631
Person to contact: Beverly Lions.
Cost to join: $10.00 per person and $15.00 per family.

Former umpire Ed Runge is the president. Under his administration there will be a monthly tailgate party during the baseball season outside Jack Murphy Stadium, trips to Yuma, Arizona—the training site of the Padres—and Anaheim Stadium, home of the California Angels.

The San Diego Madres, Inc.
P.O. 20113
San Diego, CA 92120
(619) 460-3459
Person to contact: Betty Richardson.
Cost to join: $10.00 per year.

These women help sponsor 38 Little League baseball teams (boys and girls) in San Diego. Raffles help finance the teams. Members can also mingle with ball club members at various luncheons.

San Francisco Giants

The San Francisco Downtown Ballpark Boosters Club
1550 Bay St. No. 204
San Francisco, CA 94123
(415) 931-2231

Person to contact: Daniel Woodhead, Pres.

Advocate Woodhead watchdogs the mayor's office in its handling of the relocation of Candlestick Park. He reports to the public on the relationship of city government and private-sector ballpark consultants by means of a newsletter.

San Francisco Giants Booster Club
P.O. Box 493
Los Altos, CA 94022
(415) 949-4937
Person to contact: Ken Castles.
Cost to join: $18.00 per year.

If you love to eat, there are barbecues at various haunts for only $5.00, watch Giants' games during the feasts and get a 20 percent discount at various sporting goods stores.

Tidewater Tides

The Tidewatchers
P.O. Box 12111
Norfolk, VA 23502
(804) 467-3192
Person to contact: Steve Kaba.
Cost to join: $5.00 per person or $8.00 per family.

Members raise money for trophies to recognize individual accomplishments by the Tidewater Tides, from pitching a no-hitter to hitting two home runs in a game. Also included are three banquets to honor the players during the year.

Toronto Blue Jays

Toronto Blue Jays Fan Club
P.O. Box 42, Station K
Toronto, ONT, M4P 2G1
(416) 962-3040
Person to contact: Harvey Trivett.
Cost to join: $10.00 per year.

Besides the 20 percent discount at the souvenir shop in the Sky Dome, you'll get to participate in the monthly luncheons with executives to honor the Blue Jays' Player of the Month. Includes the quarterly newsletter *Blue Jay Chatter*.   —BL

Baseball Life Begins at Thirty

Time was when a thirty-year-old ball player was washed up, especially if he was an amateur. After most of the old-fashioned town teams and industrial leagues folded in the 1950s, there simply wasn't anywhere for older men to play. Surviving semipro leagues were last-chance proving grounds for professional prospects; recreational baseball was virtually nonexistent. For thirty years the thirty-plus players could choose softball or watching.

Actually, there were a few over-thirty teams laboring in obscurity all along; the Fountain of Youth League has been in St. Louis for forty years, and a few other leagues were scattered around the country, but they were virtually unknown, even to most fans in their own cities. Then, in the mid-1980s, senior baseball surfaced.

Some credit the major league fantasy camps that started about the same time with providing the inspiration, but maybe it was the other way around. In any event, a few more clubs for men over thirty or forty formed. The Northern Vermont Old Timers' Baseball Association was among the "new" pioneers, organizing in 1985. Founder Floyd Brown, then in his late fifties, simply telephoned a lot of his old baseball buddies from decades earlier and put together a reunion. The reunion turned into a pickup ballgame; the pickup game became a series of semiweekly games which continues; the group grew large enough to have several games at different fields on any given weekend; teams formed; and now, four years later, northern Vermont has at least three six-team senior leagues, plus a number of independent town teams who frequently play the senior teams.

Unique aspects of the Vermont game are that everyone present bats, in lineups numbering as many as nineteen players (with ten to twelve the usual range); free substitution is the rule for fielders; pitchers must be over forty or even fifty in some games; courtesy runners are allowed for older players; and pitchers may work only three innings per game.

Another senior baseball pioneer was the Oxford Area Baseball Association, of Berkeley, California. Originally a neighborhood youth team that played together in 1967–1971, the members came back together for semiannual reunion games against current neighborhood youth teams, beginning in 1981. The semiannual games grew to weekly pickup games among older players by the summer of 1988. The O.A.B.A. has the three-inning limit for pitchers, but otherwise plays regulation hardball.

Although independent teams and leagues continue to proliferate, using various rules appropriate to their players, most soon join the Men's Senior Baseball League, run by Steve Sigler. The M.S.B.L. plays regulation baseball, except in the organization's World Series, held each year in Arizona. The World Series has separate divisions for players 30–39 and 40-plus.

According to Sigler, M.S.B.L. now has eighty affiliated leagues, active in forty of the fifty states, the provinces of Ontario and British Columbia, and the Dominican Republic. About 10,000 players participate. The M.S.B.L. accepts memberships from either teams or whole leagues. If a team joins, the M.S.B.L. helps it locate other teams nearby to form a league. Dues are $10 per player per year, for which teams and individuals may claim discounts on insurance and travel. Significant sponsorship comes from sporting goods manufacturers.

A few former major leaguers, most notably Bill Lee, have been playing senior baseball recently alongside the amateurs. Inevitably someone thought of organizing a senior league for ex–major leaguers, thirty-five and over. Promoters are now trying to sell that idea in both Florida and Arizona. If it ever gets going, and if the ex–major leaguers start playing against the best thirty-plus lifelong amateurs, we may discover some overlooked could-have-been superstars. As the growth of amateur running has proved, the best athletes at age twenty are not necessarily the best at age forty, when many late-bloomers reach their peak.

One no longer need be Satchel Paige to dream, "Maybe I'll pitch forever."

MEN'S SENIOR BASEBALL LEAGUE, INC.
Steve Sigler, President
8 Sutton Terrace
Jericho, NY 11753
(516) 931-2615

OVER THIRTY BASEBALL LEAGUE OF NEW JERSEY
Bob Delahant, Commissioner
P.O. Box 3080
Point Pleasant, NJ 08742
(201) 899-6664

ROY HOBBS BASEBALL ASSOCIATION
Ron Monks, President
P.O. Box 1406
Woodland, CA 95695
(916) 666-5772

OVER 40 BASEBALL LEAGUE, INC.
Terry Monroe, President
4821 Alexander Drive
Metairie, LA 70003
(504) 887-8752

FOUNTAIN OF YOUTH LEAGUE
Dave Erker, President
10011 Bellefontaine Rd., Room 101
St. Louis, MO 63137   —MC

Town Baseball

Back before television, radio, automobiles, or movies, the biggest entertainment in most small towns was the Sunday ball game—and it wasn't just a spectator sport. The millhands would take on the farmers, one side of the river would play the other, bachelors would play the married men, or, in a variant popular circa World War I, the Fats would play the Leans. The game was usually the pretext for a picnic or the other way around. Those who didn't play rooted and wagered on the outcome.

The mill teams were often well organized, with uniforms, sponsorships, and even a handful of semiprofessional players—often the ace pitcher, the catcher, and a heavy hitter. Other town teams were sponsored by local merchants. Sometimes each merchant in a small town would sponsor a different player. In their purest form, however, town teams had no uniforms, no sponsorship, no identity other than being men and boys from a particular village who played ball together against teams from other villages or against professional barnstorming teams.

Leagues tended to be highly informal, just associations of teams who met often because of geographical proximity, with neither standings nor enduring structure. Although there were neighborhood teams in most big cities that carried on the tradition, town baseball was a predominantly rural game. It thrived as a social facet of a strong sense of community, and died wherever and whenever community identity broke down.

In the late 1940s town baseball waned and all but disappeared, largely replaced by softball. The reasons were less competition from professional baseball and television, than supposed "improvements" in the game that eventually undermined what it was all about. More formal league schedules often mismatched teams of unequal caliber; business sponsorship usurped the link between team and community; and the introduction of ringers, semiprofessional players brought in from elsewhere, further eroded the notion of the town team as "our team."

Still, town baseball never died entirely. Even today, in remote regions of New England, the Northwest, Canada, Mexico, and the Deep South, traditional town baseball persists. Somewhere there's a field, where everyone knows there's a game each Sunday. Men, boys, and even a few athletic and ambitious women show up, group into teams tending to keep the same identity from week to week, and play ball. Players take turns rotating out of the lineup to umpire. Someone passes the hat to buy baseballs—and beer if there's money left over. The caliber of the game varies considerably, tending to start out at about the high school level, but dropping as heat and exhaustion take a toll.

Nonetheless, when a good local pitcher faces a good hitter with the game on the line in the ninth, there can be plenty of tension in town baseball, even if betting is largely a thing of the past. At least a couple of times a summer, the best players from town journey to another village, perhaps clear across the state, to take on the best players from there. Townball is the ideal form of baseball for players who like the challenge of competitive hardball with the spontaneity of the sandlots.

The best way to get involved, if you don't hear of a team or weekly game through your local grapevine, is to organize your own team or game and get the grapevine going. Remember to keep it as informal as possible. If you want to pretend you're in the big leagues, you belong in a senior league or semipro league. Town baseball is the game for men and women who hold the notion of baseball as a celebratory rite. If you have a respectable battery, a washed-up ex-pro at one position, a couple of promising kids at several others, a few guys over forty here and there, and a girl at second base, you have the right idea.

—MC

Picture Credits

Accolade: 309

Amateur Athletic Foundation of Los Angeles: 132

American Amateur Baseball Congress: 338

American Sports Medicine Institute: 46

American Women's Baseball Association: 326

Armchair Sports: 286

Association of Professional Ball Players of America: 336

Babe Ruth Museum: 113 (photo by John Dean), 130, 131

The Bettmann Archive: 56, 101, 146

Boston Red Sox: 332

Joe Brinkman Umpire School: 79, 89, 90

Butler Institute of American Art: 147

Collegiate Baseball: 277 (photo by Lou Pavlovich, Jr.)

Columbia Records: 4

Cryo Therapy Inc.: 34

Cybex: 35, 36–37, 38

Dizzy Dean Museum: 140

Bucky Dent Baseball School: 80, 83, 84

Dream Week: 91, 93, 94

Electronic Arts: 307

Finnish Baseball Association: 274

G.E. Lighting Systems: 16, 18 (both photos by Ronald Neilsen)

Gallery 53/Artworks: 126 (artist, Robert Houser)

Gatorade/Quaker Oats Company: 43

Henry Groskinsky: 129

Barry Halper: 2, 216

Hellmuth, Obata & Kassabaum: 23 (photo by Patricia Layman Bazelon), 26 (both)

International Baseball Association: 267, 268, 271 (photo by Luis Hernandez), 273 (right), 278, 281

International Business Machines: 283

Jaleco: 305

Lloyd Johnson: 142

Jack Kavanagh: 315 (photo by Thomas Dexter Stevens)

Kent State University: 69

Library of Congress: 31, 63

Los Angeles Dodgers: 168

Mark Ludeen: 145 (photo by Fabrice)

Major League Baseball Properties: 229

Major League Systems: 290

Mickey Mantle's Restaurant: (photo by Miller Photography) 128

Mediagenic: 310

Miami Maniac: 244

Margaret Miller: 27, 28, 143, 145, 292

Minnesota Twins: 332

Mitsubishi America: 19

National Baseball Hall of Fame & Museum: 124

National Baseball Library, Cooperstown, NY: 5 (both), 6 (both), 7 (both), 8, 9, 24, 33, 53, 54, 58, 73, 77, 78 (bottom left), 136 (photo by Frank Rollins), 171, 182, 187, 221, 222, 224, 230, 236, 247, 253, 318, 322, 353

New York State Historical Association: 353 (photo by Lori Grace)

New York State Museum, courtesy of private collection: 148 (artist, Gerald Garston)

Oakland Athletics: 332

Orion Pictures: 213 (© 1988 Orion Pictures Corporation. All Rights Reserved.)

Max Patkin: 243

Rich Pilling (*The Sporting News*): 87, 174, 175, 188

P&K Products and Major League Baseball Properties 1989: 122

Philatelic International and Major League Baseball Properties 1989: 114

Price Stern Sloan: 117

Pursue the Pennant: 296

Raintree Inc. and Major League Baseball Properties 1989: 123

Rawlings Sporting Goods: 51, 55

Replay Games: 300

Rhino Records: 13

Richmond Braves: 323

Robert Rosen Associates: 190

Rotisserie Gold Sheet: 290

Rotisserie League Stats: 285

Mark Rucker: 74, 109, 119, 141, 273

Michael Schmidt: 331

Society for American Baseball Research: 330 (photo by Dorene Thornley)

Sport Magazine: xiv

The Sporting News: 135

Sporting Views: 97 (photo by Tony Inzerillo)

Stan Musial Society: 350

Stats Inc.: 287

Strat-O-Matic Game Co.: 303

Frank & Peggy Steele: 3

The Summer Game: 127 (artist, Lance Richbourg)

Tengen: 313

Al Tielemans: 10

Tri-Star Pictures: 215

TV Sports Mailbag: 62, 219

USA Today: 285

WABC: 193

Jerry Wachter: 178

Brenda Ward: 342

Warner Bros.: 214 (both)

Western Reserve Historical Society: 138

Wide World: 15, 29, 40, 42, 44, 59, 144, 167, 173, 218, 226, 233, 235, 263, 321, 324, 328, 329

Miles Wolff: 250, 254, 258

Yankee Haters Club: 349

All other illustrations courtesy of Baseball Ink.

Index

About the Editors

John Thorn is the author/editor of more than twenty books. His baseball works include *The Game for All America, The Armchair Books of Baseball, The National Pastime, The Relief Pitcher, The Pitcher* (with John Holway) and *A Century of Baseball Lore.* He collaborated with Pete Palmer to create *Total Baseball* and *The Hidden Game of Baseball*; Bob Carroll joined them for *The Hidden Game of Football* and *The Football Abstract.*

Thorn has contributed to several periodicals, among them *The Sporting News, Sport,* and *American Heritage.* He is president of Baseball Ink, the book production company responsible for *The Whole Base-ball Catalogue.* Thorn lives in Saugerties, New York with his wife, Susan, and sons Mark, Isaac, and Jed.

Bob Carroll is the author/illustrator of many sports books. He wrote a series of books for children sponsored by the Baseball Hall of Fame and another involving the Pro Football Hall of Fame; he was a contributing writer to *Total Baseball.* He has also written *The Hidden Game of Football* and *The Football Abstract* (both with Pete Palmer and John Thorn), *100 Greatest Running Backs,* and numerous sports-related articles for magazines, including *The National Pastime, Sport, Sports Heritage, Sports History,* and *The Saturday Evening Post.* He has illustrated *The Armchair Quarterback, The Armchair Aviator,* and *The Armchair Mountaineer,* all by John Thorn.

Carroll is a long-time member of SABR, the Society for American Baseball Research. He is also the founder and Executive Director of PFRA (Professional Football Researchers Association), an organization of writers, historians, and fans with a strong interest in the history of pro football. He lives in North Huntingdon, Pennsylvania.